AGRICULTURAL LAND REDISTRIBUTION

AGRICULTURE AND RURAL DEVELOPMENT

Seventy-five percent of the world's poor live in rural areas and most are involved in agriculture. In the 21st century, agriculture remains fundamental to economic growth, poverty alleviation, and environmental sustainability. The World Bank's Agriculture and Rural Development publication series presents recent analyses of issues that affect the role of agriculture, including livestock, fisheries, and forestry, as a source of economic development, rural livelihoods, and environmental services. The series is intended for practical application, and we hope that it will serve to inform public discussion, policy formulation, and development planning.

Titles in this series:

Agricultural Land Redistribution: Toward Greater Consensus

Agriculture Investment Sourcebook

Changing the Face of the Waters: The Promise and Challenge of Sustainable Aquaculture

Enhancing Agricultural Innovation: How to Go Beyond the Strengthening of Research Systems

Forests Sourcebook: Practical Guidance for Sustaining Forests in Development Cooperation

Gender in Agriculture Sourcebook

Organization and Performance of Cotton Sectors in Africa: Learning from Reform Experience

Reforming Agricultural Trade for Developing Countries, Volume 1: Key Issues for a Pro-Development Outcome of the Doha Round

Reforming Agricultural Trade for Developing Countries, Volume 2: Quantifying the Impact of Multilateral Trade Reform

Shaping the Future of Water for Agriculture: A Sourcebook for Investment in Agricultural Water Management

The Sunken Billions: The Economic Justification for Fisheries Reform

Sustainable Land Management: Challenges, Opportunities, and Trade-Offs

Sustainable Land Management Sourcebook

Sustaining Forests: A Development Strategy

AGRICULTURAL LAND REDISTRIBUTION

Toward Greater Consensus

Editors

Hans P. Binswanger-Mkhize

Camille Bourguignon

Rogier van den Brink

THE WORLD BANK

Washington, D.C.

1818 H Street NW
Washington DC 20433
Telephone: 202-473-1000
Internet: www.worldbank.org
E-mail: feedback@worldbank.org

1 2 3 4 12 11 10 09

ISBN: 978-0-8213-7627-0
eISBN: 978-0-8213-7962-2
DOI: 10.1596/978-0-8213-7627-0

Library of Congress Cataloging in-Publication Data

Agricultural land redistribution: toward greater consensus / edited by Hans P. Binswanger-Mkhize, Camille Bourguignon, Rogier van den Brink.

p. cm. — (Agriculture and rural development)

Includes bibliographical references and index.

ISBN 978-0-8213-7627-0 — ISBN 978-0-8213-7962-2 (electronic)

1. Land reform—Developing countries—History—20th century. I. Binswanger-Mkhize, Hans P, 1943- II. Bourguignon, Camille, 1979- III. Brink, Rogerius Johannes Eugenius van den, 1958-

HD1333.5.A37 2009

333.3'1091724—dc22

2009009701

Cover and chapter opener illustration: Diego Rivera; reproduction authorized by Instituto Nacional de Bellas Artes y Literatura, 2009.

Cover design: Patricia Hord Graphik Design.

CONTENTS

BOXES, FIGURES, AND TABLES

Boxes

Figures

Tables

FOREWORD

Programs whereby governments facilitate redistribution of agricultural land are being carried out in many countries, including Brazil, Guatemala, India, Malawi, Namibia, the Philippines, South Africa, and Zimbabwe. In these countries, land redistribution is a high priority because it holds the promise of significantly reducing poverty and increasing broad-based agricultural growth. Furthermore, history demonstrates that unresolved land issues easily can spiral into crisis and conflict.

Although there is widespread agreement on the need for redistributing land in many places, there is less concensus regarding the most appropriate mechanism for implementing it, particularly concerning the mode of land acquisition. On that topic, the debate continues among land activists and researchers about "willing seller–willing buyer" mechanisms versus expropriation. These lasting disagreements point to the politically sensitive nature of land redistribution issues.

For a number of reasons, both historic and economic, redistribution of land in southern Africa is particularly important and difficult. The radicalization of the land redistribution process after 2000 in Zimbabwe indeed has highlighted the explosive nature of the land question in the region. Consequently, for both political and socioeconomic reasons, southern African governments have placed programs addressing distribution of and access to land higher on the development agenda than ever before.

The launching point for this publication arose from a series of workshops held from 2005 to 2007, during which the issues of agricultural land redistribution were discussed and debated by participants from across southern Africa. The World Bank and the Southern African Development Community Land Reform Support Facility commissioned a series of background papers and case studies prepared by key experts, government officials, researchers, and staff of international agencies, among others, to serve as the basis for workshop discussions. Selected papers and cases—expanded, revised, and presented here—deal with the history of redistributive land reforms and introduce concepts and emerging principles on how to redistribute agricultural land. The book also reflects on lessons and experiences from southern Africa and around the globe.

We hope that this publication will be an effective tool in building a common vision of the way forward for agricultural land redistribution where it can contribute to development. The vision should set the stage for implementation of programs to make property rights more secure, create fairer distribution, and foster peace and stability, while avoiding serious domestic political discord, conflict with foreign investors, capital flight, or asset stripping.

Juergen Voegele
Director
Agriculture and Rural Development
The World Bank

Inger Andersen
Director
Sustainable Development, Africa Region
The World Bank

Konrad von Ritter
Sector Manager
Sustainable Development Division, World Bank Institute
The World Bank

ACKNOWLEDGMENTS

The editors are grateful to the following people for reviewing the chapters presented in this volume: Rex Ahene, Pranab K. Bardhan, Keith Clifford Bell, Fabrizio Bresciani, Antonio M. Buainain, Frank Byamugisha, Watson C. Chidawanyika, Ed Cook, Aline Couduel, Shenggen Fan, Trevor Gifford, Markus Goldstein, Andrew Karanja, Zongmin Li, Odenda Lumumba, Xiaopeng Luo, Liberty Mhlanga, Shem Migot-Adholla, Jorge Muñoz, Mia Overall, Robin Palmer, Stefano Paternostro, Eugenio Peixoto, Idah Z. Pswarayi-Riddihough, Maria Theresa Quiñones, Claudia Romano, Dina Umali-Deininger, Trond Vedeld, and Yao Yang.

For their financial support, the editors are grateful to the Finnish, French, and Norwegian governments, the Southern African Development Community, the Southern African Regional Poverty Network, and the United Nations Development Programme. In particular, the editors thank Florence Lasbennes, Sue Mbaya, Stephen Nanthambwe, and Verity Nyagah.

The editors also wish to recognize the support of Felipe Alzir Buffara Antunes, Frédéric Bertrand, Jean-Luc Bosio, Colin Bruce, Karen McConnell Brooks, Mark Cackler, Jean-Louis Chaléard, Luis Coriolo, Chirstine Cornelius, Christine Cotting, Alain de Janvry, David Dollar, Claire Galpin, Mirella Hernani, Bert Hofman, Patricia Katayama, Alyson Kleine, Mungai Lenneiye, Christophe Lesueur, Guo Li, Lisa Li Xi Lau, Karen Macours, Jonas Mbwangue, Ritva S. Reinikka, Thierry Sanjuan, Hardwick Tchale, Janice Tuten, and Konrad von Ritter.

Finally, the editors wish to thank all those who participated in the "Land Redistribution: Toward Greater Consensus" and "Land Redistribution: Toward a Common Vision" workshops.

ABOUT THE AUTHORS

Hans P. Binswanger-Mkhize is an honorary professor at the Institute for Economic Research on Innovation, Tshwane University of Technology, Pretoria, South Africa.

Saturnino M. Borras, Jr. is the Canada research chair in international development studies at Saint Mary's University, Halifax, Nova Scotia, Canada.

Camille Bourguignon is a research fellow at the Center for the Organization and Dissemination of Geographic Information (PRODIG), University of Paris 1 Pantheon-Sorbonne, France, where he is working on land rights formalization in Brazilian cities. He is also a consultant for the World Bank on land reform and administration.

Malcolm D. Childress is a senior land administration specialist in the Latin America and the Caribbean Region of the World Bank.

Klaus Deininger is a lead economist in the World Bank Development Research Group.

Zhou Feizhou is an associate professor in the Department of Sociology at Peking University, Beijing, China.

Tim Hanstad is president and chief executive officer of the Rural Development Institute, Seattle, Washington.

T. Haque is senior land policy adviser at the Food and Agriculture Organization of the United Nations, and former chair of the government of India's Commission on Agricultural Costs and Prices.

Andrew Hilton is a fellow of the Royal Institution of Chartered Surveyors, and was a consultant to the Food and Agriculture Organization of the United Nations and the German Technical Cooperation.

Vincent Hungwe is a program director for community-driven development and sustainable livelihoods at Khanya–African Institute for Community-Driven Development. He is a former permanent secretary in the Ministry of Lands and Agriculture, Zimbabwe.

Karuti Kanyinga is a senior research fellow at the Institute for Development Studies, University of Nairobi, Kenya.

Edward Lahiff was a senior researcher at the Programme for Land and Agrarian Studies, University of the Western Cape, South Africa. He now is based at Trinity College, Dublin, Ireland, where he is a doctoral program officer for the Trinity International Development Initiative.

Stephen Machira is a former project manager for the Community-Based Rural Land Development Program in Malawi. He is currently a freelance consultant in land reform, project management, and natural resource management.

Rodrigo Fernando Maule is a consultant for Entropix Engineering Company, Brazil.

Sam Moyo is the executive director of the African Institute for Agrarian Studies, Harare, Zimbabwe.

Zander Navarro is a research fellow at the Institute of Development Studies, University of Sussex, Brighton, U.K., and associate professor at the Federal University of Rio Grande do Sul, Porto Alegre, Brazil.

Robin Nielsen is an attorney at the Rural Development Institute, Seattle, Washington.

Simon Pazvakavambwa works as a freelance consultant on various agriculture, land, and water-related issues. Formerly, he served as a permanent secretary in Zimbabwe for the ministries of Lands, Land Reform and Resettlement; Agriculture; Water Resources and Infrastructural Development; and Rural Housing and Social Amenities.

David Solomon is the head of the School of Economic and Business Sciences at the University of the Witwatersrand, Johannesburg, South Africa. He also works as a consultant with a focus on anticorruption in local government.

Gerd Sparovek is an associate professor at the University of São Paulo, Brazil.

Glen S. Thomas is a former director-general of the Department of Land Affairs, Ministry of Agriculture and Land Affairs, South Africa. Currently, he runs a consulting and investment company focusing on community and land policy development and implementation.

Rogier van den Brink is a lead economist, Poverty Reduction and Economic Management, East Asia and Pacific Region of the World Bank. He is also a former senior economist in the Bank's Africa Region.

Darryl Vhugen is an attorney with the Rural Development Institute, Seattle, Washington. He also serves as the state director for the institute's Andhra Pradesh office.

ABBREVIATIONS

AgriBee	Agricultural Broad-Based Black Economic Empowerment
AIAS	African Institute for Agrarian Studies
ANC	African National Congress
BEE	black economic empowerment
BIPPA	Bilateral Investment Promotion and Protection Agreement
CAF	Consolidation of Family Agriculture
CAMA	computer-aided mass appraisal
CARP	Comprehensive Agrarian Reform Program
CBFM	Community-Based Forest Management
CBRLDP	Community-Based Rural Land Development Project
CCP	Chinese Communist Party
CDC	Colonial Development Corporation
CF-CPR	Land Credit and Poverty Alleviation program
CFU	Commercial Farmers Union
CIMA	community-initiated, market-assisted
COC	community oversight committee
CONTAG	National Confederation of Agricultural Workers
DAR	Department of Agrarian Reform
DDF	District Development Fund
DENR	Department of Environment and Natural Resources
DLA	Department of Land Affairs
ESTA	Extension of Security of Tenure Act of 1997
EU	European Union
FDT	Farmers' Development Trust

GDP	gross domestic product
GNP	gross national product
HIV/AIDS	human immunodeficiency virus/acquired immunodeficiency syndrome
HRS	Household Responsibility System
IBRD	International Bank for Reconstruction and Development
IKP	Indira Kranti Patham
INCORA	Instituto Colombiano de la Reforma Agraria [Colombia Institute for Agrarian Reform]
INCRA	Instituto Nacional de Colonização e Reforma Agrária [National Institute for Colonization and Agrarian Reform]
IPEA	Instituto de Pesquisa Econômica Aplicada [Institute of Applied Economics]
KADU	Kenya African Democratic Union
KANU	Kenya African National Union
LAFD	Land Acquisition and Farm Development
LARP	Land and Agrarian Reform Project
LDSB	Land Development and Settlement Board
LRAD	Land Redistribution for Agricultural Development
LRRP	Land Reform and Resettlement Program
M&E	monitoring and evaluation
MDA	Ministry of Agrarian Development
MST	Movimento dos Trabalhadores Rurais Sem Terra [Landless Workers' Movement]
NCA	National Constitutional Assembly
NGO	nongovernmental organization
ODA	Overseas Development Administration
OECD	Organisation for Economic Co-operation and Development
PARC	Presidential Agrarian Reform Council
PEACE	Philippine Ecumenical Action for Community Empowerment Foundation
PMU	project management unit
PNCF	Programa Nacional de Crédito Fundiário [National Program of Land Credit]
PSIA	poverty and social impact assessment
RDI	Rural Development Institute
SAC	Special Agrarian Court
SADC	Southern African Development Community
SLAG	Settlement/Land Acquisition Grant
WSWB	willing seller–willing buyer

All amounts are U.S. dollars, unless otherwise indicated.

PART I

The Growing Consensus on the Importance of Land Redistribution

CHAPTER ONE

Introduction and Summary

Hans P. Binswanger-Mkhize, Camille Bourguignon, and Rogier van den Brink

> *Whenever there is in any country, uncultivated lands and unemployed poor, it is clear that the laws of property have been so far extended as to violate a natural right. The earth is given as commonstock for man to labor and live on. If for the encouragement of industry we allow it to be appropriated, we must take care that other employment be provided to those excluded from the appropriation. If we do not, the fundamental right to labor the earth returns to the unemployed.*
>
> —Thomas Jefferson, 1785

WHY DO WE NEED A BOOK ON AGRICULTURAL LAND REDISTRIBUTION?

Jefferson's statement in a letter to James Madison combines a profound sense of fairness with a strong economic argument for land redistribution. Jefferson was one of the earliest and most articulate spokesmen for distributing land widely to smallholders, believing that it would lay the basic foundations for democracy. Driven by similar sentiments, many countries have attempted to do land reform over the past 250 years. However, important inequalities in the distribution of landownership persist, particularly in southern Africa and Latin America.

Land redistribution has been the topic of a large body of descriptive and analytical literature. (See box 1.1 for a definition of land redistribution.) This

Box 1.1 Defining Land Redistribution, Land Reform, and Agrarian Reform

Land redistribution is an effort by governments to modify the distribution of land ownership. It is often an attempt to transform an agrarian structure composed mainly of large-scale farms into one where family farms are predominant by taking land away from large landowners, or the state, and redistributing it to tenants and landless peasants. Historically, land redistribution has been carried out to abolish feudal, colonial, or collective forms of landownership and more generally to correct old wrongs.

Land tenure reform is a program designed to change the legal and institutional framework for land administration. Other common changes attempted by land tenure reform programs include modification of the land tenure system and decentralization of the land administration and management function. In any society, the need for land reform reemerges regularly because the legislative and institutional frameworks for land administration have to be modified continually to adapt to changing political, economic, and social circumstances.

Land reform is a broader term comprising both land redistribution and land tenure reform. Land reform often takes place within an even broader strategy of *agrarian reform:* a collection of activities and changes designed to alter the agrarian structure of a country. Factors that influence the characteristics and evolution of this structure include bioclimatic conditions; socioeconomic, cultural, and political systems; population density; and technology. The objectives of an agrarian reform generally are to improve the levels of agricultural production both qualitatively and quantitatively and to improve the agricultural producers' standards of living.

Source: This information is drawn largely from Ciparisse (2003).

literature currently reflects both a growing consensus among rural development specialists and economists on the importance of land redistribution, and conflicting views among land reform practitioners on the best ways to go about it (that is, how to provide access to land and develop sustainable and prosperous new farms[1]). The roots of these controversies are to be found in ideology, politics, history, economic theory, and various efficiency and implementation arguments—a daunting list. Yet, despite these controversies, among specialists there now seems to be near consensus on the need and justification for redistribution where inequality and landlessness are widespread.

However, if there is such consensus among specialists about the need for land redistribution, why is so little actually happening, even in settings where it appears most urgently needed? And, where land redistribution actually is taking place, why is it still so controversial? There are at least three answers:

1. Land redistribution is often seen as a thing of the past, strongly associated with revolutions, and likely to generate more loss than gain. However, as

Michael Lipton (2009) points out: "The alleged death of land reform" may be premature and "substantial future land reform remains likely and desirable." Indeed, in countries where farmland and incomes are very unequally distributed, and where unemployment is widespread, "policy to cut farm size by land redistribution can slash unemployment." In short, if implemented well, land redistribution can make an important contribution toward reducing poverty (Lipton 2009).

2. Among practitioners and advocates, deep disagreements persist on how to redistribute land—that is, on the alternative paths to redistribution (such as state-led or beneficiary-led); on the mechanisms for land acquisition (such as confiscation, expropriation, negotiation, or market purchase); on who in particular should benefit from land redistribution; on who should pay for land reform; and on who should be the main players in executing it. These intense conflicts turn land redistribution into a highly sensitive political issue, despite the growing consensus about the need for it.
3. There has been little rigorous evaluation of the impact of land reform in general, and of alternative ways of implementing it in particular. Such impact analysis is necessary to convince the general public and policy makers—not simply the specialists—that public expenditures on redistribution of land are well justified. Impact evaluations also would help settle the controversies about how best to implement land redistribution.

Parts I and II of this book briefly discuss the history and the rationale for land redistribution.[2] The main focus of this book, however, is the "how" of land redistribution. To forge greater consensus among practitioners of land reform, and to enable them to make better choices among the many options, the book describes and analyzes alternative broad paths of implementation, using examples and the detailed implementation mechanisms that were used in those examples. The objectives of this book are to review and analyze

1. the growing consensus on the importance of land redistribution (this chapter)
2. the historical origins of land concentration and past attempts to redistribute land (part 1)
3. ongoing land reform programs, their mechanisms, achievements, and limitations (part 2)
4. the wide array of objectives, mechanisms, and tools for land redistribution that remain the focus of heated debate (part 3)
5. how to develop, implement, and monitor an effective national program of land redistribution (part 4).

THE PROBLEM OF LAND REDISTRIBUTION

Land distribution issues have troubled nations for ages. For instance, they were at the heart of the politics of the Roman Empire and the Chinese dynasties.

Land distribution often was unfair and unequal because it was undertaken at a period in time when a class of rulers used force and coercion to extract rents from the peasantry. Over centuries, these inequalities constantly would be challenged by countless peasant conflicts, wars, and revolutions. Even so, by the end of the 18th century, the distribution of land property rights remained highly unequal all around the world (see chapter 2).

The modern era of land reform began in Prussia and with the French Revolution. Slowly, and with many fits and starts, these reforms have led to the redistribution of land to the actual tillers. Europe completed this agenda after World War II with the land redistribution undertaken in southern Italy. The Mexican, Russian, and Chinese revolutions (to name the most important ones) led to the first countrywide redistributions of land outside of Europe.

In the communist ideology, which inspired several revolutions, land reform was the first step toward establishing a classless society. The second step, after redistributing land to the peasants, involved collectivizing farm production to achieve economies of scale. Collectivizations invariably failed to produce vibrant agricultural sectors, however, and subsequently were undone. In China, for instance, the Household Responsibility System replaced collective farming during the late 1970s (see chapter 4). Other decollectivizations were implemented in Cambodia, Ethiopia, the former Soviet Union, and Vietnam, among others.

Following World War II, peaceful countrywide land reforms were implemented in Japan, Korea, and Taiwan, China, under strong external pressure from the United States. The U.S. foreign policy position at the time was stated clearly by Isador Lubin, the U.S. representative to the United Nations Economic and Social Council (1950–53), when he introduced a resolution that would make land reform a global economic program of the United Nations: "A nation of insecure tenants and rootless laborers, who see little hope to better their lot, is an unstable society, subject to sporadic violence and easily persuaded to follow false leaders" (Lissner 1951, p. 53).

The end of colonialism triggered significant redistributions of land in the Middle East and North Africa (Algeria, Egypt, Iran, Iraq, Pakistan, Syria, and Tunisia). These reforms were carried out to liberate the agricultural sector from "semifeudal" relics and sometimes to suppress the legacy of colonialism. Similarly, attempts to strengthen tenants' and users' rights—the so-called "land-to-the-tiller" reforms—were pursued in India after independence (see chapter 9). In sub-Saharan Africa, the first land redistribution programs by an independent government were carried out in Kenya during the 1960s and 1970s (see chapter 3). Meanwhile, in Latin America, many land reform programs were initiated after the Cuban Revolution to prevent the expansion of communist revolutions. These reforms achieved modest results, leaving land distribution almost unchanged everywhere (see chapters 10 and 11). Then, during the 1980s, prospects for land redistribution became bleak and "the game of land reform" was declared lost in Latin America (de Janvry and Sadoulet 1989).

At the end of the Cold War, redistributive land reforms resurfaced. Governments in Eastern Europe and Central Asia decided to distribute collective land to the workers or, less often, to restore it to the former owners. In the meantime, in Latin America, southern Africa, and elsewhere in the world, many governments reintroduced land redistribution programs in a new attempt to address persistent inequalities in land access. But there is a major difference between past and current attempts to redistribute land. In the past, governments were particularly hostile to land redistribution. As a result, redistribution had to be an extralegal exercise or associated with profound political change. Those land reforms rarely were peaceful; more often, they were the outcome of wars or revolutions. Today, most governments have been elected democratically. They tend to be less hostile to land redistribution and are searching for ways to redistribute land at scale, peacefully and lawfully. This book focuses on that search, given advocates' pronounced disagreements on how to do it.

WHY REDISTRIBUTE LAND? THE GROWING CONSENSUS

In countries with a highly unequal distribution of land, the case for redistributing property rights from the rich to the poor or from large-scale to small-scale farmers is strong, both theoretically and empirically. The case rests on conflict prevention, equity, economic growth, jobs, and poverty reduction. Key elements of the consensus—sometimes counterintuitive and hard to understand—are discussed in this section.[3]

Fairness

Perhaps the most important reason to worry about equity is linked to the inherent political and social nature of property rights. History, culture, and many other factors can mold what a community or a nation thinks is fair use and ownership of land. As history shows, communities even may change their views on what is appropriate and fair over time.

Societies usually have strong feelings about how and by whom land should be used because the overall area of land in a country is fixed, and because agriculture is (or could be) an important source of income for many people. The matter of equity is particularly pronounced when it comes to land: communities tend to feel that land should be equitably distributed to as many people as possible. A countryside populated by small family farmers tilling the land corresponds in many peoples' minds to a system that is fair.

The fact that unresolved land issues so frequently lead to violence, civil unrest, or even civil war demonstrates how strong these notions of fairness are. In the last 50 years, land-related conflicts have plagued countries such as Algeria, Brazil, Colombia, El Salvador, Guatemala, Honduras, the Philippines, and many others. In Africa, the establishment of the settler colonies in Kenya,

Namibia, South Africa, and Zimbabwe was accompanied by fierce resistance from the displaced indigenous populations, and tension and conflict continue today. White settlers appropriated for themselves the best pieces of land. They then turned the indigenous black peasants into tenants or wage laborers, or simply expelled them (Wolpe 1972; Bundy 1979). When mechanization (subsidized by the state) made it feasible to depopulate the land, black tenants and wage laborers were removed at an even faster rate and driven away from their homes into marginal areas, designated "homelands" or "communal areas."

In southern Africa, the removal of black peasants from their land was systematic. Today, the most fertile lands in the region are occupied by very large, sprawling farms that, on average, are underused. The highest population densities—black population densities—are found in the most infertile rural areas, often close to natural parks. This density is what is called the "rural geography of apartheid," brought about by economic policies that have favored the settlers and forced the removal of black people from fertile lands over a period of more than a century. This inefficient geography continues to impose tremendous costs on the poor and on the economy as a whole; and it is highly inequitable and unfair. Because the legacy of the removal of black people from their land often is still fresh in peoples' minds, land reform is a highly emotional issue.

Similarly systematic expropriations, and sometimes outright exterminations, of indigenous people took place in many other parts of the world. In Australia, Tasmania, and most countries in North and South America, indigenous people suffered the tragic consequences of settler actions, which often were justified under variants of Herbert Spencer's philosophy of "social Darwinism." Many of these countries still are wrestling with the aftermath of these human tragedies.

Communities and nations will have to deal with this legacy. They invariably will form opinions about what is fair. They simply may look at the land issue as one of justice and of redressing old wrongs. That is as it should be. People should reflect on the existing property rights and democratically make decisions about their distribution because, as history shows, ignoring a looming land conflict is a risky economic strategy. In most of the cases discussed in this book, restoring a more equitable distribution of land will contribute greatly to more social cohesion, which will foster more inclusive institutions and policies, and hence promote better long-term development.

Equity, Growth, and Poverty Reduction

Deininger (2003) and the *World Development Report 2003* (World Bank 2002) provide evidence of the long-term implications of inequality in landholdings and development. By tracing individual countries' long-term development paths within sets of comparable countries,[4] they further illustrate how initial inequality in landholdings leads to dramatically different development outcomes in the long run. Deininger (2003) and Acemoglu, Johnson, and Robinson (2001, 2002) use cross-country time series to show the same "path-dependent" development pattern: countries with a more egalitarian distribution of land tend to have better, more inclusive institutions that, in turn, lead to higher levels of economic growth. Sokoloff and Engermann (2000) demonstrate the same patterns comparing the evolution of North America and South America, tracing political (in) equality initially to land distribution and subsequently to economic growth, democracy, and education.

Research comparing countries over time increasingly suggests that equity, in general, is good for growth (Aghion, Caroli, and García-Peñalosa 1999). In particular, equity in land distribution is associated also with overall higher economic growth (Deininger and Squire 1998; Deininger and Olinto 2000). Country case studies confirm that hypothesis. For instance, the initial phase of China's high and sustained growth and poverty reduction spurt clearly was linked to its 1979 change from collective large-scale farms to small family farms. When collective production was abandoned and key agricultural markets were liberalized, China's peasant sector initiated rapid economic growth that dramatically reduced poverty (see chapter 4).

At the other end of the equity spectrum one finds the countries that have been least successful in reducing rural poverty. These countries include, for instance, Brazil, Colombia, Guatemala, and South Africa. Not surprising, these countries are characterized by highly unequal landownership, with substantial public investments in large-scale farming. Although these large-scale farms usually have become technically sophisticated, they make little use of labor, and their mechanization leads to rapid outmigration of labor from the agricultural sector into rural or urban slums—thus creating more rural (and urban) poverty. On the other hand, small family farmers usually use more labor (their own plus hired) per hectare (or per unit of output) than do their larger peers. Hence, they generate more employment per hectare (or per unit of output) for the economy as a whole, an economywide advantage where unemployment is widespread.

Increased access to land by family farmers also can lead to more vibrant local economies. Access to land provides a good social safety net, which induces more farmers to move into nonfarm businesses, given the higher risks associated with entrepreneurship. Family farmers also spend more of their income on locally produced goods and services than do large farms, creating a positive relationship between family farms and nonfarm incomes in the local economy. In China, the broad-based access to land enabled peasants to take increased risk and move into nonfarm activities, and that then produced the boom in small-scale entrepreneurship. Other success stories are found in Costa Rica, Indonesia, Malaysia, Taiwan, China, and Thailand.

A powerful illustration of the above points is found in a seminal study of two small California towns (Goldschmidt 1947). Arvin and Dinuba, California, were selected because they were alike in virtually all basic economic factors except farm size. Although the total volume of agricultural production was about the same, the "small family farm" community (Dinuba) supported about 20 percent more people at significantly higher living standards, had twice as many businesses doing 61 percent more retail business, and boasted a substantially higher level of public infrastructure than did the "large corporate farm" town (Arvin).

Finally, half of the world's population and 75 percent of its poor people live in rural areas. In South Asia and sub-Saharan Africa, the number of rural poor people has continued to rise and likely will exceed the number of urban poor people until 2040 (World Bank 2007). In Africa, urbanization has not been associated with falling overall poverty (Ravallion, Chen, and Sangraula 2007), whereas, at a global scale, more than 80 percent of the decline in rural poverty is attributable to better conditions in rural areas rather than to outmigration of the poor (World Bank 2007). All of that stresses the importance of rural development in poverty reduction strategies. But whereas rural development undoubtedly is an effective engine for economic development and poverty reduction, its effectiveness in reducing rural poverty depends on the form that it takes. The vast majority of farmers in developing countries are smallholders: of an estimated 3 billion[5] rural inhabitants, 50 percent are in smallholder households (World Bank 2007). Therefore, although rural development holds the promise of reducing poverty significantly, its success will depend largely on smallholders and poor households participating in production (World Bank 2007).

There is significant and growing empirical evidence that well-targeted land redistribution programs have a direct and meaningful impact on poverty reduction. The history of many land redistribution programs demonstrates that when poor people are given good farmland and adequate postsettlement support, they can lift themselves out of poverty permanently. From the cases discussed in this book, we see the following outcomes: In Malawi, after one year of relocation, the average annual incomes of the beneficiary households increased by 63 percent, and food security passed from 3.6 months to 10.7 months. In Brazil, average revenues of the households who benefited from the Land Credit and Poverty Alleviation program had increased by nearly 150 percent after two years of relocation. Longitudinal household data sets on land redistribution beneficiaries of Zimbabwe's 1980s program also show that after about 10 years, "land reform beneficiaries cultivate nearly 50 percent more land than nonbeneficiaries, obtain four times as much in crop revenues, own substantially more livestock, and have expenditures that are higher by 50 percent" (Hoogeveen and Kinsey 2001, p. 132). Providing more support services to these beneficiaries would have sped up the process of establishing successful small farms even more.

Efficiency

On the one hand, a consensus has emerged on the fundamental role of small-scale farm development in the poverty reduction process (World Bank 2007);

on the other hand, there has been a lasting disagreement on the economic importance of small-scale farms.[6] For instance, it often is assumed that small-scale farms are backward and that breaking up large farms will result in a loss of efficiency in the economy. In reality, nearly a century of research by agricultural economists all over the world has produced a counterintuitive stylized fact: small-scale farmers generally use land, labor, and capital more efficiently than do large-scale farmers who depend primarily on hired labor. This "inverse farm size–productivity relationship" implies that agriculture generally is characterized by diseconomies of scale, which means that redistributing land from large farmers to family farmers can bring efficiency gains to the economy.

That fact often comes as a shock to those who equate efficiency with the visible signs of modernized, highly mechanized commercial farms that achieve very high crop yields. Indeed, yields can be raised enormously by applying lots of fertilizers and pesticides; but because that does not necessarily mean that a profit will be made, achieving high yields can be inefficient. In practice, large commercial farmers often achieve higher yields than family farmers on the land they cultivate. At the same time, large commercial farmers often use only a small fraction of their land for crops, leaving much arable land idle and forested. This practice provides lower values of output per hectare than do the crops of family farmers. Despite the advantages of leaving land fallow in some cases, the underuse of the land is the most visible sign of large farmers' inefficiency. Less visible, but consistently showing up in the research results, are the higher profits (in-kind or in cash) for every unit of investment on family farms.

All of that does not mean that family farmers are richer than large farmers. It simply means that, on average, family farmers make relatively more out of the little they have. So even if efficiency is high, wages may be very low; and sometimes the family farmer's higher economic profits per hectare do nothing to reduce his or her misery. So "small" is not necessarily "beautiful."

In many countries, the formation of the large-scale farming sector is not an expression of the efficiency of large-scale farms, but the legacy of past injustices. Although there may exist very real economies of scale for the individual producer, they are mostly "false" because usually they are the result of policies that favor larger farms over small farms (van Zyl, Binswanger, and Thirtle 1995). Under true economies of scale, marginal costs (and thus average costs) go down, and profits per hectare and the rates of return go up for each additional hectare. Such economies of scale in agriculture are limited to those crops that are highly perishable, and economies of scale exist in marketing (the banana boat) or processing (the sugar factory). Coordination between production and processing becomes critical, and the marketing or factory economies of scale spill over to the farm. In these cases, it is possible to see large plantations operated with hired labor. However, there are numerous examples where the coordination problem has been solved by contract farming with small farmers rather than by backward integration into farming.

The defining feature of family farms is not farm size per se, but rather their primary reliance on family labor instead of hired labor. What constitutes a "small" farm will vary because of differences in soil fertility, rainfall distribution, market development, technology, and the opportunity cost of capital and labor in the economy. For instance, from a profit perspective, 500 hectares of semiarid shrub can be "small" when compared with half a hectare of irrigated roses. The productive capacity controlled by the farmer matters, not size per se. Yet this increase in average farm size is not the result of economies of scale. Current U.S. agriculture still is characterized by diseconomies of scale, but average farm sizes continue to rise because of the overall increases in incomes in the U.S. economy that induce smaller owners to rent out or sell their farms if they can get higher incomes elsewhere. Rural-to-urban migration then enables the remaining farmers to earn higher incomes (Kislev and Peterson 1982; Peterson 1997).

The main reason why family-scale farms are more efficient is that their owners operate them primarily using family labor. Owners live on the farm, manage the farm themselves, and are aided by other family members who do not need a lot of supervision to work well because they care about their own property. And the owners have strong incentives to invest their savings back into their farms. Of course there are disadvantages to being small—mainly, it is more difficult to access input and output markets, financing, technical assistance, and information (especially information about new markets and technologies). However, such disadvantages can be countered if small farmers coordinate their efforts through marketing and credit cooperatives (World Bank 2005). Doing so is not easy, but it can be done. Finally, the robustness of the empirical finding of the negative farm size–productivity relationship suggests that the disadvantages to family farmers usually are more than offset by the advantages in terms of labor incentives.

Help for Land Markets

If small farmers are so efficient, why doesn't the market automatically transfer the land from inefficient to efficient users? Why don't small farmers go onto the land market and outbid large farmers for land—especially if large farmers don't use all of their land?

Land markets need help because they cannot be counted on alone to redistribute land from large to small farmers. In countries with highly unequal land distributions, land markets often need more than "help"—they need serious reform because, by historical design, they place severe restrictions on land sales to poor people.

As discussed in chapter 12, one way to help the land market is to impose a land tax. In practice, however, only a few countries use this mechanism. For instance, a land tax has existed in Brazil for a long time, but has been fully enforced only recently. It also has been introduced in Namibia, is proposed for

South Africa, and recently was raised in Malawi. The ideal land tax would tax the potential agricultural profit of a particular piece of unimproved or unused land. Unlike a property tax, a land tax would not tax the value of investments on the land or the value of the farmhouse erected on the land. Taxing investment in agriculture is probably the last thing a government should want to do in the context of a land reform program. A land tax supportive of land reform could be flat or progressive, and would exempt small farmers from making significant tax payments. Finally, the land tax revenue can be either a source of local government revenues (as proposed for South Africa) or a source of financing for land redistribution (as currently is true in Namibia).

In other instances, by historical design, land markets place severe restrictions on land sales to the poor. For instance, it may be too expensive or even impossible to break up large farms into family farms. This is because in many countries, including all settler economies of eastern and southern Africa, subdivision restrictions were imposed by the colonial powers to prevent the sale of small parcels of land to "native" people. In many countries those restrictions remain in place and make it difficult to break large farms into small farms. Notably, the restrictions impose substantial transaction costs on the beneficiaries, who need to organize themselves and pool their resources to purchase large farms. In South Africa, for instance, removing these restrictions is a longstanding and widely agreed recommendation that still has not been implemented (see chapters 6 and 7).

The cost of acquiring agricultural land in the market often is too high for the poor because investors value the land for reasons other than farming—as insurance, as an investment,[7] as a hedge against inflation,[8] as a tax shelter, or as a means by which to gain access to subsidized credit[9] or public infrastructure such as irrigation works. When subsidies in input and output markets are biased toward large farmers, they drive up the land price, too.[10] Many countries also exempt agricultural income from income tax; and even where there is no general exemption, agricultural income actually is subject to lower tax rates. These preferences will be capitalized partly or fully into land values. Thus, before any land redistribution program is introduced, the implicit and explicit distortions that drive land prices above the capitalized value of agricultural profits need to be eliminated. Governments need to intervene to boost the purchasing power of the poor and eliminate incentives for the wealthy to hold land for nonagricultural purposes.

Even when the cost of acquiring land is low, the poor rarely have the resources to acquire it in the market and often have difficulty gaining access to credit. Ironically, the political power of large landowners generally enables them to secure more credit than the poor can secure, making matters in the land market even worse. Governments need to intervene to counter this bias. To do that, they can provide poor farmers with targeted grants or subsidized loans to purchase land. Although that intervention will help poor farmers access land more easily, the downside is that purchase subsidies also may have a price-raising effect if given on a substantial scale. In Malawi, for example, land prices in the districts in which the program is operating have risen moderately since the program began (see chapter 14).

Small farmers who have land also may lose their land. In the context of imperfect markets for credit and insurance—a context typical of rural areas—droughts and other adverse shocks may force poor farmers to sell production assets (such as draft animals or land), creating even more poverty (see chapter 2). Rental markets for land could overcome some of these problems, but they rarely lead to redistribution of land access from large to small farmers in countries where there is a highly unequal distribution of land to start with (Deininger, Castagnini, and González 2004). Also, legal attempts to improve the weak economic bargaining position of the landless in land rental markets often have failed because tenants were evicted preemptively. In many cases, legislation intended to strengthen the rights of tenants has been counterproductive. Before the laws are passed, landowners evict their tenants and occupiers to preempt them from acquiring stronger rights. When the laws are in place, landowners exploit their lax enforcement. India has a long history of legally strengthening the rights of tenants; but in the end, the legislation largely has failed. Only in West Bengal was there no option for tenant eviction: tenant rights were transformed into permanent rights to use the land at a low rental rate, and those rights were documented systematically. This tenancy reform resulted in a significant redistribution of income (see chapter 9). In South Africa, laws were passed in the mid-1990s to prevent illegal evictions and confer certain land property rights on farmworkers. The laws' impact is still unknown, but only a few cases actually have been settled under those laws. The laws also have done little to stem the decline of farm employment on South Africa's commercial farms and may have contributed to preemptive evictions by landowners (see chapters 6 and 7).

HOW TO REDISTRIBUTE AGRICULTURAL LAND: EMERGING PRINCIPLES

The previous section summarized the case for land redistribution. This section focuses on the practicalities of redistribution based on wide international experience in redistributive land reform and on the case studies presented in this book. It summarizes the various debates on the "how" of land redistribution.

Building Consensus, Drafting a Policy, and Passing Laws

The objectives of land redistribution may differ vastly according to the groups that advocate it (see box 1.2). A first logical step in planning land redistribution is to try to define the objective(s) for which it is being sought.

Governments typically organize a national debate about land redistribution objectives, their relative weight, and the consequences of targeting programs to

Box 1.2 Defining the Objectives of the Redistribution

Chapter 13 of this volume identifies and discusses four broad land redistribution objectives: social, economic, political, and environmental.

1. Advocates of *social land reform* expect little overall economic gain from the reform, but see it as a way to provide some security and subsistence to a large unemployed rural labor force. To them, the main thrust of agricultural development is to come from large-scale farms and the supporting agro-industrial sectors. Social land reform advocates target rapid and direct impact on poverty and are eager to achieve social justice. They stress objectives such as decongestion of overpopulated communal areas; resettlement of squatters, destitute people, and the landless; and the associated reduction of hunger and extreme poverty (for example, in Brazil, Malawi, South Africa, and Zimbabwe).
2. Advocates of *economic land reform* stress the productive superiority of family farms; and they expect the land reform to make a significant contribution not only to agricultural production, but also to rural employment, self-employment, and poverty reduction. Economic land reform includes the specific objectives of promoting a more equitable distribution of land, thereby increasing the productivity of agriculture; and as a consequence, creating employment and self-employment and reducing rural poverty substantially (for example, in Brazil, China, India, the Philippines, South Africa, and Zimbabwe). Within this perspective, one also can find advocates for allocating land to "competent farmers" who could become small-scale, capitalist, commercial farmers (for example, in Brazil, Kenya, South Africa, and Zimbabwe).
3. Advocates of *political land reform* appreciate, for instance, the dissolution of feudal relationships of production and excessively concentrated and exploitative elite power structures. Specific objectives of political land reform include the creation of political stability and peace. In postconflict situations, this would suggest a focus on the provision of land to war veterans and other ex-combatants, and to people displaced by war (such as in Zimbabwe). In postcolonial situations, the political objectives also could include correcting the racial imbalance in land ownership (for example, in Algeria and in east and southern Africa) and empowering members of the new elite (Kenya and Zimbabwe).
4. Advocates of *environmental land reform* seek the environmentally sustainable management of land, forests, and wildlife resources by turning over their ownership and management to defined communities.

specific groups. Unless significant consensus is reached on those objectives, practice shows that lack of clarity on the goals later reemerges in the design of the land redistribution program. Design questions then often will turn into renewed dissention and debates about the underlying objectives rather than about the best way to achieve agreed objectives.

Chapter 13 describes processes that can be used in building consensus and the issues that should be resolved and negotiated between different stakeholders. Such processes can be state led (Namibia, South Africa, and Tanzania) under the pressure of land invasions and other social movements (Brazil, Malawi, the Philippines), initiated by landowners trying to forestall outcomes in which they lose all control, or facilitated by donors. These processes often involve the setting up of technical working groups or commissions to engage in fact finding and to produce initial recommendations. Their discussions inform the land redistribution policy and may touch on such issues as target groups for redistribution, beneficiary selection processes, restitution, land acquisition mechanisms, land-use planning, postsettlement support, and land tenure security.

When formulated, these policies then are translated into new laws. Such processes can be very lengthy, unless there is continued pressure either from the top of government or from landless-worker movements and their allies. For example, the land invasions of the early 1990s in Malawi led to the setting up of the Land Commission, and a land policy was produced and adopted within about five years. A land law was drafted a long while ago, but has not been approved. Such consensus-building efforts also can fail to produce laws that find favor with the legislature, as in the case of the proposed late-1990s land law in Zambia, or the Zimbabwe land law proposed after the conclusion of the land commission headed by Mandi Rukuni in the early 1990s. Finally, even when a legal framework is adopted, it may not be implemented properly, usually because resources for putting in place the structures and programs for implementation are absent or inadequate (Mozambique, Tanzania, Uganda); or laws and programs may be implemented slowly and poorly because of limited enforcement capacity or limited effective implementation systems (South Africa).

Why is the process from consensus building to implementation often so slow? The factors discussed at the beginning of this chapter play an important role: (1) the case for land redistribution is strong but based on evidence that is counterintuitive, (2) there is no agreement among the specialists on how to redistribute land, and (3) there is a lack of rigorous empirical evidence on the impact of land reform. The opposition of certain interest groups (such as large-scale farmers) and the ability of affected stakeholders to challenge new laws in court also slow down the process. Finally, there may not be enough political pressure to get the job done. In Malawi, for example, after a spate of land invasions in the early 1990s scared the government into moving forward, the invasions failed to develop into a strong landless-labor movement, and the political pressure on the government to continue its efforts virtually disappeared.

Selecting the Beneficiaries

The characteristics of the targeted beneficiaries typically come straight from the objectives of the redistribution, and they directly influence the main features of the schemes. Explicit poverty targeting has been rare (see chapter 14). More often, several objectives can be pursued at the same time, which results in defining several target groups (see chapters 3, 5, 10, and 11).

Requiring a contribution helps self-select people who actually are willing and able to run a farm. Brazil, Guatemala, Honduras, Malawi, South Africa, and many other countries ask beneficiaries to contribute in cash, in kind, or by loan. But such a request should be done within limits so as not to exclude the poor or saddle new farmers with too much debt (see chapter 3). Allowing for relatively small in-kind contributions ensures that the scheme is accessible to the poor (see chapters 6, 7, 10, 11, and 14). Governments also can ask beneficiaries to contribute implicitly to the costs of land redistribution by providing them with no or very limited postsettlement support. At the same time, the expected contribution should not exceed a certain proportion of beneficiaries' assets; otherwise, they certainly will experience difficulties ruining their farms (see chapter 5).

Schemes that provide very limited benefits are unattractive to better-off beneficiaries (see chapters 6, 7, and 14). The South African Land Redistribution for Agricultural Development program uses a sliding grant scale in which the smallest grants require no cash contribution, and larger grants require progressively larger investments by the beneficiaries. As a consequence, the program can serve the needs of both poor and nonpoor beneficiaries (see chapters 6 and 7). When beneficiaries are provided with loans, the amount lent should not exceed a certain proportion of their assets. Whereas this limit depends on the profitability and riskiness of the particular farming system adopted, a reasonably robust rule of thumb is that the loan should stay below about 30 percent of the value of assets (the so-called 30 percent debt-equity ratio).

Allowing beneficiaries to apply in groups also may enable the poor to acquire larger undivided farms, and it reduces the administrative and transaction costs (see chapter 14). By contrast, a scheme that does not allow the formation of beneficiary groups is likely to reach richer individuals (see chapter 3). Some schemes offer both options (see chapters 6, 7, 10, and 11).

Regardless of the features of the schemes, beneficiaries' eligibility for land redistribution always should be subject to screening and verification. If these mechanisms are not transparent, schemes implemented in a context of poor governance and corruption may miss the targeted individuals and/or benefit influential people instead (see chapters 3 and 5). Likewise, if there is strong pressure from social movements, the beneficiary selection process may be influenced by those political forces, and the programs may benefit mainly people from particular ethnic groups (see chapter 3) or members of the rural organizations involved (see chapters 10 and 11).

Defining the Classes of Land to Be Redistributed

As important as the issue of who should get the land is the issue of what land should be targeted for redistribution. When land is redistributed via expropriation, determining which properties are subject to expropriation is politically sensitive and hotly contested between the landless and the large farm lobbies. Law often defines the characteristics of the properties to be expropriated. These characteristics vary from country to country, and are related closely to the objectives and target groups of the reform and to whether rights-based or broader entitlements are being used (see box 1.3). A ceiling capping the amount of land one can own often is defined by law, and all agricultural land above the ceiling that is rented out or has been occupied

Box 1.3 Land Redistribution: Rights-Based and Broader Entitlement Approaches

There are two general approaches to land redistribution: rights-based and broader entitlement. Under the rights-based approach, beneficiaries already have access to land or had it at one time. Intervening through land redistribution is a way to reinstate those rights. Under the broader entitlement approach, beneficiaries have no land, or not enough land, and intervening often means taking land from "the land rich" and redistributing it to those people who need it.

STRENGTHENING TENANTS' AND USERS' RIGHTS

The most common form of rights-based land reform is transferring land rights to sitting tenants or to peaceful, long-term land users with precarious rights, as in the French and Russian revolutions. Such reforms were carried out more recently in East Asia and India under the slogan "Land to the Tillers" (see chapter 9). South Africa also has chosen to protect the rights of permanent farmworkers and "labor tenants" (that is, workers who toil in exchange for the right to housing,[1] a plot of land to farm, and/or grazing rights on the owners' farms; they receive no wages or a small wage). Before the modernization of agriculture, this form of "labor contract" had been common all over the world, but had been made illegal via various means in many countries (see chapter 2).

RESTITUTING LAND RIGHTS

Rights-based approaches also have been common where "first nations" have been dispossessed by white settlers. Australia, Canada, New Zealand, South Africa, and the United States have introduced land restitution schemes either to restitute property or to provide fair compensation to individuals or communities unfairly dispossessed. Of the countries discussed in this book, restitution of land is practiced only in South Africa, where the last

(*continued*)

Box 1.3 (Continued)

removals of black villages and townships took place as late as the early 1980s[2] (see chapters 6 and 7). In the former Soviet Union, as well as in almost all of central and eastern Europe, the issue of land restitution emerged in the early 1990s after the collapse of communism and the abandonment of collective farming.[3]

REDISTRIBUTING LAND TO THOSE WHO NEED IT

Broader entitlement approaches commonly are used to redistribute land to the landless and the land poor, as well as to wealthier individuals willing to venture into the farming sector. Such programs have been introduced in many countries, including Brazil, Kenya, Malawi, Namibia, the Philippines, South Africa, and Zimbabwe. In some countries (Brazil and Zimbabwe, for instance), programs targeting different groups are run in parallel. In other countries (such as South Africa), a single program is designed to benefit various groups.

NOTES

1. In a number of cases in South Africa, many generations would have worked the farms, or the current generation of workers would have been doing so for many years. Under the Labor Tenants Act (1996) and the Extension of Security of Tenure Act (1997), those workers are entitled to stay on the farm and acquire a portion of it. In addition, workers are protected against unfair eviction under the Prevention of Illegal Eviction Act (1999). However, all these acts have been very poorly enforced. Ironically, land redistribution itself can lead to the eviction of farmworkers. Zimbabwe, for example, provided no special protection to former workers under its Fast Track Land Redistribution, and that resulted in widespread loss of employment and destitution.
2. In Zimbabwe between 1965 and 1970, the colonial government carried out what may be considered the final land redistribution in favor of the white settlers. Still, like Namibia, Zimbabwe has opted not to include a restitution path in its land reform program. These differences may result from the fact that many of the anti-apartheid civil society groups and freedom fighters in South Africa had been deeply involved in litigation against forced resettlements and cared deeply about the people who had been removed.
3. Albania and the Commonwealth of Independent States countries opted for distributing land to the workers. Most countries in central and eastern Europe and the Baltic States took the restitution route, whereas Hungary and Romania used a mixed strategy (Lerman, Csaki, and Feder 2002).

peacefully for a long time is targeted for redistribution (Brazil, Colombia, India, the Philippines). Brazilian and Colombian programs also focus on underused or poorly used land, partly because land is abundant and much of it is underutilized. In Kenya and Zimbabwe, land redistribution focused on white-owned farms and exempted black owners from expropriation.

When land is acquired via market-assisted mechanisms, targeted properties are those available for sale. However, some properties may be judged inappropriate for resettlement—such as land that is not suitable for agriculture—and thus will be excluded automatically. In Malawi, properties that are encroached on cannot be acquired because it would encourage further encroachment and make it very difficult for alternative beneficiaries fully to possess the land they acquire. Similarly, land with unclear ownership title cannot be acquired because unresolved ownership issues could result in beneficiaries later losing their new land. Therefore, issues of unclear ownership first should be sorted out by the current conflicting claimants or via court litigation.

In Brazil, an expropriation program and a market-assisted program coexist. The former program focuses on underused land and works with support from the Landless Movement. In principle, the latter program can acquire both used and underused land, and it works primarily in tandem with the National Confederation of Agricultural Workers (CONTAG). To avoid confusion and potential conflict among different beneficiary groups and their supporters, it was decided that under the market-assisted program, land that is eligible for expropriation would not be acquired. In the Philippines, where expropriation and market-assisted programs also coexist, there are no such provisions.

Identifying Specific Land

Despite the intentions of many land reform programs to target particular types of land, identification of land for redistribution often falls to the beneficiaries.

When land is expropriated, governments have to screen every existing property and, on the basis of eligibility criteria, establish a list of properties potentially subject to expropriation. Compiling such a list often requires information that is not readily available. Legal and fiscal land records may be of limited use because they are outdated and incomplete. Therefore, compiling such lists can be a painful exercise (see chapter 5). More often, beneficiaries invade land that they perceive to be eligible for redistribution, or squat on its boundaries. This often is done with the assistance of other social actors, such as labor or landless-workers' unions (see chapters 8, 10, and 11) or war veterans and traditional chiefs (see chapter 5).

When land is transferred via market mechanisms, the land theoretically is identified by the beneficiaries themselves. In practice, the state or specific stakeholders gather information about land available for sale. Governments also can impose their right of first refusal, meaning that any landowner willing to sell his or her property must offer it to the government first. This enables the government to screen every property made available for sale and, if the land is judged suitable for the program, acquire it. If the state has no interest in the property, it can be sold to anybody else. This was the system in place in Zimbabwe under its "willing seller–willing buyer" (WSWB) approach during the 1980s and early 1990s (see chapter 5).

Acquiring Land

There are several approaches to acquiring land. Much of the controversy around land redistribution concerns the "optimum" mechanisms for land acquisition because the cost of acquiring land represents a significant share of the total cost of a land redistribution program.

One acquisition mechanism is outright confiscation or seizure of land. This occurred in the revolutionary land reforms of France, Russia, Eastern Europe, China, Cuba, and other communist countries. Only when land is acquired by confiscation is there no or little direct cost of land acquisition—but confiscation has many other undesirable consequences, such as reduced investor confidence and an international backlash. These consequences easily can lead to a devaluation of the currency, imposing the costs of land reform on the entire nation. History shows that governments have mainly two options to manage land reform without disrupting the economy and the political system: (1) expropriate the required stock of land with compensation or (2) acquire the land on a WSWB basis. In practice, these two options often coexist in the same country (see chapters 5, 6, 7, 10, and 11).

Willing Seller–Willing Buyer Approaches

Under the WSWB principle, land typically is acquired from landowners willing to sell their property by a willing buyer (usually the state), and then redistributed to groups or individuals.[11] The key to WSWB is that the land transfer is a voluntary transaction. This approach was applied in the Kenyan land reform of the 1960s and 1970s, a series of resettlement schemes to transfer land from European settlers to Africans, either landless people, smallholders, or prosperous farmers (see chapter 3). In 1980, the WSWB principle was agreed to for Zimbabwe during the Lancaster House negotiations. Since then, and until 2000 and the inception of the Fast Track Land Redistribution Program in Zimbabwe, WSWB was the predominant land acquisition principle in the Zimbabwean redistribution programs.

In many WSWB programs, the buyer of the land was the state (see chapter 3). In some cases, the state enacted laws that gave it the right of first refusal to make it easier to acquire the land needed for a land reform program (see chapter 5). But in a number of recent programs, the buyers were the beneficiaries themselves (see chapters 4, 10, and 11). In such cases, the land passes directly from the previous owner to the new owner without ever becoming state property, thus saving significant transaction costs and avoiding delays. The idea behind this approach is to simplify the process. It also aims to bring it more in line with what the beneficiaries really want because some may want a farm close to where they currently live, others may want a farm much closer to an urban center; some may want a large farm suitable for livestock production, others may want a small plot close to town for irrigated vegetable production. This variant of the WSWB approach is implemented under programs in Brazil, Malawi, India, the Philippines, and South Africa (all discussed in this volume). It also has been implemented in Mexico and various Central American countries. Most of these programs are funded partly by the World Bank.

In Zimbabwe, 3.5 million hectares were transferred from willing sellers to willing buyers between 1980 and 1998. A significant amount of land also was redistributed in South Africa, where 2,299,000 hectares were transferred between 1994 and 2007. In Brazil, although about 85 percent of the agricultural land redistributed is expropriated, 1,822,400 hectares were transferred on a voluntary basis between 1997 and 2003.

There is now enough evidence to show that the WSWB approach can be effective, but several issues have given rise to a lot of opposition to this approach:

1. Many people wonder how such a method can target poor individuals or communities who neither have the required capital nor are creditworthy enough to acquire loans. But those people are precisely the ones most in need of land. To deal with this issue, communities, families, or groups of families in these programs always receive a grant from the state and sometimes also get a subsidized loan from a development bank to buy and develop their own farms. The grants and loans, together with their own contributions in cash and/or in kind, normally (except in South Africa) are large enough to cover all the costs of farm development, not only land acquisition. In this way poor people are provided with the purchasing power they lack to enter the market (see chapters 6, 7, 8, 10, 11, and 14).
2. Even if poor individuals or communities are helped and do enter the market, some people argue that they inevitably would be at a disadvantage in bargaining with wealthy, well-informed, and well-connected landowners.To counter the information and power disadvantage of poor individuals or communities in practice, program managers, nongovernmental organizations, and farmworkers and tenants unions (such as CONTAG in Brazil) help identify, appraise, and negotiate the land purchases. They also may assist in planning the farm development (see chapters 10 and 11).
3. Some people have expressed a genuine concern that it is impossible under this approach to acquire especially desirable farms that owners are unwilling to sell. It is true that there is no direct way under the WSWB approach to acquire specific parcels of land from owners who do not want to sell them. But there are indirect ways to influence the behavior of landowners who normally would be unwilling to sell their property, including the

imposition of a land tax (discussed previously). In the end, an active and liquid land market in which sellers compete for buyers is the best way to ensure that beneficiaries can achieve their aspirations by acquiring another farm offered at a reasonable price. But if an especially desirable piece of land has to be purchased, the government will have to use negotiation under the threat of expropriation, or actual expropriation, to acquire that parcel.

Compulsory Acquisition or Expropriation

Land expropriation is the compulsory acquisition of a private property by the state, according to the strictures of the law. Governments always have a provision for land expropriation in case they need to make land available for the public interest (such as to create major public infrastructure). Every country has its own framework that reflects its history and culture. In Brazil, the Philippines, South Africa, and Zimbabwe, land reform is defined as a public purpose for expropriation. Land expropriation is a lawful process and should be used in a fair and transparent manner. That implies a clear definition of the notion of public interest, the payment of "just compensation" to the property owner, and the right of the owner to contest the level of compensation in court.

When landowners are unwilling to cede their property—and they often are unwilling—they use the judicial system to delay the expropriation process, if not to escape it altogether. Because expropriation is based on due process—an important principle of justice—the resulting litigations increase the administrative costs of land reform. By its very nature, the legal process is lengthy and costly, adding to the costs of compensation. "Just compensation," moreover, almost invariably is interpreted by courts as at least as high as the prevailing market price. Courts all over the world tend to use the market price of land as a guide in awarding compensation, and then they add something on top of it. As the experiences of Brazil and Zimbabwe show, there are ways to reduce the delays and costs. Nevertheless, expropriation in practice invariably leads to more costly land acquisition than does acquisition in the market (see box 1.4).

In Zimbabwe the early postindependence land redistribution program relied almost entirely on the WSWB principle. After a promising start in the early 1980s, the number of land offers dropped significantly, and land acquisition stalled. In the early 1990s, the government decided to use expropriation to accelerate the pace of land redistribution. However, the legal requirements of fairness, timeliness, and transparency in land acquisition made it cumbersome and expensive. By the end of the decade, 624 of the 1,471 farms listed for expropriation had been delisted, and 500 were struck off by the administrative court. In 2000, the government amended the constitution to reduce the amount of compensation to land improvement only. In 2001, it reduced the scope of judicial review by removing landowners' right to contest the expropriation order. In 2005, land was nationalized.

Box 1.4 The Cost of Land Acquisition

In South Africa, agricultural land prices on the open market approximately doubled between 1994 and 2005. During the same period, the prices paid under the redistribution program (that uses the market-assisted or community-driven land purchase approach) increased accordingly—but in every year except 1996 they were about a third lower than market prices. Some researchers suggest that land of less-than-average quality was purchased under this program, and that may explain the discrepancy.

Under restitution, however, where the state is negotiating for the purchase of parcels of land that it must buy (or expropriate), prices for land have skyrocketed, reaching as high as 2.5 times the price on the general market. It is likely that, over time, more complex and more productive farms were acquired; but the data also suggest that the sellers in those transactions have learned to exploit the state's need to acquire their land, and they have used the threat of protracted litigation to push the state to offer ever-increasing prices.

Chapter 10 argues that by the end of 2003, Cedula da Terra (the market-assisted, community-driven program) had acquired land and settled 15,200 beneficiaries for about $3,000 per family. That amount rose to $3,600 in 2006 under its successor, the Crédito Fundiário program. However, when land is expropriated or acquired through state-led negotiations, the average cost per family reaches $16,622.

Those data have led to a tense discussion (not yet resolved) about the merits of beneficiaries directly acquiring land on the market. Some advocates still oppose the Crédito Fundiário program, arguing that it promotes the land market, despite the fact that Brazil has had land markets for a long time. Nevertheless, market acquisition for land reform in Brazil has cost less than a fourth of land acquisition by expropriation or negotiation under the threat of expropriation. Again, that does not mean that the use of expropriation is not necessary in some circumstances. It simply suggests that direct acquisition of land in the market by beneficiaries is more cost effective.

With about 9 million hectares acquired since 2000, Zimbabwe certainly has "fast-tracked" land acquisition. However, many farmers whose land has been expropriated consider the compensation so low as to be akin to confiscation, while the restrictions on the right to legal recourse for landowners and the politicization of the land redistribution process have attracted severe criticism. The program has shocked anyone wishing to invest in the country, including Zimbabweans. It has led to disinvestment, devaluation of the currency, and economic contraction. Furthermore, several presidential commissions have found that the expropriation and allocation of land and other capital often were carried out poorly, leading to massive asset stripping. The program has created new wrongs and legal complications to be resolved in the future, thus prolonging the uncertainty around the land issue (see chapter 5).

Unlike the Zimbabwean situation, much more massive expropriation in Brazil created no serious domestic political conflict, and it promtped no conflict with foreign investors, no capital flight, and no asset stripping. Between 2002 and 2006, Brazil expropriated 32 million hectares for the purpose of land reform—an area equal to approximately 82 percent of the land mass of Zimbabwe (more than three times the area expropriated under Zimbabwe's Fast Track Land Redistribution between those years), or 14 times the amount of land redistributed in South Africa from 1994 onward. Brazil streamlined its expropriation legislation, and it was willing and able to pay generously for the land it acquired. Between 2002 and 2006, Brazil's federal government invested almost $2 billion to promote land reform, and there are realistic expectations that at least the same amount will be invested between 2006 and 2010.

It took a long time for Brazil to get to the point where land could be acquired in large amounts without adverse political fallout. Prior to 1964, the government was required to pay cash for land. That requirement, combined with poor political will, limited land reform. In 1964 the federal constitution was amended to require that compensation be paid in long-term public bonds, and landowners lost the right to contest the act of expropriation itself (although they kept the right to contest the level of compensation). Nonetheless, it was almost 30 years before Brazil garnered the political will to implement land reform at scale and before it finished streamlining the expropriation process.

This progress probably would not have been possible without the strong and constant pressure exerted by social movements (see box 1.5). Almost

Box 1.5 The Role of Social Movements and Civil Society

Little in the way of land redistribution has ever happened without strong peasant discontent and revolts. Thousands of such peasant rebellions have happened over the course of history, and many have been the subjects of scholarly research. The literature demonstrates that peasant revolts resulted in significant changes in extractive and repressive policies and practices only when they were carried out in association with—and with organizational help from—outside allies (often allies of urban origin, such as in the French, Russian, and Chinese revolutions). The literature also shows that the peasant gains achieved through successful revolution can be eroded subsequently by inappropriate policies, such as collectivization in communist revolutions or the lack of postreform or settlement support that is so characteristic of the land reforms done in the hacienda systems (Binswanger, Deininger, and Feder 1995).

The table in the annex is an attempt to summarize the nature and role of peasant movements, their outside supporters, and the relative focus on land of a number of historical and contemporary land reform episodes

(*continued*)

Box 1.5 (Continued)

(most of which are discussed in greater detail in this book). Only some of the historical events reviewed led to significant, countrywide redistribution of land, but peasant revolts, uprisings, and land invasions were major features of each historical event (except in South Africa). Although outsiders played a very important role in all cases, the coalition of outsiders and peasants did not always focus on land as the primary issue of the struggle. The patterns suggest that where peasant initiative was poor (South Africa), where peasants lacked support from outsiders (Malawi), and where coalitions did not focus sharply on land (China and Russia), either the subsequent redistributions were modest or the welfare gains eventually were eroded.

90 percent of expropriation processes are initiated by landless families themselves after they have invaded private land. In Brazil today, if there is no judicial contest, a new settlement may be formed in no more than a year. However, half of the landowners in Brazil go to court to contest the valuation of the farm, and this makes the process much more costly. In addition, the organized land invasions have led to organized landowner resistance. Violent conflict on a significant scale has been the result (see chapters 10 and 11).

Several other countries have attempted to use land expropriation at scale for the purpose of land redistribution, but they have done so with less success than Brazil. Mexico tried to do it, but it took the government more than 70 years to redistribute 100 million hectares—or half of its agricultural area. In India, all states adopted land ceiling legislation that limited the amount of agricultural land a person or family could own. The low level of compensation that landowners received for expropriated land made the programs unpopular with landowners, and the lack of political will to enforce land ceilings enabled landowners to use gaps and loopholes in the laws to their advantage. As a result, a rather limited amount of land has been expropriated in India to date—at least for the purpose of land reform. Since its independence in 1945, India has expropriated about 2.2 million hectares of above-ceiling land (see chapter 9). In the Philippines, too, the use of expropriation has been very limited, with 289,250 hectares expropriated over the last 30 years or so. Similarly, Colombia accomplished little through this process. In South Africa since 2003, an amendment to the Restitution Act has enabled the Minister of Land Affairs to expropriate land by ministerial order, potentially increasing the rate of private land acquisition under a restitution claim. The first expropriation orders were not issued until January 2007, and the first land was acquired by expropriation in March 2007. South Africa currently is revising its expropriation law to give effect to the constitutional provision that allows land to be expropriated below market value by deducting the value of subsidies received from the state by the landowner. However, the level of compensation needs to be deemed "fair."

In practice, even where expropriation is feasible, as in Mexico, the Philippines, and many other settings, the state often prefers to negotiate a settlement rather than to use expropriation. It does this to reduce the delays and costs associated with expropriation. In the Philippines, this mechanism is called the "voluntary offer to sell," and the incentive is the upfront cash payment of a landlord's compensation increased by 5 percent with a corresponding 5 percent decrease in the bonds portion. Since 1972, the Philippines has acquired 494,133 hectares through this mechanism, or 1.7 times the amount of land expropriated over the same period of time (see chapter 8). In many cases, expropriation is used as the "stick" in these negotiations.

Indeed, it is hard to see how countries that want to acquire specific tracts of land (either under a restitution program or as part of a planned acquisition of a particularly well-suited area) can avoid using expropriation when negotiations fail to secure a reasonably priced acquisition. Apart from acquiring land for infrastructure, such cases often will include restitution, where the state must acquire a specific parcel of land or the purchase of high-quality or peri-urban land for farmers or for housing purposes. As the Brazilian example shows, the fear of adverse economic repercussions associated with the use of the expropriation instrument should not be a deterrent to its use, provided the state is using due process and is willing to pay amounts ultimately judged reasonable by the broader class of owners and the general public, if not by individual owners.

Ensuring Security of Tenure

When the land is acquired and transferred to the beneficiaries, what property rights do they receive? It usually is argued that economic efficiency is served best if the property right is of infinite duration and fully tradable. In that way, the productivity of the resource can be exploited to the fullest extent. If a particular owner is unable to extract the maximum profits from the resource, the property could be sold to someone who would do so.

In a world of perfect markets, the argument holds. When information and credit market imperfections are considered, however, it may break down. In reality, property rights in land need not always confer full "ownership," or need not necessarily be individual for all classes of land. For instance, one of the great advantages of many common property regimes is their risk insurance, or social safety net, function. In this case, community members can claim access to land for farming when necessary. In the absence of a formal social security scheme, this insurance function of common property regimes has reduced the poverty impact of many external shocks and macroeconomic crises by enabling community members to return to the land (see box 1.6).

Whether common or individual, the rights to use land and pass it on to one's heirs or to dispose of such land—even under some restrictions—need to be transparent and secure. If beneficiaries fear losing their land against their

Box 1.6 Private, Common, and No Property

There often is a lot of confusion about "private" and "common" property. Under private property, we imagine that a person can do as he or she pleases with the property. For instance, we think of private property as a tradable right that can be sold by the individual to anyone, without asking anybody else for permission to do so. We associate it with a sign that reads "Keep Out—Private Property." In other words, it has a territorial boundary that excludes others. When we think of common property, on the other hand, we imagine nontradability: either very restricted, permissible use of the asset or the tragedy of a complete free-for-all.

Those stereotypes are misleading. Everywhere in the world, what one can and cannot do with private property is regulated by things like zoning laws, building restrictions, the obligation of the owner to allow the public access for hiking or fishing, or the obligation to allow other individuals to establish a mining operation (in the event that mining rights are sold separately from other rights). Common property regimes do the same: they may ban the sale of property to outsiders (nonmembers of the community) or may require special permission from the community. Yet, common property regimes can, and often do, allow the sale of the "shares" to others, just like private property regimes. The only difference is that in the case of private property, one needs tacit or overt permission from the state, and under common property, one asks the community.

Within a common property rights regime, a community can decide to give certain rights to an individual or to maintain them as rights of the group. It may allocate to an individual a right to produce crops on a particular plot, but allocate a grazing area to a group—for instance, all families living in the community. The individual rights within a common property regime usually can be inheritable, exchangeable, rentable, and even salable, but typically only to other members of the community or to approved outsiders with permission of the group. In "cooperative" apartment buildings in the United States, the individual purchases a right to occupy and use an apartment; he or she can sell that right only to an outsider who has been approved by the cooperative board. Common property regimes therefore can provide a high degree of security of individual ownership.

Just as it is wrong to vilify common property regimes, it is equally misguided to romanticize them. "Community failure" occurs, just as does market or government failure. Common property regimes can provide important insurance functions, but they also can be used to exclude people, especially those who are politically weak or not "real" members of the community—for instance, women (especially widows) and outsiders.

Whereas many areas in the developing world fall under common property regimes, cultivation is traditionally a family affair rather than an activity done on a collective basis. Around the world, group or collective farming often has been attempted, but it now has been abandoned practically everywhere. What

(*continued*)

Box 1.6 (Continued)

is common in Africa, though, is a system under which people set aside some time to work a particular field collectively. The output of that field is used by the traditional head of the group to provide food to members of the group or to brew beer and provide food for special occasions.

"No property," or open access, occurs when communities are no longer able to define and enforce the common property rules that apply to a natural resource. The resource then becomes free for all—open access—and everybody has a rational interest in depleting it as much as they can because if they don't do it, somebody else will. Degradation of the resource is usually a foregone conclusion. Unfortunately, this situation often is wrongly referred to as "the tragedy of the commons," giving the concept of common property a bad name. That phrase, coined by Hardin (1968), should be replaced by "the tragedy of *res nullius*"—no one's property. The tragedy of the commons is not the tragedy of common property rights; it is the tragedy of open access. When communities are able to define and enforce common property rights and rules, no tragedy of the commons need occur. The Alps in modern Switzerland demonstrate that fact, having been under common property since the Middle Ages (Netting 1976).

Source: van den Brink et al. 2006.

will, they naturally will hesitate to invest in land improvements. It therefore is essential that governments provide beneficiaries with clear land rights and then enforce them. The policy consensus on property rights in land can be summarized this way:

1. Property rights are rules that govern relationships between individuals with respect to land, and they should be defined by the community or the state to which such individuals belong.
2. Property rights must be clearly defined, well understood, and accepted by those who have to abide by them—and they must be strictly enforced.
3. Property rights can be individual, common, or public, depending on the circumstances.
4. Property rights must be deemed secure.

As important as the nature of the land rights is the state's commitment to enforce them. Land rights that are subject to chronic redistribution are likely to conflict with the objective of ensuring land users' tenure security. A difficult trade-off exists between the social security benefits of periodic redistribution in favor of new landless or land-poor families and the economic benefits of ensuring appropriate investment incentives in land (see chapter 4).

Legislation that is amended often or not implemented is likely to generate uncertainties about the value of improvements made to the land. This, in turn, will have a negative impact on overall agricultural productivity. The case of Zimbabwe's Fast Track Land Redistribution applies here. During the Fast Track phase, laws were amended repeatedly to speed the land transfer. In addition, in the absence of an agreed policy and procedures, laws were not enforced consistently. The land transfer was rapid, but the government had limited control over the process. Beneficiaries of the A1 scheme (mostly poor households) received permits, and beneficiaries of the A2 scheme (commercial farmers) received "offer letters." However, these documents do not constitute immutable rights and are in the process of being validated. Now that the land transfer is complete, clarifying the land rights situation and resolving conflicts that undoubtedly will emerge will prove a daunting task. In the meantime, without legal clarity about their new rights and proper certificates enforcing them, beneficiaries might fear further redistribution or the surfacing of restitution claims. Delays in the validation campaign, and notably in the conversion of offer letters into 99-year lease contracts, will have a significant and negative effect on the confidence of the new farmers. In addition, claims will emerge for restitution of illegally occupied land (see chapter 5).

In Brazil, under the expropriation program, land is acquired by and belongs to the government agency in charge of the land reform (Instituto Nacional de Colonização e Reforma Agrária [INCRA]). INCRA provides beneficiaries with user rights, or *direitos de posse*, until they have paid back all the costs of expropriation. Only then do they receive a title in their name. In practice, titles have rarely been given, indicating that most families settled under the expropriation program have so far acquired only user rights. Under Brazil's market-assisted program, however, beneficiaries form an association and immediately get a "joint-property title" that is a full private ownership in the name of the association. When they have paid back the loans, beneficiaries are free to keep the land as it is or subdivide it among the association's members, subject to size restrictions imposed by law (see chapters 10 and 11).

In Malawi, beneficiaries of the Community-Based Rural Land Development Project receive group titles and may apply for individual titles. Like all other farmers on commercial farmland in Malawi, they do not acquire full ownership; rather, they get a 99-year lease.

In Mexico, too, landownership was allocated to communities, the so-called *ejidos*, whereas individuals obtained inheritable usufruct rights to house plots and the arable land. Since 1992, communities decide by qualified majority under what legal form they want to hold their land. They may choose a common property regime under which they can sell their house plots to anybody; allocate their arable land to households and make it fully tradable within the community, but not to outsiders; and hold their pastures and forests as undivided common property managed under common rules. They also may decide to leave the common property regime, subdivide all of the land, and make it fully tradable. In either case, the state provides full title to the house plots and arable land that is held individually. Note that in all these cases there can be collective ownership of land, but in no case has there been collective farming on the arable land.

Dispute Resolution Mechanisms

By its very nature, land redistribution can lead to conflicts, so a system should be set up to prevent and resolve them.

Programs that transfer land rights to the tenants or restitute them to the former owners inevitably result in conflicts between the claimants and the current landowners. In South Africa, about 6 million people were dispossessed under race-based laws or practices after June 19, 1913 (the enactment of the Native Land Act). At the end of Apartheid, it was evident that no reconciliation and political stability would be achieved without ensuring equitable redress to the victims of racial land dispossession. In 1994, the government introduced a land restitution law to restore specific properties or to provide fair compensation to individuals or communities unfairly dispossessed. By 2002, the year of the last validation campaign, 79,687 claims by victims of racial land dispossession had been lodged. Five years later, 74,417 of those claims had been settled. South Africa is now entering the most difficult part of the restitution process—settling the 5,270 remaining rural claims. These claims pose major difficulties, including tracing claimants, addressing boundary disputes between communities, adjudicating disputes with current landowners on issues such as land prices or the validity of the claim, and ensuring continued production if the farms are very capital and skills intensive. The claims also raise important political considerations, especially where white landowners resist restitution and the commercial agriculture lobby opposes the "loss" of prime agricultural land.

Programs that acquire land through expropriation need to address conflicts that emerge between the parties, including the state, beneficiaries, and landowners. And, irrespective of the land acquisition mechanisms, programs that resettle groups of beneficiaries need to include mechanisms to ensure the smooth integration of the settlers with the surrounding community. Conflict may arise around boundaries or the use of natural resources. As chapter 14 shows, there are ways to minimize the risk of conflict: involving the surrounding communities, verifying that they endorse the resettlement, and ensuring that they also benefit from the program. But even with the best prevention mechanisms, conflicts are likely to arise in the course of a land reform program. This often happens when groups of beneficiaries acquire communal land rights. At some point it is inevitable that group members will develop a sense of individual ownership over the plot they are tilling. Over time, they also may want to sell plots to "outsiders." In short, the social unity that characterized the settled community may break apart.

Mexico provides an example of the accumulation of conflicts, as well as their resolution. Between 1917 and 1992, Mexico redistributed more than 100 million hectares from large farms to households organized into rural communities known as *ejidos*. Members (*ejidatarios*) held land collectively, but operated their arable land individually under inheritable usufruct rights. Land transactions within and outside the *ejidos* were extremely restricted. Partly because of these restrictions, by the early 1990s *ejidos* had become synonymous with backwardness. The inadequate development of *ejido* agriculture and the increase in land-related conflicts represented a threat to the social stability in the countryside. Since the constitutional and legal reforms of 1992, the government allows *ejidatarios* to rent land to anyone and to sell it to other *ejido* members. The *ejidos* also are free to convert to private property rights upon the choice of a qualified majority of *ejidatarios*. Also since 1992, the government has provided titles to all individually used parcels of land. Most conflicts related to landownership within the *ejidos* are being solved through a system of mediation mechanisms and agrarian courts. Between 1992 and 1999, about 350,000 land conflicts were dealt with by this mediation and court system; many of the conflicts had arisen prior to 1992. More than 50 percent of the disputes were mediated outside of court. As a result, the cost of settling these conflicts has been relatively low. Of the $50 spent on average to certify each beneficiary household, 12.5 percent was used for conflict resolution. That suggests a relatively efficient resolution mechanism. The cost of resolution is particularly low if we consider the significant and positive economic impact of this certification program. Two years after certification, a significant and quantitatively large positive impact on off-farm income was observable. By contrast, there is no evidence of a positive impact on farm income. Overall, however, the benefits of the program are clearly positive (World Bank 2001).

Developing the Farms and Supporting Them

A number of successful land rights-based reforms took place when the beneficiaries were tenants who already were farming the land (see box 1.3). They had nearby housing, implements, and farming skills. The reforms consisted mainly of reassigning the property rights in land. That made the beneficiaries notably better off by significantly improving their incentives to invest and work hard. And, as the East Asian land reforms have demonstrated amply, if smallholder services and access to input and output markets are improved, the land reform becomes even more successful. Binswanger and Deininger (1997) call these the "landlord estate systems" (see chapter 2). Such reforms were implemented in Japan, Korea, and Taiwan, China; and they were introduced in India, with West Bengal as a successful case (Bardhan and Mookherjee 2007; see chapter 9). In these cases, beneficiaries again were tenants who already were farming the land.

Most other redistribution programs face a more difficult situation: new farming enterprises need to be established by new beneficiaries. That is often the case when land redistribution is undertaken in the "hacienda systems," where large farms were managed by landowners using hired labor. In the past they may have been feudal, manorial estates in which part of the land was cultivated as the owner's home farm, and part was cultivated as the family farms of the serfs, usufructuaries, or tenants. Today, these farms often have become large-scale commercial operations, using a few hired workers with a lot of machinery. They have emerged from much more labor-intensive forms through a process of modernization described in chapter 2. Land redistribution in these systems always has been much more complicated than in the landlord estate systems, mainly because redistribution implies breaking these large estates into family-scale farms and providing beneficiaries with substantial postsettlement support. For instance, in the case of highly capital-intensive farms that produce specialized crops such as wine grapes, fruits, or milk, it may be difficult to break up the farm into family-size units. Not only the land but also all the capital has to be transferred to the collective of new owners, and those owners have to find a mode of operating a single undivided enterprise with all the incentives and conflict issues associated with collective farming. Even where land *can* be subdivided into individual family units, these farms have to be developed from scratch in a process that involves the resettlement of households into new settings.

In those cases, much more than just the land will have to be funded if land redistribution is to be successful within a reasonable time frame, say 5–10 years. To speed the process of establishing successful farms, the new owners need to receive significant immediate support after they settle on the farms and long-term support structures to ensure they have access to input and output markets, credit, and advisory services (World Bank 2007).

Unfortunately, current practices and past history are full of examples where postsettlement support has been woefully inadequate: most Latin American land reforms, and those in the Philippines, South Africa, and Zimbabwe. Providing the proper support is often made difficult by the separation of agriculture and land reform into different ministries or directorates and by the lack of incentives for those institutions to provide support jointly. To achieve redistribution targets, expenditures sometimes concentrate on land transfer–related costs, leaving inadequate budgets for nonland costs. Holding a myopic view of land reform as merely land transfer is bound to create a backlash because most politicians would agree that land redistribution is intended to create sustainable and prosperous farms and farmers, not simply to transfer land. And nonland costs will have to be financed in some way that does not saddle the new owners with unsustainable debt loads.

International experience shows that in a typical market-based land reform project, the land costs are only part (30–40 percent) of the total costs of land reform (figure 1.1). The other costs, which are essential for the success of new farms, include housing, resettlement, start-up grants, inputs, tools, equipment, farm development, and training and advisory services. Also to be factored into the cost structure is the overhead cost of managing the land reform program; or, for going specialized concerns, all of their nonland capital plus the new

Figure 1.1 Land as Part of the Cost of Typical Land Reform Project, South Africa

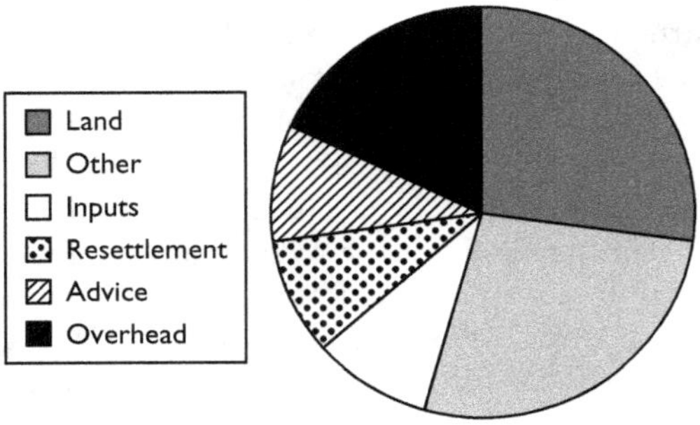

Source: van den Brink et al. 2006.

owners' housing improvements and training and advisory services. The relative importance of each slice of the cost pie varies, depending on the particular livelihood created. For instance, a rural artisan or worker who chooses to buy a homestead that has a small vegetable plot and is located close to town will need to pay more for the land slice of the project than for, say, equipment and farm development. A beneficiary who wants to acquire a farm that already has been developed substantially also will have a much bigger land cost slice than will a person who purchases a piece of undeveloped land.

In Malawi, 70 percent of the grant provided to beneficiaries goes to settlement allowance and farm settlement support. That amount does not include the resources spent on other supporting infrastructure financed separately by the government. It is not only the amount of money injected into farm development that matters; the quality of the support (particularly how responsive and accountable the support service providers are to the beneficiaries) makes a vital difference in the success of the redistribution. Chapters 6 and 7 suggest that South Africa needs to overcome important shortcomings in the way beneficiaries are assisted. Chapter 5 strongly reiterates the significance of conceptualizing land reform beyond the land transfer. Because Zimbabwe's Fast Track was implemented with virtually no funding from any donor, the government was not able to allocate adequate money to assist beneficiaries, and that left many of them incapable of producing. It is true that the state plays a fundamental role in supporting beneficiaries, but chapter 10 shows that it is not the only actor. In Brazil, social movements are extremely active in that field and provide extensive assistance to beneficiaries.

Most countries that acquire land via expropriation also leave settlement and farm planning and implementation to the responsible state agencies. Government agents subdivide the land into individual farms; lay out the roads and settlement patterns; and are in charge of infrastructure, housing, and water supply. In Malawi and in the Crédito Fundiário program in Brazil, on the other hand, the planning is done by the beneficiaries themselves, perhaps assisted by experts provided by the extension agency or by nongovernmental organizations (such as the Landless Workers Union in Brazil). The plans they prepare are screened initially by the program managers, but usually there is wide latitude left in the actual implementation. In Malawi, agricultural extension workers hired on a temporary basis now are assisting the beneficiaries in finalizing their land allocation and environmental management plans (which usually include set-asides for natural or planted forests) and they are training farmers in land conservation, integrated pest management, and production techniques. In South Africa, farm and settlement planning usually has been done by consultants or other experts—and that often has led to poorly implemented plans with little community ownership.

Monitoring and Evaluation

Finally, sound monitoring systems are necessary to identify changes in outcomes, refine programs, and plan for the mitigation of negative measures where they arise. In practice, these systems often are not developed fully at the outset of a program. They are vital, however, to inform periodic readjustments in the many implementation processes, to refine targeting, and to improve the quality of farm development. (The basic principles and practical issues that need to be considered in conducting impact evaluations are presented in chapter 15.)

Even though many redistributive land reforms have been implemented over the previous decades, there are very few reliable impact evaluations. Unfortunately, like monitoring, evaluation is often a stepchild of program implementers, as the South African and Malawi chapters in this volume reveal. When evaluations are available, the absence of a common framework for evaluating program impact makes the comparison of results between different countries extremely difficult, if not irrelevant (see chapter 8). In the absence of evaluations, arguments about objectives and implementation mechanisms often reflect ideological beliefs and assumptions rather than empirical evidence. (The need for impact evaluation is highlighted in several chapters—namely, 3, 5, 6, 7, 9, 10, and 11.) Fortunately, however, a number of impact evaluation studies currently under way in Brazil, India, Malawi, the Philippines, and South Africa should start filling the void in the near future.

CONCLUSION

From this overview of past and current experiences with land redistribution, we find a near consensus on the rationale. And although important differences of opinion on specific modalities remain, we conclude with an attempt to synthesize the lessons that have emerged from practice.

There is nearly full agreement that in countries where land distribution is skewed, redistributing land from large-scale farmers to family farmers makes sense for both political and socioeconomic reasons. It also makes sense because land markets alone cannot be counted on to transfer land between those two groups. But the objectives of land redistribution differ from county to country and according to the groups that advocate it. These objectives influence the main features of the land redistribution programs and notably the characteristics of the beneficiaries, the characteristics of the land targeted, and the type of support required to ease the land transfer and to ensure that the created farms develop and prosper. Thus, unless significant consensus is reached on these objectives, it will be very hard to design an effective land redistribution program.

Governments can transfer a fairly significant amount of land on a WSWB basis, but expropriation also plays an essential role—as a way to put pressure on landowners when negotiations fail to secure a reasonably priced acquisition or when the state must acquire a specific parcel of land. But expropriation must be a lawful process, and landowners should receive fair compensation. Also, expropriation does nothing to reduce the cost of the transfer; only outright confiscation does that. But confiscation has very adverse consequences.

Whatever the particular mix of land acquisition methods, governments need to intervene to boost the purchasing power of the poor, and eliminate the incentives for the wealthy to hold agricultural land for nonagricultural purposes. In that regard, a land tax can be used to encourage landowners to release underutilized land and to generate resources for financing the reform program.

However, much more than the land needs to be funded. In a typical land reform project, the land costs are only 30–40 percent of the total costs of land reform. Among other things, beneficiaries must be provided with significant postsettlement support. Thus, redistributing land at scale requires adequate financing; otherwise, implementation inevitably will slow down, the landowning classes will resist fiercely, and the settlers' chances of success will be undermined. Adequate financing by government can be used to leverage additional financing by beneficiaries, donors, and landowners.[12] As the experience of Brazil shows, an effective partnership with stakeholders can be built on the basis of such a commitment.

Finally, better systems to monitor and evaluate land redistribution programs must be put in place before implementation starts. Given the newness of land redistribution as a development activity, and given the importance of local context, land redistribution implementation needs to be part of a system that maximizes learning by doing.

If implemented well, a large-scale redistribution program should not create serious domestic political discord, conflict with foreign investors, capital flight, or asset stripping. Instead, land redistribution should help make property rights more secure by increasing people's perceptions that a more fair distribution has been created, and should foster peace and stability as Thomas Jefferson advocated more than two centuries ago. This book attempts to give an overview of how to bring such land reform about by summarizing the recent lessons gained from experience.

ANNEX

Table 1.A.1 Revolutions, Allies, and the Fight for Land Reform

Country	Peasant movement	Allies and organizers	Opponent	Focus of the coalition	Notable historical events	Outcome of the conflict	Land reform outcome
Brazil	Yes	Movimentos dos Sem Terra, Confederação Nacional dos Trabalhadores na Agricultura, Comissão Pastoral da Terra, other religious and social movements	Large landowners who underuse their property	Land reform (primary)	Occupation of the Fazenda Annoni (1985) and further large-scale land occupations	Constant pressure on government	Large-scale land redistribution
China	Yes	Chinese Communist Party	Ruling government (Chinese Nationalist Party)	Political reform (primary), land redistribution (secondary)	Chinese Revolution (1946–49)	Victorious	Large-scale land redistribution, followed by collectivization
France	Yes	Sans Culottes	Ruling government (absolute monarchy of Louis XVI)	Primarily political and land reform	French Revolution (1789–99)	Victorious	Large-scale land redistribution (redistribution of church land)
Kenya	Yes	Kikuyu Central Association, The Forty Group	Ruling government (British colonial power)	Primarily land and political reform	Mau Mau Revolt (1952–60)	Movement defeated	Limited land redistribution

(*continued*)

Table 1.A.1 (Continued)

Country	Peasant movement	Allies and organizers	Opponent	Focus of the coalition	Notable historical events	Outcome of the conflict	Land reform outcome
Malawi	Yes	None	Not clearly defined	No peasant allies collation	Small-scale invasions (1992–93)	Limited pressure on government	Limited land redistribution
Mexico	Yes	Villistas (led by Pancho Villa), Liberation Army of the South (led by Emiliano Zapata), Francisco I. Madero	Ruling governments (Díaz government and Huerta dictatorial regime)	Primarily political and land reform	Mexican Revolution (1910–20)	Victorious	Large-scale land reform
Philippines	Yes	Numerous militant peasant organizations (unified under the Peasant Movement of the Philippines in 1985), United Nationalists Democratic Organizations	Ruling government (Marcos administration)	Primarily political and land reform	Epifanio de los Santos uprising (1986)	Victorious	Large-scale land redistribution

Russia	Yes	Communist Party of the Soviet Union	Ruling government (autocracy of Czar Nicholas II)	Political reform (primary), land redistribution (secondary)	Russian Revolution (1917)	Victorious	Large-scale land redistribution, followed by collectivization
South Africa	No	Civil society organizations	Ruling government (apartheid)	Primarily land and political reform	Anti-apartheid fights against eviction	Constantly repressed	Large-scale land redistribution
South Africa	No	Landless People's Movement	Not clearly defined	Land reform (primary)	"No Land, no Vote" campaign (2004)	Limited pressure on government	No visible outcome
Zimbabwe	Yes	Zimbabwe African National Union, Zimbabwe African People's Union	Ruling government (Ian Smith administration)	Land reform (primary), political reform (primary)	War of Liberation (1970s)	Victorious	Large-scale land redistribution
Zimbabwe	Yes	Zimbabwe National Liberation War Veterans Association, traditional leaders	White commercial farmers	Land reform	Large-scale land invasion (2000)	Victorious	Large-scale land redistribution

NOTES

1. Recent summaries of the consensus and the contrasting views can be found in Akram-Lodhi, Borras, and Kay 2007; Bruce et al. 2006; Deininger 2003; de Janvry et al. 2001; and Moyo and Yeros 2005.
2. Michael Lipton (2009) provides more information about the history of land reforms and explains why future land reforms are likely and desirable.
3. This section is drawn from van den Brink et al. (2006) and van den Brink, Thomas, and Binswanger (2007).
4. Comparable countries were Colombia, Costa Rica, El Salvador, and Guatemala; Indonesia, the Philippines, and Thailand; states within India; and North America and South America.
5. A billion is 1,000 millions.
6. It is important to understand that the size of small farms changes, depending on the type of crop, the quality of land, the degree of mechanization, and such associated factors as marketing and credit. Thus, it is preferable to define small farmers as those who operate their farms mainly using family labor and who employ capital and machinery that they can afford or hire in rental markets.
7. With populations growing and urban demand for land increasing, the price of land is expected to appreciate, and some of this real appreciation is capitalized into the current land price.
8. In periods of macroeconomic instability, nonagricultural investors may use land as an asset to hedge against inflation, so an inflation premium is incorporated into the real land price.
9. Large owners have a transaction cost advantage in securing credit. Where, in addition, there are credit subsidies, they tend to be capitalized into land values, as shown by Feder and associates (1988), and by Brandão and de Rezende (1992).
10. For an analysis of this land price wedge in South Africa, see van Schalkwyk and van Zyl (1996).
11. Note that not all cases of restitution, even if at negotiated prices, fall under the WSWB principle. Under restitution, beneficiaries have the right to return to the specific land that was taken from them. However, the seller is most likely not a willing seller because he or she normally would not have parted with the land in the absence of the claim. And the government is not a willing buyer because it is required by the law to purchase the specific piece of land. Negotiated agreement on the price does not turn that transaction into a voluntary one for either party. The same applies to all processes in which the government must acquire a specific parcel of land for any public purpose, rather than being free to choose among different parcels of land.
12. After the end of the Cold War, many donors professed willingness to finance land reform programs, but few have done so. The World Bank is an exception, currently funding programs in Brazil, Guatemala, India, Malawi, and the Philippines. Until recently, most donors, including the World Bank, would not pay for the land, but only for the other costs. The Bank has changed that policy, and India and Malawi are among the first countries in which land actually is financed.

REFERENCES

Acemoglu, Daron, Simon Johnson, and James A. Robinson. 2001. "The Colonial Origins of Comparative Development: An Empirical Investigation." *American Economic Review* 91 (5): 1369–401.

———. 2002. "Reversal of Fortune: Geography and Institutions in the Making of the Modern World Income Distribution." *Quarterly Journal of Economics* 117 (4): 659–94.

Aghion, Philippe, Eve Caroli, and Cecilia García-Peñalosa. 1999. "Inequality and Economic Growth: The Perspective of the New Growth Theories." *Journal of Economic Literature* 37 (4): 1615–60.

Akram-Lodhi, A. Haroon, Saturnino M. Borras Jr., and Cristóbal Kay, eds. 2007. *Land, Poverty, and Livelihoods in an Era of Globalization: Perspectives from Developing and Transition Countries.* Abingdon, U.K.: Routledge.

Bardhan, Pranab, and Dilip Mookherjee. 2007. "Land Reform and Farm Productivity in West Bengal." Working Paper 314. Stanford University, Stanford, CA.

Binswanger, Hans P., and Klaus Deininger. 1997. "Explaining Agricultural and Agrarian Policies in Developing Countries." *Journal of Economic Literature* 35 (4): 1958–2005.

Binswanger, Hans P., Klaus Deininger, and Gershon Feder. 1995. "Power, Distortions, Revolt and Reform in Agricultural Land Relations." In *Handbook of Development Economics,* Volume 3B, ed. Jere Behrman and T. N. Srinivasan, 2659–772. Amsterdam, The Netherlands: Elsevier.

Brandão, A. S. P., and G. C. de Rezende. 1989. "Land Prices and Land Rents in Brazil." In *Agriculture and Governments in an Interdependent World: Proceedings of the Twentieth International Conference of Agricultural Economists, Held at Buenos Aires, Argentina, 24–31, August, 1988,* ed. Allen Maunder and Alberto Valdés. Aldershot, U.K.: Dartmouth and Gower.

Bruce, John W., Renée Giovarelli, Leonard Rolfes Jr., David Bledsoe, and Robert Mitchell. 2006. *Land Law Reform: Achieving Development Policy Objectives.* Washington, DC: World Bank.

Bundy, Colin. 1979. *The Rise and Fall of the South African Peasantry.* London: Heinemann.

Ciparisse, Gérard, ed. 2003. *Multilingual Thesaurus on Land Tenure.* New York: United Nations Food and Agriculture Organization.

Deininger, Klaus. 2003. *Land Policies for Growth and Poverty Reduction.* Washington, DC: World Bank.

Deininger, Klaus, Raffaella Castagnini, and María González. 2004. "Comparing Land Reform and Land Markets in Colombia: Impacts on Equity and Efficiency." Policy Research Working Paper 3258. World Bank, Washington, DC.

Deininger, Klaus, and Pedro Olinto. 2000. "Asset Distribution, Inequality, and Growth." Policy Research Working Paper 2375. World Bank, Washington, DC.

Deininger, Klaus, and Lyn Squire. 1998. "New Ways of Looking at Old Issues." *Journal of Development Economics* 57: 259–87.

de Janvry, Alain, Gustavo Gordillo, Jean-Philippe Platteau, and Elisabeth Sadoulet, eds. 2001. *Access to Land, Rural Poverty, and Public Action.* Oxford, U.K.: Oxford University Press.

de Janvry, Alain, and Elisabeth Sadoulet. 1989. "A Study in Resistance to Institutional Change: The Lost Game of Latin American Land Reform." *World Development* 17 (9): 1397–407.

Feder, Gershon, Tongroj Onchan, Yongyuth Chalamwong, and Chira Hongladarom.1988. *Land Policies and Farm Productivity in Thailand.* Baltimore, MD: Johns Hopkins University Press.

Goldschmidt, Walter R. 1947. *As You Sow: Three Studies in the Social Consequences of Agribusiness.* Montclair, NJ: Allanheld, Osmun.

Hardin, Garrett. 1968. "The Tragedy of the Commons." *Science* 162: 1243–48.

Hoogeveen, J. G. M., and B. H. Kinsey. 2001. "Land Reform, Growth and Equity: Emerging Evidence from Zimbabwe's Resettlement Programme. A Sequel." *Journal of Southern African Studies* 27 (1): 127–36.

Kislev, Yoav, and Willis Peterson. 1982. "Prices, Technology, and Farm Size." *Journal of Political Economy* 90 (3): 578–95.

Lerman, Zvi, Csaba Csaki, and Gershon Feder. 2002. "Land Policies and Evolving Farm Structures in Transition Countries." Policy Research Working Paper 2794. World Bank, Washington, DC.

Lipton, Michael. 2009. *Land Reform in Developing Countries: Property Rights and Property Wrongs.* Abingdon: Routledge.

Lissner, W. L. 1951. "Common and Individual Rights in Land." *American Journal of Economics and Sociology* 11 (1): 53–54.

Moyo, Sam, and Paris Yeros, eds. 2005. *Reclaiming the Land: The Resurgence of Rural Movements in Africa, Asia and Latin America.* London: Zed Books.

Netting, Robert. 1976. "What Alpine Peasants Have in Common: Observations on Communal Tenure in a Swiss Village." *Human Ecology* 4: 135–46.

Peterson, Willis L. 1997. "Are Large Farms More Efficient?" Staff Paper P97-2. Department of Applied Economics, University of Minnesota, Minneapolis.

Ravallion, Martin, Shaohua Chen, and Prem Sangraula. 2007. "New Evidence on the Urbanization of Global Poverty." Policy Research Working Paper 4199. World Bank, Washington, DC.

Sokoloff, Kenneth L., and Stanley L. Engerman. 2000. "History Lessons: Institutions, Factors Endowments, and Paths of Development in the New World." *Journal of Economic Perspectives* 14 (3): 217–32.

van den Brink, Rogier, Glen Sonwabo Thomas and Hans Binswanger. 2007. "Agricultural Land Redistribution in South Africa: Towards Accelerated Implementation." In *The Land Question in South Africa*, ed., Lungisile Ntsebeza and Ruth Hall, 152–201. Cape Town: HSRC Press.

van den Brink, Rogier, Glen Thomas, Hans Binswanger, John Bruce, and Frank Byamugisha. 2006. *Consensus, Confusion and Controversy: Selected Land Reform Issues in Sub-Saharan Africa.* Working Paper 71. Washington, DC: World Bank.

van Schalkwyk, Herman, and Johan van Zyl. 1996. "The Land Market." In *Agricultural Land Reform in South Africa: Policies, Markets and Mechanisms*, ed. Johan van Zyl, Johann Kirsten, and Hans P. Binswanger, 310–35. New York: Oxford University Press.

van Zyl, Johan, Hans Binswanger, and Colin Thirtle. 1995. "The Relationship between Farm Size and Efficiency in South African Agriculture." Policy Research Working Paper 1548. World Bank, Washington, DC.

Wolpe, Harold. 1972. "Capitalism and Cheap Labour-Power in South Africa: From Segregation to Apartheid." *Economy and Society* 1 (4): 425–56.

World Bank. 2001. "Mexico Land Policy—A Decade after the Ejido Reform." Sector Report 22187-ME. Washington, DC.

———. 2002. *World Development Report 2003: Sustainable Development in a Dynamic World.* Washington, DC.

———. 2005. *World Development Report 2006: Equity and Development.* Washington, DC.

———. 2007. *World Development Report 2008: Agriculture for Development.* Washington, DC.

PART II

The Historical Origins of Land Concentration and Past Attempts to Redistribute Land

CHAPTER TWO

History of Land Concentration and Redistributive Land Reforms

Hans P. Binswanger-Mkhize and Klaus Deininger

Most of the research on the relationship between farm size and productivity strongly suggests that farms that rely mostly on family labor have higher productivity levels than do large farms operated primarily with hired labor (see Binswanger, Deininger, and Feder [1995] for a review of the literature). If that is so, why do extraordinarily unequal distributions of ownership and operational holdings persist in many parts of the world? Why have markets for the rental and sale of agricultural land frequently not reallocated land to family farmers? Why is land reform necessary to change these landownership distributions?

The great variations in land relationships found around the world and over time cannot be understood in a simple property rights and markets paradigm. The first section of this chapter explains the idealized sequence of the emergence of property rights: increasing land scarcity leads to better definition of rights, which become tradable in sales and rental markets. The outcome should be the allocation of land to the most efficient uses and users, but that often did not happen, as observed deviations from efficiency demonstrate. Instead, rights over land and the concentration of ownership observed historically around the world were outgrowths of power relationships. Landowning groups used coercion and distortions in land, labor, credit, and commodity markets to extract economic rents from the land, from peasants and workers, and more recently from urban consumer groups or taxpayers. We describe the variety of land relationships and their consequences for the efficiency of agricultural production. We then examine how these power relationships emerged, and what legal means enabled relatively few landowners to accumulate large landholdings.

Because landownership distribution often has been determined by power relationships and distortions, and because land sales markets do not distribute land to poor people (the key point of the fourth section of this chapter), land reform frequently has been necessary to get land into the hands of efficient small family owners. (The nature, successes, and failures of reform are discussed in the third section of this chapter.) The social costs of failing to undertake reform, including losses in productivity as well as peasant revolt and civil war, also are considered. If land sales markets could allocate land from inefficient large owners to small family farmers, land reform would not be necessary. The fifth section shows why sales markets often are incapable of facilitating these efficiency-enhancing transfers—that is, covariance of risks, imperfections in credit markets, distortions in commodity markets, and subsidies to large farms. In the final section, we draw implications for land reform policies.[1]

Box 2.1 Glossary

Irrespective of their historical, cultural, or ideological origins, the following terms with these definition are used in this chapter.

***Collective farm*:** A farm jointly owned and operated under a single management with work from the members

***Communal ownership system*:** A system of land ownership in which land is assigned temporarily or permanently to members for cultivation, while other areas are held in common for pasture, forestry, collection, and hunting

***Corvée*:** Unpaid labor and sometimes the service of draft animals provided by serfs, tenants, or holders of usufruct rights

***Debt peonage, bonded labor services*:** A tribute payment or labor service originating in a defaulted loan

***Family farm*:** A farm operated primarily with family labor, with some hiring in or hiring out of labor

(*continued*)

Box 2.1 (Continued)

***Hacienda estate*:** A manorial estate in which part of the land is cultivated as the home farm of the owner and part as the family farms of serfs, holders of usufructuary rights, or tenants

***Home farm*:** That part of the manorial estate or ownership holding cultivated by the lord, landlord, or owner

***Junker estate*:** A large ownership holding producing a diversified set of commodities, operating under a single management with hired labor who usually do not receive a plot of land for their own cultivation

***Landlord estate*:** A manorial estate in which all of the land is cultivated by tenants or usufructuary rightsholders

***Land rent*:** A tenant's payment to a landowner in a voluntary contractual relationship; may be paid as a fixed or share payment in cash or in kind

***Large commercial farm*:** A large ownership holding producing several different commodities, operating under a single management with a high degree of mechanization

***Manorial estate*:** An area of land allocated to a manorial lord who has the right to tribute, taxes, or rent in cash, kind, or corvée labor from the peasants residing on the estate, either by choice or under coercion

***Rent-seeking rent*:** The additional reward received as a result of regulations and restrictions

***Reservation utility or reservation wage*:** The level of utility or wage rate that is available to a tenant or worker outside a large farm

***Residual rent*:** The payment to a productive factor in inelastic supply after all factors have been remunerated at market prices

***Share contract*:** A rental contract in which the tenant is paying a share of the crop to the landowner

***State farm*:** A farm belonging to and operated by the state

***Surplus*:** Output available beyond what is needed to preserve the energy and life of peasants, serfs, or slaves

***Tribute*:** Payment in cash, kind, or labor services to a landlord; also called rent or corvée

***Usufructuary rights*:** Rights (temporary, long-term, lifetime, or inheritable) to use the land, but not to sell it

***Wage plantation*:** A large farm specializing in a single crop, using wage labor who usually reside on the plantation

THE EMERGENCE OF PROPERTY RIGHTS IN LAND

The critical issue in land-abundant settings is access to labor, not land. At low population densities, there is no incentive to invest in soil fertility; and because fertility is restored by long tree fallow phases, ownership security is not required to induce investment. When population densities rise, fallow periods gradually are shortened until the land is cultivated continuously. Then plows, manure, artificial fertilizers, and other labor-intensive investments are required to maintain soil fertility (Boserup 1965; Ruthenberg 1980; Pingali, Bigot, and Binswanger 1987). As discussed by Boserup (1965) private rights to land emerge in a gradual process that exhibits great regularity (figure 2.1, arrows 1–4).

Virtually all the systems of land tenure found to exist before the emergence of private property in land seem to have this one feature in common: certain families are recognized as having cultivation rights within a given area of land while other families are excluded. "Free" land disappears even before the agricultural stage is reached. Tribes of food collectors and hunters believe they have exclusive rights to collect food and to hunt in particular areas.

Under the system of forest fallow, all the members of a tribe have a general right to cultivate plots of land. As long as a tribe of forest-fallow cultivators had abundant land at its disposal, a family would have no particular interest in returning to precisely the plot that it cultivated on an earlier occasion. Under these conditions, a family who needed to shift to a new plot would find a suitable plot, or have it allocated by the chief of the tribe. The situation is apt to change with increasing population, however, as good plots become somewhat scarce. Under such conditions, a family would be likely to develop an attachment to the plots they have cultivated on earlier occasions. Thus, the attachment of individual families to particular plots becomes more and more important.

As long as the general right of cultivation has not lost all its importance, a sharp social distinction exists in rural communities between cultivator families on one hand and families without cultivation rights on the other—the latter group consisting of strangers, whether they be slaves or free people. Under both long- and short-fallow systems, the land lying fallow at any given time is at free disposal for grazing by domestic animals belonging to families with cultivation rights. The cultivators' communal rights to use fallow land for grazing usually will survive long after the general right to clear new forest land has disappeared (Boserup 1965).

Boserup's discussion makes clear that property rights in land are not simple and rarely are unrestricted. As land becomes more scarce, general and inheritable cultivation and grazing rights are complemented by rights to resume cultivating specific plots after a fallow period (figure 2.1, arrow 2), to inherit specific plots rather than just general cultivation rights, to pledge or rent out the plots, to use them as collateral in informal credit transactions, and to sell them within the community (arrow 3). When the right to sell includes sales to members outside the community (arrow 4), the last vestiges

Figure 2.1 Evolution and Structure of Production Relationships and Property Rights in Agriculture

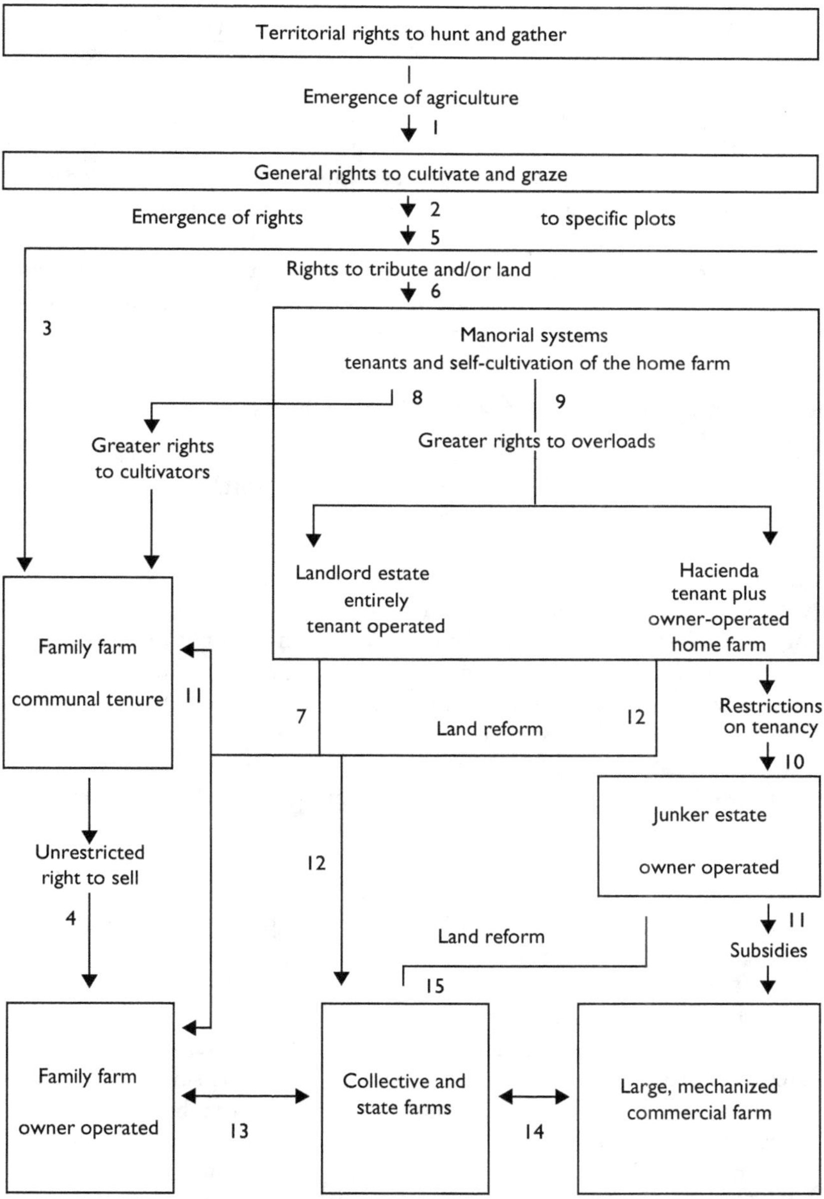

Source: Binswanger, Deininger, and Feder 1993.

of general cultivation and communal rights are lost, and private property rights are complete. General rights survive only as grazing and collection rights on communal grazing areas and in forests.

Even where communal land rights prevail, as in indigenous communities of the Americas or in tribal communities in Asia and Africa, families have strong specific land rights. These rights provide substantial "ownership" security as long as the plots are farmed by individual family units (Noronha 1985; Downs and Reyna 1988; Brasselle, Gaspart, and Platteau 1997; Otsuka and Quisumbing 2001). Land rental and sales usually occur within the community, especially among close kin. Although the internal rules and structures of these systems exhibit a bewildering variety, all communal systems have one thing in common: *sales to outsiders are either forbidden or subject to approval by the whole community.* Under communal tenure, family-owned plots can be used only for pledging in informal credit markets, not as collateral in formal credit markets.

Aggregating Land and Extracting Tribute and Rent

History has few examples of the uninterrupted transformation of general cultivation rights to land into owner-operated family farms (along arrows 1 to 4 in figure 2.1). Nearly always, there has been an intervening period under a class of rulers who extracted tribute, taxes, or rent from cultivator families (arrow 5). The landholdings of these overlords (referred to here, for expositional simplicity, as *manorial estates*, whatever the cultural or historic setting) were allocated temporarily or as permanent patrimony, along with the right to tribute, taxes, or rent (in cash, kind, or corvée labor) from the peasants residing on the estate. Frequently, peasants' freedom to move was restricted by bondage or prior claims to land by members of the ruling group. The rights of the ruling group were acquired and enforced by violence or the threat of violence, and were institutionalized in tradition, custom, and the law-and-order forces of the state. The rights took numerous forms and left historical legacies in the distribution of land. Again, Boserup (1965) says it best:

> Above the group of families with cultivation rights is usually found an upper class of tribal chiefs or feudal landlords who receive tribute from the cultivators.... Usually the position of a cultivator with regard to his rights in land does not change because a feudal government imposes itself and levies taxes and labor services. The cultivator families continue to have their hereditary cultivation rights,... and redistribution of land by village chiefs may continue without interference from the feudal landlords. Nor does land become alienable by sale; grants of land by overlords to members of the nobility and others are simply grants of the right to levy taxes, and do not interfere with the hereditary cultivation rights of the peasants. In other words, the beneficiaries of such grants do not become owners of the land in a modern sense. (pp. 82–84)

Evolution of Agrarian Relationships

Favorable agricultural conditions generate the potential for rent-seeking rent or surplus, and they provide an incentive for groups with political and military power. Under simple technology, there are no economies of scale in farming, and independent family farms are economically the most efficient mode of production (except for a very limited set of plantation crops; see the fourth section of the chapter). Compared with large farms using hired or tenant labor, owner-operated family farms save on labor supervision costs or eliminate the inefficiencies and supervision cost constraints associated with tenancy. Therefore, where peasants can establish farms of their own, they can escape paying tribute, taxes, or rent; and they will outcompete the landlord. Extracting tribute or labor requires coercion or economic distortions.

Coercion

As Boserup (1965) points out, "Bonded labor is a characteristic feature of communities with hierarchic structure, but surrounded by so much uncontrolled land suitable for cultivation by long fallow methods that it is impossible to prevent the members of the lower class from finding alternative means of subsistence unless they are made personally unfree" (p. 73). Traditionally, four ways have been used to tie labor to large farms: slavery, indentured labor contracts, serfdom, and debt peonage.

Meillassoux (1981) shows that for *merchant slavery*—in which the slaveholders purchase, rather than capture, slaves—slaveholders must produce for the market to finance the slaves.[2] In areas with sparse populations of hunters and gatherers and with ties to external markets (such as in the southeastern United States, the east coast of Brazil, and the South African Cape), large farms had to import slaves as workers (figure 2.1, arrow 6). The native hunter-gatherers were too few to provide a steady labor supply, or they simply moved away.

Large farms in areas with access to abundant labor reservoirs, such as the sugar islands of the Caribbean and Mauritius, Ceylonese (Sri Lankan) and Assamese (India) tea plantations, and Malaysia, Sumatra (Indonesia), and South Africa, were able to rely on *indentured labor* instead of slaves (arrow 7). The workers had to be indentured to prevent them from establishing plots of their own.[3] To cover the costs of bringing the workers, market production was necessary.

Serfdom or *bondage* could be used to produce primarily for local consumption in somewhat more densely populated regions (arrow 5). Overlords obtained the right to tie subsistence-oriented populations to the land and to extract tribute or labor services. This pattern arose during feudal periods in China, western Europe, and Japan, and in pre- and post-Colombian America; and it survived in eastern Europe until the late 19th century (Blum 1977).

Debt peonage or *bonded labor* survived in many areas even under high population densities. Where manorial estates had to compete with mines for labor, and therefore faced acute labor shortage (as in Guatemala and Mexico in the 19th century or in South Africa in the 20th century), vagrancy laws kept a pool of potential workers in prison for a variety of petty offenses (see table 2.1). In South Africa, the rights to prison labor could be purchased.

Economic Distortions

To get free peasants to move to the manorial estate required lowering welfare or profits in the free peasant sector. This reduced the peasants' reservation utility—the expected utility from family farming—and shifted their labor supply curve to the right. This distortion was achieved through four mechanisms that are summarized in table 2.1:

- *Reducing the land available for peasant cultivation:* Allocating rights to "unoccupied" lands to members of the ruling class only confined free peasant cultivation to infertile or remote areas with poor infrastructure and market access. Sometimes this involved forced resettlement. Farm profits and welfare of free peasant lands thus were reduced by the higher labor requirements on poor land, by increased transport and marketing costs, and by increased prices for consumer goods imported to the region.
- *Imposing differential taxation:* Free peasants were required to pay tribute, hut, head, or poll taxes (in cash, kind, or labor services); at the same time, workers or tenants in manorial estates often were exempt or were taxed at much lower rates. Such systems were used widely in western Europe during the feudal period; in ancient China, India, Japan, and the Ottoman Empire; and by all colonial powers.
- *Restricting market access:* As long as free peasants could pay tribute or taxes in kind or cash and have equal access to output markets, taxation alone might be insufficient to bring forth a supply of workers or tenants. Market access was restricted by setting up cooperative or monopoly marketing schemes that bought only from the farms of the rulers. The *prazo* system in Mozambique combined rights to labor and tribute from peasants with monopolies on inputs and outputs. In Kenya, the production of coffee by Africans was prohibited outright until the 1950s. European monopolies on sales of tobacco in Malawi and Zimbabwe were transferred directly to large farms after the countries gained independence.
- *Confining agricultural public goods and services (roads, extension services, credit) to the farms of the rulers* or subsidizing these farms directly was another means of increasing their profits, relative to peasant farms.[4]

The combination of state interventions into the allocation of land with distortions used to establish manorial estates under conditions of low population density has been remarkably similar across continents and over time (table 2.1). The most common pattern was to combine interventions in land allocation

Table 2.1 Interventions to Establish and Support Large Farms

Country	Land allocation, forced resettlement, and land market restrictions	Taxes and interventions in labor and output markets
Asia		
China (south)	No evidence of land allocation, forced resettlements, and land market restrictions	Limitations on peasant mobility, circa 500 Tax exemption for slaves, circa 500 Gentry exemption from taxes and labor services, circa 1400
India (north)	Land grants from the first century	Hacienda system, fourth century BCE Corvée labor, from second century BCE
Japan	Exclusive land rights to developed wasteland, 723 CE	Tribute exemption for cleared and temple land, 700 CE
Java and Sumatra	Land grants to companies, 1870	Indentured labor, 19th century Cultivation system, 19th century
Philippines	Land grants to monastic orders, 16th century	*Encomienda* *Repartimiento* Tax exemption for hacienda workers, 16th century
Sri Lanka	Land appropriation, 1840	Plantations tax exempt, 1818 Indentured labor, 19th century
Europe		
Prussia	Land grants, from 13th century	Monopolies on milling and alcohol Restrictions on labor mobility, 1530 Land reform legislation, 1750–1850
Russia	Land grants, from 14th century Service tenure, 1565	Restrictions on peasant mobility: - exit fees, 1400–50 - mobility forbidden, 1588 - enserfment, 1597 - tradability of serfs, 1661 Home farm exempt from taxation, 1580 Debt peonage, 1597 Monopoly on commerce, until 1830

(*continued*)

Table 2.1 (Continued)

Country	Land allocation, forced resettlement, and land market restrictions	Taxes and interventions in labor and output markets
South America		
Chile	Land grants (*mercedes de tierra*), 16th century	*Encomienda*, 16th century Labor services (*mita*), 17th century Import duties on beef, 1890 Subsidies to mechanization, 1950–60
El Salvador	Grants of public land, 1857 Titling of communal land, 1882	Vagrancy laws, 1825 Exemption from public and military services for large landowners and their workers, 1847
Guatemala	Resettlement of indigenous peoples, 16th century	Cash tribute, 1540 *Manamiento*, circa 1600 Debt peonage, 1877
Mexico	Resettlement of indigenous peoples, 1540 Expropriation of communal lands, 1850	*Encomienda*, 1490 Tribute exemption for hacienda workers, 17th century Debt peonage, 1790 Return of debtors to haciendas, 1843 Vagrancy laws, 1877
Viceroyalty of Peru	Land grants, 1540 Resettlement of indigenous peoples (*congregaciones*), 1570 Titling and expropriation of indigenous peoples' land, 17th century	*Encomienda*, 1530 *Mita*: Exemption for hacienda workers, 1550 Slavery of Africans, 1580
Africa		
Algeria	Titling, circa 1840 Land grants under settlement programs, 1871 "Settlers' law," 1873	Tax exemption for workers on European farms, 1849 Credit provision for European settlers

Angola	Land concessions to Europeans, 1838, 1865	Slavery, until 1880 Vagrancy laws, 1875
Egypt (Ottomans)	Land grants, 1840	Corvée labor, from 16th century Corvée exemption for farmworkers, 1840s Land tax exemption for large landlords, 1856 Credit and marketing subsidies, 1920, 1930s
Kenya	Land concessions to Europeans, circa 1900 No African land purchases outside reserves, 1926	Hut and poll taxes, from 1905 Labor passes, 1908 Squatter laws, 1918, 1926, 1939 Restrictions on Africans' market access, from 1930: - dual price system for maize - quarantine and forced destocking of livestock - monopoly marketing associations - prohibition of African export crop cultivation Subsidies to mechanization, 1940s
Malawi	Land allotments to Europeans, 1894	Tax reductions for farmworkers, circa 1910
Mozambique	Comprehensive rights to leases under *prazo*, 19th century	Labor tribute, 1880 Vagrancy law, 1899 Abolition of African trade, 1892 Forced cultivation, 1930
Rhodesia	Reserves, 1896, 1931	Poll and hut taxes, 1896 Discrimination against tenancy, 1909 Monopoly marketing boards, from 1924 - dual price system in maize - forced destocking of livestock, 1939
Sokotho Caliphate	Land grants to settlers, 1804	Slavery, 19th century

(*continued*)

Table 2.1 (Continued)

Country	Land allocation, forced resettlement, and land market restrictions	Taxes and interventions in labor and output markets
South Africa	Native reserves, 19th century Pseudocommunal tenure in reserves, 1894 Natives Land Act, 1912 - demarcation of reserves - elimination of tenancy - prohibition of African land purchases outside reserves	Slavery and indentured labor, 19th century Restrictions on Africans' mobility, 1911, 1951 Monopoly marketing, from 1930 Prison labor, circa 1950 Direct and indirect subsidies, 20th century
Tanganyika	Land grants to settlers, 1890	Hut tax and corvée requirements, 1896 Compulsory cotton production, 1902 Vagrancy laws (work cards), 20th century Exclusion of Africans from credit, 1931 Marketing cooperatives to depress African prices, 1940

Source: Binswanger, Deininger, and Feder 1995.

with differential taxation. Sometimes the four types of distortions were supplemented by coercive interventions in the labor market—vagrancy laws, debt peonage, and agrestic slavery, for example—to make it easier to retain workers or tenants on manorial estates. The earliest recorded incidence of this pattern that we found was in the *Arthasastra* in the fourth century BCE. Groups with widely different cultures, religions, and ethnic backgrounds—Ottomans, the Hausa and Fulani in Africa, the Fujiwara in Japan, and all European colonial powers—imposed such systems on people of the same or different ethnic backgrounds when faced with similar material conditions.

When a labor supply becomes available, large landowners can organize their operations either as *landlord estates*, with the entire estate cultivated by tenanted peasants; or as *hacienda estates*, with workers cultivating portions of the hacienda for their own subsistence as tenants or holders of usufruct rights and providing unpaid corvée labor services to cultivate the home farm of the owner. Landlord estates were prevalent in China, Egypt, Ethiopia, eastern India, Iran, Japan, Korea, and Pakistan. Haciendas emerged as the predominant form of manorial estates in Algeria, Egypt, Kenya, South Africa, and Zimbabwe; in Bolivia, Chile, Honduras, Mexico, Nicaragua, Peru, and other countries in Latin America; in the Philippines; and in Prussia and other parts of eastern Europe.

INTERVENTIONS TO ESTABLISH AND SUPPORT LARGE FARMS IN SUB-SAHARAN AFRICA

Here we provide evidence concerning the establishment and evolution of large farm systems in sub-Saharan Africa.[5]

Angola

Land Allocation and Market Interventions

In 1838 and again in 1865, all "unoccupied" land could be given as concessions to Europeans. "The settlers were given lands, seeds, tools, and slaves by the government, and measures were taken to ensure that their products could be sold" (Clarence-Smith 1979, p. 15). From 1907 to 1932, some 98 square miles were set aside for native reserves, and about 1,800 square miles were given to Portuguese and other foreign settlers (Bender 1978).

Differential Taxation and Labor Levies

After the abolition of domestic slavery in 1875, slavery continued in a variety of forms (Clarence-Smith 1979). Vagrancy laws passed in 1875 subjected all "nonproductive" Africans to nonremunerated labor contracts (Bender 1978). The laws were replaced in 1926 by native laws that provided for payments of wages but retained the provision that all Africans had to work for European landlords or could be contracted by the state.

Kenya

Land Allocation and Market Interventions

With the arrival of Europeans, all vacant land was declared to be Crown land and sold to European settlers under extremely favorable conditions. Much of the land continued to be farmed by African tenants, who were called "squatters" (Mosley 1983). Africans' land rights were limited to reserves, and a formal prohibition of African land purchases outside the reserves was codified in 1926. Subdivision of land was prohibited.

Differential Taxation and Labor Levies

The British introduced a number of regressive hut and poll taxes to "increase the natives' cost of living" (Berman 1990, p. 509). To pay these taxes, Africans initially did not seek wage labor but increased production, mainly on tenanted land. Despite repeated requests from settlers to grant tax-exempt status to Africans working on European farms, such taxes had to be paid by workers as well; therefore, large estates based on wage labor remained relatively unprofitable, compared with tenancy. The Squatter Law of 1918 required tenants to provide at least 180 days a year in labor services to their landlord at a wage not to exceed two-thirds of the wage for unskilled labor. This ordinance was amended twice (in 1926 and 1939), both times increasing the minimum amount of labor services (to 270 days per year in 1939), limiting the area that could be cultivated as well as the amount of stock owned per tenant, and making tenant eviction easier. Labor passes, which had been introduced in 1908, limited the mobility of Africans; leaving without the employer's consent was a criminal offense (Berman 1990).

Input and Output Market Interventions

A dual price system for maize, adopted in the 1930s, reduced the returns African farmers could obtain for the same produce supplied by their European counterparts, and it placed most of the price risk on Africans (Mosley 1983). Grower associations that excluded Africans were formed for most of the important cash crops. High licensing fees kept Africans out of pyrethrum production, and Africans were prohibited outright from cultivating coffee (Berman 1990). During World War II, European farmers received direct subsidies to mechanize their farms (Cone and Lipscomb 1972).[6]

Malawi

Land Allocation and Market Interventions

In 1894, Europeans were allotted more than 1.5 million hectares, or about 15 percent of total arable land, in Malawi. After independence, the Banda regime set aside large tracts of land into tobacco estates leased on a long-term basis to well-connected and better-off Malawians.

Differential Taxation and Labor Levies

Attempts to introduce labor tenancy on European-owned cotton lands were unsuccessful as farmers abandoned the land and fled to uncultivated Crown land. The situation improved only when a law was introduced in 1908 that allowed Africans to gain a significant reduction in the head tax they had to pay by working for European cotton growers at least one month a year. Africans' possibility of gaining a similar reduction of the head tax by producing cotton on tenanted land was eliminated as a result of landowner pressure (Mandala 1990). In addition, prohibitions on the production of cash crops by communal farmers were not abolished until the late 1990s.

Mozambique

Land Allocation and Market Interventions

Exclusive property rights in land and quasi-governmental authority, the institution of *prazo*, began in the 17th century. In the 19th century, such property rights often were granted to companies. The *prazo* holder had to provide minimal public services, cultivate part of the property, and pay quitrent and tithe; but he or she could levy annual tributes (in cash, kind, or labor) on the local population and was endowed with a complete monopoly on all trade within and outside the area (Vail and White 1980).

Differential Taxation and Labor Levies

Hut taxes were established in 1854. After 1880, at least half of the tax had to be paid to the local *prazo* holder in the form of labor services (Vail and White 1980). Under the Vagrancy Law of 1899, all male Africans ages 14–60 were obliged to work. Contingents of migratory labor often were "sold" to other areas (such as South Africa) where labor was relatively scarce (Vail and White 1980). Vagrancy laws were repealed in 1926—at about the time many *prazos* were expiring—and the use of forced labor for "private purposes" (that is, nonquota production) was banned. The Labor Code of 1942 instituted an obligatory labor requirement of six months for all African men.

Input and Output Market Interventions

In 1892, all itinerant African trade within *prazos* was abolished, conferring a monopoly on *prazo* holders of all commerce. *Prazos* turned into mini-states, each with its own closed economy and unlimited freedom for the *prazo* holder to determine the terms of trade. As a consequence, African producers almost completely withdrew from cash-crop productions and the *prazos* became "private labor pools from which the companies, by direct force or by indirect manipulation of the economy, could compel the labor they required" (Vail and White 1980, p. 132). Following their expiration about 1930, *prazos* were replaced by a "concession system." Concession holders received monopoly rights to purchase cotton and rice in return for enforcing Africans' work obligations and providing inputs and supervision (Isaacman and Isaacman 1983). Although exactions from Africans were still high, cultivation of all but sugar reverted to smaller-scale units rather than large-scale farms.

Sokotho Caliphate

Land Market Interventions

After 1804, the land that is present-day Burkina Faso, Cameroon, Niger, and northern Nigeria was granted to settlers by the caliphate government in the areas around defensive centers. The amount of granted land depended on the number of slaves the settlers owned. Thus anyone who had slaves could obtain enough land to start a plantation.

Differential Taxation and Labor Levies

Slaves, who made up 50–75 percent of the local population, were acquired by warfare, direct seizure, or as tribute from subjected tribes. Limited export markets and the relatively low price of slaves allowed relatively lenient treatment of slaves, who enjoyed more rights—for example, the possession of heritable house plots (Gemery and Hogendorn 1979) and self-redemption—than did the slaves acquired for cash by market-oriented plantations in the Americas. Land and the absence of economies of scale, however, meant that slave owners had to take measures to prevent slaves from escaping and establishing their own operations (Gemery and Hogendorn 1979). Eventually, these factors led to the demise of the large holdings.

South Africa

Land Allocation and Market Interventions

Native reserves were established firmly at the end of the 19th century, although they were not defined legally until 1912. For example, in the Transvaal in 1870, the area allocated to African reserves was less than a hundredth of the area available to whites (Bundy 1979). The Glen Grey Act (1894) restricted African landownership in the reserves to a parcel of no more than about 3 hectares; and it instituted a perverted form of "communal tenure" that banned the sale, rental, and subdivision of land to prevent the emergence of a class of independent African smallholders (Hendricks 1990). Various legal measures to discourage tenancy on European farms did not lead to the desired results. The Natives Land Act (1913) circumscribed the extent of African reserves and declared real tenancy on European farms illegal, forcing all African tenants either to become wage laborers or labor tenants on European farms or to move to the reserves.

Differential Taxes and Labor Levies

Prior to state intervention on European farmers' behalf, very limited market production by European farmers was based on slaves or, after the prohibition of slavery in 1834, on indentured labor. Masters and Servants laws and the Mines and Workers Act (1911) restricted Africans' occupational mobility and excluded them from skilled occupations in all sectors except agriculture (Lipton 1985). Restrictions on mobility were reinforced and tightened by pass laws (influx controls) from 1922 and the establishment of labor bureaus to enforce the legislation from 1951 (Lipton 1985). More rigid pass laws also provided a flow of cheap labor for white farmers. It is estimated that, in 1949, about 40,000 pass-law offenders were supplied to farms as prison laborers (Wilson 1971).

Input and Output Market Interventions

European farmers were assisted by a large array of monopolistic commodity marketing boards and direct credit subsidies. In 1967, the amount spent on subsidizing about 100,000 white farms was almost double the amount spent on education for more than 10 million Africans (Wilson 1971).[7]

Tanganyika

Land Allocation and Market Interventions

From the late 1890s until 1904 in present-day Tanzania, it was common practice to allocate several villages each to incoming German settlers.

Differential Taxation and Labor Levies

A hut tax payable in cash or labor services was imposed in 1896. Village headmen were required to provide a fixed number of workers each day to provide labor for the settlers. Every African was issued a work card that obligated him to render services to an employer for 120 days a year at a fixed wage, or to work on public projects (Illife 1979). In 1902, the Germans introduced compulsory cotton production in certain coastal areas; it is widely accepted that this scheme was one of the main causes leading to the outbreak of the Maji Maji Revolt in 1905 (Coulson 1982).

Input and Output Market Interventions

Africans were excluded from credit by the Credit to Natives Ordinance of 1931, which required that an African have specific government permission before he could even request that a bank lend him money (Coulson 1982). Attempts by

Africans to set up a marketing cooperative for coffee led to the attempt to outlaw traditional practices of coffee growing in 1937—and to riots. Settler-dominated marketing monopolies for African-grown crops were set up in the 1940s and skimmed off most of the profits (Coulson 1982).

Zimbabwe (Rhodesia)

Land Allocation and Market Interventions

Reserves for Africans in remote areas of low fertility were established in 1896, although their boundaries underwent some changes until 1931 (Palmer 1977), when African land purchases outside the reserves and specifically designed "African purchase areas" were declared illegal. Subdivision of farms was prohibited.

Differential Taxation and Labor Levies

Although all Africans were subject to poll and hut taxes, specific taxes discriminated against cash rental and share tenancy contracts beginning in 1909 (Palmer 1977).

Input and Output Market Interventions

Volatility and downturns in output markets were smoothed by government interventions, such as increased land bank loans; debt moratoria (especially during the depression in 1930); and after protracted lobbying by European producers, the establishment of monopoly marketing boards (for tobacco, dairy, pigs, and cotton) and of export subsidies. African maize and livestock producers were discriminated against by dual price systems. To ease the problem of land degradation in 1939, compulsory destocking was mandated; prices paid for African cattle were between one-third and one-sixth of the prices fetched for comparable European stock (Mosley 1983).[8]

Conclusions

The examples discussed here all suggest that neither the establishment nor the continued existence of large farms was the result of their superior economic efficiency or the presence of economies of scale in agricultural production. Large farms were created by government intervention in favor of large landholders through land grants and differential taxation. Withdrawal of those privileges led either to their disintegration into landlord estates or to a shift toward rent seeking and more subtle forms of support for large farms.

Manorial systems sometimes have been interpreted as the outcome of an efficiency-enhancing contract between peasants and landlords: the landlords provide protection and other public goods (which are produced with economies of scale and require some specialization) in exchange for tribute or rent (North and Thomas 1971). This is a plausible interpretation for land-abundant settings, where tribute rates or labor rents have to be set low enough to attract immigrants. However, there are two major problems with this view. First, it ignores the asymmetry between contracting parties in access to weapons, laws, and public investment budgets. The systematic use of these instruments throughout history has depressed the utility of peasants and workers to a level far below the reservation utility that would obtain in a system without such symmetric access. Moreover, there is little doubt that substantial deadweight losses and dynamic inefficiencies have been associated with taxes and tribute, with inequalities in factor ratios between farming sectors, and with restrictions on access to credit and output markets. Second, the contract view ignores the likely competition in rent seeking between landlords, which would add to the deadweight loss associated with restrictions. The literature shows that competitive rent seeking is likely to result in the dissipation of the rent into such rent-seeking costs as competitive armies, arsenals, and fortifications, which provide no consumption value. At the height of the feudal period, rents were completely dissipated into the costs of competing in the system. Periodic conflicts over the right to extract rent have caused destruction and decline in many flourishing kingdoms and empires, so the efficiency characteristics of the contractual system are only third or fourth best.

The major issue in land relationships, therefore, is the evolution of the relationship between peasants and landlords over time. The best-developed literature in this area relates to the demise of the manorial estate, corvée, and bondage and to the emergence of capitalism in Europe. Dobb (1963) interprets the emergence of capitalist farming and the loss of rights to tribute as the consequence of increased population density alone, whereas Sweezy et al. (1976) emphasize the role of increased access to markets. Hilton (1976) also discusses these issues (as well as broader noneconomic theories). In particular, Brenner (1976) stresses the importance of the cohesiveness of the peasant community in resisting attempts by the lords to increase the instruments available to them, or the intensity of their use.

SUCCESS AND FAILURE IN LAND REFORM

How did the manorial estate disappear? Boserup (1965) explains succinctly: "The process by which the feudal landlord tenure [the manorial estate] is abandoned may take different forms: sometimes the position of the feudal landlords in relation to the cultivators is weakened; they lose their power over all or most of the peasants and they end up as private owners of their home farms only [see figure 2.1, arrows 8, 10, and 11]. In other cases, the feudal landlords succeed in their efforts to eliminate completely the customary rights of the cultivators, and they end up as private owners of all the land over which they had feudal rights, while the cultivators have slipped to the status of tenants-at-will. England, of course, is the classical example of this last kind of development" (p. 87). Only in transitions of the first kind do the peasants end up with the income from land, the land rent.

Because land reform involves the transfer of rents from a ruling class to tenant workers, it is not surprising that most large-scale land reforms were initiated by revolts (Bolivia), revolutions (Mexico, Chile, China, Cuba, El Salvador, Nicaragua, Russia), conquests (Japan and Taiwan, China), or the demise of colonial rule (eastern India, Kenya, Mozambique, Vietnam, Zimbabwe). Attempts at land reform without massive political upheaval rarely have succeeded in transferring much of a country's land (Brazil, Costa Rica, Honduras) or have done so very slowly (Mexico from 1930 until the early 1990s).

The outcomes of land reforms have been conditioned by three factors: (1) whether the system was a landlord estate or a hacienda system, (2) whether reform was gradualist with compensation or took place all at once, and (3) whether reform was undertaken in a market or a socialist economy. We consider the first two factors in the context of the third, the type of economy.

Reform in Market-Based Economies

In transitions from landlord estates to family farms (figure 2.1, arrow 7), the organization of production remains the same family farm system. The only change is that ownership is transferred from large landlords to tenants who already farm the land and have the skills and implements necessary to cultivate their fields. Government involvement often has been substantial, ranging from a ceiling on the size of landholdings and the amounts to be paid for the land to the establishment of beneficiaries' financial obligations. Many reforms that followed this pattern provided stronger incentives for tenant-owners to work and invest in their farms, and led to increases in output and productivity. The resulting systems have had great stability. Since the end of World War II, landlord estates in Bolivia; Ethiopia; eastern India; Iran; Japan; Korea; and Taiwan, China, have been transferred to tenants in the course of successful land reforms.

Theoretically, the productivity gains associated with such reforms come about because of improved work and investment incentives associated with increased security of tenure. Empirical evidence shows that the reform of landlord estates led to considerable investment, adoption of new technology, and increases in productivity (Koo 1973; King 1977; Callison 1983; Dorner and Thiesenhusen 1990), and that government costs for complementary investments supporting the transition in ownership structure—such as infrastructure, housing, and training in management skills—were low because the structure of the smallholder production system already was in place.

In contrast to the relatively smooth transition from landlord estates to family farms, reform of hacienda systems has been very slow and difficult. The outcome frequently has been the emergence of large owner-operated *Junker estates*[9] (figure 2.1, arrow 10). Junker estates produce a wide variety of crops and livestock products using a hierarchy of supervisors, permanent workers who sometimes were given a house and garden plot, and external workers hired on a seasonal or daily basis. Junker estates are less specialized than plantations, which produce and process a narrow range of crops, and are less capital intensive than large-scale commercial farms.

Expansion of the landlord's home farm at the cost of land cultivated by tenants would be associated with losses in efficiency. Therefore, rational landowners would not establish Junker estates unless induced to do so by such external constraints as the threat of land reform or restrictions on tenancy. Anticipating such reforms, landowners often tried to reduce their exposure to expropriation by evicting tenants. The early rounds of land reform in Prussia gave freehold property rights to hereditary tenants, requiring them to give between one-half and one-third of their hereditary land to the Junkers as compensation for the loss of their corvée services. Fearing that further land reform would include tenants-at-will or holders of nonhereditary usufruct rights, the Junkers evicted many of the remaining tenants and reverted to cultivation with hired labor.

In Latin America, ever since the Mexican Revolution in 1910, land reform movements legally have enshrined the principles that land belongs to the tiller and that indirect exploitation of the land through tenants constitutes a cause for expropriation. The Brazilian Land Law of 1964 put a low ceiling on rental rates and crop shares, and conveyed permanent usufruct rights to tenants after a few years of tenancy by protecting them from eviction. In addition, it created a new land tax on underused properties, and made underused properties above a certain ceiling subject to land reform through expropriation. For the next two decades of military rule, however, the implementation was limited and the emphasis was placed mainly on frontier development programs.

Ceilings on rentals and crop share, and vesting of permanent rights for long-term tenants, exist in some land laws in Asia (Chuma, Otsuka, and Hayami 1990). The experience of land reform in the Philippines up to the late 1980s suffered from similar deficiencies and lack of political will, as did successive Brazilian programs up to that time. Colombia at first introduced restrictions on land rents and shares, and in 1968 made it illegal for owners to use sharecroppers, tenants, or *colonos* at all. The results in terms of tenant evictions and loss of employment have been catastrophic (Heath and Binswanger 1998). Restrictions on tenant cultivation in South Africa had different roots: they were imposed to make tenancy less attractive to Africans, who were needed as workers in the mines. Whatever the motivation, these legal restrictions on tenancy prompted owners of haciendas to evict their tenants and to expand home farm cultivation using hired labor.[10]

The inability of Junker estates to compete with the more efficient smallholder sector made Junker estates an unstable form of production relationship and led to intensive lobbying for protection and for subsidies to introduce and expand mechanization. By substituting subsidized capital for labor, the Junker estate was transformed into a large-scale, mechanized commercial farm (figure 2.1, arrow 11) that no longer depended on large amounts of labor. Intensive mechanization of large commercial farms reduces the potential for land reform because there are not enough families with farming skills and implements available on these capital-intensive farms to establish efficient small farms able to rely on low-cost family labor. A similar result can be achieved by converting haciendas or Junker farms to livestock ranches, which require very little labor.

The fact that Junker estates emerged only in response to pending land reform and tenancy restrictions supports the views that there are no technical economies of scale in nonmechanized agriculture and that the incentive problems associated with supervising hired or corvée labor far exceed the efficiency losses associated with long-term whole-farm tenancy contracts. To compete successfully with family farms, Junker estates had to find ways to reduce their labor costs or to increase their revenues. Landowners often sought to secure rents from the expanding urban and industrial sectors through trade barriers and subsidies for mechanizing production (de Janvry 1981). Examples include the German Zollverein at the end of the 19th century (Gerschenkron 1965), tariffs on beef imports in Chile in 1887 (Kay and Silva 1992), and selective price supports for products from large-scale units in Kenya, South Africa, and Zimbabwe (Deininger and Binswanger 1995).

Subsidies for mechanization led to the transformation of nearly all Junker estates into mechanized commercial farms (figure 2.1, arrow 11). Huge sums were provided either through direct mechanization subsidies, as in Kenya; or through cheap credit, as in South Africa, Zimbabwe, and practically all of South America, where real interest rates were even negative (Abercrombie 1972). Mechanization eliminated the need to rely on hired labor and resulted in widespread tenant evictions, even in countries with cheap labor—hardly an optimal transformation from a social point of view.

In some market economies, haciendas were converted to communal family farm systems (figure 2.1, arrow 11). Communal tenure was adopted first in Mexico's *ejido* system and later under land reforms in Bolivia, Zimbabwe, and elsewhere. Beneficiaries were granted inheritable usufructuary rights, but constraints on land sales and rentals often prevented using the land as collateral for credit. Attempts to provide alternative sources of credit through special banks or credit programs proved ineffective (Heath 1992). By a majority vote in Mexico, a recent constitutional amendment legalized land rental and sales within all *ejidos* and allowed each *ejido* to remove restrictions on sales to outsiders, effectively converting the *ejidatarios* to owner-operated family farms. Empirical evidence suggests that within a consistent framework of regulations enabling communities to make choices according to their needs, this helped bring about significant increases in productivity, improved governance, and had no adverse equity impacts (World Bank 2001).

In Latin America, more generally, land reforms were halting over the 60 years from 1930 to 1990; and they went through two or more farm organization models, eventually leading to large numbers of independent, small owner-operators in Chile, El Salvador, Honduras, Mexico, Nicaragua, and Peru. Only a few of them became viable farm entrepreneurs, and many still require additional support through rural development interventions to complete this transition (de Janvry et al. 2001).

Reform in Socialist Economies

In socialist economies, land reform has followed different paths (figure 2.1, arrows 10, 11, and 12). Landlord estates in China, Ethiopia, the former Soviet Union, and Vietnam were converted initially into family farms (arrow 10), in much the same way as in market economies. All or some of the redistributed farmlands were later consolidated into single-management units as state farms or collectives (arrow 13). In Algeria, Chile, the German Democratic Republic, Mozambique, Nicaragua, and Peru, Junker estates or large commercial farms were converted directly into state farms (arrows 14 and 15). In most cases, workers continued as employees, with no change in internal production relations. Over time, the organizational differences between collectives and state farms tended to disappear.

To achieve efficient production, collectives have to deal with two incentive problems. The first problem is to provide incentives to workers, a problem often addressed by adopting piece-rate systems designed to reward labor at least partially on the basis of effort. The other incentive problem concerns investment and savings decisions, which are made jointly by the collective. Bonin and Putterman (1993) show that as long as equity financing is precluded and members cannot sell their shares in the cooperative, the representative worker will not make efficient investment decisions. Mitchell (1990) also examines problems associated with the intertemporal allocation of consumption, and shows that the distribution of decision-making power between old (who would rather consume) and young (who prefer to invest) determines the rate of growth for a cooperative enterprise. McGregor (1977) provides a theoretical justification and empirical examples of the tendency of cooperative enterprises to disinvest and to reduce membership to increase current consumption by members. Barham and Childress (1992) show that Honduran collectives decreased their memberships by about one-fifth over time. Successful collectives tend to degenerate into capitalist enterprises (or wage labor–operated state farms) by substituting cheaper wage laborers for more expensive members (Ben-Ner 1984).

Thus, the problems associated with provision of workers' effort and intertemporal consumption proved at least as serious in collectives as in hacienda estates. The poor performance of agriculture under a collective mode of production is well documented, and it is not surprising that the expected increases in production from economies of scale usually were not realized for Nicaragua (Colburn 1990), for Cuba (Ghai, Kay, and Peek 1988), for Ethiopia

(Griffin 1985; Wuyts 1985), and for Mozambique (Lin et al. 1994). When given the chance to do so, members of collective farms often vote to redistribute plots to family-size farms.[11]

In China, agricultural output grew by 42 percent in the first six years following decollectivization in 1978 under the Household Responsibility System (McMillan, Whalley, and Zhu 1989; Lin 1992; Du 2006). Vietnam experienced similar productivity gains from breaking up large collective farms into tiny family units (Pingali and Xuan 1992). The family farms in these densely populated countries expanded the labor input and were able to reduce machinery and fertilizer use. Clearly, the incentive advantages of individual farming outweighed any efficiency losses resulting from the extremely small size and fragmentation of farms (Zhang and Makeham 1992). Both China and Vietnam benefited from the equal income and wealth distributions that characterized them at the outset of their decollectivization efforts (Akram-Lodhi et al. 2007).

Under different conditions, as in Algeria and Peru, the privatization and breakup of mechanized state farms or collectives has been less successful (Melmed-Sanjak and Carter 1991). Mechanization of these large farms had occurred and had reduced the number of workers or tenants before their collectivization. When those collectives were turned over to their relatively few remaining workers, the resulting family farms were relatively large and (unlike in China and Vietnam) could not be operated efficiently without additional hired workers or high levels of mechanization. But hiring additional workers dilutes the incentive advantage of the family farm, and the farms had neither the access to subsidized credit nor the large amounts of equity needed to finance hired labor or mechanization. To make reform work under these capital-constrained conditions, and to reap the efficiency benefits of family farming, it may be necessary to include more beneficiary families in the reform program than those who are employed on the highly mechanized farms, by resettling landless or near-landless workers from outside the farms.

Reforms since the End of the Cold War

In selected market economies still dominated by large farms, the end of the Cold War led to a new momentum in land reform. However, with the exception of Brazil (where the scope of land reform was large, its execution relatively rapid, and its outcome for beneficiaries largely positive), those efforts have been disappointing for the beneficiaries. The reforms now have had measurable impact on wealth distribution but only limited impact on poverty (Akram-Lodhi et al. 2007). Clearly, more agile and productive approaches to land reform need to be generalized.

The most dramatic land reform has been the Fast Track Land Redistribution in Zimbabwe. It reduced the number of white landowners from nearly 8,000 in 1998 to less than 1,000 in 2007. Several legal and constitutional reforms made expropriation much easier; but delayed or absent compensation of former landowners, combined with hyperinflation, effectively transformed most expropriations into confiscations of the farms. Farm output plummeted, and much of the capital stock (machinery, livestock, irrigation) was lost to sale, destruction, and theft. Between 2000 and 2007, more than 7 million hectares of land were redistributed to approximately 160,000 family farmers (model "A1" farmers), and 1.7 million hectares were redistributed to around 28,000 new commercial farmers ("A2" farmers). Thus the commercial farm sector now holds much less land than before, and in much smaller farms (Pazvakavambwa 2007). A disproportionate share of irrigated land and land near urban centers went to urban rather than rural owners. Former commercial farm workers and women are underrepresented among the beneficiaries, and the war veterans—key drivers of the political momentum—ended up with less land than promised. Farm output continues to decline, and Zimbabwe has become a major importer of food and recipient of food aid (World Bank 2006).

The most successful large land reform was that of Brazil, facilitated by the new constitution of 1998 but gaining momentum after 1996 as a consequence of powerful peasant movements. Economic reforms eliminated most of the privileges of large-scale farms and, together with declining output prices, made landownership less desirable as an inflation hedge. Between 1996 and 2007, Brazil transferred farms to between 700,000 and 800,000 families under two mechanisms: The bulk of the transfers of land occurred through the government's expropriation program, a demonstration that large-scale expropriation can be done without disrupting the agricultural and overall economies of a country. The Credito Fundiario program and its precursors transferred land to about 90,000 farms under the directly negotiated land reform, in which land is purchased and developed by beneficiary communities through a combination of loans and grants. Land costs under the expropriation model were approximately $16,000 per family; they were about $3,600 per family under the directly negotiated model. These cost differences suggest an enormous cost advantage to the beneficiaries' direct purchase method. The high compensation paid to the landowners by the government of Brazil may explain the peaceful outcome of the program. Leite et al. (2004) find that 90 percent of the expropriations were initiated by local landless households, and they use the acquired land intensively and derive more than 70 percent of their income from it. Beneficiaries also feel that their lot improved substantially. Similar positive findings come from beneficiaries of the directly negotiated model. In a quasi-experimental impact evaluation, the rate of return in the directly negotiated land reform program has been estimated at between 2.1 and 12.6 percent, depending on whether gross or net returns are used (Romano et al. 2008). Beneficiaries' leadership and involvement combined with state support clearly have been positive factors (Akram-Lodhi et al. 2007).

In the Philippines, the Comprehensive Agrarian Reform Program promulgated in 1998 had redistributed a total of 8.2 million hectares of land by 2007, or about 83 percent of its revised target. It has taken nearly 20 years to achieve this, rather than the anticipated 10 years to achieve the full target. Capacity constraints, legal issues, and inadequate funding explain the slow pace. The redistribution includes about 3 million hectares of private land, and nearly 4 million hectares of public land, a significant portion of which was provided under social forestry grants (Balisacan 2007). As has been the case elsewhere, distribution of government-owned land was slowed by conflicting claims over the land. Half of the private agricultural land was acquired by compulsory acquisition, and the balance was acquired by negotiation and market purchase. Funding constraints also delayed the provision of agricultural and rural development support to the beneficiaries; and several donors stepped in to provide such support, although the amount provided fell far short of requirements. Despite the redistribution of land, the Gini coefficient of the landownership distribution did not change between 1990 and 2002, and it remains between that which is typical for Latin America and that which is typical for Asian countries. Between 1990 and 2000, the real income of both land reform beneficiaries and nonbeneficiaries fell, in line with the decline in real value added in Philippine agriculture. Nevertheless, land reform beneficiaries were less likely to be poor than were nonbeneficiaries, and the more so the longer they stayed in the program (Balisacan 2007).

After the end of Apartheid, South Africa introduced ambitious reforms in agriculture that eliminated virtually all privileges of the large-scale farm sector. Land reform included land restitution (so far through negotiated land purchases by the government), redistribution under the directly negotiated or community-driven model, and recognition of labor tenants' rights. To this point, less than 4 percent of the agricultural land under white ownership has been transferred to formerly disadvantaged groups, against a target of 30 percent. Reasons for the slowness of transfers include the weakness of the landless-labor movement, initially low budget allocations, and a plethora of administrative rigidities in the programs. Outcomes for the beneficiaries often have been poor because farms rarely were subdivided into family farms; instead, they operated as group or collective farms (van den Brink et al. 2006).

A number of other countries have put in place programs for directly negotiated acquisition of land by women (India), landless workers (India), and communities (Malawi, the Philippines, and several Central American countries). The World Bank assists most of these programs.

THE SOCIAL COST OF DELAYED REFORM: REVOLTS AND CIVIL WARS

Maintaining an agricultural structure based on relatively inefficient hacienda systems is costly. In addition to the static efficiency losses,[12] there are dynamic efficiency losses associated with the lack of incentives to invest in physical and human capital. Then there are the resource costs used in rent seeking to create and maintain the distortions that support the large farms. In a competitive rent-seeking equilibrium, those costs are equal to the rents. The distortions reduce employment in the sector, imposing an additional equity cost. Finally, the social costs of failing to reform often have included peasant uprisings and civil wars.

Consider Brazil, where the emergence of an agricultural structure dominated by large farms owes much to a policy that was always biased in favor of large farms—through subsidization of immigration to relieve large farms' labor constraint in the late 19th century, various interventions to maintain high prices (especially for coffee and sugar), and subsidized credit starting in the 1950s (Graham, Gauthier, and de Barros 1987). The social costs of distortions in favor of large farms have been substantial. Between 1950 and 1980, agricultural value added in real terms grew at a remarkable 4.5 percent a year; land area expanded at 3.2 percent a year, but agricultural employment grew at only 0.7 percent annually (Maddison 1992). Large-scale farms, assisted by large amounts of subsidized rural credit, mechanized their operations and evicted most of their internal tenants and workers, many of whom migrated to urban slums or ended up as highly insecure seasonal workers (*boias frias*) (Goodman and Redclift 1982). An alternative growth path based on smaller family farms could have provided rural employment and self-employment opportunities for many of these people and gainfully absorbed a substantial share of the rapidly growing population.

In many countries, protracted and violent struggles have reduced significantly the performance of the agricultural sector and the economy as a whole. Although peasants rarely have been able to initiate radical class struggles or revolutionary movements, they have been important and sometimes the dominant movers of such struggles once they were helped to organize by outsiders (France, Russia, China). In addition, many revolutionary movements took refuge in remote areas of limited agricultural potential—sometimes designated "communal areas," "reserves," or "homelands"—where peasants have provided both active and passive support for guerrilla fighters. Many analysts have emphasized the important role of peasant discontent in incidents of regional and national violence (Moore 1966; Huizer 1972; Migdal 1974; Scott 1976; Skocpol 1979; Goldstone 1991; Wickham-Crowley 1991; Kriger 1992; Rueschemeyer et al. 1992). The losses from such conflicts are difficult to measure, of course, but some notion of their magnitude can be gauged from the duration and intensity of such struggles, as these cases show:

- In Mozambique during the colonial era, peasants escaped from forced cultivation, vagrancy laws, and forced labor to inaccessible rural areas. Some of these areas also were centers of support for the Frelimo (Liberation Front of Mozambique) guerrillas from 1961 until independence in 1975 (Isaacman and Isaacman 1983). Land reforms that were initiated after independence, however, resulted in highly mechanized collective farms. The Frelimo government did little to address the problems of the free peasant sector. The counterrevolutionary Renamo (Mozambican National Resistance Party) movement in turn took advantage of the resulting peasant discontent. Peace was not achieved until about 1990.

- In Zimbabwe, large-scale eviction of some 85,000 families from European-owned farmlands during the period 1945–51 led to a general strike among Africans in 1948, and provided the basis for peasants' support of the Zimbabwean African National Union guerrillas in 1964 (Mosley 1983; Ranger 1985; Kriger 1992). Guerrilla fighters took up the peasants' grievances and used the tribal trust areas as bases to attack European farms. Although a substantial settlement program after independence provided land to Africans, a number of shortcomings limited the success of this program (see Deininger and Binswanger 1995). Policy distortions remained in place despite evidence that large farms are not more efficient than smallholder farmers. Land reform continued to be a major issue, and it resulted in the poorly managed Fast Track Land Redistribution that contributed to the complete collapse of the Zimbabwean economy that has occurred since 2000.
- In Guatemala, communal lands in effect were expropriated in 1879 by a law giving proprietors three months to register land titles, after which the land would be declared abandoned. Most of the "abandoned" land then was allocated to large coffee growers, who evicted traditional rightsholders. Redistribution attempts in 1951–54 were reversed following a military coup in 1954, when virtually all the land that had been subject to land reform was returned to the former owners and farms expropriated from foreigners were allocated in parcels averaging more than 3,000 hectares (Brockett 1984). Since then, there has been a repeated pattern of suppression and radicalization of resistance. Suppression of the cooperative movements of the 1960s led to formation of the Guerrilla Army of the Poor in 1972, with its main base in Indian highlands. Peasants responded to a wave of government-supported assassinations in 1976 by forming the Committee for Peasant Unity in 1978. Government massacres of protesting peasants followed. Although peace was restored in the early 1990s—more than 50 years after the first attempt at reform—continuing peasant demonstrations illustrate the cost of failure.
- Smallholder land in El Salvador was appropriated in a manner similar to that in Guatemala. A decree in 1856 stated that all communal land not at least two-thirds planted with coffee would be considered underutilized or idle, and would revert to the state. Communal land tenure was abolished in 1888. Sporadic revolts led to such countermeasures as the 1888 "security tax" on exports to finance rural police forces, a 1907 ban on rural unions, and creation of a national guard force in 1912 (McClintock 1985). Areas where land pressures were particularly severe emerged as centers of the revolt of 1932, during which 10,000–20,000 peasants were killed (Mason

1986). Guerrillas promising land and other agricultural reforms gained considerable support, particularly in rural areas, following tenant evictions in the cotton-growing lowlands during the period 1961–70. These evictions led to a 77 percent decline in the number of house plots available to tenants, as the number of tenants dropped from 55,000 to 17,000. Violence continued to escalate until 1979, when reform-minded army officers engineered a coup and introduced land reform in an attempt to preempt a shift in popular support to the Farabundo Marti National Liveration Front-Democratic Revolutionary Front guerrilla forces. Narrow eligibility rules sharply limited the number of land reform beneficiaries, and more than a decade of civil war ensued. The peace accord of 1992 mandated additional land reform.

- In Colombia, conflicts over land between tenants and large-scale farmers at the frontier escalated from isolated local attacks in the early 1920s to more coordinated tenant actions by the late 1920s. Although various kinds of reform legislation were considered during the 1930s, the law finally passed in 1936 vested rights to previously public lands with large landlords rather than with the tenants cultivating the land. A series of tenant evictions followed, leading to a quarter-century of violence (1940–65) during which guerrillas recruited support from peasant groups. Land reform legislation in 1961 and 1968 regularized previous land invasions, but did nothing to improve the operational distribution of landholdings. Far fewer peasants benefited from the reforms than had been evicted previously (Zamosc 1989; de Janvry and Sadoulet 1989). Peasant land invasions intensified during the early 1970s, leading to the declaration of a state of emergency after 1974. Regional mobilizations, strikes, and blockades flared up again in 1984, indicating that the conflict was not yet resolved. Indeed, violence and conflict, partly fueled by the unresolved land question, continue today.
- Much of the rural support for the Shining Path guerrillas in Peru can be traced to the exclusion of most of the highland Indians from agricultural benefits and the benefits of the agrarian reform in 1973, which helped primarily the relatively few workers in the coastal area. As a result of the guerrilla activity, more than half the government departments in the country became practically inaccessible to government forces (McClintock 1984), and public investment in these regions was halted. Poor economic management during the 1980s and continued activity by Shining Path have led to capital flight and economywide decline. It was only under the Fujimori regime that the power of the Shining Path finally was broken.

Other countries that have experienced prolonged conflicts over land include Angola, Chile, and Nicaragua. Although the policies that created and maintained dual landownership distributions do not lead necessarily to violent struggle (because other intervening factors are likely to be important), they clearly play a significant role in many cases.

CREDIT, POLICY DISTORTIONS, AND LAND SALES MARKETS

Are Junker estates and large mechanized farms economically more efficient than smaller, family-operated holdings? If they are not, equalizing the ownership distribution or breaking up collective or state farms into family farms would enhance both efficiency and equity. A huge body of literature has emerged on this topic, and it is summarized in Binswanger, Deininger, and Feder (1995). Suffice it to say that, with few exceptions, the superior productivity and profitability of family farms over large commercial farms (in the absence of subsidies and distortions) continues today (World Bank 2007).

This leads to the second central question for land reform: If large operational holdings usually are less efficient than family farms, why do large landowners in market economies not rent or sell to family farmers? The rental market historically has been the most important mechanism to circumvent the diseconomies of scale associated with large ownership holdings. But the history of land reform shows that long-term rental of entire farms often implies a high risk of loss of land to tenants; and long-term tenancy is no longer an option. Short-term rental of parcels of land cannot create small family-operated holdings. If tenancy is no longer an option, what prevents large owners from selling their land to family farmers?

Covariate Risks and Imperfect Credit Markets

The immobility of land makes land a preferred form of collateral in credit markets. Credit can be used both for production inputs and for consumption loans that can serve as insurance substitutes when harvests fall short. Thus the collateral value of land is useful both for production and as an insurance substitute. As discussed, if landownership provides access to credit and helps in diffusing risk, the buyer has to compensate the seller for the utility derived from those services of land (Feder et al. 1988). Therefore, where land has collateral value, its equilibrium price at given credit costs always will exceed the present discounted value of the income stream produced from the land. If a buyer were to mortgage the land to pay for its purchase, he could no longer use it for production credit. With imperfect insurance markets, only unmortgaged land yields a flow of income or utility, the present value of which equals the land price. A buyer relying on credit therefore cannot pay for the land out of agricultural profits alone. Thus land sales are likely to be financed out of household savings.

This need to purchase land out of savings tends to make the distribution of landholdings more unequal. In particularly good crop years, savings would be high for all farmers, and there would be few sellers and many potential buyers of land. Good years thus are not good times for land purchases. In bad crop years, farmers would have little savings with which to finance land purchases, and many would want to sell land to finance consumption or repay debts. In particularly bad periods (perhaps after consecutive harvest failures), moneylenders would be the only ones in the local rural economy having assets with which to buy land—namely, their debt claims. Many borrowers would be unable to service those debts, and the moneylenders could foreclose on them. Moneylenders would prefer to take over such land because the price of land would be lower than average in bad years. So, in bad crop years, land would be sold mainly to moneylenders as distress sales, or to individuals with incomes or assets from outside the local rural economy. We should expect then that land sales in areas with poorly developed insurance and capital markets would be few and limited mainly to distress sales. Results from Bangladesh and India confirm this hypothesis.[13]

Historically, distress sales have played a major role in the accumulation of land for large manorial estates in China (Shih 1992) and in early Japan (Takekoshi 1967), and for large landlord estates in Punjab (Hamid 1983). The abolition of communal tenure and the associated loss of mechanisms for diversifying risk are among the factors underlying the emergence of large estates in Central America (Brockett 1984).

Although land sales markets generally are regressive for the poor (Carter and Salgado 2001), there are a few cases in which land sales markets have had a positive impact on the poor: in relatively land-abundant settings, households who received relatively less land from the family sometimes can compensate for that initial disadvantage through land purchases (see Otsuka and Quisumbing [2001] for Ghana, and Baland et al. [2007] for Uganda).

We have seen that moral hazard, covariance of income, and the collateral value of land imply absent insurance and imperfect credit markets. In such environments, land sales markets are likely to become a means for large landowners to accumulate more land. Even where markets for labor, current inputs, and land sales and rentals are perfectly competitive, weak intertemporal markets for risk diffusion may prevent land sales markets from bringing about Pareto-improving trades and an efficient farm size distribution—an illustration of the theorem of the second best.

Impact of Policy Distortions

The existence of common policy distortions intensifies the failure of the land sales market to distribute land. Consider first an idealized case of competitive and undistorted land, labor, risk, and credit markets. The value of land for agricultural use would equal the present value of agricultural profits. If the poor have to borrow to buy land at its present value, they will need to use all of the farm profits to service the debt; and the only income stream available for consumption is the imputed value of family labor. Because the poor could get the same wage in the labor market, they are no better off as landowners than they would be as wage laborers. If the poor would have to pay higher interest rates than wealthy borrowers, they would be even worse off after buying land.

We have seen that family farmers often are more efficient than large farms; therefore, they might get additional income from buying the land that we ignored in the paragraphs directly above. However, this advantage normally is more than offset by a number of factors and distortions that increase the price of land above the capitalized value of such a higher agricultural income stream. The most important factors and distortions driving land prices up above the capitalized value of agriculture are the following:

- Even where there are no credit subsidies, large landowners have a transaction cost advantage in securing credit; and transaction costs may even block access to mortgage credit altogether for small borrowers. Where, in addition, there are credit subsidies, they tend to be capitalized into land values, as shown by Feder et al. (1988) and by Brandão and de Rezende (1989). When Brandão and de Rezende simulate land prices using results of econometric estimation for Brazil (1966–89), they find that 6 percent of the increase in land value was attributable to credit subsidies and 28 percent to macroeconomic instability (inflation).
- In periods of macroeconomic instability, nonagricultural investors may use land as an asset to hedge against inflation so that an inflation premium is incorporated into the real land price.
- With populations growing and urban demand for land increasing, the price of land is expected to appreciate, and some of this real appreciation is capitalized into the current land price.
- Many countries exempt agricultural income from income tax; and even where there is no general exemption, agricultural income is de facto subject to lower tax rates. These preferences will be capitalized partly or fully into land values. Because the poor pay no taxes and so cannot benefit from the tax break, they do not receive the corresponding income stream.

Where any of these factors pushes the price of land above the price justified by the fundamentals of expected agricultural profits, the poor have difficulty buying land, even if they are provided with credit on market terms.

POLICY IMPLICATIONS FOR REDISTRIBUTIVE LAND REFORM

Most redistributive land reform is motivated by public concern about the rising tensions prompted by an unequal land distribution. The common pattern is concentration of landownership among relatively few large owners in an economy where labor is abundant and land is scarce. Thus the masses of landless laborers and tenants who derive their livelihoods from agriculture receive relatively less income because their only asset is labor. Redistributive land reform also can increase efficiency by transferring land from less productive large units to more productive small, family-based units.[14] Because of other market imperfections, however, land markets typically will not affect such transformations of ownership patterns. The value of the land to large owners may exceed the discounted sum of agricultural income that smallholders can expect to receive, despite their productivity advantages from lower supervision costs, if there are policy distortions favoring large owners or if the access of small farmers to long-term credit already has been exhausted by mortgage-based land acquisition.

Market values of land are determined in a way that prevents small farmers who lack equity from building up viable farms and improving their standards of living while repaying their land mortgages. Land reform schemes that require payment of the full market value of the land are likely to fail unless special arrangements are made. In the simplest case, beneficiaries soon default and the program ends. Many ambitious land reform programs simply run out of steam because full compensation of former owners at market prices imposes fiscal requirements that the political forces are unwilling to meet (that was the fate of programs in Brazil until the early 1990s, the Philippines, and República Bolivariana de Venezuela). Some programs try to avoid this problem by compensating landowners with bonds whose real value erodes over time. It is not surprising that landowners oppose this thinly disguised confiscation, and such programs are politically feasible only in circumstances of political upheaval (Cuba; Japan; Korea; Taiwan, China; or Vietnam). Another approach is to finance land purchases through foreign grants, from internal tax revenues or inflationary monetary expansion, or by some combination thereof.

Before any land redistribution program is introduced, the implicit and explicit distortions that drive land prices above the capitalized value of agricultural profits need to be eliminated. Otherwise, small farmers will continue to have an incentive to sell to larger farmers because the environment still will favor large ownership holdings. Political momentum for land reform normally is required to bring about such an important policy change. The poor must be provided with either the land or a grant to help them buy the land to compensate for their lack of equity. Credit to beneficiaries for land purchases can play only a subsidiary role. Removing distortions also lowers the amount of grant assistance needed by small farmers to support their land acquisition.

The type of large-scale farms influences the gains to be expected from land reform. On landlord estates, would-be beneficiaries are managing operational units already, so land reform addresses primarily the equity concerns of society, transferring the entitlement to land rents while leaving operational farm structure largely unchanged. With hacienda estates, the threat of land reform legislation often leads to the eviction of tenants and reductions in the resident workforce. The large commercial farms that result are difficult to subdivide. They involve major changes in the organization of production. The resident labor force and external workers have little or no independent farming experience; and, in many cases, neither the infrastructure nor investments in physical capital provide an appropriate basis for smallholder cultivation.

In those situations, land has to be acquired either by the state for subsequent allocation to settlers or by the settlers' direct purchase from the former owner through directly negotiated or community-driven land reform. The Zimbabwean example illustrates once again that state acquisition of land without adequate compensation—amounting to full or partial confiscation—is politically and economically costly. Instead, the state usually acquires the land through negotiation (South Africa), expropriation (Brazil), or a combination of the two. To avoid unrest and prolonged litigation, the state usually pays high prices or compensation. When settlers buy the land directly from the former owner, the problem of the state negotiating for or expropriating specific parcels of land—and the consequent delays and political risks—can be avoided. The beneficiaries usually are assisted in the negotiations by civil society organizations (Brazil) or by the ministry of lands (Malawi, South Africa), and they tend to pay much lower prices than does the state. Direct acquisition puts potential sellers in competition with each other and usually results in lower land prices than does either negotiation with the state or expropriation. And it combines purchase and land allocation to beneficiaries into a single step, simplifying and accelerating the process.

Opinions are divided on redistributive reform of wage plantations in the classic plantation crops—bananas, sugar, tea, and palm oil. The fact that contract farming in those crops is practiced successfully in many parts of the developing world indicates that converting plantations to contract farming is feasible. Indeed, Hayami, Quisumbing, and Adriano (1990) describe the successful conversion of even a banana plantation into a contract farming system in the Philippines, and they strongly argue for bringing about more such conversions through a progressive land tax. The efficiency gains from lower supervision costs associated with such a step are likely to be offset, however, by the genuine economies of scale in plantation crops.

The record of the impact of land reforms decidedly has been mixed, with few proven examples of unambiguously positive results for the settlers. Most often, this was a consequence of inadequate provision of infrastructure and support services to the new farmers. Although smallholders can prosper even with inadequate support, the availability of technology and of competitive input and output markets is critical for land reform to increase efficiency and to transform small farmers into rural entrepreneurs. Appropriate institutional arrangements are needed to ensure access to extension services, credit, and markets. Such institutions are especially important where land reform involves resettling beneficiaries on former Junker estates or large mechanized commercial farms. To reap the efficiency gains of family farming under those conditions seems to require increasing the density of family labor, and that may require resettling landless workers from outside. Reform of these systems will continue to be difficult; but where the alternative to reform is the perpetuation of large economic and social costs, including the possibility of revolt and civil war, the cost of failing to reform may be enormous.

NOTES

1. Box 2.1 provides the authors' definitions for terms used in this chapter.
2. Meillassoux distinguishes merchant slavery from systems of *aristocratic slavery*, which regularly replenished a pool of domestic slaves through warfare and raids of subsistence-oriented peasant populations.
3. The temperate zones of the Americas (Canada, the northeastern United States, southern Brazil, and Argentina) escaped slavery because their products could not be exported competitively to temperate-zone Europe until the advent of the steamship and the railroad—at a time when slavery had gone out of style. The tropical and subtropical crops—sugar, cotton, and tobacco—faced no competition in European markets.
4. In Southern Rhodesia, Africans had been encouraged to cultivate maize through the Master Farmer Program in the late 1920s, when European farmers found it more profitable to grow tobacco and cotton. When those markets collapsed, monopoly marketing and dual price systems were introduced and the Master Farmer Program was abandoned, with responsible officials publicly declaring that they had never intended to "teach the Natives to grow maize in competition with European producers" (Phimister 1988, p. 235).
5. Evidence from Asia, Europe, and North Africa can be found in Binswanger, Deininger, and Feder (1995).
6. For more detail on Kenya, see Deininger and Binswanger (1995).
7. For more detail on South Africa, see Deininger and Binswanger (1995).
8. For more detail on Zimbabwe, see Deininger and Binswanger (1995).
9. This "Junker path" was described by Lenin (1899), who considered it to be part of a necessary differentiation of the peasantry. It has been analyzed extensively by de Janvry (1981), who was the first to show the compelling impact of "reformist" land legislation in Latin America on the elimination of traditional forms of labor relations and the expulsion of internal peasants.
10. de Janvry and Sadoulet (1989) argue that the threat of land reform and large landowners' ability to lobby in coalition with the urban sector for subsidies and provision of public goods led those landowners to mechanize and make the transition from haciendas to large mechanized commercial farms in Chile (after 1972), Colombia (1961–68), Ecuador (1936–57), Peru (1964–69), and República Bolivariana de Venezuela (1959–70). In Ecuador, two separate stages can be distinguished. Widespread eviction of tenants and the formation of Junker estates until 1957 were followed by a period of increased emphasis on the family-farm sector together with widespread mechanization (1958–73).
11. Ortega (1988) offers quantitative evidence of the decline of the collective sector throughout Latin America. In Peru, the absence of economies of scale led reform beneficiaries effectively to subdivide reform collectives by concentrating effort on their private plots and to press for legal subdivisions and individual land titles (Horton 1972; McClintock 1981; Kay 1985). Collectives failed in Zimbabwe and soon were abandoned in favor of a smallholder-oriented strategy (Weiner et al. 1985). Similarly, collectives failed in the Dominican Republic and were replaced by cooperatives, with individually owned plots (Meyer 1989). Land reform cooperatives in Panama are highly indebted and use labor far below profit-maximizing levels (Thiesenhusen 1989). Algerian production cooperatives experienced low productivity, membership desertion, high use of mechanization, and considerable underemployment of the workforce (Pfeiffer 1985; Trautman 1985). The same pattern

of declining output and transformation into a "collective Junker estate" has been observed in Mozambique (Wuyts 1985).

12. Quantitative estimates of this efficiency loss are scarce, but Loveman (1976) estimates that Chile could have saved roughly $100 million a year in agricultural imports during the period 1949–64 had the 40 percent of land left uncultivated by large landlords been cultivated.
13. Farmers in India experiencing two consecutive drought years have been found to be 150 percent more likely than other farmers to sell their land (Rosenzweig and Wolpin 1993). The implications of different insurance mechanisms on distress sales and the land ownership distribution are demonstrated by a comparison of the evolution of ownership holdings from about 1960 to 1980 in Bangladesh and India (Cain 1981). These villages were characterized by distinct differences in mechanisms of risk insurance: In Maharashtra, India, an employment guarantee scheme operated throughout the period and attained participation rates of up to 97 percent of all households during disasters. Such schemes were absent after the major flood episodes in Bangladesh. Sixty percent of land sales in Bangladesh were undertaken to obtain food and medicine. Downward mobility affected large and small farmers equally. Sixty percent of the currently landless had lost their land since 1960, and the Gini coefficient of landownership distribution increased from 0.6 to almost 0.7. This result contrasts sharply with the Indian villages, where land sales for consumption purposes accounted only for 14 percent, and were incurred mainly by the rich to meet social obligations. Sixty-four percent of land sales were undertaken to generate capital for productive investment. This finding suggests that the poor not only were able to avoid distress sales, but actually could acquire some land as rich households liquidated agricultural assets to be able to pursue nonagricultural investments.
14. Under circumstances of extreme poverty and landlessness, redistribution of land also can enhance efficiency by improving the nutritional well-being and thus the productive capacity of the population (Dasgupta and Ray 1986, 1987; Moene 1992).

REFERENCES

Abercombie, K. C. 1972. "Agricultural Mechanization and Employment in Latin America." *International Labour Review 106 (1): 11–45.*

Akram-Lodhi, A. Haroon, Saturnino M. Borras Jr., Cristobal Kay, and Kerry McKinley. 2007. "Neoliberal Globalization, Land and Poverty: Implications for Public Action." In *Land, Poverty, and Livelihoods in an Era of Globalization: Perspectives from Developing and Transition Countries,* ed. A. Haroon Akram-Lodhi, Saturnino M. Borras Jr., and Cristobal Kay, 383–98. Abingdon, U.K.: Routledge.

Baland, Jean-Marie, Frédéric Gaspart, Jean-Philippe Platteau, and Frank Place. 2007. "The Distributive Impact of Land Markets in Uganda." *Economic Development and Cultural Change 55* (2): 283–311.

Balisacan, Arsenio M. 2007. "Agrarian Reform and Poverty Reduction in the Philippines." Paper prepared for the Second Regional Policy Dialogue on Agrarian Reform and Rural Development: The Case of the Philippines, Manila, May 30.

Barham, Bradford L., and Malcolm Childress. 1992. "Membership Desertion as an Adjustment Process on Honduran Agrarian Reform *Enterprises." Economic Development and Cultural Change* 40 (3): 587–613.

Bender, Gerald J. 1978. *Angola Under the Portuguese: The Myth and the Reality.* London: Heinemann Educational.

Ben-Ner, Avner. 1984. "On the Stability of the Cooperative Type of Organization." *Journal of Comparative Economics* 8 (3): 247–60.

Berman, Bruce. 1990. *Control and Crisis in Colonial Kenya: The Dialectic of Domination.* London: James Currey.

Binswanger, Hans P., Klaus Deininger, and Gershon Feder. 1993. "Agricultural Land Relations in the Developing World." *American Journal of Agricultural Economics* 75 (5): 1242–48.

———. 1995. "Power, Distortions, Revolt and Reform in Agricultural Land Relations." In *Handbook of Development Economics,* Volume 3B, ed. Jere Behrman and T. N. Srinivasan, 2659–772. Amsterdam, The Netherlands: Elsevier.

Blum, Jerome. 1977. *The End of the Old Order in Europe.* Princeton, NJ: Princeton University Press.

Bonin, John P., and Louis Putterman. 1993. "Incentives and Monitoring in Cooperatives with Labor-Proportionate Sharing Schemes." *Journal of Comparative Economics* 17 (3): 663–86.

Boserup, Ester. 1965. *The Conditions of Agricultural Growth: The Economics of Agrarian Change Under Population Pressure.* New York: Aldine.

Brandão, A.S.P., and G. C. de Rezende. 1989. "Land Prices and Land Rents in Brazil." In *Agriculture and Governments in an Interdependent World: Proceedings of the Twentieth International Conference of Agricultural Economists, Held at Buenos Aires, Argentina, 24–31, August, 1988,* ed. Allen Maunder and Alberto Valdés. Aldershot, U.K.: Dartmouth and Gower.

Brasselle, Anne-Sophie, Frédéric Gaspart, and Jean-Philippe Platteau. 1997. "Land Tenure Security and Investment Incentives: Some Further Puzzling Evidence from Burkina Faso." Working paper. Center of Research in the Economics of Development, University of Namur, Belgium.

Brenner, Robert. 1976. "The Origins of Capitalist Development: A Critique of Neo-Smithian Marxism." *New Left Review* 104 (1): 25–92.

Brockett, Charles D. 1984. "Malnutrition, Public Policy, and Agrarian Change in Guatemala." *Journal of Interamerican Studies and World Affairs* 26 (4): 477–97.

Bundy, Colin. 1979. *The Rise and Fall of the South African Peasantry.* Berkeley, CA: University of California Press.

Cain, Mead. 1981. "Risk and Insurance: Perspectives on Fertility and Agrarian Change in India and Bangladesh." *Population and Development Review* 7 (3): 435–74.

Callison, Charles Stuart. 1983. *Land-to-the-Tiller in the Mekong Delta: Economic, Social, and Political Effects of Land Reform in Four Villages of South Vietnam.* Lanham, MD: University Press of America.

Carter, Michael, and Ramón Salgado. 2001. "Land Market Liberalization and the Agrarian Question in Latin America." In *Access to Land, Rural Poverty, and Public Action,* ed. Alain de Janvry, Gustavo Gordillo, Jean-Philippe Platteau, and Elisabeth Sadoulet, 246–78. Oxford, U.K.: Oxford University Press.

Chuma, Hiroyuki, Keiro Otsuka, and Yujiro Hayami. 1990. "On the Dominance of Land Tenancy over Permanent Labor Contract in Agrarian Economies." *Journal of the Japanese and International Economies* 4 (2): 101–20.

Clarence-Smith, W. G. 1979. *Slaves, Peasants, and Capitalists in Southern Angola, 1840–1926.* Cambridge, U.K.: Cambridge University Press.

Colburn, Forrest D. 1990. *Managing the Commanding Heights: Nicaragua's State Enterprises.* Berkeley, CA: University of California Press.

Cone, L. Winston, and John Francis Lipscomb. 1972. *The History of Kenya Agriculture.* Nairobi, Kenya: University Press of Africa.

Coulson, Andrew. 1982. *Tanzania: A Political Economy.* Oxford, U.K.: Oxford University Press.

Dasgupta, Partha, and Debraj Ray. 1986. "Inequality as a Determinant of Malnutrition and Unemployment: Theory." *Economic Journal* 96 (384): 1011–34.

———. 1987. "Inequality as a Determinant of Malnutrition and Unemployment: Policy." *Economic Journal* 97 (385): 177–88.

Deininger, Klaus, and Hans P. Binswanger. 1995. "Rent Seeking and the Development of Large-Scale Agriculture in Kenya, South Africa, and Zimbabwe." *Economic Development and Cultural Change* 43 (3): 493–522.

de Janvry, Alain. 1981. "The Role of Land Reform in Economic Development: Policies and Politics." *American Journal of Agricultural Economics* 63 (2): 384–92.

de Janvry, Alain, Gustavo Gordillo, Jean-Philippe Platteau, and Elisabeth Sadoulet, eds. 2001. *Access to Land, Rural Poverty, and Public Action.* Oxford, U.K.: Oxford University Press.

de Janvry, Alain, and Elisabeth Sadoulet. 1989. "A Study in Resistance to Institutional Change: The Lost Game of Latin American Land Reform." *World Development* 17 (9): 1397–407.

Dobb, Maurice. 1963. *Studies in the Development of Capitalism.* London: Routledge and Keegan Paul.

Dorner, Peter, and William C. Thiesenhusen. 1990. "Selected Land Reforms in East and Southeast Asia: Their Origins and Impacts." *Asian-Pacific Economic Literature* 4 (1): 65–95.

Downs, R. E., and Stephen P. Reyna. 1988. *Land and Society in Contemporary Africa.* Hanover, NH: University Press of New England.

Du Run-sheng. 2006. *The Course of China's Rural Reform.* Washington, DC: International Food Policy Research Institute.

Feder, Gershon, Tongroj Onchan, Yongyuth Chalamwong, and Chira Hongladarom. 1988. *Land Policies and Farm Productivity in Thailand.* Baltimore, MD: Johns Hopkins University Press.

Gemery, Henry A., and Jan S. Hogendorn. 1979. *The Uncommon Market: Essays in the Economic History of the Atlantic Slave Trade.* New York: Academic Press.

Gerschenkron, Alexander. 1965. "Russia: Agrarian Policies and Industrialization, 1861–1917." In *The Cambridge Economic History of Europe.* Cambridge, U.K.: Cambridge University Press.

Ghai, Dharam, Cristobal Kay, and Peter Peek. 1988. *Labour and Development in Rural Cuba.* Basingstoke, U.K.: Palgrave Macmillan.

Goldstone, Jack A. 1991. *Revolution and Rebellion in the Early Modern World.* Berkeley, CA: University of California Press.

Goodman, David, and Michael Redclift. 1982. *From Peasant to Proletarian: Capitalist development and Agrarian Transition.* New York: St. Martin's Press.

Graham, Douglas H., Howard Gauthier, and Jose Roberto Mendonca de Barros. 1987. "Thirty Years of Agricultural Growth in Brazil: Crop Performance, Regional Profile, and Recent Policy Review." *Economic Development and Cultural Change* 36 (1): 1–34.

Griffin, Keith, and Roger Hay. 1985. "Problems of Agricultural Development in Socialist Ethiopia: An Overview and a Suggested Strategy." *Journal of Peasant Studies* 13 (1): 37–66.

Hamid, N. 1983. "Growth of Small-Scale Industry in Pakistan." *Pakistan Economic and Social Review* 21 (1/2): 37–76.

Hayami, Yujiro, Agnes R. Quisumbing, and Lourdes S. Adriano. 1990. *Toward an Alternative Land Reform Paradigm: A Philippine Perspective.* Quezon City, Philippines: Ateneo de Manila University Press.

Heath, John R. 1992. "Evaluating the Impact of Mexico's Land Reform on Agricultural Productivity." *World Development* 20 (5): 695–711.

Heath, John R., and Hans P. Binswanger. 1998. "Policy-Induced Effects of Natural Resource Degradation: The Case of Colombia." In *Agriculture and the Environment: Perspectives on Sustainable Rural Development,* ed. Ernst Lutz, 22–34. Washington, DC: World Bank.

Hendricks, Fred T. 1990. *The Pillars of Apartheid Land Tenure, Rural Planning and the Chieftaincy.* Uppsala, Sweden: Almqvist and Wiksell.

Hilton, Rodney, ed. 1976. *The Transition from Feudalism to Capitalism.* London: New Left Books.

Horton, Douglas E. 1972. *Haciendas and Cooperatives: A Study of Estate Organization, Land Reform, and New Reform Enterprises in Peru.* Ithaca, NY: Cornell University Press.

Huizer, Gerrit. 1972. *The Revolutionary Potential of Peasants in Latin America.* Lexington, MA: Lexington Books.

Iliffe, John. 1979. *A Modern History of Tanganyika.* Cambridge, U.K.: University of Cambridge Press.

Isaacman, Allen, and Barbara Isaacman. 1983. *Mozambique: From Colonialism to Revolution: 1900–1982.* Boulder, CO: Westview Press.

Kay, Cristobal. 1985. "Capitalist Development and the Peasant-Economy in Peru." *Journal of Development Studies* 21 (4): 659–61.

Kay, Cristobal, and P. Silva. 1992. *Development and Social Change in the Chilean Countryside: From the Pre-Land Reform Period to the Democratic Transition.* Amsterdam, The Netherlands: Center for Latin American Research and Development.

King, Russell. 1977. *Land Reform: A World Survey.* Boulder, CO: Westview Press.

Koo, Anthony Y.C. 1973. "Towards a More General Model of Land Tenancy and Reform." *Quarterly Journal of Economics* 87 (4): 567–80.

Kriger, Norma J. 1992. *Zimbabwe's Guerrilla War, Peasant Voices.* Cambridge, U.K.: Cambridge University Press.

Leite, Sérgio, Beatriz Heredia, Leonilde Medeiros, Moacir Palmeira, and Rosângela Cinarão. 2004. *Impactos dos Assentamentos: Um Estudo sobre o Meio Rural Brasileiro.* São Paulo, Brazil: Editora UNESP.

Lenin, Vladimir I. 1899. *The Development of Capitalism in Russia: The Process of the Formation of a Home Market for Large-Scale Industry.* Moscow: Progress Publishers.

Lin, Justin Yifu. 1992. "Rural Reforms and Agricultural Growth in China." *American Economic Review* 82 (1): 34–51.

Lin, Justin Yifu, F. Cai, and Z. Li. 1994. "Why China's Economic Reforms Have Been Successful: Its Implications for Other Reforming Economies." Peking University and the Chinese Academy of Social Sciences, Beijing.

Lipton, Merle. 1985. *Capitalism and Apartheid, South Africa, 1910–84.* Totowa, NJ: Rowman and Allanheld.

Loveman, Brian. 1976. *Struggle in the Countryside: Politics and Rural Labor in Chile, 1919–1973.* Bloomington, IN: Indiana University Press.

Maddison, Angus. 1992. *The Political Economy of Poverty, Equity, and Growth: Brazil and Mexico.* Washington, DC: World Bank.

Mandala, Elias C. 1990. *Work and Control in a Peasant Economy: A History of the Lower Tchiri Valley in Malawi, 1859–1960.* Madison, WI: University of Wisconsin Press.

Mason, T. David. 1986. "Land Reform and the Breakdown of Clientelist Politics in El Salvador." *Comparative Political Studies* 18 (4): 487–516.

McClintock, Cynthia. 1981. *Peasant Cooperatives and Political Change in Peru.* Princeton, NJ: Princeton University Press.

———. 1984. "Why Peasants Rebel: The Case of Peru's Sender Luminoso." *World Politics* 37: 48–84.

McClintock, Michael. 1985. *The American Connection, Vol. 1, State Terror and Popular Resistance in El Salvador.* London: Zed Books.

McGregor, Andrew. 1977. "Rent Extraction and the Survival of the Agricultural Production Cooperative." *American Journal of Agricultural Economics* 59 (2): 478–88.

McMillan, John, John Whalley, and Lijing Zhu. 1989. "The Impact of China's Economic Reforms on Agricultural Productivity Growth." *Journal of Political Economy* 97 (4): 781–807.

Meillasoux, Claude. 1981. *Maidens, Meal, and Money: Capitalism and the Domestic Community.* Cambridge, U.K.: Cambridge University Press.

Melmed-Sanjak, Jolyne S., and Michael R. Carter. 1991. "The Economic Viability and Stability of 'Capitalised Family Farming': An Analysis of Agricultural Decollectivisation in Peru." *Journal of Development Studies* 27 (2): 190–210.

Meyer, Carrie A. 1989. "Agrarian Reform in the Dominican Republic: An Associative Solution to the Collective/Individual Dilemma." *World Development* 17 (8): 1255–67.

Migdal, Joal S. 1974. *Peasants, Politics, and Revolution: Pressure toward Political and Social Change in the Third World.* Princeton, NJ: Princeton University Press.

Mitchell, Janet. 1990. "Perfect Equilibrium and Intergenerational Conflict in a Model of Cooperative Enterprise Growth." *Journal of Economic Theory* 51 (1): 48–76.

Moene, Karl Ove. 1992. "Poverty and Landownership." *American Economic Review* 82 (1): 52–64.

Moore, Barrington. 1966. *Social Origins of Dictatorship and Democracy: Lord and Peasant in the Making of the Modern World.* Boston, MA: Beacon Press.

Mosley, Paul. 1983. *The Settler Economies: Studies in the Economic History of Kenya and Southern Rhodesia, 1900–1963.* Cambridge, U.K.: Cambridge University Press.

Noronha, Raymond. 1985. "A Review of the Literature on Land Tenure Systems in Sub-Saharan Africa." Discussion Paper ARU43. World Bank, Washington, DC.

North, Douglas C., and Robert P. Thomas. 1971. "The Rise and Fall of the Manorial System: A Theoretical Model." *Journal of Economic History* 31 (4): 777–803.

Ortega, Emiliano. 1988. *Transformaciones Agrarias y Campesinado: De la Participación a la Exclusión.* Santiago, Chile: Corporación de Investigación para Latinoamerica.

Otsuka, Keijiro, and Agnes Quisumbing. 2001. "Land Rights and Natural Resource Management in the Transition to Individual Ownership: Case Studies from Ghana and Indonesia." In *Access to Land, Rural Poverty, and Public Action,* ed. Alain de Janvry, Gustavo Gordillo, Jean-Philippe Platteau, and Elisabeth Sadoulet. Oxford, U.K.: Oxford University Press.

Palmer, Robin. 1977. *Land and Racial Domination in Rhodesia. Berkeley,* CA: University of California Press.

Pazvakavambwa, Simon. 2007. "Land Redistribution in Zimbabwe." Paper presented at the Southern African Regional Poverty Network, World Bank Institute, and United Kingdom Department for International Development Course on Land Redistribution: Towards a Common Vision, Pretoria, South Africa, July 9–13.

Pfeiffer, Karen. 1985. *Agrarian Reform under State Capitalism in Algeria.* Boulder, CO: Westview Press.

Phimister, Ian R. 1988. *An Economic and Social History of Zimbabwe 1890–1948: Capital Accumulation and Class Struggle.* London: Longman.

Pingali, Prabhu, Yves Bigot, and Hans P. Binswanger. 1987. *Agricultural Mechanization and the Evolution of Farming Systems in Sub-Saharan Africa.* Baltimore, MD: Johns Hopkins University Press.

Pingali, Prabhu L., and V. T. Xuan. 1992. "Vietnam: Decollectivization and Rice Productivity Growth." *Economic Development and Cultural Change* 40 (4): 697–718.

Ranger, Terence. 1985. *Peasant Consciousness and Guerrilla War in Zimbabwe: A Comparative Study.* London: James Currey.

Romano, Claudia, Henrique D. Neder, José Maria F.J. da Silveira, and Marcelo M. Magalhães. 2008. "The Impact of a Market-Assisted Land Reform Program in Brazil: The Case of the Cédula da Terra." Unpublished manuscript.

Rosenzweig, Mark R., and Kenneth I. Wolpin. 1993. "Credit Market Constraints, Consumption Smoothing, and the Accumulation of Durable Production Assets in Low-Income Countries: Investment in Bullocks in India." *Journal of Political Economy* 101 (2): 223–44.

Rueschemeyer, Dietrich, Evelyne Huber Stephens, and John D. Stephens. 1992. *Capitalist Development and Democracy.* Chicago, IL: University of Chicago Press.

Ruthenberg, Hans. 1980. *Farming Systems in the Tropics.* Oxford, U.K.: Oxford University Press.

Scott, James C. 1976. *The Moral Economy of the Peasant: Rebellion and Subsistence in Southeast Asia.* New Haven, CT: Yale University Press.

Shih, James Chin. 1992. *Chinese Rural Society in Transition: A Case Study of the Lake Tai Area.* Berkeley, CA: University of California Press.

Skocpol, Theda. 1979. *States and Social Revolutions: A Comparative Analysis of France, Russia, and China.* Cambridge, U.K.: Cambridge University Press.

Sweezy, Paul Marlor, Maurice Dobb, Kohachiro Takahashi, and Rodney Hilton. 1976. *The Transition from Feudalism to Capitalism.* London: NLB.

Takekoshi, Yosburo. 1967. *The Economic Aspects of the History of the Civilization of Japan.* London: Macmillan.

Thiesenhusen, William C., ed. 1989. *Searching for Agrarian Reform in Latin America.* Boston, MA: Unwin Hyman.

Trautman, W. 1985. "Rural Development in Algeria: The System of State-Directed Cooperatives." *Quarterly Journal of International Agriculture* 24 (2): 258–67.

Vail, Leroy, and Landeg White. 1980. *Capitalism and Colonialism in Mozambique: A Study of Quelimane District.* Minneapolis, MN: University of Minnesota Press.

van den Brink, Rogier, Glen Thomas, Hans Binswanger, John Bruce, and Frank Byamugisha. 2006. *Consensus, Confusion, and Controversy: Selected Land Reform Issues in Sub-Saharan Africa.* Working Paper 71. Washington, DC: World Bank.

Weiner, Daniel, Sam Moyo, Barry Munslow, and P. Okeefe. 1985. "Land Use and Agricultural Productivity in Zimbabwe." *Journal of Modern African Studies* 23 (2): 251–85.

Wickham-Crowley, Timothy P. 1991. *Exploring Revolution: Essays on Latin American Insurgency and Revolutionary Theory.* Armonk, NY: M. E. Sharpe.

Wilson, Francis. 1971. "Farming 1866–1966." In *The Oxford History of South Africa, Volume II, South Africa 1870–1966,* ed. Monica Wilson and Leonard Thompson. Oxford, U.K.: Oxford University Press.

World Bank. 2001. "Mexico Land Policy—A Decade after the Ejido Reforms." Report 22187-ME. Washington, DC. http://doc.politiquessociales.net/serv1/Mexico_Land_policy_A_decade_after_de_Ejido_reform.pdf [accessed January 8, 2009].

———. 2006. "Agricultural Growth and Land Reform in Zimbabwe: Assessment and Recovery Options." Report 31699 ZW. Washington, DC.

———. 2007. *World Development Report 2008: Agriculture for Development.* Washington, DC.

Wuyts, Marc. 1985. "Money, Planning, and Rural Transformation in Mozambique." *Journal of Development Studies* 22 (1): 180–207.

Zamosc, León. 1989. "Peasant Struggles and Agrarian Reform: The Ecuadorian Sierra and the Colombian Atlantic Coast in Comparative Perspective." Meadville, PA: Allegheny College.

Zhang, Wenfang, and Jack Makeham. 1992. "Recent Developments in the Market for Rural Land Use in China." *Land Economics* 68 (2): 139–62.

CHAPTER THREE

Land Redistribution in Kenya

Karuti Kanyinga

In recent years in sub-Saharan Africa, there has been an increased resurgence of interest in access to and control of land, or what is known as the "land question." The land question has gained attention similar to what was witnessed in the 1950s and 1960s when land issues led to popular struggles for political independence. In some countries, the land question has triggered a wide range of political events, some of which are major challenges to the concept of the nation-state. There are many reasons for this growing interest in access and control of land. The land question comprises several dimensions; it concerns not only land use and economic production, but also population movements and settlement patterns, territories and identities, inequalities, and development. These issues have internal dynamics that affect access to and control of land, thereby making it an important social and economic resource in any agrarian society.

In Kenya, there has been growing interest in land because the land question was not addressed successfully at the time of independence in 1963, although issues of land access and control significantly shaped the struggle for independence. Growing landlessness, historical grievances and restitution, and demands for redistribution are some of the significant issues underlying demands for a comprehensive national land policy and a constitutional framework for the

The author wishes to thank Shem Migot-Adhola and Odenda Lumumba for their invaluable comments on the first draft of this chapter. All errors, though unintended, are the author's. Otherwise, the usual caveat applies.

administration of land. On the eve of independence, the colonial administration initiated a land redistribution program intended to prevent land-hungry peasants from destabilizing the economy and to provide opportunities for the new African elite to engage in farming. Problems arising from that initiative have become major issues for the national development process. The colonial administration facilitated the buying of land from willing European settlers in the White Highlands (land scheduled for European settlers) ostensibly to settle the landless and to assist farmers. A land purchase program also was developed to enable groups to buy land from European settlers and distribute it to group members. Land redistribution through this approach did not address the problem of landlessness successfully; instead, it triggered other sets of problems that threaten to destabilize the country.

The land question has continued to shape Kenya's political and economic life. The significance of land issues came to the fore immediately after the December 2007 general election following a flawed and hotly disputed presidential election vote count. The disputed result led to violent interethnic conflict in which locally driven evictions and mass displacement of people occurred, especially in Rift Valley Province where most of the former European farms are found. In Rift Valley, the settlement programs established through the land redistribution program in the 1960s became a theater of interethnic conflict. Mamdani's (2001) treatise of "indigenes and settlers" found expression in claims that outsider settlers (Kikuyu) wrongly and disproportionately had acquired land and political power in the territories of the indigenous Kalenjin ethnic group.

The growing significance of land in shaping political and economic events is recognized as a phenomenon of any agrarian society in Africa because land is embedded in a broader sociopolitical context. Matters of access to and control of land have a bearing on socioeconomic relationships in the society (Bassett and Crummey 1993; Berry 1993). Studies have shown that how land is held or even how access to land is regulated is important for the organization of economies and politics in agrarian societies. Any changes to rules of access and control of land amount to a restructuring of power relationships, not simply to the agrarian structure (Njeru 1978; Glazier 1985; Berry 1993; Mamdani 1996). The centrality of land in the political life of many societies has led to governments sidestepping land issues or attending only to land's economic dimension.

A related observation is that power relationships in society always determine land distribution. Tensions arising from distorted or skewed structures of land ownership may lead governments to undertake redistributive measures to address those tensions—tensions that would lead to major political upheaval if not addressed. Binswanger, Deininger, and Feder (1993) note that "most redistributive land reform is motivated by public concern about the rising tensions brought about by an unequal land distribution" (p. 77). Where political tensions are organized around the structure of inequalities in ownership, they result in violent conflicts that destabilize the basic foundation of the society. Binswanger, Deininger, and Feder also show that success and failure of land reforms depend on many factors. Land reforms without "a massive political upheaval have rarely succeeded in transferring much of a country's land. . . or have done so very slowly because of a lack of political commitment to provide funding to compensate owners" (pp. 24–25). Viewed that way, land redistribution is an intervention made to address problems arising from inequalities in the structure of land ownership, on the assumption that it will minimize social tension and prevent economic destabilization.

This chapter discusses the experiences arising from the land redistribution program in Kenya. It addresses the origins of Kenya's land question from which the land redistribution thinking evolved; and it assesses the origins of the land redistribution program, its implementation, and its economic and political outcomes. The fourth part of the chapter discusses current land distribution issues and their implications for national politics. Lessons learned from the redistributive efforts are addressed in the concluding section.

KENYA'S LAND QUESTION: THE POLITICAL ECONOMY OF COLONIAL AGRICULTURE

It is acknowledged generally that Kenya's land question developed in tandem with the establishment of the colonial settler economy when the British were setting up a colonial state in Kenya. The route to Kenya's land question had several stages, and much has been written about them (Sorrenson 1968; Okoth-Ogendo 1991). The first stage, from which others followed, was alienation and acquisition of land by the protectorate as a prelude to establishing the colonial state. The second stage involved imposition of English property law, which provided a juridical context for the appropriation of land that already had been alienated and acquired and for that which was to follow. Third was the reform of land tenure by which customary rights to land were restructured through the process of individualization or privatization of land. The main aspects of these processes and how their consequences have continued to reverberate in the Kenyan society are discussed below.

Establishment of the Colonial State and Land Alienation

A generally stable and flexible structure of access to and control of land existed in precolonial Kenya until the early 1890s, when Britain incorporated Kenya into its empire and established a colonial state (Sorrenson 1965; Okoth-Ogendo 1991; Wanjala 1996). How this colonial state was established had many effects on the structure of access to and control of land. It involved four quick stages. First, the British established the East Africa Protectorate in 1895 to gain control of present-day Kenya and Uganda. Second, after the protectorate was established, the government developed plans to link the coast of Kenya to the Uganda protectorate through a railway line. Settlement schemes for white farmers were established to support this venture. The third stage—not directly related to expropriation for settlers—was the limitation of the authority of the Sultan of Zanzibar to a 10-mile strip (*Mwambao*) along the coast of Kenya and Tanzania. The sultan had ceded *Mwambao* and land rights therein to a British company that offered to protect his dominion in return (Okoth-Ogendo 1991).

The fourth stage during which the actual land question evolved was alienation of land for establishing a colonial settler economy that would provide means to support political control of the colony. The settlers were made to feel that the land alienated for them was for permanent use; it was not a temporary acquisition (Sorrenson 1968). A land question formed, centered on expropriation of land and the dispossession of Africans. Land expropriated included land in areas along the railway line joining Kenya and Uganda. This land included part of the Ukambani region in Eastern Province, central Kenya, and the Rift Valley—agricultural land with the greatest potential. That land was chosen because white settlers had to be attracted to the area and because the land had to yield quick returns to investments on the railway.

Imposed Laws and the Evolution of White Highlands and Native Reserves

Land expropriation and alienation had to be based on law, so a legal framework was established to promote further alienation and to protect what the state already had acquired. The law had to be enforced, so a regime of force complemented this framework. First, the state introduced the Crown Lands Ordinance of 1902, which provided for sales of land by the Crown or annual rent under leases of about 99 years to the settlers. The settlers were unhappy with the ordinance because it subjected them to the control of the state (Okoth-Ogendo 1991). Because the state had to please the settlers, it introduced the Crown Lands Ordinance of 1915, which offered leases of 999 years. This ordinance declared all "waste and unoccupied" land in the protectorate to be "Crown Land" and subject to the governor's powers of alienation. The ordinance also demarcated land reserves for "natives" and land "scheduled" for European settlement—the White Highlands. Creation of what Mamdani (1996) refers to as citizens (settlers) and subjects (natives) had begun in earnest. From the outset, therefore, the colonial administration introduced a dual system of land tenure and land administration. These ordinances took away all the land rights of Africans and vested those rights in the Crown. Occupants became tenants-at-will of the Crown on the land they actually occupied. As argued by Okoth-Ogendo (1991), the occupants became tenants of the Crown.

Another set of problems arose through restructuring of the land–labor relationship. Labor had to be obtained for European settlers. The settlers had to secure a series of laws and administrative arrangements from the colonial administration to enable them to acquire African labor, directly and indirectly.

In 1918, for instance, the administration introduced the Resident Native (Squatters) Ordinance. This law provided for a labor contract, supervised by the government, by which the squatter had to work for a number of days each year before the settler could allow the squatter and his family to live on the land and cultivate a plot on the settler's farm (Van Zwanenberg 1975; Berman 1990). This ordinance destroyed any rights the squatters had by virtue of occupancy on the settler's farm, but it also created wage labor opportunities for Africans from the regions where expropriation had taken place. Population pressure in regions such as central Kenya squeezed many people into the White Highlands, where they remained without secure land rights—squatters. In the first wave of displacement between 1918 and 1928, there were about 100,000 Kikuyu squatters in the highlands (Kitching 1980).

The structure of land ownership and distribution varied considerably between the White Highlands and the Native Reserves. The land alienated for the settlers was equivalent to 3 million hectares, more than half of which was high-potential arable land suitable for cash-crop farming—coffee, tea, and sugar plantations. The rest was suited for large-scale livestock farming and other purposes. There were more than 3,600 farms, and the sizes of landholdings ranged from 400 hectares to more than 800 hectares. In the pastoral areas, one could find holdings larger than 20,000 hectares. Estimates show that the White Highlands constituted about 21,000 square kilometers of Kenya's 356,000 square kilometers (Leo 1989), or approximately 6 percent of Kenya's land. This amount was not small, considering that 68 percent of Kenya's land is remote and unsuited for farming; only 32 percent is arable. The Highlands—or 3,600 farms and, by implication, families—occupied close to 20 percent of Kenya's arable land. Six million Africans shared the rest.

The reserves occupied about 84,000 square kilometers. The land quality varied considerably, but there were some high-potential areas. Each land unit was reserved for the use of a particular ethnic group. These reservations laid a firm framework for the ethnicization of the Kenyan society. The administration placed solid sociopolitical boundaries between the various units of the Native Reserves. By doing so, it succeeded in preventing "political" interactions among the units and so prevented interethnic political relationships. The boundaries had the effect of solidifying ethnic identities and creating sociopolitical disparities through prejudices that the colonial administration propagated. The land question began to inform construction of ethnic identities. As we will see later, ethnicity in turn came to occupy a central position in matters of access to and control of land, especially in multiethnic areas where the government established settlement programs.

The Land Tenure Reform Program

In the reserves, population pressure resulted in congestion and declining productivity as the administration shifted attention toward settler farming.

Unrest among Africans built up, and colonial agronomists responded by introducing—through coercion—conservation measures and crop husbandry. The government introduced a "plan to intensify the development of African agriculture in Kenya." This plan—the Swynnerton Plan of 1954, named after the assistant director of agriculture who designed it—underlined the need to alter the collective control of land that existed in the reserves.

The plan proposed institutionalizing private property rights by giving individuals control of their individual holdings. The government assumed that doing so would make people busy in their holdings and so prevent them from organizing against the state—that is, participating in the Mau Mau rebellion. The plan sought to accelerate the displacement of customary tenure with freehold titles, to assist farmers in organizing their landholdings on a more productive basis, and to expand cash-crop farming, among others. The plan also sought to restructure landownership by introducing individual property rights. In the process of registering such rights—a process that began first in central Kenya—some people lost their rights and trooped to the White Highlands, where they joined other Kikuyus in wage labor.

The political economy of settler agriculture is the basis of Kenya's land question. How the capitalist agricultural economy developed restructured the framework of access to and control of land. People were confined to Native Reserves, where the land-carrying capacity declined because of a lack of frontiers to absorb the extra population. The change of the customary land tenure system (first among the Kikuyu) to a system of private individual holdings added to existing problems. More Africans lost land, and communal and familial conflicts over land intensified. This made the land problem a much more complex challenge for the colonial administration. Problems arising from loss of land rights generally contributed to growing resentment against the state and against the unequal structure of landownership in which European farmers controlled large holdings. This resentment rapidly grew into a peasant rebellion against the colonial structure of control of land rights. The rebellion added the pressure for land redistribution.

EARLY ATTEMPTS TO REDISTRIBUTE LAND

The above discussion suggests that there was no one single source of the land question. Problems around access to and control of land were embedded in the political economy of colonial settler agriculture. The process of establishing the colonial state and expropriating land for the colonial settler economy meant loss of land rights for many Africans. Land tenure reforms in the Native Reserves exacerbated a deepening problem of land. Several factors thus combined to build resentment against the colonial structure of land rights control. The resentment gave rise to a peasant rebellion, which the peasants organized to articulate their demands for land and political rights. It was this peasant uprising that exerted pressure on the colonial administration to prioritize land redistribution. The colonial administration also had to contend with an equally important pressure: addressing settler interests that increasingly were threatened by pressure for redistribution. The sections that follow discuss the Mau Mau peasant rebellion and its main consequence—the first settlement schemes. The discussion also shows how the government designed and implemented land redistribution in this first phase.

The Mau Mau Peasant Rebellion and Pressure for Redistribution

The Mau Mau peasant rebellion organized around the above structure of inequalities in land ownership and dispossession of the Kikuyu. Discontent among the peasantry was building through the 1940s, with open demonstrations in 1946 and 1947. By 1948, the peasants had grouped into Mau Mau and had a loose organization. The majority of the Mau Mau was of the Kikuyu ethnic group. Other members were from the Meru and Embu groups, who also had been dispossessed of their land. Members of other ethnic groups who chose to participate "did so as isolated individuals and not as part of an all-out effort on the part of Mau Mau to recruit members outside the Kikuyu cauldron" (Maloba 1993, p. 170). The Mau Mau leaders were administering oaths to create a sense of common identity and destiny. In the reserves, disaffection laid the basis for the rapid spread of the Mau Mau peasant movement and its organization (or the Land and Freedom Army, as it came to be known in the early 1960s) (Leo 1989; Maloba 1993). Mau Mau sought to disrupt the colonial administrative structures, targeting for elimination the administrators and African loyalists. The terror against the colonial establishment spread briskly throughout the White Highlands and central Kenya. Owing to increased violence against the white farmers, the colonial administration declared a state of emergency in October 1952. To the administration, the state of emergency provided a framework through which the spine of the Mau Mau insurgency would be broken and through which the Mau Mau would be isolated from the rest of society. For several years (between 1952 and 1960, when the emergency was lifted), many Kikuyu were incarcerated in detention camps.

The rebellion was organized around rights to land and political power and, therefore, was both a grievance-based and a political democracy movement. As a movement, it articulated demands for the restoration of Africans' land rights and their freedoms as well as the establishment of a social justice framework through which the society would be governed. These demands destabilized the colonial political structure and shook the structure of land ownership that existed to support the settler economy. It shook the very foundation of the capitalist settler economy and the colonial structure of political power. Efforts to contain the Mau Mau movement and maintain the state of emergency drained the government's energy and resources. White farmers also were becoming restless as the Mau Mau insurgency spread in the highlands.

The Mau Mau threat was only one problem facing the administration and farmers. An economic decline began as farmers' fears of an African government deepened. African leaders were growing impatient with the government because it was keen on protecting European interests in all negotiations that were taking place. Two African political parties, the Kenya African National Union (KANU) and the Kenya African Democratic Union (KADU), were anxious to have discussions on independence integrate deracialization of the structure of land ownership in the highlands. The leaders of the two parties had shown concern for maintaining the agricultural economy and promoting its further development. But the economy was in decline because many settlers, uncertain about the future, were not attending to their farms. Fears of an African government made some of them put pressure on the colonial government to prepare a departure package in the form of repatriation or evacuation money. The moderates among the farmers were supporting land redistribution to save themselves from the landless and unemployed Africans after an African government had come to power. Thus, threats from Mau Mau rebels and demands by African leaders to deracialize landownership in the highlands, coupled with a need to ensure the safety of white farmers when an African government took over, created some urgency in thinking about land redistribution. Settler interests and thinking, however, dominated the colonial administration, so any land reform had to be done to meet settler interests and expectations. Settlers were concerned particularly about the future of their farms under an African government.

Establishment of the First Settlement Schemes

The politics of transition to independence centered on land and, in particular, how Africans would access land and farms owned by white farmers. African leaders were concerned about landlessness and unemployment, whereas the administration and some white farmers were concerned about the future of the economy if the structure of landownership was altered. But African leaders also were divided on a number of other issues, many of which revolved around land. KADU preferred a *Majimbo* or federal structure of government in which regions were responsible for administration of land in their territories. Informing that position was the fear that numerically large communities, such as the Kikuyu, might expand into the territories of smaller communities. KADU had support from settler farmers because of its concern with the protection of minority interests. On the other hand, KANU preferred a unitary government and respect for the institution of property rights wherever established. To the union, that principle was important for national integration. Both parties agreed on the need for land reforms that addressed landlessness and unemployment. Whereas KADU preferred regional governments taking control of land administration, KANU was concerned that land redistribution under the colonial administration would protect white farmers' interests at Africans' expense. KANU did not see an administration determined to address landlessness and unemployment that had grown significantly during the emergency (Mau Mau rebellion) period. For that reason, the party preferred delaying transfer of land until an African government was in place; it was not interested in supporting a resettlement program that sought to protect the interests of the settler farmers alone.

The colonial administration was very much aware that landlessness was a key issue in the Mau Mau conflict, and this lesson became the primary factor in the formulation of subsequent land policies. In fact, the administration had failed to recognize the importance of landlessness in formulating solutions to land problems. As far back as the mid-1940s, the government established the African Land Development Board to run parallel with the Board of Agriculture for the white farmers. Little or no attention was given to landlessness. Measures to Africanize and thereby stabilize the highlands—rather than address landlessness per se—followed the Mau Mau rebellion. In 1959, the administration formulated a new policy of removing racial barriers from regulations governing ownership of agricultural land. The government also undertook to promote land purchase by Africans.

Wasserman (1976) points out that four factors motivated the government to formulate a policy on redistribution. One, the government preferred European farmers to control initiatives involving land reforms because they would ensure that their interests were protected. European farmers' desire for control of land reforms so as to protect farmers' interests was very much in line with the role that European farmers had played since the beginning of their settlement in the highlands. Two, there was a need to contain the unrest among the Kikuyu peasantry because of the threat they posed to the European farmers. Settlement schemes were needed to deal with land hunger among the Kikuyu and preempt any further insurgency. These settlement schemes became an important goal, especially as the administration began bargaining with KANU about political independence for Kenya. Third, there was a need to introduce the African landed elite into the highlands so that they could act as a buffer against agitation by the peasants (Wasserman 1976). It was assumed that landed African elites would have an interest in large-scale farming, which was crucial for maintaining the farming system in the highlands. Finally, international financial institutions had agreed to support the land transfer process. With that kind of investment, the upcoming African administration was expected to have a favorable entry point in the relationship with international financial institutions, such as the World Bank.

Those motives led to policy arrangements that favored prosperous Africans. It was hoped that such an undertaking would ease racial tensions by draining some emotion from the land issue, and would introduce confidence in the process of constitution making that was occurring at the time. It was expected that introducing settlement programs would "slow the outflow of capital from Kenya, relieve land pressure in the African areas and improve the employment position of the colony" (IBRD 1961, p. 4).

This thinking led to the evolution of land settlement institutions and the actual process of settlement. Restlessness among the African landless—the ex-Mau Mau—and growing tension between the African leaders about how to resolve the land problem compelled the administration to consider the European farmers' security. A resettlement policy had to guarantee their security. The Land Development and Settlement Board (LDSB), with a large membership of settlers, was formed to organize resettlement. (The LDSB was set up in January 1961 as a reconstituted European Agricultural Settlers Board, which the colonial government originally had established to serve only the white settlers.) Settler farmers' domination of institutions dealing with land administration made it possible to pursue a policy that would guarantee their security and maintain economic structures without significant alterations.

The government began to establish settlement schemes. The first programs were meant for the settlement of prosperous Africans (yeomen) on "Z" plots to buffer rural areas and stabilize the potentially disruptive peasantry. Land selected for settlement was to be purchased and subdivided for sale to selected African yeoman farmers. There also were schemes for farmers who were relatively prosperous but needed assistance in acquiring adequate farming skills. The plots given to these assisted farmers were similar in size to the Z plots. The African settlers had to identify their own purchasers and draw up plans for subdivision. Harbeson (1973) notes that these settlement schemes generally were meant to enrich retiring farmers, whereas other farmers helped their own tenants acquire farming skills. The first set of settlement programs sought to provide land to those Africans who were able to prosper or were able to pay for the land.

The colonial administration engineered the solution to the land question without involving KANU, which preferred to defer resettlement until independence was obtained. Nonetheless, the administration moved first to establish LDSBs with token African representation. Doing so gave the settlers and the administration, with the support of KADU, a free hand to organize land redistribution efforts. The settler community was given more voice on the board and in the resettlement efforts that followed.

The First Settlement Scheme in Practice

This first phase of resettlement during the transition to independence involved acquiring land before 1963 to settle about 1,800 yeomen (including assisted farmers) and 6,000 peasants (smallholders) on 73,000 hectares. The British government, the International Bank for Reconstruction and Development (IBRD), and the Colonial Development Corporation (CDC) financed the purchase of land. Land for the assisted farmers was to be purchased through loans, whereas a third of the land purchased for the smallholder schemes would be financed through a grant by the Commonwealth

Development and Welfare Fund and the balance would come from loans (IBRD 1961). For the purpose of the project, the LDSB would purchase only land with high potential for intensification and development. The government estimated that approximately 2 million acres in the "scheduled areas" were suited for high-potential agricultural development and so were suitable for this project. Land for yeoman farmers was purchased in the interior of scheduled areas but as noncontiguous parcels subdivided into units of about 5,000 acres (roughly 2,000 hectares). Smallholder settlements were placed on the periphery of the existing African reserves, again in solid blocks of about 5,000 acres. This form of redistribution was meant to relieve social tension and stabilize the highlands. It was hoped that this redistribution would lead to a stable African government upon independence and would perpetuate the stability of settler agricultural farming and of the economy in general.

The structure of land purchase and subsequent settlement of Africans was elaborate. However, white farmers dominated this structure of the program for the reasons discussed earlier. The government established district agricultural committees with responsibility for appraising land for sale, and the Department of Agriculture made technical assessments of soil and water capabilities to establish suitability for subdivision and intensification. The LDSB negotiated the purchase price and the Division Land Board made the final approval.

With regard to the mode of payment for land, one-third of the purchase price was to be paid in cash at the time of the title transfer, with the balance to be paid in seven equal installments carrying interest at 5 percent. Deferred payment was guaranteed by the Kenya government, which had part of the U.K. grant and loan for that purpose (IBRD 1961).

The land selected for purchase was valued at 1959 prices. Purchase was pegged on the basis of willing seller–willing buyer negotiations between the LDSB and the prospective sellers. After takeover by the board, the land was to be subdivided into holdings for the yeomen (including the assisted farmers) and the peasants. The yeoman holdings had an average of about 20 hectares, and the peasant ones had about 6 hectares. It was hoped that the program would placate the Africans by providing opportunities to alter the structure of racial ownership of land and simultaneously restore the settler farmers' confidence by supporting the land market (Njonjo 1978; Leo 1989). The administration argued that the yeomen holdings would be placed strategically proximate to the holdings of the white settlers so that the yeomen could learn farming techniques and become part of the economic life of the highlands. However, the peasants would not be integrated into the large-scale farming areas; they were placed on the periphery in the marginal areas. To the colonial administration, yeomen's access to the highlands would build yeomen's capacity to contribute to economic development through farming while motivating them to fence off the highlands from their own land-hungry groups.

The LDSB developed criteria for selecting yeomen, assisted farmers, and smallholders. The criteria for yeomen and assisted farmers centered on character, substantial farming experience, and evidence of managerial capacity, among other factors. Settlers for the smallholder schemes, however, were drawn from among farmers with fewer than 4 acres in the African areas, laborers in the African reserves who had been displaced by the individualization process, and experienced workers on the European farms (IBRD 1961). Smallholders also were expected to have working capital of approximately £50 (about K sh 1,000). District commissioners, in consultation with the appropriate personnel of the Department of Agriculture and the various agricultural committees, had responsibility for undertaking preliminary selection. The LDSB made the final selection.

The people selected got credit facilities and grants for the purchase of land and its development, as well as for purchase of livestock. Loan officers, operating under the control of an administrative committee, were responsible for the lending operations. The power of loan approval rested with the settlement board. Loans for purchase of land were made for a period of 40 years, and loans for development of the holdings were made for a period of 20 years. Average repayment, in practice, was estimated at 30 years for the land purchase loans and 15 years for the development loans. These repayment periods included a grace period (for principal only) of up to five years, depending on the length of time required to establish the cash crop. The security requirement was real estate or chattel mortgages, and interest at a rate of 6 percent was payable within the first year. These terms were meant to impress upon the settlers that they were to pay their obligations (IBRD 1961).

As noted above, implementation of the redistribution program took place in the context of anxiety among European farmers worried about the Land and Freedom Army (former Mau Mau). They were worried that ex-Mau Mau would organize to grab settlers' land forcibly or that the settlers would lose compensation when a new African government came to power. Given this context, the land purchase program was meant to demonstrate to settlers that their investment in land was secure and that they still would be able to realize their capital if they chose to liquidate their landholdings (Leo 1989).

Although settlers wanted to sell their land to the board, the terms of purchase were not attractive. They were getting one-third of the price in cash, with the balance to be paid in equal installments over a period of seven years. The settlers became increasingly worried that a new government would renege on the payment terms, or that they would lose their land completely. Negotiations with the Minister of Agriculture led to improved terms of purchase. Sellers were to receive half of the price in a lump-sum payment, and the balance would be paid in three equal annual installments over three years. Some sellers accepted the new terms; others remained worried that introducing smallholder peasant holdings and yeoman African farms into the neighborhood of large-scale farms was a threat to the settler economy. They wanted their social milieu maintained and preserved.

The Sociopolitical Outcomes of the Program

The design and implementation of the colonial land redistribution program redirected emphasis from land hunger to preserving the capitalist agrarian economy prevalent in the White Highlands at the time. Domination of settler farmers in the redistribution processes, coupled with the government's failure to involve the majority African party, meant additional challenges to the land question. Further, the government and the white farmers decided to focus on the Kikuyu, both to prevent greater migration of the Kikuyu into the Rift Valley and to get them off European farms. This emphasis on the Kikuyu led to the colonial administration excising land in Rift Valley Province, which they adjoined to the Central Province to get enough land to settle the Kikuyu.

These first settlement schemes, referred to as IBRD/CDC schemes because those entities financed the program, did not address landlessness. The people for whom the assisted or yeoman and smallholder programs were meant turned out to be the better-off Africans. Squatters' wages were so low that they could not afford to produce the required working capital of £50. Neither could they meet the administrative criterion of having sufficient experience to farm a low-density holding and generate returns to repay the loan. The majority of the people who were "actually settled were far from being absolutely landless—the people who had given political impetus for the scheme" (Okoth-Ogendo 1981, p. 332).

The settlement schemes were being established in the twilight years of the colonial administration. They all had the weaknesses of a system that was coming to an end. The settlers dominated the conception, planning, and implementation phases of the program and they failed to address the main land question at the time—landlessness and squatting. The schemes addressed only the problems involving the racial structure of landownership in the country, and they failed to address the concerns of the peasantry and of Africans in general.

RE-AFRICANIZING THE HIGHLANDS: THE ONE MILLION ACRE SETTLEMENT SCHEME

The One Million Acre Settlement Scheme differed from the previous settlement plans because its main focus was on high-density settlement; it was not designed for only a relatively small number of carefully selected farmers. What such a scheme required was huge financial support in terms of loans and grants. The World Bank and the governments of Great Britain and the Federal Republic of Germany provided that assistance. In 1962, the colonial administration negotiated terms of the plan to settle 35,000 families of smallholders—landless peasants—on more than 1 million acres of largely high-density settlement land. More land was to be purchased for those who were land hungry than for the assisted or prosperous African farmers.

The program involved purchase of about 1 million acres of land, bought in large blocks located on the periphery of the reserves—hence the name One Million Acre Settlement Scheme. About 80,000 hectares were to be bought each year for a period of five years. This purchase plan was expected to offer a market to European settlers who wanted to sell their land. To make it attractive for the settlers to sell, the administration improved the terms of payment. In July 1962, when program implementation began, a new policy was introduced stressing full cash payment at the time of sale. The European farmers had the right to choose where to be paid: London or Kenya. The settlers found this approach to the land sales more attractive than the previous arrangements.

Design and Implementation of the Settlement Program

This massive settlement program comprised both high-density peasant holdings and low-density yeoman or assisted farmer holdings. About 5,000 peasants were to be accommodated on 73,000 hectares. The initial plans provided for sharing of this amount of land between the peasants and the yeomen or assisted farmers. The total cost of the scheme was about £25.0 million, of which £19.6 million was to support the high-density settlement. The land for settlement was organized into separate units with scores of individual plots. The high-density schemes catered to low-income groups and had plots of about 25 acres each. The government expected these plots to generate incomes of between K sh 500 and K sh 1,500 a year per holding after deductions for loans and subsistence needs. When completed, this part of the scheme was expected to cover 970,000 acres. The low-density part of the plan had 40-acre holdings expected to yield a net income of about K sh 2,000 a year per holding. These holdings were expected to occupy about 180,000 acres and to benefit peasants who were interested in both subsistence and commercial farming. The assisted farmer category had plots of about 100 acres or Z plots carved around the homesteads of the former settlers. Again, the low-density areas were expected to provide stability and leadership in the high-density areas. To ensure that they remained focused on land, prosperous farmers—largely members of the African middle class—were required to hire farm managers to supervise their holdings (Leys 1975; Leo 1989).

Planning took into account the income to be produced by individual plots. The cost for the plots was based on the scheme's potential and on calculation of what the crops could yield. The new owners assumed debts in the form of settlement charges, which covered the costs of land purchase and the administration of the settlement scheme. Only individuals—not groups of people—could purchase the plots and there was no place for collective enterprises, such as cooperatives and land-buying companies.

In the One Million Acre Settlement Scheme, the government assumed control of the plan after dissatisfaction with the LDSB's management of the previous schemes, especially because the board offered high prices for less-valuable land. The board eventually was removed from the pivotal role of planning and implementing the program, and the Ministry of Agriculture took on responsibility for managing the scheme.

The settlement program structure comprised four administrative tiers. At the top of the structure was a director of settlement. Below that position were area settlement controllers, then senior settlement officers. At the base were tens of settlement officers. Each level had staff seconded from the ministry and relevant government departments, including the provincial administration. Huge amounts of land had been set aside for the program, and thousands of African families were to be settled. This structure of control was meant to ensure that many landless families were settled. At the same time, those who were given holdings in these settlement areas were given sets of incentives to ensure the program's economic success. Those people who were unsuccessful were threatened with dispossession. Selection of land-hungry people for allocation of holdings in these settlement programs was based on a system of reward and punishment to address the problem of insecurity posed by ex-Mau Mau. Concern about the former insurgents was causing fear among some of the European farmers in the White Highlands (Leo 1989).

The provincial administration, which oversaw local government in the Native Reserves throughout the colonial period, supervised the selection of farmers for the high-density schemes. The hierarchy of chiefs and headmen that reached deep into the local villages helped this process, again ensuring that only those people who genuinely were landless had access to the settlement programs. The first opportunity to own purchased land was given to those who had stayed on the purchased land longer as laborers. Other people were considered only if there was extra land available. The settlers' arrangement of selecting whom to sell to gave an opportunity to the government to punish the Land and Freedom Army. The provincial administration, comprising loyalists, vetted those who had links with the Land and Freedom Army. People convicted of offenses—and their families—were ineligible for settlement. Former Mau Mau therefore risked losing their chances of getting land in the settlement programs.

These arrangements produced several political and technical difficulties. They did not appease the politically radical groups in government who wished to find a solution to the landlessness before a new African government assumed power. Neither did these arrangements diffuse the political tension that informed the Mau Mau peasant uprising. Disaffection with the settlement program and the slow pace of land redistribution occasioned militant reorganization of the ex-Mau Mau detainees; they were mobilizing around these resentments and they became a threat to the settlement schemes. Several groups—among them the Land and Freedom Army, *Kiama Kia Mwingi* (Council of the Masses), and *Mitarukire* (the ragged ones)—emerged.

The amount of land purchased under the program was a great deal less than was needed to resettle the number of landless people. Some of the land meant for land-hungry people also was located in unproductive areas where it was difficult for poor peasants to scratch out a living. The size of plots was relatively small compared with those in low-density areas suited for the farming of high-priced cash crops and livestock (Clough 1965; Njonjo 1978). The effect of these errors in planning was more land hunger and expectation among the African landless in the highlands, the majority of whom were Kikuyu. The threats by the Land and Freedom Army and other landless groups to occupy white settlers' land called for urgent measures to come up with more land. For instance, in the Kinangop area of Nyandarua District (which was excised from Rift Valley Province to form part of central Kenya), there were threats to occupy farmers' land without waiting for the government to buy the land. Laborers also were threatening settlers with forcible occupation or outright seizure. In late 1963, Jomo Kenyatta, the prime minister of the new African government operating under self-rule from June 1963, ordered quick resettlement of the landless Kikuyu laborers in Kinangop. The Jet schemes were established and implemented through a crash program that lacked adequate preparation and planning. Although this program was done as a political necessity for the new government, it prevented a mass and violent occupation of settlers' farms just before the date set for independence—December 12, 1963.

To appease the various militant groups, in 1965 the Kenyan government established a Commission for Squatters to register and settle them. The commission "hurriedly" settled about 18,000 families on 12-acre plots in *Haraka* settlement areas (*Haraka* is a Kiswahili word for haste or hurry). These areas covered about 200,000 acres. There were no particular income targets, nor were the beneficiaries provided with loans and technical support (Leys 1975). By 1975, the *Haraka* programs had settled about 12,500 families. However, a class structure was quite evident in these programs as had been the case in previous ones. First, those people with ability to pay the 10 percent deposit for the cost of the plots and operating capital got larger plots. Because of this class bias, only those people who had capital and the local notables and elites—as well as those who were salaried—acquired plots. Furthermore, those who were able to pay had land elsewhere; they were neither landless nor unemployed. Class differentiation gradually built through the structure of the land purchase program. This differentiation ran counter to the initial objectives and demands of the rebellious peasantry.

The Commission for Squatters wound up its activities in the early 1970s, and the Settlement Fund Trustees assumed most of its responsibilities. The commission closed before settling the mass of squatters in the highlands. Some of the remaining squatters were settled in *Shirika* (Kiswahili for cooperative) settlements. The purchase of these farms was financed through an "agreement" between the British government and the Kenyan government. The agreement was based on the understanding that the farms to be involved must have been owned by British settlers.

The settlement programs attracted people throughout the 1960s and 1970s for several reasons. There was the myth of economic potential of large-scale farms (the low-density schemes). The salaried businesspeople and the politicians saw the low-density programs as a means to accumulate capital. The politicians in particular saw the programs as providing opportunity to translate political influence into ownership of capital by becoming a large farm owner (Leys 1975). But there were still others interested in accessing land in the settlement schemes because they had discovered that many people who had acquired land in the programs had not paid for it, and that it was politically difficult and sensitive to deal with defaulters. By 1970, the programs had 44 percent debt service in arrears. Total indebtedness was exceeding the ability of the small plot owners to pay (Leys 1975). A reevaluation of the scheme resulted in the government making gradual evictions—so gradual in fact that the effort did not have the desired impact.

The government also introduced a land purchase program for further redistribution. Serving as background to this program were the challenges around the settlement schemes. Notably, in the period between 1965 and early 1970, there was pressure on the government to deemphasize settlement programs and to focus instead on purchase of land and its transfer to those people who had the ability to pay for it. Part of this pressure came from the new black elite who were keen to venture into commercial agriculture. The government established the Agricultural Development Corporation and vested it with responsibility to "buy lands from private owners and to sell to 'assisted' African farmers while retaining some funds for stock breeding and for production of quality seeds to distribute to new African farmers" (Kanyinga 1998, p. 175).

This new approach meant that land redistribution would take place through the markets. Apparently this recommendation had been made by the Stamp Mission of 1966, after concluding that settlement schemes were intolerably expensive and did not contribute to increased agricultural development (Harbeson 1973). However, the farm purchase method for acceding to the highlands resulted in salaried employment and political influence becoming the main point of entry into the ownership of large landholdings. It led to formation of land purchase companies by different social classes and ethnic groups because financial institutions preferred to deal with groups rather than with individuals. To demonstrate support for the land purchase program, the government decided to give loans to those who could not raise the money to buy the farms. This decision, however, did not end the process of redistribution through the settlement schemes. In fact, settlement programs were integrated into the national development policies as a means of redistributing land. Markets emerged to become an important avenue through which those people with the ability to pay could accumulate land at the expense of the peasants.

The land redistribution and re-Africanization of the highlands appear to have had one important result: a high number of Kikuyu beneficiaries, compared with the numbers of those from other communities. These people were the most land hungry and therefore the most dangerous constituency in the highlands. But access to the White Highlands through the land purchase program also evolved a new dimension to the land question. The settlement schemes did not benefit those for whom they were meant. The landed and those with ability to pay acquired more land. This resulted in more pressure, especially by the former Mau Mau detainees who organized the Land and Freedom Army and threatened forcible occupations. The settlement schemes therefore failed to completely address the problem of landlessness.

Economic and Political Outcomes of the One Million Acre Program

After independence, the new African government preferred to maintain the structure of landholdings in the White Highlands to prevent interference with agricultural production. The design of settlement programs in which smallholdings existed alongside the assisted farmer holdings served this purpose. However, the land purchase program opened landownership to groups who could buy the farms and subdivide them among members. This was preferred as a new approach to redistribution because settlement schemes were becoming expensive and politically difficult to manage. At the same time, the government relaxed its policy against subdivisions after the International Labour Organization survey findings showed smallholdings to be superior to large-scale farming in efficient use of resources, productivity per hectare, and labor absorption (ILO 1972). The land transfer program resulted in subdivision of large farms into fragmented holdings, after which the number of holdings increased. The government allowed subdivisions to continue and supported the process by providing surveyors and facilitating the issuance of title deeds. This governmental support was provided because the program relieved pressure on the government to settle the landless, a much more difficult political task.

An important outcome was increased agricultural production, especially of some of the principal crops such as maize. The area of land under cultivation increased, but underutilized farms increased also as the process of re-Africanization and resettlement continued. For instance, from a situation in which about 17 percent of total land (nationally) was under cultivation in 1980, the area dropped to about 10 percent in 1982. Only about 12 percent was under cultivation in 1988 and 1989. This percentage dropped to 9 percent, but it rose to 11 percent in 1992 and fluctuated between 11 and 9 percent from 2000 to 2005.

In terms of output, the large farm sector trailed the small farm sector. The share production of the small farms was above 68 percent in the late 1970s. Between 1974 and 1985, the sectors had almost equal shares of gross marketed production; the whole period was characterized by interannual variability and increasing yields. In 1974, the large farms' share of gross marketed production was about 49.4 percent—that is, K sh 73.4 million out of K sh 148.4 million. This share fluctuated between 45 percent and 50 percent throughout the 1970s and early 1980s. It continued until 1986 when the share of the small sector fell by about 10 percent, and that of the large sector increased by the same margin. The share contribution of the small farms gradually picked up and attained a high of 68 percent in 1996. From then on, the share contribution of small firms in terms of their sale to marketing boards has been on the increase. It increased to 73 percent in 2004.[1]

From an economic point of view, the settlement schemes and the land purchase program, the main redistribution approaches, prevented destruction of the colonial economic structure. The settlement schemes that integrated smallholders and assisted farmers into the highlands contributed to economic stability both during and after the transition to independence. The structure of the economy remained unaltered. The government was able to meet some demands from among the land-hungry citizenry without shaking the structure of the economy and without shaking the structure of landownership itself. The land redistribution program was the avenue by which the government maintained continuity of the structure of landownership without altering it.

Politically, the settlement schemes placated the Africans' demands for altering the racial structure of landownership by providing opportunities for a new settlement pattern based on racial interaction. But that was not adequate for the ex-Mau Mau rebels, who found it difficult to pay for plots in the settlement schemes. Furthermore, the use of the provincial administration to fence off Land and Freedom Army members meant further marginalization of those who had mobilized for land rights for generations. Therefore, political tensions over land remained lodged in all the mechanisms to regulate access to and control of land. The settlement schemes in the highlands gradually were becoming an important theater where these tensions would be played out. The redistribution had an important class dimension, too. Large holdings were acquired by politicians, bureaucrats, and other people of influence. In Nakuru alone, there were 40 individually owned African farms with more than 500 acres each located on mixed farmland in the 1970s. In other cases, peasants in high-density schemes sold their land to the urban elite who had the means to raise the required deposits (Harbeson 1973). From this point of view, settlement schemes produced a relatively concentrated pattern of landownership.

THE POLITICS OF REDISTRIBUTION

In 1960, at the start of the redistribution program, political leaders from the main political parties and the government were involved in negotiations on political independence. Discussions on the transfer of political power, therefore, were taking place simultaneously with discussions on the transfer of land.

This coincidence meant that each form of negotiation had implications for the other. And because land was the fulcrum around which everything revolved, political settlement had to reflect settlement of the land question. And because ethnicity increasingly was influencing political negotiations, settlement of land issues became ethnic or developed trends toward an ethnic structure of national politics. Political discussions on the *Majimbo* system of government accelerated a trend toward this direction.

Elections for the Legislative Assembly were held in 1961, and KANU won the majority of seats. However, the party had to enter into an agreement with KADU to prevent further disagreements and delays on independence. It was that agreement that resulted in land redistribution assuming ethnic dimensions. KANU's concession to have a regional government required the drawing of regional boundaries. A Boundaries Commission was set up for that purpose. In December 1962, the commission tabled its report showing which ethnic communities should be grouped together within the various regional boundaries. The Masai preferred to be separate from the Kamba. The Meru preferred to be separate from the Kikuyu. The commission recommended putting the Kikuyu in central Kenya and putting the Meru and Kamba in Eastern Province. The Masai were placed in Rift Valley Province with the Kalenjin subgroups.

The plan for the settlement scheme followed the new ethnic boundaries. Land purchased for settlement was meant to accommodate specific ethnic groups. However, a large single settlement area (Kinangop, or present-day Nyandarua District) was excised from the Rift Valley to settle the Kikuyu, who had the largest number of squatters in the highlands and high numbers of landless peasants in their reserves. This settlement of the Kikuyu in itself aroused ethnic animosity and tensions between members of the Kikuyu ethnic community and others, including the Masai and the Kalenjin who had occupied the Rift Valley before alienation for the white farmers. The administration accelerated settlement of the Kikuyu for a number of reasons. The land consolidation program following the Swynnerton Plan of 1954 displaced many Kikuyu from their reserves. Some moved to the highlands, and others stayed landless in the reserves. At the same time, the release of more than 60,000 Mau Mau detainees after the state of emergency ended put more pressure on land in central Kenya. Many released detainees found their land had been taken by relatives or acquired by the loyalists and their relatives during the implementation of the land consolidation program (Lamb 1974). Demands for a *Majimbo* form of government also were putting pressure on the Kikuyu to return to their region, central Kenya. Combined with threats by the Land and Freedom Army to reorganize and grab land from the settlers, these factors accelerated the settlement of the Kikuyu (see Wasserman [1976] for details). Excising land to settle the Kikuyu added to political tension that accompanied hostility around negotiations for political independence in which the land question featured prominently.

The early face of redistribution, coupled with hostile positions that the two political parties adopted, framed the structures for ethnic conflicts at the outset. But the redistribution that followed the 1970s did not prioritize the Kikuyu as the group to be attended to in haste and hurriedly. This preference for Kikuyu in the settlement program applied to the One Million Acre, Jet, and *Haraka* settlement schemes. The government continued to alienate public land to settle the landless, including those from other communities. The settlement scheme policy was emphatic that 60 percent of plots in the settlement schemes should be given to the local residents, and the remaining 40 percent should be allocated to deserving people from other parts of the country. This division was intended to give priority to the landless from the region in which the settlement scheme had been established and to give opportunity to people from other parts of the country for the purpose of national integration. Kenyatta heralded that approach as early as the mid-1960s when he applauded the schemes and the purchase program as a success in enabling people from different communities to live together.

Redistribution and Interethnic Relationships

The settlement schemes contributed to the building of ethnopolitical tensions from the 1960s. In Rift Valley Province, local communities resented the land redistribution exercise because the program skewed in favor of the Kikuyu people. As early as 1960, when the first program of redistribution began, some Kalenjin leaders mobilized against it on the grounds that they could not buy their own land—land that belonged to them prior to colonial settlement (Klopp 2001). In the 1970s, as land pressure began to bear on the Kalenjin people, they became more resentful of the government's approach to the land redistribution efforts—the settlement scheme and the land purchase programs. Aware that they were losing out to the Kikuyu and other groups, the Kalenjin organized land-buying companies and began to compete against the Kikuyu. The Kalenjin people began to experience political difficulties as they organized to buy settler farms. Kikuyu elite had overwhelming influence on officials in the Ministry of Lands and Settlement as well as the financial institutions that were providing loans for the land purchases. The Kalenjin, however, had no senior officials in these institutions or in the government. They had Daniel arap Moi as a vice president to President Kenyatta, but he lacked the influence required to commit himself to competition with the powerful Kikuyu elite. Both groups were competing to purchase settler farms, but the Kalenjin were standing on relatively weaker ground. Each group nonetheless mobilized support from the political elite in its respective ethnic region to bring political influence to bear on the land control boards, which authorized transactions in the land market (Njonjo 1978).

Settlement schemes in Rift Valley remained sites of intense competition between the Kikuyu and the Kalenjin communities. In Coast Province, the local residents also were resenting the high numbers of Kikuyu who found their way into the settlement schemes through both sales and allocation by the government. Settlement schemes in Western Province experienced similar grievances although the magnitude of grievances was less than that in Rift Valley. The manner in which the government administered the allocation of land in some of these areas also affected interethnic relationships. In Coast Province, for instance, local residents complained about biases in the selection of settlers, abuse of procedure, and nepotism (Kanyinga 2000).

In the redistributive programs that followed the One Million Acre program, the Ministry of Lands and Settlement identified land for settlement; the Settlement Fund Trustees played a technical role in subdividing the land, following up on repayments, and monitoring the programs in general. The provincial administration identified the landless people who qualified for plot allocation in the settlement schemes and drew a list of allottees. In many instances, the number of people qualifying for plots was more than the total holdings. Where this was the case, the administration used a lottery to allocate the plots.

The transparent process of allocating plots changed with time when the process was placed under the direct control of the provincial administration's Office of the President, where district commissioners chaired the allocation committees. The administration would identify people qualified for plots through the District Plot Allocation Committee, which comprised the district commissioners, heads of departments in relevant ministries, and local leaders. This procedure raised complaints of irregularities, with many people complaining that undeserving people got plots in the settlement schemes. Even after allocations had been made, some allottees quickly sold their land to new buyers. In parts of Coast and Rift Valley Provinces, these sales resulted in an ethnic mix of allottees in some settlement schemes, even where the schemes would have benefited a homogenous ethnic group. Sales through the markets also produced a new class structure; those with ability to pay accumulated more plots through this process.

The skewed nature of the policy in favor of the Kikuyu was an issue of concern. Some of the settlement schemes were designed to satisfy Kikuyu land hunger because they had the organization to destabilize the structure of landownership and the economy. A review of the regional pattern of settlement schemes reveals the source of this tension: By early 2004, there were about 418 settlement schemes in the country, 154 (or 37 percent) of them in Rift Valley. Nakuru and Laikipia districts, the largest home of the Kikuyu in the diaspora, have about one-third of the 154 settlement schemes. This implies that more than one-third of settlement schemes in Rift Valley Province have relatively more Kikuyu than other communities. Central Province has about 90 schemes, 60 percent of which are in Nyandarua District (an area excised from Rift Valley in the early 1960s to settle the Kikuyu). In other settlement schemes in different parts of the country, the Kikuyu settled after acquiring land either through the markets or through government allocation. The point to note is that the land redistribution process in the early 1960s aimed at ensuring stability of the postindependence economy by addressing the possible source of political unrest—the Kikuyu. Doing so produced new social tensions; the redistribution process became a site of protracted ethnic conflicts. Thus land redistribution shifted attention from inequalities in the structure of landownership to ethnic dimensions of occupation and settlement.

Redistribution, Electoral Politics, and Conflicts

The political tension arising from the settlement schemes and the land purchase program did not break into open and widespread violence throughout the 1970s and 1980s. The land purchase program provided opportunities for the political elite to mobilize their respective landless groups into land-buying companies, as long as there was land to buy. The program relieved much of the pressure generated by tensions over skewed allocation of land to the Kikuyu. As long as land for sale existed and the Kalenjin could organize to buy it, there was little interest in outright violence against the Kikuyu.

In 1978, Moi ascended to the presidency—a position previously held by a Kikuyu. Although Moi was a Kalenjin, that minority's grievances against the Kikuyu could not be expressed openly because Moi had promised to promote a unitary government, a policy position that Kenyatta and KANU held dear when Moi and others in KADU advocated for a *Majimbo* government. In the 1970s and 1980s, therefore, although the settlement schemes were contested, there were no organized forms of violence to evict the Kikuyu from the area. That changed, however, in 1991 when multiparty politics was reintroduced in the country.

The struggle to bring multiparty politics back onto the political stage in the early 1990s was promoted especially by leaders from some of the numerically large communities who had been marginalized from power during the Kenyatta consolidation of political power and the Kikuyu political interests. Moi and KANU responded violently to their demands. Kalenjin politicians allied with Moi and KANU picked the land question to mobilize ethnic support in Rift Valley Province. Those people demanding reintroduction of multiparty politics aimed to remove President Moi from office. They argued that those in opposition to their demands, and the Kikuyu in particular, got land in Rift Valley in settlement schemes meant for the settlement of the Kalenjin and the Masai ethnic communities. From that point forward, political campaigns were built on the land question and the need to reintroduce a *Majimbo* system of government so that groups in Rift Valley could take control of their lands. A discourse developed concerning the ethnic homogeneity of the Rift Valley for Kalenjins and other pastoralists. This discourse fueled campaigns in which those opposed to KANU were labeled "foreigners." Pursuing that campaign and at the urging of Moi, senior politicians in KANU declared Rift Valley a "KANU zone." They carved Rift Valley into an exclusive political territory for

KANU and Moi, and they fenced it off from opposing parties and Kikuyu and Luo politicians. The provincial administrators quickly picked up on this and similarly declared Rift Valley an administrative KANU zone from which anyone critical of the government was excluded. Both forms of exclusion had one goal: violently to eliminate from the area those opposed to Moi, evicting them from the land they had occupied in the settlement schemes. In one particular incident, a senior KANU leader in Nakuru ordered KANU supporters to chop off the fingers of anyone raising a two-finger salute, the symbol used by multiparty advocates to campaign for pluralism. In line with the campaign against "foreigners," this campaign turned violent in October 1991 when *Majimboists* and KANU supporters invaded a farm in Nandi District to evict non-Kalenjin shareholders. With the support of the provincial administration and local KANU leaders allied with Moi, gangs of Kalenjin youth ("Kalenjin warriors," as they were known popularly) evicted outsider groups from the farms (National Council of Churches of Kenya 1992; Parliamentary Select Committee 1992). Politicians allied with Moi paid for the services of the warriors, and encouraged them to settle on the land of the departing Kikuyu. Many of these politicians came to occupy senior positions in government after the December 1992 general election.

In the 1997 election, politicians in KANU again played a similar role. Kikuyu landholders (some of whom had returned to their land in 1993 when KANU again won the election) again were evicted from their farms. In the 1997 period, however, other areas outside Rift Valley Province experienced similar violence. In Coast Province, local residents organized to evict "outsiders" from their properties, including holdings in the settlement schemes. Violence related to land continued to follow election cycles, with Kikuyu peasants being the main victims of all the waves of evictions.

During the 2002 general elections, there were no threats against the Kikuyu in Rift Valley. Having completed his constitutionally permitted terms in office, Moi was not a candidate, and there was no pressure on the Kalenjin elite to fight for him. Second, Moi had identified Uhuru Kenyatta, a Kikuyu and the son of the first president, as KANU's candidate for the presidency—a strategy that combined the interests of the Kikuyu and the Kalenjin. On one hand, Uhuru Kenyatta would protect Moi's and the Kalenjin interests when Moi retired from political life; on the other hand, Kikuyu interests would be safeguarded under a Kikuyu presidency and KANU leadership. KANU, however, lost the election. A coalition of political parties, the National Rainbow Coalition, won the election on a platform of comprehensive reforms, including land and constitutional reforms. A new government was formed, headed by President Mwai Kibaki, a Kikuyu. The new government represented various regional interests, and there were no complaints of political exclusion. In 2004, the coalition disintegrated following disagreements on power sharing. Those disagreements spilled over to the constitution-making process where those people allied with the government watered down proposals made in the Constitutional Assembly. Their actions were viewed as an attempt to consolidate the Kikuyu's hold on power and to exclude other groups politically. A new draft constitution, which provided a framework for land administration and access to/control of land in general, was presented in a referendum in November 2005, but it was rejected.

In 2006, following the disintegration of the national coalition and the defeat of the proposed new constitution, there were violent conflicts over land in several areas, including outside of Rift Valley Province. The most protracted conflicts have been those in Mount Elgon District in Western Province and in Kuresoi in Rift Valley. In the Mount Elgon case, the cause of the conflict centered on the allocation of plots in one settlement scheme in which local residents complained about outsiders being allocated land at the expense of local residents. In Kuresoi, the conflict centered on disputes between the Kikuyu and the Kalenjin ethnic communities over ownership of farms in the area.

Conflict over land recurred after the disintegration of the coalition because the disintegration signified a loss of opportunity to address the question of land rights endemic to these areas. Furthermore, the opportunity to address grievances on land was lost when people rejected the draft constitution in the referendum. It was the perception that the Kikuyu political elite, who were in central positions in government, were not keen to share political power with other tribes that defeated the proposed constitution. Issues of land and the domination of Kikuyu in settlement schemes in Rift Valley shaped those perceptions. The ensuing conflicts, therefore, were an expression of local resentment over wrongs arising from how land issues—including redistribution—were addressed.

Land and the Violence Following the December 2007 Election

Political grievances over land redistribution and land reform in general continue to inform Kenya's local and national politics whenever political circumstances change. That was true in the December 2007 general election. The background to the election was the political tension arising from the fall of the earlier political coalition and the defeat of the constitution in the November 2005 referendum. Most important, a few months before the December 2007 general elections, the *Majimbo* debate and the land question surfaced again in the debate over the future of Kenya—whether to have a *Majimbo* or a unitary system of government. The main opposition supported the *Majimbo* system. They argued that devolution would be pursued as a policy to enable people to make decisions on matters around their region. The government's party, however, argued against *Majimbo,* describing it as bad policy for the country because it would undermine national cohesion.

Against that background, Kenyans went to the polls on December 27, 2007. Voter turnout was relatively higher than in the three elections conducted since December 1992; about 70 percent of registered voters went to the polls. During the vote counting, the opposition complained that the Electoral Commission of

Kenya was rigging results in favor of the government. The final vote count and result were hotly disputed by the opposition political party. Notwithstanding that, the Electoral Commission announced the results late on December 30. Within hours of declaring Mwai Kibaki the winner of the disputed presidential poll, violence broke out in Nairobi, Rift Valley, Coast, Western, and Nyanza Provinces—regions where the opposition had huge support. In Rift Valley Province, many Kikuyu families were evicted from their landholdings. Also evicted were members of the Kisii ethnic community who were argued to have voted in support of Kikuyu candidate Kibaki. The Kalenjin evicted the Kikuyu and assumed control of areas on which the Kikuyu had settled both through the land purchase program and through allocation of plots in settlement schemes. The Kalenjin occupied these settlements and gave them local Kalenjin names to erase their Kikuyu identity. In the first quarter of 2008, the violence produced more than 300,000 internally displaced persons. Through the efforts of the African Union and the United Nations, an international mediation team intervened, and the two parties agreed to a power-sharing arrangement.

Although the international mediation process returned calm to these areas, the coexistence of the Kikuyu and the Kalenjin has become overpoliticized, and sustainable cordial relationships will depend on how the land question is addressed. Crucial for this purpose is further redistribution of land to the Kalenjin landless. The success of such redistribution depends on a commitment of the government to change the structure of landownership in the Rift Valley by buying underused large farms for redistribution.

The land redistribution policy of the 1960s and its outcome clearly shaped the outcome of the December 2007 presidential election dispute. Both the procedure by which land settlement schemes were established and the skewed bias in favor of certain groups are responsible for the recurrence of violence. Notably, there is a clear link between land, territory, and politics. Land gives meaning to politics so communities carve and claim territories in a manner that will advance their political interests.

Land Redistribution in Policy Debates

Problems arising from redistribution efforts have made land an important factor in national development debates. Matters of land became important because of the manner in which they integrated into and altered the local and national political circumstances. As shown above, land issues became important political resources around which the elites built their political and economic fortunes. Land became a patronage resource. Successive governments gave land to loyal individuals, who would sell the same land to public institutions at inflated prices (Republic of Kenya 2004). This gave rise to the grabbing of public land and the subsequent reduction of the amount of land available for distribution to the landless. Grabbing of public land and increased politicization of the resettlement program led to continued underprioritizing of land redistribution for the landless, creating room for redistribution to a small group of economically and politically powerful elites.

The government responded to some of those issues by appointing a Commission of Inquiry into the Land Law Systems of Kenya in 1999. The Njonjo Commission (named for the person who chaired it) identified the lack of a national land policy as a major shortcoming of the framework for regulating control of land. The commission made several observations: First, there had been a systematic breakdown in land administration and land delivery procedures. The breakdown made the land question much more complex than had been the case earlier. Second, there was no policy to guide the administration of land or to regulate land access and control. Formulation and implementation of a national land policy therefore were important. Third, matters of land were so crucial that they required constitutional guarantees to provide a basis for landownership and administration (Republic of Kenya 2002). The commission's findings were tabled in late 2002.

However, a land policy process already had started and was anchored on the constitutional review process begun in 2001. With the leadership of a coalition of civil society organizations, the Kenya Land Alliance, nongovernmental bodies provided their input to the process, while the Ministry of Lands coordinated the administrative aspects of the process. Through these efforts, land became one of the priority themes at the National Constitutional Conference.

The pace toward a national land policy increased when a new government came to power in 2003. Alarmed by the complexity of the land question and the impunity with which public land had been grabbed over the years, the new government established another commission to look into land allocations over the years. With regard to the land redistribution program through settlement schemes, the commission found that allocation of land in some of the settlement schemes lacked a clear legal, policy, and regulatory framework. This lack of a framework had provided opportunities for civil servants, politicians, and other elites to acquire public land illegally and irregularly in the settlement schemes. The commission noted that settlement schemes established in the early years of independence conformed to the original objectives, but they later deviated from those objectives. In some cases, land was allocated to people who were not deserving; neither were they landless nor did they have "unique skills and facilities to be able to use the land in an agriculturally productive manner" (Republic of Kenya 2004, p. 126). Such people included officials in the provincial administration, their relatives, members of parliament, Ministry of Lands and Settlement officials, and other influential individuals. The commission also found cases in which some influential people obtained far greater amounts of land than the landless peasants or more than the recommended acreage. The commission recommended revoking all illegal and irregular allocations made since the early 1960s (Republic of Kenya 2004).

The process of developing a national land policy incorporated findings from the commissions and from the constitutional review process, which began about 2001. In 2006, the government produced a draft policy that recognized people as owners of land. It provided for land redistribution, restitution, and resettlement; alteration of the structure of landownership; and taxation. The policy sought to restore rights to those who lost their land rights through unfair government policies, and to settle disadvantaged groups to ensure they had secure rights to land. The policy also underlined the need to establish a land bank for purposes of accessing resources to acquire land for settling the landless.

The draft policy was developed in anticipation of a new constitution, but that constitution was rejected in 2005. The draft constitution contained provisions reflecting the principles articulated in the draft national land policy. In the absence of a national policy to guide land reforms and in the absence of comprehensive constitutional reform to facilitate development of laws on land, land distribution has tended to rely on political patronage rather than on government policies. The government has been responding to problems of landlessness both on an ad hoc basis and at the urging of leading political elites. Influential political elites have been directing the government toward excising public areas, such as forests, for allocation to their landless constituencies. Political patronage also has intertwined with ethnicity and land redistribution efforts. The elite tend to mobilize their own ethnic groups in demands for land or in opposition to settling people in their territories—people who do not share the same ethnic identity. Those efforts have resulted in land redistribution becoming increasingly politicized and ethnicized; they have built a base for local political conflicts where land redistribution is taking place.

CONCLUSION: SOME KEY LESSONS

Land redistribution reforms in Kenya have not addressed the challenges of landlessness adequately. Through the resettlement efforts of the earlier period of independence, new political and economic elites acquired more land at the expense of landless people. The redistribution efforts resulted in a concentration of land. The elite acquired more land while the poor continued to hold onto small patches of land that were insufficient even for subsistence farming. Large holdings were in the hands of the new political and economic elites, who acquired many of them through the markets and/or through political patronage.

The land reform program failed to address the problem of landlessness because the objectives of the initial phase of reform centered on economic interests: how to maintain a stable economy after independence. The reform prioritized issues of equity and economic efficiency on the assumption that giving Africans access to holdings in the White Highlands would reduce social tension. Furthermore, the reform had to be carried out in the best interest of the European settlers so that they could protect themselves against an independent government. Access to the highlands was skewed in favor of the Kikuyu land-hungry people. That bias laid a framework for recurrent interethnic conflicts that repeatedly threaten national cohesion. The objectives of land redistribution, therefore, first ought to examine the possible unintended consequences of land being anchored in a continually changing socioeconomic and political context. This also suggests that equity and efficiency as objectives in land reform are not compatible with the objective of addressing social tensions. Contradictions in how equity is addressed can give rise to new tensions and new land questions. In the case of Kenya, these contradictions led to interethnic conflicts.

Land redistribution in Kenya has been a gradual process. The military defeat of the Mau Mau peasant rebellion removed the possibility of a radical alteration of the structure of landownership. If examined from the perspective of Binswanger, Deininger, and Feder (1993), the Mau Mau upheaval was not so major that it would have altered the structure of landownership radically. Mau Mau nonetheless forced some urgency on how the administration had to deal with the land question.

There are several lessons to be learned from the Kenyan experience. First, markets are not necessarily the most viable mechanism for redistributing land. Through the land purchase program, those who had the ability to pay bought more land at the expense of land-hungry people. Markets result in a skewed structure of landownership and so do not address problems around issues of access to and control of land. Second, landlessness is a political issue, and land redistribution efforts should be seen from a political perspective; those efforts require a political solution. The government has been addressing landlessness from an administrative and technical point of view, thus losing sight of the numerous competing interests around issues of land. Those interests cannot be satisfied through administrative and technical procedures. They require political negotiations.

That second point leads to the third point: political interests, however, should not override the technical and administrative requirements of a solution to land problems. Land redistribution procedures, if abused, can undermine the reform process. People can lose confidence in the administrative and technical arrangements of land reforms if the mechanisms for the reforms are not transparent or if the key actors are not accountable to the society. Democratizing the process of redistribution and establishing mechanisms through which people can participate in decision making on key aspects of a reform program are crucial to the success of land reforms. Fourth, a clear policy on land redistribution is needed to address the political and economic challenges around issues of land. Lack of a clear policy has meant shifts in ideas as well as interests in addressing the land question.

NOTE

1. These data were gathered from the *Kenya Statistical Abstracts*, 1974–2005, published annually by the Kenya National Bureau of Statistics.

REFERENCES

Bassett, Thomas J., and Donald E. Crummey, eds. 1993. *Land in African Agrarian Systems.* Madison, WI: University of Wisconsin Press.

Berman, Bruce. 1990. *Control and Crisis in Colonial Kenya: The Dialectic of Domination.* London: James Currey.

Berry, Sara. 1993. *No Condition Is Permanent: The Social Dynamics of Agrarian Change in Sub-Saharan Africa.* Madison, WI: University of Wisconsin Press.

Binswanger, Hans P., Klaus Deininger, and Gershon Feder. 1993. "Power, Distortions, Revolt, and Reform in Agricultural Land Relations." Policy Research Working Paper 1164. World Bank, Washington, DC.

Clough, E. S. 1965. "Some Notes on a Recent Economic Survey of Land Settlement in Kenya." *East African Economic Review* 1 (3): 78–83.

Glazier, Jack. 1985. *Land and the Uses of Tradition among the Mbeere of Kenya.* Lanham, MD: University Press of America.

Harbeson, John W. 1973. *Nation-Building in Kenya: The Role of Land Reform.* Evanston, IL: Northwestern University Press.

IBRD (International Bank for Reconstruction and Development). 1961. "Project for Development and Settlement of Land in the Scheduled Areas, Kenya." Report TO 303a, Department of Technical Operations, Washington, DC.

ILO (International Labour Organization). 1972. *Unemployment, Incomes and Equality: A Strategy of Increasing Productive Employment in Kenya.* Geneva, Switzerland.

Kanyinga, Karuti. 1998. "The Land Question in Kenya: Struggles, Accumulation and Changing Politics." Unpublished PhD diss., Roskilde University, Denmark.

———. 2000. *Re-Distribution from Above: The Politics of Land Rights and Squatting in Coastal Kenya.* Research Report 115. Uppsala, Sweden: Nordic Africa Institute.

Kitching, Gavin. 1980. *Class and Economic Change in Kenya: The Making of an African Petite-Bourgeoisie.* New Haven, CT: Yale University Press.

Klopp, Jacqueline M. 2001. "Ethnic Land Clashes and Winning Elections: The Case of Kenya's Electoral Despotism." *Canadian Journal of African Studies* 35 (3): 473–517.

Lamb, G. 1974. *Peasant Politics: Conflicts and Development in Murang'a.* New York: St. Martin's Press.

Leo, Christopher. 1989. *Land and Class in Kenya.* Harare, Zimbabwe: Nehands.

Leys, Colin. 1975. *Underdevelopment in Kenya: The Political Economy of Neo-Colonialism 1964–1971.* London: Heinemann.

Maloba, Wunyabari O. 1993. *Mau Mau and Kenya: An Analysis of a Peasant Revolt.* Bloomington, IN: Indiana University Press.

Mamdani, Mahmood. 1996. *Citizen and Subject: Contemporary Africa and the Legacy of Late Colonialism.* Princeton, NJ: Princeton University Press.

———. 2001. *When Victims Become Killers: Colonialism, Nativism and Genocide in Rwanda.* Princeton, NJ: Princeton University Press.

National Council of Churches of Kenya. 1992. *The Cursed Arrow: A Report on Organised Violence against Democracy in Kenya.* Nairobi.

Njeru, Enos H. N. 1978. "Land Adjudication and Its Implications for the Social Organisation of the Mbeere." Research Paper 73. Land Tenure Center, University of Wisconsin, Madison.

Njonjo, A. 1978. "The Africanization of the 'White Highlands': A Study in Agrarian Class Struggles in Kenya, 1950–1974." PhD diss., Princeton University, Princeton, NJ.

Okoth-Ogendo, W.H.O. 1991. *Tenants of the Crown: Evolution of Agrarian Law and Institutions in Kenya.* Nairobi: ACTS Press.

Parliamentary Select Committee. 1992. Report of the Parliamentary Select Committee to Investigate Ethnic Clashes in Western and Other Parts of Kenya. Nairobi: Government Printer.

Republic of Kenya. 2002. Report of the Commission of Inquiry into the Land Law System of Kenya on Principles of a National Land Policy Framework and Constitutional Position of Land and New Institutional Framework for Land Administration. Nairobi: Government Printer.

———. 2004. Report of the Commission of Inquiry into the Illegal/Irregular Allocation of Public Land. Nairobi: Government Printer.

Sorrenson, M.P.K. 1968. *The Origins of European Settlement in Kenya.* Nairobi, Kenya: Oxford University Press.

Van Zwanenberg, R.M.A. 1975. *Colonial Capitalism and Labour in Kenya, 1919–1939.* Nairobi, Kenya: East African Literature Bureau.

Wanjala, Smokin. 1996. "Recurrent Themes in Kenya's Land Reform Discourse since Independence." Paper presented at the Eastern and Southern Africa Regional Conference on Experiences, Perspectives and Strategies on Land Reform and Land Rights in Rural and Urban Settings, Johannesburg, South Africa, June.

Wasserman, Gary. 1976. *The Politics of Decolonization: Kenya, Europeans, and the Land Issue, 1960–1965.* Cambridge, U.K.: Cambridge University Press.

CHAPTER FOUR

Land Reform throughout the 20th Century in China

Zhou Feizhou and Camille Bourguignon

Throughout the 20th century, many large-scale land redistribution programs were carried out by communist governments. These programs were part of broader efforts to establish a classless society. In this process, land redistribution was only the first step, and it often was followed by the abolition of land property rights and the collectivization of the agricultural production system. Forced collectivization invariably failed, notably because it removed fundamental production incentives, and new reforms were introduced to correct these mistakes. China is perhaps one of the most relevant examples to illustrate this path of land reforms.

By presenting land reform in China throughout the 20th century, this chapter will show how land redistribution takes place in the broader development process, and how constant changes in land ownership are closely related to economic, political, and social transformation. The first part of the chapter presents the first land redistribution in modern China. The second part discusses the subsequent collectivization of agriculture and its socioeconomic consequences. It then describes the new changes in land institutions in the wake of China's economic reform that began in the 1980s. The third part looks at the influence of current industrialization and urbanization on land institutions. The conclusion discusses possible future changes in China's land institutions.

THE FIRST LAND REDISTRIBUTION IN MODERN CHINA

By promising radical land redistribution, the leaders of the Chinese Communist Party (CCP) gave millions of peasants a reason to stand and fight with them against the ruling party. When in power, the CCP carried out large-scale land redistribution. Because the reform was violent, it is impossible to call it a success. Nevertheless, it would have been a "productive miracle."

The Chinese Communist Revolution

Defeated by the British in the First Opium War in 1842, China was forced to sign the Treaty of Nanjing whereby five Chinese ports were opened for trade to British merchants and the Island of Hong Kong was ceded to the British Crown. Trade between China and the West intensified and western countries kept pressing the Qing authorities to open further to the West. This pressure was the cause of a second outbreak of hostilities, also known as the Second Opium War. Defeated once again in 1858, China was forced to open 11 more ports to western trade. Among Chinese officials and intellectuals, this increasing foreign influence was perceived as a threat to China's sovereignty. Many people also were convinced, however, that China would have to adopt the technological and commercial advancements of the West if it were to remain a sovereign nation. In 1895, the Qing Dynasty's prestige was damaged further when it was defeated in the First Sino-Japanese War. As a result, the capacity of the Qing Dynasty to unify the country and stand against foreign assaults came under serious question.

With the opening of China to the West, new ideas had penetrated Chinese society, and many intellectuals were convinced that time for deep political reform had come. During the 1890s, intellectuals started advocating for a revolution to overthrow the ruling dynasty and establish a republic. During that decade, tensions mounted between conservative and reformist forces. On the verge of being overthrown, the government started carrying out important reforms, including the 1905 abolishment of the Imperial Examination. But many people held the firm view that a radical political change was necessary.

In 1911, the government was overthrown, the Republic of China was founded, and the groups that had orchestrated the revolution formed the Kuomintang (also known as the Chinese Nationalist Party). The 1911 Revolution, or Xinhai Revolution, was a political revolution. It established a new political system but did not prompt fundamental social changes in Chinese society. Even as a political revolution, it was partly a failure; and by 1915 the Kuomintang had been dissolved.

After a failed attempt to reestablish an empire, the country was left without a strong political figure and in the hands of warlords. Many people thought that a second revolution was needed to bring deeper political and social transformation. In 1919, World War I officially ended with the Treaty of Versailles, which transferred German concessions in China to Japan. This "unfair" treatment of China by foreign powers and the incapacity of the central government to defend the interest of the Chinese nation provoked indignation among Chinese intellectuals who unified around the May Fourth Movement.

The May Fourth Movement of 1919 involved huge student demonstrations held in Peking to denounce a pro-Japanese government. The movement was both anti-imperialist and anti-warlord, and was the reaction of the Chinese people to the turbulent new forces unleashed by World War I. It is also considered the beginning of the Chinese modern revolutionary era (Chen 1970). China's political and social organization was widely thought to be the main cause of the country's fragmentation, which was exploited constantly by foreign nations. Intellectual discussion became more radical. And in that context the Kuomintang was resuscitated in 1919 and the CCP was founded in 1921. In 1922, the CCP was a small party of 195 members, but it grew rapidly; by 1927, it comprised nearly 60,000 members.

Following the directives of the Comintern (also known as the Communist International), the CCP encouraged its members to join the Kuomintang. Together, the CCP and Kuomintang formed the First United Front; by 1925 they had established a Kuomintang government in Guangzhou and had funded the National Revolutionary Army. Then began a military campaign to suppress warlords' control and to unify the country. Soon, however, this cooperation fell apart. For the CCP, revolution in China had to be *agrarian*. Members of the CCP believed that radical land reform had to be carried out to achieve the Marxist ideal of a classless society. The leaders of the Kuomintang rejected their radicalism.

In 1927, Kuomintang leaders organized the "Purge of Communists in the Party" in an attempt to destroy the influence of the CCP. The party suffered severe losses and was forced to organize a massive military retreat (the Long March). This was the beginning of the Chinese civil war that pitted the CCP and the Kuomintang against one another for more than two decades. Between 1937 and 1945, the CCP and the Kuomintang collaborated one more time under the Second United Front to resist Japanese invasion, but the civil war resumed full scale in 1946; and on October 1, 1949, Mao Zedong proclaimed the People's Republic of China. By 1950, isolated pockets of resistance had been destroyed and the civil war was over.

The Land Reform Promise and the Victory of the CCP

Initially, the CCP was a movement led by urban revolutionary intellectuals and supported by urban workers. However, it was the ability of the CCP to rally peasant masses around the promise of land reform that eventually ensured its overwhelming victory over the Kuomintang.

Life in the countryside was harsh for the peasant masses. Chinese communist historians tend to stress human responsibility and denounce the exploitation of the peasantry by "local tyrants and evil gentry." By contrast, other historians argue that economic and demographic conditions in rural China were enough to make the misery of the vast majority inevitable. To those historians, discontent and the bankruptcy of the rural society created an inexhaustible supply of potential revolutionaries. Thus the strength of the CCP was that it gave this blind force purpose and direction (Bianco 1971).

Other historians argue that peasant living standards declined during the modern era simply as a result of population growth. China's population had increased very rapidly during the 18th and 19th centuries, reaching 426 million in 1901. China remained a predominantly rural society, and the average size of the landholding was decreasing. During the Song Dynasty, the land per capita ratio was about 0.53 hectares. At the end of the 19th century, it had dropped to 0.19 hectares. Despite evident regional disparities, there is no doubt that Chinese peasants had very small plots of land to cultivate by the beginning of the 20th century. On the eve of the Communist Revolution, land pressure was greater than it ever had been (Bianco 1971).

Although Chinese agriculture was far from primitive, it belonged to the prescientific era. Furthermore, the excessive land fragmentation hampered capital investment in land. It obstructed both drainage and irrigation, and limited the use of animal and machine power in agricultural production. Finally, the labor surplus caused by demographic growth tended to be used to cultivate the land because of the lack of alternative sources of employment. These factors were at the bottom of the tradition of intensive cultivation in Chinese agriculture. At the same time, they also were at the base of a labor overinvestment called "involution," in reference to a continuous labor input even after marginal returns to labor sink below the subsistence level (Huang 1985).

China always has had one of the world's highest outputs per unit of land. For instance, according to a nationwide survey conducted in the 1930s, the output per unit of land in China was twice as great as that in the United States. However, that output was achieved at the cost of extremely high labor investment. In fact, the amount of labor put into a unit of land in China was 23 times the amount in the United States (Buck 1937). But the fact that Chinese peasants produced relatively more per unit does not mean that they were better off than their American counterparts. They simply produced relatively more out of the little they had.

The malaise of the Chinese peasantry was accentuated further by the prevalence of tenant farming. Very large landowners were rare in China, and rich individuals rarely owned more than 20 hectares (see box 4.1). During the 1920s and 1930s in the wheat-producing area of northern China, landlords owned between 6.5 and 13.5 hectares, on average. In the rice-producing area of southern China, however, landholdings were larger, and the percentage of tenant peasants was higher. Land rights there were distributed relatively equally among tenants, and landlessness was rare. Nonetheless, tenancy was widespread overall, and in the early 1940s, the top 10–15 percent of the wealthiest families would have owned approximately 40–60 percent of the land (Zhang 1988).

Box 4.1 Land Distribution from China's Song Dynasty to the Republican Era

The conventional theory of the origin of Chinese Revolution in 1949 assumes that during the Republican Era (1912–49), land distribution in China was extremely skewed. Among scholars, however, there actually is no full agreement on whether there was a long-term trend toward land concentration from the Song Dynasty to the Republican Era. Opponents of the Marxist theory argue that these social institutions, combined with wars and natural disasters, would account for the fact that China's land distribution did not have any obvious tendency toward a high degree of concentration throughout history. Some scholars even argue that the Gini coefficient of land distribution kept decreasing from the Song Dynasty to the Republican Era. According to them, land distribution at the beginning of the 20th century would have been at its most equal state in China's long history.

Source: Chao 1986.

For the mass of tenant farmers, land rents and land taxes were a huge burden. In the late 1930s, land rent probably averaged around 45 percent of the total harvest. Many landowners also asked their tenants for advance payments and required deposits. Land tax was incomparably lower than land rents; but there were frequent abuses, such as surtaxes or tax collection long in advance (Bianco 1971). Social mobility was possible, and a poor peasant could hope for a rise in status. Nonetheless, inequalities were pronounced. Peasant masses were chained in economic servitude. There was a real malaise in the countryside, and the CCP soon understood that this mass of discontented peasants was potentially "a force so swift and violent that no power, however great, will be able to hold it back" (Mao 1927[1]).

The Nationwide Land Reform Movement

In 1947, the CCP adopted the "basic program of the Chinese Agrarian Law," a program of 16 basic points to "wipe out the agrarian system of feudal and semi-feudal exploitation" and implement Sun Yat-sen's slogan, "He who tills the land shall own it" (Lee 1948, p. 20). This was the inception of a nationwide land reform movement that started in northern China and initially was called "Land Reform in the Old Liberated Areas." When the CCP took power in 1949, the movement spread farther south. It then became "Land Reform in the New Liberated Areas."

According to the CCP regulations, "complete reallocation" was implemented in the old liberated areas of northern China (Zhou 2000). Land redistribution was carried out at the village level and executed by the village peasant assemblies and committees. Land holdings were seized and equally redistributed among peasants. Each beneficiary acquired exactly the same amount of land.[2] In the new liberated areas of southern China, however, land redistribution was carried out differently. Based on household property in general, but landholding in particular, the population of the village was classified as landlords and as rich, middle-level, and poor peasants. Rich peasants were allowed to retain land up to a ceiling defined by the central government. The surplus of land then was redistributed to landless and land-poor peasants.

In the end, 46.7 million hectares of land were redistributed to approximately 300 million peasants, or 60 percent of the total rural population (Prosterman, Li, and Hanstad 1996). In the old liberated areas of northern China, land reform was radical and often violent. "Struggle sessions" against the landlords and rich peasants were common, and many of those people were executed (Hinton 1966, chs. 13 and 15). By contrast, in the new liberated areas of southern China, land was redistributed in a relatively milder fashion. Analysis of the agrarian structure in the different parts of China before the nationwide land reform movement shows that land distribution was not as skewed in northern China as it was in southern China (Zhang 1988). Land reform was, however, more radical and violent in northern China.

Thus, if the peasant malaise was real, the nationwide land reform movement was essentially a political movement. The CCP leaders' principal objective was to acquire the power needed to implement their ideology. So as long as the CCP was not in power, radical land reform was seen as necessary to modify the political structure of the villages, secure the support of a mass of poor peasants, and suppress the opposition. All of that suggests the economic goal of the land reform would have been only secondary. But regardless of its initial objective, land redistribution produced an "economic miracle." From 1949 to 1952, rural incomes increased by 48 percent and food production rose by 36 percent.

LAND COLLECTIVIZATION AND THE PEOPLE'S COMMUNE

As soon as the CCP had completed large-scale land redistribution, it moved on its broader objective of establishing a communist society. That meant abolishing private property rights and collectivizing the agricultural sector. A few years later, China was stricken by the Great Famine.

Premises of the Collectivization Movement

By 1952 the nationwide land reform movement was complete. The priority of the CCP had shifted to developing the economy through industrialization, and the role of the agricultural sector was to serve the development of heavy industries.[3] During the early 1950s, China was industrializing, but at a slow pace. In the late 1950s, light industry was backward technically; in the other industrial sectors in general, and particularly in heavy industries, there were hardly any signs of development. Chinese energy and transportation industries—not to mention large infrastructure—also were very underdeveloped.

When land had been redistributed, peasants were encouraged to form "mutual aid teams"—small production teams of about a dozen households. To this point, land, livestock, and farm tools were privately owned by the peasants themselves. Only in busy seasons (such as during cultivation, seeding, irrigation, and harvesting) would the households work and cooperate as a team. Peasants received the produce from their own plots of land. To encourage the formation of mutual aid teams, the government gave them "economic and technical help and preferential treatment" (Doak 1953). By 1952, according to the CCP, 35 million peasant families (40 percent of all peasant families in the country) belonged to one of the 6 million mutual aid teams (p. 192).

Soon after the CCP took power, peasants were encouraged to form agricultural producer's cooperatives. These cooperatives were three to four times larger than small production teams, and the nature of the cooperatives was quite different from that of the teams. Peasants decided to pool their assets, including land, livestock, and farm tools. In exchange, peasants were entitled to a profit share in the cooperative. Of the net profit made, about 8 percent was retained as public savings, 40 percent was distributed to members as dividends on the land in which they invested, and 52 percent was distributed as wages. Land put into the cooperative no longer was identified with individual households—peasants partly had lost their land ownership. There were 3,000 agricultural producer's cooperatives operating in China by 1952 (Doak 1953).

The nationwide land reform movement was followed by a rapid increase in agricultural production. Even with an expanding population, underdeveloped economy, and low living standards, the market price for grain remained high. From 1950 to 1953, the central government had to purchase grain at a high price to provide food for urban workers employed in the heavy industries. This need to procure grain at elevated prices placed a high fiscal cost on developing heavy industries, and the CCP was seeing it as a constraint to achieving fast development of those industries.

In November 1953, the CCP introduced the Unified Grain Procurement system. Under this system, the private grain market was suppressed and peasants were obliged to sell their grain to the state at a price established by the state. Only when they had fulfilled grain procurement quotas could the peasants sell any surplus, either on the state-controlled market or informally. Similar systems followed for cotton in 1954 and for various other farm products in 1956 and 1957. The mandatory state purchase subsequently was extended to more than 130 items, including live pigs, eggs, sugar, silk, flue-cured tobacco, and aquatic products (Du 2006).

In 1956 the government introduced advanced cooperatives. These entities were much larger than the earlier elementary cooperatives and included several hundred households. They functioned in a manner similar to the elementary cooperatives; but in advanced cooperatives, the amount of land that peasants initially owned had nothing to do with the profit share they received. The share depended exclusively on the number of days a peasant worked for the cooperative. The top leaders of the CCP regarded the advanced cooperatives as "completely socialist" in nature because incomes were distributed "to each according to his labor."

By the end of 1955, Mao Zedong called for a "socialist upsurge" to upgrade all the elementary cooperatives to advanced cooperatives. Farmers were forced to join advanced cooperatives, and Mao's goal was achieved in the next year. During the first half of 1957, many rich and prosperous peasants demanded to quit the cooperatives (Lin 1990). Following this nationwide "tide of withdrawal," the central government (led by CCP Vice-Secretary Liu Shaoqi) made some adjustments and requested that local governments adopt an "anti-rush" collectivization policy. However, Mao responded by calling for an "anti-anti-rush" campaign. He said, "Some comrades want to anti-rush, but I propose to anti-anti-rush, and to anti-anti-rush is to leap forward" (Chen 1993). That statement set the stage for the Great Leap Forward Campaign in 1958.

From the Great Leap Forward to the Great Famine

The most important institutional change came in 1958, during the Great Leap Forward, when cooperatives were consolidated into 24,000 people's communes, representing 99 percent of China's rural households (Lin 1990). The communes regrouped dozens of advanced cooperatives, thousands of households. Virtually all peasants' personal properties were collectivized, including houses, furniture, and jewelry. Incomes were distributed according to the Marxist principle, "From each according to his ability, to each according to his need." Every member received food at no cost. The central government obliged cooperatives and people's communes to sell food in the quantities and at the prices the government set. Whatever was left was distributed according to the number of labor days each member had put into the production.

The establishment of people's communes was followed by a severe agricultural crisis: peasants' incentives to produce were dampened, and the amount of cultivated acreage declined rapidly. Soon China was struck by severe famines. Between 1959 and 1961, about 30 million people died of "unusual causes" (Chang and Wen 1997). The Chinese government first claimed that the Great Famine was mainly the result of a series of natural disasters. But a large body of literature suggests that the radical political choices made by the CCP were its main cause (Bernstein 1984; Yang 1996). There were important differences in death rates between different regions, and the number of deaths by starvation was much smaller in the cities. All of the evidence points to serious problems in grain distribution (Kung and Lin 2003).

People's communes were subdivided into production brigades and production teams. After the Great Famine, responsibility for the distribution of profit shares to the peasants was transferred from the people's communes either to the production brigades or to the production teams. Nevertheless, landownership remained in the hands of the production brigades, and peasants kept working under the supervision of the heads of the production teams. This mode of agricultural production was maintained until the late 1970s. During those 20 years, China's agricultural production and labor productivity both sank, and peasants' incomes stalled. Involution was as serious as it had been before the nationwide land reform movement. At the same time, because of the severe lack of incentives to produce, the labor surplus was not invested systematically in agricultural production. Peasants adopted opportunistic behavior, such as shirking, to deal with the system.

In the field of development economics, there has never been enough evidence to show that collectivization would work, especially in East Asia with its tradition of family farming and intensive cultivation. Nonetheless, some scholars believe that it was not land collectivization per se that caused the stagnation of China's agricultural economy, but rather the widespread egalitarianism in distribution (Putterman 1993). Most scholars, however, are convinced that the high transaction costs and supervision in densely populated agricultural regions inevitably led to the failure of collectivization (Bradley and Clark 1972).

DECOLLECTIVIZATION AND REINTRODUCTION OF INDIVIDUAL LAND RIGHTS

In 1972, two years after Mao's death, 18 households from Xiaogang village, in the Anhui Province, secretly signed contracts with their production team whereby collective land was assigned to individual households. This was the very beginning of the decollectivization process.

Introducing New Land Institutions

At the time of the Great Famine in 1960 and 1961, in some places the production brigades started contracting collective land to individual households. As long as the households fulfilled the terms of the contract, they were allowed to retain the production surplus. This system proved to be very effective in terms of agricultural production and surplus distribution. At the same time, it was regarded as a form of "capitalism." As such, it was banned by Mao right after the Great Famine.

Mao died in 1976. On the national level, after several years of power struggles, Deng Xiaoping tightly controlled the new generation of CCP leaders. Deng's pragmatic ideas contrasted with Mao's radicalism and, under his leadership, China initiated an era of comprehensive reforms that were to transform the socialist planned economy into a socialist market economy.

In the early 1980s, the central government introduced the so-called Household Responsibility System (HRS; *baochan daohu*). According to the HRS, production brigades were allowed to assign collective land to families. Where the HRS was adopted, land was distributed according to household size. The agricultural output no longer was turned over to the production brigades, and production teams no longer supervised agricultural production. Excluding state tax and the collective fund, the households kept all income generated from land cultivation. With state tax and the collective fund generally being of a fixed amount, the HRS was essentially a fixed-rent contract system.

The HRS was adopted voluntarily. Some local cadres were convinced that the system would bring little in terms of economic efficiency, but the central government supported it and peasants were entitled to choose (Du 2006). They adopted it with enthusiasm. By the end of 1983, nearly 98 percent of the production teams in China's rural areas had adopted the HRS (Lin 1992). The introduction of the system prompted huge progress in agricultural production, notably because it restored fundamental production incentives that had been swept away by collectivization (Lin 1992; Zhang 2000). From 1957 to 1978, the average annual agricultural production growth rate was 2.3 percent. From 1980 to 1985, it soared to 8.2 percent, and by 1985 Chinese peasants produced huge surpluses (Lin 1992).

After 1985 the growth rate of agricultural production slowed and eventually stalled at an average of 4.8 percent for the subsequent five years, slightly better than half what it had been during the previous six years. Some scholars believe that this slowdown indicated the end of the momentum released by introduction of the HRS. To continue the progress, further reform—and technological innovations—became necessary.

Maintaining an Equal Distribution of Land Rights

When the HRS was introduced, land use rights were contracted for periods of three years or less. In practice, most villages in rural China undertook periodic readjustments of land in response to demographic changes in the village. Many local officials considered these repeated land redistributions necessary to follow one of the collectives' basic rules: each peasant is entitled to a plot of land to cultivate. Local officials could decide when and how to redistribute land; and by the mid-1990s, more than 60 percent of the villages had readjusted land distribution frequently (Kung and Liu 1997). In some villages, redistribution occurred every year; in others, it was done every three or five years. Only in a few villages was land never redistributed. And the methods of redistribution varied: at times, all the land was taken back and reapportioned among peasants by lottery; at other times, only the surplus of land from households that had reduced in size was taken back and redistributed to households that had grown.

For many poor peasants, land readjustment would have played the role of a safety net. Most Chinese peasants had very low incomes and no social benefits. For them, land was the main source of livelihood, and the practice of periodic land redistribution was the warranty to access land equally, regardless of their incomes. Although this system may not have supported the long-term development of agricultural production, it did help maintain a stable social order in the countryside (Zhao 2007). In recent years, the possibility of introducing a nationwide social security system has been discussed. If new social benefits for rural residents are established in the future, the safety net function of rural land may weaken.

There is still no full consensus on whether peasants are in favor of, or against, the practice of periodic land readjustment (Kung and Liu 1997). However, there are genuine reasons to believe that the practice of chronic land redistribution is likely to conflict with the objective of providing land tenure security. If peasants know that they may lose their land, they logically will have little incentive to invest in long-term improvements to it. This lack of incentive would hamper agricultural development. Thus, from an economic perspective, the practice of recurring land readjustment may be harmful for the long-term development of the agricultural sector.

In 1984 the government issued Rural Work Document No. 1, urging local officials to prolong the land-use term to at least 15 years. In 1994 it became possible to extend land-use rights another 30 years after the original 15-year term expired. These directives, however, were not widely implemented by local officials. By 1998, fewer than 10 percent of all villages nationwide had extended usage rights for another 30 years (Prosterman et al. 1998).

In 1995, acknowledging the importance of providing farmers with long-term and stable transferable land rights, the government issued a policy document discouraging further land reallocation (the State Council, "To Stabilize the Land Contract System," Document No. 7, 1995). In 1998 it adopted new land readjustment principles requiring that reallocated or contracted land must be approved by at least two thirds of the villagers' representatives and by the government of the county (NPC 1998, art. 14). Since then, the practice of land readjustment gradually has been abandoned. In 2002, the Rural Land Contracting Law was passed to offer better protection of peasants' land use rights. According to a nationwide survey in 2003, more than half of the villages in the country had stopped readjusting land.

CONVERSION OF RURAL LAND TO URBAN USES

China nationalized urban land in 1949. Whereas rural land is owned by the collective, urban land is owned by the state—that is, the central government or local governments. Rural and urban lands are subject to different rights regimes and are administered by separate institutions under different rules. Before 1988, when the Land Management Law was passed, the government allocated urban land to nongovernment institutions (including business enterprises, schools, and hospitals) for a limited period of time free of charge. After 1988, the government began to cover the fee.

Today, urban land can be acquired for a specified period of time in two ways: "sale transfer" and "listed auction." When land is required for public use (for example, for roads, bridges, schools, and hospitals), the government conducts a sale transfer (*hua bo*). Land rights are allocated free of charge or provided for a very low fee. When land is required for the installation of business enterprises for commercial development and housing (for example, for commercial, office, and residential apartment buildings), it is allocated through a listed auction (*zhao pai gua*). The land is sold by public bidding for a period not to exceed 70 years.

Since the late 1990s, with China's rapid industrialization and urbanization, the demand for urban land has soared. To satisfy the need for land in the cities, local governments increasingly have relied on the conversion of rural land to urban uses. To do this, urban authorities first must acquire rural land from the village committees.[4] The land is obtained through compulsory acquisition with compensation.[5] When a local government has formalized the acquisition, the land can be developed. Utilities such as roads, running water, and electricity are installed and, if necessary, the land is leveled. It then can be transferred to developers through one of the two means mentioned above. Through this process, local governments not only satisfy the demand for urban land, but also make huge profits in the sale of the land-use rights.

China's Pacific coast is by far the most industrialized and urbanized part of the country. In this region, the transfer acquisition of rural land by local governments is extremely frequent. It is interesting to note that the conversion of rural land to urban use is an important source of profits for local governments, but these revenues are not categorized as fiscal income. They do not appear in the entire budget and do not need to be shared with upper-level governments. Thus, the central government does not have sound knowledge of the actual amount of these revenues. A few case studies (notably of the provinces of Guangdong, Jiangsu, and Zhejiang) suggest that these revenues would be tantamount to the budget of the local governments (Zhou 2008). Local governments, therefore, would seem to have great incentives to convert rural land to urban use.

Making such a conversion is particularly lucrative for local governments for two main reasons: First, the demand for urban land keeps increasing and its value is soaring. Second, local governments acquire land from the village committees at very low prices.[6] The amount paid hardly ever exceeds RMB100,000 per mu,[7] and it averages between RMB30,000 and RMB50,000 per mu. The amount that local governments charge when they transfer the land to developers usually reaches several million renminbi per mu. Thus, even after deducting the development costs, the net income that local governments generate from this conversion equals 30–60 percent of the total land transfer price (Liu and Jiang 2005).

For the peasants, the conversion of rural land to urban uses results in the definitive loss of their land rights. The problem is that the low compensation they receive is not only paltry compared with the benefits local governments derive from the operation, but it also is insufficient to secure future income. It is only logical that these practices fuel peasants' discontent. Many peasants have appealed to higher authorities to contest the level of compensation. It is not surprising that the province in which the number of court appeals is highest is the province of Zhejiang, where the economy is booming and where the local government has acquired huge tracts of rural land.

The fact that converting rural land to urban use causes discontent among peasants suggests that the current mode of administering collective landholding allows very little, if any, room for peasants to take part in the negotiation process and secure fair compensation. The legal status of collective ownership is weaker than that of public ownership. In addition, peasants, as users of the land, seldom have the opportunity to participate in negotiations between the local government and the village. Under China's current political system, the head of the village committee represents the village collective and negotiates with the local government. However, the committee head is often the party secretary, who generally has a close and subordinate relationship with the local government, so the local authorities easily can use administrative means to compel the village party secretary to agree to sell the land at a low cost, even though that may not be in the interest of the villagers.

Since 2002 the central government has made many efforts to protect farmers' land rights. For instance, the Rural Land Contracting Law and the Property Law were passed in 2002 and 2007, respectively. According to the Rural Land Contracting Law, "any organization or individual is not allowed to expropriate or illegally limit the land contracting rights of farmers." More recently, with Document No. 1 of 2008, the central government encourages the establishment of rural land registries. Such a system, whereby the farmers would hold the legal certificates to their contracted land, should provide better protection of farmers' land rights (upgraded to the status of property rights under the 2007 Property Law).

CONCLUSION

China's land institutions have undergone drastic changes during the past 100 years, and have accounted for profound economic and social transformations. The defining feature of this process of change is its instability. Table 4.1 shows that peasants were dispossessed of their land rights progressively after the 1949 land reform. Since the early 1980s, individual land rights have been reintroduced, and the level of tenure security these rights confer has increased gradually. Today, although the nominal ownership is still in the hands of village collectives, peasants have access to relatively secure land rights. At the same time, the urbanization of China is having an important impact on land property rights in the countryside, and there are strong reasons to believe that peasants' interests are not represented fairly in the current mode of rural land administration.

Table 4.1 Structure of Land Property Rights since 1949

Period	Years	Ownership	Right to Use	Right to Receive Income	Right to Transfer
Land reform	1949–54	Farmer	Farmer	Farmer	Farmer
Collectivization	1955–56	Farmer	Collective	Farmer	Collective
People's communes	1957–80	Collective	Collective	Collective	Collective
HRS	1981–present	Collective	Farmer	Farmer	Collective and farmer

Source: Author's compilation.
Note: HRS = Household Responsibility System.

China has a long way to go to strengthen peasants' negotiating power and ensure that they truly share the benefits of urbanization and economic development. It sometimes is argued that land privatization would be the most direct way to provide peasants with secured land rights. Given the current political context in China, however, land privatization is not a realistic proposal. Furthermore, there are other ways to provide farmers with an adequate level of tenure security. For instance, the Rural Land Contracting Law could provide Chinese rural peasants with stronger land rights, perhaps similar to those of their urban counterparts. Also, the Land Management Law that regulates compulsory land acquisition could be revised to ensure more fair compensation.

NOTES

1. "Report on an Investigation of the Peasant Movement in Hunan," available at http://www.marxists.org/reference/archive/mao/selected-works/volume-1/mswv1_2.htm.
2. This policy was based on The Outline of Land Reform issued by the CCP in 1946. The policy of land reform in new liberated areas was based on The Land Reform Law issued in 1950 when the CCP took control of all of China.
3. The strategy adopted by the CCP was based on the principles of (1) "low distribution" (the salary part in the output value for distribution in industries should be kept to a low percent), and (2) "high accumulation" (the percentage of reinvestment in the output value should be kept high).
4. In 1983, the State Council changed the names of the three grassroots levels of governmental organizations. The previous people's commune, production brigade, and production team were renamed "township," "village," and "village group," respectively. A village committee generally is similar to the previous production brigade–leading group.

5. Some scholars call this process land acquisition or land expropriation. It actually is a set of procedures with compulsory "purchase" of the land and low compensation fees to the landowners.
6. According to the Land Management Law, local governments should compensate village committees for land, improvements, and resettlement. Land compensation has to equal 6–10 times the average annual land output value of the previous three years. Resettlement compensation must equal four to six times this annual average land output value. The compensation for land improvement is based on the estimated original cost of construction and of the crops already planted. The law also stipulates that the basis for the calculation of land output value should be the original farm production and that the total amount of the compensation fees should not exceed 30 times the average land output value.
7. One hectare equals 15 Chinese mu.

REFERENCES

Bernstein, Thomas P. 1984. "Stalinism, Famine, and Chinese Peasants." *Theory and Society* 13 (3): 339–77.

Bianco, Lucien. 1971. *Origins of the Chinese Revolution, 1915–1949.* Palo Alto, CA: Stanford University Press.

Bradley, Michael E., and M. Gardner Clark. 1972. "Supervision and Efficiency in Socialized Agriculture." *Soviet Studies 23*: 465–73.

Buck, John L. 1937. *Land Utilization in China. Volume 2, Atlas: A Study of 16,786 Farms in 168 Localities, and 38,256 Farm Families in Twenty-Two Provinces in China, 1929–1933.* Nanjing: University of Nanking.

Chang, Gene H., and Guanzhong J. Wen. 1997. "Communal Dining and the Chinese Famine of 1958–1961." *Economic Development and Cultural Change* 46: 1–34.

Chao, Kang. 1986. *Man and Land in Chinese History: An Economic Analysis.* Palo Alto, CA: Stanford University Press.

Chen, Ji-yuan. 1993. *The Social and Economic Transformation in China's Countryside (1949–1989).* Shanxi, China: Shanxi Economics Publishing House.

Chen, Joseph T. 1970. "The May Fourth Movement Redefined." *Modern Asian Studies* 4 (1): 63–81.

Doak, Barnett A. 1953. "China's Road to Collectivization." *Journal of Farm Economics* 35 (2): 188–202.

Du Run-sheng. 2006. *The Course of China's Rural Reform.* Washington, DC: International Food Policy Research Institute.

Hinton, William. 1966. *Fanshen: A Documentary of Revolution in a Chinese Village.* New York: Vintage Books.

Huang, Philip C.C. 1985. *The Peasant Economy and Social Change in North China.* Palo Alto, CA: Stanford University Press.

Kung, James K., and Justin Y. Lin. 2003. "The Causes of China's Great Leap Famine, 1959–1961." *Economic Development and Cultural Change* 52 (1): 51–73.

Kung, James. K., and Shou-ying Liu. 1997. "Farmers' Preferences Regarding Ownership and Land Tenure in Post-Mao China: Unexpected Evidence from Eight Counties." *China Journal* 38 (July): 33–63.

Lee, Frank C. 1948. "Land Redistribution in Communist China." *Pacific Affairs* 21 (1): 20–32.

Lin, Justin Y. 1990. "Collectivization and China's Agricultural Crisis in 1959–1961." *Journal of Political Economy* 98 (6): 1228–52.

———. 1992. "Rural Reforms and Agricultural Growth in China." *American Economic Review* 82 (1): 34–51.

Liu, Shou-ying, and Xing-san Jiang. 2005. "Urbanization, Land Institution, and Economic Sustainable Development." Unpublished manuscript. World Bank, Washington, DC.

NPC (National People's Congress). 1998. Land Administration Law of the People's Republic of China. Beijing.

Prosterman, Roy L., Tim Hanstad, Brian Schwarzwalder, and Ping Li. 1998. "Rural Land Reform in China and the 1998 Land Management Law." Foreign Aid and Development Report 98, Rural Development Institute, Seattle, WA.

Prosterman, Roy L., Ping Li, and Tim Hanstad. 1996. "Can China Feed Itself?" *Scientific American* 275 (5/November): 70–78.

Putterman, Louis G. 1993. *Continuity and Change in China's Rural Development: Collective and Reform Eras in Perspective.* Oxford, U.K.: Oxford University Press.

Yang, Da-li. 1996. *Calamity and Reform in China: State, Rural Society, and Institutional Change Since the Great Leap Famine.* Palo Alto, CA: Stanford University Press.

Zhang, Jun. 2000. "China's Economic Reform and Development: The Influence of Value Change." *Jiangsu Social Science* 4: 1–5.

Zhang, Youyi. 1988. "Re-estimating the Land Distribution in 1920–1930s." *Studies on Chinese Economic History* 2: 3–9.

Zhao, Yang. 2007. *Communal Ownership and Private Use: An Economic Analysis on China's Rural Land Institutions.* Beijing: Sanlian Shudian.

Zhou Feizhou. 2000. "The Political Economy of the Land Reform." Working paper. Hong Kong University of Science and Technology, China.

———. 2008. "Land Seizure, Local Government and Farmers." In *Creating Wealth and Poverty in Postsocialist China,* ed. Deborah S. Davis and Wang Feng. Palo Alto, CA: Stanford University Press.

PART III

Ongoing Land Reform Programs, Their Mechanisms, Achievements, and Limitations

CHAPTER FIVE

Land Redistribution in Zimbabwe

Simon Pazvakavambwa and Vincent Hungwe

Zimbabwe has been working on land redistribution since independence in 1980. Taken as a whole, land redistribution transferred 12.3 million hectares of land to 203,000 small-scale farmers and led to the establishment of 30,000 indigenous black commercial farmers within a period of 25 years. Despite these seemingly laudable achievements, land redistribution in Zimbabwe has brought mixed fortunes. From a world-appreciated program of the 1980s to a world-condemned program since 2000, Zimbabwe provides important lessons on how to plan and manage land redistribution under situations of bitter conflict.

The post-2000 period, known as the Fast Track Land Redistribution Program, has attracted a lot of attention and criticism from the international community. Many writers have tended to blame current events on the government of Zimbabwe, without locating the argument in its proper context. The early land redistribution program was hailed as a success largely because of the particular context in which it was implemented and because all parties played their roles as envisaged. The Fast Track was different because the overall context had changed and the parties failed, or were reluctant, to honor their obligations. Though concentrating on the Fast Track, this chapter reflects on the interplay of historical factors in shaping the nature, scope, and purpose of land

The views expressed in this chapter are those of the authors and do not necessarily reflect the views of the government of Zimbabwe.

redistribution in Zimbabwe. It explores the evolution of land redistribution under the colonial state, reviews the postindependence experience from 1980 to 2000, and then focuses on the Fast Track.

LAND REDISTRIBUTION UNDER THE COLONIAL STATE

Prior to the colonization of the country by the British, the people of Zimbabwe lived in communities where the traditional chiefs were the recognized land authorities. That custom was ignored by the British government in 1889 when the Crown granted the British South Africa Company the right to administer and govern the region.

Land Policy under Colonial Rule

In 1890, the British South Africa Company sent a group of settlers (also known as the Pioneer Column) with the hope that they would find gold and diamond mines north of the Limpopo River. When the discovery of gold and diamonds failed to materialize, the settlers focused on the fertile land and its high prospects for agriculture. The settlers identified land suitable for commercial agriculture and large-scale ranching; and they displaced the local people, resettling them with their chiefs in what are now known as "communal lands." Those lands therefore are a creation of the very early land redistribution program carried out by the colonialists.

The Shona and Ndebele peoples fiercely opposed the onslaught of land displacement under colonialism, but were defeated in 1897 during the "First Chimurenga" (First War of Independence). Thereafter, the transfer of land rights from the indigenous majority to the European settlers, and the confinement of indigenous Africans to Native Reserves by the British South Africa Company continued and progressively accelerated through much of the 20th century. From 1908 to 1915 alone, 1.5 million acres of land were alienated from the indigenous Africans and given to white settlers. Of that total, 1 million acres were transferred in a single year by the Native Reserves Commission of 1914–15 (Moyana 1984). In the wake of the crushing of the 1885–96 Shona and Ndebele uprisings and the passing of an array of statutes legitimizing the expropriation and ownership of land, by 1914 Africans had been restricted to a mere 23 percent of the worst land in designated Native Reserves. By 1919, a dual system of land ownership had been enshrined in law: whites enjoyed private titles and access to land while blacks continued to be governed by customary law (Lawton 2002). Subsequently, provisions were adopted to create and give constitutional protection to property rights. These provisions were intended to give a veneer of juridical protection and legitimacy to land and property rights that had been expropriated through conquest.

In 1923, Southern Rhodesia became a self-governing territory. The colonialists strengthened the white settlers' outright expropriation of land owned by indigenous people by enacting entrenched legislation. The Land Apportionment Act was passed in 1931, designating land in terms of who lived on and farmed it.

Under this legislation, 51 percent of land was allocated to about 3,000 white farmers, and 1.2 million indigenous Africans were confined to Native Reserves that constituted 30 percent of the country's poorest agricultural land (Jennings and Huggins 1935; Palmer 1977; Moyana 1984). In 1951, the Land Husbandry Act was introduced to improve the rural economy in the African reserves. This act was not passed through universal suffrage because Africans were not allowed to vote, and it didn't have the expected impact. This was to be a main reason for the protracted armed struggle that ensued later.

During the 1950s and 1960s, local people were driven from Tengwe in Mashonaland West Province. The area was pegged into massive commercial farms and distributed to World War II veterans, largely those of British and Dutch descent. To this day, the subsequent generations of the British and Dutch descendants occupy some of the farms in Tengwe, but they are being displaced in the current land redistribution program. It should be remembered that none of the beneficiaries of the colonial land redistribution paid for the land; they simply moved in with their families and started farming the land. For that reason, the government of Zimbabwe similarly has declined to compensate them for the land itself, although it has agreed to compensate the settlers' descendants for capital improvements to the land.

The Unilateral Declaration of Independence of 1965 reaffirmed the dualism in land ownership through the Land Tenure Act of 1969 (Jennings and Huggins 1935; Moyana 1984; Scheuermaier 2006). Between 1965 and 1970, the colonial government carried out what may be considered the final land redistribution before the war forced them to the negotiating table. Hundreds of families were removed from the area between Mvuma and Kwekwe to create massive ranches that were allocated to members of the Rhodesia Front party, then in power. The people removed were resettled in the Gokwe and Silobela areas where they had to start new lives with very few assets salvaged from their previous homes. People were moved in groups according to their chieftainships. No compensation was paid. Establishing new homes was a difficult task and, depending on when people moved, some lost whole cropping seasons. Transit camps included makeshift homes at government schools. The forced removal of black people from their land to make way for white settlers added to the bitterness that later fueled anxiety for land restitution. Many of the African families were not allowed to move their cattle to new areas because of tsetse infestation. The abandoned livestock either was sold to new white settlers at suboptimal prices or was transferred to relatives living in areas where livestock was still allowed. The resulting bitterness eventually would prompt the call for a liberation struggle to restore lost land rights to the people of Zimbabwe.

The War of Liberation

The land redistribution program carried out in the 1960s provided the spark for confrontation. Although some of the land expropriated from the Africans was for urban expansion, it was the inhuman removal of indigenous people from their land to make way for white settlers and the intolerable deprivation that eventually led to the armed struggle. Land inequalities, inequitable access to economic opportunities, blatant racism (the color bar), and political repression fomented African nationalism that became the rallying cry for the war of liberation. The war displaced large numbers of African people, some of whom were enclosed in so-called protected villages in an attempt to starve liberation fighters. The conflict was bitter, and the bitterness carried over into the independence era. Therefore, it is important to understand and appreciate that the land redistribution programs that were introduced after independence in Zimbabwe were carried out against this background of historical bitterness.

The war of liberation was fought over the land issue. The local indigenous people had no access to land in their country of birth. Although there were other repressions meted out to the black population, such as prohibition from owning and improving the land in certain areas as well as subtle separate development, land constituted the major bone of contention. Africans had no rights to any land, even land in communal areas where the majority of them lived. Instead, land rights were held on their behalf by the administrative machinery set up by colonial governments, such as the district commissioners. Traditional chiefs, who were the true representatives of the people, were stripped of their powers, and most of those powers were exercised by the district commissioners. There was even a separate education system for the blacks. The whole idea was to keep blacks subordinate and to exploit their labor. The protracted war of liberation eventually forced the colonialists to negotiate, and those negotiations resulted in the Lancaster House Constitution in 1979, the initial supreme law for postindependence Zimbabwe.

At independence in 1980, the new government inherited a skewed agricultural sector consisting of three distinct subsectors:

- A large-scale commercial subsector with about 6,000 white farmers who owned 15.5 million hectares, comprising more than 45 percent of prime agricultural land, mainly in the high-potential natural regions I, II, and III.
- A small-scale commercial farming subsector with about 8,500 black farmers who had 1.4 million hectares, comprising 5 percent of agricultural land. More than 50 percent of this land was in the drier natural regions IV and V. A distinct feature of the small-scale commercial farming areas was that most of these were created as buffer zones between communal and commercial areas.
- A communal subsector with approximately 700,000–800,000 peasant farmer families on 16.4 million hectares, comprising less than 50 percent of agricultural land. Seventy-five percent of this land lay in the lower-potential regions IV and V.

The national pattern of land distribution, ownership, and control in Zimbabwe in 1980 (table 5.1) therefore belied an economy anchored on a domestic white

Table 5.1 Land Redistribution Pattern and Targets, 1980

Tenure Category	Area (millions of hectares)	Target area (millions of hectares)
Large-scale commercial farming sector	15.5	5.0
Small-scale commercial farming sector	1.4	1.4
Resettlements	n.a.	8.3
Communal areas	16.4	16.4
State farms	0.3	2.5
National parks and urban settlements	6.0	6.0
Total	39.6	39.6

Source: Ministry of Lands, Agriculture and Rural Resettlement.
Note: n.a. = not applicable.

landowning class that was linked to and supported by international capital. That class directly and indirectly controlled the financial, agro-input, processing, and marketing subsectors of the Zimbabwean economy (Moyo 1995).

EARLY ATTEMPTS TO REDISTRIBUTE LAND, 1980–99

Government adopted the early land redistribution program at the time of independence. The program initially aimed to resettle 18,000 families on 1.1 million hectares over a period of three years. In 1982, however, this objective was revised to resettle 162,000 families on 10.5 million hectares over a period of 12 years. Of the 10.5 million hectares to be acquired from the commercial farming sector, 8.3 million would be redistributed to landless people, and 2.2 million would constitute the state farming sector. Retention of 5 million hectares in the large-scale farming sector indicated a desire to maintain a viable large-scale commercial farming sector (see table 5.1). The program had a social and political focus. It was meant to benefit primarily three groups: (1) refugees and people displaced by the war, including extraterritorial refugees, urban refugees, and former inhabitants of protected villages; (2) people without land who were residing in the overcrowded communal areas; and (3) people with insufficient land to maintain themselves and their families.

In 1979, at the Lancaster House conference, the British government had agreed to support the implementation of a program based on the willing seller–willing buyer (WSWB) principle through a reimbursable expenditure grant. Land could be acquired on a WSWB basis or, if it was underutilized and derelict land, it could be expropriated. In either case, compensation in the landowner's currency of choice had to be paid promptly. Expropriation had to be financed by the government of Zimbabwe because Britain had agreed to finance land purchases only on the WSWB basis. The requirements for compensation were to prove quite onerous for the Zimbabwean government, especially in the context of the immediate need for postwar reconstruction and rehabilitation. A large share of the rural population had fled to urban areas and forcibly had been confined to protected villages. In that process, they had lost about 30 percent of their livestock to rampant disease. The displacement of the rural African population resulted in severe dislocation of peasant production (Palmer 1990).

The early land redistribution program was executed with the almost exclusive use of the WSWB approach. By 1985, the program was anchored by a well-targeted policy of right of first refusal by the government. This policy dictated that all land released on the market had to be offered first to the government. Only after the government had refused to acquire that land could it be offered to other interested parties. In practice, the use of the right-of-first-refusal option was based on consultations whose primary objective was to ensure that commercial agricultural land remained consolidated and intact. The policy shows that government was interested in ensuring the continued consolidation of commercial agricultural land and in avoiding fragmentation. As a result, the quantity, quality, location, cost, and pace of land redistribution were driven by landowners rather than by the state and the beneficiaries, in accordance with their needs and demands. Fortunately, there was an agreed program with responsibilities shared among the parties who delivered on their promises.

Early resettlement was undertaken using four models. Model A was individual allocations of approximately 5 hectares with village settlements and communal grazing. Most beneficiaries were displaced people who could not go back to their original homes for a variety of reasons. They were the landless and poor households in overcrowded areas and the retrenched farmworkers. Beneficiaries were grouped together and allocated land as communities. This process prompted the establishment of new communities that did not have tribal ties or ethnic characteristics. Some of the farms with developed infrastructure, such as irrigation facilities, were allocated under model B, which was for groups on a cooperative basis whereby all property, land, and equipment were held cooperatively. Under the model C plan, farms with export potential or those that could produce major industrial crops were converted into core estates with out-growers who were expected to grow their crops outside the boundaries of the estate and market them through the core estate. Each core estate was run by a cooperative community or by the Agriculture and Rural Development Authority, and provided services to the out-growers who were required to contribute some of their labor to the core estate. Whereas models A, B, and C were used in the major crop-producing areas, model D was implemented in areas where livestock was the major form of agricultural production. This model was based on communal grazing of cattle, without necessarily relocating people.

The four models had varying levels of success. Model A was successful in the crop-producing areas of Manicaland, Mashonaland, Masvingo, and Midlands Provinces. Because it was individual-based, the model had popular appeal. Model B had mixed success, mainly because people were not familiar with the cooperative approach to agricultural production. A few of the model B farms collapsed, and the former cooperative members allocated themselves land units similar to those of model A. Because of the failure of most cooperatives in model B, implementation of new plans using that model was discontinued by the late 1980s. Model C was implemented only in one case; it soon was abandoned and the estate was allocated to the Agriculture and Rural Development Authority. Model D plans never moved beyond the conceptual and pilot phases. Although deemed suitable for livestock-producing areas of Matabeleland, the long distances involved and the peoples' reluctance to relocate made the model untenable. Until the Fast Track Land Redistribution Program began, farms intended for model D implementation remained in the hands of their former owners.

Beneficiaries did not pay for land, and the government established a line of credit (the Resettlement Credit Scheme) for cropping and cattle-stocking purposes to give new settlers a head start. The Resettlement Credit Scheme had a 5 percent interest rate, and the loans were accessed through the Agricultural Finance Corporation, which was transformed into the Agricultural Development Bank of Zimbabwe in 2002. Seasonal loans had to be repaid within 18 months, and the cattle-stocking loans were repaid over five years.

Achievements and Impacts

By 1989, about 52,000 families (420,000 beneficiaries) had been resettled on 2.8 million hectares of land. That total number of resettled families represented a crude success rate of 32 percent. Added to the total were 400 black commercial farmers who leased state land, and an equal number who had purchased land directly from white landowners under the principle of right of first refusal by the government. The number of commercial farmers had decreased from 6,000 to 4,300, and the share of land they owned decreased from 42 percent to 30 percent (Palmer 1990). According to the evaluation report of the land resettlement program commissioned in 1988 by the British Overseas Development Administration (ODA), the program had been orderly; had been impressive in achieving its principal objectives; and had generated an economic return of 21 percent, which made it one of the most successful aid programs in Africa (Cusworth and Walker 1988).

Overall, the early land redistribution program was well executed. It is estimated that more than 80 percent of its beneficiaries fell into the category of people with the greatest need—refugees, people affected by war, landless peasants, and those whose land was inadequate for generating a livelihood (Kinsey 1999). Planning moved ahead of settlement, and beneficiaries moved only after the planning process had been done. The essential social infrastructure to service the new settlers, such as schools, clinics, dip tanks, and rural service centers (albeit suboptimal), was established in tandem with the redistribution program. Getting this infrastructure in place reduced or removed potential settlers' hesitation about relocating because they did not have to maintain two homes to keep their children in school. There was proper agricultural planning that took into account the potential of the area to be resettled. The program was transparent and suffered little political influence. The small-scale farmers succeeded despite the program's shortcomings—there may have been too many constraints on new small-scale farmers; settlers may have received only permits that constituted some form of rights instead of fully secured land titles; and they may not have been given sufficient extension, input supply, and output market services.

The transfer of 2.8 million hectares of land from the large-scale commercial farming sector to the small-scale sector did not have any negative impact on agricultural production. By 1990, in fact, the large-scale commercial farming sector recorded significant increases in productivity. Throughout the 1980s, white large-scale commercial farmers accumulated significant capital through enhanced agricultural productivity and higher land values (see table 5.2 and figure 5.1). Those outcomes greatly enhanced the standing of the government as the most farmer-friendly government the country had ever had (Palmer 1990). That standing resulted from a combination of favorable agricultural support services; the opening of international markets; and a structural shift from a focus on traditional crops, like maize and cotton, to high-value and export-oriented legumes, horticultural crops, and meat exports. If anything, the developments of the 1980s seem to vindicate the findings of Weiner et al. (1985) that only 33–35 percent of the land in the large-scale commercial farming sector was fully used at the time of independence. The land redistribution program therefore could target a total of 10.5 million hectares of land without any significant negative impact on the national economy in general or on agriculture in particular.

Table 5.2 Purchase Prices for Land Acquired for Resettlement between 1980 and 1988

Financial year	Land (hectares)	Purchase price (Z$)	Average price (Z$/hectare)
1980/81	223,196	3,517,198	15.76
1981/82	900,196	18,803,158	20.88
1982/83	939,925	22,009,187	23.42
1983/84	159,866	4,536,168	28.37
1984/85	75,058	2,966,849	39.53
1985/86	86,187	4,444,610	51.57
1986/87	133,515	3,898,335	29.20
1987/88	20,319	1,874,200	92.24
Total	2,538,262	62,049,705	24.45

Sources: Adapted from Palmer (1990) and Government of Zimbabwe, Ministry of Lands, Land Reform and Resettlement (2006).

Figure 5.1 Amounts and Purchase Prices of Land Acquired, 1980–88

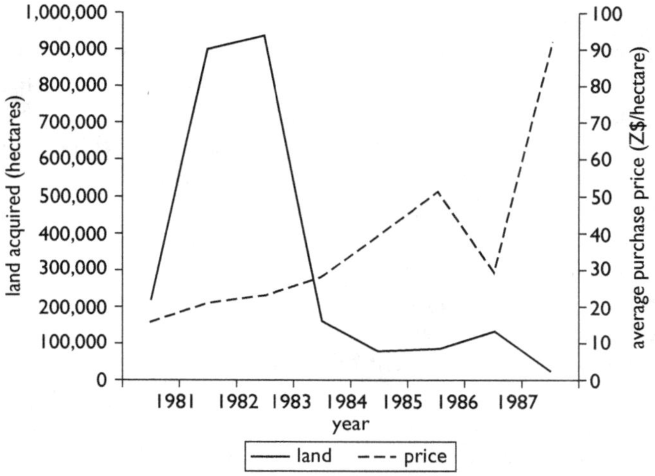

Source: Palmer 1990.

The program resulted in visible gains in productivity and production in the resettlement areas. Comparing farm incomes in resettlement areas with those in communal areas, Kinsey (1999) finds that by 1997, the crop output of the average resettled family was worth more than 4.5 times that of the average communal area household. Resettled farmers earned from their crop sales 6.8 times what communal area farmers earned. However, some observers and investigators may have been too quick to establish a direct link between the early land redistribution program and the postindependence boom in peasant agricultural production. Analyses of production trends, especially with respect to cotton and maize production, have shown that the productivity increases were neither a widespread national phenomenon nor exclusively the result of the land redistribution program. Studies by Cliffe (1988) and Weiner (1988) suggest that the dramatic increase in peasant production and sales (from 12 percent of total in 1979 to 22 percent in 1988) was confined to the more fertile areas of Mashonaland and was realized by peasants belonging to the "master farmer" category who responded positively to market price incentives and the credit, extension, and research facilities that previously were the preserve of white farmers.

The 1980s program was quite successful and is often hailed as the perfect example of how land redistribution could be done. At the same time, as far as the land transfer mechanism is concerned, the transfer of 2.8 million hectares on a voluntary basis would have been impossible without particular circumstances: In the 1980s, large tracts of land had been abandoned during the war of liberation, and those tracts constituted the bulk of the land used for resettlement. Although some previous owners who had long abandoned their farms came to lay claim for compensation, that was done without delaying the redistribution program's planning and subsequent settler emplacement. Not surprising, about 81 percent of land redistributed during the 1980s was acquired during the three years following independence. Finally, these achievements may not have been possible without strong pressure from the beneficiaries themselves, as the early redistribution program coincided with the emergence of groups of families who identified land by "squatting" on it. The government purchased the land at market prices to support community-based "self-provisioning" of land (Moyo 2000, 2003, 2004a; Alexander 2003).

The almost-exclusive use of the WSWB approach to land redistribution meant that the state had very limited control over the amount, location, and quality of land acquired. Thus, although the amount of land transferred is significant, only about 25 percent of it was prime land. The rest was agro-ecologically marginal and therefore not suitable for grazing and crop cultivation. That land was available mainly because some of the positive land transfer outcomes realized during this phase coincided with the willingness of some white landowners to sell their marginal land and relocate to the more fertile natural regions I, II, and III.

Some commentators also argue that the early land redistribution program was riddled with encumbrances that inevitably slowed it down. To them, during the 1980s the new state of Zimbabwe had to deal with the discomfort of sharing power in a postwar partnership (cast in the form of a reconciliation pact) with a surrogate white domestic landowning class allied with international capital (Mandaza 1986a; Sibanda 1988). Consequently, the new government ruled within neocolonial structures underpinned by a neoliberal economic and democratic framework that placed constitutional restraints on the radical transfer and transformation of property rights. The social forces that demanded radical land redistribution were outweighed by the dominant political alliance interested in maintaining the inherited economic structures (Mandaza 1986b; Moyo 2004a). Given their focus on social welfarism, their neoliberal developmental values, and their parasitic dependence on links to international aid, civil society land reform advocacy and nongovernmental organization activists focused on marginal and status quo apologetic conservationist and agronomic improvements within communal area reorganization precepts, not on radical land redistribution.

Despite the notable progress of the 1980s, the need for further land redistribution remained evident. With 68 percent of the families yet to be resettled, the program was far from complete. Meanwhile, the population density in the "communal areas" continued to increase, and it exacerbated the dualistic inequalities in the economy. From its promising start, the case for land redistribution to address the more than 1 million families who still eked out a miserable existence on 16 million hectares of poor land in communal areas remained a source of social, economic, and political disquiet in 1990, as it had been in

1980. The ODA report observed in 1988 that it was both equitable and economically sound to continue with further resettlement, provided such resettlement was linked directly to communal area rehabilitation.

The Stall in Land Redistribution

By 1990, land redistribution had stalled. To deal more decisively with the glaring land redistribution imperatives, the government adopted a national land policy in 1992. The policy represented a significant shift in the conceptualization of land redistribution in the country. The objectives of redistribution were recast in terms that went beyond restitution of lost lands to (1) ensuring equitable and socially just access to land; (2) democratizing land tenure systems and ensuring security of tenure for all forms of landholdings; (3) providing for participatory processes of management in the acquisition, planning, and use of land; and (4) promoting sustainable and efficient use and management of land.

During the 1980s, land redistribution attempted to restore political stability by rehabilitating families displaced during the war of liberation, restoring lost land, and promoting equity in land rights. With the adoption of the 1992 national land policy, land redistribution effectively was to take place in the broader context of agrarian reform. The program intended to address not only the issues of equitable land distribution and historical justice, but also matters of tenure security, agricultural investment, and sustainable land use. It targeted the establishment of small and efficient landholdings and the retention of a core large-scale commercial agricultural sector. The Zimbabwe Agricultural Policy Framework also sought to increase agricultural productivity in the context of the country's changing structure of land ownership (Government of Zimbabwe 1995). A complementary program, the Agricultural Services Management Program, also was designed with the support of donors to restructure the agricultural sector and enhance the provision of support services to small-, medium-, and large-scale farmers. At the executive level, the conceptualization of land redistribution as a key component of a national agrarian reform agenda resulted in the merging of the "land and agriculture portfolios" under the same ministry. This shift was anchored in the dominant neoliberal macroeconomic, trade, investment, and export-oriented agricultural policies. It was part of the economic structural adjustment programs peddled at the time by the World Bank and the International Monetary Fund (Moyo 2000a, 2000b).

Despite these efforts to carry out an orderly land reform, further land redistribution efforts were undermined by the state's inability to acquire land. By the early 1990s, the circumstances that had made possible the acquisition of land on a voluntary basis had faded away. The existing legislation on land acquisition came under tremendous challenge, and most of its weaknesses were exposed as farmers sought to exploit the loopholes in the law. Even those farmers who had willingly offered their land for resettlement approached the courts to seek a reversal of the process. With the favorable climate for agricultural investment and production, white landowners became increasingly unwilling to release land. Through their representative, the Commercial Farmers Union (CFU), commercial farmers facilitated offers to the government for land in areas of limited potential. Meanwhile, CFU members purchased land in areas of high potential. In essence, this dual approach enabled the commercial farmers to consolidate their landholdings in high-potential areas.

The pressure exerted on white commercial farmers to release land for the purpose of land redistribution was extremely weak. This situation was worsened further by the British government's refusal to support a program based on land expropriation. Despite the favorable evaluation of the early land redistribution program by the ODA mission of 1988, and even after the 1990 expiration of the "sunset clauses" in the constitution, the British government still insisted on making financial resources available for land acquisition exclusively on a WSWB basis. The WSWB arrangement had to be done at a time when land prices were at their highest, in large measure as a result of the political and economic stability created by the government. As shown in table 5.2, land values increased sixfold, from Z$15.76 per hectare in 1980 to Z$92.24 per hectare in 1988.

The problem here was that the WSWB approach was no longer delivering, even on the most marginal of land. It is against this background that the government promulgated the Land Acquisition Act of 1992 (a slight revision of the 1985 Land Acquisition Act). The act empowered the state to designate land for compulsory acquisition and provided regulations to impose a land tax; reduce the sizes of farms; and regulate ownership of land, especially ownership by foreigners. These provisions were perceived as impinging on ownership rights. Thus, combined with the relaxation of land subdivision and consolidation regulations, the provisions resulted in a significant reduction of land prices. The reduction became even more evident after the CFU's challenge to land designation was defeated in the high court. Nevertheless, the government did not embark directly on a comprehensive land redistribution program to address the acute land hunger in the country. At that time, the Zimbabwean government remained confident that a deal to unlock the impasse could be struck with the British government.

In 1997 the British government stopped paying land compensation. Subsequently, the number of land offers dropped significantly. Commercial farmers, who had consolidated themselves in the most fertile part of the country, rallied and prepared themselves for legal challenges to the government's land resettlement program. The original intention of reconciliation now appeared to be rejected by the farmers; they preferred instead to take the government to court. Taking advantage of the weaknesses in the Land Acquisition Act of 1985, farmers mounted relentless challenges. Meanwhile, the courts reversed or reserved judgment on a number of farms, which led to anxiety among newly settled people. With these developments, the Zimbabwean government felt let down and betrayed by both the British government and local commercial farmers, and an increasingly political element started to creep into the land redistribution program.

Between 1990 and 1997, an additional 800,000 hectares of land was redistributed, less than the amount of land acquired during the two years that followed independence. Land was redistributed under the Commercial Farm Settlement Scheme—with a decided bias toward better-off black farmers, including medium-scale producers and poor but capable farmers from the overcrowded communal areas (Moyo 2000a). By 1997 the land redistribution program in Zimbabwe had transferred 3.5 million hectares to about 71,000 beneficiaries, 93 percent of whom were resettled according to model A. Given the targets set in 1982 to resettle 162,000 families and to transfer 10.5 million hectares, these transfer totals represented achievement rates of 44 percent and 33 percent, respectively. After 17 years of independence, the land redistribution program had failed to address the land question in the country.

Mounting Pressure for Land Redistribution

In 1997 the Zimbabwean government tried once again to speed up land redistribution. This time it attempted to expropriate 1,471 farms. The effort was made under pressure from an increasingly agitated constituency of war veterans, restive rural communities and their leaders, local politicians, and a generally contested national political space wrought by the emergence of the National Constitutional Assembly (NCA). However, the effort was frustrated by a confetti of statutory and constitutional encumbrances, burdensome administrative procedures, bureaucratic ineptitude, a lack of resources, and an international constituency ill disposed to land expropriation. The situation worsened when Britain's new Labour government announced that Britain had no historical obligation arising from colonialism to support land redistribution in Zimbabwe. For all of these reasons, 1997 was a defining year for Zimbabwe's land redistribution. The ruling party and its government metaphorically had to cross the Rubicon and muster the requisite political resolve to challenge the legacy of settler land and property rights enshrined in existing national law. Land redistribution became the object of increasing attention. The World Bank eventually stepped in, although apart from recommending the introduction of a land tax, it had not supported Zimbabwe's land reform directly. Land reform had taken a decisive turn, and the government's 1998 pronouncement that it would take no action to remove war veterans or communities and their traditional leaders who had occupied white-owned land in the Svosve area indicated that a more radical approach to land redistribution was in the offing.

In June 1998, the government published the Land Reform and Resettlement Program (LRRP), which incorporated land redistribution into a broader agriculture-driven national strategy for economic growth and development. The program approximated a national agrarian reform strategy. It conceptualized land redistribution beyond the transfer of land. It supported such other agriculture-based development interventions as provision of agricultural credit, agricultural input supply and marketing, extension services, and land tenure arrangements to facilitate the enhanced use of redistributed land (Adams 1995; Maroleng 2004). More precisely, the objectives of the LRRP were cast as (1) to restore balance in land ownership by removing the racial inequalities created by colonialism and to empower indigenous people; (2) to decongest overcrowded communal areas whose economic and environmental value was in continuous and rapid decline; (3) to tackle rural poverty and improve food security at the national and household levels; (4) to increase the contribution of the agricultural sector to the GDP; (5) to promote environmentally sustainable use of land; (6) to develop commercial agriculture within the indigenous community; and (7) to create conditions for sustainable economic, political, and social stability.

In September 1998, the government convened a donors' conference. This conference was an attempt by national stakeholders, including the government and the international partners, to forge a consensus on a land redistribution program that would be planned and implemented within market principles and the rule of law. The program would go beyond the global restitution of lost land paradigm and address the imperatives of poverty reduction and agriculture-based national economic growth and development. It broadened the scope of land redistribution and thus exposed it to a wider, perhaps unrealistic, evaluation framework. One can argue that the 1998 donors' conference became the defining moment for international capital, with the inadvertent support of the neocolonial state, in subverting the historical legitimacy of land redistribution in Zimbabwe.

Donors at the conference agreed to implement an Inception Phase Framework Plan—a two-year "learning-by-doing" transition phase during which 1 million hectares of land were to be acquired using both expropriation and a World Bank–inspired voluntary land redistribution program. In the Office of the President, a donor-funded technical support unit was established with responsibility for piloting this "twin-track" approach over a period of two years. Unfortunately, the twin-track Inception Phase Framework Plan floundered shortly after its launch. Fissures developed among the partners, particularly concerning the availability of money to buy land. On one hand, the World Bank could not finance land purchase because doing so would run counter to its lending policy at that time. On the other hand, the British government insisted on making financial resources available to acquire land on a WSWB basis and anchored its support for land distribution in its poverty reduction strategy. To many observers, Britain's actions were reminiscent of its earlier "kith-and-kin" arguments that had culminated in Minister Clare Short's pronouncement that the British government had no historical obligation to provide adequate resources for land acquisition.

The Zimbabwean government had to craft an alternative strategy to carry forward its land redistribution imperative. Crafting that strategy grew more urgent in light of the increasingly contested political space in which the NCA and a new political entity—the Movement for Democratic Change—combined to create a "no-vote campaign" in the constitutional referendum of February 2000. Rejection of the draft constitution had far-reaching consequences for land redistribution. First, it put to rest the hope that land redistribution could be managed as part of a national macroeconomic stabilization and agriculture-based development agenda under the veneer of the LRRP. Second, despite policy pronouncements and public utterances to the contrary, compulsory acquisition of land became the only practical and central plank on which the land redistribution program could stand. Finally, government recognized the futility of implementing the land redistribution program within a rule-of-law regime that was status quo apologetic. Thus, the government took steps to locate the program within the compass of an evolving system of "national law." President Robert Mugabe then declared, "We must deliver the land unencumbered by impediments to its rightful owners. It is theirs by birth. It is theirs by natural and legal right. It is theirs by struggle. Indeed, theirs by legacy" (Scheuermaier 2006, p. 1). This is the context in which the Fast Track Land Redistribution Program started in 2000.

THE FAST TRACK LAND REDISTRIBUTION PROGRAM, 2000–05

The first year of the Fast Track phase clearly was characterized by the radicalization of land redistribution. Forces that sought to challenge the vestiges of the neocolonial state had been unleashed. They defied a rule-of-law regime embodied by property rights laws and a judiciary that had been established to protect the interests of a white landowning class supported by international capital. In national politics, opposition to land redistribution was represented by a status quo apologetic compliant and elitist class masquerading as a local domestic political opposition. Thus, the year 2000 marked the beginning of the process by which national laws and their concomitant administrative processes were aligned to respond to the imperatives of the national land redistribution program.

During the Fast Track phase, the objectives and targets of the LRRP were further revised: (1) to acquire from the large-scale commercial sector more than 11 million hectares of land for redistribution; (2) to decongest the overpopulated and overstocked wards and villages; (3) to enable local indigenous people to take control of the large-scale commercial farming sector through the model A2 scheme[1]; (4) to reduce the intensity and extent of poverty among rural families and farmworkers by providing them with adequate land for agricultural use; (5) to increase the contribution of the agricultural sector to the GDP and to foreign currency earnings; (6) to promote environmentally sustainable use of land through agriculture and ecotourism; (7) to develop and integrate small-scale farmers into the mainstream of commercial agriculture; and (8) to create conditions for sustainable economic, social, and political stability. It is pertinent to note that there was a deliberate attempt under Fast Track to focus on land acquisition and redistribution as articulated in objectives (1) to (4). Indeed, the development and review of national legislation, including the constitution, during this phase largely were meant to give the state more power to facilitate the land acquisition process.

The first shot in Fast Track was fired through the Constitution of Zimbabwe Amendment (No. 16) Act (No. 5) of 2000, which principally empowered the government to acquire compulsorily the agricultural land needed for resettlement purposes. The amendment placed the responsibility for paying for the land acquired for purposes of resettlement firmly into the hands of the former colonial power, Great Britain, but obligated the Zimbabwean government to pay full compensation for any improvements that had been made on properties that were acquired (Coldham 2001). In May 2000, the Temporary Powers Amendment Act (1986) was used to amend the Land Acquisition Act (1992) so as to clarify and streamline the land acquisition process and to prescribe new compensation rules. This amendment effectively reduced the administrative requirements in land acquisition and provided for the staggered payment of compensation for improvements through a combination of cash, bonds, and bills. In November 2000, the Land Acquisition Act was amended further to vest the ownership of land in the state as the acquiring authority upon the serving of acquisition orders, notwithstanding any challenges in the courts. That amendment was followed by regulations limiting farm sizes in the country to units ranging from 250 hectares to 400 hectares in natural regions I, II, and III; and to 2,000 hectares in natural regions IV and V.

Land was to be redistributed on a "one person–one farm" basis. However, the Fast Track program was implemented with limited resources. Thus, unlike during the 1980s when proper technical assessments were done, the listing of farms for acquisition, serving of acquisition orders, and transferring of title to the land from current white owners to the state as the acquiring authority took place prior to, during, or after beneficiaries had occupied the land. The white commercial farmers saw these occupations as illegal, and many of the owners tried to reverse them in court. However, the Rural Land Occupiers (Protection from Eviction) Act was passed to protect people who had occupied land not yet acquired by the government. In December 2000, the Supreme Court weighed in on the side of the white landowners, declaring that the land reform and resettlement process was illegal because it was not informed by a planned program. A new judiciary sworn in the following year reversed that legal position.

Whereas land redistribution in the previous phases was driven by technical assessments and administratively cumbersome procedures, the Fast Track phase was highly politically charged (see box 5.1). This tension posed a major challenge for government and for the technicians responsible for implementing the redistribution program. In many instances, disagreement regarding which land should be acquired and who should receive it resulted in the allocation of land

Box 5.1 The Role of War Veterans during the Fast Track Phase

War veterans have been a distinct group since independence, through the establishment of the Zimbabwe National Liberation War Veterans Association. Membership comprises former combatants and serving members from the security forces. During the first phase of land redistribution, war veterans were considered part and parcel of the landless people. They did not have a distinct quota. Events leading to the Fast Track Redistribution Program saw war veterans emerging as the prime movers behind farm demonstrations. A specific quota of 20 percent at all designated model A1 farms was set aside for war veterans. Although there was no quota for war veterans under the A2 model, some provincial governors and resident ministers allowed such a quota.

under unclear circumstances outside the framework of the institutional machinery. Even when settled, some people moved from one farm to another, often leaving a trail of vandalized equipment. Apart from sheer greed, the major reason for such movement was the search for better homesteads or better infrastructure. This lack of settlement discipline led to conflicts among beneficiaries, and some farmers who had been allocated land in time for the season still failed to grow crops.

The government wanted to see orderly land redistribution taking place, and it took measures to stop the spontaneous redistribution of land by various categories of people, including traditional chiefs and war veterans. Because of the prevailing atmosphere and the fact that tempers had been allowed to reach the boiling point, however, it was difficult for the government to ensure that discipline was established and maintained. Furthermore, it soon became clear that when settlement had preceded planning, it was difficult to implement plans retrospectively—no matter how good the plans were—because some settlers had staked themselves and were not willing to move. In a politically charged environment, implementing plans retrospectively is almost impossible. Correcting for proper technical assessments on the ground proved difficult in some cases because people who thought they had been allocated better land refused to give way for plan revisions.

The Fast Track was undertaken with virtually no funding from any donor. The government concentrated on providing mobility for demarcation teams and the initial resources required for planning. Unlike the previous phases in which lines of credit were established, the Fast Track phase relied to a large extent on new farmers funding themselves. Government did provide some incentives through subsidized inputs, including seed, fertilizer, and chemicals. Fuel for tillage also was provided, at a subsidized cost, and conscious efforts were made to increase the producer prices for maize and wheat. Lines of credit required for agricultural production were offered at subsidized interest rates through the Agricultural Sector Productivity Enhancement Facility. Unlike earlier programs, the Fast Track phase was not preceded or accompanied by the development and establishment of social infrastructure, such as schools and clinics. Although some schools and clinics were already established, they could not cope with the large numbers of people now settled on the land. The government addressed the shortage of schools and clinics by transforming some of the homesteads into temporary schools and health care facilities. The lack of social infrastructure was cited as one of the major reasons that some settlers delayed taking up their plots because doing so in areas where there were no school facilities meant they would have to maintain two distant homes so their children could continue their education.

Some farms had Bilateral Investment Promotion and Protection Agreements (BIPPAs). These agreements between the government of Zimbabwe and foreign governments stated that any investment either party made in its respective country would be protected from expropriation. Furthermore, compensation would be payable in the affected party's currency of choice. Professional and technical people knew of the existence of BIPPAs, but politicians were not aware or pretended not to know of them. A cost–benefit analysis would have indicated that the farms protected by BIPPAs contributed less than 2.3 percent of the targeted land under the Fast Track program. However, the political fallout from the international community, including from some countries that sympathized with the land redistribution program, was too high a price for Zimbabwe to pay. The process of honoring the existing BIPPAs meant that either those people settled on farms with such agreements had to be moved or the owners had to be compensated according to the terms of the agreements. The government expressed its commitment to BIPPAs through the budget speech delivered to parliament by Herbert Murerwa, the Minister of Finance (box 5.2).

The major emphasis during the Fast Track phase was on allocating land to as many people as possible, regardless of the land's agricultural potential. Planning was minimal. There was not enough time to do proper assessments, so settlement was haphazard. Politicians gave instructions on how many people were to be accommodated on a particular farm, regardless of the land's capacity or suitability. Many demarcations were done on outdated maps. There was no time to check and verify plans on the ground, and the basis for settlement was variable. This lack of preparation led to numerous boundary disputes and to the demarcation of many plots in marginal and fragile environments. One does not expect such land to yield much.

Looking at the present and to the future, the lack of proper planning will continue to influence the performance of the land redistribution program. The government will have to cope with massive areas that were allocated and are now under the plough without proper conservation or land protection measures having been taken. There is also a need to develop the capacity for

Box 5.2 Bilateral Investment Promotion and Protection Agreements

- Government recognizes the indispensable need to nurture and preserve an investor-friendly environment.
- Consistent with this, Government is actively laying the foundation for stronger business relations between Zimbabwe and its regional and international cooperating partners.
- BIPPAs have a significant bearing on the ability of the country to mobilize financial and material resources from other countries for the much needed foreign direct investment.
- Where Zimbabwe has ratified BIPPAs, Government is committed to honoring all its commitments and obligations as provided for by our Constitution. This includes payment of compensation for BIPPA-related farms that were acquired for resettlement.

Source: Minister of Finance Herbert Murerwa, Budget Speech, 2006.
Note: BIPPA = Bilateral Investment Promotion and Protection Agreement.

planning through such units as the Agricultural Research and Extension Department, the Department of Livestock Planning and Production, and the Department of Veterinary Services.

Most of the farms that were subdivided now need conservation plans that recognize the subdivisions. Conservation planning is essential if land is to be preserved for sustainable production. In addition to the Agricultural Research and Extension Department, which carries out conservation planning, Zimbabwe has established the Environmental Management Agency as the watchdog for the environment in the country. The agency currently is strengthening its capacity to carry out environmental impact assessments to ensure that all projects conform to the principle of land conservation. New farmers are being encouraged to construct contour ridges to reduce erosion and fire guards to inhibit the loss of flora and fauna. Preservation of ecosystems will enable production to take place in a sustainable manner. It is essential that land conservation measures be accorded top priority to maintain the land's productive potential.

The Fast Track experience has shown that adequate funding must be provided for activities associated with land redistribution. The financial constraints associated with the program made some critical activities unaffordable. The government tried to fund the land redistribution program to the extent available resources would permit, but there were notable shortcomings: lack of vehicles to enhance the mobility of planning officers; lack of funding for subsistence and travel allowances; and shortages of planning materials, such as paper, survey equipment, computers, and other associated consumables. The government could not afford to allocate more resources because there were competing requirements. Prioritizing adequate funding of the land redistribution program for a given number of years could have enhanced the government's implementation capacity.

Toward an Evaluation of Land Redistribution in Zimbabwe

By far the greatest achievements of the Fast Track Land Redistribution Program are that the number of farms has increased and that the racial imbalance in access to land has been addressed. The program gave access to land to a large number of people who had been deprived of land rights through historical injustices. With the Fast Track, they acquired land they can cultivate on a subsistence or commercial basis. They now are poised to contribute in various ways to agricultural production and to the development of the country.

Precise figures on the number of farms and amount of land acquired and redistributed during the Fast Track program vary from one source to another. According to the program implementation report produced by the Presidential Land Review Committee—the Utete Report—6,422 farms had been listed for acquisition by July 2003. Of those farms, 1,012 had been delisted, and 2,652 farms covering a total area of 4.23 million hectares had been redistributed to 127,192 households under model A1. During the same period, an additional 1,672 farms covering 2.2 million hectares had been redistributed to 7,260 beneficiaries under model A2. There are no more recent accurate figures, but there is an emerging consensus that by the end of 2005, about 5,200 farms had been listed and acquired (see table 5.3). These farms represented about 9.0 million hectares out of the 11.7 million hectares occupied by the large-scale commercial farming sector in 1997. As for the number of beneficiaries, about 160,300 smallholder farming households would have been allocated 7 million hectares, while 28,000 black indigenous commercial farmers received 2 million hectares.

The Fast Track significantly altered the agrarian structure of the country. It increased the average land units in the commercial farming subsector by 64 percent, and reduced the share of agricultural land the sector occupies by

Table 5.3 Progress in Land Redistribution by the End of 2005

Resettlement phase	Families resettled	Area (hectares)
1980 to 1998	72,000	3,498,444
1998 to June 2000	4,697	144,991
Fast Track model A1	160,340	7,269,936
Fast Track model A2	27,854	1,680,197
Total	232,738	12,500,000

Source: Ministry of Lands, Agriculture and Rural Resettlement.

42 percent. By contrast, the share of total agricultural land occupied by the smallholder subsector increased from 56 percent to 70 percent. The distribution and quality of transferred land varied as a function of the agro-ecological potential of, and the water and irrigation infrastructure on, the land (Moyo 2004a). Taken as a whole, during the 25 years from 1980 to 2005, the land redistribution program in Zimbabwe resulted in the transfer of 12.5 million hectares of land, benefited about 232,000 small-scale farming families, and created about 30,000 black commercial farmers. Those black commercial farmers since have swelled the ranks of the country's medium- and large-scale commercial farming sector.

The program would have had a limited impact on the decongestion of communal areas, but it would have been more successful in reaching the poor, because the rural poor constituted about 87 percent of the beneficiaries. Nonetheless, some people have expressed concern that many urbanites would have received land at the expense of their rural counterparts, rural workers, or occupants of communal areas. The level of women's participation has been relatively low. They account for 18 percent of the beneficiaries of the A1 scheme and for 12 percent of the A2 scheme. However, the "letter of offer" issued for the A2 scheme provides for joint allocation of land between spouses. The level of participation of previous farmworkers also has been relatively low. They represent about 2 percent of the beneficiaries. Commercial farmers were asked to provide severance packages to their farmworkers. Some workers received the packages and returned to their places of origin; but a sizable number remained on the resettled farms, refusing to work for the new farmers. According to the Utete Report, "Their continued presence on the farms has created numerous problems arising from illegal gold panning, misuse of farm facilities and resources and general criminal activities" (Government of Zimbabwe 2003, p. 6).

Some observers have expressed concern about the program's lack of transparency, its lack of respect for the one person–one farm principle, and thus for the possible introduction of new wrongs in the land redistribution process. One of the objectives of the Fast Track was to enable local indigenous people to exercise control of the large-scale commercial farming sector. It targeted not only poor people but also wealthy people willing to venture into commercial farming. However, the allocation process for commercial farms did suffer from political interference, and the A2 farms' low take-up rate may suggest opportunistic behavior. Only 66 percent of the model A2 beneficiaries effectively had taken possession of their farms by 2003, which means that large tracts of land lay fallow or unused. By contrast, the take-up rate among model A1 beneficiaries averaged 97 percent (Government of Zimbabwe 2003). As far as the issue of multiple acquisitions of farms is concerned, 400 influential individuals would have been allocated more than one A2 plot by 2003 (Moyo 2004a). Since that time, the government has issued several presidential orders to relinquish these farms.

There is no doubt that Zimbabwe's agricultural productivity has been severely challenged for a wide range of reasons:

- New farmers were poorly equipped and, even though they may have been experienced in farming, they could not produce without equipment. This situation was worsened by shortages of seed, fertilizer, chemicals, and fuel.
- Some white commercial farmers were allowed to take their equipment and dispose of it as they wished. However, many facilities and much equipment were destroyed by both former commercial farmers and some of the new settlers who sought to "get rich quick" through disposal and sale of equipment. Of particular significance were facilities for irrigation, tobacco curing, horticulture processing, water storage, and fuel storage, as well as tractors and other essential equipment.
- Government's assumption that the A2 farmers had enough resources to develop their farms has proven to be false. It soon became evident that the new farmers needed government support, but the government lacked sufficient resources to support them. Banks and financial institutions were reluctant to lend support because of the lack of collateral security.
- Given the country's lack of political and economic stability, beneficiaries could not engage in productive agriculture. Frequent policy changes and numerous land audits by the land authorities unsettled new farmers, thus significantly reducing their productive potential. Furthermore, most of the new farmers did not have permanent homes on the allocated land, and long-distance farming has never been successful.
- New farmers in horticulture have had to establish new markets—and that takes time. White commercial farmers had neither the desire nor the time to hand over any marketing infrastructure and connections they had established. Many of the land redistribution beneficiaries had no training in farming, and the absence of an intensive training program continues to be a major negative factor.
- The government took time to introduce incentives for production through producer price reviews. The amount of money that government offered for controlled crops—maize, wheat, and sorghum—could not match the prices paid for crops such as soybeans, sugar beans, sunflower, and barley.
- Negative media reports have created uncertainty and despondency among some of the new farmers and have misinformed the international community about the true situation in the country.

Instability in the resettlement areas, either as a result of people's frequent movements or because verifiable land rights are lacking, also has played a part in the country's decline in production and productivity. Beneficiaries face insecurity of tenure because displaced commercial farmers are still contesting farm acquisitions, and most of the beneficiaries have not received leases or permits. There also are uncertainties about how government will implement the new maximum limits on farm size and the one person–one farm policy, including whether the estimated 145 farmers—both black and white—who still own multiple farms acquired on the open market will be allowed to retain them (Moyo 2004a). Most farmers have not invested in their new acquisitions, citing an uncertain future. The early land redistribution program conferred permits to beneficiaries as a form of right. The permits, although not conferring rights that could be registered, were sufficient proof of possession of a piece of land in a resettlement area, and they protected their holders from arbitrary eviction. Under the Fast Track phase, district authorities provided A1 beneficiaries with permits similar to the one provided during the early redistribution program. Model A2 beneficiaries—the commercial farmers—were issued letters of offer describing the physical location and size of the piece of land offered. It also specified the purpose for which the offer was made. Conditions are attached to the offer letter, the most important of which is the requirement to develop the land, based on a defined program. The letter also provides for joint allocation of land between spouses, and it confers succession rights to spouses and heirs. In an attempt to improve land tenure security, the government introduced a 99-year lease as a basis for land rights in the newly redistributed areas. The 99-year leasehold interest can be registered, traded, or used as collateral to access capital for agricultural production. Delays in issuing the 99-year leases has been cited as a major drawback in the current land redistribution program—one that causes instability and a lack of confidence, and that prompts new farmers to delay their development efforts.

Critics of the Fast Track have been quick to point out that it was "chaotic" and that it resulted in drastic reductions in the production of maize and other food crops. Available statistics do indicate a decline in production across the board. In general terms, the decline in production ranged from 20 percent in the traditional food crops to 70 percent in the export crops, such as tobacco. At the same time, the decline in the productivity of food crops cannot be attributed entirely to the Fast Track program. During the early years of the land redistribution program (the 1980s), there was a distinct shift among commercial farmers away from food crops—maize, wheat, sorghum, millet, and beans—and toward such nonfood crops as tobacco and cotton, horticulture products such as flowers, and other export-oriented products. The gap this shift created was filled somehow by the communal farmers. That distinct group was untouched by the Fast Track program. However, because communal farmers did not have access to drought mitigation facilities, such as irrigation systems, their ability to fill the gap completely was severely impaired. The productive potential of the communal farmers always has depended on the weather. The extreme variation in maize production shown in table 5.4 suggests that maize production trends took a dip not only because of the unavailability of critical inputs and limited tillage capacity, but also because of droughts.

The Fast Track program has received mixed reviews and assessments that range from low-intensity recognition of its radical approach in resolving what

Table 5.4 Maize Deliveries to GMB and Producer Price Trends, FY1994/95–2006

Marketing season	Area planted in maize (hectares)	Maize harvested (tons)	Delivered to GMB (tons)	Price per ton (Z$)	Average yield per hectare (tons)
1994/95	1,397,900	839,600	1,248,000	900	0.6
1995/96	1,535,000	2,609,000	64,000	1,050	1.7
1996/97	1,641,000	2,192,170	872,485	1,200	1.3
1997/98	1,223,800	1,418,030	258,082	1,200	1.2
1998/99	1,446,400	1,519,560	222,007	2,400	1.1
1999/2000	1,416,700	2,148,110	376,969	4,200	1.5
2000/01	1,223,100	1,476,240	338,462	5,500	1.2
2001/02	1,239,988	498,540	154,847	8,500	0.4
2002/03	1,379,418	929,619	49,418	28,000	0.7
2003/04	1,620,788	1,300,000	244,187	300,000	0.8
2004/05	1,715,152	1,058,786	186,661	750,000	0.4
2005/06	1,790,397	1,686,151	181,219	2,748,024	0.9
2006/07	1,800,000[a]	915,366	543,655	52,350	0.5

Source: GMB, Zimbabwe.

Note: GMB = Grain Marketing Board.

a. This figure is an estimate; data were not available at the time of writing.

otherwise was an intractable postcolonial national question, to unqualified depictions of it as a failure that brought the economic downfall of the country. It is important to understand, however, that although the early land redistribution program was introduced in the early 1980s as an alternative to a land restitution program, by the late 1990s it had morphed into a sustainable agriculture-driven national economic development strategy progressing at a snail's pace. As land redistribution stalled in the 1990s, and pressure from civil society mounted, the government refocused on the initial objective of land restitution to the people of Zimbabwe. Commentators have tended to evaluate the Fast Track against criteria normally designed to evaluate more comprehensive national agrarian reform interventions. At the same time, although there is a conceptual link between the mechanisms for land redistribution and the objectives of agrarian reform, redistribution can—and perhaps should—be evaluated in relation to the extent to which it achieves its land redistribution targets. Redistribution in Zimbabwe restored 12.3 million hectares of land to 232,000 small-scale farmers and led to the establishment of 30,000 indigenous black commercial farmers within a period of 25 years—a laudable achievement.

The few examples of successful large-scale land reform (such as those in Japan, the Republic of Korea, and Taiwan, China) were implemented under strong pressure from the international community and with its financial support. In Zimbabwe, after 20 years of implementation and persistent disagreement on the optimum mechanisms for land acquisition, the hopes for a massive land transfer undertaken with the support of the international community continued to recede. It is not stretching the imagination to note that the international community underestimated the importance of such an intervention for the people of Zimbabwe. Apparently, the wounds caused by a century of white domination had not healed. As El-Ghonemy (1999) notes, perhaps no other policy issue is more susceptible to shifts in ideology and balance of political power than the transfer of land property rights. Before, during, and after the Fast Track, land redistribution in Zimbabwe remained a national process that impinged on and was affected by the interests of dominant players in the international community. Clearly, the national interests that the government of Zimbabwe sought to address with the Fast Track program did not coincide with the interests of the dominant international agenda. Therefore, the program could not be underwritten ideologically and financially or recommended as good practice for replication elsewhere.

While recognizing the theoretical case linking land redistribution and agricultural production, the lessons to be drawn from Zimbabwe's experience suggest that there is merit in developing a conceptual framework that recognizes land redistribution as a distinct but related process that can be planned, implemented, and evaluated apart from an agriculture-based national development strategy. Indeed, examples of land redistribution programs that have been structured and subsequently passed evaluation tests based on the extent to which they achieved agrarian reform targets or objectives are few and far between. At best, the implications of land redistribution on agricultural production are real, but they certainly are not inevitable in all circumstances. Where they are likely to occur, their effects can be minimized in terms of time and space through careful program planning. In Zimbabwe, land redistribution was informed by studies establishing that it was technically possible to plan and implement the transfer of about 10.5 million hectares of land to landless blacks in the small-scale farming sector and to subdivide part of the large-scale farms and allocate them to emerging black commercial farmers without negatively affecting agricultural production in any significant way. It is a curious irony of history that 25 years of land redistribution in Zimbabwe seem to have validated the facts that were in evidence at the beginning of the program but were ignored in preference for a more protracted and destructive course of action.

The Future of Land Reform in Zimbabwe

Zimbabwe's land redistribution program cannot be reversed. What remains is for government to devise a program for strategic recovery of the agricultural sector. The land redistribution program has made land available to more people than ever before, but not all the people who have accessed land are competent farmers—although most of them have a passion to farm and produce crops. The government can learn from what the colonialists did to develop agriculture during the colonial era. To reestablish agriculture firmly on its feet, the following actions need to be taken:

1. *Define an appropriate agricultural policy framework*—The agricultural sector has changed significantly, so it is necessary to define and adopt a new agricultural policy framework that takes into account what has been spawned by the land redistribution program over the last 25 years. The technical assistance of international development partners should be sought to attract, retain, and support critical local staff to bridge Zimbabwe's human resource gap in agriculture.
2. *Strengthen agricultural support services*—Such services are not adequate to meet the needs of the expanded agricultural sector. Government deliberately should allocate more resources to the agricultural sector to strengthen its capacity to deliver services. If the fruits of the land redistribution program are to be enjoyed in a sustainable manner, the capacity of organizations charged with service delivery must be bolstered. In particular, there is a need to strengthen agricultural extension services because most of the new farmers look to the Agricultural Research and Extension Department for assistance.
3. *Provide financial resources for agriculture*—Agriculture has been poorly funded since independence. Current efforts by the Agricultural Sector Productivity Enhancement Facility through the central bank are commendable, but the central bank cannot continue to do the work of commercial banks. In the past, banks and financial institutions provided funds to commercial farmers. New criteria for funding and new methods of defining collateral security must be developed. Institutions, such as the Agricultural Development Bank of Zimbabwe, should play a leading role in providing financing to the agricultural sector. The Zimbabwe Infrastructure Development Bank also should play a significant role in restoring infrastructure in the agricultural sector.
4. *Invest or provide incentives for investment in agriculture*—In the last 10 years there has been very little investment in agriculture. Among the reasons for this dearth of investment have been the uncertainty brought about by the land redistribution program and the lack of investment funds available for new farmers. These were compounded by the destruction of infrastructure caused both by the former commercial farmers who did not want to see the new farmers benefiting from it and by the new settlers who destroyed infrastructure mainly out of ignorance and an urge for self-enrichment. The infrastructure that previously had served the agricultural sector is no longer available. Of particular concern is irrigation infrastructure, including pumps, motors, main delivery lines, center pivot systems, pipes, and sprinklers—items that were vandalized, stolen, or simply rendered unusable. Given the droughts endemic to the region, massive

investment in irrigation systems is required if agriculture is to be revived with some measure of sustainability. Alongside investment, farmers should be trained in the proper use of irrigation systems. The irrigation equipment manufacturing industry is currently import dependent, and investment should be made to revive it. Although some of the existing irrigation systems have been restored, sustainability remains doubtful because service and spare parts capacity are limited. New farmers should be encouraged to invest in their new acquisitions—especially A2 farmers who have the means.

5. *Develop and maintain a competent base of agricultural staff*—The agricultural sector has not avoided the brain drain that has swept through the country. Most agriculture professionals either have left Zimbabwe or are devoting their energies to better-paying jobs. The net loss of trained agriculture practitioners has reduced the capacity of the advisory services considerably. There are sufficient training facilities for both the diploma and degree levels at various colleges and universities in the country, but the sector has failed to maintain staff because of low remuneration levels and, in some cases, poor opportunities for advancement. Agricultural experts who have left the region or gone to other occupations should be lured back into agriculture.
6. *Set up an appropriate legal framework that promotes agricultural development*—The focus of land redistribution since 1980 has been the restoration of land rights to the indigenous people of Zimbabwe. Now that the land redistribution is winding down, it is essential to look into other aspects of the law that will strengthen the gains achieved so far. Presently, legal provisions for proper land management are extremely weak. Although the Environmental Management Act has been passed, and the Environmental Management Agency has been set up as the watchdog, land abuses remain rampant. The increase in the number of farmers and the destruction of infrastructure on the farms are fueling deforestation. Zimbabwe needs an all-embracing consolidated land act to address current and anticipated shortcomings. The act should instill discipline among farmers and preserve agricultural land for posterity. Most of the legislation used in agriculture was derived from the colonial era. Such legislation has not kept pace with developments in the sector, and should be amended or overhauled completely to reflect the sector's transformation.
7. *Provide security of tenure to landowners*—New farmers have expressed concern over their lack of tenure security. Some of them have cited the absence of a secure tenure system as the main reason for not investing in their new farms. Government has made tremendous progress in developing the 99-year leasehold regime under which land is held, but leases have not been finalized. Although the leases were launched in 2006, legal hitches have been identified. Issuing the leases will go a long way in giving new farmers the confidence to make investments in their holdings.

CONCLUSION

It is tempting to draw lessons from the land redistribution program in Zimbabwe. The temptation, however, runs foul of the fact that there is neither a silver bullet nor a magic wand that can ensure the success of a land redistribution program. Land redistribution invariably is dogged by historic, social, political, economic, and ideological peculiarities and cultural idiosyncrasies that are context specific. Those factors render substantive and procedural replication hazardous. Thus, the discourse on the so-called contagion effect of Zimbabwe's land redistribution program—particularly in countries like Namibia and South Africa—may be misplaced because the conditions in those countries are different and warrant the evolution of different strategies.

Some lessons, however, can be drawn from the Zimbabwean experience. First, it is necessary to develop and use policy intervention options whose content is informed by the context in which the land redistribution program has to take place. Ideally, the policy framework for land redistribution should create an environment where different land acquisition options can operate in a collaborative way and can change over time to meet changing circumstances. Second, regardless of the overall approach adopted, a combination of local, national, and international interests and power relationships invariably operate to promote, hinder, and/or undermine land redistribution programs. Third, land redistribution is a distinct means to achieve agricultural production, national economic growth and development, poverty reduction, sustainable livelihoods, and so forth. But those outcomes are not dependent on land redistribution modalities per se. They are underpinned by post-settlement agriculture-related and macroeconomic interventions. To use a common framework to evaluate land redistribution and the efficacy of post-settlement support will expose land redistribution to a test that it cannot pass. It therefore is necessary to conceptualize land redistribution as a distinct program that can be planned, implemented, and evaluated against the purposes it is intended to achieve.

What remains of greatest importance in Zimbabwe is for the international community to recognize that it would be foolhardy to reverse the new structure of access to and ownership of land. Efforts now should be directed toward strengthening the security of land tenure as an integral component of the national agrarian reform agenda.

NOTE

1. Model A1 is a communal type of arrangement where individuals obtain 6 hectares for cropping and where cattle graze communally. Model A2 is an allocation based on commercial farming attributes, except that land sizes are smaller than former commercial farms. Typical model A2 allocations range from 50 hectares for horticulture to 1,500 hectares for ranching. These allocations are wholly self-contained units.

REFERENCES

Adams, Martin. 1995. "Land Reform: New Seeds on Old Ground." *Natural Resource Perspectives* 6 (October). http://www.odi.org.uk/resources/details.asp?id=2163&title=land-reform-new-seeds-old-ground [accessed January 24, 2009].

Alexander, Jocelyn. 2003. "'Squatters,' Veterans and the State in Zimbabwe." In *Zimbabwe's Unfinished Business: Rethinking Land, State and Nation in the Context of Crisis,* ed. Amanda Hammar, Brian Raftopoulos, and Stig Jensen. Harare, Zimbabwe: Weaver Press.

Binswanger, Hans P. 1996. "The Political Implications of Alternative Models of Land Reform and Compensation." In *Agricultural Land Reform in South Africa: Policies, Markets and Mechanisms,* ed. Johan van Zyl, Johann Kirsten, and Hans P. Binswanger. New York: Oxford University Press.

Bryceson, Deborah. 2000. "Peasant Theories and Smallholder Policies: Past and Present?" In *Disappearing Peasantries? Rural Labour in Latin America, Asia, and Africa,* ed. Deborah Bryceson, Cristobal Kay, and Jos Mooij. London: Practical Action Publishing.

Cliffe, Lionel. 1988. "Zimbabwe's Agricultural Success and Food Security in Southern Africa." *Review of African Political Economy* 43: 4–25.

Coldham, Simon. 2001. "Land Acquisition Amendment Act, 2000 (Zimbabwe)." *Journal of African Law* 45 (2): 227–29.

Cusworth, J., and J. Walker. 1988. "Land Resettlement in Zimbabwe: A Preliminary Evaluation." Evaluation Report EV34. Overseas Development Administration, London.

El-Ghonemy, M. Riad. 1999. "The Political Economy of Market-Based Land Reform." Discussion Paper 104, United Nations Research Institute for Social Development, Geneva, Switzerland.

Food and Agriculture Organization of the United Nations. 2005. *Access to Rural Land and Land Administration after Violent Conflicts.* Rome.

Government of Zimbabwe. 1995. "Zimbabwe Agricultural Policy Framework 1995–2020 (ZAPF)." Ministry of Lands and Agriculture, Harare.

———. 2001. "Land Reform and Resettlement Programme: Revised Phase II." Ministry of Lands, Agriculture and Rural Resettlement, Harare.

———. 2002. "Fast Track Land Resettlement Program: Progress Report, July 2000 to October 2002." Ministry of Lands, Agriculture and Rural Resettlement, Harare.

———. 2003. "Report of the Presidential Land Review Committee on the Implementation of the Fast Track Land Reform Programme, 2002–2004" (the Utete Report). Harare.

———. 2005. "The National Budget Statement, 2006." Ministry of Finance, Harare.

———. 2006a. "National Development Priority Plan." Ministry of Economic Development, Harare.

———. 2006b. "Response to the Portfolio Committee on Lands, Agriculture, Water Development, Rural Resources and Resettlement: 2006, Budget Performance Report." Ministry of Land, Land Reform and Resettlement, Harare.

Izumi, Kaori. 2006a. *The Land and Property Rights of Women and Orphans in the Context of HIV and AIDS: Case Studies from Zimbabwe.* Pretoria, South Africa: HSRC Press.

———, ed. 2006b. *Reclaiming Our Lives: HIV and AIDS, Women's Land and Property Rights and Livelihoods in Southern and East Africa, Narratives and Responses.* Pretoria, South Africa: HSRC Press.

Jennings, A. C., and G. M. Huggins. 1935. "Land Apportionment in Southern Africa." *Journal of the Royal African Society* 34 (136): 296–312.

Kinsey, Bill H. 1999. "Land Reform, Growth, and Equity: Emerging Evidence from Zimbabwe's Resettlement Programme." *Journal of Southern African Studies* 25 (2): 173–96.

Lawton, Steve. 2002. "British Colonialism: Zimbabwe's Land Reform and Settler Resistance." Portland Independent Media Center.

Mandaza, Ibbo. 1986a. "The Political Economy of Transition." In *Zimbabwe: The Political Economy of Transition 1980–1986*, ed. Ibbo Mandaza. Dakar, Senegal: CODESRIA.

———. 1986b. "The State and Politics in a Post-White Settler Colonial Situation." In *Zimbabwe: The Political Economy of Transition 1980–1986*, ed. Ibbo Mandaza. Dakar, Senegal: CODESRIA.

Maroleng, Chris. 2004. "Zimbabwe; Reaping the Harvest." Situation Report. Institute for Security Studies, Pretoria, South Africa.

Moyana, Henry V. 1984. *The Political Economy of Land in Zimbabwe.* Gweru, Zimbabwe: Mambo Press.

Moyo, Sam. 1995. *The Land Question in Zimbabwe.* Harare, Zimbabwe: SAPES Books.

———. 2000a. "Interaction of Market and Compulsory Land Acquisition Processes with Social Action in Zimbabwe's Land Reform." Paper presented at the Southern Africa Regional Institute for Policy Studies' Trust Colloquium, Harare, Zimbabwe, September.

———. 2000b. *Land Reform Under Structural Adjustment in Zimbabwe; Land Use Change in Mashonaland Provinces.* Uppsala, Sweden: Nordiska Afrika Institutet.

———. 2000c. "The Political Economy of Land Redistribution in Zimbabwe: 1990–1999." *Journal of Southern African Studies* 26 (1): 5–28.

———. 2004a. "The Land and Agrarian Question in Zimbabwe." Paper presented at the Conference on Agrarian Constraint and Poverty Reduction: Macroeconomic Lessons for Africa, Addis Ababa, Ethiopia, December 17–18.

———. 2004b. *The Land Question in Africa: Research Perspectives and Questions.* Dakar, Senegal: CODESRIA.

Nyapokoto, Kudzai, and Ruth Hutchinson. 2004. Dorset: A Survey of New Settlers and Their Needs on a Former Commercial Farm in the Midlands of Zimbabwe, June 2004. Harare, Zimbabwe: Independent Office Machines.

Palmer, Robin. 1977. *Land and Racial Discrimination in Rhodesia.* London: Heineman.

———. 1990. "Land Reform in Zimbabwe." *African Affairs* 89 (355): 163–81.

Roth, Michael J., and Francis Gonese, eds. 2003. *Delivering Land and Securing Rural Livelihoods: Post-Independence Land Reform and Resettlement in Zimbabwe.* Harasre, Zimbabwe: Centre for Applied Social Science, University of Zimbabwe; Madison, WI: Land Tenure Center, University of Wisconsin-Madison.

Rukuni, Mandivamba, Patrick Tawonezvi, and Carl K. Eicher, with Mabel Munyuki-Hungwe and Prosper Matondi, eds. 2006. *Zimbabwe's Agricultural Revolution Revisited.* Harare, Zimbabwe: University of Zimbabwe Publications.

Scheuermaier, Markus. 2006. "Should Land Be Returned to White Farmers in Zimbabwe?" *Africa Policy Journal* 2: 1–12.

Sibanda Arnold. 1988. "The Political Situation." In *Zimbabwe's Prospects: Issues of Race, Class, State and Capital in Southern Africa,* ed. Colin Stoneman. London: Macmillan.

Thompson, Carol B. 2003. "Globalizing Land and Food in Zimbabwe: Implications for Southern Africa." *African Studies Quarterly.*

van Onselen, Charles. 1976. *Chibaro: African Mine Labour in Southern Rhodesia, 1900–1933.* London: Pluto Press.

Weiner, Daniel. 1988. "Land and Agricultural Development." In *Zimbabwe's Prospects: Issues of Race, Class, State and Capital in Southern Africa,* ed. Colin Stoneman. London: Macmillan.

Weiner, Daniel, Sam Moyo, Barry Munslow, and Phil O'Keefe. 1985. "Land Use and Agricultural Productivity in Zimbabwe." *Journal of Modern African Studies* 23 (2): 251–84.

CHAPTER SIX

Land Redistribution in South Africa

Edward Lahiff

This chapter provides an overview of land reform in South Africa since the advent of democratic government in 1994, with a particular emphasis on land redistribution. It begins with a brief sketch of the historical background, before outlining the main aspects and achievements of the land reform program to date. The final sections of the chapter briefly discuss some new policy proposals and the key challenges facing land reform in the country.

LAND REFORM SINCE THE END OF APARTHEID

Land reform in South Africa seeks to address more than 350 years of race-based colonization and dispossession, as part of the transition to a democratic society.

Origins and Patterns of Land Concentration

The extent to which the indigenous people of South Africa were dispossessed by European colonists—mainly Dutch and British settlers—was greater than in any other country in Africa, and it persisted for an exceptionally long time. European settlement began around the Cape of Good Hope in the 1650s and

The author wishes to thank Rogier van den Brink for his valuable comments on the draft of this chapter. The final comments and the opinions expressed are, however, the responsibility of the author alone.

progressed northward and eastward over a period of 300 years. By the 20th century, most of the county, including most of the best agricultural land, was reserved for the minority white population, with the African majority confined to the Native Reserves (later, African Homelands or Bantustans), which constituted just 13 percent of the country. Because the European decolonization of Africa was resisted strenuously and delayed by the settler-colonies of southern Africa, South Africa did not make the transition to democratic, nonracial government until 1994.

At the end of Apartheid,[1] approximately 82 million hectares of commercial farmland (86 percent of all farmland, or 68 percent of the total surface area) was in the hands of the white minority (10.9 percent of the population), and was concentrated in the hands of approximately 60,000 owners.[2] More than 13 million black people, the majority of them poverty stricken, remained crowded into the former homelands, where rights to land generally were unclear or contested and the system of land administration was in disarray. These areas were characterized by extremely low incomes and high rates of infant mortality, malnutrition, and illiteracy, relative to the rest of the country. On private farms, millions of workers, former workers, and their families faced severe tenure insecurity and lack of basic facilities. South Africa today has one of the most unequal distributions of income in the world, with income and quality of life being correlated strongly with race, location, and gender (May 2000).

The transition to democracy in South Africa (1990–94) occurred under circumstances very different from those of its neighbors, through a negotiated settlement rather than an all-out war of liberation. This political compromise left intact much of the power and wealth of the white minority, including their property rights. The international political and economic climate also was changing rapidly; and the old certainties that had informed both the nationalist and the socialist wings of the liberation movement, led by the African National Congress (ANC),[3] were fading fast. The new constitution created the basis for a liberal democracy, albeit with an emphasis on socioeconomic rights and a clear mandate on the state to redress the injustices of the past. The constitutional clause on property guaranteed the rights of existing owners, but also granted specific rights of redress to victims of past dispossession and set the legal basis for a potentially far-reaching land reform program.

South African agriculture is of a highly dualistic nature, where a developed commercial sector coexists with large numbers of small farms on communal lands (OECD 2006; Government of South Africa, National Department of Agriculture 2007). The commercial sector generates substantial employment[4] and export earnings, but contributes relatively little to GDP in this highly urbanized and industrialized economy: agriculture's share of GDP fell from 9.12 percent in 1965 to just 3.20 percent in 2002 (Vink and Kirsten 2003). Although close to half of the African population continues to reside in rural areas, most of the people are engaged in agriculture on a very small scale, if at all; and they depend largely on nonagricultural activities, including migration to cities, local wage employment, and welfare grants, for their livelihoods. South Africa had a thriving African peasant sector in the early 20th century, but this was destroyed systematically by the white settler regime on behalf of the mines (which demanded cheap labor) and white farmers (who demanded access to both cheap land and cheap labor) (Bundy 1979).

The Legal and Policy Basis for Land Reform

Since 1994, South Africa has embarked on a multifaceted program of land reform designed to redress the racial imbalance in landholding and secure the land rights of historically disadvantaged people. Progress in all areas of the program generally is considered to have fallen far behind expectations and official targets. This section of the chapter provides an overview of the main developments in land policy, touching briefly on restitution and tenure issues but concentrating on redistribution policy.

The Constitution of the Republic of South Africa sets out the legal basis for land reform—particularly in its Bill of Rights, which places a clear responsibility on the state to carry out land and related reforms and grants specific rights to victims of past discrimination: "the public interest includes the nation's commitment to land reform, and to reforms to bring about equitable access to all South Africa's natural resources" (section 25, 4). The constitution allows for expropriation of property for a public purpose or in the public interest, subject to just and equitable compensation.

The framework for land reform policy was set out in the "White Paper on South African Land Policy," released by the Department of Land Affairs (DLA) in April 1997, and it can be divided into three broad areas:

1. *Land restitution,* which provides relief for certain categories of victims of dispossession
2. *Tenure reform,* intended to secure and extend the tenure rights of the victims of past discriminatory practices
3. *Redistribution,* based on a system of discretionary grants that help certain categories of people acquire land through the market.

The state's land reform program thus aims to achieve objectives of both equity (in terms of land access and ownership) and efficiency (in terms of improved land use), while contributing to the development of the rural (and ultimately the national) economy. These objectives, and the preferred means of achieving them, are described in the White Paper: "The purpose of the land redistribution program is to provide the poor with access to land for residential and productive uses, in order to improve their income and quality of life. The program aims to assist the poor, labor tenants, farm workers, women, as well as emergent farmers. Redistributive land reform will be largely based on willing-buyer willing-seller arrangements. Government will assist in the purchase of land, but will in general not be the buyer or owner" (Government of South Africa, Department of Land Affairs 1997, p. 38).

Land Restitution: Reclaiming Historical Rights

The legal basis for restitution was created under the Restitution of Land Rights Act (Act 22 of 1994), which provided for the restitution of land rights to people or communities dispossessed under racially based laws or practices after June 19, 1913. The Commission on Restitution of Land Rights was established under a chief land claims commissioner and seven regional commissioners. A special court, the Land Claims Court, with powers equivalent to those of the High Court, was established to deal with land claims and other land-related matters. Legally, all restitution claims are against the state, rather than against past or current landowners; and provision is made for three broad categories of relief: restoration of the land under claim, grant of alternative land, or financial compensation.

The cut-off date for lodgment of restitution claims was December 31, 1998; and the total number of claims lodged was 63,455, including individual (or family) and community claims in both urban and rural areas. Following a validation campaign during 2002, the total number of claims in the system was revised to 79,687 (Government of South Africa, Ministry of Agriculture and Land Affairs 2003), and the settlement of claims accelerated dramatically. By August 2006, only 8,107 claims were still waiting to be settled, 6,975 of which were classified as rural and 1,132 as urban (Government of South Africa, Department of Land Affairs 2006b).

Having settled a large proportion of urban claims, mostly by cash compensation, the Commission on Restitution of Land Rights is now dealing with the backlog of rural claims, many of them on prime agricultural land. The processing of rural claims poses major administrative challenges for the commission in terms of land acquisition, resettlement of communities, and negotiation of long-term development support. Although more than 8,000 rural claims have been settled, it would appear that less than half have been settled through the restoration of land, suggesting that the process still has a long way to go. The current approach to restitution also raises important political considerations, especially where white landowners resist restitution and the commercial agriculture lobby opposes the "loss" of prime agricultural land. The manner in which such claims are settled, particularly the politically sensitive question of whether to expropriate land in certain circumstances, will have major implications not just for the restitution program but also for the whole process of land and agrarian reform in South Africa.

Until 2006, the state relied entirely on voluntary agreements with landowners to purchase privately owned land on behalf of claimants. Substantial areas of state-owned land also were restored. A 2003 amendment to the Restitution of Land Rights Act allows the Minister of Land Affairs to expropriate land by ministerial order, potentially greatly increasing the rate of acquisition of private land under claim. The first expropriation orders were not issued until January 2007, and the first land was acquired by expropriation in March 2007.

Following much adverse criticism arising from the perceived failure of a number of high-profile settled restitution claims, the state recently has begun exploring the use of "strategic partnerships" with commercial farmers and other operators, particularly in areas of high-value agriculture and ecotourism. Under this system, communities that regain their land will be required to enter into long-term profit-sharing relationships with commercial partners as a means of securing access to working capital and management expertise.

Although there have been a number of "success stories" in restitution—such as the Zebediela Citrus Estate in Limpopo Province, and the Makuleke claim on part of the renowned Kruger National Park—these have been outmatched greatly by the number of settled claims that effectively have collapsed or have failed to generate any benefits to date.[5]

Tenure Reform: Securing Land Rights

Tenure reform in rural South Africa refers both to the protection and strengthening of the rights of occupiers of privately owned farms and state land (for example, farmworkers and tenants), and to the reform of the system of communal tenure prevailing in the former homelands.

Almost all land in the rural areas of the former homelands still is legally owned by the state, in trust for particular communities. These areas are characterized by severe overcrowding and numerous unresolved disputes in which the rights of one group of land users overlap those of another group. Today, the administration of communal land is spread across a range of institutions, such as tribal authorities and provincial departments of agriculture, but it is in a state of collapse in many areas. There is widespread uncertainty about the validity of documents (such as permission-to-occupy certificates), the appropriate procedures for transferring land within families, and the legality of leasing or selling rights to land (Ntsebeza 2006; Cousins 2007). Numerous cases have been reported concerning development initiatives that are delayed by a lack of clarity on the ownership of land in the former homelands. Larger settlements and towns within the homelands generally have undergone a process of "formalization," whereby title to residential sites is transferred to individual owners, and services and infrastructure are provided by local municipalities; but this process has not been applied to rural villages and agricultural land. These "urban" areas effectively are removed from the formal authority of traditional leaders (chiefs) and no longer are considered part of the communal lands.

Attempts to draft a law for the comprehensive reform of land rights and administration in communal areas were abandoned in mid-1999 in the face of stiff opposition from traditional leaders. A revised Communal Land Rights Act was passed by parliament in 2004, but it has yet to be implemented. The act is intended to give secure land tenure rights to communities and individuals who occupy and use land previously reserved for occupation by African people and registered in the name of the state or held in trust by the Minister of Land Affairs or the Ingonyama Trust (which operates in the province of KwaZulu-Natal). According to the DLA, "The Act seeks to reverse this historical legacy of colonialism and apartheid by strengthening the land tenure rights of the people living in these communal land areas and to give their land tenure rights the full protection of the law" (Government of South Africa, Department of Land Affairs 2004). Among its provisions, the act grants land tenure rights in communal areas the recognition and protection of the law, permits the vesting of land and land tenure rights in communities and persons, and allows for registration of land rights in the deeds registry. The act aims to transfer ownership of land from the state to local structures, which in most areas are likely to be tribally based traditional councils set up in terms of the Traditional Leadership and Governance Framework Act of 2003. Although supported by the traditional chiefs, these measures have been criticized by a range of trade unions, women's organizations, the South African Human Rights Commission, and land rights nongovernmental organizations (NGOs) as perpetuating the undemocratic rule of tribal chiefs and failing to secure the rights of individuals, especially women (Claassens 2003; Walker 2003). Nongovernmental voices have warned of the dangers of overlooking countless informal land rights and strengthening the hand of unaccountable local leaders. They have called for a more gradual approach that safeguards existing rights, allows for a range of democratic landholding structures to evolve, and provides administrative and dispute resolution mechanisms during what is likely to be an extended period of transition (Cousins 2007). Local government structures also have entered the debate, raising the contentious question of which institution will be responsible for the delivery of infrastructure and services when communal land has been "privatized."

The Extension of Security of Tenure Act of 1997 (ESTA) has had little success in preventing evictions on commercial farms. In theory, ESTA provides protection from illegal eviction for people who live on rural or peri-urban land with the permission of the owner, regardless of whether they are employed by the owner. Although the act makes it more difficult to evict occupiers, evictions within the law are possible, and illegal evictions remain common. A study by Wegerif, Russell, and Grundling (2005) finds that more than 2 million farm dwellers—many of them tenant farmers engaged in independent production—were displaced between 1994 and 2004, more than had been displaced in the last decade of Apartheid (1984–94) and more than the total number of people who had benefited under all aspects of the official land reform program since it began.[6] In theory, ESTA allows farm dwellers to apply for grants for on-farm or off-farm developments (for example, housing) and gives the Minister of Land Affairs powers to expropriate land for such developments—but neither of those measures has been used widely to date. Where grants have been provided, they usually have involved farm residents moving off farms and into townships rather than farm residents being granted agricultural land of their own or secure accommodation on farms where they work.

In theory, one category of farm dwellers—labor tenants—has acquired much stronger legal rights. The term *labor tenant* refers to black tenants on white-owned farms who pay for their use of agricultural land through the provision of labor, as opposed to cash rental. The Land Reform (Labour Tenants) Act of 1996 aims to protect labor tenants from eviction and gives them the right to acquire ownership of the land that they live on or use. Approximately 19,000 claims have been lodged under the act, mostly in the provinces of KwaZulu-Natal and Mpumalanga; only a minority of those claims has been settled to date. Neither the Labour Tenants Act nor ESTA has succeeded in meeting its chief objectives of preventing illegal evictions and securing land rights—failures that can be attributed largely to a lack of dedicated budgets for tenure reform on the part of the DLA and a lack of enforcement of the law by police, prosecutors, and the courts (Hall 2003; Xaba 2004).

A total of 126,519 hectares of land has been provided to people under the tenure reform program since 1994, mainly to farm dwellers and labor tenants removed from commercial farms. As with other land provided under the reform program, this land is held by the beneficiaries in freehold title, either as individuals or as part of a communal property association[7] or a legal trust.

Redistribution: Shifting the Balance of Landholding and Production

Whereas restitution and tenure reform cater to specific groups of people who have legally enforceable rights (the programs generally are referred to as "rights based"), redistribution is a more discretionary program that seeks to redress the racial imbalance in landholding on a more substantial scale. The legal basis for redistribution is the Provision of Certain Land for Settlement Act of 1993 (amended in 1998 and now titled the Provision of Land and Assistance Act), but that is no more than an enabling act that empowers the Minister of Land Affairs to provide funds for land purchase. The details of the redistribution program thus are contained in various policy documents rather than in legislation.

Redistribution policy has undergone a series of shifts since 1994, focusing on provision of grants to assist suitably qualified applicants to buy land in rural areas, mainly for agricultural purposes but also for residential purposes ("settlement"). Provision of land in urban areas, to date, largely has been pursued by local government under its housing programs.

The methods chosen by the state to bring about redistribution are based mainly, although not entirely, on the operation of the existing land market. Other measures, such as expropriation, are available to the state, but have not been used widely so far. The role of the state has thus been limited to the provision of grants and other measures to assist people who otherwise might be unable to enter the land market to purchase property of their own.[8]

The concept of willing seller–willing buyer (WSWB) gradually entered the discourse around land reform in South Africa during the period 1993–96, reflecting the ANC's rapid shift in economic thinking from left-nationalist to neoliberal (Lahiff 2007). The principle was absent entirely from the ANC's "Ready to Govern" policy statement of 1992, which instead advocated expropriation and other nonmarket mechanisms; and from the Reconstruction and Development Program, the manifesto on which the party came to power in 1994. An extensive program of consultation by the new Department of Land Affairs, both within the country and with international advisers, led to a new policy direction, outlined in the 1997 White Paper on South African Land Policy, which made a market-based approach—and particularly the WSWB concept—the cornerstone of land reform policy (World Bank 1994; Williams 1996; Government of South Africa, Department of Land Affairs 1997; Hall, Jacobs, and Lahiff 2003). Such an approach was not dictated by the South African constitution but can be seen as a policy choice in line with emerging international trends and with the macroeconomic strategy (the Growth, Employment, and Redistribution strategy) adopted by the ANC in 1996.

Until 2000, redistribution policy centered on the provision of the Settlement/Land Acquisition Grant (SLAG), a grant of R 16,000 to qualifying households with an income of less than R 1,500 a month. This phase of redistribution generally was described as targeting the "poorest of the poor," which it appears to have done with some success. However, it also was criticized widely for "dumping" on former commercial farms large groups of poor people without the skills or resources necessary to bring those farms into production. Since 2001, SLAG effectively has been replaced by a program called Land Redistribution for Agricultural Development (LRAD), which was introduced with the explicit aim of promoting commercially oriented agriculture, but claimed to cater to other groups as well. The new policy offers higher grants paid to individuals rather than to households; and it makes greater use of loan financing through institutions, such as the state-owned Land Bank, to supplement the grant. LRAD offers a single, unified grant system that beneficiaries can access along a sliding scale from R 20,000 to R 100,000. All beneficiaries must make a cash or in-kind contribution, the size of which determines the value of the grant for which they qualify. The minimum contribution is R 5,000 (which may be in the form of the applicant's own labor), with which an applicant can obtain a grant of R 20,000. Under LRAD, grants are provided by provincial land reform offices and, under an agency agreement with the DLA, have been disbursed through the offices of the Land Bank. In its approach to land acquisition, LRAD retains the market-based, demand-led approach of previous policies. Since 2006, however, the state has been directly (proactively) purchasing some land on the market without first identifying potential beneficiaries.

Most redistribution projects have involved groups of applicants pooling their grants to buy formerly white-owned farms for commercial agricultural purposes. This emphasis on group projects has resulted largely from the small size of the available grant relative to the size and cost of the typical agricultural holding and the many difficulties associated with the subdivision of land (see "Farm Planning" below). Also, many rural communities view redistribution as a means of extending their existing system of communal landholding, and they favor collective ownership. Under LRAD, however, there has been a move toward smaller groups, including extended family groups, because of the increased availability of financing in the forms of grants and credit (van den Brink, Thomas, and Binswanger 2007). In addition, removing the income ceiling for grants has facilitated entrance into the redistribution program of black businesspeople able to engage more effectively with officials and landowners to design projects and obtain parcels of land that match their needs.

Less commonly, groups of farmworkers have used grants to purchase equity shares in existing farming enterprises, especially in areas of high-value agricultural land, such as the fruit and wine lands of the Western Cape. Although these share-equity schemes often are described as being among the more successful aspects of land reform in South Africa, they have been criticized for perpetuating highly unequal relationships between white owner-managers and black worker-shareholders, and for providing few material benefits to workers (Deininger and May 2000; Mayson 2003; Kleinbooi, Lahiff, and Boyce 2006).

Since 2001, state land under the control of national and provincial departments of agriculture also has been made available for purchase. More than 700,000 hectares of land have been provided in this way, much of that total transferred (in freehold title) to black tenants who previously had been renting it from the state (Wegerif 2004). A separate grant—the Grant for the Acquisition of Municipal Commonage—has been made available to municipalities wishing to provide land for use by the poor, typically for grazing purposes.

In 2007, the DLA reported that a total of 2,299,000 hectares had been transferred through the redistribution program, with an additional 1,897,000 hectares transferred through disposal of state land—almost 4.2 million hectares in all (see table 6.1). As with other areas of the land reform program, however, detailed statistics on beneficiaries, geographical spread of projects, type of land acquired, and types of financing used (that is, the mix of grants, loans, and "own contributions") generally are unavailable.

Since 2005, two new programs have been implemented in response to demands for greater support to new and emerging farmers. The Comprehensive Agricultural Support Program is a grant targeted to existing black farmers and the beneficiaries of land reform, largely intended for the development of infrastructure. In addition, the Micro-Agricultural Finance Schemes of South Africa has been established by the state to provide small loans to farmers.

Table 6.1 Land Transfers under South Africa's Land Reform Programs, 1994–2007		
Program	**Hectares transferred**	**Percent of total amount transferred**
Redistribution	2,299,000	54.79
Restitution	1,897,000	45.21
Total	4,196,000	100.00

Source: South Africa, Department of Land Affairs 2007.

Achievements to Date

In terms of overall achievements, land reform in South Africa consistently has fallen far behind the targets set by the state, and behind popular expectations. In 1994 virtually all commercial farmland in the country was controlled by the white minority, and the incoming ANC government set a target for the entire land reform program (restitution, tenure reform, and redistribution) to transfer 30 percent of white-owned agricultural land within a five-year period (ANC 1994). The target date subsequently was extended to 20 years (that is, to 2014); but at current rates of land transfer, meeting even that target is most unlikely. Government has tended to attribute this slow progress to resistance from landowners and to the high prices being demanded for land,[9] but independent studies point to a wider range of factors, including complex application procedures and bureaucratic inefficiency (Hall 2004a).

By March 2007, almost 4.2 million hectares had been transferred through the various branches of the land reform program, benefiting an estimated 1.5 million people (see table 6.1). The greatest amount of land (54.79 percent) was transferred under the redistribution program (including state land disposal and tenure reform), with the balance transferred through restitution.[10] The total transferred is *equivalent* to 5 percent of the agricultural land under white ownership in 1994. However, the actual impact on white-owned land is considerably less than this because much of the land transferred under restitution and tenure reform, some of the land under redistribution, and all of the land under state land disposal was land formerly owned by the state. Missing from these statistics are the amount of "pure" market redistribution (that is, land sales unconnected with the official land reform program)[11] and, more significant, the large number of farm dwellers (workers, tenants and their dependents) who have lost access to land on white-owned commercial farms since 1994. It must be stressed that the precise achievements of the land reform program are a matter of intense debate, largely because of poor reporting by the state agencies involved.

KEY EMERGING POLICY ISSUES IN SOUTH AFRICA'S LAND REFORM

The first part of this chapter has sketched the background to land reform in South Africa and outlined the land reform program to date. In this section, attention is given to some of the key challenges facing the land reform program, particularly in the area of land redistribution, drawing on a range of official documents, qualitative case studies, and gray literature. It also considers some recent proposals for policy changes.

Land Acquisition

The manner in which land is to be selected, acquired, and paid for has been the most contentious issue in South African land reform policy since 1994. The WSWB model was based on the World Bank's recommendations for a market-led reform, emphasizing the voluntary nature of the process; payment of full market-related prices, up front and in cash; a reduced role for the state (relative to previous "state-led" reforms elsewhere in the world); and removal of various "distortions" within the land market. The WSWB approach also fit well with the general spirit of reconciliation and compromise that characterized the negotiated transition to democracy, although it goes considerably farther than the requirements of the 1996 constitution. However, the South African approach to redistribution diverges from the model promoted by World Bank thinkers in several important respects—particularly in the failure to introduce a land tax to discourage speculation and dampen land prices, the absence (until 2007) of an element of expropriation to deal with difficult cases, the failure to allow beneficiaries to design and implement their own projects, and the failure to promote subdivision of large holdings.

The WSWB approach has remained at the center of South African land reform despite widespread opposition and recurring promises of "review" from government leaders. At the National Land Summit in July 2005, for example, abandonment of that approach was the uppermost demand from civil society and landless people's organizations, and it was the subject of criticism by both the president and the Minister of Land Affairs. Representatives of large-scale landowners remain broadly in favor of the approach, especially the payment of market-related prices, although they have been critical of protracted processes around land purchase and payment (Lahiff 2007).

South Africa has an active land market and well-developed market infrastructure (deeds registry, financial system, professional surveyors and valuers, and so forth), which undoubtedly presents many opportunities for land acquisition. The weaknesses that have become apparent in the current approach are largely in three areas: the suitability of land being offered for sale, the prices being demanded, and bureaucratic delays (including budgetary shortfalls) in funding purchases. The market-led approach being implemented in South Africa offers landowners absolute discretion in deciding whether to sell their land, to whom they will sell it, and at what price, with the result that most land that comes onto the market is not offered for land reform. Many landowners are politically opposed to land reform or they lack confidence in the process, especially the slow process of negotiation and payment. If possible, they prefer to sell their land to other buyers. There have been widespread reports suggesting that land being offered for land reform purposes is of inferior quality (Lyne and Darroch 2003; Tilley 2004).[12] In addition, there have been recurring complaints—from land reform beneficiaries, officials, and politicians—that where land is offered, excessive prices are being demanded (Government of South Africa, Ministry of Agriculture and Land Affairs 2005a).

Average prices paid for land under both the redistribution and the restitution programs have diverged considerably from the pattern for the general market trend (see figure 6.1). With the exception of one year (1995), prices paid for land under the redistribution program have been below those of the general land market—by an average of 33 percent since 1997. By contrast, prices paid for land under the restitution program, having remained below market for the period 1994–99, have exceeded market prices every year since 2000, reaching as high as 2.5 times the general market price in 2004. In the absence of more detailed data that would enable one to control for land quality and location, these data are open to a number of interpretations. For

Figure 6.1 Land Prices for Redistribution, Restitution, and the General Market, 1994–2004

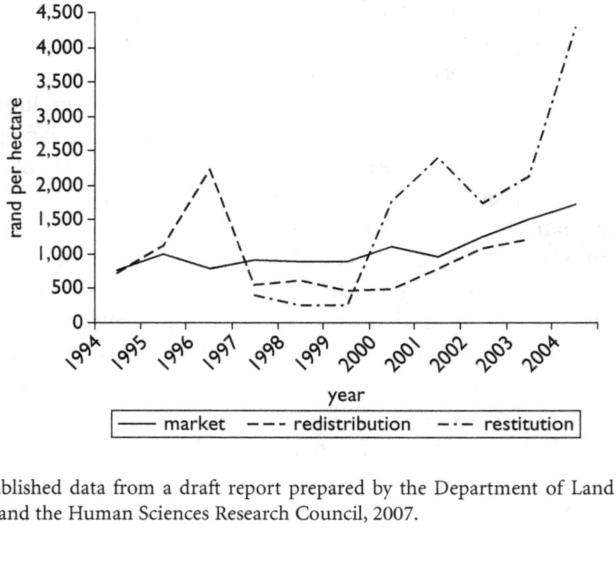

Source: Unpublished data from a draft report prepared by the Department of Land Affairs, the World Bank, and the Human Sciences Research Council, 2007.

redistribution, given the voluntary nature of the transactions, the below-average prices being paid would suggest that land purchased is below the average quality of land traded on the market—but that does not exclude the possibility that above-market prices are still being paid for land of this quality. Regardless of cost considerations, the purchase of land that is much below average in quality obviously gives cause for concern. For restitution, the escalation in prices in recent years probably reflects, in part, the acquisition of many high-value farms, but whether the prices paid represent value for money again is open to question. In the absence of a realistic threat of expropriation to date, it would appear that landowners facing restitution claims are in a strong position to demand prices equal to or exceeding prevailing market rates.

Demands for the abandonment of WSWB have included calls for removal of landowner discretion over sales (that is, routine use of expropriation or compulsory purchase), especially in areas of high land demand; and the payment of below-market prices—measures that are explicitly provided for in the constitution (Ntsebeza 2007). Since 2005, the DLA has been exploring a number of alternative policy options, including proactive land acquisition and area-based planning (see "New Policy Issues under Consideration" below). These options imply a more active and strategic role for the state in land purchase negotiations, rather than leaving it to uncoordinated negotiations between individual landowners and landless people. Although these approaches might go some way toward accelerating the pace of land transfer, no measures have been introduced to restrict the discretionary power of landowners or to pay below-market prices.

Beneficiary Targeting

From the outset of land reform, its intended beneficiaries have been defined in very broad, and almost exclusively racial, terms. The 1997 White Paper cast a very wide net that included the poor, labor tenants, farmworkers, women, and emergent farmers, but no specific strategies or system of priorities have been developed to ensure that such groups actually benefit. As in other areas of land reform, there is a critical shortage of data from government or independent sources, leading to much speculation on the socioeconomic profile of beneficiaries, especially since the introduction of LRAD in 2001. The limited evidence, however, would suggest that young people, the unemployed, and farmworkers have been served particularly poorly.

Because the redistribution program is based on beneficiaries' self-selection, there effectively is no targeting of applicants in terms of income or agricultural experience (beyond their ability to conform to the application procedures and, in the case of LRAD, to produce the necessary "own contribution").[13] Under SLAG (from 1995 to 2000), a household income ceiling of R 1,500 per month was set (but not always enforced). The low level of the grant and the requirement that people acquire land in groups (often comprising more than 100 people) probably were effective in targeting relatively poor people and deterring those who are better off.

DLA's Quality of Life Survey conducted in 1999 found that 75 percent of beneficiaries fell below the poverty line, levels of participation by female-headed households were high (31 percent nationally), and more than 20 percent of household heads were unemployed (May and Roberts 2000, p. 12). The Quality of Life Survey in 2002 found an illiteracy level of 61 percent for all respondents (Ahmed et al. 2003, p. 196), and supported the earlier survey's general findings that land reform was successfully targeting the poorer sections of rural society: "If employment levels, access to human capital and reliance on social security are used as proxy measures of poverty, then the results indicate that the program is still targeting the right beneficiaries" (p. xxi).

The switch to LRAD in 2001, however, with its larger grant sizes and its emphasis on more commercial forms of production, undoubtedly shifted the emphasis toward small groups (often family based) of better-off applicants—although again the data are extremely sparse. This change, and the emphasis on relatively large-scale commercial farming (in the absence of subdivision), also shifted land reform toward a simple deracialization of commercial agriculture rather than the radical restructuring that had been pictured by many people in the land sector in the early years of the program. The greater emphasis now paid to economic "viability" also was in line with an emerging policy direction centering around black economic empowerment (BEE), which emphasized the participation of black people in all sectors of the economy.[14]

Farm Planning

Apart from the ways in which land is acquired and beneficiaries are selected, South African land reform has been shaped by the type of farm (or project) planning that it has employed. Although the type of planning has varied somewhat over time, and has given rise to a range of outcomes (not all of them intended), its broad characteristics can be discerned.

First, farm planning in practice tends to be about the farm, not about the beneficiaries who are due to take it over. Great attention is paid to the physical features of the land, its recent history, and its agricultural potential, as seen through the eyes of the commercially oriented consultants appointed by the DLA. Little or no attention is paid to the resources, skills, and even the expressed wishes of the beneficiaries themselves. Many such "business plans" fail even to mention the size of the group concerned. It is quite clear that the beneficiaries must adapt to the needs of the farm, and not the other way around.

Nowhere is this more evident than in the official opposition to subdivision of farms. This opposition has deep roots in South African history, and it has been a persistent feature of land reform since 1994, spanning SLAG and LRAD as well as restitution and even the tenure reform program.[15] The failure to subdivide is arguably the single greatest contributor to the failure and general underperformance of land reform projects because it not only foists inappropriate sizes of farms on people (and absorbs too much of their grants in the process), but also forces them to work in groups, whether they want to do so or not.[16] The World Bank long has argued for subdivision, but its argument has been opposed consistently by most of the South African agricultural "establishment" (including DLA and the Department of Agriculture) (see box 6.1).

It is difficult to explain this failure to contemplate subdivision, and the topic rarely has been debated during the first decade of the South African land reform program, but a number of factors may be contributing to this phenomenon. Group acquisition has not been questioned openly by organizations representing the landless, perhaps in the belief that beneficiaries will fare better in a mutually supportive group. The limited evidence from existing land

Box 6.1 Restrictions on Subdividing Land

South Africa ... still has explicit legal and policy restrictions against the subdivision of farms into smaller units. . . . South Africa's subdivision policy—the Subdivision of Agricultural Land Act, 1970 (Act No. 70 of 1970)—was inspired by the danger of *"die verswarting van het platteland"*—literally, the *"blackening of the country side."* The official reason given at the time was that farms should not be allowed to decrease in size below the so-called "viable" size. This begs the next question: what is a "viable" size? The first thing to realize is that "viability" is not a notion related to production economies of scale. Instead, it is linked to a minimum income target. In former settler colonies, the "viable" size was calculated by setting a minimum income target for white farmers. On the basis of this income target, a simple calculation followed which determined the size of the farm. Efficiency considerations, such as economies of scale, or employment generation, did not enter the calculation. The viability policy was a social policy which ensured that white farmers earned an income acceptable to white society. . . .

To date, unfortunately, neither Zimbabwe nor South Africa has removed such subdivision restrictions. The result is that the restriction on subdivision functions as a powerful barrier to racial integration in the commercial farm areas and in the peri-urban areas. . . . It makes it difficult for a black person—in Southern Africa, on average, poor—to legally buy a small plot in a formerly white area—simply because no small subdivisions are on offer. . . . In other words, a policy that had been designed with the sole purpose of ensuring white living standards and segregating the races is still in place in the democratic, non-racial South Africa of today. This policy lacks any economic, let alone social, rationale. It restricts the land market and makes it difficult for small farmers to buy small farms.

Source: van den Brink et al. 2006, p. 31.

reform projects, however, suggests that large groups do not translate into effective production units or into benefits for members, and many groups collapse into individual production, usually at a very low level of output and with little tenure security for such individuals. The collective ("community") basis of many restitution claims, and the requirement that people organize themselves into groups to access grants under the redistribution program, also appear to have contributed to the prevalence of collective landholding and the attempts at collective production.

This progression from applying for land as a group to using land collectively is not inevitable, however, especially if beneficiaries were to be given (or insisted upon getting) greater freedom of choice. The most immediate explanation for the lack of subdivision is thus the requirement that groups implement "whole-farm" plans that conform to the imagined norms of large-scale commercial farming. That requirement is imposed by officials of the DLA, provincial departments of agriculture (responsible for vetting land reform applications), and the regional land claims commissioners (responsible for restitution settlements), as a condition of grants and settlement awards. The state is supported in that requirement by the vast majority of agricultural economists and commercial farmers in the country who clearly are hostile to a radical restructuring of the existing commercial agricultural sector based on large farms. Grant applications that propose small-scale production or the breakup of existing farm units—especially for noncommercial (that is, subsistence) purposes—have little or no hope of being approved under the current system.

Retaining former commercial farms as undivided properties, however, is only one (albeit important) aspect of the farm model being imposed as part of the South African land reform. In many other ways as well, groups of generally resource-poor, risk-averse, and inexperienced black farmers are required to conform to the imagined ideal of an individual commercial farmer. This demand starts with the "business plan" typically drawn up by consultants or officials of the Department of Agriculture who have been exposed only to large-scale commercial farming and, as argued above, relate almost entirely to the physical properties of the land and hardly at all to the socioeconomic characteristics of the new landowners. Production for market usually is the only objective; and plans typically require substantial loans from commercial banks, purchases of heavy equipment, selection of crop varieties and livestock breeds previously unknown to the beneficiaries, hiring of labor (despite typically high rates of unemployment among members themselves), and often the appointment of a full-time farm manager. Much of that typically fails to materialize.

Thus, a defining characteristic of South African land reform policy is that beneficiaries—no matter how poor or how numerous—are required to step into the shoes of former white owners and continue to manage the farm as a unitary, commercially oriented enterprise. Alternative models, based on low inputs and smaller units of production, actively are discouraged. That inappropriate model, and the tensions within beneficiary groups that emerge from it, largely are responsible for the high failure rate of land reform projects.

Postsettlement Support

In terms of market-led land reform, beneficiaries should not rely exclusively on the state for postsettlement support services, but should be able to access services from a range of public and private providers. Indeed, the past two decades have seen a major reduction in the overall state services available to farmers. Whereas large commercial farmers generally have managed to overcome this service decline through their access to a range of commercial and cooperative services, land reform beneficiaries and other small-scale farmers largely are left to fend for themselves (Vink and Kirsten 2003). Recent studies show that land reform beneficiaries experience numerous problems accessing services—such as credit, training, extension advice, transport and plowing services, veterinary services—and input and produce markets (HSRC 2003; Hall 2004b; Wegerif 2004; Bradstock 2005).

Services that are available to land reform beneficiaries tend to be supplied by provincial departments of agriculture and a small number of non-NGOs, but the evidence suggests that these providers serve only a minority of projects. In a study of LRAD projects in three provinces, the Human Sciences Research Council reports that "... in many cases there is still no institutionalised alternative to laying the whole burden of training, mentoring and general capacitation on the provincial agricultural departments" (2003, p. 72). In a study of nine LRAD projects in the Eastern Cape Province, Hall (2004b) finds not one had obtained any support from the private sector and most had not had any contact with the DLA since obtaining their land; two had received infrastructure grants from the Department of Agriculture, but none was receiving any form of extension service. In November 2005, the Minister for Agriculture and Land Affairs told parliament that 70 percent of land reform projects in Limpopo Province were dysfunctional, a situation she attributed to poor design, negative dynamics within groups, and a lack of postsettlement support (*Farmers Weekly* 2005).

For Jacobs (2003), the general failure of postsettlement support stems from a failure to conceptualize land reform beyond the land transfer stage, and from poor communication between the national DLA (responsible for land reform) and the nine provincial departments of agriculture (responsible for state services to farmers): "The rigid distinction in South Africa's land policy between land delivery and agricultural development has resulted in post-transfer support being largely neglected. There is no comprehensive policy on support for agricultural development after land transfer and the agencies entrusted with this function have made little progress in this regard. Agricultural assistance for individual land reform projects is ad hoc ..." (p. 7).

This lack of coordination between the key departments of agriculture and of land affairs is compounded by poor communication with other institutions (such as the Department of Housing and the Department of Water Affairs and Forestry) and local government structures (Hall, Isaacs, and Saruchera 2004). The need for additional support for land reform beneficiaries was acknowledged by the Ministry of Agriculture and Land Affairs, and that acknowledgment led to the introduction in the fiscal 2004/05 national budget of both the Comprehensive Agricultural Support Program, with a total of R 750 million allocated over five years, and the Micro-Agricultural Finance Schemes of South Africa, intended to provide small loans to farmers (Hall and Lahiff 2004).

The well-developed (private) agribusiness sector that services large-scale commercial agriculture has shown no more than a token interest in extending its operations to new farmers who, in most cases, would be incapable of paying for such services anyway. The assumption that the private sector would somehow "respond" to demand from land reform beneficiaries with very different needs from the established commercial farmers has not been supported by recent experience. The principal explanation for that, of course, is that cash-strapped land reform beneficiaries generally are not in a position to exert any effective demand for the services on offer, even if those services were geared to their specific needs.

THE FUTURE OF LAND REFORM IN SOUTH AFRICA

There is widespread concern that the South African land reform program is failing to meet its objectives in terms of both equity and efficiency. The following section addresses some of the key challenges that will need to be tackled if it is to deliver a substantial amount of land to landless people in a sustainable manner.

Program Monitoring and Evaluation

The need for ongoing monitoring and evaluation (M&E) of a major national program such as land reform has been recognized widely from the outset. As the scale and complexity of the land reform program developed, however, the official M&E functions within the DLA have not kept pace. As a result, major information gaps now exist across all aspects of the program. "A lack of good quality systems to generate information on the poverty impact of reforms is a program design flaw and demonstrates a lack of focus on the processes meant to transform land into sustainable livelihoods . . ." (Chimhowu 2006, p. 31). This raises concerns about the DLA's ability to manage its programs effectively, about the reliability of statistical information coming into the public domain, and about the prospects for determining the impact of reforms on their intended beneficiaries.

At the most basic level, for many years no reliable or standardized systems were in place to record project data in provincial offices or to report such data to the national office. Fundamental problems with the collection, analysis, and reporting of statistics run across all aspects of the land reform program (Hall 2004a).

Between 1997 and 2003, three DLA Quality of Life surveys were conducted to investigate the impact of land reform on beneficiaries nationwide. The first[17] and third[18] surveys in the series have been criticized widely for their sampling methods and the quality of their findings, and they are considered unreliable. The second survey used a more robust methodology and provided some useful findings, but because it was conduced at a relatively early stage in the land reform process, its findings on the impact of land reform were very limited (May and Roberts 2000). Changes in research design between surveys also created severe difficulties in comparing the results from each of them.

A comprehensive and effective M&E system will require a number of components that presently are not in place, including

- Collection of information on all applicants to the program (including those who are refused funding)
- Socioeconomic profiling of all beneficiaries entering the program (to throw light on targeting and to provide a baseline for subsequent livelihood impact assessment)
- Information on land transferred (agro-ecological conditions, size, cost)
- Consumption, expenditure, and asset data for beneficiary households and an appropriate control group
- Adherence to a standardized process of project planning, implementation, and support (with reporting of all milestones)
- Effective centralized management, processing, and reporting of all data emerging from the program
- Recurring national studies to include systematic panel surveys, case studies, and so forth
- Structured processes for feeding M&E data into policy making.

Impact of Land Reform

Very few data are available on the impact of land reform on agricultural production or on the livelihoods of beneficiaries. The data that are available, however, point to widespread underutilization of land and minimal benefits for most program participants. Vink and Kirsten (2003) argue that conditions in the communal farming areas have remained largely unchanged or even may have worsened after eight years of land reform. They suggest that there is "no evidence that the supposed beneficiaries of land reform are better off because of their participation in the program" (p. 16). Similarly, Seekings and Nattrass (2005) explicitly link changes in the agricultural economy with increasing poverty, and then link that to failures in the land reform program. Instead of increasing employment in agriculture, they argue, government's macroeconomic policies have caused it to fall dramatically, swelling the ranks of the unskilled unemployed:[19] "Overall . . . government policy has not succeeded in being pro-poor. Farm workers have experienced continued retrenchments and dispossession, despite supposedly protective legislation. Land reform has not benefited the poor significantly. The reforms that have been implemented have generally been to the benefit of a constituency that was already relatively advantaged. In this crucial sector, the post-apartheid distributional regime has not resulted in improved livelihoods for the poor" (p. 357).

On the more positive side, authors such as Deininger and May (2000) point to the *potential* of smallholder agriculture to contribute to agricultural employment and poverty alleviation. Other than demonstrating that land reform was targeting the poor successfully, however, those authors were unable to provide evidence that such potential was being realized in practice: ". . . the fact that economically successful projects reached significantly higher levels of poor people suggests that increased access to productive assets could be an important avenue for poverty reduction. Given the importance of developing a diverse and less subsidy-dependent rural sector, a suitably adapted land reform could play an important role in the restructuring of South Africa's rural sector" (p. 17).

DLA's 1999 Quality of Life Survey found that only 16 percent of projects were delivering "sustainable" revenues (May and Roberts 2000, p. 14), whereas the 2002 survey found that "in many projects no production is happening and some beneficiaries are worse off" (Ahmed et al. 2003, p. xxvi).

Most studies to date have considered the impact of land reform at a project or household level, paying less attention to the wider impacts of land reform on agricultural production and local economies. In a study from Eastern Cape Province, Aliber, Masika, and Quan (2006) find a drop in production (compared with production by previous owners of the same farms) alongside modest improvements in the livelihoods of those who now own the land. Thus, welfare (equity) objectives were being achieved to some degree, but at the expense of growth (efficiency). In a district study from a high-value wine and fruit belt in the Western Cape, Kleinbooi, Lahiff, and Boyce (2006) show that land reform has not led to any major changes in land use and to only very modest contributions to livelihoods. Of the 12 projects established in the area, only 2 have involved the transfer of land ownership; the rest have been farmworker equity programs and tenure projects. The impact on beneficiaries has been "limited, but not negligible" (p. 3), largely taking the form of improved housing quality or stronger tenure rights to existing houses on farms. Cash dividends—the major benefit anticipated in equity schemes—have been paid out only in one scheme and only on one occasion.

Budgets

Allocations in the national budget have imposed overall limits on the redistribution program, but the inability of the DLA to spend its budgetary allocation in successive years has been a greater problem. Overall, the budget for land reform has grown dramatically year after year (figure 6.2), but DLA consistently failed to use all of its funds until fiscal 2002/03. This exhausting of the budget led to DLA approving projects for which funds were not available and being unable to process new projects. In both the Western Cape and the Eastern Cape, for example, provincial offices of DLA discouraged new grant applications during 2003 because of the backlog of existing commitments. By February 2004, the total backlog of redistribution and tenure projects that had been approved, but for which no funding was available, amounted to R 587 million—more than double the funds available for land purchase during that fiscal year (Hall and Lahiff 2004). By fiscal 2005/06, however, DLA spending again was unable to keep up with an increasing budget. Out of a total budget of R 3.8 billion,[20] the allocation for restitution was underspent by R 800 million (30 percent), and redistribution was underspent by R 150 million (21 percent). This underspending led to the projected allocations for fiscal 2006/07 and 2007/08 being revised downward.

Rising budgets and substantial underspending suggest that finance is not the main constraint to speeding up the delivery of land reform in South Africa. Figure 6.2 shows the growth in the budget for land reform since 1995: the trend generally has been upward, with a dramatic increase for restitution since fiscal 2005/06 and much slower growth for the rest of land reform. Note that the land reform trend line includes both redistribution and tenure reform programs, whereas restitution is a separate trend line. Restitution is expected to decline

Figure 6.2 Budgets for Land Reform and Restitution, Including Estimates for the Medium-Term Expenditure Framework

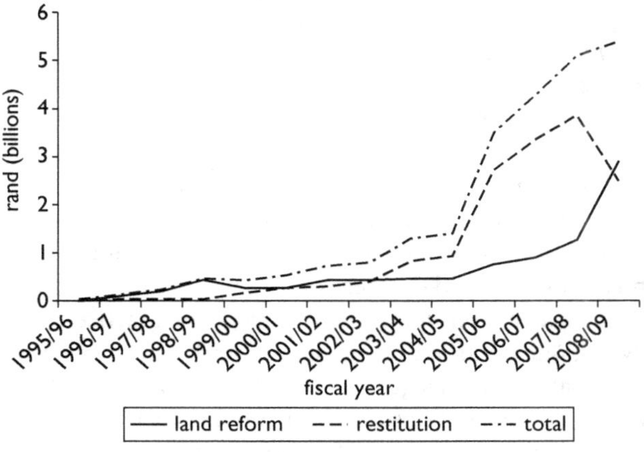

Source: South Africa National Treasury, Estimates of National Expenditure 2006; statistics are drawn from pages 667–92.

dramatically after 2008—assuming that the program is largely complete by then—with substantial shifts in resources into the redistribution program.

New Policy Issues under Consideration

Over the years, various changes to land policy have been proposed. This section looks briefly at some of the main proposals from within and outside government, not all of which have become official policy.

- *Scrap the WSWB approach*—Strong opposition to this approach has been expressed by much of civil society since the beginning of the land reform program, but clear policy alternatives have yet to emerge. Opposition largely has centered on the payment of full market price, with proposed alternatives ranging from payment of a "productive" (that is, agronomic) price to confiscation without compensation. Less attention has been paid to the questions of land targeting and ending the landowner veto over sales (for example, by granting the state the right of first refusal on all land sales). Nationalizing land has been proposed from time to time, but it does not appear to enjoy popular or political support.
- *Restrict land ownership*—Civil society organizations have proposed various measures to restrict landownership, but none of the ideas has been translated into policy. These proposals have included ceilings on land ownership (that is, maximum sizes, related to agro-ecological zones), "one person–one farm" rules, and restrictions on foreigners' ownership rights. In 2006, an expert panel was appointed to look into the possibility of placing legal restrictions on foreign ownership of land. Presenting its report to the minister in August 2007, the panel recommended a number of regulatory measures, the most controversial of which was the inclusion of race (along with nationality and gender) on all title deed records.
- *Impose a land tax*—The absence of a land tax in South Africa has drawn attention over the years, especially from economists and from the World Bank. Within South Africa there appears to be no significant support for such a measure from civil society or from government, which tends to see it as an extra administrative burden that counteracts efforts to reduce the overall tax take. Needless to say, landowners strongly oppose it. The matter has been further complicated recently by the introduction of municipal levies on agricultural land—levies widely seen as a form of land tax.
- *Develop a proactive land acquisition strategy*—In practice but perhaps not inevitably, the "demand-led" approach to land reform has led to a highly reactive approach to land acquisition on the part of the South African state. Civil society's calls for the state to take a more proactive approach to identifying and acquiring land in areas of high demand have been resisted by DLA (Lahiff 2007), but in 2006 the department began developing policy in this area. According to the department, "The [proposed] focus is on the State as

a lead driver in land redistribution rather than the current beneficiary-driven redistribution. This means that the State will proactively target land and match this with the demand or need for land" (Government of South Africa, Department of Land Affairs 2006a, p. 3). Under this approach, the state—or an intermediary trust such as a Section 21 nonprofit company—would become the initial owner of the land, rather than the beneficiaries. In this way, the state might lease land to targeted beneficiaries on a trial basis while they become established, prior to the transfer of title. To date, this approach has been piloted only in Mpumalanga Province. The system of land acquisition, however, remains voluntary, with full market-related prices being paid. In the national budget for fiscal 2007/08, the allocation for proactive land purchase was fully one-third of the total provision for land acquisition.

- *Adopt area-based land reform (or areas-based planning)*—The uncoordinated approach to land acquisition and the difficulties it has presented for the provision of support services have prompted proposals for a more integrated, area-based approach to land reform, with a greater role for local government. Such an approach has been attempted in the Makhado local municipality, with the cooperation of a local NGO (Nkuzi Development Association) and support from the U.K. Department for International Development. DLA currently is considering implementing it in a number of pilot sites, based on local municipality boundaries (Government of South Africa, Department of Land Affairs 2006a).
- *Adopt the Agricultural Broad-Based Black Economic Empowerment Charter*—Like other initiatives to transform the economy and society, land reform now is considered a means of achieving black economic empowerment, as required by the Broad-Based Black Economic Empowerment Act of 2003. A draft of the Agricultural Broad-Based Black Economic Empowerment (AgriBEE) charter was released in July 2004, and further modified at the AgriBEE Indaba (summit meeting) in November 2005. The process leading to the release of the draft charter involved two years of consultations between AgriSA (the main organization representing large-scale landowners), the National African Farmers' Union, and the National Department of Agriculture. The consultations have been going on since the Agricultural Sector Plan was adopted by the Presidential Working Group on Agriculture in 2002. However, key groups, such as the trade unions organizing in the agricultural sector and the Landless People's Movement, complain that they have not been consulted (Hall 2004a). The draft charter reiterates the existing target of redistributing 30 percent of agricultural land to black South Africans by 2014; and it sets ambitious targets for deracializing ownership, management, and procurement in the agricultural sector, including 35 percent black ownership of existing and new enterprises by 2008 (Government of South Africa, National Department of Agriculture 2004). The targets apply all along the value chain, rather than just at farm level, including

value-adding and processing industries in secondary agriculture. However, the BEE focus on deracializing demographics in shareholding, management and procurement is relevant mainly to larger farms and other enterprises in the agribusiness sector. In that context, the charter effectively is an agribusiness charter. It is not clear what measures are envisaged for smaller commercial farms or how BEE might empower farmworkers and smallholders who remain marginalized within the sector (Government of South Africa, Ministry of Agriculture and Land Affairs 2005b). In April 2008, the charter finally was launched.

- *Implement the Land and Agrarian Reform Project (LARP)*—In October 2007, the Minister of Agriculture and Land Affairs launched LARP, which is being promoted as a joint venture between different spheres of government, including the DLA, provincial departments of agriculture, and local municipalities (Government of South Africa, Ministry of Agriculture and Land Affairs 2008). The initiative aims to better integrate agencies and promote both agricultural production and agribusiness. Although the project sets ambitious targets—such as the redistribution of 5 million hectares of land in two years—it has no budget of its own. Rather, it depends on existing land reform allocations. LARP project documents emphasize promoting commercial farmers working on a substantial scale. Political pronouncements on the project have stressed the inclusion of farmworkers as a priority group.

Emerging Partnerships among Stakeholders

Given the "negotiated" basis of land reform in South Africa, there has been a remarkable lack of formal agreement among the main players—the state, landowners, and targeted beneficiaries. As noted above, within the agricultural sector the Presidential Working Group on Agriculture has brought together AgriSA, the National African Farmers' Union, and the National Department of Agriculture, and that led to the adoption of the Agricultural Sector Plan in 2002. However, organizations of the landless were not included in the consultations of that group, and the group generally avoids matters of land reform policy. No equivalent forum exists for the land sector. The July 2005 National Land Summit, and the resolutions emerging from it, revealed the isolation of white landowners from virtually all other parties, including the state, at least at the rhetorical level (see box 6.2).

At a more local level, however, a range of partnerships has emerged among stakeholders in the land sector, within and outside of the formal land reform program. Notable examples include the sugar industry and the wine industry, but individual examples may be found across the country (see box 6.3).

Share equity schemes also represent a form of partnership but, as discussed above, secured land rights or other material benefits gained by workers under these schemes have been very limited. In a number of cases, white farmers

Box 6.2 Summary of Resolutions Adopted at the National Land Summit, July 2005

On land restitution:

- Speeding up the process of settling rural claims and restoring land to claimants
- Expropriating land under claim where negotiations with current landowners fail
- Reopening the lodgment process for eligible restitution claimants who missed the 1998 deadline
- Improving development planning for claimants who have returned to their land
- Developing a holistic approach to restitution of mineral rights and rights to water and forests, as well as land
- Creating a restitution truth and reconciliation commission to hear people's experiences of dispossession and to bring healing and closure.

On redistribution:

- A proactive role for the state to acquire land through negotiated purchase and, where necessary, expropriation
- Increased resources to appoint new staff and enable state agencies to take on this new role
- Regulation of land markets through a moratorium on foreign land ownership, a ceiling on the size of landholdings, a right of first refusal for the state on all sales of agricultural land, and the imposition of a land tax to curb speculation and bring underutilized land onto the market
- Proactive subdivision of farms to make available parcels of land appropriate to the needs of smallholders
- A focus on the poor, specifically women, farmworkers, and youth
- Payment of "just and equitable" compensation for land, in line with the constitution rather than market prices
- A social obligations clause in the constitution, legally to protect landless people who occupy certain categories of land
- Local governments' identifying land needs and the land to meet those needs, and stopping the rental of municipal commonage to commercial farmers
- State support for small-scale farming by the poor and a moratorium on "elitist" developments, such as golf courses and game farms.

On tenure reform:

- A new law to secure farm dwellers' tenure rights, independent of their employment status, and to create a class of "non-evictable occupiers"
- A moratorium on evictions of farm dwellers until a new law and effective systems for its enforcement are in place
- Provision of basic services to farm dwellers, including water and sanitation
- Land for farm dwellers so that they can become farmers in their own right.

Source: Hall 2005.

Box 6.3 A Silent Revolution in Agriculture?

Throughout South Africa, small, local, private sector and civil society initiatives are working to make the agricultural sector more equitable, stable, and profitable for everyone involved. Additional research into these initiatives is needed, but it could be that, working quietly and locally, they are doing at least as much for sustainable land reform as the government programs are doing. Initiatives recorded over the past five years include the following:

- The Land for Peace Initiative, a loose coalition of commercial farmers, landowners, and private sector individuals, is working to encourage greater private sector involvement in land reform.
- The Red Meat Producers' Organization has established the National Emergent Red Meat Producers' Organization, and has recommended that a "strategy should be implemented to provide technical services and credit services to emergent red meat producers."
- The Grain Producers' Organization has embarked on production and marketing support for emergent farmers in North West Province, and is active in other provinces. It also has a development office in Zeerust, and holds regular information and training sessions where expertise with regard to the planting, fertilization, chemical treatment, and harvesting of oil seeds is offered.
- Boeresake, Bellville—an organization of mostly white commercial farmers in the Western Cape—has donated tractors to emergent farmers, and provides them with ongoing assistance.
- The Coastal Farmers' Co-operative in KwaZulu Natal has established three subdepots for delivering services to small cane growers.
- MKTV-Tobacco, an organization of mostly white commercial tobacco farmerss in North West Province, assists new farmers in the Vryheid, Klerksdorp, Rustenburg, and Ventersdorp areas.
- SOK Holdings Ltd., an agri-marketing and trading company, is financing 94 emergent farmers, at a cost of R 2.4 million. New farmers are established on 1- to 2-hectare farms planted with apple orchards.
- Senwes, a large maize milling company, is involved in establishing emergent farmers at Odendaalsrus, Koppies, and Oppermansgronde.

Source: CDE 2005, p. 16.

(neighbors or former landowners) have served as mentors to land reform beneficiaries, but that tends to occur on an isolated and ad hoc basis.

Under the restitution program, a range of so-called strategic partnerships has been established as previously dispossessed communities lay claim to a range of valuable—and often well-developed—resources. One notable example is the Makuleke claim on a portion of the Kruger National Park, where the community has entered into profit-sharing agreements with the National Parks Board and with a number of private tourism operators who have established up-market lodges on the restored land. At Zebediela Citrus Estate, in Limpopo, the Bjatladi community has entered into a 10-year management and shareholding agreement with a private agribusiness company; the agreement promises revenue for the community through dividends and land rental, plus opportunities for employment, training, and participation in management. This model of strategic partnership is set to be extended over many of the larger claims on high-value agricultural land in Limpopo, although it has been criticized for the lack of certainty around community benefits and the fact that it effectively excludes community members from direct access to their land for at least 10 years (Derman, Lahiff, and Sjaastad 2006).

CONCLUSION

Land reform is an important aspect of social and economic transformation in South Africa, as a means both of redressing past injustice and of alleviating the pressing problems of poverty and inequality in the rural areas. The South African land reform program is founded on the country's constitution and has the potential for far-reaching change through restitution, tenure reform, and redistribution. The policies that have been adopted by the state, however, are problematic from a number of perspectives, and they have fallen far short of their delivery targets. Even where land has been transferred, it appears to have had minimal impact on the livelihoods of beneficiaries, largely because of inappropriate project design, a lack of necessary support services, and shortages of working capital leading to widespread underuse of land. There is no evidence to suggest that land reform has led to improved efficiency, job creation, or economic growth.

Some gains undoubtedly have been made, but they remain largely at a symbolic level. Where real material advances have occurred, they often can be attributed to the involvement of third parties—individual mentors, agribusiness corporations, NGOs, or ecotourism investors.

The evidence of the last 14 years suggests that the current approach—based on acquisition of land through the open market, minimal support to new farmers, and bureaucratic imposition of collectivist models loosely based on existing commercial operators—is unlikely to transform the rural economy and lift people out of poverty. What clearly is missing at present is any small-farmer path to development that could enable the millions of households residing in the communal areas and on commercial farms to expand their own production and accumulate wealth and resources in an incremental manner. Without doubt, making this happen would require radical restructuring of existing farm units to create family-size farms, and more realistic farm planning, appropriate support from a much reformed state agricultural service, and a much greater role for beneficiaries in the design and implementation of their own projects. Recent policy proposals—which focus mainly on the process of land acquisition—do not seem to offer much in that direction. Much more will be required if the land-based economy is to contribute significantly to economic growth and to the redistribution of wealth and opportunities to the majority of the population.

NOTES

1. *Apartheid* is an Afrikaans word meaning "separation," and it implies strict racial segregation in all areas of life. It was the official ideology of the white minority regime that held state power from 1948 to 1994.
2. In 1996, the South African Census reported a total population of 40.5 million, broken down in the following categories: African = 76.7 percent; White = 10.9 percent; Colored = 8.9 percent; Indian/Asian = 2.6 percent; unspecified/other = 0.9 percent (Statistics South Africa).
3. The ANC was founded in 1912. During the struggle against Apartheid (1948–94), it contained both nationalist and socialist factions, and it has long-standing alliances with the South African Communist Party and the Congress of South African Trade Unions. The ANC was victorious in the general elections of 1994 (when it formed the multiparty Government of National Unity under the leadership of Nelson Mandela), and again in 1999 and 2004 (under the leadership of Thabo Mbeki).
4. Agriculture accounted for 10 percent of formal employment in 2002 (Vink and Kirsten 2003, p. 6).
5. High-profile projects that have collapsed include Elandskloof in the Western Cape and Komani-San in Kalahari Gemsbok National Park in the Northern Cape.
6. Of an estimated 2,351,086 people displaced from farms since 1994, a total of 942,303 (40 percent) were evicted; others left for a variety of social and economic reasons (Wegerif, Russell, and Grundling 2005, p. 7).
7. A communal property association is a legal entity, created in terms of the Communal Property Associations Act of 1996, which allows groups of people to own land collectively.
8. Strictly speaking, the WSWB policy applies only to the (discretionary) redistribution program. In practice, negotiated purchases at market prices have been a feature of the restitution and tenure programs as well, despite their rights basis. Recent moves by the state to invoke powers of expropriation in cases where negotiations have deadlocked apply only to restitution claims, and have no direct bearing on the application of the WSWB principle in redistribution.
9. Report by the director general of DLA to the Parliamentary Portfolio Committee on Agriculture and Land Affairs, quoted in *Farmers Weekly*, November 4, 2005.
10. Much of the land transferred (or "delivered," to use the official term) under the restitution program has been transferred in nominal ownership only, as the land remains incorporated into nature reserves and state forests, and, in terms of the restitution agreements, is not accessible for direct use by the restored owners (Hall 2003).
11. Lyne and Darroch (2003) find that of all farmland acquired by historically disadvantaged people in KwaZulu-Natal between 1997 and 2001, private, nonmarket

transfers (mainly bequests) accounted for 16,097 hectares (13 percent), government-assisted purchases 45,121 hectares (37 percent), and private purchases (cash and mortgage loans) 60,266 hectares (50 percent). This total area of 121,484 hectares means that 2.3 percent of white-owned farmland was transferred to disadvantaged owners during those five years.

12. Lyne and Darroch argue that, for KwaZulu-Natal Province, "farmland redistributed by private market purchases . . . comfortably exceeded that redistributed by the government-assisted transactions . . . *and consisted of higher quality land* (greater weighted farmland price per hectare)" [emphasis added] (2003, p. 13).
13. Unlike the situation in such countries as Brazil, India, and Malawi, the self-selection process in South Africa lacks a strong element of oversight by communities, labor unions, and other civil society organizations, reflecting the generally low level of popular participation in the implementation of land reform in the country.
14. A specific BEE policy on agriculture—known as AgriBEE—has been in preparation for some time. It is not clear how this policy—which emphasizes share ownership, new business opportunities, and participation in management—will relate to land reform.
15. For example, labor tenants (that is, tenant farmers) in Mpumalanga, with a long history of family-based farming, have been resettled in groups on specially acquired farms, which they hold collectively in undivided shares—effectively, a forced collectivization.
16. This discussion focuses on the failure to subdivide farms after they have been acquired. However, a policy of acquiring portions of farms, in sizes appropriate to the needs of identified beneficiaries, could make the acquisition process itself much quicker and the land reform program more attractive to more people. Thus, the failure to subdivide contributes not only to postacquisition failures of production, but also to the slow pace of land transfer.
17. "An independent assessment of the report concluded that the study was not sufficiently detailed to permit the assessment that was required by DLA. The assessment also questioned the sampling procedures that were used, and the way in which these were implemented, raising the concern that the study may not be representative or sufficiently rigorous for the purposes of monitoring" (May and Roberts 2000, p. 2).
18. The research was contracted to a Cape Town-based social survey company with no experience in the land sector. Major problems were reported with sampling, with the redesign of the research instruments, and with the analysis of the data. The most worrisome aspect was the inability to locate *any of the beneficiaries* in the sample provided by DLA (Ahmed et al. 2003).
19. Some of the dimensions and outcomes of these processes are well captured in the work of Du Toit and Ally (2003) and Wegerif, Russell, and Grundling (2005).
20. A billion is 1,000 millions.

REFERENCES

Ahmed, A., Peter Jacobs, Ruth Hall, W. Kapery, R. Omar, and M. Schwartz. 2003. "Monitoring and Evaluating the Quality of Life of Land Reform Beneficiaries: 2000/2001." Technical report prepared for the Department of Land Affairs, Directorate of Monitoring and Evaluation, Pretoria.

Aliber, Michael, P. Masika, and J. Quan. 2006. "Land Reform at Scale: A Case Study of Land Redistribution in the Elliot District, Eastern Cape." Unpublished report for the National Treasury, Pretoria.

ANC (African National Congress). 1994. *The Reconstruction and Development Programme: A Policy Framework.* Johannesburg, South Africa: Umanyano.

Bradstock, Alastair. 2005. *Key Experiences of Land Reform in the Northern Cape Province of South Africa.* London: FARM-Africa.

Bundy, Colin. 1979. *The Rise and Fall of the South African Peasantry.* London: Heinemann.

CDE (Centre for Development and Enterprise). 2005. *Land Reform in South Africa. A 21st Century Perspective.* Research Report 14. Johannesburg, South Africa.

Chimhowu, Admos Osmund. 2006. "Tinkering on the Fringes? Redistributive Land Reforms and Chronic Poverty in Southern Africa." Working Paper 58. Chronic Poverty Research Centre, University of Manchester, U.K.

Claassens, Aninka. 2003. "Community Views on the Communal Land Rights Bill." Research Report 15. Programme for Land and Agrarian Studies, University of the Western Cape, Cape Town, South Africa.

Cousins, Ben. 2007. "More Than Socially Embedded: The Distinctive Character of 'Communal Tenure' Regimes in South Africa and Its Implications for Land Policy." *Journal of Agrarian Change* 7 (3): 281–315.

Deininger, Klaus, and Julian May. 2000. "Can There Be Growth with Equity? An Initial Assessment of Land Reform in South Africa." Policy Research Working Paper 2451. World Bank, Washington, DC.

Derman, Bill, Edward Lahiff, and Espen Sjaastad. 2006. "Strategic Questions about Strategic Partners: Challenges and Pitfalls in South Africa's New Model of Land Restitution." Paper presented to the Land, Memory, Reconstruction and Justice Conference, Cape Town, South Africa, September 13–15.

Du Toit, Andries, and Fadeela Ally. 2003. "The Externalisation and Casualisation of Farm Labor in Western Cape Horticulture." Research Report 16. Programme for Land and Agrarian Studies, University of the Western Cape, Cape Town, South Africa.

Farmers Weekly. 2005. "Didiza Offers Reasons for Limpopo Failures." November 18.

Government of South Africa, Department of Land Affairs. 1997. "White Paper on South African Land Policy." Pretoria.

———. 2004. "The A-Z of the Communal Land Rights Act, 2004 (Act No. 11 of 2004)." Pretoria. http://land.pwv.gov.za/tenurereform/.

———. 2006a. "Media Briefing by Minister of Agriculture and Land Affairs, Lulu Xingwana." September 7. http://land.pwv.gov.za/publications/news/press_releases/KEYMES~2.DOC.

———. 2006b. Presentation to Nedlac by Mduduzi Shabane, Deputy Director-General, Rosebank, Johannesburg, August 24.

———. 2007. *Annual Report 2006/07.* Pretoria.

Government of South Africa, Ministry of Agriculture and Land Affairs. 2003. Address by Thoko Didiza, Minister for Agriculture and Land Affairs, on the budget vote of the Department of Land Affairs, April 1. Pretoria.

———. 2005a. "Delivery of Land and Agrarian Reform." Report to the National Land Summit, Johannesburg, July 27–31.

———. 2005b. Speech by the Minister of Agriculture and Land Affairs, Thoko Didiza, to the AgriBEE Indaba, Midland, South Africa, December 6.

———. 2008. "Land and Agrarian Reform Project: Concept Document." http://www.info.gov.za/view/DownloadFileAction?id=80105 [accessed December 30, 2008].

Government of South Africa, National Department of Agriculture. 2004. "Broad-Based Black Economic Empowerment in Agriculture." AgriBEE Reference Document. July. Pretoria.

———. 2007. *Abstract of Agricultural Statistics 2007*. http://www.nda.agric.za/docs/Abstract_07.pdf [accessed December 30, 2008].

Hall, Ruth. 2003. "Farm Tenure." Evaluating Land and Agrarian Reform in South Africa Series, Report 3. Programme for Land and Agrarian Studies, University of the Western Cape, Cape Town, South Africa.

———. 2004a. "Land and Agrarian Reform in South Africa: A Status Report 2004." Research Report 20. Programme for Land and Agrarian Studies, University of the Western Cape, Cape Town, South Africa.

———. 2004b. "LRAD Rapid Systematic Assessment Survey: Nine Case Studies in the Eastern Cape." Unpublished manuscript. Programme for Land and Agrarian Studies, University of the Western Cape, Cape Town, South Africa.

———. 2005. "The National Land Summit: A Turning Point?" *Umhlaba Wethu* 4 (November). http://www.plaas.org.za/publications/newsletters/umhlaba-wethu/Umhlaba%20Wethu%204%20-%20November%202005.pdf/[accessed December 30, 2008].

Hall, Ruth, Moenieba Isaacs, and Munyaradzi Saruchera. 2004. "Land and Agrarian Reform in Integrated Development Plans: Case Studies from Selected District and Local Municipalities." Unpublished manuscript. Programme for Land and Agrarian Studies, University of the Western Cape, Cape Town, South Africa.

Hall, Ruth, Peter Jacobs, and Edward Lahiff. 2003. "Final Report." Evaluating Land and Agrarian Reform in South Africa Series, Report 10. Programme for Land and Agrarian Studies, University of the Western Cape, Cape Town, South Africa.

Hall, Ruth, and Edward Lahiff. 2004. "Budgeting for Land Reform." Policy Brief 13. Programme for Land and Agrarian Studies, University of the Western Cape, Cape Town, South Africa.

HSRC (Human Sciences Research Council). 2003. "Land Redistribution for Agricultural Development: Case Studies in Three Provinces." Unpublished manuscript. Integrated Rural and Regional Development Division, Pretoria, South Africa.

Jacobs, Peter. 2003. "Support for Agricultural Development." Evaluating Land and Agrarian Reform in South Africa Series, Report 4. Programme for Land and Agrarian Studies, University of the Western Cape, Cape Town, South Africa.

Kleinbooi, Karin, Edward Lahiff, and Tom Boyce. 2006. "Land Reform, Farm Employment and Livelihoods. Western Cape Case Study: Theewaterskloof Local Municipality." Programme for Land and Agrarian Studies, University of the Western Cape, Cape Town, South Africa, and Human Sciences Research Council, Pretoria, South Africa.

Lahiff, Edward. 2007. "State, Market or the Worst of Both? Experimenting with Market-Based Land Reform in South Africa." Occasional Paper 30. Programme for Land and Agrarian Studies, University of the Western Cape, Cape Town, South Africa.

Lyne, Michael C., and M.A.G. Darroch. 2003. "Land Redistribution in South Africa: Past Performance and Future Policy." BASIS CRSP Research Paper. Department of Agricultural and Applied Economics, University of Wisconsin-Madison.

May, Julian. 2000. "Growth, Development, Poverty and Inequality." In *Poverty and Inequality in South Africa: Meeting the Challenge*, ed. Julian May, 1–18. Cape Town, South Africa: David Philip.

May, Julian, and Benjamin Roberts. 2000. "Monitoring and Evaluating the Quality of Life of Land Reform Beneficiaries: 1998/1999. Summary Report prepared for the Department of Land Affairs." Department of Land Affairs, Pretoria, South Africa.

Mayson, David. 2003. "Joint Ventures." Evaluating Land and Agrarian Reform in South Africa Series, Report 7. Programme for Land and Agrarian Studies, University of the Western Cape, Cape Town, South Africa.

Ntsebeza, Lungisile. 2006. *Democracy Compromised: Chiefs and the Politics of the Land in South Africa.* Cape Town, South Africa: HSRC Press.

———. 2007. "Land Redistribution in South Africa: The Property Clause Revisited." In *The Land Question in South Africa: The Challenge of Transformation and Redistribution,* ed. Lungisile Ntsebeza and Ruth Hall, 107–31. Cape Town, South Africa: HSRC Press.

OECD (Organisation for Economic Co-operation and Development). 2006. *OECD Review of Agricultural Policies: South Africa.* Paris.

Seekings, Jeremy, and Nicoli Nattrass. 2005. *Class, Race, and Inequality in South Africa.* New Haven, CT: Yale University Press.

Tilley, S. 2004. "Why Do the Landless Remain Landless? An Examination of Land Acquisition and the Extent to Which the Land Market and Land Redistribution Mechanisms Serve the Needs of Land-Seeking People." Research Report. Surplus People Project, Cape Town, South Africa.

van den Brink, Rogier, Glen S. Thomas, and Hans Binswanger. 2007. "Agricultural Land Redistribution in South Africa: Towards Accelerated Implementation." In *The Land Question in South Africa: The Challenge of Transformation and Redistribution,* ed. Lungisile Ntsebeza and Ruth Hall, 152–201. Cape Town, South Africa: HSRC Press.

van den Brink, Rogier, Glen Thomas, Hans Binswanger, John Bruce, and Frank Byamugisha. 2006. *Consensus, Confusion, and Controversy: Selected Land Reform Issues in Sub-Saharan Africa.* Working Paper 71. Washington, DC: World Bank.

Vink, Nick, and Johann Kirsten. 2003. "Agriculture in the National Economy." In *The Challenge of Change: Agriculture, Land and the South African Economy,* ed. Lieb Nieuwoudt and Jan Groenewald, 3–20. Scottsville, South Africa: University of Natal Press.

Walker, Cherryl. 2003. "Piety in the Sky? Gender Policy and Land Reform in South Africa." *Journal of Agrarian Change* 3 (1-2): 111–48.

Wegerif, Marc. 2004. "A Critical Appraisal of South Africa's Market-Based Land Reform Policy: The Case of the Land Redistribution for Agricultural Development (LRAD) Program in Limpopo." Research Report 19. Programme for Land and Agrarian Studies, University of the Western Cape, Cape Town, South Africa.

Wegerif, Marc, Bev Russell, and Irma Grundling. 2005. *Summary of Key Findings from the National Evictions Survey.* Polokwane, South Africa: Nkuzi Development Association.

Williams, Gavin. 1996. "Setting the Agenda: A Critique of the World Bank's Rural Restructuring Programme for South Africa." *Journal of Southern African Studies* 22 (1): 139–67.

World Bank. 1994. "South African Agriculture: Structure, Performance and Options for the Future." Working Paper 12950. Washington, DC.

Xaba, Zanele. 2004. "Living in the Shadow of Democracy." *AFRA News* 57 (May). http://www.afra.co.za/default.asp?id=1015 [accessed December 31, 2008].

CHAPTER SEVEN

Land Reform in South Africa: Additional Data and Comments

Rogier van den Brink, Glen S. Thomas, and Hans P. Binswanger-Mkhize

The previous chapter on South Africa provided a comprehensive overview of land reform as it has been designed and implemented in that country since 1994. This chapter provides data and comments that complement the discussion in the previous chapter.[1] The topics selected here do not attempt to develop an independent line of argument; rather, they offer additional insights to interested readers.

ALARMING TRENDS IN RURAL INCOME AND AGRICULTURAL EMPLOYMENT

In addition to redressing past injustice, land reform in South Africa has the potential to improve rural incomes and employment, even though it has not yet lived up to that potential. The alarming trends in rural incomes and agricultural employment in South Africa since the political transition in 1994 only make this case more compelling.

Census data reveal that 46 percent of South Africa's population of 40.6 million people lived in rural areas in 1996—the areas where 70 percent of the country's poor people live. Despite the dramatic political, economic, and social reforms that have taken place, rural areas seem to have benefited less than urban areas from the policy changes introduced after 1994. When changes in household expenditure, poverty, and inequality between 1995 and 2000 were examined,[2] the following trends emerged: slow consumption growth (less than 1 percent per capita annually); no change in the overall poverty headcount; and increases in the poverty gap, the severity of poverty, and overall inequality. The data show a deterioration of real expenditures at the bottom end of the distribution and an improvement at the top. Because most of the poor live in rural areas, this finding implies that the rural black population is becoming more impoverished both in absolute and in relative terms.

Data on poverty trends for the period between 2000 and 2004 are limited, but most observers tend to agree that poverty has been reduced, probably as a result of the massive increases in social transfers. The declining trend also is supported by the results of the third wave of the KwaZulu-Natal Income Dynamics Study, which reports a decline in all poverty measures between 1998 and 2004 in both urban and nonurban areas (May et al. 2007).

What are the trends in agriculture? Parts of commercial agriculture responded well to the devaluation of the currency and to trade liberalization, exploiting the new opportunities for South African products abroad. Agriculture now contributes 4.5 percent to exports—a share that has been growing rapidly since the liberalization process started in the late 1980s. However, the increased export orientation was not matched by increased labor intensity of production in the sector as a whole. Employment in commercial agriculture declined from about 1.1 million in 1995 to 0.9 million in 2003 (or roughly 10 percent of total employment).[3] It is now estimated that about 1 million farm dwellers, or approximately 200,000 households, were evicted between 1994 and 2004, continuing the trend established under Apartheid.[4]

This trend needs to be reversed, given the imperative to reduce overall unemployment in South Africa (currently measured at about 30 percent). In 1993, a joint South African and World Bank team estimated that reaching the land redistribution target would cost between R 22 billion and R 26 billion[5] in total (about R 1.5–1.7 billion a year) and would create more than 1 million rural livelihoods (or the net equivalent of 600,000 full-time farm jobs at about R 35,000 per job).

Laid-off and evicted farmworkers would be an important target group for South Africa's land reform program. Even some of the unemployed urban youth, without any farm experience, will find it worth their while to join the beneficiaries of land reform and work on these new farms. Yes, a job in town is much more desirable to them; but if there are no jobs in town, working on a farm may be better than permanent unemployment in South Africa's sprawling squatter camps. In the former homelands, where about 12.7 million people—31.4 percent of South Africa's population—live,[6] subsistence farming bucked the general jobs trend and added a respectable 0.4 million livelihoods between 1995 and 2003.[7] This is all the more remarkable because of the limited potential for agriculture, low consumption growth, lack of investment (and maintenance of existing investments) in irrigation infrastructure, and poor agricultural support services. Much more can be done to promote farming in these areas, and land reform beneficiaries could be drawn from them.

EXPLOITING MULTIPLE SOURCES OF LIVELIHOOD AND PERIURBAN FARMING

Debates about land reform often assume that all new farmers should be full-time farmers. However, family farm communities the world over typically consist of households that obtain only *part* of their income from farming. For instance, the contribution from farming to the average farm household in the United States is only 11 percent, although this contribution rises to 60 percent on large family farms.[8] Land reform in South Africa should take note of such well-established international stylized facts and set as its goal the creation of both full-time *and* part-time farming livelihoods.

In the short term, creating sustainable "pluri-activity" households with only a small portion (say, up to 25 percent) of income resulting from farming is especially feasible and attractive in the periurban areas where there is a dearth of small-scale agricultural production for the informal urban markets nearby.[9] In the medium term, stimulating pluri-activity households at higher income levels and with a higher contribution from farming could be achieved in the rural areas. However, much more will be needed here in terms of support services and rural infrastructure investments to stimulate the farm and nonfarm incomes of rural households. Those investments will need to be undertaken as part of the integrated local development plans and fiscal transfer systems underpinning decentralized development in South Africa. Therefore, the main economic impact of a well-executed land reform program would come not only from a more intensive use of agricultural land, but also (perhaps more important) from the multiple livelihoods created by a more dynamic local periurban and rural economy based on a substantial increase in the number of small family farms.

ECONOMIES OF SCALE IN SOUTH AFRICAN AGRICULTURE

South Africa's farms confirm the international evidence that organizational form and the associated farm size matter (as discussed in chapter 1). Within the commercial, formerly "white" farm areas, smaller farms consistently have higher profits and employ far more labor per hectare than do large farms (Christodoulou and Vink 1990; van Zyl, Binswanger, and Thirtle 1995). It would be unfair—and virtually impossible considering the general lack of data on black farming—to compare the formerly white farming areas with the formerly black areas (the so-called homelands) because of the centuries of suppression of black farming. However, there do exist case studies in the tea and sugarcane industries that compare black small-scale farmers benefiting from support services under contract farming with their large-scale black counterparts. Those case studies confirm the higher efficiency of the small farms. Moreover, in dryland cotton, black small-scale farmers were more efficient than were white farmers, even under Apartheid (Wheeler and Ortmann 1990).

LAND REFORM OPPORTUNITIES IN ARID AND SEMIARID AREAS

In the South African context it would be easy to assume that land reform is not going to create viable new farming or enterprise units in arid and semiarid areas, and therefore that much of South Africa is unsuitable for land reform. International comparison, however, shows that South Africa does not have a higher proportion of arid and semiarid areas than, for example, do China (where small farms predominate), Mexico (where much of the land made available through land reform was in arid and semiarid areas), or northeast Brazil (where most of that country's land reform occurred). Arid and semiarid lands are excellent livestock production areas (for example, think of Texas) because of the lower risk of disease compared with more humid areas. This comparative advantage remains after land reform, but production costs can go down as a result of the lower labor supervision costs on the new family farms.

Breaking up large-scale, fenced-in ranches would improve efficiency in several other ways. First, in arid and semiarid areas, there is great variability in rainfall (and in the availability of water and fodder), which puts a premium on flexibility. The benefits of flexibility increase with rainfall variability (van den Brink, Bromley, and Chavas 1995). Given highly variable rainfall, fenced-in areas never will be large enough, forcing owners during severe droughts either to move or to sell their herds at significant costs to the household. Those costs sometimes are transferred to the surrounding areas (that is, common property is turned into open access) or are transferred to the state (special subsidies are accorded to prevent livestock prices from plummeting). Getting rid of fences, and organizing more flexible grazing systems in other ways, would increase the efficiency of production.

Second, the suppression of bushfires to protect the costly ranching infrastructure leads to so-called bush encroachment, thereby reducing the area under pasture.[10] As figure 7.1 shows, following this pattern, Namibia's commercial cattle herd has shrunk by 70 percent over 40 years. This clearly is not an efficient production system. If the lost grazing land were to be recovered, the bush-encroached areas would need to be destumped manually or mechanically. Land redistribution from large to small farmers would make available the extra labor required to destump the areas affected by bush encroachment.

Figure 7.1 Cattle Numbers in Commercial Ranch Areas, Namibia, 1958–2000

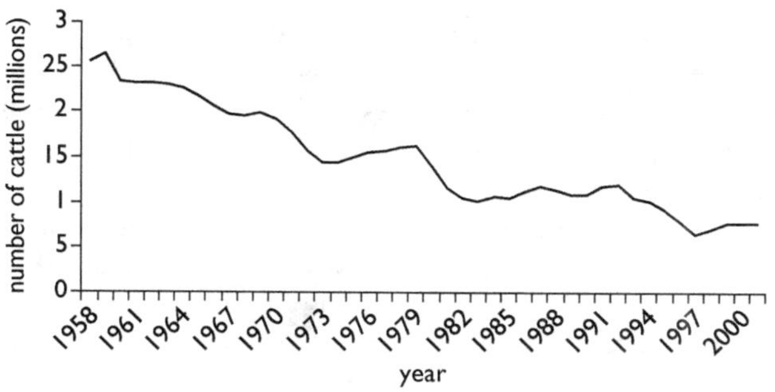

Source: de Klerk 2003, p. 20.

Third, at higher population densities, the depressions in the terrain where good soil and water accumulate will be cultivated with crops, resulting in the very beneficial interaction between crops and livestock (through the exchange of fodder and manure).

In conclusion, livestock production is characterized by the same diseconomies of scale as is crop farming, associated with farm size and the need to hire additional labor. It is true, of course, that arid lands are not very suitable for crop production and that lumpy investments to wells and pumps will tend to favor larger units. But "dryness" does not reverse the inverse farm size–productivity relationship, which is based on labor supervision costs rather than on rainfall. Furthermore, land reform in dry areas does not imply a wholesale switch from livestock to crop farming.

In summary, even though the empirical evidence for the higher efficiency of family farms in South Africa remains scarce, the existing data confirm the international evidence. There is no reason to believe that arid and semiarid areas are unsuitable for land reform, although the farm and enterprise models need to be adapted to these areas; and there is a case for land reform on efficiency grounds, including in dry areas.

NEGOTIATED TRANSFERS VERSUS EXPROPRIATION

South Africa's restitution process started in 1994 when the first law that the new democratic government passed was the Restitution of Land Rights Act. The act operationalized the clause in the constitution that allowed for the restitution of property (physically or financially) to people who had been dispossessed based on racially discriminatory laws after June 19, 1913. Initially each restitution case had to be dealt with by a specialized court—the

Land Claims Court. This requirement caused the process to slow to a trickle, with only 41 of 79,000 land claims settled between 1995 and 1999. When the act was amended to allow for an administrative, out-of-court settlement, the pace picked up dramatically. A total of 75,000 claims had been settled by September 2008.

Nevertheless, the escalation of prices in the restitution program, and the protracted and lengthy negotiation processes involved with some landowners, now have compelled the government to start using expropriation—but on a modest scale. However, the restitution legislation still has not been adapted fully to the needs of land reform, as discussed in the previous chapter. Clearly, having such an improved legal framework is a high priority for South Africa, both for restitution and for targeted land acquisition of especially desirable plots for redistribution. As the Brazilian example discussed in chapter 1 shows, effective and transparent expropriation need not lead to adverse economic consequences, such as massive capital flight. Even if better expropriation or restitution legislation is in place, an out-of-court settlement always is far easier and cheaper for all parties involved. The mechanisms for such settlements can range from mediation via nonbinding arbitration to fully binding arbitration. Expropriation should be a credible commitment that can be used in a timely manner as a last resort.

UNDERUSED FLEXIBILITY IN THE LAND REDISTRIBUTION FOR AGRICULTURAL DEVELOPMENT PROGRAM

A land redistribution program that tries to change an agrarian structure such as the one in South Africa—which is dominated completely by large farms—will need to be flexible enough to fill in a large spectrum of farm sizes. It will need to accommodate periurban gardens, medium-scale commercial farms, irrigated vegetable plots, and small livestock ranches. It will need to cater to poor, vulnerable, and marginalized groups as well as to emerging commercial farmers.

The design of the Land Redistribution for Agricultural Development (LRAD) program attempts to incorporate such flexibility, both by offering a sliding scale of grants and by allowing projects to allocate more or less to land acquisition and more or less to agricultural development of that land. Although purely residential projects are not supported under LRAD (rather, they are supported by the Settlement/Land Acquisition Grant [SLAG]), beneficiaries seeking to establish household gardens at their new residences can be supported by LRAD. In addition, beneficiaries can use the LRAD grant to participate in so-called equity schemes and become shareholders in existing agricultural enterprises. Farmworkers can use LRAD to participate in employee-ownership enterprises. Other beneficiaries enter LRAD to engage in commercial agricultural activities, accessing the grant and combining it with normal bank loans approved under standard banking procedures and their own assets and cash to purchase a farm. Finally, although many people living in communal areas already have secure access to agricultural land, they may not have the means to make productive use of that land. Those people would be eligible to apply for assistance to formalize their tenure and make productive investments in their land.

Initial fears that LRAD had abandoned the poor are unfounded. The self-selection using the sliding scale of grants seems to have been effective in reaching poor people as well as emerging farmers. Women and youth also are participating effectively in the program. The distribution of the number of grants (figure 7.2) and the total value of transfers approved by the provincial offices follow a distribution in favor of the poor.[11]

Both LRAD and SLAG experienced slow starts, as systems were being developed and officials were becoming familiar with the implementation procedures. But both programs also demonstrated their ability rapidly to accelerate land transfers in subsequent years.

SALES OF PARCELS BY DEVELOPERS

There is likely to be a number of beneficiaries who would prefer individual acquisition to acquisition as members of communities. For such beneficiaries, developers could be encouraged to acquire farms on the market (or from the state as a result of compulsory acquisition) for subsequent subdivision and development. Although that approach often is discussed as an option for land redistribution, we are not aware of actual experience with it, and therefore we suggest the developer model be tried first on a pilot basis.

Figure 7.2 Distribution of LRAD Grants by Size of Grant, FY2001–FY2002

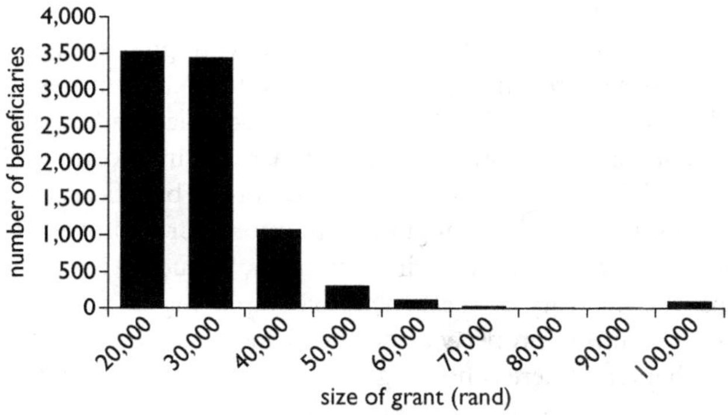

Source: Data from the Department of Land Affairs.

INADEQUATE DECENTRALIZATION AND COMMUNITY EMPOWERMENT

Many land redistribution programs in the world are hampered by very bureaucratic and slow approaches to resettling farmers once land has been acquired. Centralized planning and execution of individual land reform projects, whether by a single line ministry or a dedicated parastatal, invariably have slowed the process to a snail's pace. Centralizing all aspects of land reform into specialized land agencies usually has not been able to speed up the process, as examples from Colombia, Honduras, Mexico, and the Philippines show. Instead, these one-stop land reform shops have spawned costly and paternalistic bureaucracies. As an alternative, several ministries have to work closely together—an effort that also is very difficult to coordinate.

The implementation of both SLAG and LRAD has been constrained by excessive centralization, lack of community empowerment, and overreliance on consultants. SLAG adopted an implementation strategy under which each project needed the approval of the minister of land affairs. That approval, in turn, would be based largely on a perusal of farm and business plans drawn up by consultants hired by the ministry. As a result, the program was extremely slow in taking off and reaching significant numbers, and it became consultant driven. Many of the business plans may have looked quite compelling on paper, but they were not "owned" or even understood by the beneficiaries themselves. Under LRAD, project approval was delegated from the minister at the national level to the provinces—the main factor explaining its faster delivery. LRAD started in 2001, but by late 2002 several provinces had exhausted their budgets in the middle of the fiscal year. Until 2006 the program remained severely budget constrained. Lack of community empowerment and difficulties in providing postsettlement support continue to this day. For instance, the current design of the land purchase, agricultural support, and housing developments in separate "silo" programs—each with its own application procedures and timetables—creates insurmountable coordination problems.

The programs also sideline their beneficiaries. Government is reluctant to allow beneficiaries to manage much of the land reform process themselves, even though doing so has proven successful in several other countries, including a much less developed country like Malawi. Instead, officials and consultants enter bilateral agreements during project preparation, sometimes completely marginalizing the beneficiaries. Government officials, not the beneficiaries, present the project proposal to the provincial grant committees for approval. Even though beneficiaries are free to choose their legal entity, including individual title on subdivisions, the majority of the beneficiaries applying as a group have been steered toward common property associations and trusts, even under LRAD. As discussed in chapter 1, there is nothing inherently problematic with these forms of ownership, but one would expect a much wider variety of legal entities if beneficiaries truly were empowered to make there own decisions.

Community empowerment is inadequate not only in the project design phase; communities also are not allowed to implement their own projects. Community procurement of goods and services is not permitted under the program; rather, all procurement has to be undertaken by the government, from selection of design agents, technical advisers, and trainers to purchase of agricultural inputs, such as seeds and fertilizers or plowing services. The lack of community procurement has constrained the flexibility of beneficiaries to make their own choices, and thereby has disempowered them. Because government departments simply do not have the capacity to deal with hundreds or thousands of procurements at the same time, this centralized approach also has made scaling up the program very difficult, if not impossible.

The lessons learned so far during the implementation of LRAD- and SLAG-supported projects suggest that flexibility in design rarely has resulted in flexibility in practice. This rigidity not only slows implementation, but also results in projects for which the beneficiaries feel no ownership, and that explains much of the poor production performance of the transferred farms.

LARGE-SCALE FARMERS' OPPOSITION TO LAND REFORM

South Africa today has a relatively favorable agricultural policy environment for land reform. After the political transition in 1994, South Africa liberalized agricultural marketing and reduced most commercial farm subsidies to very low levels in one of the most complete agricultural liberalizations in the world.

Other restrictions remain, however, demonstrating the considerable political power of the large-farm lobby in South Africa. One can hardly find a better demonstration of the strength of that lobby than the fact that South Africa has not abolished its anti-subdivision law, and has only partly relaxed the subdivision rules, with the resulting adverse impacts on land reform that were discussed in chapter 6.

Why is there still so much opposition to land reform? If there were uncertainties about compensation, opposition of the farm lobby to land reform would be understandable and rational. Such uncertainties would present personal financial risk and would influence expectations, thus immediately reducing land prices. However, there is another reason for the opposition by large-scale farmers to land reform: a reluctance to integrate poorer black neighbors into a less racially integrated farm community. Instead of viewing integrated rural communities as providing increased long-term security, parts of the white farming community in Southern Africa view an influx of black families as a cause for more insecurity. Some of these farmers whose lands border the former homelands have experienced theft and vandalism.

Political theory and history suggest that these anti–land reform lobbies may switch strategy only when they perceive that a large-scale land reform program is the price they have to pay for peace. Unfortunately, by then the situation already may have deteriorated to such an extent that an "orderly" land reform program is impossible, as the example of Zimbabwe so amply shows.

LAND REFORM FUNDING

International experience shows that a sound financing plan must rest first on a country's own fiscal resources. In South Africa's case, the prospects look good. Based on estimates of present budget trends, South Africa's fiscal support for land reform is increasing significantly. In the current three-year national budget, the FY2007/08 land reform budget rises to R 5.7 billion. If we assume that this level of financing is not reduced until 2014 (the year by which the 30 percent target needs to be reached), a cumulative budget of R 56.0 billion will be available for land reform. Estimates of the total costs based on current land reform costs per hectare put the total around R 35.0 billion. As explained above, however, in the current program the nonland costs are underfunded. Another way of demonstrating that the projected fiscal resources for land reform seem about right is to start with the value of commercial farm assets and then take 30 percent of that value—about R 30 billion.[12] That value constitutes more than just the land because it also includes houses, buildings, and fixed improvements.

The adverse consequences of inadequate funding are severe, including slowing program implementation, creating strong political resistance among the landowning classes, and undermining the settlers' chances of success—consequences we already have seen in South Africa. Adequate funding by government, however, can be used to leverage additional financing by beneficiaries (enabling them to borrow safely and increase their productivity), donors, and landowners. Fortunately, South Africa's current land reform budget trends put the national targets within reach. International experience shows that an effective partnership with stakeholders can be built on the basis of this commitment.

RECOMMENDATIONS

We suggest four areas for improvement, based on the assessment made above. First, rather than trying to opt for the "best" way of acquiring land, put in place several operational options that can be implemented effectively as circumstances require. Second, put a stop to the proliferation of centralized, supply-driven silos. Because of the complexity it creates, this proliferation is undermining the implementation capacity of all parties concerned. Third, reestablish accountability in the system—accountability seriously undermined by the same proliferation of programs and beneficiaries' lack of decision-making power. And fourth, do more to create the type of partnerships that may "agree to disagree" on certain issues, but nonetheless work together on the ground to achieve the objective shared by all: a successful land reform program.

Create a Choice of Land Acquisition Methods

The overall land reform policy objective should be to have a ready set of complementary land acquisition methods that have been tested and are operational. If the government prefers to use negotiated approaches and market-assisted and community-driven land acquisition approaches, it still will be necessary to have a flexible and tested expropriation tool available to give government an alternative option when negotiations fail. As discussed previously, having options is particularly important in the case of restitution. Being able to use both a market-assisted and an expropriation option sometimes is referred to as the "sandwich" or "carrot-and-stick" approach. The improved policy framework thus would consist of a package of at least three options for land acquisition: compulsory acquisition, market-assisted or community-driven land acquisition, and negotiated land transfer. In addition, the government should promote the testing of a developer model capable of delivering right-size farms to individual beneficiaries.

In implementing compulsory acquisition pilot projects, the government could test—and improve on—the Expropriation Act of 1975, ensuring that it is consistent with the constitution. It also is advisable to find a legal mechanism that transfers ownership directly, or almost directly, from the former owner to the beneficiaries and avoids a span of time during which the state has to ensure the security of the asset "in transit."

Unify the Grant System, Decentralize Decision Making, and Empower Beneficiaries

Whatever land acquisition method is used, much can be done to redistribute and resettle land in a faster and less bureaucratic way. The first imperative is to unify the separate grant systems for project planning, land acquisition, farm development, and housing into a single grant that, combined with additional credit and beneficiary contributions in cash or in kind, covers the entire cost of fully developing the new farm. The other imperative is to decentralize the support and decision-making process at least to the level of the district municipality.

In a unified and decentralized grant and implementation system, beneficiaries of restitution and redistribution should have much more say in the way in which resettlement—*their resettlement*—is carried out. They should be in charge of farm planning, of choosing all needed inputs, and of selecting service providers. Why not let beneficiaries choose who helps them plan the farm, provides access roads, ensures water supply, and so on—for example, by giving them the financial resources to procure these factors themselves? Government ministries can provide such services, but there may be private sector providers or nongovernmental organizations (NGOs) that can deliver them at a lower cost and more efficiently. Why not provide much more flexibility in getting this done? Why not permit and encourage much more decentralization and community participation? Why not allow for much more private sector and NGO involvement? Why not define national standards and procedures for how this should be done, but decentralize implementation and supervision to the local level?

In South Africa, land reform and many other development programs that try to deliver services in a decentralized fashion suffer from the prohibition on community procurement that the Public Financial Management Act of 1998 seems to have created. The Municipal Finance Act explicitly allows for community procurement, however, and the Department of Land Affairs now has issued guidelines that permit community procurement in land reform projects. Under these guidelines, communities will be able to manage resources directly, following such simple and transparent rules as gathering three quotes before making purchases and documenting their democratic decision making.

Strengthen Accountability

Central ministries frequently resist decentralization on the grounds of transparency and accountability. It often is felt that vertical accountability to a strong center reduces opportunities for collusion and corruption with regard to the selection of beneficiaries, the farm price, and the procurement and allocation of goods and services. Decentralization speeds up decision making, but indeed could lead to more corruption if the more limited "vertical accountability" is not supplemented by more "horizontal" and "downward" accountability. Horizontal accountability should be to the beneficiaries themselves in the first instance, and be supplemented by additional stakeholder participation (both government and nongovernment) in the decision-making process.

As vertical accountability is relaxed, horizontal and downward accountability and integration between programs should be strengthened. All land reform programs should be channeled through the same screening and approval processes. Those processes should be managed by local-level multisectoral committees that allow for stakeholder participation. The land reform programs then can become integral parts of the local development plans, which in South Africa are the basis for local development budgeting and implementation. District land reform committees could be constituted as subcommittees of the district councils.

Strengthen the National Implementation Strategy

At this point, a broad-based consensus is emerging among the various stakeholders that South Africa needs to solve its land question as a matter of urgency. What government needs to do now is build on this emerging consensus and involve stakeholders in a dialogue on policy implementation. Stakeholders, including local government structures, farmers' associations, NGOs, and churches, can assist in a number of ways. They can identify urgent land needs, support beneficiaries in accessing the various land reform programs, and provide technical assistance as needed by the beneficiaries. NGOs and research institutions can perform valuable monitoring and evaluation services and assist in policy improvement. An emerging consensus should be captured in an implementation strategy that has widespread support.

NOTES

1. The data and comments presented in this chapter are drawn from van den Brink, Thomas, and Binswanger (2007).
2. Analysis of the changes used comparable consumption aggregates from the income and expenditure surveys.
3. One explanation for this trend is as follows: In the commercial farm areas (86 percent of the total area), the legacy of Apartheid often strains labor relations. Expanding agriculture means expanding the labor force, and that is accompanied by increased supervision problems—not a preferred option for many white farmers. The commercial farmers' expectations that the post-1994 government would provide increased protection against the eviction of labor tenants and farmworkers often resulted in their preemptive expulsion. These expectations proved to be true; and although exact numbers are not available, anecdotal evidence suggests that the eviction of labor tenants and farmworkers has been quite dramatic.
4. Briefing to the Parliamentary Portfolio Committee for Agriculture and Land Affairs by the Nkuzi Development Association and Social Surveys Africa, August 30, 2005. The estimate is a national extrapolation based on a random sample of 300 communities and 7,759 households.
5. A billion is 1,000 millions.
6. The data come from Statistics South Africa's 1997 rural survey.
7. The data come from the annual October Household Survey/Labor Force Survey of Statistics South Africa.
8. These data come from the Web site of the U.S. Department of Agriculture, http://www.ers.usda.gov/Briefing/FarmIncome/forenew.htm. In 2003, a large family farm was defined as one with farm sales between $250,000 and $499,999.
9. The absence of such high-intensity, small-scale farming "rings" around all of South Africa's cities is the direct result of Apartheid in the past, and the continued restrictions on subdivision and absence of a land tax (leading to unused periurban land for speculative reasons) in the present.
10. The suppression of fire has had similar negative effects on the ecology of the prairie grasslands of North America (Licht 1997).
11. During FY2001/02 and FY2002/03, the average grant per beneficiary was R 27,696—only about R 7,500 above the minimum grant—while the distribution of grants administered by the Department of Land Affairs followed a pro-poor pattern. The pattern for the Land Bank–administered grants showed that the prospective farmers targeted by the Land Bank benefited from a higher average grant, consistent with the bank's targeting objective.
12. The value of total commercial farm assets in 2002 was R 98.4 billion; and 30 percent of that is R 30.0 billion (see http://www.statssa.gov.za/publications/Report-11-02-01/CorrectedReport-11-02-01.pdf). To put that number in perspective: current annual spending on social welfare is R 73.0 billion.

REFERENCES

Christodoulou, Nicholas T., and Nick Vink. 1990. "The Potential for Black Smallholder Farmers' Participation in the South African Agricultural Economy." Paper presented at the Newick Park Initiative's Conference on Land Reform and Agricultural Development in South Africa, October, United Kingdom.

de Klerk, J. N. 2003. *Bush Encroachment in Namibia: Report on Phase 1 of the Bush Encroachment Research, Monitoring and Management Project.* Windhoek, Namibia: Ministry of Environment and Tourism. http://www.met.gov.na/programmes/napcod/encroachment.htm [accessed February 14, 2009].

Licht, Daniel S. 1997. *Ecology and Economics of the Great Plains.* Lincoln: University of Nebraska Press.

May, Julian, Jorge Agüero, Michael Carter, and Ian Timaeus. 2007. "The KwaZulu-Natal Income Dynamics Study (KIDS) 3rd Wave: Methods, First Findings and an Agenda for Future Research." *Development Southern Africa* 24 (5): 629–48.

van den Brink, Rogier, Daniel W. Bromley, and Jean-Paul Chavas. 1995. "The Economics of Cain and Abel: Agro-pastoral Property Rights in the Sahel." *Journal of Development Studies* 31 (3): 373–99.

van den Brink, Rogier, Glen S. Thomas, and Hans Binswanger. 2007. "Agricultural Land Redistribution in South Africa: Towards Accelerated Implementation." In *The Land Question in South Africa: The Challenge of Transformation and Redistribution,* ed. Lungisile Ntsebeza and Ruth Hall, 152–201. Cape Town, South Africa: HSRC Press.

van Zyl, Johan, Hans Binswanger, and Colin Thirtle. 1995. "The Relationship between Farm Size and Efficiency in South African Agriculture." Policy Research Working Paper 1548. World Bank, Washington, DC.

Wheeler, M. W., and G. F. Ortmann. 1990. "Socio-economic Factors Determining the Success Achieved among Cotton-Adopting Households in Two Magisterial Districts of Kwa-Zulu." *Development Southern Africa* 7 (3): 323–33.

CHAPTER EIGHT

Land Redistribution in the Philippines

Saturnino M. Borras, Jr.

One of the most important causes of persistent poverty in the Philippines has been the peasants' and rural workers' lack of control over land resources. The preexisting agrarian structure in the Philippines has shaped the character of political power distribution in society and state, and has provoked periodic peasant upheavals (see Kerkvliet 1977; Putzel 1992; Boyce 1993; Putzel 1995; Aguilar 1998; Anderson 1998; Rutten 2000). A combination of repression, resettlement, and limited reform has been the traditional way in which the elites and the state have responded to these cycles of peasant mobilization and revolt (Abinales 2000). None of those reforms significantly addressed the underlying cause of peasant unrest—rural poor people's widespread lack of control over land. As a result, unrest remained an important part of rural politics throughout the 20th century.

By the late 1980s, the distribution of agricultural lands[1] was extremely skewed. In 1988, the Gini coefficient for landownership distribution was calculated by Putzel at 0.64 (1992, pp. 27, 29).[2] That year, more than a third of the agricultural land was owned by about 25,000 individuals—a mere 1.6 percent

This chapter draws on the author's article published in the *Journal of Agrarian Change* (Borras 2006a) and, more generally, on the author's recent book (Borras 2007). I thank the publishers of those works (Blackwell and the University of Ottawa Press) for allowing me to revise from those works for the current publication. I thank the editors of this volume as well as an anonymous reviewer for their helpful comments.

of the total number of landowners (see figure 8.1). In contrast, another third of the agricultural land was owned by about 1,341,000 individuals—86.3 percent of the total number of owners. Seventy-five percent of these smallholders each owned an area of less than 3 hectares.

After 1986, the regime transition opened new political opportunities for partial democratization that led to a heated policy debate on agrarian reform. After initially dragging its feet on the issue, the administration of Corazón Aquino was forced to act on peasants' demands for land reform. In 1988, the Philippines initiated the Comprehensive Agrarian Reform Program (CARP), under which approximately 8.1 million hectares of agricultural land were to be redistributed over 10 years. (See box 8.1 for a discussion of CARP's budget and timeframes.) Objectives have been revised since then, and the reform was extended by 10 years. By 2004, two out of every five people were poor, and three-quarters of the poor were rural poor (ADB 2005). Needless to say, the outcomes of this reform are highly contested.

This chapter presents CARP's basic features, including its main objectives, institutional framework, and land transfer mechanism. It also discusses the dynamics of its implementation process and, notably, the fundamental role that social movements play in it. Finally, it presents the overall outcomes of the program and explains why there is so much controversy around their interpretation.

Figure 8.1 Concentration of Agricultural Landownership, 1988

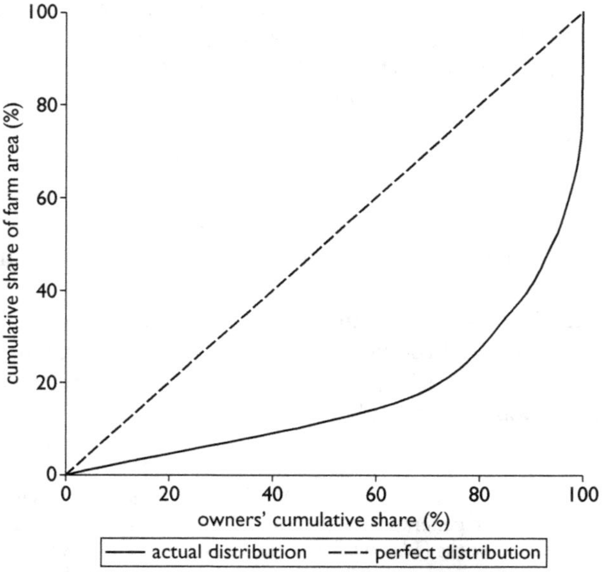

Source: Putzel (1992, p. 29), based on "Listasaka I: Final Report on Landholders Registration by Regions as of July 18 1988."

Box 8.1 CARP's Budgets and Timeframes

The Philippines Comprehensive Agrarian Reform Program (CARP) was given a fund of ₱50 billion[1] in 1988, and its charge was to finish the land acquisition and distribution components within 10 years' time (by 1998). All proceeds of the government's effort to recover the so-called ill-gotten wealth of Ferdinand Marcos and his cronies were supposed to be transferred automatically to the CARP fund, supplementing its regular fund allocation from the General Appropriations Act. By the end of 1997, it was clear that the program would not be completed within the time allotted. After a series of complex political events, a new law was passed that extended the implementation period for another 10 years, or until 2008, with a new budget cap of ₱50 billion.

1. A billion is 1,000 millions.

KEY FEATURES OF CARP

While landlessness, poverty, and exploitation have marked the condition of the rural poor since the colonial era (under both Spanish and American rule), peasant revolts and overt peasant collective actions have occurred in an uneven manner marked by periodic ebb and flow. The elite response to peasant unrest traditionally has been a combination of repression, cooptation, resettlement, and limited land and tenancy reforms. There have been several dozen such periods in the past, with the peasants gaining only intermittent concessions from the state. None of the past tenancy and land reform programs significantly addressed rural poor people's widespread lack of control over land—an important part of Filipino rural politics throughout the past century. The most important peasant-based revolution since World War II has been the insurgency led by the Communist Party of the Philippines, together with its armed wing, the New People's Army.

The transition from an authoritarian regime to a "national clientilist electoral regime" in 1986 did not lead to complete democratization of the countryside. Even now, entrenched political elites continue to dominate the rural polity, although in recent years there has been some erosion of these rural "local authoritarian enclaves" in a political process that can be traced back mainly to two factors: the series of highly constrained elections held during and immediately after the period of authoritarian rule, and sustained social mobilization "from below" (Franco 2001). But the regime transition opened new political opportunities for a partial democratization that led to a heated policy debate on agrarian reform. The Aquino administration was forced to act on peasants' demands for land reform, and the subsequent land reform policy-making process led to the passage of CARP (Hayami, Quisumbing, and Adriano 1990; Lara and Morales 1990; Putzel 1992; Riedinger 1995).

Basic Principles and Objectives

CARP was introduced in 1988 with the three major official goals: (1) social justice or equity in terms of access to, use of, and control of land; (2) an increase in productivity and income; and (3) development of beneficiaries into self-reliant farmers, using a variety of instruments. The program intends to achieve those objectives through three broad types of reform: (1) redistribution of private and public lands, (2) leasehold reform (including leasehold on lands legally retained by landlords and stewardship contracts for some public lands) on a small scale and limited to the first few years of CARP implementation, and (3) stock distribution for some large commercial farms.

Based on the original 1988 scope, CARP intended to reform tenure relations on 10.3 million hectares of the country's farmland through land redistribution (and to a limited extent, stock distribution), reaching an estimated 4 million landless and land-poor peasant households (close to 80 percent of the agricultural population). Additionally, some 2 million hectares of farms smaller than 5 hectares (farms retained by landlords) were made subject to leasehold reform that would benefit an estimated 1 million poor tenant households. Though landlords had the right to retain 5 hectares, they also could hold 3 hectares for each legitimate heir on the condition that any such heir should be 15 years of age by June 1988 and willing to work directly on or manage the farm. It should be noted that the average farm size in the country is 2 hectares, and the land reform award ceiling is fixed at 3 hectares. This 1988 land redistribution scope, however, was reduced over time through a series of legal-technical and administrative reasons that have since been questioned by observers (Borras 2003). By 2006, the land redistribution scope was down to 8.0 million hectares, from its original 10.3 million hectares, effectively removing an estimated 1 million peasant households from the list of potential land reform beneficiaries (Borras 2003).

Institutional Framework

More than 20 state agencies, large and small, are directly involved in land redistribution processes for different purposes. Private lands and some government-owned lands are redistributed by the Department of Agrarian Reform (DAR), whereas redistribution of public alienable and disposable lands and forest lands under the Community-Based Forest Management (CBFM) program is implemented by the Department of Environment and Natural Resources (DENR). Within the DAR bureaucracy, various bureaus are involved at different levels in land reform implementation. These bureaus are of three broad types: quasi-judicial, policy, and executive. The quasi-judicial body is the DAR Adjudication Board, which functions as the main adjudicator of legal cases related to agrarian disputes. The board has representatives at the regional and provincial levels, the regional adjudicator and the provincial adjudicator, respectively. Among other legal cases, the Adjudication Board handles disputes about just compensation, although a landlord can opt to apply to a Special Agrarian Court (SAC) for such appeals. SAC is a special arm directly linked with the regular courts; a SAC judge is a regular court judge. DAR decisions on agrarian disputes can be appealed to the Office of the President, and decisions made there can be appealed to the Supreme Court. (See box 8.2 for further discussion of agrarian dispute resolution.) But the CARP law states that the land acquisition and distribution process can proceed despite pending appeals by landlords. The processes of land value assessment, compensation to landlords, and amortization payments by peasants are handled by the government-owned Land Bank of the Philippines. Meanwhile, the highest oversight, policy-related body for CARP is the Presidential Agrarian Reform

Box 8.2 Occurrence and Resolution of Agrarian Conflicts

There are two broad types of agrarian disputes: the "application cases" and the "implementation cases." Application cases, handled by the Department of Agrarian Reform (DAR) Adjudication Board include disputes regarding land valuation, preliminary determination and payment of just compensation, definition and collection of lease rentals, disturbance compensation, and amortization payments, among others. Implementation cases, under the jurisdiction of the DAR executive arm, include conflicts over classification and identification of landholdings for coverage under the Comprehensive Agrarian Reform Program (CARP), exercise of the right of retention by landowners, applications for exemption, and other matters strictly involving the administrative implementation of CARP. A full list of the nature and handling of agrarian disputes can be found in the table in the annex. The incidence of agrarian disputes has increased over time, in general, and particularly during the Fidel Ramos administration (1994–98) (see figure). Not only did agrarian conflict substantially increase during that period (which is known as the "reformist period"), but the resolution rate improved as well. Between 1988 and 1992, only 45 percent of the cases reported (15,302) to the DAR Adjudication Board were resolved. By contrast, from July 1992 to the end of 1997, almost eight times more cases were filed (117,487) and 95 percent were resolved. The board apparently improved its conflict resolution mechanisms over time. The higher case resolution rate, despite the increased number of legal cases, shows that a mutually reinforcing reformist alliance between state actors "from above" and autonomous rural social movements' actions "from below" can overcome even the most difficult legal and administrative obstacles put up by resistant landlords.

(*continued*)

Box 8.2 (Continued)

Number of Agrarian Cases Resolved Per Year, 1988–2000

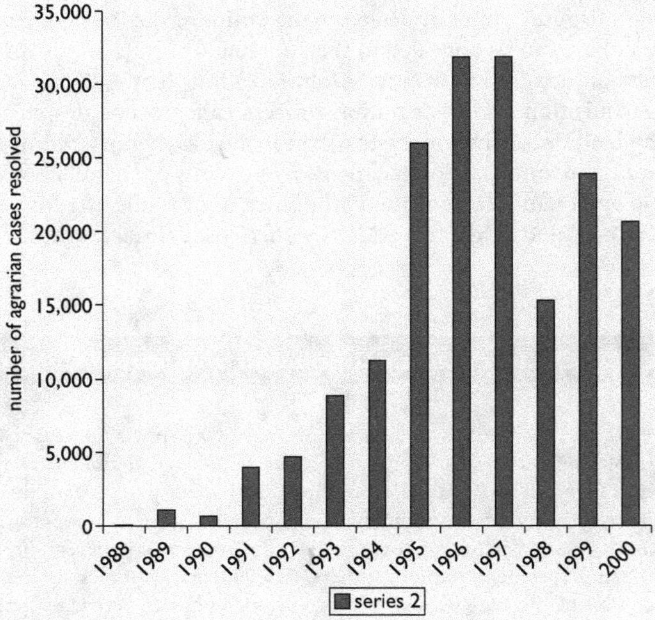

Source: Franco 2005, pp. 15–16.

Council (PARC), a multiagency and multisectoral body formally headed by the President of the Republic. PARC is anchored at the DAR and comprises all of CARP's implementing agencies, with representation of the landlord group and the peasant sector. It functions as a consultative council at the national level. At the provincial level, PARC takes the form of the Provincial Agrarian Reform Consultative Committee; at the village level, it is the *Barangay* Agrarian Reform Committee. In 1994, PARC's Audit Management and Investigation Committee was created to conduct annual comprehensive internal program audits. The bulk of implementation tasks, however, rests with the main executive body of the DAR, headed by the department secretary, down through the regional directors, provincial agrarian reform officers, municipal agrarian reform officers, to the lowest-ranked employee, the agrarian reform program technician. There are 15,000 DAR employees nationwide.

Land Targeting

The CARP law mandates that all private and public farmlands, regardless of tenurial and productivity conditions, be subject to agrarian reform. The program contains a number of exclusions, however; among them are military reservations, penal colonies, educational and research fields, timberlands, and some church areas. "Undeveloped" hills with a slope of 18 degrees or more also are excluded. In the mid-1990s, further exemptions were introduced, namely, agricultural sectors that are "significantly less dependent on land" (for example, poultry, livestock, salt beds, and fishponds). But these exemptions are not automatic. The owners of these lands must be able to demonstrate at all times that the lands indeed are used for the purposes cited. For cattle ranches, a ratio of one head for every hectare of land must be upheld; otherwise, the land will be expropriated and redistributed. These farms also are compelled by law to implement labor-related reforms, including compulsory production and profit sharing.

Landholdings under the control of government also are subject to redistribution; they include (1) previously private lands that have been foreclosed by various government financial institutions; (2) public lands earlier segregated and earmarked for the Marcos livelihood program, *Kilusang Kabuhayan at Kaunlaran;* (3) the remainder of the friar lands (landed estates); and (4) public lands set aside for settlement programs before and after the CARP law was enacted. Finally, other public lands under different legal classifications can be distributed via DENR's alienable and disposable lands and CBFM programs (Borras 2006b).

Some related acquisition and distribution policies and mechanisms are important to note. For one, the stock distribution option (allowed during the first few years of CARP implementation) is a distinct mode designed for very large corporate farms. CARP exempts such lands from redistribution if the owner opts for corporate stock sharing with peasant beneficiaries through the option. Moreover, in 1988 the acquisition of other large commercial/corporate farms, specifically banana and rubber plantations, was deferred for a 10-year period, ostensibly to allow plantation owners to recoup their investments and to prepare farmworkers for their eventual takeover (Borras and Franco 2005). During this deferment period, the plantation owners were compelled by law to implement production and profit-sharing schemes. Under certain conditions, peasant beneficiaries are allowed to lease back awarded lands to an investor. Acquired landholdings can be transferred to individuals or cooperatives, although the bias is to the former (de la Rosa 2005).

Transfer Mechanisms

During implementation, CARP has been brought to the crucible of state-society relations, where various dynamic factors influence policy processes and outcomes. The implementation process has been a tale of struggle between the advocates for voluntary transfer and for compulsory transfer. The four land acquisition mechanisms for private lands reflect this conflict internalized within CARP:

1. *Compulsory acquisition*—This is the mechanism by which land is acquired with or without the landlord's consent. Compensation is based on "just compensation." For the land, it generally is interpreted at slightly below the market value. Valuation is based on various criteria, such as land productivity and tax declaration. Landowners receive 30 percent of the compensation in cash. The other 70 percent is disbursed in equal payments over 10 years at an interest rate equal to the prevailing 91-day treasury bill rate. When land has been acquired by the state, it is redistributed to the peasant recipients, who pay for the land parcels at rates determined by "affordability." Government subsidizes the difference between the cost of acquisition and the price beneficiaries can afford to pay. Beneficiaries are issued Certificates of Land Ownership Award. Beneficiaries of the CBFM program receive stewardship contracts that are good for 25 years and are renewable for another 25 years. Beneficiaries of the public alienable and disposable land program can secure similar instruments, free patents, or Certificates of Land Ownership Award, depending on the actual condition of the land transferred to them. Awarded landholdings cannot be sold or rented out by the beneficiary for 10 years after the award. CBFM beneficiaries do not have to pay for the awarded lands. If uncontested, compulsory acquisition can be completed within a year. When contested, however, it drags on for years.
2. *Operation and transfer*—This mechanism was used for tenanted rice and corn lands under the Marcos-era land reform program, and later integrated into CARP. The process is the same as that in compulsory acquisition, with some differences in the bases for computing the value of the land. These differences generally result in lower land prices for rice and corn lands, compared with lands dedicated to other crops.
3. *Voluntary offer to sell*—This mechanism was devised to reduce landlord resistance to reform and to expedite the transfer process. With this mechanism, the up-front cash payment of landlord's compensation is increased by 5 percent, with a corresponding 5 percent decrease in the bonds portion. Land transfer can be fast (about a year), but in many cases it is actually prolonged (Borras 2005; de la Rosa 2005; Borras, Carranza, and Franco 2007). Voluntary offer to sell operates in the context of expropriation; that is, if a landlord is unwilling to sell his or her estate, it can be expropriated.
4. *Voluntary land transfer*—In the same vein as the voluntary offer to sell, the voluntary land transfer aspires to court landlord cooperation. By this mechanism, land is transferred directly from the landlords to the peasants. Terms of the transfer are mutually agreed by peasants and landlords, with the

government's role confined to providing information and enforcing contracts. Landlords and beneficiaries directly discuss and negotiate the transaction terms (that is, land price, mode of payment, and set of beneficiaries). When full agreement is reached, the parties submit a proposal to the DAR, which approves or rejects the plan. If the proposal is rejected, the process has to be reinitiated. Depending on the case, the DAR then may take the expropriation route.

Skepticism among Academics and Activists

Critics of CARP—academics and activists—predicted that no significant redistribution of land would be achieved through the program because of its various flaws. Among the key criticisms are the following: (1) the 5-hectare retention limit is too high and will exempt a substantial portion of agricultural lands, (2) the additional 3-hectare award for every qualified heir of the landlord will exempt more lands from redistribution, (3) the adoption of the principle of just compensation essentially means full market price and thus will make the program unaffordable for the government and beneficiaries, (4) the inclusion of the stock distribution option as an alternative for landlords effectively will exclude large corporate farms from reform, (5) the leaseback option will facilitate awarded lands reverting to landlords, and (6) the deferment of the land acquisition and distribution process on large commercial farms will give plantation owners a way to evade land reform eventually. Such criticisms are firmly grounded in concrete analysis of the historical political and economic conditions of the country. However, there were important CARP processes and outcomes, especially during the short-lived but reformist 1993–2000 period, that were unanticipated by earlier critics.

CARP IMPLEMENTATION DYNAMICS

This section discusses the role of social movements and state–civil society interaction in the implementation of land reform.

The Role of Social Movements

As most studies on peasant behavior in the Philippines and elsewhere have concluded, it is not landlessness and poverty per se that prompt peasants to mobilize and eventually revolt against landlords and governments. Rather, the spark to revolt is caused by the deep feeling and realization at given points in time that injustice committed against them has reached an intolerable level, as in the numerous uprisings during the Spanish era, in the 1930s, the 1950s, and the 1970s (see Scott 1976).

The emergence and availability of allies has been a crucial factor determining whether the rural poor engage in covert collective actions or even revolt.

Allies can come in the form of charismatic people who become leaders; on most occasions these leaders are from the peasant class but have urban and/or higher educational exposure, or they might come from the middle class and have sympathy with the rural poor. Sympathetic political parties are other typical allies for the peasants—for example, the communist parties in the 1930s, 1970s, and 1980s. At times and under certain conditions, progressive elements within churches can be crucial allies to peasants—for example, there was widespread church-based effort to organize the rural poor in the 1960s and 1970s. Since the 1980s, the emergence and proliferation of various types of progressive nongovernmental organizations (NGOs)—local community-based organizations, national policy think tanks, and international donors—have provided the rural poor a pool of allies. Broader alliances, either sectoral or multisectoral, have been important allies for peasants, especially those organized in local and singular associations. Such alliances have provided the vertical and horizontal links necessary to extend the political reach of peasants' collective actions. Some examples of these coalitions are the alliances between peasant associations and trade unions in the 1930s, and ideologically broad national coalitions like the Congress for a People's Agrarian Reform in the late 1980s and early 1990s, and the Partnership for Agrarian Reform and Rural Development Services from the 1990s onward.

Grievances around and demands for land and tenancy reforms generally have been centralized within the state. State laws increasingly have become the defining parameter within which grievances are voiced and collective actions launched. Hence, the Filipino state has become an important arena within which such grievances are partly defined and where different social classes and interest groups debate with, compete against, or coalesce with each other to influence or control the state and its public policies. Therefore, decisions made by peasants and their allies on the type of actions to engage in (overt or covert, armed or unarmed) and the set of demands put forward (tenancy and labor reforms or land redistribution) have been calculated partly against their perception of the balance of forces within and outside the state. This is seen in the calibration of peasant demands of the state from the colonial era to the present—always trying to capitalize on state official promises and then to push the official boundaries farther than what state actors originally intended.

The state is a principal source of political opportunities for peasants and their allies against which they plan and launch collective actions. Filipino state laws, dormant or otherwise, have been crucial contexts and objects of peasant mobilizations: they influence the level, scale, and nature of peasant demands; in turn, such demands have influenced subsequent state policy making and choices. They always have been mutually reinforcing. Hence, the Filipino state's pronouncements on land and tenancy reforms, even when state actors really did not mean to implement them, historically became rallying points for peasants' claim-making mobilizations. During the past century in the Philippines, there appears to have been a "ratchet effect" in the cycles of reforms or reform promises: from the most limited (and essentially flawed) friar land reform, to homestead and resettlement, to tenancy reforms in selected land types, to land redistribution of some land categories, to land redistribution of and tenancy reforms in all types of farmland. Peasant demands have tended to be calculated on the basis of actual political opportunity structure, including the way that Filipino state laws pertaining to land and tenancy reforms and to public/community forested lands have been (re)formulated at different periods of time (see Putzel [1992]; Franco [2008]). Thus, in this context perhaps the most important unintended outcome of Marcos' largely unimplemented land reform was that it set the benchmark in the popular discourse on land reform: expropriationary land redistribution. Succeeding peasant mobilizations would be anchored in that period and the level of reform discourse it promoted; there was no turning back the nature and scale of demands from the peasants and their allies. Hence, although the history of land and tenancy reforms in the Philippines has been quite protracted and marked by dozens of state laws, it has to be understood in the context of an upward calibration of reform content and extent.

The escalation of peasant mobilization for reforms, on one hand, and state actors' initiatives for land and tenancy reforms on the other usually occurred during an important national political transition or administration turnover: the Commonwealth era in the mid-1930s to the post-World War II transition, the Macapagal assumption of power to the 1972 shift to authoritarian rule, the 1986 regime transition, and periodic changes of administration since then. The efforts of competing elites to court peasant votes and/or to shore up eroded political legitimacy might have been keenly perceived and taken advantage of by poor peasants and their allies to put forward, or even increase, their demands for reform.

Peasants' decisions to pursue covert actions to advance their demands and interests have been premised on their collective perception that there was a good chance that their goals could be better realized in that way. This also partly explains why, on most occasions, peasant demands have tended to match what the state already offered, at least formally and legally, such as tenancy reforms during the first three quarters of the 20th century or the contemporary demand to implement CARP.

Having explained the various ways in which peasants launched their collective actions to engage the state overtly on issues of rural reforms, it is important to note that Filipino peasants usually have not engaged in overt mass actions. Instead, they have used "everyday forms of resistance," from pilferage to misdeclaration of crop harvests, from foot dragging to arson (see Scott 1976, 1985, 1990; Scott and Kerkvliet 1986; Kerkvliet 1990). Decisions to engage in open collective mass action usually are calculated against the weight of their gains through everyday forms of resistance or claim making. This calculus is demonstrated in Kerkvliet's (1993) explanation of the 1980s peasant land occupations.

State–Society Interactions in Land Reform Implementation

The interactions between state reformists from above and social movements from below contributed to the relative success of CARP in the mid- to late 1990s. State reformists—that is, state actors who were tolerant and even supportive of social mobilizations—became entrenched within DAR. With some degree of autonomy from antireform currents within the state and society, they built up DAR's capacity to implement reforms. Most important, they recognized the role played by autonomous social movements. By 1994, DAR had to begin moving into the more contentious components of CARP, and for this it found an alliance with autonomous peasant organizations to be indispensable. Meanwhile, the political landscape of the rural social movements also had been altered dynamically. New players had emerged and built up their political and legal capacities, alignments had shifted, and traditional coopted peasant organizations increasingly had become isolated.

There were at least three ways in which this new interface could be seen. The first was the emergence of one-on-one dialogue in which an individual case would be taken up and handled by government officials. Although inherently time consuming, this process can produce concrete results. It happens when local cases are elevated to the DAR national office for speedy resolution in favor of the peasants, and is most likely to occur in cases that are politically explosive in character. The second way in which to see the interface was in the civil society-initiated campaigns. Rural social movements initiated nationally coordinated campaigns in which state actors were enticed or forced to engage. An example of this was "Task Force 24" (see box 8.3). The third illustration of the new interface was DAR-initiated campaigns or programs begun by state actors in which rural social movements were obliged to engage. An example of this was "Operation Sugarland," in which DAR planned to fast-track land redistribution in the sugarcane sector. This initiative, however, was unsuccessful.

There were several other important areas in which DAR reformists and autonomous peasant organizations and NGOs interacted positively, as well as more informal interfaces. DAR reformists also actively checked tendencies within the military to repress autonomous peasant organizations, and even used the military and police to defeat landlords' violent resistance. The pro-reform state–society relationship that began during the term in office of DAR Secretary Ernesto Garilao continued during the term of Secretary Horacio Morales Jr.—but not without major shifts in alignments and political biases on both sides. Under the Macapagal-Arroyo administration that began in 2001, however, the top leadership at DAR was given to politicians who had no serious agenda in carrying out land reform. That was the end of the pro-reform state–civil society alliance. The land reform processes and outcomes largely are determined by the character of state–society

Box 8.3 Task Force 24: An Example of Civil Society-Initiated Campaigns

In 1994, the Philippine Ecumenical Action for Community Empowerment (PEACE) Foundation and its network of local, autonomous peasant organizations and nongovernmental organizations (NGOs) initiated a dialogue with the Department of Agrarian Reform (DAR) regarding land reform issues in 24 provinces. A joint PEACE-DAR working group was established—called Task Force 24—and its main objective was fast-track land acquisition and distribution in those provinces. The task force's work entailed collective efforts to identify major landholdings or ongoing local land disputes, and joint strategizing on how to defeat landlords' resistance to expediting land expropriation and redistribution. The dynamic and often conflict-ridden interaction among local DAR officials, NGOs, and peasant organizations was mediated by national-level DAR officials and NGOs. Toward the end of Ernesto Garilao's time as DAR secretary (1992–98), this interface mechanism was consolidated further, then expanded and renamed "Project 40 Now!" Also at that time the local expression of this pro-reform, state–society alliance—the Provincial Campaigns on Agrarian Reform and Rural Development—became more coherent and widespread.

interaction dynamics over time. This can be detected partly in the data presented in table 8.1 and figure 8.2.

The mutually reinforcing state–civil society reformist alliance strategy that pushed for reformist gains in the 1990s has been referred to popularly in the Philippines as the "*bibingka* strategy" to make the point that the state and society are marked by often heated simultaneous conflicts between pro- and anti-reform forces at different levels (Borras 2001).[3] This strategy involved combining autonomous and militant social mobilization from below with initiatives by state reformists from above (Borras 2007). Its forms of collective action have ranged from forcible land occupation to dialogues, from street marches to legal offensives, from petition letters to occupation and padlocking of DAR offices and gates to dramatize their protest. By persistently navigating between "outright opposition" and "uncritical collaboration" with the state on the issue of land reform (Franco 1999), however, the main adherents of this strategy among rural social movements attempted to maximize the reformist potential of CARP, while remaining strategically concerned about redistributive land reform beyond the institutional limits of that program. The strategy proved to be a path-breaking one. Discussions in this chapter concerning this strategy draw partly from Jonathan Fox's (1993) notion of "sandwich strategy" in the context of rural Mexico.[4] However, forging such a coalition does not automatically guarantee successful land redistribution because antireform

Table 8.1 DAR Land Redistribution, 1972–2005

Comparative aspect	Marcos administration (1972–86)	Aquino administration (1986–92)	Ramos administration (1992–98)	Estrada administration (Jul. 1988–Dec. 2000)	Macapagal-Arroyo administration (Jan. 2001–present)[a]	Total
Duration (years)	14	6	6	2.5	5	35.5
Share in land reform output (%)	1.86	22.51	52.34	9.24	13.86	99.88

Source: Borras and Franco 2007.

Note: DAR = Department of Agrarian Reform.

a. Data for the Macapagal-Arroyo administration consider only the period 2001 through 2005.

Figure 8.2 Land Redistribution Outcomes by National Administration, 1972–2005

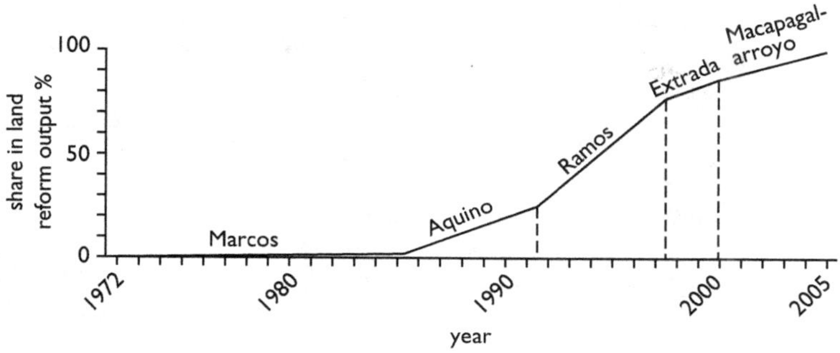

Source: Borras 2007.

forces block the reform process through their own state–society alliances. It is when the antireform forces are fragmented and the pro-reform alliance remains strong that the chances of successful land redistribution are higher.

LAND REFORM ACHIEVEMENTS AND THEIR INTERPRETATIONS

The discussion in this section includes conflicting interpretations of land reform law, redistribution in public lands, leasehold reform, and redistribution in private lands.

Conflicting Interpretations

By 2006, based on official records, 5.9 million hectares of private and public lands—about half of the country's 10.3 million hectares of farmland—were redistributed to 3 million rural poor households, representing two-fifths of the agricultural population (table 8.2), and 1.5 million hectares of land were subjected to leasehold, benefiting about 1 million tenant-peasant households. However, the land reform outcome in the Philippines (table 8.3) has been the subject of competing interpretations and debates. On one hand, CARP's implementers claim very significant success for the land redistribution component of the program; on the other hand, critics dismiss such official claims. The optimistic view suggests that all officially reported statistics are correct, and the only challenge now is to complete the remaining land redistribution balance. The pessimistic view advanced by many civil society organizations suggests that the claims of land redistribution involving private land are "padded reports" and that most of the accomplishments involve public, not private, land and leasehold reform—so should not be considered land reform accomplishments. Although there are valid points in

Table 8.2 CARP's Land Redistribution Accomplishments, in Hectares, 1972–2006

Agency	Type of land	Program	Land area (hectares)
DAR	Private land	Operation land transfer	576,556
		Compulsory acquisition	289,250
		Voluntary offer to sell	494,133
		Voluntary land transfer	514,277
		Government financial institutions	161,985
		Subtotal (private land)	2,036,201
DAR	Government-owned land	*Kilusang Kabuhayan at Kaunlaran* lands	737,512
		Landed estates	70,658
		Settlement	722,620
		Subtotal (government-owned land)	1,530,790
DENR	Government-owned land	Alienable and disposable	1,295,559
		Community-based forest management	1,042,088
		Subtotal (public and state land redistributed by DENR)	2,337,647
		Total	5,904,638

Source: Borras 2007.
Note: CARP = Comprehensive Agrarian Reform Program; DAR = Department of Agrarian Reform; DENR = Department of Environment and Natural Resources.

Table 8.3 Number of Land Reform Program Beneficiaries, 1972–2000

Program	Number of beneficiary households
Land Transfer under DAR	1,697,566
Land Transfer under DENR	1,273,845
Leasehold Operations	1,098,948
Stock Distribution Option	8,975
Total	4,079,334

Source: Reyes 2002, p. 15.
Note: DAR = Department of Agrarian Reform; DENR = Department of Environment and Natural Resources.

each camp's positions in this debate, interpreting the land reform outcome remains quite problematic, demanding an alternative interpretation. It is most likely that CARP's actual land redistribution outcome by 2006 was somewhere in between the optimistic and pessimistic claims. The key point, however, is to specify the basis for including or excluding official data about land reform outcome.

There certainly are problems with the official statistics on CARP's land redistribution accomplishments. It is most probable that the program's real levels of accomplishment in redistribution and leasehold are far below the official claims of 6 million hectares transferred (plus another million hectares under leasehold). Meanwhile, the critics' dismissive assertion that CARP has achieved nothing significant also is unconvincing. But the entire range of these claims and counterclaims is not captured and explained fully by the dominant critique that, like the official view, is fundamentally flawed itself. There is no real way to measure CARP's exact land redistribution and tenure reform accomplishments. The most critical starting point, however, is to specify in precise terms how a real redistribution of land-based wealth and power actually can happen—if it can happen. In discussing this issue, it is important to explain the three basic problems with both the official claim and its critique.

Redistribution in Public Lands

Following the dominant convention in land reform scholarship, Riedinger, Yang, and Brook (2001) for example, have argued for the exclusion of public lands from any accounting of land redistribution accomplishments: "This figure . . . reflects the area distributed by the DAR (2,562,089 hectares) in the period 1972–1997 net of lands distributed as settlements (662,727 hectares), and *Kilusang Kabuhayan at Kaunlaran* (606,347 hectares). . . . The two elements of the distribution program are netted out because they do not involve *re*-distribution of *private* agricultural lands" (p. 376). That sweeping conclusion presumptively excludes from analysis two-thirds of the total scope of land redistribution and the potential peasant beneficiaries thereof. Such a view cannot capture and explain cases of real redistributive reform in public lands where these did occur.

We may illustrate this problem empirically. A 201-hectare farm tilled by 76 tenants, planted with coconut and citrus trees, located in Mulanay, Quezon, and "owned" by a family presents a relevant empirical example. The landlord was able to secure a private title to this piece of land, despite its official "timberland" classification. Since the 1960s, the landlord has imposed share-tenancy relationships between 70-30 and 80-20 in his favor, while the peasants have shouldered the bulk of production expenses. It was a hard life for the peasants. In 1995, the tenants petitioned for leasehold reform and the landlord vehemently opposed the motion. The tenants elevated their demand to land redistribution. Then they discovered that the landholding was officially classified as "timberland," and thus could not be titled legally to any private individual. But they had mixed feelings: they were elated that the landlord did not own the land legally, but were wary because timberlands are not supposed to be covered by land redistribution. The landlord launched a legal opposition against expropriation. Joined by ally NGOs and emboldened by their findings on the nature of the property, the peasants decided to declare a boycott on land rent. The landlord filed numerous criminal charges (108 counts of *estafa* [fraud] and theft) before the municipal court. There were several waves of arrest and detention of the tenants and peasant leaders: peasants were in and out of the municipal jail. Assisted by their ally NGOs, the peasants elevated their case to the DENR central office and the Office of the Solicitor General in Manila. Their demand was changed to the cancellation of the landlord's private land title on the grounds that it was illegal in the first place. In the peasants' opinion, a declaration that the landlord's private title was illegal would make all the criminal charges filed against them "moot and academic." The tenants were involved in a series of actions in the national capital, joining other militant peasant movements from elsewhere in the country in street marches, dialogues, and pickets at the DENR and the Solicitor General's office. Finally, in 1998 the Solicitor General filed for cancellation of the title, and in 2001 the DENR awarded the estate to the peasants under CARP's CBFM program: the peasants received a 50-year stewardship contract and they were not to pay for the land. The case entered the official CARP records as a land distribution accomplishment in the CBFM program—that is, as a public land transfer. The peasants achieved a decisive victory because there was a real transfer of land, wealth, and power.

Unfortunately, most scholars exclude that case from their accounting and analysis of redistributive land reform. The reform of land-based production relationships in the farm as presented in that case is not captured by and explained in dominant land reform scholarship. But there is an abundance of empirical experience in the Philippines that is similar to that case, and it has been analyzed elsewhere by the author (for example, Borras [2006b]).

Leasehold Reform

Most activists and academics tend to downgrade the importance of leasehold reform in redistributive reform. In cases where an agrarian reform program has a leasehold component, even the policy implementers often treat it marginally, and systematic analysis of it often does not figure in land reform scholarship. When share tenancy reform is made part of the analysis, often there is no critical examination of whether it is a type that is (1) merely formal or (2) real. Moreover, studies seldom take into account the context within which such a policy is thought about or carried out—that is, whether it is an alternative/substitute or a complementary/parallel reform policy relative to land redistribution. Thus, the dominant view often misses a significant portion of the preexisting agrarian structures—and some reforms therein where these did occur. The following case illustrates the point.

The estate involved is the Dimakuhaan (pseudonym) property owned by the 18 heirs of the family. The 126-hectare farm is devoted to coconut farming and is worked by 26 tenant farmers. For a long time, the tenants were under a 60-40 sharing arrangement (favoring the landlords). The tenants shouldered all production costs, which mostly were related to labor. The tenants were convinced that a leasehold contract would be better than either a perpetual 60-40 sharing scheme or a full land redistribution. Under CARP's leasehold, the tenant–landlord relationship is "formalized" (documented) through the lease contract, and so provides the tenants security of tenure. The terms of relationship also change to a leasehold contract, with fixed land rent at 25 percent of the average harvest of the principal crop. Under leasehold, the peasants can pursue more intensive farming by intercropping but the lease rental is computed only on the harvest of the principal crop (in this example, coconut).

The Dimakuhaan tenants contacted with an NGO working on agrarian reform in the municipality. Through the NGO's legal literacy program, they were fully able to understand that share tenancy already was illegal and that leasehold must be enforced on their farm. They petitioned for leasehold. In early 1999, the provincial agrarian reform adjudicator, a quasi-judicial body in charge of agrarian disputes, supported and confirmed the application of the 26 tenants. The leasehold contract was formalized, shifting the sharing arrangement to 75-25 in favor of the tenants, and the peasants started to pay 25 percent of the net harvest to the landlords. The amount each beneficiary paid varied according to the amount of land each received and the number of coconut trees on that land. However, the landlords petitioned for a review of the terms of the leasehold contract, arguing that the secondary crops (corn, vegetables, and citrus trees planted between the coconut trees) must be included in the leasehold contract. The landlords also argued that they were not provided due process during the preliminary process for leasehold conversion. Later that year, the adjudicator ordered a return to the "status quo ante," meaning that the terms of relationship should revert to the 60-40 sharing arrangement favoring the landlords while the landlords' petitions were studied. The peasants refused to abide by the adjudicator's order, arguing that share tenancy is illegal, as declared by CARP law, and therefore the order to revert to the 60-40 share tenancy was illegal as well. The peasants continued to "forcibly pay" the landlords (via escrow at a bank) during the subsequent harvest, but they based their payments on the leasehold contract. The landlords retaliated by filing criminal charges against the peasants (the usual *estafa* and theft) in the municipal trial court. Only the assistance of their NGO allies and some sympathetic municipal officials who provided bail kept the peasants out of jail. Because of their fear of being dragged to jail again, the peasants tactically agreed to return to the 60-40 arrangement. While doing so, the peasant group and its ally NGO escalated their campaign all the way to the regional and national DAR offices, putting heavy pressure on the adjudicator to decide in their favor. Eventually, in early 2002, the adjudicator issued an order in favor of the peasants. The leasehold contract was upheld and reinforced—redistributive reform was achieved.

The case shows a clear redistribution of land-based wealth and power. But such a gain is ignored or given scant attention by most scholars and activists; CARP's leasehold component generally is absent in their analyses and political advocacy. The Philippines case, however, demonstrates that a leasehold reform can be radical when it is taken as a *complementary* policy—a policy that has the potential to radically restructure the terms of land-based production relationships, to affirm the tenants' tenure security, and to be applied to all lands that are under the legal retention rights of the landlords. It is not a matter of an "either/or" choice between land redistribution and leasehold. Moreover, because there is hardly any serious examination of leasehold reform in the Philippines, the very likely padding in the official statistics on leasehold has escaped critical scrutiny, as the author has explained in detail elsewhere (see, for example, Borras [2007]).

Redistribution in Private Lands

Both scholars and activists generally are wary of official data on redistribution involving private lands. But such apprehension often is confined to the issue of possible government padding of official statistics. And because these anomalous practices actually occur often, such critical examination is welcome and important. Other forms of "apparent-but-not-real" redistributive land reform, however, are not captured by the dominant scholarship, and among the most significant and relevant examples of these are reforms involving problematic voluntary land transfer schemes. We may consider an example.

The Floirendo family holds one of the largest elites in the domestic banana sector, with links to multinational companies. The family controls thousands of hectares of land, both privately owned and leased from government. For their privately owned plantations, they first tried to frustrate land reform by setting a sky-high asking price for their lands—$15,000 per hectare in 1997. In 1998, however, the state land bank assessed the value at only $5,500 per hectare. In 2001, a local court declared the value of a banana plantation similar to that owned by the Floirendos to be $26,000 per hectare. Therefore, it was a big surprise when, in the following year, the Floirendos sold their plantation for $1,900 per hectare. The sale was made through the voluntary land transfer scheme integrated within a leaseback contract. The key features of the contract were these: (1) the land was to be bought directly by the farmworkers from the landlord, (2) the worker-beneficiaries would lease the land back to the Floirendos for 60 years, (3) direct payment for the land to the Floirendos was to be amortized over 30 years[5] and automatically deducted from the lease rental due to the worker-beneficiaries, (4) the annual lease rental was set at $100 per hectare, (5) the worker-beneficiaries would remain employed as workers on the plantation, and (6) the Floirendos would have the sole right to buy back the land of any beneficiaries who gave up their land or were later disqualified as beneficiaries. The terms of such a contract reveal the absence of real redistributive reform. The landlord's decision to radically lower the asking price for the land was tied to the leaseback arrangement: the lower the land price, the lower the lease rent would be. The prevailing land lease rental rate in adjacent banana plantations was as much as $1,200 per hectare, or 12 times greater. The 60-year lease contract virtually covers a lifetime; before the 60th year, most beneficiaries would have died without ever owning the land they were supposed to have obtained via land reform. It is expected that should a beneficiary decide to abandon the farm and "sell" the land to the Floirendos (who have the right to purchase the land), the sale price will not be based on market price but rather on the same benchmark established earlier ($1,900 per hectare).

The Floirendos, known for their violent repression of farmworkers' rights historically, were able to impose this kind of arrangement through a variety of tactics: promises, deceit, coercion, and violence (as examined in detail in Franco [2008] and de la Rosa [2005]). There was no real transfer of wealth and power from the landlord to the farmworkers in this particular case, but it has been listed as a land redistribution accomplishment in the private lands category, and has been included in what is considered a land reform achievement in both official government claims and scholars' analyses, despite the absence of real reform therein. This case of problematic voluntary land transfer is not an isolated one. Many variations of this voluntary approach are treated at full length elsewhere, most particularly in Borras (2005), Borras, Carranza, and Franco (2007), and Putzel (2003). Those authors have argued that there is a general pattern of "antipeasant" and "pro-elite" processes and outcomes in such a voluntary approach. In June 2008 the same voluntary land transfer approach was used by the big landlord lobby in the Philippines congress to block a third extension of the land reform law. The program will continue, but can use only the voluntary land transfer method. In the Filipino context, this essentially puts an end to the land reform program.

CONCLUSION

By 2006, according to official records, 5.9 million hectares of private and public lands, accounting for about half of the country's total farmland, were redistributed to 3 million rural poor households, representing two-fifths of the agricultural population; 1.5 million hectares of land were subjected to leasehold, benefiting about 1 million tenant-peasant households. Those findings are subject to competing interpretations, with the official story being far more optimistic, and critics being dismissive altogether. This chapter has shown that both interpretations have a certain degree of validity, but both have flaws.

It has been shown here that the tendencies of conventional land reform scholarship and practice to focus only on lands that are formally classified as private, and to focus solely on the "right to alienate," have produced a problematic analytic perspective that presumptively has excluded from enquiry any real redistributive reforms in public/state lands and through leasehold reform. The problems associated with excluding realities from, and including nonexistent reform in, an accounting of land reform accomplishments are not only (research) operational in nature, but also involve basic conceptual and methodological issues.

Making clear and explicit the bases for exclusion/inclusion in calculating land reform accomplishments helps us see the outcome of the Philippines land reform from 1972 to 2006 from a more accurate perspective. We do not accept uncritically the optimistic official claim of nearly complete, successful land reform, nor do we embrace uncritically many critics' position that nothing significant has been achieved by the Philippines land reform. It is our argument that the likely land reform accomplishments are somewhere in between these two opposing views. Following Putzel, the most authoritative scholar on Filipino agrarian reform, we argue in this chapter that from 1972 to 2006, the Philippines has achieved a *significant partial land reform* (Putzel 2003).

To date, the reform achieved has been the result of a reformist state–civil society coalition. The main lesson drawn from this chapter is that the effects of land reform policy are not determined either by structural or institutional factors alone, or by the actions of state policy elites alone; rather, the political actions and strategies of a wide range of state and societal actors also have a bearing on the outcomes of the reform process. The symbiotic interaction of autonomous societal groups from below and strategically placed state reformists from above (the "sandwich strategy") provides the most promising strategy to offset strong landlord resistance to land reform, facilitating state expropriation and redistribution of highly contentious private estates to previously landless and near-landless peasants. The Philippines had its reformist peak between 1993 and 2000. By 2001, under the Macapagal-Arroyo presidency, the reformist trend was over.

ANNEX

Table 8.A.1 Agrarian Disputes and Their Legal and Administrative Jurisdictions

Application Cases Jurisdiction: DAR Adjudication Board	Implementation Cases Jurisdiction: DAR
■ Rights and obligations of persons, whether natural or juridical, engaged in the management, cultivation, and use of all agricultural lands covered by CARP and other agrarian laws	■ Classification and identification of landholdings for coverage under CARP, including protests or opposition thereto and petitions for lifting of coverage
■ Valuation of land and the preliminary determination and payment of just compensation; definition and collection of lease rentals; disturbance compensation, amortization payments, and similar disputes concerning the functions of the Land Bank of the Philippines	■ Identification, qualification, or disqualification of potential farmer-beneficiaries
■ Annulment or cancellation of lease contracts or deeds of sale or their amendment involving lands under the administration and disposition of the DAR or Land Bank	■ Cases involving the subdivision surveys of land under CARP
■ Cases arising from or connected with membership or representation in compact farms, farmers' cooperatives, and other registered farmers' associations or organizations related to land covered by CARP and other agrarian laws	■ Issuance, recall, or cancellation of Certificates of Land Transfer Award or CARP Beneficiary Certificates in cases under the purview of Presidential Decree 816, including the issuance, recall, or cancellation of Emancipation Patents or Certificates of Land Transfer Award not yet registered with the Register of Deeds
■ Cases involving the sale, alienation, mortgage, foreclosure, preemption, and redemption of agricultural lands under the coverage of CARP or other agrarian laws	■ Cases involving the exercise of the right of retention by landowner
■ Cases involving the issuance, correction, and cancellation of Certificates of Land Ownership Award or Emancipation Patents that are registered with the Land Registration Authority	■ Applications for exemption
■ Cases previously falling under the original and exclusive jurisdiction of the defunct Court of Agrarian Relations (it is understood that said cases, complaints, or petitions were filed with the DAR Adjudication Board after August 29, 1987)	■ Issuance of certificates of exemption for lands subject to voluntary offer to sell and compulsory acquisition

(continued)

Table 8.A.1 (Continued)

Application Cases Jurisdiction: DAR Adjudication Board	Implementation Cases Jurisdiction: DAR
■ Other agrarian cases, disputes, matters, or concerns referred to it by the DAR secretary	■ Applications for conversion of agricultural lands to residential, commercial, industrial, or other nonagricultural uses, including protest or opposition thereto
	■ Cases involving the right of agrarian reform beneficiaries to home lots
	■ Disposition of excess area of the farmer-beneficiary's landholdings
	■ Transfer, surrender, or abandonment by the farmer-beneficiary of his farmholding and its disposition
	■ Cases involving the increase of awarded area by the farmer-beneficiary
	■ Cases involving a conflict of claims in landed estates and settlement
	■ Other matters not mentioned above but strictly involving the administrative implementation of CARP and other agrarian laws, rules, and regulations, as determined by the DAR secretary

Source: Franco 2005, p. 11.
Note: CARP = Comprehensive Agrarian Reform Program; DAR = Department of Agrarian Reform.

NOTES

1. Agricultural lands count for about a third of the Philippines' land area (30 million hectares).
2. The Gini coefficient, one of the most common measures of income inequality, is on a scale of 0 (least unequal) to 1 (most unequal). In his study, Putzel looked at the land that is identified officially as privately owned. Such land represents about one-third of the agricultural land. His study does not capture public land informally controlled by individuals, which is likely to cover a significant area. The issue of such contested public land is discussed elaborately in Borras (2006b).
3. *Bibingka* is a native Filipino rice cake baked in a homemade oven having two layers, with charcoal embers in each layer, on top of and underneath the cake.
4. Also see Herring (1983) in the context of South Asia.
5. Under the compulsory acquisition scheme, the land reform beneficiary is to amortize payment to government for the land over 15 years. But under the voluntary land transfer scheme where the payment is directly paid to the landlord, the payment period can be adjusted.

REFERENCES

Abinales, Patricio N. 2000. *Making Mindanao: Cotabato and Davao in the Formation of the Philippine Nation-State.* Quezon City, Philippines: Ateneo de Manila University Press.

ADB (Asian Development Bank). 2005. *Poverty in the Philippines: Income, Assets and Access.* Manila, Philippines.

Aguilar, Filomeno V. Jr. 1998. *Clash of Spirits: The History of Power and Sugar Planter Hegemony on a Visayan Island.* Honolulu: University of Hawaii Press.

Anderson, Benedict. 1988. "Cacique Democracy in the Philippines: Origins and Dreams." *New Left Review* 169 (May-June): 3–29.

Borras, Saturnino M. Jr. 2001. "State–Society Relations in Land Reform Implementation in the Philippines." *Development and Change* 32 (3): 545–75.

———. 2003. "Inclusion-Exclusion in Public Policies and Policy Analyses: The Case of Philippine Land Reform, 1972–2002." *Journal of International Development* 15 (8): 1049–65.

———. 2005. "Can Redistributive Reform Be Achieved via Market-Based Land Transfer Schemes? Lessons and Evidence from the Philippines." *Journal of Development Studies* 41 (1): 90–134.

———. 2006a. "The Philippine Land Reform in Comparative Perspective: Conceptual and Methodological Implications." *Journal of Agrarian Change* 6 (1): 69–101.

———. 2006b. "Redistributive Land Reform in Public (Forest) Lands? Rethinking Theory and Practice with Evidence from the Philippines." *Progress in Development Studies* 6 (2): 123–45.

———. 2007. *Pro-Poor Land Reform: A Critique.* Ottawa, Ont.: University of Ottawa Press.

Borras, Saturnino M. Jr., Danilo Carranza, and Jennifer C. Franco. 2007. "Anti-Poverty or Anti-Poor? The World Bank's Market-Led Agrarian Reform Experiment in the Philippines." *Third World Quarterly* 28 (8): 1557–76.

Borras, Saturnino M. Jr., and Jennifer C. Franco. 2005. "Struggles for Land and Livelihood: Redistributive Reform in Philippine Agribusiness Plantations." *Critical Asian Studies* 37 (3): 331–61.

———. 2007. "The National Land Reform Campaign in the Philippines." Paper prepared for the "Citizens' Participation in National Policy Processes Project," Institute of Development Studies, and the Ford Foundation. http://www.ids.ac.uk/ids/Part/proj/pnp.html.

Boyce, James K. 1993. *The Political Economy of Growth and Impoverishment in the Marcos Era.* Quezon City, Philippines: Ateneo de Manila University Press.

de la Rosa, Romula. 2005. "Agrarian Reform Movement in Commercial Plantations: The Case of Banana Plantations in Davao." In *On Just Grounds: Struggling for Agrarian Justice and Exercising Citizenship Rights in the Rural Philippines,* ed. Jennifer C. Franco and Saturnino M. Borras Jr., 35–82. Quezon City, Philippines: Institute for Popular Democracy; Amsterdam, Netherlands: Transnational Institute.

Fox, Jonathan. 1993. *The Politics of Food in Mexico: State Power and Social Mobilization.* Ithaca, NY: Cornell University Press.

Franco, Jennifer C. 1999. "Between Uncritical Collaboration and Outright Opposition: An Evaluative Report on the Partnership for Agrarian Reform and Rural

Development Services, PARRDS." Occasional Paper 12. Institute for Popular Democracy, Quezon City, Philippines.

———. 2001. *Elections and Democratization in the Philippines.* New York: Routledge.

———. 2005. "Making Property Rights Accessible: Movement Innovation in the Political-Legal Struggle to Claim Land Rights in the Philippines." Working Paper 244. Institute of Development Studies, Brighton, U.K.

———. 2008. "Making Land Rights Accessible: Social Movement Innovation and Political-Legal Strategies in the Philippines." *Journal of Development Studies* 44 (7): 991–1022.

Hayami, Yujiro, Agnes R. Quisumbing, and Lourdes S. Adriano. 1990. *Toward an Alternative Land Reform Paradigm: A Philippine Perspective.* Quezon City, Philippines: Ateneo de Manila University Press.

Herring, Ronald J. 1983. *Land to the Tiller.* New Haven, CT: Yale University Press.

Kerkvliet, Ben. 1977. *The Huk Rebellion: A Study of Peasant Revolt in the Philippines.* Berkeley, CA: University of California Press.

———. 1990. *Everyday Politics in the Philippines: Class and Status Relations in a Central Luzon Village.* Berkeley, CA: University of California Press.

———. 1993. "Claiming the Land: Take-overs by Villagers in the Philippines with Comparisons to Indonesia, Peru, Portugal, and Russia." *Journal of Peasant Studies* 20 (3): 459–93.

Lara, Francisco Jr., and Horacio Morales Jr. 1990. "The Peasant Movement and the Challenge of Democratisation in the Philippines." *Journal of Development Studies* 26 (4): 143–62.

Putzel, James. 1992. *A Captive Land: The Politics of Agrarian Reform in the Philippines.* New York: Monthly Review Press.

———. 1995. "Managing the 'Main Force': The Communist Party and the Peasantry in the Philippines." *Journal of Peasant Studies* 22 (4): 645–71.

———. 2003. "The Politics of Partial Reform in the Philippines." In *Agrarian Studies: Essays on Agrarian Relations in Less-Developed Countries*, ed. V. K. Ramachandran and Madhura Swaminathan, 204–12. London: Zed Books.

Reyes, Celia M. 2002. "Impact of Agrarian Reform on Poverty." Discussion Paper 2002–02. Manila, Philippines: Philippine Institute for Development Studies.

Riedinger, Jeffrey M. 1995. *Agrarian Reform in the Philippines: Democratic Transitions and Redistributive Reform.* Palo Alto, CA: Stanford University Press.

Riedinger, Jeffrey, Wan-Ying Yang, and Karen Brook. 2001. "Market-Based Land Reform: An Imperfect Solution." In *Power in the Village: Agrarian Reform, Rural Politics, Institutional Change and Globalization*, ed. Horacio Morales and James Putzel, 263–378. Quezon City, Philippines: University of the Philippines Press.

Rutten, Rosanne. 2000. "High-Cost Activism and the Worker Household: Interests, Commitment, and the Costs of Revolutionary Activism in a Philippine Plantation Region." *Theory and Society* 29: 215–52.

Scott, James C. 1976. *The Moral Economy of the Peasant: Rebellion and Subsistence in Southeast Asia.* New Haven, CT: Yale University Press.

———. 1985. *Weapons of the Weak.* New Haven, CT: Yale University Press.

———. 1990. *Domination and the Arts of Resistance: Hidden Transcripts.* New Haven, CT: Yale University Press.

Scott, James C., and Ben Kerkvliet. 1986. "Everyday Forms of Peasant Resistance in Southeast Asia." *Journal of Peasant Studies* 13 (2): special issue.

CHAPTER NINE

Learning from Old and New Approaches to Land Reform in India

Tim Hanstad, Robin Nielsen, Darryl Vhugen, and T. Haque

India contains both the largest number of rural poor people and the largest number of landless households on the planet. The two statistics are closely related: landlessness—more than either caste or illiteracy—is the best indicator of rural poverty in India (World Bank 1997, pp. xiii–xiv).

At both national and state levels, India has made significant efforts to reduce rural poverty through attention to the inequalities of land access and the insecurity of land tenure. India's land reform efforts initially employed a range of approaches, including elimination of intermediate interests in land, restrictions on tenancy that included land-to-the-tiller provisions, the imposition of land ceilings, and land distribution programs. In the course of these efforts, India has encountered challenges, confronted problems, and experienced some successes. In recent years, some Indian states absorbed the lessons of those initial efforts and reconsidered ways in which land policies and legislation could reduce rural poverty. Those states have designed and implemented new approaches to increase land access for the poor and marginalized—with encouraging early results.

Dina Umali-Deininger and Edward Cook made comments on an early version of the chapter.

This chapter briefly reviews the country's land reform history and its promising future. The hope is that India's experience may help policy makers and civil society members committed to alleviating rural poverty in developing countries. Following this introduction, the next section provides an overview of the historical context in which India began reforming its land policies and laws. The section describes India's key postindependence legislative land reforms and the results of those initial efforts. The following section highlights the critical role women's land rights play in land-based efforts to reduce poverty, and it identifies the unique issues and challenges arising from efforts to strengthen women's rights to land. The third section of the chapter discusses how three Indian states have taken lessons learned from those early efforts and created new routes to increase rural poor people's access to land and enhance the security of land rights. The final section offers some lessons learned from India's extensive experience.

FIRST-GENERATION REFORMS TO LAND POLICY AND LAW

At independence in 1947, India's policy makers focused substantial attention on reforming the agrarian structure in an effort to increase equality of land access, eliminate the exploitation of farmers, and improve agricultural productivity (Behuria 1997). With guidance from the central government, the states enacted legislation aimed at (1) abolishing intermediate interests in land, (2) regulating tenancy, (3) limiting the size of landholdings and redistributing the above-ceiling surplus, and (4) distributing government wasteland to those without agricultural land and houses.[1] This section discusses each of these types of reform in turn. In addition to a general countrywide discussion, the chapter focuses on three states that have had notable success in implementing land reform legislation and programs: Andhra Pradesh, Karnataka, and West Bengal.

Land Systems at Independence

At independence, India inherited an agrarian structure that was distinguished by highly inequitable land ownership, chronic insecurity of tenure among farmers, and low agricultural productivity. A small percentage of wealthy and politically well-connected individuals owned most of the country's agricultural land, leaving approximately 68 percent of the rural population landless or nearly landless (Dantwala 1950, p. 240). Absentee landowners delegated operational control of their land to managers. Cultivating tenants and sharecroppers had no tenure security; they answered to layers of intermediaries who controlled their terms of employment while siphoning off production and income to meet personal needs and state revenue requirements.[2]

The intermediary interests responsible for much of the exploitation of farmers arose from the three colonial land revenue systems: the *zamindari*, *ryotwari*, and *mahalwari* systems. These systems (briefly described below) defined relationships among the state, landowners, landlords, tenants, and laborers (Kotovsky 1994; Appu 1997).

In eastern and northern India, the *zamindari* system gave feudal lords and tax collectors permanent rights to and control of the land in exchange for collecting tax from peasant tenant farmers. These landlords (*zamindars*) freed themselves from the burden of managing their estates and collecting rents from cultivators by leasing out the rent-collecting rights. In some areas, many layers of intermediary rent-collecting rights (as many as 50) were created between the *zamindar* and the cultivator (Kotovsky 1964, p. 19).

The *ryotwari* system of southern India initially rejected the presence of intermediaries. In this system, farmers were considered proprietors of the land they cultivated, paid tax directly to the state, and had rights to transfer and mortgage their land. However, many of the farmers under the *ryotwari* system leased out their land to tenants and sharecroppers, creating layers of interests akin to the *zamindari* system (Appu 1997).

The *zamindari* and *ryotwari* systems together governed in 95 percent of the country. In the remaining 5 percent, the *mahalwari* system prevailed. Under the *mahalwari* system, all residents contributed to a collective tax payment passed by the village to the state.

As time passed, all three systems gave numerous individuals rights to control land and land revenue, placing increasing pressure on those cultivating the land. The layers of intermediary interests, coupled with exploitation of tenants and inequitable landholdings, set the stage for India's first generation of land reforms (Dantwala 1950; Appu 1997).

Abolition of Intermediaries

The abuses of the system of intermediaries attracted attention during the struggle for independence. The injustices imposed by *zamindars* and the landowners' support of the British colonial administration fueled the political will to reduce or eliminate intermediary rights to land.[3] In the period immediately following independence, almost every Indian state passed laws restructuring the systems of landholdings and land revenue to abolish intermediate interests. Most legislation granted intermediaries absolute, proprietary rights to portions of their land for personal cultivation, and divested them of control over the remainder. The state compensated the intermediaries for loss of land rights at high rates. According to the National Planning Commission's "Report of the Committees of the Panel on Land Reforms," the compensation paid to the lowest layer of ex-intermediaries reached as high as 15–30 times their annual net income (Appu 1996, p. 64).

In general, these legislative efforts were effective: state laws eliminated the large population of intermediate interests in land, and 20–25 million tenants became landowners.[4] The achievements were not without costs, however. In anticipation of the new legislation, landlords evicted sharecroppers and tenants at will to prevent them from gaining rights. In addition, shortcomings in the laws limited opportunities for the state to protect and empower the poorest tenants. That said, however, the states implemented this phase of India's land reforms more comprehensively than they did the land ceiling and tenancy reforms that were to follow. As a result, despite the deficiencies in the legislation abolishing intermediary interests, that effort is judged among the most successful of India's land reforms.

Regulation of Tenancy

In the period immediately after independence, tenant farmers constituted an estimated 35 percent of India's rural population (Dantwala 1950, p. 240). The tenancy system favored powerful landlords at the expense of their tenants. Most tenancies were verbal, and the landlord could terminate them at will. Laws provided virtually no protection for the most vulnerable tenants.

Recognizing the exploitative nature of tenancy relationships, in the 1960s and 1970s every Indian state passed tenancy reform legislation. These laws affected both existing and future tenancies and were intended to give tenants greater security.

In most states, tenants who remained on tenanted land became entitled to permanent rights, with one large exception for "resumable" land (see box 9.1). The legislative approaches varied by state. For example, certain existing tenants in Karnataka, West Bengal, and the Telangana area of Andhra Pradesh were entitled to ownership or permanent occupancy rights. In the Andhra area of Andhra Pradesh, the law gave many existing tenants perpetual rights to tenanted land. In West Bengal, only share tenants were entitled to permanent rights, and at a regulated share rent.

Perhaps the most controversial aspect of the tenancy laws was whether states permitted the creation of new tenancies. The laws fall on a continuum, with Karnataka, West Bengal, and Andhra Pradesh as representative:

- Karnataka's law prohibits tenancy, with a few minor exceptions. The state has the power to seize leased-out land without compensation to the landowner and to distribute the land to land-poor families.
- With some narrow exceptions, West Bengal does not allow fixed-rent (cash) tenancies, but does permit sharecropping (although, because the law gives permanent rights to such sharecroppers, the law discourages landowners from future sharecropping relationships).
- The Telangana area of Andhra Pradesh prohibits new tenancies unless the landowner is a smallholder (defined as holding less than 18 acres of irrigated land) or is deemed "disabled" (a status defined to include women). Where tenancies are permitted under these exceptions, they must meet precise requirements for the duration of the tenancy and the rate imposed.
- In the Andhra area of Andhra Pradesh, the law permits tenancy relationships but they must meet strict requirements regarding duration, rates, and renewal that grant substantial rights to qualifying tenants.[5]

Box 9.1 Loophole Undermines Reform

The "resumable" land exception in the tenancy reform laws was the largest legal loophole used to prevent tenants from obtaining ownership rights. Essentially, landowners were permitted to evict tenants if they resumed farming the land themselves. Even on nonresumable land, tenants' permissible "voluntary" surrenders of tenancy rights frustrated the objectives of tenancy reform. Many landlords took back their land by persuading their tenant(s) to give up tenancy rights "voluntarily." Most states amended their laws to protect against such coercive tactics, but by that time the damage had been done.

Impact of Tenancy Reform

India's tenancy reform legislation largely failed to achieve its goals of protecting tenants and providing landownership rights to landless rural poor people. In the decades following enactment, the laws provided 12.4 million tenants with rights to 15.6 million acres of land. Those totals constitute about 8 percent of rural households and 4 percent of India's agricultural land, as shown in table 9.A.1 in the annex. Although the achievement cannot be discounted for those who benefited, significant negative impacts experienced by a far larger group offset the positive results:

- *Evictions*—Tenancy reform caused the large-scale eviction of tenants. One study estimates that the legislation caused landlords to evict tenant families from as much as 33 percent of India's agricultural land (Appu 1997, p. 187).
- *Passive dispossession*—In addition to causing evictions, the tenancy laws prevented poor farmers from accessing land through tenancy. Most rural landless and landholding households believe that landowners risk losing some rights to their land when they rent it out. As a result, (1) some landowners let their land lie fallow rather than assume risks associated with leasing it out; (2) landowners who rent out land rent only to those whom they trust not to assert rights, and they may rotate tenants to different parcels, often every year, for added protection; and (3) land-poor households often report that they wish more land was available for rental. The rural poor do not fear exploitation as much as they fear not being able to access land to meet their needs and improve their lives.

Recent studies show that the laws prohibiting or placing substantial restrictions on agricultural tenancies both constrain productivity and prevent landless and marginal farmers from accessing land (World Bank 2007). Thus, relaxing these tenancy restrictions now is likely to serve the interests of the landless and poor farmers. (The chapter discusses this opportunity in the "New Approaches" section below.)

Agricultural Landownership Ceilings

All Indian states adopted land ceiling legislation that limited the amount of agricultural land a person or family can own. The laws equalize landholdings by authorizing the states to take possession of land in excess of the ceiling, and to redistribute the excess land to poor, landless, and marginal farmers.

Ceiling laws vary by state. In Andhra Pradesh and Karnataka, the law permits a family of five to hold between 10 and 54 acres of land, depending on the quality of the land held. In both states, the laws permit the state to buy land that exceeds the ceiling, but the required payment to the landowner is set at only a fraction of the land value (Behuria 1997).

The states prioritize distribution of surplus land among landless and disadvantaged households. State laws vary in the type of land rights received by the beneficiaries and the parcel size. Many states (including Andhra Pradesh and West Bengal) permanently prohibit transfers by beneficiaries. Other states, such as Karnataka, prohibit beneficiaries from transferring their land for a period of time (ranging from 10 to 20 years). Still other states allow such transfers only with the permission of the local revenue authority. In Andhra Pradesh, the state grants surplus land to beneficiaries in parcels of up to 2.5 acres of wetland and up to 5.0 acres of dryland. The state has redistributed a total of 582,319 acres of ceiling-surplus land to 50,344 beneficiaries. Karnataka redistributed 68,745 acres (0.5 percent of the state's arable land) to 33,610 beneficiary households (Government of India, Ministry of Rural Development 2006, annex XXXVII).

West Bengal set a relatively lower landownership ceiling than did the other states, and it redistributed the surplus land in smaller plots. The ceiling area ranges from 6 to 17 "standard acres," depending on family size. A "standard acre" is 1 acre of irrigated land and 1.4 acres of other land. The government must pay landowners for land taken by the state. Again, however, the payment is less than market value. A landowner also can lose his or her land if the landowner fails to farm it personally. The state distributes the land to local residents who own less than 1 acre of farmland. The law gives preference to specific disadvantaged groups and persons who form a cooperative society, and it prohibits beneficiaries from transferring the land.[6] West Bengal has redistributed 1.04 million acres of ceiling-surplus land to 2.54 million land-poor households (see box 9.2) (Government of India, Ministry of Rural Development 2006, annex XXXVII).

Overall Impact of Ceiling Laws

With some exceptions, the ceiling laws have not been effective. The laws fell short of expectations for several reasons: (1) the governments paid inadequate compensation for the land taken, which made the programs unpopular with landowners; (2) landowners used gaps and loopholes in the laws to their advantage; (3) states often distributed the relatively small amount of land obtained in relatively large parcels, benefiting only a small percentage of landless families;

Box 9.2 Benefiting More Families in West Bengal

West Bengal's land allocation practices emphasize distributing available land to as many landless families as possible, rather than trying to give each beneficiary family a "full-size" farm. In recent years, the state has been allocating the dwindling supply of ceiling-surplus lands in very small plots, averaging less than one third of an acre. Field studies have shown that even a fraction of an acre can provide important supplementary benefits to a landless family. For example, in one study covering two districts in West Bengal, the Rural Development Institute interviewed 34 previously landless people who had received plots averaging 0.16 acre (ranging from 0.07 to 0.38 acre). Nearly all farmed their plots intensively and reported significant increases in food consumption, income, and social status attributable to the plots.

Source: Hanstad and Lokesh 2003.

and (4) outdated and incomplete land records made implementation of the ceiling legislation more difficult.

By the end of 2005, state governments across India had declared 7.34 million acres to be above ceiling (approximately 1.8 percent of India's agricultural land). Of that land, the governments had taken possession of 6.50 million acres and had distributed 5.39 million acres to a total of 5.64 million households. The total acreage distributed amounts to approximately 1 percent of India's agricultural land and 4 percent of rural households (see table 9.A.1 in the annex) (Government of India, Ministry of Rural Development 2006, annex XXXVI).

The only states where more than 5 percent of agricultural households benefited are West Bengal, Jammu and Kashmir, and Assam. West Bengal leads India: the state distributed ceiling-surplus land to 34 percent of all agricultural households, and the state accounts for 40 percent of the country's beneficiaries who received ceiling-surplus land. The state's relative success is based on several factors. First, the law has fewer loopholes than do most other state land reform laws. Second, the state government's political will led to more effective implementation. Finally, the state government's emphasis on distributing the benefits widely (but in smaller plots) led to more grassroots support for the process.

The disappointing impact of ceiling laws in other states largely results from a lack of political will. In many cases, ceiling legislation was incomplete and allowed large landowners to avoid the law. What is most significant, however, is that the laws failed to provide fair compensation to landowners. Thus, even after policy makers revised the laws, government officials lacked the will to make compulsory land purchases from the relatively powerful landowning class. The lack of adequate land records also complicated redistribution efforts.

The lack of political will to confront and dismantle existing power structures, to trace land rights through dated (or nonexistent) recordkeeping systems, and to dedicate time and resources to unpopular programs persists to the present day. Under these somewhat dismal circumstances, reconsideration of ceiling laws is unlikely to contribute significantly to providing India's rural poor with greater access to land. Other strategies, such as those discussed in the "New Approaches" section below, are more likely to succeed in improving land security for India's rural poor.

Government Land Allocation Programs

In addition to the legislative abolishment of intermediaries, tenancy reform, and ceiling laws, some Indian states conducted major efforts to allocate government land to land-poor families. Under various programs, states have allocated government land as both house sites and agricultural plots.

Some states have provided house sites or homestead plots to landless laborers or other land-poor households. Land used for such programs has included government land, ceiling-surplus land, residential land under tenancy, and purchased land. Incomplete data indicate that an estimated 4 million households have received ownership of house sites India-wide. The plots typically range in size from 0.02 acre (about 900 square feet) to 0.10 acre (about 4,300 square feet), with the majority at the smaller end of the range (Das 2000, p. 38).[7]

Karnataka provides an example. That state's land reform law gave agricultural laborers the legal right to apply for and receive ownership of their house and house site.[8] The law initially limited to 2,180 square feet the amount that the state could grant a beneficiary, but a 1982 amendment eliminated that ceiling. On average, each applicant received 5,880 square feet of land.

However, more recent rural housing programs designed to assist the rural poor allot plots averaging approximately 1,200 square feet.[9] These plots provide space for little more than a house. Recent studies show that larger homestead plots provide other important benefits, particularly when the plots are large enough to include a garden and space for a few animals (Hanstad, Brown, and Prosterman 2002). Plots that are 0.07 to 0.10 acre (about 3,000 to 4,500 square feet) in size have been shown to provide the following benefits to farmworker families:

- Most or all of the families' fruit and vegetable needs
- Space to keep livestock that can provide all of the families' dairy needs
- Income (from the sale of products) equivalent to the wages of one full-time adult farmworker
- A chance to create wealth through the growth of valuable trees and/or labor-intensive improvements to the plot
- A valued boost in social status

- Improved access to credit
- The basis for ending a family's dependency on a large landowner (Hanstad, Brown, and Prosterman 2002).

Those findings from India are consistent with evidence from other developing countries (Mitchell and Hanstad 2004). Moreover, many of these benefits of house plots are directed toward and received by women, and thus benefit the family as a whole. When women have some control over a house plot and its use and production, they will tend to use the benefits of that plot (including increased amounts of food and surplus income) to benefit the children and family (Agarwal 1994, 1998; Deininger 2003).

Programs granting house plots have enormous potential to improve the livelihoods of the poor. Unfortunately, the vast majority of rural housing programs India-wide provide the poor with very limited space, leaving little room beyond the footprint of a small house. As discussed in the section on "New Approaches" below, Karnataka and West Bengal have recognized the opportunity in small plots. Both states recently adopted programs designed to provide landless and other poor families with plots that can benefit them substantially.

Wastelands are lands that either are entirely barren or are producing significantly below their economic potential (Sharma 2000). An estimated 150 million acres of India's 810 million acres are wastelands, and most are owned by state governments. Not surprising, India has tried a variety of ways to use its wastelands to provide the poor with access to land.

State governments have allocated 14.7 million acres of government wasteland to poor rural households through land reform programs (Government of India, Ministry of Rural Development 2003, annex XL). Six states account for 80 percent of this land, led by Andhra Pradesh (see table 9.A.1 in the annex).[10] Most of the allocations took place in the 1970s and 1980s, and most beneficiaries received between 2 and 3 acres of land.

In recent years, wasteland distribution programs have slowed or stopped altogether. In addition to the lack of new allocations, recent field studies show that a significant portion of the government land supposedly given to poor families actually is not in their possession. In Andhra Pradesh, for example, observers estimate that many of the reported recipients of government wasteland are not in legal or physical possession of their land. In some cases, the lands were distributed "on paper" but not on the ground. In other cases, the state distributed land, but without formal legal documentation. In still other cases, more powerful interests in the village forced the beneficiaries off the land (Akella, Hanstad, and Nielsen 2007). Indeed, in many states the general failure of governments to maintain accurate, current land records also has undermined their ability to undertake effective redistribution of land, including government land (for example, see Akella 2005).

The Andhra Pradesh state government, with World Bank support, is now taking steps to identify and correct cases where the beneficiaries are not in secure legal and physical possession. Moreover, the state government is pursuing the allocation of unallocated wasteland and other innovative and decentralized methods for providing secure land rights to the rural poor. The state's efforts may offer useful models for other states and countries (see the discussion of the Indira Kranti Patham (IKP) project below).

Summing Up and Moving Forward

Overall, India's first-generation land reform efforts have had some positive results, particularly in a few states where they were well implemented. As of 2002, state governments had transferred 17.7 million acres under ceiling-surplus and tenancy reform legislation (Government of India, Ministry of Rural Development 2003, annexes XXXVI and XXXVII). Results of a nationally representative survey of approximately 5,000 rural households interviewed in 1982 and again in 1999 reveal that land reforms had a positive impact on livelihoods. In particular, households in states that implemented tenancy reforms and land ceiling legislation experienced higher growth in income, asset accumulation, and childhood education than did those in states with lower levels of land reform effort (World Bank 2007).

Overall, however, land reforms did not fully accomplish their objectives and, significantly, the positive impacts of the reforms that beneficiaries realized have declined as implementation efforts have slowed over time. The negative impacts of reforms now may be outweighing the positive effects (World Bank 2007). Furthermore, research indicates that the reform programs have not benefited the poorest and the landless in a uniform manner. For example, ceiling laws often induced landowners to transfer land to relatives and to rent land to better-off tenants who had the capacity to farm the land more effectively (World Bank 2007). In addition, the neediest beneficiaries lost some of the potentially beneficial impacts of reform because the state failed to provide essential supporting nonland inputs.[11] (See box 9.3 about the continuing challenges facing India's tribal population.)

Finally, the first-generation reforms missed a significant opportunity to give rural women rights to land. However, as the next section discusses, some states in India understand the substantial impact women's access to and control of land can have on their families' well-being, and they have learned from the missed opportunities of the past. With women's land rights as the foundation, these states have created and implemented programs that lead the second generation of land reforms in India.

WOMEN'S LAND RIGHTS: OVERCOMING PAST INEQUITIES AND LEADING NEW APPROACHES

Although women in India have the legal right to own land, very few do. Moreover, for those women who do own land, ownership rarely means control of

Box 9.3 Tribal Land Rights: A Need for New Approaches

India's indigenous population, known as tribals or *adivasis*, makes up 7 percent of India's population. Tribals are among the poorest and most land-dependent of India's people, but their land rights are among the least secure. Land that tribals rely on for their livelihoods has been encroached, seized, transferred, and acquired—too often without adequate compensation or provision for comparable other land.

For decades, policy makers and civil society alike have struggled to preserve tribal land rights. Efforts include (1) laws restricting tribal land transfers, (2) recent extension of local governance authority to tribal areas, and (3) new legislation granting forest land rights. Historically, these efforts have suffered from the same gaps between law and reality, lack of political will, and lackluster implementation that plagued India's first-generation land reforms. However, state governments and civil society are trying new approaches, including targeting tribal areas for legal aid services and integrating land programs with development programs. Such new approaches to combat the persistent problem of tribal land rights are sorely needed.

the land or of the assets flowing from it (see Agarwal 1994; Mukund 1999; Deere and Leon 2001).

Government land allocation programs are one means by which women can gain rights to land. Under first-generation reforms, men received title to the vast majority of transferred lands because programs almost uniformly gave land rights to the heads of households or the farmer of the land—roles traditionally filled by men (Agarwal 2002).[12] This section discusses the opportunity missed to affect rural livelihoods positively through those reforms, and new efforts to provide women with access to land and control over the benefits attendant to land rights.

Poverty-Reducing Potential in Women's Land Rights

The harmful effect of women's unequal rights to access and control of rural land has been well documented (Agarwal 1998; Deininger 2003). The impact on livelihoods is particularly strong in India, where men migrate to expanding nonfarm employment opportunities and women constitute a growing percentage of the rural population.[13] Women's literacy rates, child care obligations, and cultural constraints make them less qualified and less available than men for nonfarm employment (Agarwal 2002). As a result, 86 percent of female workers in rural India—the majority of whom are among the poorest and most vulnerable in the population—are dependent on agriculture for their livelihoods (Gopal 1993).

Despite their growing dependence on agriculture, rural women's ability to access land and manage the benefits from the land to which they are tied remains highly restricted. Excluding women from control of agricultural land and its production harms not only the individual women, but also their children, families, and communities.[14] Where men control the use of land and household assets, they are more likely to spend income on personal items, status-seeking activities, and the fulfillment of individual desires. In contrast, women tend to use income and production from land to meet the basic nutritional, welfare, and educational needs of their children and families. In short, if women have secure access to land and can control its production, the benefits to the family can be life changing (Agarwal 1994; da Corta and Venkateshwarlu 1999; Deininger 2003).

State Programs to Increase Women's Land Rights

Several Indian states have tried to increase women's land rights through policies dictating how title should be granted in land distribution programs. The results have been mixed. Fourteen years after its land distribution programs began, West Bengal started requiring government land to be issued jointly in the name of husbands and wives, or to women individually "to the extent possible" (Gupta 2002, p. 7). Unfortunately, the state already had distributed most of the land, and the policy did not have retroactive effect (Gupta 2002). In addition, even in the case of new land allocations, implementation of the policy by local officials has been spotty.[15]

The problems encountered in West Bengal also threatened a government housing program in Karnataka. That state is among a small group of states that have attempted to increase women's land rights through ownership of government-distributed housing benefits. Beginning in 1993, the state ordered officials to put government housing benefits (houses and often house plots) in the names of both husbands and wives. As in West Bengal, implementation of the requirement was uneven at best. In 2000, Karnataka attempted to address the problem of implementation and further enhance the rights of women by requiring officials to title housing benefits in the name of women individually, with limited exceptions.

Karnataka's experience with this housing program yields critical lessons. Since 2003, local officials statewide have titled houses and house plots assigned to poor rural families in the name of a female family member (usually the wife of a married couple). In some areas, however, local officials did not understand the purpose of the titling requirement. In those areas, officials met the technical titling requirement of the program but were unable to assist women in realizing the economic, physical, social, and psychological benefits of ownership. In those areas, the titling requirement had little impact on the lives of the beneficiaries.

Elsewhere the situation is much different. In some areas of the state, local nongovernmental organizations (NGOs) are working actively with the community, providing capacity-building, savings, and income-generation programs for rural women. Partnering with the local government in its implementation of the housing program, the NGOs

- Teach the community about the benefits to the entire household when women have land rights
- Provide education programs on issues of gender equality for men and local leaders
- Train women to create kitchen gardens, raise livestock, and develop home-based businesses, such as tailoring and food preparation
- Assist women in developing credit relationships with local banks.

The impact of those efforts is uniformly positive. Where the NGOs are working actively with the housing program, the women beneficiaries, their husbands, and their families recognize the value of land rights. The women understand how their ownership of the house and house plot can be used to obtain a bank loan. They see how they can use the plot to improve their families' nutrition and generate additional income. The women participate in newly formed action committees that, together with other community members, identify local problems and discuss possible solutions. In short, the women, their families, and their communities are receiving all of the benefits of property ownership.

NEW APPROACHES

Karnataka's recent efforts in its housing program to put land titles in the names of women are fueled by a number of potentially powerful new approaches to land reform: (1) changing existing laws and drafting new regulations and rules narrowly tailored to objectives; (2) designing focused land-based programs; (3) using local, decentralized government institutions for implementation; (4) getting support for land-based programs from capable NGOs and community organizations; and (5) planning for legal aid and support for rights enforcement and education.

This section highlights some further examples of these new approaches. The first two examples involve legislative reforms. The proposed reforms are designed to support the creation of a land rental market that meets the needs of both landless people and landowners, and to facilitate the desires of sharecroppers to purchase the land that they farm. The third and fourth examples are descriptions of state programs that operate under existing law to increase land access and tenure security for the rural poor.

Removing Restrictions on Tenancy

Current tenancy restrictions now largely have a negative impact on the poor families they were intended to benefit. The negative effects of laws that prohibit or strictly limit tenancy are becoming more widely recognized. Several Indian states, including Andhra Pradesh and Karnataka, are considering relaxing these restrictions. Through carefully designed changes in the law, tenancy legislation could grant poor households access to substantial amounts of underutilized land and could ensure that tenancy relationships are recognized and regulated appropriately.

The specific content of these amendments will differ from state to state. In general, however, policy and legislative changes under consideration include the following:

- Where tenancy is now prohibited, allow for tenancy but include enforceable regulation that balances the interests of the tenants and landlords.
- Require lease agreements to be in writing, using a standardized form that forces the parties to state the rent amount, the lease length, and other important terms of the lease. Guarantee the tenant the right of exclusive possession for the duration of the agreement, but avoid unenforceable maximum rent payments or minimum length of terms.
- Expressly provide that neither the law nor any practice will grant new tenants any long-term rights to land or other rights beyond what may be mutually agreed by the parties, as evidenced in a written agreement.

Turning Protected Tenants into Landowners

West Bengal provides a second opportunity for improving land rights through legislative change. In its initial legislative reforms, West Bengal gave its sharecroppers (known as *bargadars*) substantial rights and protections. Under the West Bengal Land Reforms Act, sharecroppers are entitled to permanent and nontransferable (except by inheritance) rights to farm the sharecropped land and to keep a legally determined share of the production.[16] In addition, sharecroppers have a right of first refusal to buy the sharecropped land. Thus, if a landowner wants to sell his or her land, he or she first must offer it for sale to the sharecropper. A sharecropper keeps his rights even if the owner sells the land to a third party.

For many years sharecroppers were unable to enforce these rights. In an effort to help them realize the benefit of the law, in the late 1970s the West Bengal government initiated Operation Barga—a campaign to register and enforce sharecropper rights. The state has registered more than 1.4 million sharecroppers, and field studies confirm that their rights under the law now generally are respected and enforced.

However, although West Bengal's sharecroppers have benefited from stronger tenure security and lower crop share payments, virtually all of them would prefer to have ownership of the land. In addition, as nonagricultural opportunities have increased, many landowners would like to sell their land and engage in other business activities. The law has not kept pace with these changes. Instead, it has frozen sharecroppers in their positions as tenants and effectively prevents landowners from selling the sharecropped land to third parties.

West Bengal can expand its already significant land reform achievements by allowing its protected sharecroppers to become landowners. However, land sales between the many landowners and sharecroppers who want to do business often are prevented by legal restrictions on the transferability of sharecropped land and by the sharecroppers' lack of purchasing power.

The West Bengal government now is exploring legislative revisions and other steps to support the sharecroppers who wish to become owners (and helping those landlords who want to sell). These legal revisions and other efforts include

- Funding a land corporation to help sharecroppers purchase the land they farm
- Adopting a simpler and less costly process for the sale or exchange of sharecropped land to sharecroppers that includes safeguards to prevent abuse by landowners
- Setting a standard or minimum price to be used when a sharecropper wishes to sell or purchase sharecropped land.

Expanding Land Access through Land Purchase

A third new approach assists the rural poor with land purchases. The state governments in Andhra Pradesh, Karnataka, and West Bengal have initiated projects to transfer microplots of land to landless laborers through land purchase programs. In these programs, the land is obtained only through voluntary purchase. The voluntary nature of the programs avoids the problems of past land reform approaches that relied on involuntary takings of land. The programs in all three states purchase land in large parcels and divide the land for multiple beneficiaries. The amount of land provided for each recipient varies from 0.10 acre (in Karnataka) to as much as 1.0 acre (in Andhra Pradesh).

The programs in Karnataka and West Bengal are focused in part on providing house and/or garden plots. Beneficiaries of these programs can choose to use the plots for a house site (if needed) as well as for income-generating purposes, such as farming and keeping livestock.

Providing a 0.10-acre house-and-garden plot may be the most practicable method of giving meaningful land rights to India's 17 million landless rural families. Because land in most village areas is scarce and expensive, the Karnataka and West Bengal governments are buying land parcels of 1 or more acres situated within 1 kilometer of a village. They divide the parcels into house and/or garden plots. The programs also provide some basic infrastructure, such as a road, drinking water, and an electricity line, if those are needed (see box 9.4).

Andhra Pradesh's land purchase program, which is part of the state's pro-poor IKP program, aims to provide up to 1 acre of irrigated land per beneficiary. Whereas Karnataka's program operates through village governments, and West Bengal's operates through the state government line departments, Andhra Pradesh's program operates through women's self-help groups. It has the following features:

- *Beneficiary-driven process*—Beneficiaries, not government officials, initiate the land purchase activity. Self-selected beneficiaries who have shown the capacity for a land purchase identify the land, negotiate a price, and develop a business plan for farming the land.
- *Purchase plus improvements; business plan requirement*—The program requires beneficiaries to consider what improvements are necessary (such as irrigation) and to include those improvements in the business plan. The requirement of a business plan focuses the beneficiaries on the economic feasibility of their land purchase and requires consideration of options.
- *Cost-recovery plan*—The program includes a substantial grant component and reasonable repayment terms so beneficiaries do not end up with too much debt. The program allows up to 75 percent of the total cost of the land purchase and any improvements to be paid with grant funds. The beneficiary is responsible for 25 percent of the total costs, no less than two fifths of which must be the beneficiary's personal contribution in cash or in kind. Beneficiaries can pay the balance with loans advanced from the self-help group or project. Repayment of any loan can be spread over 15 years and carries a market rate of interest (Government of Andhra Pradesh 2005, pp. 8–9). The debt repayment plan is included in the business plan so beneficiaries can understand their financial obligation and how it affects the overall economics of the land purchase option.

Box 9.4 Microplots: Low Cost and High Impact

The land costs per family for microplots are affordable. If nonirrigated agricultural land is targeted, typical costs of such land in India range from $450 to $2,000 per acre, or $45 to $200 to benefit each family with a one-tenth–acre plot. Thus, governments need not be constrained by insufficient existing government land. They also can avoid the political and administrative difficulties of taking land involuntarily. The amount of land needed in India is not large—giving such plots to each of the 17 million landless families would require only about 0.5 percent of India's agricultural land.

The early experience of Andhra Pradesh's program is promising. One study shows beneficiary households enjoyed significantly higher levels of food security, improvements in health and education, and less migration (Panth and Mahamallik n.d.). However, the possibility of providing a majority of the landless poor with 1 acre of land through land purchase is in question, both because of the relatively high costs per beneficiary (about $1,200) and because of the limited supply of land available for sale.

Land-Related Legal Aid in Andhra Pradesh

In the final example, a legal aid program developed in Andhra Pradesh as part of its IKP program ensures that land rights reach intended beneficiaries. Many of those whom the state intended to benefit from land reforms, as well as other small and marginal farm families, have not fully realized the land rights to which they are entitled. Often they are unaware of their rights, or barriers related to poverty and marginalized social and economic status prevent them from asserting those rights. Legal aid can bridge the gaps.

Andhra Pradesh recently began a statewide legal assistance program to help individuals and families realize their land rights. Most land cases involving the poor are not complex and may be resolved satisfactorily with relatively modest attention and resources. Andhra Pradesh's program seeks to (1) advise the poor of their rights, (2) collect and evaluate the facts of existing land cases, and (3) empower the poor to assert their rights effectively.

The program primarily operates through village-based paralegals. It trains local young people to serve as paralegals in their communities, with the support of a lawyer. The paralegals conduct legal literacy campaigns and train women's self-help groups and local activists to identify land cases in which the poor may not have received justice, and they assist in resolving those cases. Because many of the land cases require surveys, and the government has a shortage of surveyors, the program also trains educated youth from the villages to become community surveyors who work with the paralegals to resolve cases requiring survey work.

The program's benefits extend beyond the resolution of land cases on behalf of the poor. The program increases the capacity of local youth through the skills training programs. In addition, the self-help groups and their communities gain increased legal awareness and they experience the collective strength that enhances their empowerment.

LESSONS LEARNED

The following lessons can be drawn from India's experience with land reforms, to date:

1. *Define the issues narrowly in legislation*—Legal reform strategies and land legislation benefit from efforts to define issues and terms narrowly. In an

attempt to end exploitative relationships, India's tenancy laws often broadly prohibited all tenancy relationships or imposed excessive restrictions, resulting in unintended negative impacts. The overly expansive laws failed to allow for the evolving and diverse nature of rural livelihoods or to recognize the role land rental markets can play in providing land access for the poor while meeting the legitimate needs of landowners.

2. *Look for unanticipated impacts*—India's first-generation land reforms suffered in their effectiveness because they failed to take into account the vulnerability of the tenants and sharecroppers on the land. Legislation that successfully abolished intermediary interests in land unintentionally caused the eviction and resulting landlessness of some of those most dependent on the land. If policy makers had possessed greater knowledge of the rural realities and likely responses of all groups to the new legislation, governments could have designed protections for these populations, such as the protections West Bengal gave its *bargadars.*
3. *Give attention to the rights of women and other marginalized groups at all stages of any reform process, and provide capacity-building opportunities*—India's land reform legislation failed to recognize the importance of equitable land rights for women and men. States taking steps to address inequities are learning that increasing women's land rights involves fundamental social change. To facilitate and ease the process of social change, program staff must study every aspect of a program—from concept to design to development to implementation to evaluation—to identify problem areas and act to avoid inequities. In addition, considerable time and resources must be devoted to sensitization, education, and capacity building at all levels.
4. *Respect existing land rights*—The needs of those with existing land rights cannot be ignored in efforts to help the beneficiaries of land reform. India has been unable to implement its ceiling laws primarily because the laws do not provide fair compensation to larger landowners. The inadequate compensation caused landowners (who otherwise might be willing sellers) to evade the law, and local officials lacked any incentive to enforce the ceiling. In the process of reform, existing land rights should be protected with clear legal authority to retain existing rights or to obtain fair compensation for those rights acquired by the state.
5. *Seek opportunities to decentralize power*—India's decision to give states power over land matters generally has served the objectives of land reform well. Each state has the authority to adopt legislation and develop programs for the circumstances unique to its region and population. Where local officials are trained in land matters, such as through Andhra

Pradesh's IKP program or West Bengal's Operation Barga, the results are more likely to benefit the intended communities.

6. *Challenge assumptions and settled thinking*—India's early land reform planning was paralyzed by the belief that government land distribution programs must provide families with at least 2 acres of land. Karnataka and West Bengal's small-plots programs are examples of projects based on current knowledge about rural livelihoods and increased understanding of the benefits available with small plots. The first step for policy makers creating such promising programs is being willing to question old beliefs regarding land reform.
7. *Prioritize and fund implementation of new legislation*—Much can be lost between legislative intent and implementation. Upon investigation, officials in Andhra Pradesh discovered that as much as 30 percent of the intended benefits of government land allocation programs had not reached the intended beneficiaries. In many areas, Karnataka's effort to title land in women's names was unknown and had no impact. A well-planned program for implementation can make an enormous difference. West Bengal's *bargadars* benefited enormously from Operation Barga, the government's program to educate communities about *bargadar* rights and to register *bargadars*. Twenty years later, *bargadars* almost always report that they learned about their land rights from Operation Barga. They identify registration of their rights through the program as one of the most important factors in their power to negotiate with landowners.
8. *Improve land records to provide more secure tenure to the poor*—Inadequate and incomplete land records are a substantial obstacle to conducting meaningful land redistribution or to strengthening poor people's existing land rights. Improving land records administration benefits the poor by reducing the time, cost, and petty corruption associated with land transactions (World Bank 2007). Although modern and complete land records are not always a prerequisite for effective land reform, they do make the task much easier. Before attempting reform, attention must be given to the state of current land records, with consideration given to updating and improving those records and the mechanisms used to manage them.
9. *Plan dispute resolution and rights enforcement systems*—Land rights are valuable only if they can be enforced. In India, the judicial and administrative institutions charged with enforcing land reforms are inadequate in number, capacity, and funding. As a result, hundreds of thousands of land rights cases are stuck in the courts and administrative bodies, usually to the disadvantage of the poor. Land reforms must include methods and institutions for dispute resolution and the enforcement of rights that are accessible to the poor.

ANNEX

Table 9.A.1 Shares of Households and Agricultural Area Affected by Land Reforms in Major Indian States

State	Tenancy Area (%)	Tenancy Population (%)	Ceiling Area (%)	Ceiling Population (%)	Wasteland Area (%)
Andhra Pradesh	1.67	0.75	1.64	3.80	11.80
Bihar	—	—	1.84	3.25	7.92
Gujarat	10.80	20.25	0.58	0.51	5.75
Haryana	—	—	1.16	0.93	—
Himachal Pradesh	Unknown	33.62	0.25	0.52	—
Karnataka	8.65	8.65	0.41	0.48	4.51
Kerala	37.40	56.91	1.77	3.34	11.70
Madhya Pradesh	—	—	0.46	0.80	0.19
Maharashtra	8.36	12.63	1.25	1.19	1.99
Orissa	0.78	2.49	1.25	2.11	5.70
Punjab	—	—	1.05	0.96	1.10
Rajasthan	—	0.26	0.88	1.17	0.17
Tamil Nadu	4.03	4.52	1.05	1.30	1.20
Uttar Pradesh	—	—	0.58	1.33	5.60
West Bengal	—	12.00	7.76	21.79	3.15
All India	3.96	8.40	1.37	3.82	37.32

Sources: Agricultural area figures used to calculate percents are the "all holdings" from Government of India, Ministry of Agriculture (2006). Population figures used to calculate percents are the "estimated number of rural households" from Government of India, Ministry of Agriculture (2005, p. 211). Beneficiary figures used to calculate percents are from the Government of India, Ministry of Rural Development (2003, annexes XXXVI, XXXVII, and XL).

Note: — = not available.

NOTES

1. In addition to these government land reform tools, civil society used another tool that achieved some redistribution success. Vinob Bhave, a disciple of Mahatma Gandhi, started the *Bhoodan* (land gift) movement in Andhra Pradesh in 1951, when an armed landgrab upsurge was gathering momentum. Bhave asked landowners to donate a portion of their land for peaceful distribution to the landless. The *Bhoodan* ultimately received donations of 39.16 million acres of land across multiple states for redistribution to the poor. Of the land donated, only 21.75

million acres have been distributed formally to the poor. The remainder have not been distributed for a variety of reasons, including that land was unfit for agriculture or had been encroached on, the donation was contested by heirs, or the donation documents were either missing or not in order (Government of India, Ministry of Rural Development 2003, annex XXXIX).

2. For background on India land tenure systems, see Kotovsky (1964) and Appu (1996).
3. For example, in Andhra Pradesh, peasants banded together in formal and informal associations; and through marches, demonstrations, and other public education efforts, they protested the abuses by intermediaries. Their efforts ultimately resulted in a string of legislative acts that transferred the land that previously had been controlled by intermediaries into *ryotwari* or state land (Reddy 2002).
4. Haque and Sirohi state that "nearly 20 million" cultivators were brought into direct contact with the government between 1950 and 1960 (1986, p. 30). Appu estimates that "about 25 million" former tenants were brought into direct relationship with the state (1996, p. 73).
5. Other measures adopted by Indian states include (1) complete prohibition and (2) leasing permitted but with the tenant getting a right of ownership or a right to purchase ownership after a period of one to six years.
6. West Bengal Land Reforms Act, 1955, § 49.
7. West Bengal reports allocating approximately 500,000 such house sites.
8. Karnataka Land Reforms Act, 1961, as amended, § 38(a).
9. The Rajiv Gandhi Housing Corporation maintains records of the state housing programs on its Web site, www.ashraya.*kar.nic.in*; see also the discussion in ICRW/RDI (2006).
10. The state-level revenue departments still control about 50 million acres of wasteland (Chambers, Saxena, and Shah 1989, p. 44).
11. West Bengal recently has initiated a new microfinance program to provide financial support for land purchase by the landless poor in that state. Loans of up to Rs 6,000 are available at an annual interest rate of 4 percent.
12. Even where women actually were heads of households, title often was given to a male family member (Gupta 2002).
13. Most recent statistics suggest that females are de facto heads of 20–30 percent of rural households (Agarwal 2002, p. 3).
14. The debilitating effect of women's unequal rights to access and control land is well documented (see Agarwal 1998; Deininger 2003).
15. In three rounds of field research, the Rural Development Institute (RDI) encountered few cases of government-granted land allocated in the joint names of husband and wife or in the independent name of a woman. RDI found several examples of families who had received government-allocated land after the adoption of this policy and who stated that the land was granted solely to the male head of household (Brown and Das Chowdhury 2002). RDI did not view the land documents in these cases, so it is possible that the land in these situations had been granted jointly, and the female grantees were not aware of their ownership status.
16. The sharecropper's share is 50 percent if the landlord provides inputs, 75 percent if not (West Bengal Land Reforms Act, §§ 15[2] and 15A).

REFERENCES

Agarwal, Bina. 1994. *A Field of One's Own: Gender and Land Rights in South Asia.* Cambridge, U.K.: Cambridge University Press.

———. 1998. "Disinherited Peasants, Disadvantaged Workers: A Gender Perspective on Land and Livelihood." *Economic and Political Weekly* 33 (9/March 28).

———. 2002. "Are We Not Peasants Too? Land Rights and Women's Claims in India." SEEDS (pamphlet series published by the Population Council), November 21. http://www.popcouncil.org/pdfs/seeds/seeds21.pdf [accessed January 2, 2009].

Akella, Karuna Vakati. 2005. "Building on Political Will: The Next Step for Land Reform in Andhra Pradesh." Unpublished manuscript. Rural Development Institute, Seattle, WA.

Akella, Karuna Vakati, Tim Hanstad, and Robin Nielsen. 2007. "New Life for Land Reform: The Potential in a Decentralized Approach." Unpublished manuscript. Rural Development Institute, Seattle, WA.

Appu, P. S. 1996. *Land Reforms in India: A Survey of Policy, Legislation and Implementation.* New Delhi, India: Vikas Publishing.

Behuria, N. C. 1997. *Land Reforms Legislation in India.* New Delhi, India: Vikas Publishing.

Brown, Jennifer, and Sujata Das Chowdhury. 2002. "Women's Land Rights in West Bengal: A Field Study." Reports on Foreign Aid and Development, No. 116. Rural Development Institute, Seattle, WA.

Chambers, Robert, N. C. Saxena, and Tushaar Shah. 1990. *To the Hands of the Poor: Water and Trees.* Boulder, CO: Westview Press.

da Corta, Luci, and Davuluri Venkateshwarlu. 1999. "Unfree Relations and the Feminization of Agricultural Labour in Andhra Pradesh, 1970–1995." *Journal of Peasant Studies* 26 (2/3): 71–139.

Dantwala, M. L. 1950. "India's Progress in Agrarian Reform." *Far Eastern Survey* 19 (22): 239–44.

Das, Sukumar. 2000. "A Critical Evaluation of Land Reforms in India (1950–1995)." In *Land Reforms in India: An Unfinished Agenda,* Series Volume 5, ed. B. K. Sinha and Pushpendra, 29–44. New Delhi, India: Sage.

Deere, Carmen Diana, and Magdalena Leon. 2001. *Empowering Women.* Pittsburgh, PA: University of Pittsburgh Press.

Deininger, Klaus. 2003. *Land Policies for Growth and Poverty Reduction.* Washington, DC: World Bank.

Gopal, Gita. 1993. "Gender and Economic Inequality in India: The Legal Connection." *Boston College Third World Law Journal* 13 (63): 63–86.

Government of Andhra Pradesh, Rural Poverty Reduction Project. 2005. "Operational Guidelines: Increasing the Rural Poor's Access and Rights to Rural Land." September. Society for the Elimination of Rural Poverty, Hyderabad.

Government of India, Ministry of Agriculture, Agricultural Census Division. 2005. "Agricultural Statistics at a Glance, 2005."New Delhi.

———. 2006. "Agricultural Statistics at a Glance, 2006." New Delhi.

Government of India, Ministry of Rural Development. 2003. *Annual Report 2002–2003.* New Delhi.

———. 2006. *Annual Report, 2005–2006.* New Delhi.

Gupta, Jayoti. 2002. "Women Second in Land Agenda." *Economic and Political Weekly,* May 4.

Hanstad, Tim, Jennifer Brown, and Roy Prosterman. 2002. "Larger Homestead Plots as Land Reform? International Experience and Analysis from Karnataka." *Economic and Political Weekly,* July 20.

Hanstad, Tim, and S. B. Lokesh. 2003. "Findings from Micro-Plot Research in West Bengal." Memorandum. Rural Development Institute, Seattle, WA.

Haque, T., and A. S. Sirohi. 1986. *Agrarian Reforms and Institutional Changes in India.* New Delhi, India: Concept Publishing.

ICRW (International Center for Research on Women) and RDI (Rural Development Institute). 2006. "Women's Property Ownership: An Examination of the Process and Impact of Karnataka's Rural Housing Program Titling Directive." Unpublished manuscript. Rural Development Institute, Seattle, WA.

Kotovsky, Grigory. 1964. *Agrarian Reforms in India.* New Delhi, India: People's Publishing House.

Mitchell, Robert, and Tim Hanstad. 2004. "Small Homegarden Plots and Sustainable Livelihoods for the Poor." Livelihood Support Programme Working Paper 11. Food and Agriculture Organization of the United Nations, Rome. ftp://ftp.fao.org/docrep/fao/007/J2545E/J2545E00.pdf [accessed January 2, 2009].

Mukund, Kanakalatha. 1999. "Women's Property Rights in South India: A Review." *Economic and Political Weekly,* May 29.

Panth, Ananth, and M. Mahamallik. n.d. "A Report Submitted to the Society for Elimination of Rural Poverty, Government of Andhra Pradesh, by Indian Institute of Dalit Studies." Rural Development Institute, Seattle, WA.

Reddy, G. B. 2002. *Land Laws in Andhra Pradesh.* Hyderabad, India: Gogia Law Agency.

Sharma, S. C. 1990. "Wastelands: Definition and Classification." In *Utilization of Wastelands for Sustainable Development in India: Proceedings of the National Seminar on Utilisation of Wastelands for Sustainable Development in India, Balrampur, 1987,* ed. S. C. Sharma, R. B. Chaturvedi, and O. P. Mishra, 41–53. New Delhi, India: Concept Publishing.

World Bank. 1997. *India: Achievements and Challenges in Reducing Poverty.* World Bank Country Study. Washington, DC.

———. 2007. *India: Land Policies for Growth and Poverty Reduction.* New Delhi, India: Oxford University Press.

PART IV

The Wide Array of Objectives, Mechanisms, and Tools for Land Redistribution that Remain the Focus of Heated Debate

CHAPTER TEN

Expropriating Land in Brazil

Zander Navarro

Land reform is an age-old debate in Brazil, whether as a government policy or as an imperative to enhance social development defended by various political actors. Since the end of the 19th century, one finds in the literature vigorous demands to reform one of the most skewed land structures in the world. However, perhaps it is correct to point out that land reform, in fact, was made visible only in two well-defined periods in the country's political history. First, it emerged on the public agenda in the late 1950s and was abruptly interrupted soon after by the military coup of 1964 (see Martins [1981]). The second historical moment gradually materialized after the adoption of the 1988 constitution, when strong political pressures and a growing social demand developed. Two of the hottest topics when legislators drafted the new constitution were increased access to land for the rural poor and the promotion of land redistribution because of many disagreements about their mechanisms. As a result of the post-constitution capacity of rural organizations and social movements to exert pressure, by the mid-1990s an ambitious process of land expropriation was under way. If measured by the implementation of actual initiatives, therefore, that second historical moment covers the period 1996 onward, when four successive mandates (including the current one) prompted several actions to make land reform a reality in Brazil.

This chapter summarizes the history of land reform in Brazil and its most decisive facts, moments, achievements, and current challenges. The first section following this introduction briefly sketches the origins of land concentration and the main aspects of that first historical moment when land reform emerged as a heated political issue. It also highlights the military cycle that followed it, when land reform in practice was replaced by projects of colonization and land regularization in several still sparsely populated and remote regions of the country. The second section discusses how land reform was structured legally in Brazil after the Land Statute of November 1964, covering its main formal stipulations and the definition of the expropriation program. After an account of how land reform principles evolved and were adjusted over time, the third section discusses recent years, especially those after 1995, and the main achievements of the land reform program implemented since that year. Finally, before concluding, the fourth section analyzes the most pressing challenges facing this policy now that it probably is reaching its historical end for reasons including diminishing social demand. In various sections, the chapter also discusses the links between the expropriation program and the actions of social and political organizations, and the pressures exerted (especially land occupations) to reach greater results in the implementation of land redistribution.

LAND REFORM IN THE 1950s AND THE YEARS OF THE MILITARY CYCLE

Social demands for land redistribution became a politically disputed theme in the late 1950s and, in particular, in the years before the military coup of 1964. But all attempts to promote land reform were blocked by constitutional barriers and insufficient clout. Reflecting this social pressure, the new rulers after the coup approved comprehensive new legislation to implement land redistribution in the country. However, these legal measures were not used, and the military regime reverted to colonization as a favorite mechanism to ensure that poor families gained access to land.

Origins of Land Concentration in Brazil

Brazilian land structure, well known as one of the most skewed land distributions in the world, has an historical justification, starting with the Portuguese colonization and decisions made over time by that empire, before independence in 1822. The justification relates to a dual movement favoring aristocratic groups, on one hand, and a persistent effort to deny access to land by nonelite members of the white poor population. Later in the 19th century—after the rise of coffee as a major international commodity, the end of slavery in 1888, and the inauguration of the republic a year later—those measures were an attempt to keep former slaves from securing land and to maintain a large permanent pool of cheap rural labor to serve the agrarian oligarchs. As a result, the main facet of agrarian history is the formation and permanence of underutilized large estates throughout rural Brazil, usually termed "unproductive *latifundia*" in local legislation and general literature. This was the historical background that established land concentration and was the pattern at least until the period following World War II. It was a time when Brazil experienced a cycle of democratization that started with elections in 1945 but came to a blunt end with the military coup of 1964.

Emergence of a Demand for Land Redistribution

The first historical moment when struggles for access to land took center stage gradually developed from the mid-1950s onward—in step with the process of political openness that was typical of that period—until the military takeover in 1964 (see Medeiros [1989]). Land reform then was seen as a fundamental policy that would liquidate the political domination of land elites; contribute to improved patterns of income distribution in rural areas; and, in particular, boost industrialization in Brazil after the formation of an enlarged internal market. Land reform at that time reflected an international concern and a policy considered crucial to ease social tensions and respond to political demands. Those demands were inspired by the Cuban Revolution and a reform proposed by a then-influential United Nations Economic Commission for Latin America and the Caribbean. Both perspectives had an implicit idea for a national process of capitalist development. In Brazil, the idea entered the political agenda after peasant leagues formed and promoted a series of actions in some of the traditional sugarcane estates in northeastern Brazil, particularly in the states of Paraiba and Pernambuco (see Hewitt [1969]). Contemporaneously and for the first time in the country's history, inspired by a then-semilegal Communist Party of Brazil, rural trade unions were forming in rural areas known for their commercial activities—for example, the state of São Paulo (see Houtzager [2004]). Stimulated by these social forces, pressure gradually mounted on the national government to implement rural labor rights and land reform. The pressure was even more radicalized during the brief mandate of the reformist government of João Goulart (1961–64), who eventually was deposed by the military coup in April 1964. In his term, for example, the number of pro-poor rural trade unions spiraled upward and political spaces for protest and political pressures were more open than ever (see Camargo [1981]). To illustrate, in 1963 the biggest strike ever held by rural workers in the history of Brazil occurred when the majority of workers in some northeastern sugarcane-producing areas stopped working to demand that labor rights be implemented in rural areas.

In the period 1955–64, however, two special barriers had to be overcome if any attempt to implement land reform was to be successful. The first barrier was the political conservatism of that period, when right-wing parties and political forces were powerful in congress and had large majorities that blocked any discussions—let alone proposals—to change the legal precepts of land reform and labor rights in rural areas. Specifically in the case of land reform, however, the second and main impediment was the 1946 constitution itself. It stipulated in article 176 that any land expropriation eventually signed by the government should compensate the former landowner in cash before any eviction—and, moreover, the amount paid should reflect the fair market price. Land reform was impossible in practice under those requirements, and no feasible attempts were made to change the constitution or to expropriate land under the impracticalities of those stipulations.

The 1964 Military Coup

Although many actions were taken and much political pressure was brought to bear in the period, land reform was merely a subject of heated debate in that first historical moment; land expropriation never materialized. It should be mentioned, however, that agrarian tensions were a major factor affecting the climate that eventually led to the 1964 military coup. After that institutional rupture, five successive military presidents made no serious attempts to implement land reform because of their conservative natures; and only occasional expropriations were made, usually in specific situations of strong social tension. According to official statistics, in the period 1964–85 (that is, during the military regime), only 77,000 families were settled—in Brazilian terms, a negligible number. As a rule, the military governments preferred to design a policy of colonization in rural backlands, justifying it under the political imperatives of forming new human settlements in frontier regions to colonize remote areas of the country. During that period, in addition to that colonization, the military implemented a land titling and registry program. Until the end of the military period in March 1986, however, no substantial attempts were made to bring land reform back onto the political agenda.

BRAZIL'S LEGAL STRUCTURE FOR IMPLEMENTING LAND REFORM

Especially because of the political turmoil in the years before the military coup, the new rulers found it necessary to devise new legislation to implement land reform in the country. The idea perhaps was to enforce rules that would place any change in the land structure under the strict control of the state. Any farm to be expropriated, for example, would be subjected to a long judicial procedure, and the final decision required a presidential decree. After some years, however, this legislation (enacted at the end of 1964) no longer was used, and the mark of the military regime was not land reform but a huge process of agricultural modernization with no tangible changes in patterns of landownership. For landless families, access to land came under ambitious policies of colonization in new areas on the agricultural frontier—particularly in the center-west region of Brazil.

A Legal Framework for Land Redistribution

The most striking characteristic of land reform and related social struggles is a dualism that is rarely understood by external observers unaware of Brazilian politics. On one hand, after the 1960s the country developed detailed and extensive agrarian legislation that, in principle, enables any government to implement ambitious programs of land reform if there is the political will to do so. On the other hand, the country's political history has demonstrated a vigorous and as yet invincible alliance among large landowners, politicians, and conservative sectors capable of preventing the enforcement of law in due course should a significant process of land reform become a reality. Brazilian history is a paradigmatic example of the political power of elites to block the state and law enforcement when those entities' policies are against their interests.[1]

The basic legal framework that still sustains land reform in Brazil is the Land Statute signed November 30, 1964, just after the military coup (Law 5604). Its main focus was to devise ways of dealing with unproductive *latifundia*, apart from creating conditions to force agricultural modernization and increasing access to land for the rural poor. Because the primary barrier to overcome was the existing constitution and its stringent financial requirements to expropriate land, the first military government signed a constitutional amendment (in December 1964) that scrapped the need for pre-eviction "fair" payment for land expropriated to be paid in cash. It stipulated that from that time forward, land expropriation would be paid for with public bonds that could be fully redeemed only 20 years after issue (their values periodically updated in accordance with indexes of inflation). Also crucial was the amendment's unifying all existing legal possibilities and permitting only the federal government to decree expropriations for the purpose of land reform. As a result, at least at the level of legal requirements, no factor could prevent the implementation of this policy because it now depended only on political decisions. The constitutional amendment even declared that landowners would be incapable of disputing in court any decisions to expropriate their land; proprietors would be able only to demand renegotiation of monetary compensations for the investments and buildings existing on their properties—not for the act of expropriation itself.

The Land Statute also established, for the first time, a mechanism to formalize a typology of establishments in rural areas. All landowners, no matter the size of their farms, were invited to declare details about their properties. After that information was collected, private farms were classified into one of four types of landholdings: (1) small "*minifundia*," (2) typically medium-size rural enterprises, (3) the *latifundia* on which more than 50 percent of the potentially productive acreage was unused, and (4) *latifundia* based solely on the absolute size of the property.

All those categories were defined according to objective criteria listed in the approved statute. The criteria basically were centered on the concept of a so-called rural module, a fixed unit of minimum land size in any specific region of the country that, in principle, would be enough to secure subsistence for an "average family" involved in agricultural activities. Depending on the region, proximity to markets, soil quality, rainfall regimes, and so on, the module size was defined for a given region and then all rural establishments were classified into one of the four categories. For example, landholdings smaller than the module fixed for their region would fall into category 1—*minifundia*—and obviously would be exempt from expropriation. Legislation later was modified, and currently no farm that is smaller than 15 times the fixed rural module for its region can be expropriated legally. With its new databank, the federal government gradually had a clearer idea about land use, types of rural properties, their main characteristics, and an approximate picture of land structure in the country. The rationale was that land reform could be implemented without much tension because decisions to expropriate would be based on objective facts and all farmers would know the rules of the game in advance. In particular, the biggest land estates (category 4) would be expropriated without any legal chance of their avoiding the action; those estates of significant but not immense size (category 3) would risk expropriation only if they did not cultivate a substantial part of their agricultural land. Rural enterprises and small farms (categories 1 and 2), on the other hand, were strictly protected under the new law and could not be expropriated at all.

A Progressive Land Tax

It is also relevant to mention that the Land Statute of 1964 established a progressive scale of "rural land taxation" that, on paper, would penalize large landowners, forcing them either to sell their estates or radically rearrange their agricultural activities to cultivate most of their land. If most of the land was not productively crop-cultivated, the biggest landholdings would be taxed at an annual rate of 20 percent of the property's market value. If that tax were imposed, in a few years it would be economically meaningless for the owner to keep such a property. This taxation, however, has proven to be hard to collect. The basic problems with the tax are its direct incidence on "nonused land" and the lax and insuperable disinterest of governments at all levels to collect it. In relation to the first aspect, for example, there is a growing contradiction facing an economic activity that in many areas is becoming strongly technologically organized and more productive and, as a result, is capable of producing more on less arable land. It means that rural land taxation in Brazil is reaching a curious state where it is a burden on those farmers who seek higher productivity through technology (see Oliveira [2007]). The main evidence of this contradiction is that the area cultivated with crops in Brazil (ranging from 48 million to 54 million hectares) has not increased substantially between 1988 and 2008, whereas the national production of grains, for example, has risen remarkably. In the period 1990–2005, the area under cultivation observed an annual growth of 1.2 percent, whereas the total agricultural output increased 6.5 percent a year. Whereas Brazilian agriculture is experiencing an impressive growth in production and gradually is becoming highly modernized, this taxation still relies on a moral argument based on historical legacies (that is, land taxation was supposed to force the use of land because there were so many unproductive *latifundia*). Many landowners avoid providing information to the tax authorities and, according to official estimates in 1992, more than 1 million rural landholdings were not declared officially as required by law, constituting a territory of about 110 million hectares. As a result, the relationship of the total area of all officially recognized and registered landholdings to the total surface of the country was only 39 percent (see INCRA [1996]). Also according to official estimates, when comparing all sources of revenues collected by the government, the highest proportion obtained in recent years was 0.2 percent in 1996 (INCRA 1996).

The Land Statute: A "Dead Letter"

The main goal of most legal changes adopted was to make land productive and, as a consequence, to prompt rural farms to fulfill their "social functions." The Land Statute and subsequent legislation, though representing an unprecedented rupture with past agrarian history, were extremely generous with large landowners because the criteria used to classify land estates were too tolerant, and because only immense holdings with most of their acreage unproductive theoretically were under the threat of the law.

Even so, the Land Statute—despite its innovations and potential capacity to transform land use and rural structures—stayed for most of the military cycle as a dead letter, enforced only as a last recourse by the federal government. For most of the period, all military presidents preferred to avoid it (and its resulting political disputes) and to follow policies of colonization on new agriculture frontiers of the Brazilian center-west region, where poor families, specially recruited in the south of the country or in the poverty-stricken northeast region, were offered plots of land in an area still largely unoccupied. As a consequence, in the period 1964–85, land reform virtually was ignored and the number of new settlements was rather modest. Not only was colonization one of the major rural policies of the military period intended to freeze land reform; efforts to privatize former public lands on the agricultural frontier also were implemented in those years. Approximately 30 million hectares were transferred to private hands through the mechanism of "fiscal incentives" adopted by the military governments. Under the promise of productive investments (especially cattle ranching) in the agricultural frontiers of the center-west region, the backlands of the northeast region, or in the Amazon state of Pará, it was the main policy of land occupation in those years. Especially in the 1980s, this transference of land rights was the main source of land conflicts in those areas of the country because it eventually opposed local and scattered social groups of indigenous populations and dispersed small farmers in support of the interests of powerful economic groups who claimed vast expanses of land.

THE SECOND MOMENT OF LAND REFORM: 1995 ONWARD

Conditions for implementing land reform on a massive scale improved enormously in the mid-1990s. The new constitution of 1988 opened the space for political pressure from various groups in Brazilian society, and the vigorous process of democratization observed in the country throughout the 1990s created conditions to force the federal government to launch reform. Especially after 1996, land reform came to be a reality for the first time in Brazilian history.

The Return of Democracy

Political conditions surrounding the subject of land reform changed after the end of the military cycle, and the country began a process of political democratization that eventually made Brazil one of the most democratic countries in the world.

Land reform returned to political center stage sometime in the second half of the 1980s, especially during the legislative period leading to the signing of the new constitution in October 1988. Two of the most disputed themes when representatives to congress were preparing the new constitution were the legal requirements to redefine properties available for land expropriation and to separate them from those protected from the action. The debates galvanized social forces, emerging social movements, and several public figures—usually in favor of land reform—but the new constitution did not improve the legal possibilities to prompt it (see da Silva [1988]). Therefore, in the 1990s when social movements and organizations representing rural poor people became increasingly vocal and capable of mobilizing support for their demands, they faced legal stipulations that were similar to those they had faced in the past.

Congress did approve some, albeit modest, progressive changes, however, and they were made part of the new constitution. The generic principle of the "social function of [rural] properties" launched by the Land Statute was incorporated in the constitution (articles 184 and 186). Two other important decrees were signed in 1993 (decree 8629 in February and Law 76 in July), which defined faster legal procedures for expropriation of rural properties for the land reform program. After these new stipulations, landowners whose properties had been expropriated had fewer opportunities for legal opposition. Expropriation procedures were placed under a quicker schedule and the scope for bargaining and delaying the due course of justice was made narrower, thus facilitating the juridical arrangements of land expropriation. In short, these new laws imposed on the involved courts shorter periods of time to decide on several aspects of a given property expropriated for the purpose of land reform. Even with these changes intended to enlarge the scope of land reform, outcomes did not improve much over the outcomes that were typical during the military cycle. Official statistics indicate, for example, that in the first civilian government (1985–90), only 83,000 families were settled; and in the period 1991–94, only 57,000 landless families were offered plots of land in different parts of the country (Scolese 2005).

The Land Situation in the Late 1990s

Land structure in late-1990s Brazil still reflected the legacies of the past, with an immense concentration of land assets in the hands of a few owners. Although income concentration in the country is high relative to international patterns (the Gini index for income is currently around 0.6), land concentration is almost absurdly skewed and official estimates based on censuses place the current index at 0.843. Given the continental size of Brazil, this index suffers some variations, being lower as an average of those states constituting the south region (0.712) and the center of the country (0.757), but higher in the center-west (0.810) and north (0.851) regions. In the northeast, the index reaches 0.811. The resulting picture is one of dramatic asymmetries in Brazilian rural land ownership: although 31.6 percent of all rural properties are in the 0–10-hectare group (and the sum of their areas corresponds to only 1.8 percent of total area owned by all landowners), at the other extreme one finds the opposite to be true—that is, all properties with 2,000 hectares or more constitute only 0.8 percent of all landholdings (and the sum of those properties corresponds to 31.6 percent of the total area owned by all Brazilian landowners). Under these social differences it is no surprise that rural poverty is rampant in the Brazilian countryside, with approximately 5 million families living on less than two official minimum wages per month (at the end of 2008, the standard wage corresponded to $190 a month) and infant mortality rates the highest in the country. If these figures were analyzed per region, it would be possible to demonstrate that the most dramatic levels of poverty and illiteracy in the western hemisphere exist in the rural northeastern areas of Brazil.[2] Table 10.1 summarizes the 2003 structure of land ownership in Brazil.

Table 10.1 Structure of Landownership, 2003

Size of rural landholdings (hectare)	Landholdings (%)	Area owned (%)
0 to 25	57.6	6.3
25 to 100	27.6	13.7
100 to 500	11.4	23.8
500 and more	3.4	56.2

Source: Instituto Nacional de Colonização e Reforma Agrária.

Pressure and the Start of Land Redistribution

A new and favorable juncture occurred during the two terms of former president Fernando Henrique Cardoso (1995–2002), when opposition parties and rural organizations defending land reform were stronger and, in particular, when a difficult economic context significantly affected agricultural activities and made many large landowners offer their estates for the national program of land reform.[3] Especially in the years 1995–2002, this program experienced an extraordinary increase, and approximately 400,000 families were settled. For the first time in Brazil's history, land reform became a substantial investment of the central government and made headlines for most of those years.

In the second part of that decade, the Landless Workers' Movement (*Movimento dos Trabalhadores Rurais Sem Terra* [MST]), in association with the National Confederation of Agricultural Workers, representing smaller and poor farmers, came to the forefront and was able to promote a growing series of actions intended to push forward the struggle for land reform and to exert pressure on the federal government. The record of the MST is impressive, particularly from the second part of the 1990s onward, and is reasonably well documented in the literature (for example, see Branford and Rocha [2002]; Navarro [2002]; Wright and Wolford [2003]). It must be noted, however, that the historical role of these organizations and their actions to stimulate social mobilization in rural areas around land reform and the agrarian question, notwithstanding the relevance, are beyond the scope of this chapter. Despite the importance of peasant struggles in many telling situations in the past, their political impact in recent times has diminished. Such diminishment is inevitable, given the many social and economic transformations experienced in the country, especially after the profound structural economic changes promoted in the 1970s during the so-called Brazilian miracle. After that decade of high rates of economic growth, Brazil emerged as a country destined to be urban and industrial. The agrarian question suffered a fatal blow; it was only a matter of time before the onset of intense urbanization prompted the reduction of agriculture's contribution to GNP and the loss of the political clout enjoyed in the past by the agrarian elites. Those were expected changes after nearly 40 years of growing urban and industrial dominance. In fact, the current claims of the "centrality of the agrarian question" in Brazil represent either a corporatist defense or merely myopic academic readings of reality, seen through an ideological lens. I argue at the end of this chapter, however, that in the absence of any visible "agrarian question," land reform still can be an important policy tool to reduce poverty if a concerted effort is made, particularly in the poorest rural northeastern regions.

It was in the period 1996–2002 that a clear strategy to promote land reform was in place for the first time in Brazilian history, mobilizing several state ministries (including the armed forces), and there was a detailed plan to break social and political resistance to reform. The most spectacular result of the period—apart from a huge rise in the number of families settled and the total area expropriated for the national program—was the elimination in most rural areas of local large landowners' capacity to use all means (licit or otherwise) to avoid expropriation and interrupt the continuity of government procedures. If any observer compares the mid-1980s with the political conditions for land reform in Brazil in more recent years, he or she will find the difference to be remarkable. In most parts of Brazil now, every large landowner knows that land must be farmed intensely or the risk of land occupation rises. If land occupation happens, there are good chances that swift legal actions sanctioned by local authorities to evict invaders will not be enforced and eventually that property will be lost to expropriation. These facts constitute an extraordinary political achievement resulting from that late-1990s combination of government strategy and pressure from rural organizations to keep land reform on the political agenda.

Despite these visible political gains in the implementation of land reform and advances in legal procedures, expropriated farmers still are able to enjoy some bargaining space, and several actions may be used to avoid or delay expropriation. For example, even if laws signed in the 1990s promoted faster legal procedures, the local judge in charge of the geographical jurisdiction of a given land that the government decides to expropriate may allege various reasons either to block the government evaluators' access to the land or to deter landless families trying to reach the property. Given the common political alliances involving the local elites (including local judges), judicial decisions often are not fair and result in controversial readings of legal stipulations. As a consequence, the act of expropriation frequently does not occur for a long period of time. Also, because the state actually is absent in many rural regions, landowners threatened by expropriation may use direct action to avoid, for example, visits by government evaluators trying to check the viability of land for expropriation. Such direct action is illegal, of course, but there have been occasions when the state was not able (or did not wish) to mobilize police to protect their evaluators, and the evaluations either took a longer time or did not occur at all. Additionally, if a time delay is granted to the farmer whose property is due to be expropriated, there is a chance that underused land rapidly will be transformed into "productive economic activity." For example, this happens in cattle ranching, where neighboring farmers rush part of their cattle to the soon-to-be-expropriated farm before any official evaluator checks the actual use of the land. The most common action taken by proprietors of large holdings when their land is expropriated (or an expropriation is announced after an examination of land records) is using legal recourses ad infinitum because Brazilian law offers countless loopholes for legal challenges, especially when the threatened farmer is rich and able to hire the best lawyers. In these cases, the process of expropriation may be delayed for some years and the costs will spiral out of control because the government's lawyers must counter each legal act the farmer takes until a final decision is made by a higher court. To date, no study has been made to estimate the costs of such legal disputes, however, and there is enormous variation within the country in terms of the costs of legal procedures.

In the administration of President Luiz Inácio Lula da Silva, elected in 2002 and reelected for a second term four years later, the national program was maintained with a single but crucial difference: more financial resources were invested. The logistics of the program, however, remained almost the same. In President Lula's first term, it was possible to settle 381,000 landless families in an area of approximately 32 million hectares (an area equivalent to the size of Belgium, Denmark, Portugal, and Switzerland put together). The federal government invested almost $2 billion[4] to promote land reform between 2002 and 2006, and there are solid expectations that at least those amounts will be repeated in the second presidential term. That means that by 2010, Brazil will have experienced a period of 15 years when approximately 1.5 million landless families were settled.

Also in the 1990s, another important change in rural politics was taking shape: the emergence of the notion of "family-based agriculture," which previously did not exist under that name in Brazil. There is not space here to discuss the reasons for this change; suffice it to say that from the mid-1990s onward, rural organizations defending family farmers were able to entrench new policies directed exclusively to family farming. Consequently, this new policy created a crucial cleavage in public funds commonly invested in agriculture, formerly under the sole control of powerful agrarian sectors. Because landless families eventually form new groups of family farming in new settlements, this new initiative was in practice a decisive change not only to reduce the political clout of large landowners, but also to put forth additional arguments in favor of land reform.[5] To illustrate the point, in the current decade when the number of new jobs created by economic growth has not been high and unemployment has been a trademark of the Brazilian economy, the very fact that family farming in the new settlements offers at least three new jobs on each plot of land and creates a list of indirect new jobs related to the settlements has been an important justification for this social policy.

Controversy around Redistribution Mechanisms

It must be noted that in January 2009 the Brazilian program of land reform is structured along two complementary mechanisms. The first mechanism is the conventional scheme based on expropriation in accordance with the legal framework referred to above. The second mechanism usually is referred to as "market-based land reform." Of the two alternative means of acquiring land for redistribution, expropriation is by far the one used most often; it corresponds to approximately 85 percent of all land transferred for land reform in Brazil. In fact, the paths are made complementary merely by ideological constraints; otherwise, the tendency would be to avoid the complex, costly, and bureaucratized route of expropriation in favor of negotiated alternatives.

Given its political composition and under the intense pressure of left-inspired social organizations, the government has not yet promoted any serious discussion of these options. The expropriating mechanism often is defended on purely moral grounds, responding to an "historical social debt" owed by large landowners, presumably because of excessive land concentration, social exploitation, and a record of impunity typical of Brazilian agrarian history. In short, the two paths are complementary not because one indeed complements the other, but because political conditions impose their dual existence. Given this reality, as explained in an earlier section of this chapter, properties susceptible to land expropriation are to be found under the legal stipulations of the Land Statute; and properties that can be negotiated under the second existing mechanism actually are not limited by many restrictions.

The market-based land reform route is a mechanism born of a small project in place in the state of Ceará (Projeto São José) that in 1996, under the name Cédula da Terra, was extended to four states in the northeast region and to the northern areas of Minas Gerais (see Navarro [1998]). After a project in Colombia, it was the second market-based land reform project approved by the World Bank, and it followed a new format under which beneficiary associations of poor families obtained financing to purchase suitable agricultural properties after negotiations with willing sellers. At that time, following the program of monetary stabilization that launched the "Real Plan," macroeconomic conditions prevailing in the country were especially favorable. As a result, land prices plummeted, thus creating a new context in which promoting efficient land markets could be an important instrument to facilitate access to land. By the end of Cédula (in 2003), an estimated 15,200 families had settled on 609 separate properties at a cost of approximately $3,000 per family. It is worth noting, however, that economic conditions at that juncture were exceptional because declining agricultural credit subsidies and low inflation reduced the incentives to hold land as a hedge, increased the supply of land available for sale, and lowered its price. This program involved loans to landless families or poor smallholders (renters, sharecroppers, and tenants) prepared to form an association and buy a property that suited their interests and was available for sale. Additional grants were offered for complementary investments. The main requirement for access to this program was the claimant's level of poverty; individuals outside the associations also applied for funds on their own behalf. Before its discontinuation, this project briefly was transformed into a World Bank–financed program implemented in several states (a program now called Crédito Fundiário or Land Credit), which offered credit to acquire land under a rationale mainly destined to alleviate poverty. In 2000, on a parallel initiative, the Land Bank was established by the Brazilian government to provide loans for small farmers interested either in buying new properties or only in seeking to increase their landholdings. Loans from the Land Bank have been sought particularly by more modernized small farmers in the south. Until 2003, credit sources available through Cédula (for a brief period, Land Credit) and the Land Bank had been the two possibilities open to people searching for access to land not based on the traditional program of expropriation.

In the initial year of President Lula's first term (2002), paying tribute to pressures based purely on ideological justifications (because Cédula resulted from World Bank loans), both initiatives mentioned above were abolished and soon were replaced by a new program displaying few substantial differences from the ones they replaced. The new program was called the National Program of Land Credit (*Programa Nacional de Crédito Fundiário*). It had several components, the most important ones being land credit to combat rural poverty (cofinanced with the World Bank) and the consolidation of family-based agriculture. In their time, Cédula had been concentrated mainly in the states of the northeast region, whereas the Land Bank was decentralized and active in most states. States—especially in the south—encouraged farmers to access the Land Bank (particularly the state of Rio Grande do Sul). Taken together, Cédula (with World Bank cofinancing) and the Land Bank (operating strictly with federal funds) settled 42,000 families in the period 1999–2004, and identified 1.5 million hectares to be bought to establish new settlements.

Despite political pressures, the National Program of Land Credit was implemented in 2004, and the federal government has set a goal of settling 120,000 families under this scheme during the two terms of the current president (2003–09). Although there is a subsidy embodied in this second mechanism, it usually is expected that monetary results coming from most agricultural activities in Brazil do not produce net financial results capable of repaying the loan amounts and interest rates that are a part of this second route opened to landless families. Analysts do not yet agree on the financial viability of this program for poor farmers; further research is necessary to clarify that viability. Conditions stipulated for loans were rather favorable on paper, but some studies insisted that most farmers would not be able to repay those loans, especially because of the low profitability observed in Brazilian agriculture in recent years. Notwithstanding those doubts, however, the experience of Cédula and, more recently, of the National Program, have demonstrated that usually the market route to land is cheaper than the conventional process of expropriation. In 2006, the specific credit fund for poor rural families set up under the National Program (Land Credit—Combating Rural Poverty, cofinanced by the World Bank), which follows the principles of market-based land reform, found that the national average cost was an estimated $3,600 per family, with a great range of variation among the states (in some richer states, the figure was approximately $16,000 per family).

In contrast, Marques (2007), who has written the most complete study of costs of land reform under the traditional expropriation method, has found much higher costs when analyzing the conventional route to land reform in Brazil. He concludes that when land is expropriated, the national average cost per family reaches $16,081, with specific states ranging from $10,622 in the poverty-stricken states of the northeast region to $23,919 in the states of the prosperous south. When land is bought by the government through the Land Bank project (instead of expropriated) to form new settlements, the national average skyrockets to $26,938 (again varying statewise from $16,564 in the northeast to $32,372 in the south). Finally, Marques also finds that when land is public and the state simply decides to form new settlements in those areas (such as in states in the Amazon region), the national average cost is $7,824 per family, varying across states from $7,466 per family in the northeast and $6,751 per family in the south). These data (all using 2005 U.S. dollar values) also demonstrate the crucial importance of land prices when the traditional method of expropriation is the main one used in land reform. Occasional comments by those who favor the expropriation route (rather than market-based initiatives) tend to dispute these figures, insisting instead that the real figures are much lower. Given these differences, there is a tense discussion about the continuity of land reform based on the acquisition of properties by groups of landless families. This matter, however, suffers from strong pressures based on mere ideological perspectives. In particular, the rural organizations mobilized by the Via Campesina (a left-leaning coalition that is commanded by the MST) combat this second option on rather controversial arguments. Although land acquisitions do not stimulate a dynamic market, it is curious that the Via Campesina organizations are demanding that the option based on market negotiations be scrapped because "it promotes a land market" when Brazil has lived under capitalism for such a long time. It must be emphasized, however, that additional studies are needed to clarify all aspects of these two mechanisms to facilitate access to land by rural poor families in Brazil. For example, we do not know the precise costs of land and nonland expenditures in new settlements established in different regions of a country so heterogeneous as Brazil. Only after these details are known will it be possible to devise a better, more effective strategy for a national program of land reform.

Land Expropriation in Practice

The national land reform program now has an automatic operational framework. Land for expropriation is found through various modern techniques, from aerial images taken by satellites to the formal databases organized on statements of ownership by landowners forced to make them because of the land rural tax they are supposed to pay. If a specific property appears to fall under the existing criteria and may be expropriated, there is a standard and normative set of procedures applicable in all cases, regardless of the region, starting with an analysis of the actual conditions of the property to be expropriated recorded in official databanks. The procedures also include an official visit by agricultural specialists who produce a technical assessment that is shared with the landowner, who then may decide to contest it legally. Only after these procedures are final does the president sign a decree of expropriation. Thereafter, a financial evaluation is carried out, because land is paid for with public bonds to be redeemed in 20 years, with all existing improvements to the farm compensated in cash. The former landowner also may decide to contest the decisions that have been made in the run up to expropriation. If there is no further legal dispute by the expropriated farmer, then the government agency in charge of land reform (Instituto Nacional de Colonização e Reforma Agrária, or National Institute for Colonization and Agrarian Reform [INCRA]) is issued an authorization to enter the area and start additional measures to establish the new rural settlement. These steps all told, it may take more than a year for a new settlement to be formed if there is no judicial contest. If the former landowner contests the expropriation, then the actual formation of the settlement could be postponed even longer. The main difficulties of expropriating rural property are not in the operational process, but in judicial maneuvers that owners sometimes are able to use to delay expropriation. In recent times, however, public bonds issued in exchange for an expropriated farm have been accepted in financial markets, and many large landowners have opted to avoid litigation. When these disputes occur, they are decided by the Supreme Court, according to a long list of decrees, laws, and legal norms.[6]

Beneficiaries, in turn, are expected to be selected under formal rules and to be able to register their interest in the public branches of the executive agency in charge of land reform. In practice, however, the selection of new settlers often is made under a tacit agreement with rural organizations representing the poor families—such as the MST or the rural trade unions. Often this cooperation creates distortion and undue preferences because those organizations select loyal members and do not pay much attention to more reasonable objective criteria when forming a list of candidates for new settlements. On paper, the new settlers must pay for the land and for the credits they receive after taking over their piece of land in the new settlement. In practice, however, things may be far different. For example, land will be paid for only when the settlement is officially "emancipated," and when the settler receives a formal land title to the property and is able to dispose of it as he or she wishes. But social movements and rural organizations representing the rural poor strongly have opposed that final step of making settlers private proprietors. They allege that the settlers face many difficulties and will be severely affected if emancipated (for example, many would not resist the land markets and would sell their plots in the settlement), so they oppose any attempt by the federal government to offer land titles to settlers. The cases where it has happened are rare, and it means that land has not been paid for in the vast majority of settlements throughout Brazil.

After occupying their plots of land in the new settlement, all families are entitled to different forms of credit for different purposes to secure postsettlement support. For example, an initial credit is offered to a settler to build his or her house, and "basic food baskets" are offered to every family at least during the first year. A more substantial form of credit called Pronaf A also is available through the National Program to Support Family-Based Agriculture (which is specifically for rural settlers in the land reform program); it covers expenses to cultivate the area (seeds, fertilizers) in the first two years. There are other forms of credit to which some settlements are entitled because of specific circumstances. The settlers repay the nonland loans they take, but substantial discounts are common when the time for payment is reached. Many times, there is also space for negotiation, and payments may be postponed. Although there are national rules for all these forms of credit offered to settlers, it has been observed that part of the debts may be reduced—or even cancelled—in the face of political pressures or the patronage of a given political actor, under specific circumstances.

Impacts of New Settlements

One controversial aspect of land reform in Brazil concerns its overall impact. Several studies were carried out in recent years and, in general, there are more findings in favor of the national land reform program than there are arguments against it or analysts who propose different social policies to replace it (see Sparovek [2003]). Perhaps the study by Leite et al. (2004) is an ideal illustration of the contributions made by new settlements in Brazilian rural areas. The authors selected six regions where there is a concentration of new settlements formed by the national land reform program in different parts of Brazil, and interviewed 1,568 settlers in 92 settlements over a period of almost two years. Some of their findings are worth mentioning here.

They find, for example, that in almost 90 percent of land transfers, the initiative to request the land expropriation came from the landless families themselves, after they invaded private land or exerted other pressures. State action in support of land reform has been rather slow; if rural organizations do not promote actions, state agencies rarely will offer land in advance to an interested group of landless families, despite the updated information available and more reliable administrative procedures. However impressive the number of landholdings expropriated between 1996 and 2006, land structure did not change in any visible aspect throughout Brazil. After analyzing data, Leite et al. conclude that new rural settlements in Brazil do not alter patterns of land ownership, and the Gini indexes for most regions remain the same after the new settlements are counted in specific municipalities. Usually this fact also implies that the local power and influence of large landowners in the regions of new settlements are still as strong as ever, and that a process of political democratization does not transform local realities. The survey also indicates that approximately 80 percent of the population settled lived formerly in the same region, and 94 percent worked in rural activities. These statistics show that although Brazil is a country of migrants, new rural settlements usually attract landless families of the same region, and they are farmers. The usual accusations that land reform is mobilizing nonfarmers from urban centers who want to escape the high unemployment rates prevailing in urban Brazil are not true—the national land reform program indeed is offering land for families with a tradition in agriculture. Those facts also highlight the crucial importance of land reform offering a reasonable, productive occupation to a large population of unemployed rural families formerly living in very unstable social and economic situations. After being settled, these families usually use their plots of land intensely to produce a long list of crops (and animals); approximately 70 percent of their income eventually is produced on the land they cultivate. This ambitious survey also demonstrates that conditions of life improved substantially, in all aspects. Not only is there housing and a better diet for all; rural settlements also create stable conditions for the members of a given kinship, including relatives who were not formally settled but who are invited to live with the family that was offered the land. New settlements stimulate local commerce when they sell their products. Farmers seek credit to implement new initiatives and become active "economic actors," especially when they establish organizations (for example, cooperatives) and make their presence visible in the local economy. After some time, they adapt to local society and become involved in politics and other social dimensions of those municipalities where the settlements were established. If the town is small, a medium-size settlement (80–150 families) might make a substantial impact on the local economy because many settlers will be entitled to receive government grants and pensions; they search for new credits and eventually there is a new economic dynamism in the municipality.

All findings taken into consideration, this important study by Leite et al. (2004) clearly demonstrates the social and economic relevance of new settlements formed under the national program of land reform for most rural areas of Brazil. Its most relevant finding is exactly the feeling of the vast majority of the people settled—that their lot has improved substantially and that they have a much better quality of life.

CURRENT CHALLENGES AND DILEMMAS

In recent years, despite the formation of an institutional framework to implement land reform and an increasingly favorable political context, this policy is becoming uncertain and is facing growing dilemmas and difficulties. The first aspect to highlight is the diminishing social demand in most Brazilian regions, especially because an unstoppable process of urbanization has reduced the number of landless families demanding access to land.[7] The structural spatial change of the Brazilian population is impressive: whereas in 1960 the rural population was an estimated 55 percent of the total population, the 2007–08 demographic census certainly demonstrated that the rural population now constitutes roughly only 15 percent of the total Brazilian population. Industrial and service sectors dominate the economy, and agriculture does not produce jobs in the same proportions as it did in the past, because of mechanization and an increasingly technological rationale prevailing in agricultural activities. The actual number of possible beneficiaries for the national program of land redistribution is highly disputable because of different statistical sources that—in this case—often are unreliable. It is also controversial because social demand is not always publicly demonstrated. However, when the demographic census or the National Survey of Households is taken into account, the approximate estimated number of potential beneficiaries is 3.1–3.5 million poor families. These are landless families, but it would be possible to include poor small producers (sharecroppers, renters, and small farmers with very small plots of land). The total then would reach approximately 5 million poor rural families as potential clients for the national program. This was, in fact, the figure established by the most recent National Plan for Land Reform, most probably representing an overestimated parameter. This figure does not mean, however, a proper social demand that is expressed politically in all regions.

A second factor affecting land reform is the cost of implementing it. There is a growing argument that, given the diminishing number of landless families, it would be cheaper to offer a monthly payment to the rural poor instead of the costly process (costly in administrative and financial terms) of land reform. At the moment, the federal government is in charge of a host of social policies for the Brazilian poor—the most effective one being Bolsa Família, a conditional cash transfer program in which poor families receive a monthly payment on the condition that their children attend school. Because most studies demonstrate that new settlers in most regions of Brazil are not capable of producing a monthly income bigger than a minimum wage, there are suggestions that instead of maintaining a complex process of land reform, it would be better to enlist these poor families in that social program. However, it must be recognized that the rationale behind each of these programs is distinct, and different areas of the federal government administer the programs. Access to land creates a multifaceted impact in the life cycles of landless families, whereas access to additional income provided by Bolsa Família may be simply an occasional benefit. In other words, that comparison would be too narrow and purely financial, disregarding other social factors associated with land reform.

Perhaps some of the most crucial factors that affected the implementation of land reform in Brazil from 1996 onward are the indexes of land productivity stipulated in law for all regions and agricultural activities in the late 1970s under then prevailing technological conditions. Those parameters were very low and, even if Brazilian agriculture showed impressive development after that decade, the parameters were not updated and landowners were not encouraged to improve their general productivity. If the required low levels of productivity were reached, owners would escape land expropriation. With the passing of time, even if political pressure was brought to update those indexes, the federal government always resisted it. Eventually the stock of land for land reform decreased because the government was unable to find available landholdings in line with legal requirements to submit to the process of expropriation, particularly in the most modernized agricultural regions. This is especially true in the technologically modern agricultural regions of the central-south where land prices have soared in recent years. In those regions the federal government has been forced to buy land, and it is unable to revert to expropriation measures because of legal impediments. In the less-developed northeast and north regions, there are still a great many underutilized *latifundia* that are subjected to legal expropriating decrees, and the government has concentrated its efforts to settle landless families in those regions (especially in the northern state of Pará). That factor, associated with the reduction of social demand, most probably means that land reform in Brazil is agonizing in these years and going through its final phase.

These facts notwithstanding, there is scope and there are justifiable reasons to implement land reform in Brazil. For example, if a massive effort were made to concentrate land reform in the Brazilian northeast, the reform could produce significant poverty reduction and economic prosperity for a very important proportion of the rural poor population. Approximately half of the Brazilian rural poor live in that region, but the most economically important areas of agricultural production lie outside the northeast region. If a concentration of financial and human resources were applied in that region to expropriate most of its large landholdings (which exist in great number in the region), a formidable stock of land would be made available and the vast majority (if not all) of the Brazilian landless families could be settled there (see Navarro [2001]). It would be possible then to enforce a process of land distribution that is qualitatively different from the traditional pattern of policies implemented to date. This suggestion usually is received with skepticism because the northeast region is plagued by a central and large area of semiarid conditions where agricultural activities are strongly affected. However, defense of this suggestion takes into account an enormous area encompassing the northern half of the state of Minas Gerais in the Brazilian center toward the state of Maranhão, bordering the northern state of Pará. Within this larger region there are many relevant areas with satisfactory environmental conditions where agriculture easily could prosper. If this region is the object of an intensive process of land reform, government agencies will find land enough to settle all landless families still demanding access to land in Brazil.[8]

CONCLUSION

Land reform in Brazil is approaching its Rubicon—its moment of truth when crucial decisions will be needed. With a social demand that is reduced every passing day, the development of several social policies that could be cheaper while producing better results for the rural poor (in terms of income), the opening of new agricultural frontiers at the hands of large landowners, and the country becoming a major player in international markets, it appears that reasons for land reform are no longer quite clear.

The recent expansion of the national program of land redistribution has produced satisfactory results in many areas and has been justifiable after social pressures and a rationale of offering land to the rural landless poor in times when the rate of growth of the Brazilian economy has been dismal and unemployment is too high. With a slight change in these macroeconomic circumstances, however, there is a strong probability that land reform will become an even more controversial policy, perhaps unjustifiable when its costs and its complex operational implementation are considered. If that situation occurs in the years to come, then a host of new policies devised to promote rural development must be discussed, including an enlarged role for negotiated projects to foster access to land by the rural poor.

NOTES

1. It reminds us of the famous 19th-century Argentine author José Hernández, who wrote, "The Law is like a knife; it does not hurt who holds it" (*El Gaucho Martín Fierro*, verse 1093).
2. It must be noted, however, that poverty in Brazil was reduced substantially in recent years, especially after the expansion of social programs like Bolsa Família, a huge conditional cash transfer program that now benefits approximately 11 million poor families in the country. This program was launched in 2003. If taken as a measure of income distribution, for example, in 2004 the country observed the lowest level of income inequality in its history. For a detailed discussion, see a recent article published by the government think tank Institute of Applied Economics, which is a part of the Planning Ministry (IPEA 2007).
3. In fact, that period is more complex than this mere indication. For example, some large landowners also were attracted by the policies of privatization carried out by the Cardoso government. It was announced that the federal government would accept land public bonds (*títulos da dívida agrária*) from private buyers trying to acquire public enterprises—that is, promises of payment by the state to be redeemed in 20 years. These documents were received by proprietors whose land estates were expropriated in the second part of the 1990s, and they were devalued historically because of their long-term conditions. When the government announced that the bonds would be accepted when state enterprises were privatized, these *títulos* gained an immediate chance to be cashed at their face values. Thus, landowners affected by an economic crisis because prices of agricultural commodities had plummeted in those years saw an opportunity to sell their properties and enter the privatization process to reap huge gains. Political factors also influenced the decision to implement a more ambitious program of land redistribution. The killing of landless workers in Corumbiara in 1995 and the following year in Eldorado dos Carajás (both states of the northern region) had an enormous impact on public opinion. That was particularly true for the second killing, which was filmed and which produced commotion in the country: state police murdered 19 landless workers when those workers obstructed a regional road to put pressure on the government. These tragic events also ignited a growing sympathy for the

Landless Movement, which took advantage and promoted the famous "March to Brasília" in April 1997—perhaps the only moment when then-incumbent President Cardoso actually was put against the wall. On the day the march reached the capital, it is estimated that 100,000 people gathered in the main square of that city to protest impunity for those charged with the crimes and to exert strong pressure in favor of land reform in Brazil. (For additional details, see Navarro [2002].)

4. A billion is 1,000 millions.
5. After the notion of family farming became institutionalized in the second half of the 1990s, several studies were made to differentiate it from so-called agribusiness. These studies demonstrated, for example, that family farming accounts for 84 percent of all rural establishments and employs 77 percent of all rural labor. This sector also accounts for approximately 40 percent of agricultural production and cultivates 30 percent of the total agricultural land utilized in the country. If the 15 most important agricultural commodities are considered (in value), family farming produces a significant proportion of 12 of those commodities. However, this enormous agricultural sector has access to only a quarter of government credit for agriculture, while large properties reap the bulk of credit (mostly subsidized) for agricultural activities.
6. This picture, in practice, is not as rosy as it might seem. As an example, land records in many states are a mess, and many presumptive proprietors dispute the same land. According to official estimates, only 51 percent of the total rural area in Brazil is registered formally. This fact most likely means that a vast area is being used illegally, especially for extensive cattle ranching scattered in the remote regions of the country.
7. "Demand" here is a political expression—that is, when potential beneficiaries are able to organize themselves and make public their interests. It does not refer to what social scientists would call "potential demand." The latter obviously is higher but also is diminishing with the passing of time, for the same reasons pointed out in the text.
8. I have defended this argument for some years (Navarro 2001), but a recent article by an influential economist reinforced the rationale of this policy in the existing conditions of Brazilian rural areas (see da Silva [2007]).

REFERENCES

Branford, Sue, and Jan Rocha. 2002. *Cutting the Wire: The Story of the Landless Movement in Brazil.* London: Latin America Bureau.

Camargo, Aspasia. 1981. "A questão agrária: crise de poder e reformas de base (1930–1964)." In *História Geral da Civilização Brasileira. O Brasil republicano,* Volume 3, Number III, ed. Boris Fausto. São Paulo, Brazil: Difel.

da Silva, José Gomes. 1988. *Buraco negro. A reforma agrária na Constituinte.* Rio de Janeiro, Brazil: Paz e Terra.

da Silva, José Graziano. 2007. "Uma nova agenda para a reforma agrária." *Valor Econômico,* June 27.

Hewitt, Cynthia. 1969. "The Peasant Movement of Pernambuco, 1961–1964." In *Latin American Peasant Movements,* ed. Henry A. Landsberger, 386–97. Ithaca, NY: Cornell University Press.

Houtzager, Peter. 2004. *Os últimos cidadãos. Conflito e modernização no Brasil rural (1964–1995).* São Paulo, Brazil: Editora Globo.

INCRA (Instituto Nacional de Colonização e Reforma Agrária). 1996. *Atlas fundiário brasileiro.* Brasília, Brazil.

IPEA (Instituto de Pesquisa Econômica Aplicada). 2007. "Sobre a recente queda da desigualdade de renda no Brasil." Technical note. Ministério do Planejamento, Brasília, Brazil.

Leite, Sérgio, Beatriz Heredia, Leonilde Medeiros, Moacir Palmeira, and Rosângela Cinarão. 2004. *Impactos dos Assentamentos: Um Estudo sobre o Meio Rural Brasileiro.* São Paulo, Brazil: Editora UNESP.

Marques, Vicente P.M. 2007. "Aspectos orçamentários e financeiros da reforma agrária no Brasil (2000–2005)." Ministério do Desenvolvimento Agrário/INCRA, Brasília, Brazil.

Martins, José de Souza. 1981. *Os camponeses e a política no Brasil.* Petrópolis, Brazil: Editora Vozes.

Medeiros, Leonilde S. 1989. *A história dos movimentos sociais no campo.* Rio de Janeiro, Brazil: Federação de Órgãos para Assistência Social e Educacional.

Navarro, Zander. 1998. "O projeto piloto 'Cédula da Terra.' Comentário sobre as condições sociais e político-institucionais de seu desenvolvimento recente." Unpublished manuscript. World Bank, Brasília, Brazil.

———. 2001. "Desenvolvimento rural no Brasil. Os limites do passado e os caminhos do futuro." *Estudos Avançados* 15 (43): 83–100.

———. 2002. "Mobilização sem emancipação. As lutas sociais dos sem-terra no Brasil." In *Produzir para viver,* ed. Boaventura de Sousa Santos, 189–232. Rio de Janeiro, Brazil: Civilização Brasileira. (English edition published by Verso Editions, Santa Barbara, CA, 2006).

Oliveira, Mauro Márcio. 2007. "Qual o destino histórico do imposto territorial no Brasil?" Unpublished manuscript. Brasília, Brazil.

Scolese, Eduardo. 2005. *Reforma agrária.* São Paulo, Brazil: Publifolha.

Sparovek, Gerd. 2003. *A qualidade dos assentamentos na reforma agrária brasileira.* São Paulo, Brazil: Páginas & Letras Editora e Gráfica.

Wright, Angus L., and Wendy Wolford. 2003. *To Inherit the Earth: The Landless Movement and the Struggle for a New Brazil.* Oakland, CA: Food First Books.

CHAPTER ELEVEN

Negotiated Agrarian Reform in Brazil

Gerd Sparovek and Rodrigo Fernando Maule

The initial concept for negotiated agrarian reform originated with the World Bank's "Land Reform Policy Paper" (1975; Deininger and Binswanger 1999), and it was implemented first in Colombia in 1994.[1] Practical adoption of the policy's principles was carried out worldwide under different institutional arrangements, political designs, motivations, operating rules, targeting methods, and objectives, and its results have varied. In some cases (such as Brazil, Colombia, Guatemala, Honduras, and Malawi), the World Bank partially supported the initiatives.

The Brazilian experience with negotiated agrarian reform is the most comprehensive, long-standing, and diverse program of any in the world. In Brazil, the reform has gone through four phases since its beginning (table 11.1 and figure 11.1). It was introduced as a pilot project in 1997. The pilot project was followed by a rolled-out phase (Cédula da Terra) before going through two national consolidation phases. In at least two phases of the negotiated agrarian reform, independent surveys were conducted to measure its achievement and evaluate its impact, notably in terms of poverty reduction. Understanding how the reform has operated and what outcomes it has produced in Brazil permits an assessment of its possibilities and restrictions in a scenario where the model is mature and comprehensively adopted.

This chapter aims to present a synthesis of the historical origins of agrarian reform in Brazil, with a focus on the point in time at which negotiated agrarian reform was initiated. It also describes the four phases of this reform program,

Table 11.1 Negotiated Agrarian Reform in Brazil, 1997 Onward

Period	Beginning	End	Beneficiaries	Federal state	Source
São José	1997	1998	700	Ceará	Garcia 1998
Cédula da Terra	1997	2002	15,000	Ceará, Maranhão, Pernambuco, Bahia, Minas Gerais	World Bank 2003
Banco da Terra	1999	2003	34,500	All Brazilian states (Brazil)	Teófilo and Garcia 2002
CF-CPR + PNCF	2002	n.a.	30,583[a]	Brazil minus Acre, Amapá, Rorâima, Pará, and Amazonas	Government of Brazil, Ministry of Agrarian Development 2007
Total			80,783		

Note: CF-CPR = Land Credit and Poverty Alleviation program; n.a. = not applicable; PNCF = National Program of Land Credit. CF-CPR includes the initial period of the program (2001–03). PNCF started in 2003, with the modalities CF-CPR, Consolidation of Family Agriculture, and Our First Land.

a. The Ministry of Agrarian Development has an online monthly bulletin that reports CF-CPR information; the data shown were taken from that bulletin.

followed by the empirical survey results that covered each of those phases. The conclusion summarizes both the achievements and impact of the negotiated reform in Brazil and its strengths and weaknesses, and suggests some challenges to be faced in an effort to improve the model.

AGRARIAN REFORM IN BRAZIL

The country's negotiated agrarian reform is part of a much broader agrarian reform effort initiated in 1964 with the Land Statute. This section highlights the concepts and historical events that are important in understanding the agrarian reform and that, to some extent, have influenced it.

History

Agrarian reform in Brazil started with the adoption of the Land Statute and the establishment of the Brazilian Institute for Agrarian Reform at the beginning of the military regime in 1964 (Gomes da Silva 1971). At that time, the military leaders were anxious to reduce agrarian conflicts and respond to the demand of the peasant organizations that were behind the political turmoil of the early 1960s. During nearly 30 years that followed the adoption of the Land Statute, however, no large-scale land redistribution was carried out. Instead,

Figure 11.1 Brazilian States and Coverage of the Different Periods of Negotiated Agrarian Reform

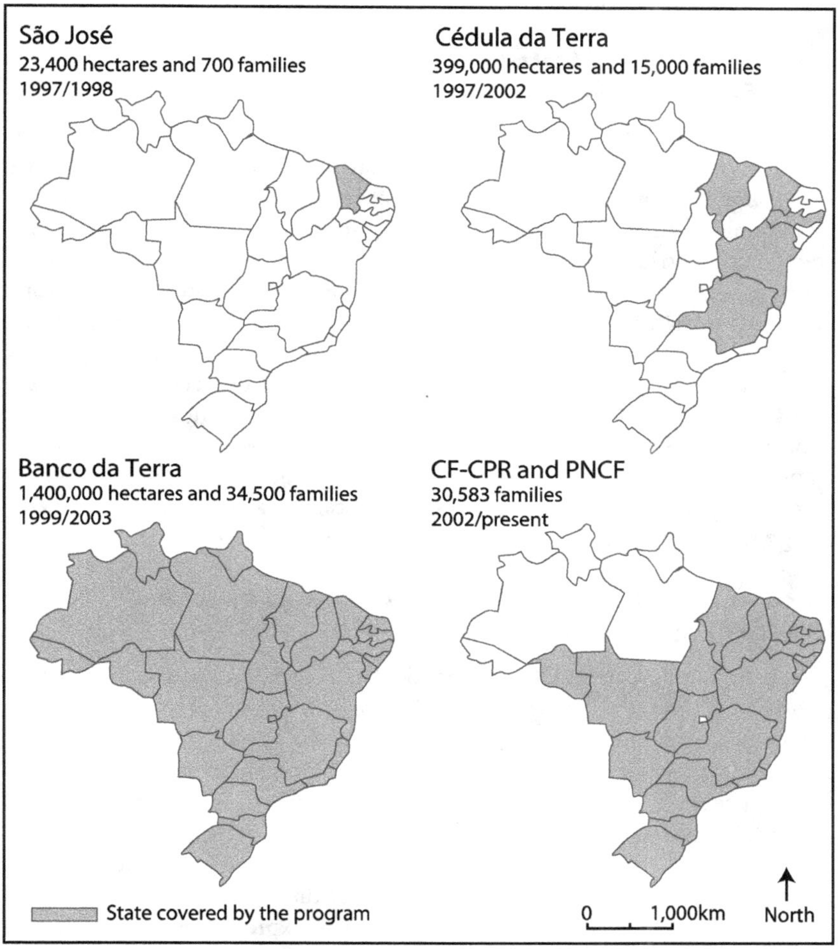

Sources: Garcia 1998; Teófilo and Garcia 2002; World Bank 2003; Government of Brazil, Ministry of Agrarian Development 2007.

the military regime preferred to promote colonization and an expansion of the agricultural frontier into remote areas of the country. As a result, during that period the contribution of agrarian reform to promoting profound changes in land distribution is questionable. By the early 1980s, the country's skewed land distribution remained almost unchanged (Hoffmann 1998). This slowly changed after the early 1980s. The military regime was living its last moments, and peasant movements were resurging. After the end of the military regime in

1985, these peasant movements, and notably the Landless Workers' Movement (MST), started to have a more expressive role in intermediating and conducting the agrarian reform process.

Conceptual Basis of State-Led Agrarian Reform Using Expropriation

In Brazil, the conceptual basis of the state-led agrarian reform using expropriation is the social function constitutionally attributed to land ownership. Since 1964, large land properties (*latifundia*) that are not productive, promote land or natural resource degradation, do not conform to labor legislation or contracts, and contribute nothing to the well-being of employed workers may be expropriated with compensation for land, improvements, and infrastructure. Once expropriated, land is redistributed to rural landless workers to create family-based agricultural operations. Land expropriation often is resisted by landowners who use legal means to contest expropriation decrees. But there is also a strong popular base of organizations constantly pushing the land redistribution process forward.[2] Occupation of unproductive areas by these organizations is common practice, and such actions frequently are met by violent reactions from the landowners. The state is a central actor, leading and mediating the reform process.

Circumstances Existing When the Negotiated Agrarian Reform Program Was Established

At the beginning of President Fernando Henrique Cardoso's term of office (1995–2002), the construction of a "new Brazil" was concerned with restoring democratic principles under a neoliberal and globalized logic. Democracy had returned for 10 years and popular movements for agrarian reform were extremely strong. The MST, one of the largest movements, was organized nationally.

It was in this context that the negotiated agrarian reform was introduced in 1997 to meet the demands of these movements. The reform not only fit in ideologically, but also aimed to handle some of the weak points in the expropriation model by (1) avoiding the high cost of expropriation, (2) reducing the overblown bureaucracy, (3) accelerating access to land and productive resources, (4) promoting a decentralized operation at the federal state level, and (5) establishing direct self-selection and volunteer pathways for land redistribution applications. The suggested design also promised an alternative way to gain access to land—one that was fast, efficient, and based on market logic, and one in which the conflicts (land occupation) and expropriation were not essential elements.

The MST and other popular movements related to agrarian issues immediately opposed the new model, interpreting it as part of a strategy to weaken and becalm them. In this same period, the massacres of MST militants in Corumbiara (1995) and in Eldorado dos Carajás (1996) (Oliveira

2001) dramatically focused attention on agrarian reform both in Brazil and internationally. After those massacres, President Cardoso immediately established the Ministry of Agrarian Development (MDA), with the mandate to speed up the execution of the state-led agrarian reform whereby land is acquired via expropriation. Since then, both expropriation and negotiation models have continued to be implemented separately.

EVOLUTION OF NEGOTIATED AGRARIAN REFORM

This section describes the four phases of negotiated agrarian reform in Brazil. Some phases have been analyzed comprehensively, allowing the selection of published articles to report them. Others scarcely are studied, and in those cases, unpublished reports have been used as sources of information.

First Pilot Project: São José

Negotiated agrarian reform was implemented first in Brazil in the northeastern state of Ceará in February 1997. It began as a pilot project named Reforma Agrária Solidária, better known as the São José Project. This project financed the purchase of land for landless rural workers organized in associations that negotiated and traded directly with landowners. To participate in the project, an association had to design and submit a proposal for land acquisition and farm development. Once the proposal had been reviewed and approved by the project management unit, resources required for its execution were transferred to the association. The financial arrangements offered by the project had two components: a loan component to be repaid by the association according to the terms of a collectively signed contract, and a grant component for the establishment of physical and social infrastructure (Garcia 1998; Pereira 2004; Sauer 2004).

Over a period of two years, the São José Project financed the purchase of 23,400 hectares of land, settling 700 families at an average per-family cost of R$6,083, or R$179 per hectare. Because of the grant component and other compensation measures, only part of this cost was paid back by the beneficiaries. The Brazilian government, the World Bank, and the project coordinator considered the results of the first phase of the São José Project positive and promising in relation to administrative efficiency and costs. Because of these results, the Brazilian government suggested to the World Bank a scaled-up project, named Cédula da Terra (World Bank 2000).

Second Pilot Project: Cédula da Terra

The "Land Reform and Poverty Alleviation Pilot Project," better known as Cédula da Terra, was approved in April 1997 and executed between July 1997 and December 2002 (Pereira 2004). Its coverage was restricted to four federal states (Bahia, Ceará, Maranhão, and Pernambuco) and the northern part of

Minas Gerais (Pereira 2004; Sauer 2004). The project's beneficiaries were landless rural workers (contract laborers, sharecroppers, tenant farmers) or farmers with less land than necessary to provide subsistence. Over a period of six years (1997–2002), the project resettled approximately 15,000 families on 399,000 hectares of land, at a per-family cost of R$11,975, or R$191 per hectare (World Bank 2003).

Cédula da Terra introduced an important mechanism to stimulate the bargain during the land sale negotiation. As in the São José Project, the total amount of credit, ruled regionally by limits, was divided in two parts—part 1 consisted of a loan for the land purchase, and part 2 was a grant component for improving physical and social infrastructure. The innovation was that a credit limit applied to the sum of parts 1 and 2. Thus, buying cheaper land, or reducing its price during negotiation, would result in a greater share of the grant that could be invested immediately in infrastructure. The debt of the loan was based exclusively on the cost of land, stimulating buyers to bargain more vigorously. The exact impact of this mechanism is not clear, but empirical evidence indicates that the cost for land purchase during the Cédula da Terra phase was equivalent to or lower than market prices.

Transition to a Consolidated Phase

An important moment in the history of Brazil's negotiated agrarian reform is the institution of the Land Bank (Banco da Terra) and the Land Fund. In February 1997, parliament issued Law 25 creating both entities, although they were not fully approved and regulated until February 1998. With this law, negotiated agrarian reform was no longer a pilot project, nor was it entirely dependent on resources from the World Bank. From this point, the reform was secured by a national fund constitutionally mandated to finance the purchase of land by rural workers. In other words, the basic principle of the reform—voluntary transfer of land purchased under market conditions instead of state-led expropriation—formally was incorporated in the national agrarian policy within the frame of a legislative regulation approved by the absolute majority of the parliament (Pereira 2005). Although the World Bank did not finance the Land Bank, the Brazilian government used federal resources from the Land Fund as a counterpart fund for Cédula da Terra.

First Consolidated Phase: Banco da Terra Project

Shortly before the creation of Banco da Terra in 1995, more than 30 social movements—including MST, the National Confederation of Rural Trade Unions (CONTAG), the Pastoral Land Commission, and the Brazilian Association for Agrarian Reform—had established the National Forum for Agrarian Reform and Rural Justice (Pereira 2005). The forum was responsible for several actions in Brazil and abroad aimed at compelling the international community to support the creation of an inspection panel to oversee World

Bank actions regarding negotiated reform in Brazil. Their main actions included (1) denouncing Cédula da Terra to the National Department of Justice for corruption and intentional purchase of land at prices exceeding market value; (2) supplying the World Bank with documents to show that during execution of Cédula da Terra, essential operational rules were not followed completely; and (3) informing the international community about irregular and political use of Cédula da Terra.

In May 1999, the inspection panel rejected the arguments presented by the National Forum for Agrarian Reform and Rural Justice, and concluded that an investigation into the matters alleged was not warranted. However, the turbulent opposition had delayed negotiations with the World Bank for additional funds, and ultimately Banco da Terra was established and run totally on the resources of the Land Fund.

As for the Cédula da Terra project, although associations were allowed to acquire any type of rural land until 1999, after the ruling of the inspection panel, project funds could not be used to acquire unproductive land—that is, land suitable for expropriation.

Whereas the São José and Cédula da Terra projects clearly were targeting poor and landless people, Banco da Terra targeted families with higher incomes. Unlike the São José and Cédula da Terra projects, Banco da Terra had no grant component. The funding—including the money for infrastructure—was amassed in the loan amount. Also different was the maximum loan amount for which a family could qualify: whereas a Cédula da Terra family could receive up to R$15,000, a Banco da Terra family could receive up to R$40,000 (or more in exceptional cases). Most of the resources allocated through Banco da Terra were used in the three federal states of the more developed south region of Brazil (Rio Grande do Sul, Santa Catarina, and Paraná), and the individual cost per family was significantly higher than in the Cédula da Terra phase (Teófilo and Garcia 2002). Banco da Terra was discontinued in 2003 as one of the first actions of the government of President Luiz Inácio Lula da Silva.

Restart of World Bank Investments: Land Credit and Poverty Alleviation Program

Because of this turbulent opposition, the World Bank delayed for almost two years the requested additional support for negotiated agrarian reform in Brazil. Also, securing the legitimate support of at least one organization representing the rural workers had become essential to overcome the resulting alienation of parties and to open a space for new initiatives. That support materialized in 1999 when the national leaders of CONTAG decided to support the negotiation of a new program, named Land Credit and Poverty Alleviation (CF-CPR). Those negotiations resulted in additional financial support from the World Bank (Pereira 2005).

CF-CPR started operating in 2002 at the end of the Cardoso government. Its territorial coverage included the nine federal states of the northeast region, Espírito Santo in the southeast region, and (experimentally) the states of Rio Grande do Sul, Santa Catarina, and Paraná in the south region. CF-CPR aimed to benefit 50,000 families divided thus: 40,000 in the northeast, 5,000 in the southeast, and 5,000 in the south (World Bank 2000). Access to the program was through workers' associations, as was true in Cédula da Terra. In exceptional cases, individual proposals were considered, as they were in Banco da Terra. In CF-CPR, areas that qualified for expropriation under the state-led agrarian reform (that is, unproductive *latifundia*) could not be purchased.

Second Consolidated Phase: National Program of Land Credit

In November 2003, the MDA launched the National Program of Land Credit (*Programa Nacional de Crédito Fundiário* [PNCF]), which consolidated the CF-CPR and the Land Fund (Banco da Terra) under the same name. At this time a new subprogram was created—the Consolidation of Family Agriculture (CAF)—for established family farmers. CAF offers higher loan amounts and has no grant component for physical or social infrastructure. Unlike CF-CPR modalities related to the poverty alleviation program, CAF is not supported by the World Bank (Government of Brazil, Ministry of Agrarian Development 2005). Finally, for young rural workers (those aged 18–28) and for the children of farmworkers, another subprogram called Our First Land was created.

When the PNCF was established, its aim was to benefit 50,000 families from the northeast, southeast, and south regions. It was implemented first from July 2002 to the end of 2004; then it was postponed until August 2006 and again until December 2007. The beneficiaries, whether as individuals or as members of associations, apply directly for credit (land purchase and investments). CONTAG—and in some cases, technical extension services or nongovernmental organizations—will help with organization and with navigating the bureaucracy. The land purchase price is paid directly to the selling landowner. The grant part of the credit (if applicable, depending on the PNCF subprogram) is deposited in the bank account belonging to the beneficiary (individual or association) to use for specific investments previously agreed to with PNCF officials. When the beneficiary has repaid the land loan completely (planned to occur over 20 years), a land title is issued in the beneficiary's name. This general process may vary according to the PNCF subprogram, the time at which the credit was established, and in line with minor regional requirements.

There were no significant changes in land reform policy during the first term of President Cardoso's successor, President Lula da Silva (2003–06). No concrete political measures affecting agrarian reform were adopted until President Lula da Silva's second term (2007–10) when, on December 2, 2008, a presidential act (Decreto 6.672) established the legal framework and design to allow negotiated agrarian reform to operate independently of external funds—that is, without World Bank credits. The most important aspect of this act is that it allows the allocation of investment grants for beneficiaries of CF-CPR. Such allocation was not possible before because all federal credits had to be paid back. The grant for investments is an essential benefit for the consolidation of new projects in poor regions and thus is necessarily part of any agrarian reform initiative. It is too early to analyze the effects of this act, but it is likely that the ability to execute negotiated agrarian reform with a grant component, and without external funds, will consolidate the policy even more and ensure its continuation for a longer time.

MAIN RESULTS OF NEGOTIATED AGRARIAN REFORM EVALUATIONS

The results presented in this section cover the existing articles and reports (published and unpublished) and summarize their findings. Considering the nonuniform methods and research designs used by the researchers, the results are only partially comparable between phases.

São José Project

The only evaluation that comprehensively describes São José was the preliminary evaluation of the rural component of the São José Project (Garcia 1998). Field data were collected in seven settlements during its initial period. The evaluation's principal objective was to guide the formulation of Banco da Terra with information on economic impact and the payment capacity of the beneficiaries. The survey was expeditious (a total of three weeks) but it coincided with a year of severe drought in the project areas that limited the fullness of its findings. The evaluation revealed that the program had positive economic effects on the incomes of the beneficiary families, mainly because of the increase in consumption of agricultural production. The increase in income varied from 450 to 800 percent when compared with income previous to the project. Only in a few cases, however, was the monetary income sufficient to ensure loan repayment—despite the use of optimistic indexes during modeling to avoid the bias of data collected in a severely dry year. The restrictions were related to climatic conditions (semiarid climate) and the low technological level adopted for agricultural production. The evaluation suggested changes and improvements for the program, including (1) a longer contract term, (2) a reduction in the rate of interest, (3) a reduction in the time allowed to access physical and social infrastructure resources, (4) an increase in the participation and the responsibilities of the associations, (5) provision of expert support for the elaboration of land purchase and farm development proposals, (6) production and distribution of informative material concerning the project, and (7) inclusion of a grant component for technical assistance contracts.

Cédula da Terra Project

There have been more evaluations and academic studies of Cédula da Terra than of any other phase of Brazil's negotiated agrarian reform. The main evaluations are (1) the preliminary evaluation of projects from Cédula da Terra in the state of Bahia (Garcia, Paranhos, and Machado 1998), (2) the preliminary evaluation of projects from Cédula da Terra in the state of Ceará (Corrales 1998), (3) the evaluation of preliminary results, challenges, and constraints by Buainain (1999), and (4) the impact evaluations by Buainain (2002, 2003).

The preliminary evaluation of Cédula da Terra was carried out in the state of Bahia. The first survey was launched in 1997, and field studies were conducted in 1998 (Garcia, Paranhos, and Machado 1998). Based on a sample of 16 associations, the results showed good targeting, with most beneficiaries being landless rural workers, temporary workers, or small farmers (smallholders or sharecroppers). In most cases, the family income before the project was below one minimum wage. Land was purchased at market prices or lower. The production systems resembled local and regional family agriculture, and, eventually, crops that were expanding in the region. In some cases, beneficiaries suggested technically dubious production systems that were not adopted by other farmers. In such cases, there was always a need for high-priced investments that were not accessible to the families. The prediction models based on the suggested production systems estimated a considerable increase in income, but one that was not enough in all cases to guarantee repayment of the debts.

The preliminary evaluation in the state of Ceará aimed the assessment of Cédula da Terra's implementation at the institutional and field levels (Corrales 1998). A case study methodology was used, selecting five settlements in distinct ecological zones to permit the comparison of different production systems. The study evaluated (1) the institutional arrangement, (2) the criteria for selecting beneficiaries and land, (3) the components of the definition of land price, (4) the agricultural system types, and (5) the beneficiary repayment capacity. The experimental design comprised 23 interviews: 13 for economic and projection assessment, 5 aiming at the analysis of the origin and trajectory of the workers' associations, and 5 describing the agricultural systems.

As main results, the study showed that the institutional design was not well defined and not working in a cooperative and efficient way. The result was a sullen procedure, mainly followed to secure approval for the infrastructure grant. There were noticeable effects on agricultural production and family well-being. Infrastructure and estate deficiencies were noticed. The associations had limited experience in trading and in planning agricultural production. They were not capable of organizing the collective work adequately and they did not participate actively during the land purchase negotiations that were led by the Cédula da Terra representatives. Most of the beneficiaries were sharecroppers and rural workers, thus in the targeting group of Cédula da Terra. However, there were some leaks in the target group. In the semiarid and arid regions, beneficiaries had insufficient capital to completely occupy and produce on all the land that was purchased. The production, organization, and financial conditions of the beneficiaries were considered to be mostly precarious. Corrales (1998) believes the beneficiaries would not be able to repay their debt unless they received additional investments, improved their agricultural production, and received appropriate technical assistance.

Buainain's (1999) survey of Cédula da Terra's preliminary results, challenges, and constraints was carried out between December 1998 and July 1999. Field data were collected in 116 settlements covering the five federal states in which the program was active. The president or director of the workers' association responded to one questionnaire, and a random selection of families in each project was surveyed. Also, the analysis considered information from local administrators of Cédula da Terra. Of interest here are the results of the socioeconomic profile of the beneficiaries and some important findings about the projects' establishment period. Cédula da Terra showed good targeting, with almost no leaks in relation to the defined beneficiary profile. In the five federal states, most beneficiaries were temporary workers, small producers (sharecroppers, tenant farmers), and others cultivating a little land with subsistence crops. They were experienced rural families with no or little land and incomes that placed them below the poverty line (in some cases, below the extreme poverty line). Average annual beneficiary income was R$958 during 1998, equivalent to 73 percent of a minimum wage at the survey time. The average annual family income was estimated at R$2,057 in 1998. Considering the mean number of residents per family (5.2 people), the monthly per capita income was R$33 (an amount below the poverty line). The illiterate members of the family represented 14 percent, another 45 percent had formal education between the first and fourth grades, and 14 percent had education between the fifth and eighth grades. Only 25 percent of the beneficiaries lived on the purchased land; 23 percent lived in other rural areas close to the purchased land, 21 percent lived in villages located near the purchased land, and 31 percent lived in urban areas.

Each federal state organization, locally responsible for Cédula da Terra, influenced its project's establishment and administration in a different way, according to prevailing local priorities. The normative and operational procedures were not always aligned with the high intensity of program implementation, thus were not followed completely. Local organizations preferentially selected the poorest within the eligible group, and Buainain suggests that future surveys should evaluate the payment capacity of this selection bias. Regarding social and organizational capital, the associations were not prepared to achieve the goals they aimed to reach.

Buainain's (2002) impact evaluation of Cédula da Terra is important because it compares negotiated agrarian reform with state-led agrarian reform based on expropriation and executed by the National Institute for Colonization and Agrarian Reform (INCRA). The beneficiaries' selection under both programs showed a differentiation between these two groups and the regional rural poor population. In both cases, the beneficiaries were in more precarious socioeconomic conditions than was the regional population outside the programs (before joining the agrarian reform programs). Also in both cases, most of the beneficiaries were landless rural workers with migration and nonrural employment experience. Targeting was efficient in both cases. The positive impact on income was greater for INCRA beneficiaries who also started with a lower level of income (R$982 per year for Cédula da Terra and R$871 per year for INCRA) in 1997. After three years, income was similar for both groups: in 2000, R$3,273 for Cédula da Terra and R$3,334 for INCRA. The income comparison had methodological restrictions, however, because INCRA settlements were created before Cédula da Terra projects and therefore were not completely comparable. Unfortunately, no other survey offers a better assessment on this topic.

Buainain's (2003) impact evaluation of Cédula da Terra complements the earlier study and focuses on the socioeconomic effects of Cédula da Terra, agricultural production and productivity, and the income of the beneficiaries compared with that of the 1999 reference period (the beginning of Cédula da Terra). No control group was established for a complete impact assessment because the study aimed mainly at identifying the progress trend. The families showed progress in both establishing agricultural production and increasing income. The families' total annual income was R$2,057 in 1998, R$2,672 in 1999, and R$5,777 in 2003. The increase from 1998 (before Cédula da Terra) to 2003 was an average of 181 percent. Net annual income in 2003 was R$4,913. During the same period, the mean income of the rural poor population slightly decreased regionally. The main agricultural systems were based on annual crop and subsistence production, but with an increase in production trade starting at 13 percent in 1998 and reaching 33 percent in 2003. Buainain suggests increasing the amount of credit and technical assistance offered to reduce production inefficiencies. The production activities in the projects were sufficient to occupy the beneficiaries and their families, as evidenced by a reduction of income from outside employment. New association members often were substituted for initially selected beneficiaries, either officially or informally.

Banco da Terra Project

Despite the comprehensiveness of Banco da Terra, which benefited 34,500 families, only a few studies focus on it. One survey that should be noted was made by the Department of Rural Socioeconomic Studies. It evaluated the payment capacity of the beneficiaries from the south region, where the program was more active (Nunes 2006). Banco da Terra operated between 1999 and 2003 (when it was replaced by the CAF modality of PNCF), and in that period financed 17,886 projects, covering 1.4 million hectares and 34,500 families. In total, R$731 million in loans were distributed. Approximately 54 percent of this budget was used in the south region, which comprises 48 percent of the beneficiaries. The experimental design selected six municipalities (three in the state of Rio Grande do Sul, two in Santa Catarina, and one in Paraná), in each of which approximately 30 beneficiaries were interviewed (for a total of 181 questionnaires). The results indicated that access to land increased. Before Banco da Terra, the farmers had an average 0.5 hectare of their own land and leased another 2.5 hectares. After receiving the credit, farmers increased their own farmland to an average of 12.9 hectares and decreased the amount of land leased to 0.7 hectare. Sixty-four percent of the interviewed beneficiaries declared that the debt parcels were not yet due. From the almost 40 percent who declared parcels due, 18 percent declared they had no financial means to pay the debt (7 percent of this group preferred not to respond about their capacity to repay). Projections taking into account the yield of crop year 2004/05 indicated that 60 percent of the Banco da Terra beneficiaries had the means to repay the program debts together with Pronaf-A (a special production credit available after joining agrarian reform projects). These projections deducted from income the expenses of maintaining the family. Also, 62 percent of the beneficiaries had monetary savings at the time the survey was taken. The beneficiaries from Banco da Terra formed a very heterogeneous group with a large variance in income.

Land Credit and Poverty Alleviation Program

With World Bank support, CF-CPR was evaluated comprehensively on two occasions: (1) in a diagnosis of the CF-CPR projects by Sparovek et al. (2003) and (2) in the evaluation of the trajectory of CF-CPR from establishment to consolidation (Government of Brazil, Ministry of Agrarian Development 2006).

Sparovek et al.'s 2003 evaluation reflects the condition of 174 projects out of the 226 existing on July 6, 2003, with field interviews conducted between October and November 2003 covering the initial establishment period of the projects. Targeting was adequate in two aspects: (1) the selection of beneficiaries followed the rules defined in the program's operational manual and (2) in the large universe of eligible families, lower-income profiles prevailed. The poorest people in the poor population were selected by the self-selection procedure. Illiterate people had less access to the credit when compared with the average rural population. The average age of the beneficiaries was 39 years; the average family had 6 members, of whom 3.6 were occupied with production in the project areas. Approximately one-third of the total number of beneficiaries resided in the project areas. The associations were stable, with few members leaving, and most comprised members with previous communal experience or kinship. On average, it took 15 months to purchase the land; approximately 4 months after the purchase, the first families occupied the land and began agricultural production or infrastructure implementation. Most families came from neighborhood areas, and only one option of land was considered for purchase, usually located close to urban areas. The representative of the rural workers' union participated during the association's organization and the representative of CF-CPR administration participated in the land price negotiation, but in a noncontinuous way. Technical assistance was present, but only available for a third of the families. The mean education level of beneficiaries was in the cycle between the first and fourth grades. Agricultural production was not implemented in most areas, but where present, it was concentrated in individual areas. The income, considering conditions before and after the credit, was similar because most production activities in the new areas had not been started and the previous agricultural sites were still in use. Considering only the group that occupied the areas with production, an increase in agricultural production income was evident. This increase was the result of land ownership because it entailed a lower cost than did leasing land or sharecropping. The standard of living increased in all analysis items, such as housing conditions, access to electricity, sanitary conditions, garbage disposal, telephone, refrigerator, and own transport by car or motorcycle.

The survey results reported in 2006 were developed by the same research group who worked in 2003 (Government of Brazil, Ministry of Agrarian Development 2006). A sample of the projects visited in 2003 (the establishment period) was revisited in 2005 (the initial consolidation period). The evaluation was based on the evolution over this period. The transition from establishment to the consolidation period produced important changes in the dynamics and structure of the projects. The families occupied and transferred housing to the new areas; infrastructure improved, especially housing and sanitary conditions; individual agricultural production was present in almost all cases; and new initiatives in postharvest processing and value aggregation were more frequent. The rapid and important changes that were reflected in an increase in well-being were highly dependent on the grant part of the credit designated for social and physical infrastructure investments. The consolidation phase also increased significantly the incomes of beneficiaries who changed their positions in relation to the regional condition. The incomes of the beneficiaries were inferior to the regional level of the eligible rural population at the time CF-CPR began (2003); after the beginning of the consolidation period (2005), the incomes of the beneficiaries were significantly superior. This increase in income was related directly to the new land occupation, to better agricultural production conditions, and to better insertion of the families into the local labor market (salaries and temporary work). That better insertion into the labor market also can be attributed to families' greater stability regarding housing and future prospects. External effects—such as income transfer programs, pensions, retirement funds, and other nonagricultural income sources—taken together represented an important income increase. The intensification of agricultural income (that is, increases in area, productivity, and more profitable trade) and the better performance in the labor market also were considered to offer the greatest potential for income increase in the future. Quantitatively, some changes in the condition of the projects in 2003 and 2005 were (1) 8 percent of the beneficiaries in 2003 lived exclusively in the project areas, whereas 66 percent lived there in 2005 (in 99 percent of the cases, the houses were built of masonry); (2) the average annual income per family in 2003 was R$1,656, whereas it was R$4,064 in 2005 (the latter exceeding the mean regional rural income at the time); (3) agricultural production was undertaken by 37 percent of the beneficiaries in 2003, whereas 82 percent had undertaken it in 2005; (4) annual income from agricultural production in 2003 was R$460, whereas it averaged R$1,210 in 2005; and (5) the number of beneficiaries who traded agricultural products doubled over the period.

CHALLENGES TO THE PERMANENCE OF NEGOTIATED AGRARIAN REFORM

Despite the long history and the large scale of implementation, we identify some challenges that negotiated agrarian reform still has to face to establish itself more permanently in Brazil. These challenges include political structures and organizational issues.

The Political Climate Supporting the Permanence of Negotiated Agrarian Reform

The political climate and the institutional arrangements favor the permanence of negotiated agrarian reform in Brazil, and possibly its intensification. The factors that confer its stability are these:

- Negotiated agrarian reform is independent of international financing and of specifically negotiated national budgets. With the creation of the Land Fund in 1998, the financial resources for the reform were guaranteed constitutionally.
- Negotiated reform is supported by CONTAG, whose members are spread over the entire country. As a legitimate representative of rural workers, CONTAG historically has been responsible for rural workers' important victories.
- Except in some federal states, negotiated reform has a diverse and decentralized supporting network—an extensive cooperative chain comprising municipalities, state governments, official and private technical assistance institutions, and nongovernmental organizations. All these entities act together with the official partner from CONTAG.
- Since 1997, two models of agrarian reform (negotiated reform and state-led reform based on expropriation) have coexisted, with their implementation supported most of that time by the same ministry, the MDA. The ideological

disputes between the two models were not strong enough to discontinue one or the other, and there is institutional space for both.

- The positive results of independent research to evaluate at least two periods of negotiated reform (Cédula da Terra and CF-CPR) indicate its feasibility and the repayment capacity of its beneficiaries. Eighty-five percent of the Cédula da Terra associations were up-to-date with their debt payments in 2004, and several were negotiating credit contract changes. More comprehensive and official data on debt repayment are not available, and most contracts negotiated during the recent reform periods are not due. With these payments, the cycle of the Land Fund, with decreasing input of external resources, will be initiated, providing a more independent investment capacity in a short time.

Challenges for the Future

Within the permanence scenario, several important questions remain unanswered, and important issues will have to be addressed. The issues that pose challenges are these:

- *Comprehensiveness*—Because negotiated agrarian reform has a market-based credit approach, an important issue always will be the repayment capacity of the beneficiaries. As a social inclusion policy, considering that most of the negotiated reform is conducted under the frame of a poverty alleviation program, the inclusion of the poorest of the poor should be prioritized. Combining these two concepts in a model that is driven by self-demand is still a challenge. Conducting negotiated reform in extremely poor regions where there is reduced social and organizational capital, great deficiency in institutional support, and limited natural resources (such as the semiarid part of the northeast region) may compromise repayment capacity and may not occur by self-demand because of low organizational capacity, thus requiring induction mechanisms that are not present in the current implementation in Brazil.
- *Self-demand*—Recent evaluations of CF-CPR indicate that even the poorest of the eligible, and the least educated (illiterate) people progressed in a manner similar to that of more favored beneficiaries, considering income and well-being indicators (Government of Brazil, Ministry of Agrarian Development 2006). People with better education and more social and organizational capital have more privileged access to negotiated reform through its self-demand mechanism. Considering the program's poverty alleviation objective, such bias is not desirable.
- *Credit limits*—The credit in all modalities of negotiated agrarian reform is limited regionally. The limits exclude more developed regions in which the market price of land is high. Increasing these limits to adjust to the market may attract nonpoor beneficiaries. Maintaining low credit limits reduces

the territorial coverage of the reform program, excluding the more developed regions and, consequently, the poor rural workers and farmers from those regions.

- *Evaluation and monitoring*—Despite the presence of negotiated agrarian reform in Brazil for more than 10 years, empirical studies of the program are limited, and almost all of the pertinent literature consists of case studies. No systematic, comprehensive, and continuous monitoring is performed. Operational problems and deficient institutional designs or arrangements therefore are not detected in time to avoid problems that may generate liabilities (including environmental impacts, inclusion of ineligible beneficiaries, or a compromise of agricultural production performance that may reduce beneficiaries' repayment capacity). Increased monitoring is essential for improving the program, for validating it in the very diverse regions in which it is active, and for publicly justifying the resources invested. Performance is expected to vary across regions. In the year 2006, two robust surveys started with a complete project impact assessment design (including control group and probability sample)—one for Cédula da Terra and the other for PNCF; results are not yet available.
- *Land market*—In regions where negotiated reform is used intensively, suitable land (relative to credit limits) tends to become scarce, thereby raising market prices. Monitoring land markets is important to identify and quantify this trend and to facilitate payment conditions for the beneficiaries. In all modalities of negotiated reform, the credit for land acquisition is considered a loan, not a grant. The purchase of land above its market price may compromise the beneficiaries' ability to repay the loan.

CONCLUSION

The comprehensiveness of its future targets and its past implementation rates suggest that negotiated agrarian reform will not change the extreme land property concentration significantly in Brazil. Its actions will be localized, will be included in a poverty alleviation context (mainly in the northeast and north regions), and will be important for sustaining a family farm–based rural landscape in some parts of the south and southeast regions (through the CAF modality that operates with higher credit limits).

Serving those objectives and aims, Brazilian negotiated agrarian reform has evolved over time from a pilot project phase dependent on international resources (1997–99) to a national policy supported constitutionally (1999 to the present). Its performance has improved over those years. Since 2002, the reform has been supported by the strong rural workers' union movement, and a broad cooperative network has been constructed. Despite methodological weaknesses, data collected so far indicate that beneficiaries' repayment capacity is guaranteed (probably with the exception of a greater part of Banco da

Terra beneficiaries), ensuring the effectiveness of the Land Fund. All of this supports the approach's continued independence and stability.

The greatest challenges are related to its expansion in regions of extreme poverty and restricted natural resources, to the improvement of monitoring and evaluation procedures, to the maintenance of its targeting the poorest among the eligible (considering the poverty alleviation modalities), and to a non-negative interference in land market prices in regions where the program is present more intensively.

NOTES

1. Colombia was the first country that regulated negotiated agrarian reform, passing Law 160 in 1994 (Hollinger 1999).
2. These organizations include the MST, the Roman Catholic pro-peasant movement (for example, the Pastoral Land Commission), rural workers' unions, and other popular supporting efforts.

REFERENCES

Buainain, Antonio M., Jose M. Silveira, Marcelo M. Magalhães, Rinaldo Artes, and Hildo M. Souza Filho. 1999. "Programa Cédula da Terra: resultados preliminares, desafios e obstáculos." Unpublished report. Ministry of Agrarian Development, Brasília, Brazil.

———. 2002. "Estudo de avaliação de impacto do Programa Cédula da Terra." Unpublished report. Ministry of Agrarian Development, Brasília, Brazil.

———. 2003. "Estudo de avaliação de impactos do Programa Cédula da Terra." Unpublished report. Ministry of Agrarian Development, Brasília, Brazil.

Corrales, Hérnan M. 1998. "Avaliação do projeto cédula da terra: estado do Ceará." Unpublished report. Ministry of Agrarian Development, Brasília, Brazil.

Deininger, Klaus, and Hans P. Binswanger. 1999. "The Evolution of the World Bank's Land Policy: Principles, Experiences, and Future Challenges." *World Bank Research Observer* 14 (2): 247–76.

Garcia, Danilo P. 1998. "Avaliação preliminar do componente fundiário do Projeto São José." Unpublished report. Ministry of Agrarian Development, Brasília, Brazil.

Garcia, Danilo P., Marcelo G. Paranhos, and Gustavo B. Machado. 1998. "Avaliação preliminar dos projetos do programa Cédula da Terra no Estado da Bahia." Unpublished report. Ministry of Agrarian Development, Brasília, Brazil.

Gomes da Silva, José. 1971. *A reforma agrária no Brasil.* Rio de Janeiro, Brazil: Zahar Editores.

Government of Brazil, Ministry of Agrarian Development. 2005. *Programa Nacional de Crédito fundiário. Operatoins Manual.* Brasília.

———. 2006 "Trajetória do Crédito Fundiário: da implantação à consolidação." Brasília.

———. 2007. Management Indicator Panel, Bulletin 08/07, Year II, April 10. Brasília.

Hoffmann, Rodolfo. 1998. "A estrutura fundiária no Brasil de acordo com o cadastro do Incra: 1967 a 1998." Unpublished report. Ministry of Agrarian Development, Brasília, Brazil.

Hollinger, Frank. 1999. "Del mercado de tierras al mercado de reforma agraria." In *El mercado de tierras em Colombia: una alternativa viable?* ed. Absalon Machado and Ruth Suárez, 137–96. Santa Fé de Bogotá, Colombia: Tecer Mundo Editores.

Nunes, Sidemar P. 2006. "Capacidade de pagamento dos beneficiários do banco da terra na região Sul do Brasil." In *Estudos de Reordenamento Agrário,* IICA/MDA/PCT-Crédito Fundiário.

Oliveira, Ariovaldo U. 2001. "A longa marcha do campesinato brasileiro: movimentos sociais, conflitos e Reforma Agrária." *Estudos Avançados* 15 (43): 185–206.

Pereira, João M.M. 2004. "O modelo de reforma agrária de mercado do Banco Mundial em questão: o debate internacional e o caso brasileiro. Teoria, luta política e balanço de resultado." Master's thesis, Federal University of Rio de Janeiro, Brazil.

———. 2005. "A disputa política no Brasil em torno da implementação do modelo de reforma agrária de mercado do Banco Mundial (1997–2005)." *Revista Nera* 8 (6): 92–117.

Sauer, Sergio. 2004. "A terra por uma cédula: estudo sobre a reforma agrária de mercado." In *O Banco Mundial e a terra: ofensiva e resistência na América Latina, Ásia e África,* ed. Mônica Dias Martins, 101–20. São Paulo, Brazil: Viramundo.

Sparovek, Gerd, Rodrigo F. Maule, Alberto G.P.O. Barretto, Sergio P. Martins, and Ludwig A.E. Plata. 2003. "Diagnóstico dos projetos do Crédito Fundiário e Combate à Pobreza Rural (CPR-CF)." Unpublished report. Ministry of Agrarian Development, Brasília, Brazil.

Teófilo, E., and Danilo P. Garcia. 2002. "Políticas de terra, pobreza e desenvolvimento rural: o caso do Brasil." Paper presented at the World Bank Workshop on Land Issues, Latin America Region, Brasília, Brazil, April.

World Bank. 1975. "Land Reform Policy Paper." Washington, DC.

———. 2000. "Project Appraisal Document to Brazil for Land-Based Poverty Alleviation Project." Report 19585-BR. Washington, DC.

———. 2003. "Implementation Completion Report (CPL-41470)." Report 25973. Brazil Country Management Unit.

CHAPTER TWELVE

Agricultural Land Tax, Land-Use Intensification, Local Development, and Land Market Reform

Malcolm D. Childress, Andrew Hilton, David Solomon, and Rogier van den Brink

A "land tax" is a tax on the value of land paid by the owner. It is different from a "property tax" in that a land tax taxes only the value of the land, whereas a property tax taxes the value of the land *and* the fixed improvements made on it (for example, a house, a farm building, an irrigation canal).

The main arguments in favor of land taxation are based on economics, land use, and administrative and social justice considerations. The principal economic argument is that a pure land tax does not distort economic behavior negatively because it has no negative effects on investment or production. Because the land tax is a fixed cost that must be paid whether or not the land is used for production, it does not penalize production and it creates an incentive to

This chapter was reviewed by Peter Hansen (World Bank). It is based on a discussion document prepared by the Department of Land Affairs of South Africa and the World Bank, written by David Solomon, Hans Binswanger, Rogier van den Brink, Andrew Hilton, and Michael Love.

develop land to its most profitable use. In this regard, land taxation discourages underutilization of land and land speculation.

Administratively, it is a preferred type of taxation because of its transparency: land is immobile and cannot be hidden or disguised as a bookkeeping transaction. From a social justice perspective, it captures the economic rent that arises from a scarce natural resource or due to population presence and public infrastructure investments that increase its market value. As such, it is inherently equitable to tax such "unearned increments" that arise from public actions. The tax can be viewed as a payment to society for the benefits conferred to the landowner for the guarantee of private property.

In the land taxation literature from around the world there is evidence to support those arguments in favor of a land tax. For instance, when the rate at which the land is taxed is economically significant and the taxation procedures are well administered, the effect of land taxation on intensifying land use is strong. Nevertheless, it also is apparent that achieving such an effect in the developing world has been difficult, mainly because of low tax rates, low assessed values, and limited administrative capacity. Fortunately, several improvements in land tax administration—such as area-based valuations and (community) self-assessments—have proved to be effective answers to the administrative challenges.

The idea that the intensification of land use as a result of more effective taxation will lead, through markets, to some redistribution of land from less efficient to more efficient farms is supported by international experience, but not necessarily in a way that will benefit small farmers. This is true because small farmers usually must cope with disadvantages in land and credit markets (vis-à-vis large-scale commercial farmers) and in access to new technology and marketing. By reducing the nonagricultural value of land, however, the land tax *does* assist small farmers in reducing one of their disadvantages in the land market.

Hence, improved land taxation is an important element of a package of land policies geared toward achieving greater rural employment and less concentrated land distribution. But it can never be the *only* instrument to address structural inequalities in assets and opportunities within pluri-active rural communities linked in diverse ways to urban- and global-scale economies and environmental services.

THEORY OF LAND TAXATION

Land and its *taxation* are topics that have received the theoretical attention of economists from the age of David Ricardo until the writing of Henry George in the 19th century. The topic has lost prominence in modern economic theory, but is receiving new attention in the urban planning and development literature because practical considerations of municipal finance and pressures on land use are serious concerns being taken up across many jurisdictions worldwide.

Economic Theory of Land Taxation

The taxation of the unimproved value of land long has been considered an "ideal tax" by a wide range of scholars and politicians, including 17th-century philosopher John Locke, 18th-century revolutionary Benjamin Franklin, and 19th-century politician Henry George. In 1990, several leading economists—including four Nobel Prize winners—wrote to the then president Mikhail Gorbachev and suggested that the Russian Federation use land taxation in its transition to a free market economy.[1]

The attractiveness of a land tax is attributed to the following factors:

- It does not distort economic incentives because the overall supply of land is fixed.
- It is fair because it specifically targets *unearned* income (a rent); it taxes the value improvements of land caused by *public* investment, not by an economic activity of the owner.
- It provides a disincentive to land speculation in both urban and rural areas.
- It is relatively easy to administer because the land cannot be hidden.

The value of fertile land is composed of both its direct capacity to produce goods and services (such as crops and accommodation) and the broader advantage of providing a domicile among and membership in a specific human community. The amenities and infrastructure directly provided by the community, whether through a governmental structure or by other means, contribute a major and significant portion of the land value. Since Ricardo elaborated his theory of value, economists have referred to this as "rent" in order to make a useful distinction between this part of the value and the more conventional element of productive or income value, the returns derived from the next best opportunity. Incremental efforts by society to improve the economic and amenity environment inevitably are reflected in increased land rents and value.

Failures—in which community resources are spent in ways that restrict development, harm the environment, or improve it less than the costs incurred—will have a negative impact on land values. In other words, the land tax also works in reverse. The owner of the property is compensated automatically for such failures by a reduction in the land tax paid.

This process of embedding social actions, both positive and negative, in the value of land located in the community was identified, measured, and named by Wallace Oates (1969) as "capitalization." He pointed out that public actions, whether on the expenditure or on the revenue side, promptly are reflected and capitalized in local property values.

Since the 1970s, hundreds of studies have confirmed and measured in hard currency the contributions that local and national communal facilities (and the contributions that funded them) have made to land value. Property valuers the world over use variables reflecting collective services—including proximity to public transportation, quality of infrastructure, and local schools—as key determinants of property values. It is commonly held that a significant component of land value is not earned by the efforts of the landowner or occupant, but results directly from collective actions (even from the mere presence) of an organized community, regardless of the quality of services it currently provides for its members. As such, in this updating of the positions of Henry George, the incumbent owner of the land has no moral right to claim increments in the value as his or her own, nor any cause for complaint if a tax on land value is instituted to capture such value for the benefit of the entity that was responsible for its creation: community government and its partners.

A land tax is considered a progressive tax in that wealthy landowners normally should be paying relatively more than poorer landowners and tenants. Conversely, a tax on buildings can be said to be regressive, falling heavily on tenants who generally are poorer than the landlords (Netzer 1973). That progressivity occurs because the local supply of land is inelastic, compared with the demand for it. Hence, owners cannot adjust their behavior easily to minimize the tax in the short term by reducing the supply of land to the market. The tax on the site value therefore falls on the suppliers, not the demanders; on the owners of the land, not the tenants.

The equity argument posed above is made in the seminal work on property tax incidence by Peter Mieszkowski (1972). His basic point is that a property or land tax that is common to all jurisdictions and cannot be avoided by moving will fall on the owners of fixed and mobile capital, on immobile labor, and local consumers. He concluded that because owners of capital generally also are wealthy, the property or land tax is progressive. He qualified that conclusion by pointing out that the tax differentials between jurisdictions can be avoided by the act of moving, and therefore finally fall on those economic actors who cannot easily do so—immobile labor, consumers, or tenants. This portion of the tax therefore is an excise tax rather than a capital tax, and generally is regressive.

Slack (2002) supports Mieszkowski's conclusion by pointing out that because the imposition of or increase in a land tax (site value) will be capitalized into lower property values, and because the tax is borne proportionately more by owners of land than is the case with a property tax (which would include the value of the buildings), the tax should be more progressive (borne relatively more heavily by high-income taxpayers than by low-income taxpayers).

Land Tax and the Intensity of Land Use

Economic intuition supporting the land intensification effect of land taxation is the observation that any increased cost of holding land at a suboptimal rate of return (for example, by foregoing a shift into a higher-return agricultural technology) creates an incentive to increase intensity. If land is not used at its optimal intensity, then raising the cost of holding land through a tax should induce greater effort for land utilization (see figure 12.1).

Figure 12.1 Effects of a Property Tax on the Demand for Property While Supply Is Inelastic

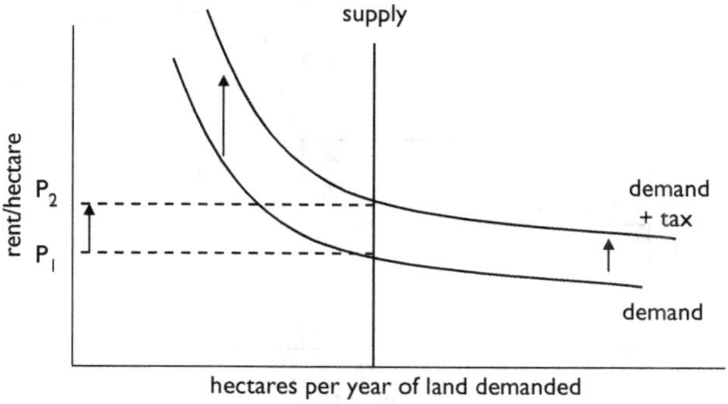

Source: Mieszkowski 1972.

In many countries with a highly inegalitarian distribution of land, there usually are significant quantities of agricultural land that are not used at their optimal intensity for a variety of historical and institutional reasons. More effective land taxation thus would lead to more intensive land use. Figure 12.2 illustrates a situation in which the supply of land used at optimal intensity is elastic over some range.[2] This curve could apply to either an individual landholder or an economy. As the tax is imposed (the move from C to C'), the landholder increases the quantity of land used at optimal intensity (the move from Q to Q').

That observation is supported empirically. In a survey of agricultural land taxation in the United States, Wunderlich (1993) concludes from an exhaustive review of time-series data that there is "a positive relationship between higher property tax rates and more intensive use of farmland, which in turn is associated with more equal distribution of farmland" (p. 24). Yamamura (1986) makes the same case for Japan, linking the imposition of a land tax to increased agricultural productivity. Strasma (2000) points out how the structure of Chile's agricultural land taxation system successfully encourages full use of the land by basing assessments on the potential profitability of each land parcel—assessments that are updated regularly according to a table of actual market transactions.

Other economists have expressed skepticism about the land use–intensifying effect of agricultural land taxation, but their skepticism hinges on the specific circumstances under which the tax is applied. Skinner (1991a, 1991b), for example, believes that it is not clear at a theoretical level why a land tax should encourage more productive use of land, unless the tax is tied to a reduction in export taxation (which would increase domestic output prices) because "by definition an efficient tax should not affect land use decisions" (p. 501). But

Figure 12.2 Increase in Land Use Intensity as a Result of Land Tax

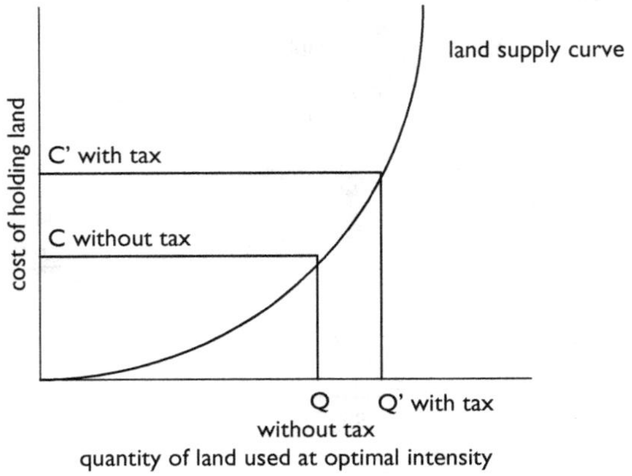

Source: World Bank 2007, figure 3.1, p. 38.

he goes on to say that "it is possible that a sufficiently large land tax could spur landowners to work harder (an income effect) or to break away from reliance on traditional methods of production and seek new and more efficient methods" (p. 501). In effect, Skinner counters his own critique by pointing out the incentive that an agricultural land tax creates to intensify effort, especially in places where there is reliance on traditional methods or, even more pointedly, where land is being held for nonproductive reasons involving imperfections in other markets (such as a store of value due to low confidence in the financial system).

Skinner also expresses doubts that land taxes reduce speculation in land because the tax only results in a one-time land price reduction. That critique is valid when land is the only asset the investor holds. But when an investor has the opportunity to invest in a variety of assets, and the rate of return on one of them (for example, land) is lowered, the investor will shift investment away from that asset. Especially in a progressive land taxation scheme, such shifting of incentives could induce market transfers of land.

Finally, the actual valuation level at which a property is assessed matters for land-use decision making. Although typically somewhat lower in Latin America than in countries of the Organisation for Economic Co-operation and Development (OECD), tax rates are much less critical than below-market-value assessments in the failure of Latin American rural land taxes to have significant impact on land-use decisions. The issue for Latin American land-use intensification thus is what level of assessment and what tax rates together could change behavior and the willingness to intensify land use through technical change or by renting out or selling the land to more intensive users. Most of the observed rates in Latin America's agricultural land are somewhat lower than those in OECD countries, but combined with very low assessments they generate amounts of tax that are scarcely worth collecting and have little presumed economic relevance to landholders. Were Latin American valuations do rise closer to market levels, the effects of land taxation on land-use decisions would be expected to be greater.

Land Tax and Land Redistribution

The effect of agricultural land taxation as a mechanism for inducing redistributive market transfers is not as clear as its effect on land-use intensity. Considering Brazil, Assuncão and Moreira (2005) note that the land tax (rural property tax) there is intended to support public policies for land redistribution, but it has had little success. They note that there is a high level of evasion and default that hinders its efficiency as an instrument of landholding policy. The tax is collected by local governments, and large landowners often exert substantial lobbying power in those local areas. In addition, the tax is based on "unused" land, which is notoriously difficult to define. Despite these drawbacks, the authors still conclude that "appropriate land taxes might correct land prices in economies where they are above the discounted present value of agricultural inflows, inducing land redistribution from large landowners to more productive small peasants" (p. 15). Similar tax policies have been applied in the Caribbean—for example, St. Lucia and Jamaica—and have had mixed results.

Strasma et al. (1987) conclude that the use of agricultural land taxes to stimulate redistribution has not succeeded because land taxes are imposed at too low a rate to affect the decisions of property owners. Shearer, Lastarria-Cornhiel, and Mesbah (1991) are guardedly optimistic about land taxation as a policy tool to encourage redistribution in the Latin American context, but they call for more research.

Skinner (1991b) also objects to land taxation as an instrument for land reform. He says that "efforts to encourage land reform though this channel in Colombia and other countries have generally been unsuccessful for two reasons: First, commonly administered land tax rates have been neither large enough nor progressive enough to affect land use. In one study of Colombia, L. Harland Davis concluded that: 'Because of low rates the tax burden is a relatively small percentage of income and this fact means that there is little opportunity for the nonfiscal effects to operate . . . particularly . . . among the larger farmers, where the tax burden is lightest'" (p. 501).

Low tax rates are the problem noted here, not the economic incentives created by the land tax.

LAND TAXATION IN PRACTICE

Whereas the theoretical economic reasoning for promoting land taxation is relatively strong, in practice various policy goals have been put forward as the motivating force for programs of land taxation. A number of developing and transitional countries have embraced new land taxation programs as a part of their policy tool kits, using a variety of valuation methods. However, practical implementation of land taxation in developing-country contexts—and rural areas in particular—typically faces daunting political challenges, and the performance record of land taxation systems in these circumstances is weak.

Countries' Rationale for Land Taxation

Why have countries adopted land taxes? The levying of public charges based on some measure of land value has been an element of economic life in every part of the world for most of recorded history. It is almost inevitable that where there are human communities with organized governments, there will be some mechanism for generating funds for collective use, based on a measure of land itself or the products of land.

In this section, we discuss some of the motives behind several countries' recent moves to strengthen land taxation. These efforts are most notable in Eastern Europe, where many land policy innovations are emerging.

Land Tax as a Source of Local Government Revenue, Independent of National Government

Taxes on agricultural land typically constitute a declining share of total national revenues because agricultural land values typically become a smaller proportion of national wealth as economic growth changes the economy's sectoral structure. Despite this trend, land taxes remain a significant source of subnational revenues. In the United States, property taxes have been used extensively to give local governments an independent source of revenue collection to finance important services, such as education. In countries such as Armenia, Estonia, Poland, and Russia, among others, national governments have created land value taxes as part of their fiscal reform packages rather than employing the land taxes for revenue (see Malme and Youngman [2001]).

Land Tax to Ensure Productive Use of Restituted Land

In a number of Eastern European countries, land taxes have been imposed to ensure the productive use of land transferred for restitution purposes—for example, in Estonia. Given that land was returned to the previous owner as a matter of principle, the government did not impose any conditions on the capacity of the owner to use the land productively. The land tax was seen explicitly as part of this process, and was established to encourage the productive use of restituted land as a process over time. Much of this land was restored to heirs and owners who, through force of circumstance, had moved away from agriculture or other land-based activities during the 50 years of state ownership. Many former owners, or their heirs, had moved to other parts of the world or other areas in the former Soviet Union. It was hoped that a land tax would encourage them either to return and resume their land-based work or to transfer the land to higher-intensity users by way of sale or lease.

Thus, Malme and Youngman (2001) suggest that the commitment of countries such as Estonia to a land tax was less motivated by fiscal considerations or concerns of neutrality than by the effect of the tax on a range of strategic issues. They point out that the tax yield in urban areas was less than 2 percent of local revenue, an insignificant fiscal contribution. The real contribution, they suggest, was in the facilitation and support of the social changes that were being pushed forward in that country, especially those having to do with land and property rights and land restitution.

Land Tax to Define Property Rights

In most of the transitional countries, there had been no well-defined property rights in land for several decades. The land tax and the property tax, based on clear assessment and valuation processes, were seen as mechanisms that would assist in the development of local land markets and a local brokering and property-based lending industry, in both urban and rural areas.

Land Tax to Create Land Valuation Capacity

Conducting formal, well-organized valuations requires a cadre of trained officials who have knowledge and active understanding of the markets. This base of knowledge and expertise provides a mechanism for transmitting an understanding of the transformation more widely, and it creates a process for training and supporting a valuation industry that will be a core requirement of the development of urban and agricultural property markets.

Land Tax to Defuse Transitional Tensions

The transitional reform process in Eastern Europe naturally created tensions between the widely held belief in the association of land with the "national interest" and the pursuit of the ideal of individual rights to land and other forms of property. A land tax was seen as the appropriate retention by the state of some land rights with which it was empowered during the time of communism. "Clarification of a continuing public claim on a portion of land value in the form of an annual tax can help reconcile these competing claims" (Malme and Youngman 2001, p. 3).

Land Tax to Build on Existing Taxation Systems

In Armenia, the fiscal system was shifted away from business income taxes to an enhancement of the existing property tax system, which was based heavily on land values. Saving on assessment costs was one of the reasons for adopting a land taxation system in Kenya and South Africa (before the recent shift away from "land only" to "land and improvements"; see below). Authorities were encouraged in its use by the fact that the specifics of each property would not need to be captured and used in the valuation. In general, land valuation is much cheaper than the valuation of buildings in both urban and rural areas because it requires fewer data and fewer site visits by valuers.

Land Tax to Discourage Foreign Absentee Ownership

Van den Brink (2002) suggests that a land tax could be used to discourage the vacant holding of land by foreign buyers. This motivation is particularly well reflected in the practices in Queensland, Australia, where foreigners are taxed both beginning at a lower threshold ($350,000 instead of $450,000) and with a higher rate.

Land Tax to Discourage Speculative Landholding

Brazil has used a land tax as an incentive to put pressure on idle land without imposing measures leading to expropriation. In addition, Jamaica and Singapore both intend their use of land taxes or land-based surcharges on property taxes as a means of discouraging vacant landholdings and land speculation.

Land Tax to Manage Political Tensions around Land

A land tax can diffuse political tensions around land in a number of different ways. In China and the transitional states of the former Soviet Union, the once-dominant rights of the state are being dismantled in favor of individual property rights. A similar scenario is playing out in a number of African countries, such as Kenya, Madagascar, and Mozambique. In South Africa, in particular, there are strong calls for the state to adopt a more forceful approach to the land reform process, more swiftly restoring rights to historically dispossessed black men and women.

In all these cases, land—more than any other form of property—is associated politically, emotionally, and often even linguistically with the nation itself. There is a keenly felt sense of contradiction between the belief in the need for a public stake in the permanent fixed heritage of the country—the land—and the simultaneous enthusiasm for reform, manifested via an assertion of individual property rights, especially individual private rights over land. Participants at a recent Land Summit in South Africa reflected this tension in demands for land to be expropriated under the assertion of state rights, and simultaneously to distribute the land to "those who work it," creating individual rights that are sustainable and defensible.[3]

Appropriately implemented with valuations reflecting true social and environmental value, land taxation offers one readily available policy tool to cross this divide, especially if embedded in a context of other policies that also address structural inequalities in assets and opportunities. By reserving a claim on the land for the state in the form of a land tax, different social negotiations about the rights and responsibilities of landholding may be possible, thus creating a new combination of land rights involving both the state and private owners in ways that are politically feasible.

The same theme plays itself out in the South African context: a land tax represents the state's assertion of rights over land, within certain limits. In this sense, tax policy is one of a larger set of institutional and policy decisions that shape the ways in which individual private rights of ownership, or other ownership arrangements, are expressed and treated by society. Land taxes reflect a combination of state and personal rights in the land heritage of the nation and the public goods inherent within it.

Land Tax Administration

A land tax usually is based on a regular assessment of the value of the land, and the value often is determined by the prevailing market value. Certain rebates and exemptions sometimes are granted.

A land tax is a public policy instrument of value capture and revenue collection. "Value capture" means any attempt to recapture increases in the value of land that were not created by either the investment or the labor of the landowner—especially public investments, such as roads and bridges.

In agricultural contexts, the land tax is based on the unimproved value of the land in its agricultural use. This value does not include any agricultural improvements to the land, such as fencing, drainage, or dams. Moreover, this value does not incorporate any nonagricultural opportunity cost—that is, the value of the land if it were used in another capacity, such as for a residence or for industry.

The base of a land tax is the monetary value of the site component of the total value of the property. A seminal study defines the value of a site as "the market value of the freehold with vacant possession free from any encumbrances other than easements or restrictions on user imposed by or under an Act of Parliament on the assumption that there are no buildings or works upon the land or anything growing except natural growth" (Turvey 1957, p. 83).

Assessing the market value of a site requires a number of practical rules and assumptions before it can be made operational. It should be noted that differentiating the agricultural site value from the buildings/works in this exercise becomes more complicated than it is when evaluating land and structures together or estimating the value of improvements to the land.

In practice there is a range of definitions and terminologies applied, each of which makes certain assumptions about how land markets and land values operate. Some of these terms are defined here:

- *Market value*—The property is valued as if the rights over it were sold currently in a hypothetical market reflecting all current conditions in the location, without any duress by a willing seller to a willing buyer, unencumbered by any loans or other financial obligations.

- *Prairie value*—This is the value of the land as if there were no improvements or any geographical advantages relating to infrastructure or improvements, as if on a virgin prairie beyond the frontier of public infrastructure.
- *Use value*—This is used in favor of "highest and best use" in situations where the value of the land includes the potential for future development, usually for urban residential use. Agricultural land often is valued only on the current use (that is, agriculture), not on the basis of potential future uses.

Administrative systems used to implement a land tax also vary in their methodology for generating valuations, managing revenue collection, resolving disputes, and updating information. Several approaches that are used to administer valuations and collections at reasonable cost, with accuracy within a local standard of fairness, and with manageable processes for appeal, dispute resolution, and information management are (1) area-based land taxes, (2) self-appraisal, (3) community valuation, (4) banding, (5) computer-assisted mass appraisal, and (6) thresholds. Each of those approaches is described below:

1. *Area-based land tax*—In some countries, the land tax is not based on the actual land value of each individual farm, but on a standardized price per hectare, adjusted by a fertility or location factor. In effect, this is a simplified valuation aimed at reducing the cost of assessment.
2. *Self-appraisal*—When taxpayers themselves assess the taxable value of their property, the process is known as self-appraisal. It has the advantage of simplicity, as the cost of appraisal is shifted to the taxpayer. In practice, taxpayers often have access to this information, having conducted valuations for such other purposes as acquiring the property or taking out a loan. Self-appraisal gives taxpayers the voluntary opportunity to provide this otherwise confidential information. Underappraisal can be discouraged by a provision that makes expropriation possible at the declared value and by auditing values that deviate significantly from benchmarks.
3. *Community assessment*—International experience shows that, in practice, local populations always have a highly accurate knowledge of land values, even if this information never is reflected in legal documents. Local knowledge always is the most fully informed about land. The local mayor (or tribal chief) and agricultural extension agent are involved in many transactions within the community, and they know what land is worth. "Community perception" is a promising tool for handling valuation legitimately, fairly, and cheaply; it has been tested successfully in several countries (Bell, Bowman, and Clark 2005).
4. *Banding*—A method of lowering the cost of appraisal, banding requires the assessing officer to assign each property to one of several value bands, instead of performing a detailed valuation in each case.

5. *Computer-aided mass appraisal (CAMA)*—This means of performing valuations en masse determines the variables that are key to creating value by using statistical analysis and applying the estimated statistical coefficients to locally collected data. CAMA is much less expensive than are individual valuations. The range of computer-assisted methods is continually expanding.
6. *Thresholds*—Many jurisdictions set a minimum threshold of land value below which no tax is charged. This approach has a dual function: it provides relief for the poor and lowers the cost of administration by avoiding the need to conduct a detailed valuation on a very large number of small properties. It also eases the transition when an area is absorbed into the tax base.

For a land tax to deliver on its promise of fairness, it must be administered in a way that ensures assessments genuinely reflect the market value of land, or at least diverge from that ideal in a generally consistent way. In a practical context, the equity and efficiency of a tax depend more on the nature and quality of administration than on the design and architecture of the tax system itself.

From an equity perspective, it is less important whether assessments understate or overstate land values, as long as they do so in a way that is consistent from one taxpayer to the next. The essential point is that the tax share paid by each household should be determined by the proportion of the land value each one holds. To ensure this, it is a common practice for assessment quality to be monitored by statistical tests in which the assessed value of a sample of properties is compared with the actual value at which the properties changed hands. A mean or median of these values (the assessment-to-sales ratio) is taken, and divergences from the mean or median are measured (Bell and Bowman 1998).

A crucial component of this and other similar quality assurance tests is the ability to compare the assessment with the outcome of an observable market transaction. Pure land taxation does not lend itself well to this kind of quality control. If the land is valued in isolation from the buildings, this is inevitably a notional valuation that must be adjusted by the addition of building values to derive a figure that is comparable with the only tangible data available—the market value of the improved plot. This makes it difficult and unreliable to test the consistency of assessments. Without such tests and monitoring, the quality of assessments depends entirely on the appeal processes and the courts that underpin them. In the context of political and social transition, the appeal process generally will be relatively inaccessible and not fully trusted. Appeals alone cannot be relied on either as a means of testing assessments or as a mechanism for quieting discontent, and that places a heavy burden on the monitoring process. Therefore, the land tax needs to be equipped with particularly effective monitoring and appeal processes to enable them to meet the expectations of their designers.

The most important administrative challenge to the land tax is to maintain an up-to-date, judicially defensible roll of land titles and values. An institutional infrastructure of chartered valuers is needed (supported by appropriate legislation)—valuers who broadly are perceived by taxpayers to be legitimate, fair, and reasonable, and whose valuations can withstand inevitable legal challenges.

Especially in areas with few formal market transactions, many taxpayers feel more secure with an officially determined number, such as that generated by the tax assessor, than with a number generated by reference to markets. In this context, a land tax initially relying on an area-based valuation can create a system that has a high degree of transparency and offers a vehicle of transition to more location-specific valuations, as warranted. As markets in real estate develop and as market-based evidence becomes available, this information will begin to support and, in some cases, replace the simplified area-based value determination.

Because defining the overall land value can be complex, the annual rental value of a site, rather than a direct measure of its capital value, often is used as a base for taxation. Easily observed, annual rental value is the basis for the economic measure of capital value (that is, capital value is the discounted present value of expected net rental flows). The use of rental values also has the advantage of not being incentive neutral in the medium term because rental levels are not immediately eroded or enhanced by the tax (Prest 1981). The choice of rental or capital value as the unit of valuation is one of administrative cost and information management, except in areas where an expected change of use makes current rental flows an inaccurate guide to future value.

In the agricultural context, some countries have implemented extensive land-tax relief mechanisms to take account of local stresses, such as droughts, fluctuations in commodity prices, and other market conditions. All these stresses will have a dramatic bearing on farmers' earnings, and they have led some countries to provide for "relief," or "circuit breakers." However, the exposure of the farm income to these risks should be reflected already in the land price. Hence, economic theory would argue against providing such relief. And given farmers' (in)famous lobbying powers the world over, practical considerations also would support this position.

Exempting the poor from the land tax is a more defensible policy recommendation. A minimum threshold could be established to accommodate this policy principle. Low-value properties should be exempted, or zero-rated. In Africa, a combination of factors has worked to make the land tax a familiar, if not popular, institution: the low level of improvement to most land, the lack of capacity to monitor and value improvements, the popularity of a tax that burdens absentees and others, and the high cost of administering improvement taxes compared with the low yield of doing so.

McCluskey (1999) finds in general that there has been a recent trend away from the taxation of land only to the inclusion of capital improved value. Table 12.1 compares the use of land and improvements as the basis for property taxation (or rates) in selected countries.

Table 12.1 Use of Land and Improvements as the Property Rates Base, Selected Economies

Economy	Rates based on value of site and improvements	Rates based on value of site only	Other rates basis
Australia		X	
Botswana	X		
Brazil	X		
Cyprus	X		
Czech Republic			X
Estonia		X	
Hong Kong, China			X
Hungary			X
Ireland			X
Jamaica		X	
Kenya		X	
Malaysia	X		
Netherlands	X		
New Zealand	X	X	
Pakistan			X
Philippines	X		
Poland			X
Singapore			X
South Africa	X	X	
Thailand		X	
Zimbabwe	X	X	

Source: Adapted from McCluskey (1999), p. 13.

Land Tax in South Africa

The South African government is seeking to improve and accelerate the impact of its land reform strategy. One element of this effort, following the recommendations of the 2005 National Land Summit, involves imposing a land tax. Participants at the summit concluded that such a tax could be instrumental in achieving the following objectives: (1) increasing the supply of land to the market and for various land reform programs; (2) intensifying agricultural land use; (3) reducing the price of land, especially its speculative value; and (4) contributing to the financing of land reform by the current owners of land.

Before 1994, many municipalities did not tax agricultural land at all, whereas others used a highly regressive tax system (dating from 1939) under which the first hectare was taxed 100 times more than the 20th hectare. The right of municipalities in South Africa to tax all land, including agricultural land, was confirmed when the 1994 constitution was passed. In 1998, a special subcommittee of the so-called Katz Commission on Taxation issued its findings on the implications of introducing a land tax in South Africa. Subsequently, the commission proposed a tax on agricultural land, including stipulations for its collection and retention at the local government level. However, although the Municipal Property Rates Act that passed in 2004 provided a national legal framework for taxing agricultural land, it also required local governments to tax the improvements on it for reasons of administrative uniformity and simplicity. Property would be taxed in the same way in both urban and rural areas.

As of July 2007, only three of the 283 municipalities had implemented the Municipal Property Rates Act. In the other municipalities, the old system was still in place. Many local governments have been hesitant to implement the municipal rates on agricultural land, although it is their statutory right to do so because of the extension of municipalities to include rural areas. One of the main reasons for this lack of implementation is the absence of practical guidelines. Although the national government has issued general guidelines on rate policies (which municipalities must issue annually), there is little guidance on the imposition of an agricultural land tax or on the effect this tax is likely to have. The following concrete suggestions can be made.

The purpose of an agricultural land tax should be to augment own-source revenues at the local level, with a decrease in land prices and the discouragement of vacant possession being welcome bonuses. In South Africa, the maximum extent of negative impact on land values—the so-called land tax capitalization—has been estimated at less than 5 percent, for an effective tax rate of 1 percent.

To ensure the conservation of areas with high biodiversity values, the existing system of declaring specific public and private lands conservation areas will impact appropriately both the land's taxable value and the liability of the owner or taxpayer. The current tax legislation already excludes from taxation conservation lands that are not used for commercial purposes. No further special exemption from the land tax is required.

Tax collection should be conducted at the local level if the purpose of the tax is to provide for an own-source of revenues at that level. International evidence clearly demonstrates that taxation systems are most efficient when imposition of the tax and expenditure of the revenues gathered are done at the same level of government. This also boosts tax morale because the benefits provided by the collected revenue will be seen within the community being taxed.

Certain tax relief measures should be implemented. There should be thresholds and a process of phasing-in to lower administration costs, improve acceptance, and exempt the poorest landowning cohorts. However, there should be no relief for low agricultural prices or high input costs because these risks already are discounted in the land price, and catastrophic and unanticipated risks are better dealt with through special dedicated mechanisms. In addition, blanket relief or exemption should not be given for farmers who provide certain services to farmworkers living on their farms. Other mechanisms for compensating such employers are available in the Housing Code and in the procurement processes of local government.

As for communal areas, innovative methods must be found—and have been tested in several other parts of the world—to put a value on this land and to fairly assign shares of the collective tax bill to residents who can afford to pay the tax. Thresholds and use-value assessment will keep administrative costs down while they provide relief to the rural poor.

Land Tax in Namibia

The rural land tax system of Namibia is particularly relevant to this discussion, given that Namibia and South Africa share a common history and that the land tax there has been introduced only recently as a completely new tax.

Since Namibia's independence in 1990, land and land reform have been among the most prominent of its political issues. As in South Africa, the pattern of ownership of commercial agricultural land skewed in favor of a small minority of predominantly white owners has led to pressure for redistribution of ownership. The introduction of a land tax on such properties is considered to be one of the cornerstones of the land reform program, along with the state's right of first refusal to purchase commercial farms at market value for the purpose of resettlement.

The two main objectives of the land tax are to encourage greater efficiency in the use of commercial agricultural land and to generate revenue for a Land Acquisition and Development Fund, which is used to purchase appropriate commercial farms coming on the market. The tax is levied against assessments of the market value of the bare land for each property listed in a valuation roll prepared by the Ministry of Lands, Resettlement, and Rehabilitation, through its Directorate of Valuation and Estate Management. The legal framework for the tax is provided by the Commercial Land Agriculture Reform Act of 1995. This act provided for the introduction of a commercial agricultural land tax (as subsequently detailed in the Land Valuation and Taxation Regulations), and it enabled the state to acquire agricultural land by preferential right or, in certain circumstances and subject to adequate compensation, by compulsory acquisition for the purpose of land reform. It also regulated the purchase of land by non-Namibian citizens, and provided for the creation and administration of the Land Acquisition and Development Fund to finance farm purchases.

That policy context is important because it influenced both the design of the tax and the institutional arrangements for administering it. The Ministry of Lands, Resettlement, and Rehabilitation was appointed as the responsible body for developing and implementing the land tax, land acquisition, and resettlement program. In 2001, it created the Directorate of Valuation and Estate Management as a centralized unit responsible for land tax and land acquisition. The Resettlement Program is administered separately in collaboration with the Land Reform Advisory Commission, Lands Tribunal, and Interministerial Land Use and Environmental Board.

The objectives of Namibia's land tax are to

- Encourage the efficient use of land
- Discourage speculative landholding
- Discourage multiple ownership of farms through the application of a "progressive rate"
- Encourage redistribution and diversification of ownership
- Reduce land prices and thus broaden the base of, and access to, ownership
- Redress the skewed pattern of land ownership
- Support successful communal farmers in their efforts to farm commercially
- Relieve poverty indirectly through resettlement and by lessening pressure on communal land
- Raise revenue for the Land Acquisition and Development Fund to facilitate and accelerate the process of land purchase, distribution, and development
- Create an environment of political acceptance of change and appease pressure groups.

Because the tax is a dedicated one used by the Land Acquisition and Development Fund to acquire and resettle land, the specific objectives of the tax are linked inextricably to the objectives of the government resettlement policy.

Institutional and Technical Issues

Although the main regulatory framework was largely in place at an early stage, establishing a new Directorate of Valuation and Estate Management with only limited staffing levels was—and still is—a major constraint. Furthermore, the technical difficulties of designing, developing, and introducing the tax with minimal resources and within a relatively short time frame were considerable. Those challenges led to some delay in implementing the tax, but the delay was not considered to be excessive under the circumstances.

Fundamental to the implementation process is whether the tax should be administered at a national, regional, or municipal level. Notwithstanding the various regional and municipal jurisdictions, a number of arguments influenced the decision to implement the tax at a national level. These arguments included the following:

- Although individual municipalities had well-established property taxation systems for urban properties located within their boundaries, no experience and only limited resources existed at the local level to institute a rural land tax.
- It was politically important that the land tax be introduced throughout the country at a single point in time, not willy-nilly depending on the different resources and efficiencies of regional or local authorities.
- As a new tax, and one that was politically sensitive, it was important that there be consistency, transparency, and fairness in the assessments; and that the system could be easily understood by the taxpayer.

- A comprehensive database of properties had to be compiled from scratch, and much of the required information concerning details of property holdings and land ownership could be sourced only from the central deeds registry office.
- It was essential that the land tax be cost effective—that is, that it generate substantially more in revenue than it cost to administer. This requirement meant that mass-appraisal techniques would need to be adopted, and such an approach lends itself to centralization.
- Much of the data relating to land productivity, which were used in assessing market value, were held at the central offices of the Ministry of Agriculture, Water, and Rural Development.
- The assessment of land values is notoriously difficult on a practical level, given the rarity of unimproved land sales. Valuation skills, necessary for the assessment of individual farms, were extremely limited and mainly confined to the Directorate of Valuation and Estate Management in Windhoek.
- The process for issuing statutory notices, the creation of the new Valuation Court responsible for arbitrating on appeals by the general public, and the development of a computerized financial system for billing and collecting the taxes could be coordinated more easily at a central site.
- The revenue from the land tax was to be dedicated to the Land Acquisition and Development Fund, rather than incorporated into central or local budgets. In addition, this fund was to be administered by a central committee in accordance with the National Development Plan.

Implementation of the Land Tax System

A comprehensive list of all commercial farm properties in the country was compiled and mass assessments were conducted on the basis of the land's unimproved market value (capital value). The assessments were based on the analysis of a sample of 295 farms sold between 1999 and 2002. An iso-value map (a form of value banding, or zoning, in which farmland was grouped according to its value per hectare) covering the whole commercial farming region was created to form the basis of the mass-valuation model. Part of this valuation process, including the development of computer-assisted mass-appraisal software, had to be outsourced to the private sector because the needed human resources were lacking within government.

The mass-appraisal model is recognized to have limitations in terms of how well it reflects local soil conditions and topographical, geological, hydrological, meteorological, and locational variations that affect individual farm valuations; however, the nature of mass-appraisal systems is such that an acceptable level of averaging is necessary. Meanwhile, there is scope for improvement as more sophisticated models are developed over time.

The provisional valuation roll proceeded through the appeals process, which included the newly appointed Valuation Court hearings, and gained the minister's approval in 2004. The tax was collected for the first time in 2005, raising approximately N$4 million in revenue.

Namibia's National Assembly debated the level of the "general rate" that would be applicable, the appropriate "progressive rate" (to discourage taxpayers who own more than one property, foreign nationals, and absentee landlords), and the issue of exemptions. A resolution was passed setting the general rate at 0.75 percent of assessed value, a progressive rate of 0.25 percent for each additional property, and a rate of 1.75 percent for foreign absentee landlords. Although there are sound economic arguments for setting the tax rate at significantly higher levels, the relatively low level of the general rate was agreed in order to gain taxpayer acceptance. The efficacy of that decision was largely borne out in practice; and although the levels of tax rates remain unchanged to date, it is intended that further consideration will be given to these in the future when the tax and its implications are established more firmly.

In addition, it has been recognized that the incremental charges for additional farm ownership do not always provide equitable results because they do not account for the aggregate size of the farms. For example, an individual holding several farms may be penalized unduly if his total acreage is less than that of an individual owning a single larger farm. This issue and the issue of what may constitute an "economic farming unit" are the subjects of further study.

Notwithstanding certain imperfections in the system, annual revenue generation has been on target, with few defaulters, and the system overall is improving with use. The tax generally has been accepted by the commercial farmers, mainly because of the relatively low amounts they have to pay. The Land Acquisition and Development Fund has received sufficient revenue to meet its current acquisition needs. This is a contentious issue, however, because not all farms offered for sale are suitable for government purchase and resettlement, and government has shown some dissatisfaction with the pace of change. Nevertheless, this has less to do with the functioning of the land tax than with the difficulties associated with the wider issues of land reform.

In accordance with statutory requirements, the valuation roll underwent its first review in 2007 (to keep pace with inflation and changes in market conditions) and received the minister's approval. The new roll went into effect on April 1, 2008, and will remain valid for the next three years.

Summary

Although it is too early to assess the full implications of the land tax in Namibia, indications are that there is reason for some optimism. The impact of some of the broader goals—such as increased land use, reduced speculation and foreign ownership, lower land prices, and so forth—has yet to be assessed. However, the introduction of the tax in a transparent and equitable manner, widely accepted by taxpayers, generating revenue at a relatively low administrative cost, and serving as a cornerstone of the land reform process, has taken place relatively smoothly.

The recent experience of introducing a rural land tax in Namibia illustrates the need not only for the initial political will but also for continued prioritizing of and support for the tax to ensure its smooth implementation. Notwithstanding this, the time and technical resources required to implement a new land tax successfully should not be underestimated. There is a need for adequate resource planning, a comprehensive and detailed implementation program, and an environment that facilitates the interaction and collaboration of all major stakeholders.

CONCLUSION

The case for taxing the unimproved value of agricultural land is strong, both economically and socially. However, just as a land tax should not be the *only* tax—the original argument of the followers of Henry George—it also should not be put forward as the *only* instrument to redistribute land from large to small farmers and to intensify land use. A land tax will take away one of the disadvantages that small farmers have vis-à-vis large farmers and speculative landowners, but will not remove all of them. And if large landowners are able to evade the tax, or if low rates and value assessments are made, it is no wonder that land taxation does little to redistribute land. These observations, however, illustrate the political power of large landowners, not any inherent flaws in land taxation. Presumably, the landowners' lobbying power could be used to thwart *any* redistribution instrument, not just a land tax.

In addition to the key economic and social arguments for a land tax (intensifying land use and taxing unearned capital gains), many other justifications have been found. These justifications range from providing a source for local revenues to establishing a property rights registry.

Earlier arguments that a land tax would be too difficult to administer have not withstood the test of time. Valuation and collection can be done at reasonable levels of cost, accuracy, and fairness; manageable processes for appeal, dispute resolution, and information management have been put in place around the world, including area-based land taxes, self-appraisal, community valuation, banding, computer-assisted mass appraisal, and the use of thresholds.

The cases of South Africa and Namibia were discussed in some detail in this chapter. Both countries share a similar land distribution issue, but the role that land taxation has played in each country is quite different. In South Africa, a decision was made to tax urban and rural properties in much the same way, with a tax on the combined value of the land and its improvements. In Namibia, only the value of unimproved rural land is taxed. In South Africa, the tax's main objective is to create a source of revenue for local government, which also administers the tax. In Namibia, the tax is one of the main instruments to effect and fund land reform, driven by the national government.

It is too early to draw firm conclusions about the experience of the two countries. South Africa faces the challenge of implementing the tax in such a way that it does not hurt investment in agriculture, but does support land reform and put a premium on speculative landholding. Namibia has done remarkably well in introducing the tax as a broadly supported land reform policy instrument, as a means to discourage foreign land ownership, and as a source of revenue for its redistribution program. What is clear from both cases, however, is that taxing agricultural land is a useful and practical policy instrument within a broader menu of options for achieving land redistribution.

NOTES

1. See http://en.wikisource.org/wiki/Open_letter_to_Mikhail_Gorbachev_(1990).
2. This situation occurs commonly in a dualistic agrarian structure with low-intensity uses predominating, even though the total supply of land is fixed.
3. Malme and Youngman noted this tension in the Eastern European transitional nations they surveyed: "The economic advantages of a system of private ownership . . . frequently conflict with deeply held beliefs in the need for a continuing public interest in the permanent and irreplaceable heritage of immovable property" (1997, p. 3).

REFERENCES

Assuncão, Juliano J., and Humberto Moreira. 2005. "Land Taxes in a Latin American Context." Discussion Paper 497. Department of Economics, Pontifícia Universidade Católica de Rio de Janeiro, Brazil. http://www.econ.puc-rio.br/pdf/td497.pdf [accessed February 11, 2009].

Bell, Michael E., and John H. Bowman. 1998. "Local Property Tax Administration in South Africa." Paper prepared for the Department of Constitutional Development, South Africa.

Bell, Michael E., John H. Bowman, and Lindsey C. Clark. 2005. "Valuing Land for Tax Purposes in Traditional Tribal Areas of South Africa Where There Is No Land Market." Working Paper 05MB1. Lincoln Institute of Land Policy, Cambridge, MA.

Malme, Jane H., and Joan M. Youngman. 1997. Property Tax Developments in Transition Economies." Presentation to the Fourth International Conference on Local Government Taxation, Institute Rating Revenues, and Valuation, Rome.

———. 2001. *The Development of Property Taxation in Economies in Transition: Case Studies from Central and Eastern Europe.* Washington, DC: World Bank.

McCluskey, William J., ed. 1999. *Property Tax: An International Comparative Review.* Aldershot, U.K.: Ashgate Publishing.

Mieszkowski, Peter. 1972. "The Property Tax: Excise Tax or Profits Tax." *Journal of Public Economics* 1 (1): 73–95.

Netzer, Dick. 1973. "The Incidence of Property Tax Revisited." *National Tax Journal* 30: 515–35.

Oates, Wallace. 1969. "The Effects of Property Taxes and Public Expenditure on Property Values." *Journal of Political Economy* 77 (6): 957.

Prest, Alan R. 1981. *The Taxation of Urban Land.* Manchester, U.K.: Manchester University Press.

Shearer, Eric B., Susana Lastarria-Cornhiel, and Dina Mesbah. 1991. "The Reform of Rural Land Markets in Latin America and the Caribbean: Research, Theory and Policy Implications." Research Paper 12761. Land Tenure Center, University of Wisconsin-Madison.

Skinner, Jonathan. 1991a. "If the Agricultural Land Tax Is So Efficient, Why Is It So Rarely Used?" *World Bank Economic Review* 5 (1): 113–33.

———. 1991b. "Prospects for Agricultural Land Taxation in Developing Countries." *World Bank Economic Review* 5 (3): 493–511.

Slack, Enid. 2002. "Property Tax Reform in Ontario: What Have We Learned?" *Canadian Tax Journal* 50 (2): 576–85.

Strasma, John. 2000. "Chile: Economic Aspects of Land Use." *American Journal of Economics and Sociology* 59 (5): 85–96.

Strasma, John, James Alm, Eric Sherar, and Alfred Waldstein. 1987. "The Impact of Agricultural Land Revenue Systems on Agricultural Land Usage in Developing Countries." Associates in Rural Development, Burlington, VT.

Turvey, Ralph. 1957. *The Economics of Real Property: An Analysis of Property Values and Patterns of Use.* London: George Allen & Unwin.

van den Brink, Rogier. 2002. "Land Reform Policy in Sub-Saharan Africa: Consensus and Controversy." Paper presented at the Regional Workshop on Land Issues in Africa, Kampala, Uganda, April 29–May 2.

World Bank. 2007. "Paraguay Real Property Tax: Key to Fiscal Decentralization and Better Land Use. Volume 1: Main Report." Report 37456-PA. Washington, DC.

Wunderlich, Gene, ed. 1993. *Land Ownership and Taxation in American Agriculture.* Boulder, CO: Westview Press.

Yamamura, Kozo. 1986. "The Meiji Land Tax Reform and Its Effects." In *Japan in Transition: From Tokugawa to Meiji*, ed. Marius B. Jansen and Gilbert Rozman. Princeton, NJ: Princeton University Press.

PART V

How to Develop, Implement, and Monitor an Effective National Program of Land Redistribution

CHAPTER THIRTEEN

Designing and Implementing Redistributive Land Reform: The Southern African Experience

Sam Moyo

The importance of land reform, beyond the short-term reprieve that it offers to poor people living in rural areas, lies in its potential to reorganize the political structures that impede development, including defining the fate of the peasantry or small farmers. A successful land redistribution hinges on (1) defining a clear strategy and effective goals and procedures to guide the acquisition of land to be redistributed, (2) determining who gets the land, (3) giving beneficiaries secure land rights (tenure), and (4) providing appropriate support to help beneficiaries resettle and commence productive use of the land. Postsettlement policies and programs to support beneficiaries—infrastructure and technical/social services—are not unique to land redistribution because these services typically are provided in communal areas. The difference is that resettled lands tend not to have such services, and providing them entails new investment.

This chapter discusses the overall designing and implementing of redistributive land reform experiences in Zimbabwe. Land reforms had been initiated in southern Africa during the late 1960s and 1970s, and then returned to the development agenda in Zimbabwe in 1980, in Namibia and South Africa in the 1990s, and in Malawi in the early 2000s. Access to land was recognized as an important poverty alleviation issue, and rightly so. Access to land for the rural poor, and especially for women, is crucial to improving the social reproduction of the household. The significance of these land reforms, however, lay not only in poverty alleviation, but more fundamentally in their larger political-economic objectives. Yet, current initiatives have sought to obtain land redistribution *within* the given national political structures, which not only are hostile to reform, but also tend to be committed to "accumulation from above." The later experience of Zimbabwe deviated from that strategy.

We first examine the various strategies and objectives of land reform used in the Southern African Development Community region, and we provide a stylized overview of land reform approaches in southern Africa. The key processes and mechanisms (and their principles) for executing land redistribution are discussed in the second section. The third section addresses the legal framework required, the implementation strategy and institutional arrangements, and the need for policy review and adjustment based on effective monitoring and evaluation.

SETTING THE AGENDA: OBJECTIVES, TRAJECTORIES, AND STRATEGIES

Land reforms are implemented using various strategies, which are informed by disparate elements of social, economic, and political objectives. In southern Africa, these objectives have tended to focus on redressing the past colonial land injustices and on meeting new land demands, increasing agricultural production, and rationalizing settlement patterns.

Overall Objectives of Land Reform

The broad consensus today is that land reform is a necessary but not sufficient condition for national development, as was acknowledged widely during the period from 1950 through 1970. From the 1970s onward, under the influence of international finance and neoliberal economics, land reform was removed from the development agenda and replaced by a concerted market-based land policy. That policy focused on privatizing and commercializing land and confining land transfers to the market. This framework abandoned integration of agriculture and industry on a national basis, instead promoting their integration into global markets.

The end of the Cold War and the reemergence of organized rural movements returned land reform to the development agenda. However, the literature on land reform does not yet agree on a coherent purpose for land reform in national development. Land reform is an inherently conflictive process, for it challenges established economic and political structures and dominant cultural identities. Although peaceful land reform is always the objective of public policy, such policy must be informed by a realistic assessment of the sources of conflict and the implications of different models of land reform. The following three views on the purpose of agrarian reform compete (see Moyo and Yeros [2005]).

Social Land Reform

The social version of land reform is based on the argument that agro-industry is sufficiently modern and competitive, as well as highly rewarding in its export capacity, to permit any intervention in the sector to be confined to the purpose of providing a measure of security to dispossessed and unemployed workers until employment can be generated elsewhere in the economy. The related argument is that the problem of unemployment can no longer be dealt with by means of agrarian reform (as had been the formula in the past) because that would destroy agro-industry. This version of land reform also argues that smaller-scale production is inherently unproductive, and that the urbanization trends since the 1980s are irreversible.

Economic Land Reform

The economic version of land reform has various tendencies, drawing on diverse arguments. Its agreed positions are that smaller-scale agriculture could reach a reasonable level of productivity and that urbanization is partly reversible or can be slowed. The dominant current in this debate emphasizes the role of the "family farm" (perhaps a misnomer for middle-size capitalist farms of 20–100 hectares employing some wage labor). This current also argues that the benefits of large-scale farming are overestimated, given their historical privileges, social costs, and environmental unsustainability. This side of the debate therefore would demand a generalized shift in the national policy framework that would challenge the historical privileges (in terms of credit, services, electricity, irrigation, and marketing infrastructure) enjoyed by the large-scale farming sector. This current sees the modern small or part-time farm and the middle-size farm as having the potential to absorb labor in the form of self-employed and wage-employed workers (Binswanger, Deininger, and Feder 1995). However, labor absorption could correlate inversely with the level of technological development; in itself, that is not a sufficient rural employment policy. The middle-size farm also has the potential to redirect production to the national market, and hence to synergize dynamically with domestic wages; but again this would be contingent on a concerted national policy framework seeking the integration of the home market. Some among the advocates of economic land reform see economic potential in a bifurcated agricultural sector where large-scale farming specializes in the export of high-value crops and smaller-scale farming specializes in the domestic provision of low-value crops for domestic consumption (Rukuni and Eicher 1994; Rukuni et al. 2006).

A second current in this economic version of land reform places more hope on large-scale land redistribution, the promotion of collective/associative forms of production, the redirection of agriculture to the home market, and the creation of intersectoral links (see Moyo and Yeros [2005]). This current sees value in a national strategy of partial "delinking" from the global market, but faces the chronic foreign-exchange dilemma, as well as national and international reaction.

Political Land Reform

The political version of land reform also has various tendencies and is not necessarily distinct from the economic version. The political version may be subdivided into micro and macro tendencies, the latter being the most closely associated with economic thinking. The micro tendency sees political value in land reform as a means to dissolve noncapitalist relations of production or excessively concentrated power structures where they continue to exist at the local/regional level. Land reform, in this case, should be confined to a targeted local/regional democratization project, not to a national project of structural transformation. By contrast, the macro tendency views land reform as a means of dissolving the political power of large agrarian capital that operates in tandem with international capital and has an interest in maintaining an extroverted model of accumulation (NEAD-AIAS 2003). This tendency sees large-scale land reform as a political precondition for implementing a national development policy whose objective is the integration of the home market.

Objectives of Land Reform in Southern Africa

The objectives of land reform in southern Africa tended to combine various elements of the wider social, economic, and political objectives, focusing on stabilizing the postcolonial nations by assuaging historical grievances and accommodating immediate land needs. Although there are subtle variations in the objectives, which are reviewed periodically, those variations mainly have been functionalist efforts to alleviate poverty, promote rural development, and rehabilitate displaced people. The objectives have combined some of the following: (1) to decongest and reorganize overpopulated communal areas; (2) to increase the base of productive agriculture; (3) to reduce poverty; (4) to rehabilitate people displaced by war; (5) to resettle squatters, the destitute, and the landless; (6) to promote equitable distribution of agricultural land; (7) to correct the racial imbalance of land ownership; (8) to empower and benefit members of the new black elite; (9) to provide land to war veterans; (10) to provide land to "competent farmers" and indigenous capitalists; (11) to promote environmentally sustainable land use; and (12) to create political stability and peace.

Creating space for the reorganization of communal areas also has been a common goal, inspired by environmentalists, to address land degradation and create order through land-use plans overseen by state planners. This has been prioritized in land programs in Namibia and Zimbabwe (and partially in Malawi), but not in South Africa's beneficiary selection system.

The initial objectives of land redistribution were modified later to support experienced farmers willing to give up their communal land rights and to develop indigenous "commercial" (capitalist) farmers. The rationale veered toward advancing decasualized "commercial" agricultural development, rather than toward assuaging landlessness or promoting smallholders (in whom most policy makers have had less faith and whose advocacy is weaker).

The agitation and strong organization of war veterans in Namibia and Zimbabwe have influenced land policy in a way that tends to specify them as a target for support. In Zimbabwe, for instance, the government in 1995 reserved a 20 percent quota of resettlement land for war veterans, while master farmers and agricultural graduates were to benefit from the land allocations of medium- to large-scale farms under the newly established tenant farmer scheme.

The broader objectives of redistributive land reform programs have tended to include institutional developments such as these: (1) building the institutional and implementation capacities of institutions involved in land reform, (2) enhancing learning among all parties, and (3) leveraging resources from multiple sources.

Macroeconomic policy objectives also have tended to circumscribe the objectives of land redistribution, given that agricultural growth and its links to industry and other sectors have been seen as critical. Most countries sought to preserve current production systems, including their direction toward exports. Indeed, arguments against land redistribution have been based largely on the wrong assumption that small-scale farmers either are unable to contribute to such an export strategy or cannot contribute to an equally productive development strategy based on expanding domestic markets.

Macroeconomic policy incentives thus promoted the switching of land use and natural resources toward new exports (tourism), such as wildlife (extending land use). This switch generated emotional agitation in a number of the countries because land redistribution was perceived to be prejudiced by such land uses, while policies downplayed investments into developing land, water, and new technologies for the growing number of small farmers in communal regions and resettlement areas (despite the increasing poverty and demands for land therein).

Other purported preconditions of market-assisted land reforms are the need to eliminate distortions that drive up the price of land and the need to improve the functioning of land markets in terms of the transfer of land to efficient users and the deconcentration of land ownership. Combined with giving grants to land-poor or landless people, land markets are expected to reflect effective and social demand for land when instruments such as land taxation and improved land subdivision procedures are adopted. Some advocates also argue for the complementary instrument of compulsory state land acquisition where the market fails (van den Brink et al. 2006).

Land reform also has entailed acquiring land for the state to promote strategic estate farming (for example, in Zimbabwe, and in the 1970s in Malawi), as well as to promote nuclei for "development" in communal areas, as in the case of the Agriculture and Rural Development Authority in Zimbabwe. Some of this state land then was transferred to indigenous commercial farmers and to "out-grower" beneficiaries in both countries.

Land Reform Trajectories

Land reform generally has been characterized by five trajectories, or paths (see Moyo and Yeros 2005). The five paths are these:

1. *A dominant "junker path"* of landlords-turned-capitalists in Latin America and Asia (outside of East Asia), with its variant in the white settler societies of southern Africa. This path matured in the course of the 20th century, and was reinforced by the green revolution, combined with massive subsidies to modernize inefficient large-scale farms. In economic and political terms, this path of large-scale commercial farming now operates in tandem with transnational corporations (whether landowning or not). More recently, large landowners have expanded/converted land away from farming and onto wildlife management or ecotourism ventures (for example, in eastern and southern Africa).
2. *A "merchant path"* of nonrural capital, including merchant capital, petty-bourgeois elements, bureaucrats, military personnel, and professionals who have gained access to land, whether leasehold or freehold, via the state, the market, or land reform. They farm on a smaller scale than does the traditional commercial farm sector, but they are integrated properly into export markets and global agro-industry. This path is present across the periphery (poor countries in the south) and in many parts of Africa.
3. *A "state path"* involving land appropriated by states in the course of nation building, present across the periphery. This path is now being reversed by privatizations, concessions to national and international capital, or conversion to ecotourism; and it is feeding directly into the junker and merchant paths.
4. *A limited "middle-level to rich-peasant path"* of petty-commodity producers created by a combination of generic tendencies to rural differentiation and active state policies in the postwar period. During nation building, this class of producers was subject to contradictory policies of low producer prices, subsidy, and land reform (for example in Kenya). Under neoliberalism, this class of producers has been augmented by parcelizing and decollectivization, but also forced to sink or swim on its own. It operates in a variety of tenurial arrangements, including freehold and communal; during liberalization, it also has diversified investments to off-farm activities, such as transport, trading, and small-scale hospitality services.
5. A *"rural-poor path,"* including the masses of peasants who are fully or partially proletarianized (semiproletarianized) laborers. This path is characterized by

the contradictory tendencies of full proletarianization and retention or acquisition of a family plot for petty-commodity production and social security (consistent with functional dualism). The rural proletariat and semiproletariat migrate within rural areas, from rural areas to urban centers, and across international boundaries; they enter the informal economic sector, both rural and urban, through such activities as petty trading, craft-making, and part-time/casual employment; and they struggle to become peasants again, sometimes successfully. Under privatizations associated with structural adjustment, this path has been joined by retrenched workers from mines, farms, and urban industries. This large underclass of displaced, insecurely employed, and unemployed people also provides foot soldiers for many economic/nonemancipatory wars for control of the production and trade of high-value resources, including oil, timber, diamonds, and coca.

Land reform has combined mainly the merchant and rural-poor paths, with elements of the junker path in Malawi and Zimbabwe; in Namibia and South Africa, the same is true but with less emphasis on the rural-poor path because the choice has been made to preserve large-scale agriculture.

Overall Land Reform Strategies

There are three different models of land reform in existence, and they interact in a politically dynamic way. These are the "state," "market," and "popular" models, and they entail five elements of land reform: (1) the selection of land, (2) the method of acquiring land, (3) the selection of beneficiaries, (4) the method of transferring land to the beneficiaries, and (5) support to beneficiaries.

The State Model

In the state model, the state plays a prominent role in the land reform process. It may acquire land compulsorily or on a "willing seller–willing buyer" (WSWB) basis. In the radical scenario of compulsory acquisition, the state selects the land (unless it is already occupied by landless people without formal rights), confiscates it without compensation (or with token compensation), selects the beneficiaries (if they have not self-selected already), and transfers the land directly to them through collective or individual title. In the WSWB scenario, the landowners offer the land (if and when they see it to be to their advantage), the state purchases it at market price and compensates the landowners (sometimes with external aid), the state selects beneficiaries (again unless they self-select by occupying the land), and the state transfers title to them. The state also may seek to stimulate land transfers by imposing land taxes, by stipulating a minimum productivity requirement on land, or by evaluating the price of the land administratively by taking the market into account. Variations of the state model may coexist in a country's constitution and, in fact, may compete for prominence in the social and political process. This was the case in Zimbabwe in the 1990s when both expropriation and WSWB strategies were implemented, a conflict that was resolved in favor of expropriation. This is also the case in Brazil, where expropriation and WSWB approaches are implemented in tandem, although the great majority of redistributed land is acquired through expropriation. Variations of the state model exist in many other places, such as Namibia Nicaragua, El Salvador, the Philippines, and South Africa.

The Market Model

The market model, although present within the state model throughout the postwar period, sought to consolidate itself in the 1990s by displacing the state from various processes and putting the beneficiaries in charge of part of the land reform. The model—described as "community-initiated, market-assisted" (CIMA)—operates as follows: "communities' (the rural poor) select themselves, enter negotiations with landlords over the location and price of land, purchase the land, and receive the title from the landlord. This process is monitored at arm's length by the state, which also facilitates the process through taxes imposed on or incentives given to landlords to encourage them to dispose of land. Nongovernmental organizations (NGOs) provide technical assistance to the communities for identifying land and their legal recourse; and states and development agencies in joint ventures provide a variable mix of loans and grants to the rural poor to buy the land, build infrastructure, and set up viable farming operations. The model has been tested in Brazil, Colombia, Guatemala, Malawi, South Africa, and Thailand (Barros, Sauer, and Schwartzman 2003).

The Popular Model

The actions of the landless and land-poor historically have been critical to agrarian reform, so land reforms have always been "popular." Attempts to influence the state and market are made mainly through land occupations and are the first steps in land transfer. The landless and land-poor people self-select as beneficiaries; they choose the land; acquire it de facto, and await their legal formalization by the state. The state may or may not acquire the occupied land. More generally, the low-profile (illegal "squatting") tactic is known to exercise influence over the policy process, but mainly in a much more diffuse manner. The dominant phenomenon in land movements is not the interests of the middle-level peasant (Moyo and Yeros 2005). The coexistence of petty-commodity production and wage labor underlies these movements (for example, in Brazil). What the two groups of workers need from land includes sources of sustenance that cannot be exchanged; the use-values derived from the land and its natural resources, such as food, water, and wood-fuel; and the security that the rural residence provides against economic fluctuations, sickness, and old age. The coexistence is dynamic, as petty-commodity producers and wage-laborers struggle for a living against richer peasants, large-scale commercial farmers, and other employers who hire semiproletarians at wages below the cost of living. This indicates entrenched class struggles over land, although survival strategies under pressure of impoverishment are varied (Raikes 2000).

Interaction between Models

In some circumstances, these three models may combine in different ways that make them not easily distinguishable. For instance, where the WSWB approach has worked, it has been under the influence of militant action. In Zimbabwe's early land reform experience within the WSWB framework, the only land with high agro-ecological value that was redistributed to the poor was the land of white settlers who had been evicted from the liberated zones during the war. This is also true for the expropriation approach used in Brazil. It often is initiated when social movements engage in land occupation actions. The experience of Brazil corroborates the significance of militant agency (Fernandes 2005). Localized occupations in Malawi, Namibia, and South Africa have had more remote influence on policy. The role of rural movements in these sociopolitical dynamics—and such other issues as the roles of finance, security forces, the justice system, mass media, civil society, and state functionaries—remains to be explored in a more systematic manner in relation to state-based reform (Moyo and Yeros 2005).

Land Reform Strategies in Southern Africa

The land question in southern Africa is tied closely to the colonial legacy, especially in the countries with histories of large-scale farming/landlordism. The pertinent issues include land redistribution, tenure, and use. These issues often are treated synonymously, and compounded with questions of indigenous rights or racial imbalances. Integration into generalized commodity production has seen pressures and trends of land alienation and capital concentration, both within the communal areas and outside them (where state and freehold tenure predominate), deepening with liberalization and demographic pressure to create situations where the land question could become explosive. Within communal areas, the key issues are (1) tenure insecurity, land subdivision, and informal land markets; (2) land alienation and concentration, combined with externally determined land-use changes; and (3) undemocratic, patriarchal systems of local government to adjudicate land disputes and administer the resulting decisions. Agrarian reforms without land redistribution in southern Africa are unrealistic because political and economic demands for structural transformation and broad-based development of the home market, and the inclusion of the majority poor, persist.

Attaining independence or majority rule did not lead most southern African states immediately to affirm their sovereign right over land, except in the cases of Zambia (1968), Mozambique (1974), and Angola (1975). Such an approach to nationalization was followed in 2005 only by Zimbabwe's Fast Track Land Redistribution Program in which a militant land occupation movement led by veterans of the national liberation war brought about a radical redistribution of land.

"State-Centered But Market-Based" Approach

In Zimbabwe in the 1980s, prior to the radical period, and in Namibia, resource, constitutional, and legal constraints led to state-centered models of land redistribution whereby governments took responsibility for gradually acquiring or supporting the purchases of land through the market and redistributing it to the needy and "competent." They used persuasion and force to restrain communities from initiating spontaneous action to repossess land. Their policies rejected the legal restitution of particular private or community land rights that had been expropriated during colonial rule, as in the restitution program of South Africa. In southern Africa, a mixture of land reform mechanisms (redistribution, tenure, resettlement, state farming, capitalist farmer development, and so forth) has been used, depending on the reforms' various objectives (as depicted in eight selected countries in table 13.1). Most dominant among the land reform mechanisms used in most of the countries since the 1960s is a state-centered but market-based approach. In this approach, land is purchased by the state for redistribution, following WSWB procedures. The private sector led the land identification and supply, and central government was a reactive buyer choosing land on offer. The governments controlled local land occupations. In Namibia and Zimbabwe, government provided land to beneficiaries chosen mainly by its officials; in contrast, South Africa's land redistribution to date has been driven by demand—that is, it has been based on self-selection.

Thus the market defines the nature, location, and cost of land to be acquired for redistribution, such that neither the government nor the beneficiaries have driven the land acquisition. Moreover, the state having been a key buyer of land on offer has conditioned the parameters of the land market, in terms of land prices and a procurement process that is amenable to the government settlement planning system.

"Community-Initiated, Market-Assisted" Approach

The CIMA approach to land redistribution has been implemented slowly in South Africa (beginning in 1994) and abortively in Zimbabwe (as a result of its slow pace in redistributing land and of fiscal constraints in 1998/99). Its proponents have argued that it could be more cost effective, transparent, fair, and speedy if the entire process were led by the private sector, communities, and NGOs within a market framework. Such actors would identify and purchase land, plan its use, and settle themselves; the government's role would be to provide a public grant to the beneficiaries and otherwise facilitate the transactions.

Table 13.1 Trajectories of Land Reform

Country	Type of Reform	Type of Problem	Source of Reform	Type of Land Acquisition	Role of State/Market
Botswana	Tenure: land boards	Black capitalists and traditional authority	Elite needs	Local land board allocations	State liberalization policy
Malawi	Estates-transition	State/estates	Social/political pressure	Market pricing	Community demands
Mozambique	Tenure/redistribution	Settler/state alienation	Postwar crisis	Expropriation	Not applicable
Namibia	Redistribution	Settler alienation	Political pressure/squatting	State market purchases	State driven
South Africa	Restitution/redistribution/tenure	Settler alienation	Political pressure/squatting	State compensation for restitution; state grants	State and community
Swaziland	Tenure	State/estates	Social/political pressure	Chiefs	Low
Zambia	Tenure: statutory leasehold	Black capitalists and traditional authority	Elite needs	Chiefs	Low
Zimbabwe	Redistribution	Settler alienation, black capitalists	Political pressure/squatting	State market and state compulsory purchases	State driven

Source: Moyo 2007.

Beneficiaries could use such a grant as they chose: purchase more land or make other investments within the resettlement scheme. The grant would be equal to the average amount of money that government provides in the programs it leads. Those benefiting in this approach would have to fit the criteria for target groups established by government policy. In South Africa, the approach has been judged "not proactive."

Compulsory Acquisition with Compensation at Market Price Approach

This approach to land redistribution uses compulsory methods of state land acquisition and the payment of market prices for both the land and its improvements. It was used by Zimbabwe in the 1990s and has been used on a few farms in Namibia and South Africa since 2000. In Zimbabwe, such acquisitions attempted in 1992, 1995, and 1997 were unsuccessful because of litigation and failed negotiations; and they were superseded in 2000 by land expropriations based on compensation only for improvements. In the latter approach, land occupations and confrontations with landowners and farmworkers supported the expropriations, and continued litigation stalled the acquisitions until 2005 (when land was nationalized) and slow, inadequate compensation limited the finalizing of land transfers.

Popular Approach

The popular or community land occupation–led approach to land reform has been experienced mostly in Zimbabwe, although scattered attempts at land invasions have been seen in South Africa (mainly on urban land in the 1980s), Malawi (1990s), and Namibia (2000s). In this approach, which is extralegal, land identification is led by communities through "squatting." During the 1980s in Zimbabwe, the government stepped in to purchase such land at market prices in what was officially termed the "Accelerated Resettlement Program." Local squatter communities self-selected as beneficiaries by occupying mainly abandoned and underused lands, most of which were in the liberation war frontier zone of the Eastern Highlands. The government subsequently used forced evictions to restrain this approach. Land occupation reemerged in Zimbabwe during 1998 and in 2000, when many farms that had been identified for compulsory acquisition were occupied by squatters who then conformed to government resettlement guidelines. After 2000, the government of Zimbabwe gazetted in law its intention to acquire compulsorily about 90 percent of large-scale commercial farms. Most of these farms were acquired and distributed to A1 and A2 beneficiaries. Thus we can see that within a single country, two or three types of approaches can be used over time or concurrently, as is proposed in Namibia and South Africa. The first three approaches to land redistribution have been used at times in combination on a smaller scale in Zimbabwe during the 1990s—although by 1997 the government attempted to acquire land compulsorily on a large scale and has proceeded to do so from 2000 onward.

LAND REFORM POLICY: PRINCIPLES AND MANAGEMENT

The core principle of land reform centers on approaches to the selection of beneficiaries of land redistribution and on the methods of acquiring the necessary land.

Beneficiaries' Eligibility Criteria

Defining who benefits from land redistribution is a key effort informed by reform objectives and available land. The issues involved are the fairness and transparency of the process and the need for accountability in regularly informing the public about the benefits available through land reform. Beneficiary selection principles in southern Africa are converging around a two-prong approach: transferring some land to competent farmers, and transferring some land to the landless or poor people in overcrowded areas. Most of the poorer beneficiaries are selected to gain access to village-based schemes of mixed and livestock farming, whereas the more "competent" beneficiaries are chosen to gain access to individual self-contained dryland or irrigated farms.

In Zimbabwe, several resettlement schemes targeting different beneficiaries coexisted. With the A1 model and its variants, the government targeted as its main beneficiaries poor families from overcrowded communal areas, displaced farmworkers, women, former combatants, agricultural graduates, master farmers, and people with means and ability who intended to engage in agriculture.[1] The government also introduced the A2, or commercial farm, scheme initially for agricultural graduates and master farmers. Those beneficiaries also had to be able to sustain themselves (as indicated by possession of cattle), be married or be widowed with dependents, and be unemployed. Finally, in the 1980s, the cooperative resettlement schemes were reserved mostly for young and unemployed people, but these programs also benefited many former combatants and former farmworkers who were believed to be capable of adapting to scientific farming on collective farms.

Process for Selecting Beneficiaries

Implementing the selection criteria—that is, fairly managing the lists of those who apply for a land transfer program and actually selecting those people who finally will benefit—is another controversial aspect of land redistribution policy consensus building. In Zimbabwe during the early stage of the land reform (1980), schemes were announced in the media and individuals were invited to apply. Beneficiaries also were identified in various other ways, including through central government planning and selection from waiting lists; the compilation of lists of potential beneficiaries by traditional leaders, rural district councils, and different government structures; and the organization of field-based studies of congested areas. To increase the chance of reaching the targeted beneficiaries, local-level authorities (village leaders, ward assemblies, councilors, and other stakeholders) were made aware of beneficiary selection criteria. Sometimes, registries of potential beneficiaries—notably the landless, war veterans, and squatters—were compiled and the lists publicly displayed. Those people who were willing to participate in the program submitted an application form—thus showing they were literate and had access to printed media or at least access to help from local authorities. They also had to pay application fees. Some groups (including Women and Land in Zimbabwe) argue that this approach screened out many potential beneficiaries, especially those in remote areas.

Candidates then were selected through a scoring system that gave more points to larger unemployed married families and then to those who were gender disadvantaged (for example, widows); in the commercial schemes, more points were awarded for evidence of farming experience and resources that could be invested. Individuals ages 25–50 and women scored higher, thus in theory they had greater chances of benefiting from these programs. For the commercial program, the short-listed candidates were interviewed.

During the late 1990s, a decentralized process for selecting beneficiaries was introduced, ostensibly to involve locals in decision making, to include more landless locals, to promote social cohesion, and to reduce the logistical costs of resettlement. With this process, the role of rural district councils and traditional leaders was strengthened, although it involved functionaries from the central government. At the same time, because the government of Zimbabwe determined which lands were to be decongested and which farms were to be purchased, the overall approach remained state-centered until the inception of the Fast Track Land Redistribution Program in 2000.

In practice, these decentalized beneficiary selection mechanisms were not implemented fully, the transparency of the actual selection often was contested, and the selection was considered to be unfair. Involvement of local community-based organizations, farmers' unions, women's clubs, and NGOs could have contributed to a more fair and transparent selection process within a decentralized framework, but these groups have not engaged adequately with land redistribution in most countries.

There is a genuine concern that the beneficiary selection process for some commercial farm schemes since 2000 has been unfair, although it certainly was more equitable than in the colonial context. The finding of unfairness comes from those with some influence having gained larger and better resource plots (see Moyo [2007]). More broadly, it is not clear whether traditional leaders and rural district councils are best placed to be fair and transparent. Using traditional chiefs, an apparently legitimate local structure (albeit not a democratic governance system), aims at ensuring that resettled communities form cohesive groups. In Zimbabwe, however, it was reported that some families unofficially were charged money to obtain registration forms or to be wait-listed for land (Moyo 2007). Another matter of contention is squatters' eligibility as potential beneficiaries. In most countries, squatting has been regarded unofficially as a sign of landlessness. However, the selection of squatters is considered by some to be an acceptance of jumping the resettlement queue, and this tends to encourage further land occupation. Thus, although people occupying land illegally were resettled in the early 1980s in Zimbabwe, squatting was repressed until 2000, when it was encouraged and/or condoned by the state.

By far the most controversial aspect of beneficiary selection is its tendency to discriminate against and even exclude farmworkers. In South Africa and Zimbabwe, farmworkers often are citizens of foreign origin. As such, they have no ensured land rights in communal areas, towns, or large-scale farm and resettlement areas. Furthermore, land policies generally lack sound provisions to protect the rights of migrant farmworkers who are removed from their communities and dependent for their residential rights on their employers. In Zimbabwe, the land rights of farmworkers were not covered in any law. When the state or donors plan to invest in social services for farmworkers, they depend on voluntary permission to use land segments of given farms as granted by landowners.

Finally, regarding the participation of women in land redistribution schemes, in Zimbabwe and many other countries the certainty and security of women's land rights are rather vague, as are their chances of being equally selected to benefit from resettlement schemes. Women seeking land in their individual right—whether married or not—typically are discriminated against in practice when they apply for land. The inclusion of women and farmworkers increased during the land occupations of 2000, but land reform still excludes many of them.

Mechanisms for Identifying Land

Targeting land to be redistributed starts with the defining of land eligibility criteria. During the 1980s, the government of Zimbabwe announced that it would expropriate only (1) derelict land, (2) underused land, (3) multiple tracts of land owned by the same person, (4) foreign-owned land, and (5) land contiguous to communal areas. However, there were no clear-cut operational definitions of how these criteria would be applied by the government-appointed land acquisition committee. Nor was there an order of priority in applying the criteria used to identify farms. Before the Fast Track Land Redistribution Program, the government had proposed various additional criteria for land to be acquired,[2] but these criteria never were defined legally. The absence of a land management information system also severely limited land identification and acquisition. For instance, there was no comprehensive computerized database of farms that systematically defined their tenurial and productive features.

Once land eligibility criteria have been defined, it is possible to evaluate the amount of land available for redistribution. Such an evaluation was done during the 1980s in Zimbabwe through land-use studies. The government then was committed to redistributing land without reducing large-farm production, so it commissioned a study whereby large-scale commercial farming areas were rated across agro-ecological regions, and the amount of underused land that could be transferred from that sector without losing its strategic role in national agricultural production was estimated.

During the early 1980s, the government adopted an approach that consisted of first estimating the number of households needing land and then assessing the amount of land required. The type and amount of land were defined on the basis of actual need. The findings of this study were presented publicly in the Riddell Report. The initial estimate was that 162,000 households would receive an average of 6 hectares, as well as common areas for grazing. The specific land needs per beneficiary later were expected to vary in scope, depending on the agro-ecological attributes of the land and the degree to which water could be harnessed to intensify the land use. For instance, the size of the irrigated plot was estimated at less than 1 hectare.

In the mid-1990s, land redistribution stalled, mainly because of the difficulty in identifying and acquiring land. To speed up land redistribution, the government dramatically decentralized land identification. Farms were now to be identified for expropriation and market purchases at the provincial level. By 1997, a total of 1,470 farms had been identified for expropriation. Geographic, economic, social, and tenurial data on each farm then were sought from various sources. In line with the expropriation process, the potential impacts or implications of acquiring the listed farms were examined. Each farm was checked post facto by the central government at the deeds registry to rid it of possible inaccuracies regarding ownership status, property description, location, and size. Planners next had to find data sources to provide production, land use, and other socioeconomic information on each farm.

The experience of land acquisition in Zimbabwe suggests that land identification should be done systematically, by first examining the qualities and suitability of the land, before announcing land for acquisition. The problems in the process as it stands are compounded when many farms are being acquired simultaneously. In 1998, still committed to expropriating only underused land, the Zimbabwean government delisted a large number of farms—including indigenous large farms, farms approved as new investment projects, and some highly productive farms. Church lands also were not to be acquired.

During the Fast Track Land Redistribution Program, and until 2001, land identification was led by war veterans who directly occupied farms. The government of Zimbabwe later coopted this movement and announced that most large-scale commercial farms would be acquired. Thus, the government led farm identification after 2001.

Land Acquisition: Market, Expropriation, and Negotiation

In the final analysis, the method of acquisition chosen—WSWB, negotiation, expropriation, or occupation—tends to define the amount and quality of land actually acquired and the scale and scope of beneficiaries. The complexities of land acquisition policies and practices are well illustrated by the history of Zimbabwe since 1980.

Throughout the 1980s, the government of Zimbabwe was strongly committed to redistributing land on a WSWB basis and to making limited use of expropriation. Under the WSWB approach, land identification was led by the market, with the state and/or private actors entering transactions with landowners offering land for sale. In other words, the state mostly acquired land from owners willing to sell it. Therefore, it had relatively limited control over the geographical distribution of the 71,000 beneficiaries who gained close to 3 million hectares. As a result, the land acquired was spread unevenly across administrative regions and agro-ecological zones. This uneven spread led to critical distributional imbalances in land quality accessed, in relative levels of access across regions, and in infrastructural endowments. Furthermore, under the WSWB principle, it was difficult to acquire large tracts of land that would enable government to plan and deliver viable schools, clinics, and so forth to larger communities.

This weakness strengthened the case for compulsory acquisition rather than voluntary sales. Therefore, between 1989 and 1993, at least 428,936 hectares were expropriated in a bid by the Zimbabwean government to get large blocks of land that were contiguous to abandoned and occupied farms for the accelerated resettlement program (Government of Zimbabwe 1999). Landowners were compensated at market prices.

During 1997 and 1998, attempts were made to expropriate 1,471 farms (about 4 million hectares). The attempts failed because of successful litigation by landowners and a retreat on some acquisitions in compliance with stated policy. That exercise revealed that the criteria for acquiring land on efficiency grounds (underused land that tends to be held as oversized and multiple-owned landholdings) could have yielded the bulk of the 5 million hectares of land that then were required for redistribution by the policy, without affecting production (Moyo 1998). About 80 percent of the identified farms were underused and oversized. Only 200 farms could deliver 2 million hectares, 90 percent of which was sparsely grazed by cattle and wildlife and had no crops. One multinational held 25 farms, amounting to about 500,000 hectares, which mostly were not cropped.

During the Fast Track Land Redistribution Program, the government expanded its use of expropriation, with the support of "illegal" land occupiers. By 2006, a total of 8,000 farms (owned by 3,500 farmers and representing 10 million hectares) was subjected to expropriations based on compensation for improvements only. Most of those expropriations were resisted unsuccessfully in the courts. Donor funding also was not available for those expropriations. The land effectively was nationalized and redistributed to more than 150,000 households.[3]

After 2000, the centralized management of land acquisition was abandoned. Under Fast Track, provincial governors and district land committees, as well as local war veterans' association and land occupiers, became key actors in identifying land for acquisition and recommending formal expropriations by central government agencies.

Land restitution processes through squatting became visible in Zimbabwe during 1998, and were critical to negotiations for a renewed land redistribution program. This approach to land transfers reflected a certain level of political alliance between the state and local forces in opposition to what was seen as landowner resistance to redistribution, and international conditionalities against land reforms, being perceived to be in defense of narrow (racial) interests in land. When Zimbabwe reached independence, the government did not commit to restituting land to those who had been dispossessed unfairly. That alternative was rejected on grounds that it was too legalistic, bureaucratically cumbersome, and likely to lead to conflict. Until 2000, the government did not formally sanction attempts to repossess land through illegal land occupations. Nonetheless, it failed to appease popular discontent and, in 2000, land occupations emerged as a populist mechanism in support of land expropriation.

Proponents of "alternative" land transfer, commonly opposed to expropriation, argue that such transfer reduces the overall cost of the reform by minimizing the transaction costs. By contrast, they also argue that the cost of expropriation often is higher because of administrative and judicial procedures. At the same time, for a voluntary transfer to occur at scale, the land market needs to be fluid and competitive, encouraged by more effective rules to allow the subdivision of oversized holdings and an effective rate of land taxation that could force underused land onto the market. However, these land size regulations were not in place by 2000, although technical proposals had been made in Zimbabwe, nor was the environment favorable for such approaches. It was conducive, however, in Malawi, Namibia, and South Africa.

The need for the government and landowners to develop an effective negotiation strategy that would lead to more land purchases by the state was never realized in Zimbabwe. Some Zimbabweans believed that approach to be a ploy aimed at "enriching" elites who were speculating on the land market. They felt it was unfair to compensate these landowners at market prices. Hence, there have been few attempts to negotiate land transfers. For instance, in 1998 and 1999, the Commercial Farmers' Union promised to offer the government 1.5 million hectares of land as a collective representing the large-scale white farmers, but that did not happen. Subsequently, the Farm Community Trust of Zimbabwe proposed to develop a settlement model whereby farmworkers would gain ownership of their own residential and garden plots. A few private organizations with developmental and financial interests in the land and the related financial markets also expressed interest in engaging in negotiated land transfers. They included large and small farmers' unions, banks, and NGOs. Numerous alternatives based on the Zimbabwean settlement and farming projects could have been examined, but initiatives were slow to come and were overtaken in 2000 by large-scale land occupations. The proponents of alternative approaches in southern Africa do not promote land occupation as an instrument of the community-led redistribution approaches because they generally believe that land reform in a democratic state should not entail extralegal measures. At the same time, some people do recognize the importance of land occupation as a tactic to place pressure on governments and as a counter to the lobby of large-scale farmers who generally oppose land redistribution.

Land Settlement and the Use-Planning System

When beneficiaries are settled on former large farms, the entire settlement has to be reorganized. Too often, governments tend to predetermine and impose rigid guidelines concerning the types of farms created rather than allowing for participatory and flexible planning approaches. As a result, the scope of farming options for the beneficiaries is narrow. Indeed, large farms should be subdivided into viable small-scale farms. In southern Africa, however, the definition of the viable farm is based on static notions of technology. It is based on a form of dryland farming without irrigation, with meager artificial inputs and weak markets for small-scale intensive horticulture. That type of agricultural planning for dryland mixed farming based on field crops and cattle also underlies the farm modeling for most resettlement programs. This is why the type of available resettlement models tended to exclude a range of possible land uses, such as ecotourism, agro-forestry, and other natural resource–based land uses, and a range of possible irrigation and out-grower resettlement models that could be developed in conjunction with the subdivision of large farms.

In Zimbabwe, the 1980 Intensive Resettlement Policies and Procedures Document spelled out three resettlement models. In model A, beneficiary households were allocated 0.5–2.0 hectares in a village of 20–25 households. They shared common grazing land, woodlots, and water points. The target beneficiaries were the landless and poor households in overcrowded areas and retrenched farmworkers who opted for resettlement. In model B, land and equipment were held cooperatively, but the livestock was privately owned. In model C, beneficiaries were out-growers. They provided labor to an estate run by a cooperative community or by the Agriculture and Rural Development Authority. The estate supplied essential services to setters at economic rates (mechanical draft power, load transport, seedlings and processing for specialized crops, and marketing). For the cattle-focused people of natural regions IV and V (Matabeleland), a fourth model—model D—was added by the revised 1985 Intensive Resettlement Policies and Procedures Document. The beneficiary community in this model had access to grazing land on ranches, especially during times of grazing shortages (during the dry season and during periods of drought). Beneficiaries contributed toward the costs of maintaining ranches and paddocking their grazing areas.

Those four models were used throughout the 1980s, with model A accounting for 90 percent of the beneficiaries and land redistributed, and model D pilot-tested on one farm. In 1990, models B and C were abandoned. A model A2 was introduced later, and the original model A became model A1. Under model A2, beneficiary households were allocated self-contained farm units for cropping, residential, grazing, and woodlot use. Beneficiaries settled in natural region II received 50 hectares; those settled in natural region III were allocated 150 hectares; and those settled in natural regions IV and V received 300 hectares. Model A2 plots were considered self-contained plots and classified as a new small- to medium-scale commercial scheme rather than a resettlement model. The most popular resettlement scheme in Zimbabwe was model A/A1, apparently because it is similar to the communal area land allocation system, and because it provided each beneficiary more land on average. Many existing model A/A1 schemes have been opened to numerous additional "informal occupants" by the official beneficiaries subletting portions of their arable plots. Thus, it is possible that the actual number of people benefiting from land reform is double the official count.

Finally, there was a resettlement model that combined both the government and the private sector. The Farmers' Development Trust (FDT) was established in 1994 as a private sector organization related to the Commercial Farmers' Union. The FDT complements government agricultural extension efforts and provides support services for resettled farmers in model A/A1 resettlement schemes. The FDT also has developed a resettlement model for commercial tobacco farming by adapting model A and by training graduates in diploma courses at government-owned training centers. The FDT was partly funded by government.

In Zimbabwe, beneficiaries have not participated fully in the design of most resettlement models, whereas the schemes in South Africa tended to be more self-designed. Namibia and Malawi slightly mirror the Zimbabwe planning process (with Malawi perhaps more liberal), largely because resettlement models mirror communal area practice. Namibia and South Africa have stepped up research and support for building nonfarm settlements, based on Zimbabwe's earlier experiences with the Communal Area Management Program for Indigenous Resources (a program designed on a concept of sharing and co-managing natural resources). It is in this context that the use of incentives, subdivision of land, planning support, reduced capital gains charges, grants, and penalties (for example, land taxation and compulsory purchases) could guide more effective approaches to land acquisition and transfers and to the planning of land use and farm models.

Postsettlement Support

A major requirement for successful postsettlement support is the coordination and mobilization of funds for newly settled farmers. Various training institutions and financiers—government, the private sector, NGOs, church groups, farmers' organizations, local development associations, and specialized commodity organizational parastatals—are expected to be encouraged to play a greater role in postsettlement farming support across the region. There is little evidence of best practices on this, however, other than the Zimbabwean experience of the 1980s when required services were delivered. In Malawi, the Community-Based Rural Land Development Project resettlements appear to address the issue of postsettlement support.

In Zimbabwe, the most effective way to deliver the required services had been through partnerships with the private sector (seed, fertilizer companies), leading to the peasant boom starting in 1984. During the early 1980s, the Agricultural Finance Corporation of Zimbabwe provided credit for development and working capital under its Farm Input Credit Scheme and Resettlement Credit Scheme through loans in the first year of settlement. Start-up grants to cover part of a beneficiary's initial production needs were provided. But those funds dried up by 1987. Private sector financial institutions were not keen to provide credit to beneficiaries. Informal sector financial institutions, which could act as rural financial intermediaries, hardly were involved. The government created an enabling environment for marketing agricultural commodities, including access roads, depots, and marketing information during the 1980s. The state gave beneficiaries support to demarcate the plots according to a land-use zoning design and individual beneficiary allotments of the model. Then, depending on resources available to the relevant government department, the state built roads, schools, clinics, and other infrastructure, mainly through the District Development Fund (DDF).

During the economic structural adjustment program in the 1990s, the government reduced its budget allocation for postsettlement support. Similarly, the extension and training packages that were developed during the 1980s to meet the specific needs of beneficiaries diminished in quantity. The training needs of beneficiaries (such as training in agronomic and animal husbandry skills) hardly have been met since 2000. Beneficiaries of the model A2 program were expected to have proven competency in farming and thus to be more self-reliant in mobilizing their own finances and training, and in taking advantage of other services—especially refresher courses to develop new enterprises and training in water and irrigation management. The problem was that, given the mass beneficiary selection procedure followed from 2000, many new farmers did not have the means and experience expected.

Postsettlement social services also were crucial for improving beneficiaries' livelihoods during the 1980s in Zimbabwe. Delivery of these services was approached through the creation of rural service centers. Initially, programs planned to build a center for every 500 families. Beneficiaries would have access to clinics and to industrial, commercial, and residential plots of land over a period of five years. The centers acted as nuclei for off-farm employment and as incubators for the development of small and medium-size enterprises. They also provided for the people's residential needs for homes and small gardens. The centers were to have the following facilities: telephone, electricity, and reticulated water systems to attract further investment. The health, education, and social services of the beneficiaries would be met by various government ministries and local authorities using program funds. The DDF would build its capacity to provide tillage and other mechanical services to farmers, and farmers or private operators were expected to establish tillage services for the benefit of beneficiaries. In practice, these ideas were implemented only partially and minimally in Zimbabwe. The experience with social services in Namibia and South Africa has not yet been assessed. The Malawi land redistribution program began in 2006.

Postsettlement support was planned as part of the resettlement model designs in Malawi, Namibia, and Zimbabwe, but not in South Africa. The key principle of postsettlement support is to develop a more democratic, gender-neutral, disability-sensitive, and former farmworker–sensitive multiform regime that guarantees greater security for owners of a variety of interests in land. It also should encourage investment in land and generally facilitate the implementation of a wide range of land distribution models. Numerous policy statements, procedural guidelines, and related legal instruments for implementing specific land tenure policy changes are required to promote postsettlement support with adequate resources.

The main policy issues of concern in the southern Africa region are questions both of principle and of the effectiveness of approaches to providing support services. Policy debates raise various questions, including these:

- Taking into account the diminishing state subsidies to farming, how can government provide beneficiaries with the bulk of adequate infrastructure and services both cost effectively and in a timely manner?
- Given the trend toward decentralization, and despite private investment in smallholder agriculture being limited, how can community initiatives, private-public partnerships, and outsourcing or subcontractual approaches to infrastructure provision be more effective?
- Should communities be allowed or should they be required to take responsibility for such services?
- Given that local capital and financial markets tend to be urban biased and donor dependence is high in most of the countries, how can government promote private sector and NGO stakeholder participation in infrastructure delivery, with facilitative technical and financial support from the government?
- How can government reduce the burden and cost of providing support services and encourage local initiatives to enable speedier provision of services?

It has been argued that promoting beneficiary and stakeholder participation in planning and improving the design of government resettlement models would result in more beneficiary families gaining access to land. That is what happened in Zimbabwe's Fast Track Land Redistribution when more beneficiaries gained access to land because occupiers and local planners reduced the sizes of plots, in opposition to the A1 and A2 farm size models. Reductions varied among districts.

In a spirit of participation, prospective beneficiaries in South Africa are expected to select the farming system or economic activity they prefer, and to take part in the detailed design and planning of their own scheme by identifying the suitability of the land for their chosen enterprises, evaluating the land and its infrastructure (both current and planned), identifying its resource base, and planning the overall scheme and their settlement. Beneficiaries also participate in environmental action planning, including conducting an environmental impact assessment. In practice, however, consultants largely determined the options chosen. Truly participatory and user-driven approaches to farm planning and implementation have been tested only in Malawi.

Land Tenure Security

Securing land tenure entails marking land allocations, establishing the nature of tenure or land rights, and developing effective systems to administer those rights. Laws are crucial to this process, as discussed below in the section titled "Legal Frameworks for Implementing Land Reform Policy."

The administrative costs associated with planning, marking, subdividing, surveying, and registering title to the land usually are high. In Namibia and Zimbabwe these costs are borne by the state, although there are expectations to recover these costs from beneficiary households through appropriate land and administrative fees in model A2, the commercial scheme. The tenure system in Zimbabwe's newly resettled areas depends on the nature of the settlement model in question. After the 2005 nationalization of land in Zimbabwe, the tenure system for A2 beneficiary families provides them with a long-term leasehold (99 years) without an option to buy the land, but with an option to purchase the improvements. Individual or group farmlands, especially in large conservancies, are being designed to allow for collective leasehold. In A1 schemes, tenure provides a group permit for communally owned land (for grazing, as an example) and individual permit titles for individually owned arable land. The Namibian and Malawian resettlement schemes for A1 beneficiaries are similar to the one in Zimbabwe, but commercial schemes in South Africa and Namibia provide beneficiaries with freehold titles.

During the Fast Track Land Redistribution Program, beneficiaries in Zimbabwe are given both self-contained units of land in A2 schemes and individual arable units with common grazing land in A1 schemes. Beneficiaries in the latter scheme include divorced women and widows, and they are provided with a permit form of title. The majority of land permit titles, however, have been issued to married couples, and some are now being registered in the names of both spouses. Where the disposal of interest in land is to be effected, the consent of both spouses is expected to be sought before ownership is transferred. The formula for those in polygamous relationships has not been worked out adequately. In A2 land allocations, currently people in polygamous relationships hold "letters of land offer" that entitle them to occupy and use the plots, while the National Land Board slowly is offering 99-year leases to them.

Often during land reform, disputes will arise between landowners and the state, between landowners and new beneficiaries, among beneficiaries, between beneficiaries and farmworkers, and between the state and beneficiaries. A strategy to mediate or arbitrate such disputes is required.

To lower the costs of managing dispute, increase access to dispute resolution mechanisms, and tailor the resolution mechanisms to the various peculiarities in the different regions of a country, it may be more efficient to establish local (district-level) mediation structures. These structures would involve various actors, including government, landowners, beneficiaries, NGOs, and legal professionals. Staff development (including paralegal training) and adequate administrative capacity would have to be made available.

The legal regime for establishing state-level adjudicating bodies should be amended to permit the establishing of village and district land courts to improve local access to community-based conflict resolution authorities. The village land courts would function as village-level land registries as well. The district land courts would work with the village assemblies and the Department of the Surveyor General to set village boundaries. In the event of conflicts over village boundaries, the district land courts would act as the courts of first instance.

Most institutional arrangements and legal instruments for land reform management tend to reside in different ministries and departments. All the laws that deal with land management should be consolidated into a single comprehensive land act administered by one form of a central land authority, such as the National Land Board.

Under compulsory land acquisition in Zimbabwe, most of the beneficiaries came from a few communal areas because land acquisition emphasized the nearness of communal areas to the land being sought. Ethnoregional grievances have surfaced in these communities because it is feared that a self-reinforcing distributional distortion occurs in favor of those communal areas located adjacent to the large commercial farms.

LEGAL FRAMEWORKS FOR IMPLEMENTING LAND REFORM POLICY

Land reforms tend to be implemented within a specific legal framework. The framework addresses rights and obligations of the state, landholders, and beneficiaries in specified procedures related to the acquisition of, allocation of, and tenures assigned to land. These laws also establish the executing agencies involved, within a given policy framework.

Building Consensus for Land Reform Policy and Laws

Managing land reform requires building consensus among various actors on a vision, objectives, and strategy, as well as on the implementation framework. Implementation approaches in Zimbabwe varied, depending on whether the process was purely state led or one with multiple stakeholders. During the 1980s and 1990s, the process involved few private actors.

In Zimbabwe, for example (during the period 1997–99), the Inception Phase Framework Plan was produced jointly and consultatively by various stakeholders and experts within and outside government, through a joint technical subcommittee of the Inter-Ministerial Committee on Resettlement and Rural Development and the private sector–engaged National Economic Consultative Forum's Land Reform Task Force. Numerous formal consultative meetings, forums, and workshops were organized to gather input and gain consensus on the plan. Various donors also provided solicited and unsolicited input. A Cabinet Committee on Resettlement and Development and the government-donors' consultative forum negotiated the plan, which aimed at combining a state-led land acquisition program with a market-led alternative approach and at involving various stakeholders in both models. However, this process had collapsed over wider political conflicts by 2000.

The Namibia land reform policy formulation process was initiated first through various technical studies from the South West Africa People's Organization (SWAPO) and external experts (1989–91), followed by a national land summit involving numerous stakeholders, and then through government-led policy development and legislative reforms. South Africa experienced a similar but more elaborate consultative approach, within a context of homegrown constitution making. Some of the planning in all countries was done centrally and up front, while other aspects (such as land identification and land-use planning) were done through decentralized structures.

Redistributive land reform challenges the landowners' existing land rights, and in Malawi it reallocates estates owned by the state. The controversy is over how to expropriate land legally because the loss of rights requires some level of compensation—and the pricing and the payment method frequently are disputed. Compulsory acquisitions require an appropriate constitutional provision (which already is in place in Namibia, Malawi, South Africa, and Zimbabwe) and an enabling land acquisition law. Because landowners will challenge acquisitions in court, laws have had to be amended to be effective, and the states have had to create legal and administrative capacity to manage the land acquisitions.

Land reform also introduced new land market regulations (the right of first refusal on land sales, land taxation, land subdivision, and so forth), which required amendments to various laws and regulations (land acquisition laws, environmental laws, planning regulations, and the like). Concurrently, land acquisition created new (or expanded) state land property or estate holdings, and generated new land rights among land redistribution beneficiaries—all of which require laws that define and enforce the new rights and ensure tenure security. These laws and regulations were developed earlier in the process in South Africa and Namibia; but during the Fast Track Land Redistribution in Zimbabwe they were not formulated until after the land acquisitions.

Effective implementation of land reforms also requires effective negotiating with the powerful landowner lobbies and orienting conservative media, as well as existing judicial structures, toward the longer-term benefits of land reform. As argued in earlier sections, however, the strong land movements are crucial in shaping the policy and legal environment for land reform. They are necessary to pressure governments to make proactive efforts and to insist that landowners negotiate in positive terms.

Coordinating and Sequencing Implementation of Land Reforms

There is no hard-and-fast programming strategy that can be identified in southern Africa. Namibia, South Africa, and Zimbabwe appear to have opted for a loose coordination of land reform within a ministry of lands, and to have chosen to procure other services from various departments. South Africa separated its programs into three components (restitution, redistribution, and tenure), highlighting the restitution and tenure components. The other countries did not adopt those latter two components. Malawi has one authority dealing with its few schemes. The major choice made so far by that authority has been to disaggregate land reform program components to be implemented by various government agents under a central coordinating authority rather than implementing the entire program as one integrated activity bringing all agents into a single (if decentralized) authority (as Brazil has done).

Given the high costs of land reform, a major implementation principle relates to the need to craft an acceptable and feasible program of phasing implementation to provide a road map for state and nonstate actors engaged in making specific projects operational. A gradual learning approach to implementation has been tried in all the countries, including the use of pilot projects.

In addition to leading policy formulation, the governments' role in land reform could be extensive, as in the Zimbabwe case. The ministries of land and agriculture acquired land and exercised an overall land-use inspectorate role on all land reform (sometimes through the services of decentralized departments), and they provided technical and professional services to the whole farming sector. Parastatals such as the Agricultural Finance Corporation (now AgriBank) in Zimbabwe have been responsible for providing credit. The Ministry of Local Government and National Housing supervised beneficiary selection and administered schemes prior to handing over completed schemes to local authorities, and was responsible for conducting land evaluations and for planning service centers. The rural district councils supported such local planning. The Ministry of Rural Resources and Water Development provided infrastructure services to beneficiaries—roads, dip tanks, and boreholes—through the DDF. The cabinet office coordinated land identification and the resettlement program.

The roles of nonstate stakeholders in land reform have varied according to their own priorities and interests: landowners, potential beneficiaries, service providers, local councils, and leaders. They have fomented social pressure for redistribution, lobbied for specific policies, participated in planning, and so forth. Other than traditional leaders in Namibia and Zimbabwe, and some NGOs in South Africa, few nonstate actors have been involved in selecting beneficiaries. Participatory monitoring and evaluation systems to ensure compliance with acceptable selection norms (such as gender mainstreaming to ensure that men and women have equal access to the program) also have been limited. Some civil society organizations have focused on educating and training beneficiary communities and supporting resettlement activities. In the four countries discussed here, however, these organizations (especially NGOs) have been spread thin and weak in program implementation.

A major challenge in the countries of southern Africa has been one of building adequate capacity at the state level (executive branch of government and the judiciary), among representatives of new landholders (farmers' associations), and in other stakeholders (NGOs, valuers, surveyors, and so forth) to make them effective participants in policy formulation and the administration of land reform. Popularizing the policy and laws also lagged behind implementation, leading to various delays, errors, and disputes over land. Most of the countries have had limited resources to build adequate organizational, legal, and administrative structures and procedures, and that has led to delays in implementing reform. Most of the countries have tried programs to improve the skills and enhance the capacities of executing agencies and practitioners involved in valuation, planning, extension services, management, and monitoring, but these have not be enough to meet their needs.

Financing Land Reforms

The main costs of land reform programs in the countries of southern Africa have been those of land acquisition (at roughly 30 percent), infrastructure development, farming support, social services, and overhead. These costs have been spread over many years, with investments in infrastructure and social services delayed. For instance, in Zimbabwe's state-based land reform, resettlement communities were not expected to contribute much in cash or in kind toward land acquisition and infrastructure construction. The market-assisted approach in South Africa, in contrast, has argued that requiring little or no investment from beneficiaries makes land redistribution unduly expensive.

However, when dealing with the landless poor, the ethical choice of making them pay—given their historical disadvantage—has been a controversial matter in the region. South Africa has tried to spread the costs, as Zimbabwe's inception phase proposed and as was done in 2006. It also has been argued that beneficiaries receive much more government support per family than do their communal area counterparts, and this has led to calls for beneficiary communities to contribute more in cash and in kind to reduce the costs of land reform (van den Brink et al. 2006). There is general agreement in the region that some cash contributions should be paid fully by new commercial farm schemes that target the nonpoor, but there are countering arguments that credit and loans, as well as beneficiaries' own savings, could be used to pay those costs that demand cash rather than labor or materials—land purchase costs (which could be paid for either at the time of purchase or through a mortgage and leasehold fees), land titling costs, and basic administrative program overhead (van den Brink et al. 2006).

Providing flexible grants to beneficiaries has been rolled out slowly in Malawi and South Africa. In the latter case, it remains uncertain whether a greater role for government in financing and building infrastructure would speed up the land reform process. Zimbabwe's experience of the early 1980s was relatively speedier, however, and was found to be cost effective (ODA 1989)—but it was delayed by diminished funding in the 1990s.

Finally, the nature of international funding of land reform is a controversial aspect of establishing an overall land reform framework. The issue of colonial obligations has dogged Zimbabwe and, to a lesser extent, Namibia. Although South Africa has its own resources, donor financing restrictions and wider economic policy conditionalities have been problematic for adequate funding of land reform.

Policy Review, Monitoring, and Evaluation

It is critical when implementing land reforms to learn systematically from one's experience by capturing new demands and controversies that arise, and to use that knowledge to adjust and refine the policy in a flexible and consensual manner. Knowledge capture and appropriate responses require participatory and effective systems for assessing prior conditions and post facto program developments through effective systems of land information management, monitoring, and impact assessment. Moreover, these systems should be transparent and their findings should be shared in a timely manner through periodic policy reviews. To this point, capacity restrictions and a lack of best-practice models for involving all stakeholders in a cost-effective but representative manner while pooling evaluative resources have limited the needed impact assessments of land reform.

Land information systems have been a key weakness in land management decision making in all the countries discussed here, mainly because of technical weaknesses and resource shortages. Land reform agencies in all four countries aspire to establish a comprehensive land information system to facilitate state management of beneficiaries, renewal or cancellation of leases, granting of concessions and titles to land, rent collection, and land-use monitoring. They also seek to inform all the participants about the quality of land available in various areas, and the nature of the demand for land. Existing systems do not support those goals.

Detailed impact assessments, as elements of critical policy adjustments or refinements, have been limited. Thus, there is little knowledge of such elements as the social and economic returns to land reform, and that has led to difficulties in mobilizing resources. Such analyses require effective methodologies suitable to the situation. A framework for impact assessment that also guides the monitoring process should include income changes; numbers and types of livelihoods created; and financial/fiscal, technical, social, and environmental effects that need a wider social and pro-poor economic policy design. Monitoring of land reform programs generally has excluded input from communities, stakeholders, and subsidiary government agencies, let alone aspects of gender sensitivity.

CONCLUSION

Setting up a framework for land reform requires extensive consultation, consensus building, and negotiation within governments; among governments, landowners, and potential beneficiaries; and with other stakeholders who provide funding and a variety of other services. A consultative approach is key in setting an agenda, defining objectives, choosing implementation mechanisms and defining their principles, creating the legal framework, conducting the actual implementation and making its institutional arrangements, and assessing progress and program impact. A participatory process of setting up the framework is the best guarantee of success.

NOTES

1. The Namibian approach to identifying beneficiaries is broadly similar to the Zimbabwean approach prior to 1997.
2. Criteria for identifying land for acquisition included these: (1) farms can be partially identified and excised for acquisition based on negotiations to capture the underused land segments needed for redistribution; (2) farmers owning only one farm located near communal areas can have their farm exchanged for another farm more appropriately located, but in consultation with them; (3) owners of multiple farms are able to select which farm they want to keep; (4) indigenous (black)-owned farms generally will not be acquired compulsorily, except in cases where multiple-owned farms are underused; (5) farms owned by institutions, such as NGOs, churches, and trusts, will not be acquired compulsorily; (6) government-owned parastatal farms will not be acquired compulsorily; (7) no farmer will be left without a residence and land for his or her commercial livelihood (if these

were productively used); and (8) farms with a record of abusing farmworkers are likely to be more frequently targeted for compulsory acquisition.

3. A total of 141,656 A1 households were allocated 5.7 million hectares, with an average land size of 40 hectares. About 15,572 A2 beneficiaries were allocated 1.9 million hectares, with an average farm size of 125 hectares. However, 1,500 of those A2 farms (medium to large) had an average farm size of 600 hectares, while the remaining 14,072 farms averaged 71 hectares.

REFERENCES

Barros, Flávia, Sérgio Sauer, and Stephan Schwartzman, eds. 2003. *The Negative Impacts of World Bank Market-Based Land Reform.* São Paulo, Brazil: Comissao Pastoral da Terra/Movimento dos Trabalhadores Rurais Sem Terra/FoodFirst Information and Action Network.

Binswanger, Hans P., Klaus Deininger, and Gershon Feder. 1995. "Power, Distortions, Revolt and Reform in Agricultural Land Relations." In *Handbook of Development Economics,* Volume 3B, ed. Jere Behrman and T. N. Srinivasan, 2659–772. Amsterdam, The Netherlands: Elsevier.

Fernandes, Bernardo Mançano. 2005. "The Occupation as a Form of Access to Land in Brazil: A Theoretical and Methodological Contribution." In *Reclaiming the Land: The Resurgence of Rural Movements in Africa, Asia and Latin America,* ed. Sam Moyo and Paris Yeros, 317–40. London: Zed Books.

Government of Zimbabwe, Ministry of Land and Agriculture. 1999. "The Inception Phase Framework Plan of the Second Phase of the Land Reform and Resettlement Programme." Harare.

Moyo, Sam. 1998. *The Land Acquisition Process in Zimbabwe (1997/8).* Harare, Zimbabwe: United Nations Development Programme Resource Center.

———. 2007. "Emerging Land Tenure Issues in Zimbabwe." Unpublished manuscript. African Institute for Agrarian Studies, Harare, Zimbabwe.

Moyo, Sam, and Paris Yeros. 2005. "The Resurgence of Rural Movements under Neoliberalism." In *Reclaiming the Land: The Resurgence of Rural Movements in Africa, Asia and Latin America,* ed. Sam Moyo and Paris Yeros, 8–64. London: Zed Books.

NEAD/AIAS (Nucleo de Estudos em Agricultura e Desenvolvimento/African Institute for Agrarian Studies). 2003. "NEAD-AIAS Research Collaboration Draft Proposal—7 September 2003." Harare, Zimbabwe.

ODA (Overseas Development Administration). 1989. "Evaluation of the Resettlement Program." London.

Raikes, Philip. 2000. "Modernization and Adjustment in African Peasant Agriculture." In *Disappearing Peasantries? Rural Labour in Latin America, Asia, and Africa,* ed. Deborah Bryceson, Cristobal Kay, and Jos Mooij, 64–80. London: Practical Action Publishing.

Rukuni, Mandivamba, and Carl K. Eicher, eds. 1994. *Zimbabwe's Agricultural Revolution.* Harare, Zimbabwe: University of Zimbabwe Publications.

Rukuni, Mandivamba, Patrick Tawonezvi, and Carl K. Eicher, with Mabel Munyuki-Hungwe and Prosper Matondi, eds. 2006. *Zimbabwe's Agricultural Revolution Revisited.* Harare, Zimbabwe: University of Zimbabwe Publications.

van den Brink, Rogier, Glen Thomas, Hans P. Binswanger, John Bruce, and Frank Byamugisha. 2006. *Consensus, Confusion and Controversy: Selected Land Reform Issues in Sub-Saharan Africa.* Working Paper 71. Washington, DC: World Bank.

CHAPTER FOURTEEN

Pilot-Testing a Land Redistribution Program in Malawi

Stephen Machira

For decades, colonial and postindependence land allocation policies in Malawi supported the concentration of landownership in the hands of a few people. In 2002, however, a National Land Policy was adopted by the government of Malawi to bring parity between tenure categories and hence to check the willy-nilly conversion of land under customary tenure into other tenure categories. Malawi being largely an agrarian economy, access to land has a direct impact on the livelihoods and quality of life for the majority of its people. The land access problem is particularly pronounced in the southern part of the country where population densities in some districts are among the highest in Africa.

On one hand, it is recognized that existing land distribution issues constrain poverty reduction efforts and fuel social tensions. On the other hand, with the liberalization of the tobacco sector in the early 1990s,[1] an increasing number of estates became unprofitable, resulting in an increasing number of landowners or leaseholders willing to sell their land. This conjunction of factors created a context favorable to the introduction of a land redistribution program based on voluntary/negotiated land transfers between landowners (willing sellers) and land-poor people (willing buyers). First implemented at large scale in Brazil, this willing seller–willing buyer (WSWB) approach has been undergoing pilot-testing in Malawi since 2004, under the aegis of the Community-Based Rural Land Development Project (CBRLDP). Whereas beneficiaries in Brazil buy land through loans, in Malawi they acquire it though grants. The Malawi project is only the second one in which International Development Association resources are being used to purchase land for resettlement purposes; the other such project is in India.

This chapter outlines the history of land issues in Malawi, presents the design principles of the CBRLDP, describes how the program is implemented, summarizes what has been achieved so far, and shares the preliminary results of the impact evaluation. Finally, the chapter discusses the limitations of the WSWB approach and raises the need for alternative approaches to land acquisition and broader land reform.

THE LAND SITUATION IN MALAWI

The existing land situation in Malawi is a reflection of colonial influence and failure by postindependence administrations to address the land issues. The government of Malawi operated without a comprehensive land policy until February 2002. This lack exacerbated the inequality in land distribution and the ineffective land administration.

The British Protectorate of Nyasaland

Prior to the creation of the British protectorate of Nyasaland in 1891, European settlers, missionaries, and companies started acquiring land from African chiefs or headmen under a "master–servant" kind of relationship. Under the African Orders in Council 1889 and 1892, the British government appointed a commissioner who was responsible for formalizing these agreements and making new land grants in the name of the Crown. European settlers were provided with "certificates of claim."[2] They acquired some of the best land, most of it in the Shire Highlands located in the southern part of the country. Through this process, the Crown allocated to European settlers and companies about 15 percent of the total land in Malawi, or 27 percent of the total land suitable for cultivation. In fact, 73 percent of the granted land went to a single company, the British South Africa Company (Government of Malawi 1999).

Granted land was not necessarily vacant, and the Crown soon had to deal with the issue of African natives' status on granted land. Certificates of claim originally included a nondisturbance clause that protected the rights of the African occupants. However, settlers needed a workforce to cultivate their lands, and extracting rent in the form of compulsory labor became common practice. A second attempt to regulate the relationship between settlers and natives was the Lands Ordinance (Native Location) in 1904. In exchange for labor services, native occupants could receive an 8-acre plot. In practice, the ordinance was ignored by the settlers, who were unwilling to divide their estates and found it more convenient to keep thinking of natives as tenants-at-will. Their attitude fueled discontent among native Africans. Tensions were heightened rapidly by demographic growth, and they culminated in 1915 with the Chilembwe uprising. This uprising resulted in the abolition of labor tenancy in 1917. At the same time, natives remained weakly protected against eviction, and proprietors retained great power (Pachai 1973).

With 10 percent of the population living on private estates in 1926, the status of Africans settled on estates remained a sensitive issue (Ng'ong'ola 1990). Government tried to tackle the issue one more time in 1928 by granting native occupants the right to a site, materials for a hut, and a cultivable plot of land. In exchange, occupants had to sell part of their crops to the landlord or offer him their labor to pay a rent fixed by a district board (Pachai 1973). This new tenure arrangement never worked, mostly because settlers found it difficult to employ occupants or to buy their crops when the world was wracked by the Great Depression of the 1930s. At the same time, labor tenancy that had been abolished in 1917 was reestablished.

Tobacco rapidly became one of the most lucrative businesses in Nyasaland. In 1926, the National Tobacco Board was appointed and charged with regulating the production and trade of tobacco. Measures taken by the board gave birth to a segmented tobacco market where independent peasants were discouraged from producing the most profitable tobacco. The board also controlled the tobacco market by setting prices and authorizing growers to sell their product at a limited number of places. Those measures were to foster an increase in growth production, but they openly favored the development of an estate sector over the smallholder one.

During the early phase of the colonization process, the Crown paid little attention to the status of Africans living outside of the estates. In practice, these Africans enjoyed little security of tenure and could be evicted at will. In 1936, an ordinance differentiated Crown, reserved land, and native trust land. Crown land included "all lands and interest in land acquired or occupied by or on behalf of his Majesty" (Ng'ong'ola 1990, p. 51). Reserved land mainly included forest reserves and land occupied under certificates of claim. Native trust land encompassed all the rest. Africans had the right to occupy and use native trust land, but the governor was in charge of administering the land "for the use and common benefits of the natives" (p. 51). In 1951, these categories of lands were denominated as public, private, and communal lands, respectively.

During the 1940s, it became increasingly difficult for the Crown and settlers to evict natives. In 1946, some 31 percent of the native population was living on private estates in the Shire Highlands (that is, 11 percent of the total area of the country). The colonial power started encountering strong resistance in trying to evict natives when land available for resettlement was becoming scarce. Convinced that the only solution was the full emancipation of the natives, the Crown began reacquiring privately owned land. Whereas about 15.0 percent of the country had been granted to European settlers during the early 1900s, by 1954 that figure had dropped to 3.7 percent. At independence in 1964, it was only 2.4 percent.

Malawi's Independence

At independence in 1964, Malawi inherited a dualistic agricultural sector comprising a few export-oriented estates and a large number of smallholder subsistence farmers, most of them poor. Following the land reallocation policy of the 1950s, the share of private land had decreased substantially. Post-independence land administration was faced with two challenges: how to deal with freehold land that was largely in the hands of foreigners, and how to effectively manage customary land. In 1967, the government adopted a series of acts that were to bring public, private, and communal lands under a unified administration system.[3] It was expected that with this new legal framework, a vibrant small-scale farm sector would develop quickly. That expectation arose from the assumption that customary tenure was insecure, and because the new framework mainly focused on formalizing individual property rights on customary land, small-scale farmers would feel more secure and would produce more broadly. The framework was first pilot-tested in Lilongwe West, as part of the Lilongwe Land Development Project. However, the pilot test fell short of expectations, was not expanded to the entire country, and thus remained an incomplete experiment.

During a short period of time after independence, "tobacco seemed destined to become a smallholder crop" (van Donge 2002, p. 101). However, the government eventually preferred to favor the expansion of large-scale agriculture. The 1965 Land Act allowed the government to alienate customary land without compensation; and during the 1970s and 1980s, the government nationalized or privatized large tracts of customary land for burley tobacco production. In the early 1980s, estates occupied about 8 percent of the total land area in Malawi. One decade later, they occupied 12 percent. As had been the case under British rule in the colonial era, the government maintained a dualistic agricultural sector. Estates held the monopoly on burley tobacco, the most lucrative export crop, while smallholders were forced to sell their product to the state-owned Agricultural Development and Marketing Corporation. This dualistic system remained in place until the liberalization of the tobacco economy in the 1990s.

In 1993, the ruling Malawi Congress Party was voted out in a referendum. It was the end of a three-decades-long authoritarian regime and the beginning of profound policy changes. Between 1993 and 1994, Malawi liberalized the tobacco sector. Smallholders became eligible to grow burley tobacco, and many workers left the estates to cultivate tobacco on their own land. As a consequence, tobacco production on the estates began to decline. In 1997, "representatives of the two largest companies growing tobacco declared that it was no longer profitable to grow tobacco" (van Donge 2002, p. 103). This decline of estate production commonly is referred to as the "estate crisis."

Efforts Toward a New Land Policy

Until 2001, Malawi still lacked a comprehensive land policy. The failure of past governments to resolve land policy concerns properly is believed to have contributed to current problems of poverty, food insecurity, and persistent inequities in access to arable land. Poverty is acute in Malawi. About 60 percent of the population lives below the poverty line. More than 80 percent of the population lives in rural areas, and the large majority depends on subsistence farming for its livelihood. Poverty is most severe in the southern and central regions of the country, which also are the most densely populated areas. For the rural poor, accessing land represents one of the rare opportunities to generate income, have a decent life, and eventually move out of poverty.

Filling the country's "land policy gap" became a priority of the newly elected government. In 1996, a Presidential Commission on Land Policy Reform was appointed and charged with organizing a review of the land issues in Malawi. The commission report was released in 1999 (Government of Malawi 1999). From that document, a national land policy was drafted, publicly discussed, and eventually approved by the cabinet in 2002. This approval was the starting point for important policy changes in Malawi (see box 14.1). This was followed by the development of a Land Reform Program Implementation Strategy that was adopted by the government in 2003. The government appointed a Special Law Commission to review the legal framework in light of the new policy principles. In this context, in 2004 the government—with the support of the African Development Bank, the European Union, and the World Bank—started implementing a series of land programs, including the CBRLDP that is discussed in this chapter.

Overview of the Land Issues

The problems associated with land in Malawi are numerous, varied, and in many ways symptomatic of much deeper social discontent and economic hardship. Specific land pressure concerns vary widely around the country, between regions, districts, communities, and individuals. The southern region has the most severe land pressure problems. Although not intended to be exhaustive, a summary of some of the main land problems prevalent in Malawi is presented here.

Increasing Pressure for Land

With an estimated population of 13,757,883 in 2007[4] and a total land area of 94,276 square kilometers, population density in Malawi is one of the highest in Africa. In 1998, population density was approximately 105 people per square kilometer. That figure, however, masks important disparities; and in the southern part of the country, population density reaches 146 people per

Box 14.1 National Land Policy Objectives

- To ensure secure tenure and equitable access to land, without any gender bias and/or discrimination, to all citizens of Malawi, as stipulated under article 28 of the constitution
- To instill order and discipline in land allocation and land market transactions to curb encroachment, unapproved development, speculation, and racketeering
- To ensure accountability and transparency in the administration of land matters; and to guarantee that existing rights on land, especially customary rights of the smallholders, are recognized, clarified, and ultimately protected by law
- To facilitate efficient use of land under market conditions to ensure optimum benefits from land development
- To provide formal and orderly arrangements for granting titles and delivering land services in a modern and decentralized registration system that supports local governments throughout Malawi
- To promote community participation and public awareness at all levels so as to ensure environmentally sustainable land-use practices and good land stewardship.

Source: Government of Malawi, Ministry of Lands, Physical Planning, and Surveys 2002.

square kilometer, in contrast to 105 in the central region and 46 in the northern region. The population keeps growing at an average rate of 3.3 percent a year, one of the highest rates in Africa. Current demographic trends are provoking rapidly increasing pressure for land.

Land Fragmentation and Degradation

Mounting land pressure has led to the fragmentation of landholdings. In the northern and central regions, farms comprise an average of 10–15 hectares and 5–10 hectares, respectively. In the southern region, the average farm size falls to 0.1 hectare. As land has become scarce, people have started cultivating more intensively, but because many of them cannot afford to use better farming techniques, production remains low. Peasants tend to reduce the period of fallow, and that is a serious threat to sustainable agriculture. Smallholder agriculture is mainly subsistence oriented, but smallholders also are contributing significantly to cash-crop and export production in burley tobacco, cotton, tea, paprika, groundnuts, and chilies (World Bank 2004). The production of tobacco tends to be an important cause of land degradation and decline in soil fertility. It also requires an extensive use of wood and therefore fuels deforestation—the greatest environmental problem facing Malawi.

Underuse of Land

On the basis of 1994's estimates, 2.6 million hectares of suitable agricultural land remain uncultivated in the rural areas. Hence, approximately 28 percent of the country's total land area is laying idle. The northern and central regions have more arable vacant land than does the southern region because of an extremely skewed population distribution across the country and because of colonial and postindependence land allocation policies. By leasing large estates to European settlers and, after independence, to "Malawian young pioneers," the state has favored the concentration of the most fertile and well-watered lands within the hands of relatively few people. About 1.1 million hectares of land is held in some 30,000 estates, with the average size of landholding ranging between 10 and 500 hectares (World Bank 2004). Since the estate crisis, however, a large number of those estates have become underutilized.

Tensions and Encroachments

As land pressure increases, social tensions around land inequalities intensify. In the southern region, overcrowded customary lands border large tracts of abandoned, underused, or idle lands belonging to individuals or government agencies. In these areas, rural tensions and land encroachments have become chronic. Squatting in forest reserves or national parks, on private land, and on other protected areas in land-pressure districts also has become more frequent—sometimes violent. The fact that the creation of some national parks and protected areas involved the displacement of entire villages, some of which were forced to move into valleys and uncultivable areas, remains a source of grievance that makes those parks and protected areas vulnerable to encroachment (Government of Malawi, Ministry of Lands, Physical Planning and Surveys 2002).

Land Tenure Insecurity

Most of the land in Malawi is owned communally, and the great majority of the landholdings are not registered formally. There is increasing evidence that, as the economy develops and becomes less dependent on subsistence agriculture, the need to secure individual land rights becomes stronger. However, in the absence of a clear and transparent policy to enable the conversion of customary land to individual land, attempts by communities to consolidate land access rights both physically and legally have shown limited results. This is a source of tenure insecurity. In its turn, tenure insecurity undermines agricultural development. It is difficult for most citizens to understand the evolving "rules of the game," and in that game, the poor, who generally are the least informed, also are too often the losers. Particularly prone to illegal development is the lakeshore, which from time immemorial has been under the jurisdiction of traditional authorities. Since the early 1990s' rush by individuals and corporations to erect private leisure cottages and hotels, planning and development problems have gone unchecked.

THE COMMUNITY-BASED RURAL LAND DEVELOPMENT PROJECT

The CBRLDP was designed to address the plight of landless and land-poor Malawians. The project offers them an opportunity to own and develop land for agriculture. The project also is testing community demand-driven principles.[5]

The Need to Pilot-Test a Resettlement Project

Prior to the current relocation initiatives, the government had bought estates for redistribution to needy citizens. There is no sound impact analysis for these past redistribution schemes, but it is commonly admitted that they suffered from lack of transparency and understanding between parties, as well as from insufficient planning. In one instance, at the Makande estate in Thyolo District, the resettlement was hasty and not well coordinated. The selection criteria for beneficiaries were not clearly laid out and explained to the communities; promises to provide social amenities and loans for housing were made by the authorities, but never fulfilled. A number of undeserving beneficiaries were given plots, while deserving beneficiaries were unable to keep their plots because they did not have resources with which to bring the plots to productivity within a reasonable time. Consequently, they sold their plots and went back to their places of origin.

Given the level of tension in the southern region of Malawi, land redistribution moved up in the national political agenda. Past experience provided lessons, but there was no approach that had proved workable and could be used in a more systematic way. Firmly convinced that the land issue should be tackled in a peaceful way, in 2004 with the support of the World Bank, the government of Malawi started pilot-testing under the CBRLDP a project that is a transparent, voluntary, legal, and resource-supported approach to land redistribution. The project is community driven and focuses on rural areas where poverty is most pervasive. The estimated total project cost is $27,307,192. The World Bank, through the International Development Association, has provided a grant of $27 million; the government has contributed the balance. (The project was retrofitted in December 2005, thereby removing the government contribution altogether.) Implementation started in July 2004 and is expected to be complete in June 2009.

Pilot Project Districts

The project is being tested in four districts of the southern region of Malawi, namely, Machinga, Mangochi, Mulanje, and Thyolo (see figure 14.1). According to a preliminary report of the 2008 Population and Housing Census, the total population for the four districts stands at slightly more than 2.4 million, representing 18.4 percent of the national population (Government of Malawi 2008). In March 2008, the government extended the project to two neighboring

Figure 14.1 Pilot Project Districts in Malawi

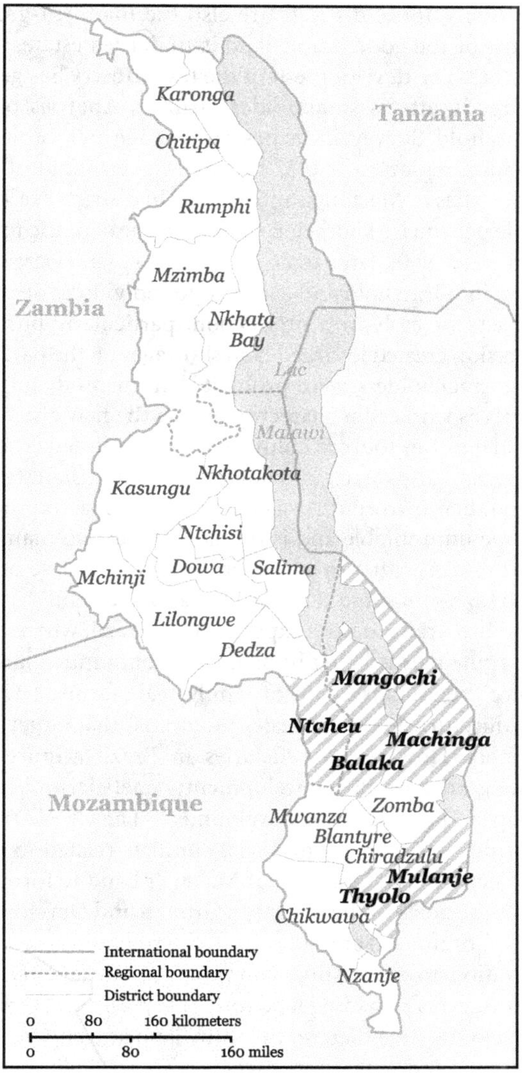

Source: World Bank.

districts, Balaka and Ntcheu, with a combined population of 623,847, thus bringing the total population in the project area to about 3.2 million (24.5 percent of the country's population; in both totals, using 2008).[6] Land pressure is intense in southern Malawi, in general, but particularly so in Mulanje and Thyolo. Those two districts have very high population densities: 208 and 268 inhabitants per square kilometer, respectively (Government of Malawi 1998). Coincidentally, those districts are also the main tea-growing areas of the country. Most of the good arable land is under tea estates, largely owned by foreign investors. The development of the tea industry has generated a land scarcity that directly affects smallholder farmers. Analysis of the 1997–98 Integrated Household Survey indicates an average per capita landholding size for the southern region to be 0.37 hectare (Government of Malawi 2000).

Population densities in Machinga and Mangochi districts are lower, averaging around 97 people per square kilometer. During the peak of the tobacco industry in the 1980s and early 1990s, large tracts of customary land were converted from customary tenure into leasehold and allocated to individuals deemed able to use the land effectively for cash-crop production, particularly burley tobacco. In effect, that conversion created localized land shortages on the part of smallholder farmers. Because smallholders were prohibited from producing tobacco, they offered themselves as workers or sharecroppers on the new estates. The prohibition on smallholder burley tobacco cultivation was abolished around 1995 (with repeal of the Special Crops Act), and smallholders left the estates to cultivate burley tobacco on their own land. As a consequence, tobacco production on the estates has become unprofitable and is on the decline; and many estate owners want to sell their estates, either in whole or in part. Underuse of land leased to the estates is also high—in some cases, as high as 50 percent.

The CBRLDP has drawn on the experience of Brazil, where a project based on similar core principles is being implemented on a much larger scale. Both programs finance the establishment of family-scale farms. They are "market-assisted, community-driven land transfer programs" that target land-deprived, small-scale farmers. However, beneficiaries in Brazil acquire land through loans and receive grants for farm development; beneficiaries in Malawi receive grants for buying land and for farm development. The CBRLDP is designed to make a start in addressing emerging social conflicts related to unequal access to land. The project is an integral part of Malawi's Land Reform Program, and is consistent with the goals of the country's Growth and Development Strategy. The redistribution of unused arable lands to the poor also is expected to make a direct contribution to increasing economic growth and reducing poverty. Specifically, the project is providing land to 15,000 poor rural families organized into beneficiary groups. Together, they identify land and engage in negotiations with the government and with estate owners who are willing to sell or donate lands. The government eases the process by (1) empowering beneficiaries through advisory help and training, (2) providing grants to facilitate land purchase and the transportation of beneficiary groups who travel more than 50 kilometers, and (3) supporting on-farm development through grants for the establishment of shelter and the purchase of basic inputs and necessary advisory services. If successful, it is expected that the approach will be scaled up.

The CBRLDP's Core Principles

The project design and implementation are based on the following core principles:

- Land redistribution will take place only on farm lands acquired from willing sellers, on land transferred from government administration, or on land acquired through private donations.
- The project explicitly will exclude protected or fragile areas, or areas with restricted/limited agricultural potential.
- Beneficiaries will be self-selected, formed in groups on a voluntary basis, and subject to predefined eligibility criteria.
- Implementation will be decentralized, through the existing and emerging District Assembly institutions, consistent with decentralization policy.
- Project resources for the Land Acquisition and Farm Development (LAFD) project will be transferred directly to beneficiaries, and will be managed by them.
- Land given to a beneficiary household should be sufficient to meet subsistence and economic viability.
- Beneficiaries will decide the property regime under which they will hold the land (leasehold, freehold, or customary estate).
- Enhanced capacity at all levels is a prerequisite for successful implementation of this project.
- Lessons learned from the pilot districts will determine the scope of future interventions.

The typical target beneficiary is a self-selected, organized group of individuals and households that is defined and identified by an expressed need for land and a willingness to move as a group to newly acquired land. Vulnerable and disadvantaged groups, such as women, orphans, and poor displaced farmworkers, are encouraged to participate. Women are expected to constitute at least 30 percent of the beneficiaries. To qualify for funding under the project, beneficiaries should meet two-tier predetermined eligibility criteria, as shown in table 14.1.

It is the responsibility of the beneficiary group to identify the land that it proposes to acquire and to negotiate the price directly with the landowner. To ensure equitable distribution and easy administration of the LAFD grant, each beneficiary receives a uniform amount of $1,050 for land acquisition, resettlement allowance, and farm development (figure 14.2). For groups of beneficiaries traveling more than 50 kilometers to their farms, the cost of transportation also is provided. Beneficiaries are required to make a 10 percent contribution toward the development of their farms. This is an in-kind contribution made through household labor as they prepare their gardens and conduct communal work on the estate.

Table 14.1 Beneficiary Selection Criteria

Individual Applicant	Beneficiary Group
■ Malawi citizen ■ Landless, land-poor, and food-insecure ■ Least amount of land, but with excess labor ■ Lowest income ■ Chronically dependent on external assistance ■ Vulnerable and disadvantaged ■ Not encroaching on the farm of interest	■ No member assisted before ■ Cohesive group (10–35 households) with a common purpose, constitution, and identifiable leadership ■ Willingness to relocate and to engage in farming ■ Adherence to transparency and accountability principles ■ All members will participate actively ■ Adherence to sectoral norms and recommended practices

Source: Adapted from Government of Malawi, Ministry of Lands, Physical Planning and Surveys (2004).

Figure 14.2 Apportioned Shares of Each Beneficiary's $1,050 LAFD Grant

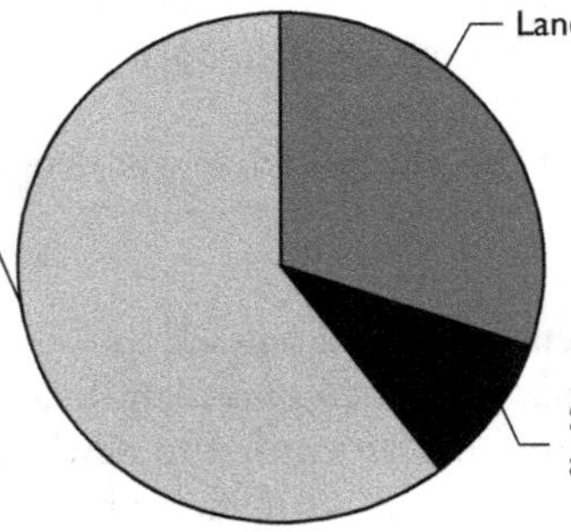

Source: Government of Malawi, Ministry of Lands, Physical Planning and Surveys 2004.
Note: LAFD = Land Acquisition and Farm Development.

Institutional and Implementation Arrangements

The project has been designed to fit in the institutional framework that is in place in Malawi. The main executing agency is the Ministry of Lands and Natural Resources. At the national level, a project management unit (PMU) and a project steering committee have been established. The PMU is responsible for overall management of the project; and the project steering committee provides overall guidance for the project and a mechanism for addressing cross-sectoral issues, such as gender, environment, HIV/AIDS, and policy harmonization. Members of the project steering committee represent key stakeholders, including ministries, civil society, the private sector, and donors. The project also is implemented in close collaboration with the Malawi Social Action Fund, established in 1995 to finance self-help community projects, which is responsible for managing LAFD funds. At a local level, the project is implemented by self-selected rural beneficiary communities. In participating communities, community oversight committees (COCs) are created; they encourage poor and land-poor people who are willing to farm to organize themselves into beneficiary groups, and vet the eligibility of would-be beneficiaries. Once created, a beneficiary group forms a project management committee that identifies land, negotiates acquisition, prepares a farm development plan, oversees the activities of the group, signs all documents on behalf of the group, and opens a bank account and withdraws funds for the group.

Nongovernmental organizations (NGOs) also are playing a role in project implementation. When land has been identified, agreement has been reached for the land transaction, and a general farm plan has been prepared, the beneficiary group submits a proposal for land acquisition and farm development to the Lands Project Officer in the District Assembly where the estate is located. Once submitted, the proposal is appraised by a field appraisal team led by the Lands Project Officer. If the proposal passes appraisal, it goes to the District Executive Committee for approval. The committee reviews it and, if necessary, seeks help from the PMU. If approved, the proposal then goes to the National Technical Advisory Committee for further review and ultimately reaches the ministry for final approval. Upon approval, the beneficiary group signs an LAFD Grant Agreement with the Malawi Social Action Fund. From then on, the main occupation of beneficiaries becomes farm development. Figure 14.3 shows institutional and functional links among project management subsystems.

The Process for Developing Subprojects in a Community

Members of a beneficiary group participate in the development of subprojects, working through a series of interrelated activities. Those activities are described in this section.

Mobilizing Beneficiaries and Arousing Interest

The project management team regularly holds sensitization[7] meetings with District Executive Committees and estate owners in the pilot districts. Thereafter, District Executive Committees hold mass meetings at area and village levels where area development committees, village development committees, and the general public are sensitized. This is being augmented by radio programs, episodes, and jingles, and by print media. Occasionally, documentary programs about the project are televised. After people learn about the project, individual

Figure 14.3 CBRLDP Institutional and Implementation Arrangements

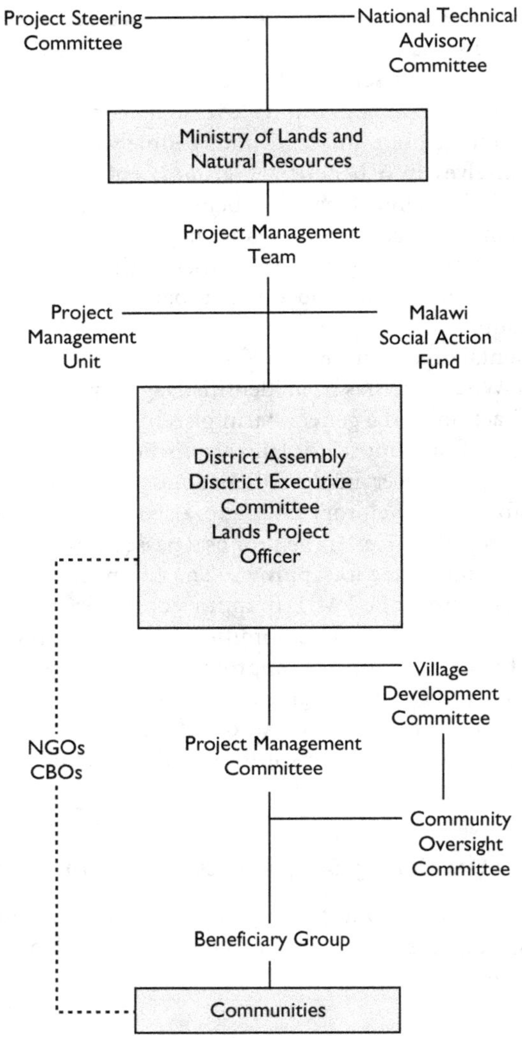

Source: Adapted from Government of Malawi, Ministry of Lands, Physical Planning and Surveys (2004).
Note: CBO = community-based organization; NGO = nongovernmental organization.

expression-of-interest forms are given to group and village heads to distribute to persons who may wish to participate in the project. The public is advised to form COCs as subcommittees of village development committees. Among other things, a COC is responsible for distributing individual expression-of-interest forms and vetting applicants at the village level.

Vetting Individual Expressions of Interest and Forming Beneficiary Groups

When the COCs receive and register all completed individual expression-of-interest forms, the forms are checked for eligibility against preset criteria. Applicants either are accepted or are rejected on the basis of those criteria. The accepted forms are submitted to the village headman for endorsement. The COCs advise people whose forms have been approved to form a beneficiary group of 10–35 households. The group then appoints an interim committee comprising a chairperson, a secretary, and a committee member. This committee completes a group expression-of-interest form. All individual expression-of-interest forms are attached to the group form and sent to the district commissioners.

Endorsing the COC and Beneficiaries

Once the group forms are received, checked, and registered at the district commissioners' office, the Lands Project Officer and members of the District Executive Committee organize meetings with the village development committee. The community members endorse the eligibility of each member of the beneficiary group. When endorsements are completed, the group elects a project management committee in a participatory manner, taking into consideration individual trustworthiness and the committee's gender balance. After those elections, the beneficiary group is acquainted with the LAFD project cycle (figure 14.4). A list of estates on sale in the pilot districts is distributed to the group for consideration and selection. Some leaflets on HIV/AIDS voluntary counseling and testing also are distributed at this time.

Training the COCs and Project Management Committees

The COCs and the project management committees are trained in their roles. Trainings are based on identified needs, and are coordinated by the capacity-building component of the project. District training teams play a pivotal role. Training sessions vary in duration, depending on the subject—project cycle, leadership skills, group dynamics, communication skills, conflict management, or gender and HIV/AIDS mitigation.

Verifying the Eligibility of the Beneficiary Group

When the District Assembly receives the group interest forms, a field appraisal team, led by the Lands Project Officer, scrutinizes the documents to ensure all applicants are in compliance with eligibility criteria. This is done in a transparent manner through meetings with communities, village development committees, and extension agents. At those meetings, the eligibility of individual applicants is vetted and applicants' gardens are visited on a sample basis.

Identifying Farms and Negotiating Price

Once an estate is offered for sale, the PMU and officials from the District Assembly where the estate is located inspect the farm to verify its existence,

Figure 14.4 LAFD Project Cycle

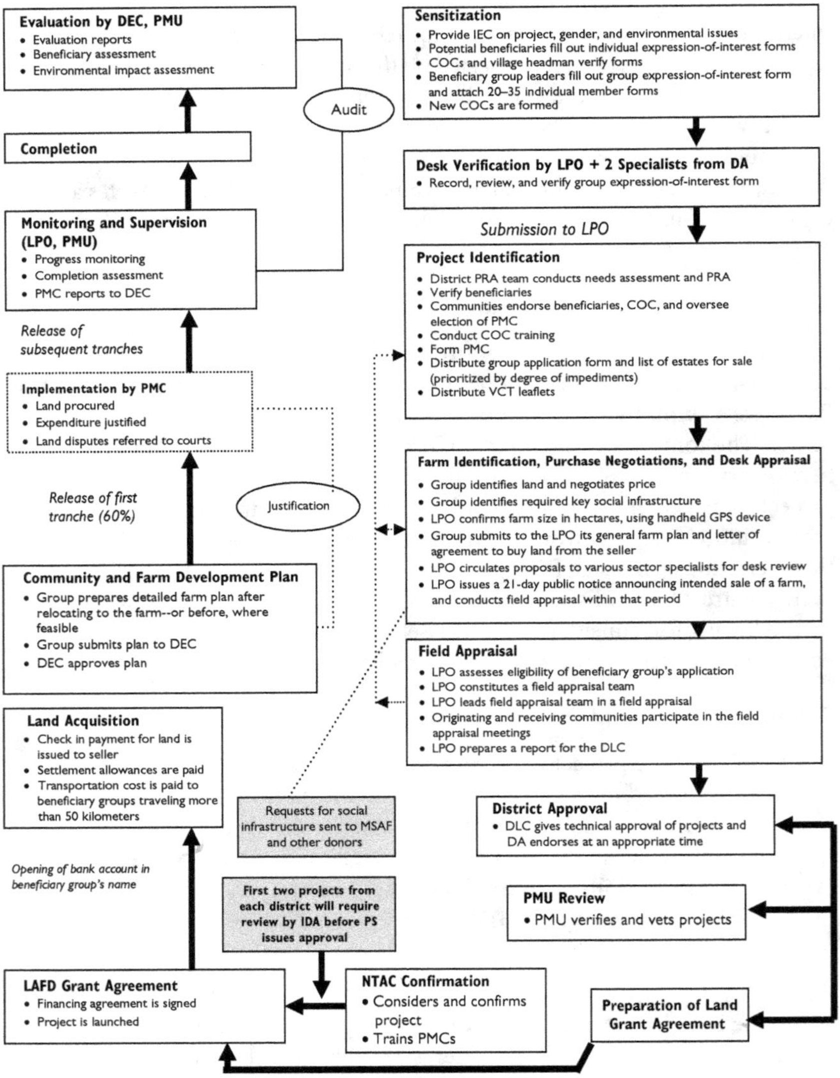

Evaluation by DEC, PMU
• Evaluation reports
• Beneficiary assessment
• Environmental impact assessment
Audit
Completion
Monitoring and Supervision (LPO, PMU)
• Progress monitoring
• Completion assessment
• PMC reports to DEC
Release of subsequent tranches
Implementation by PMC
• Land procured
• Expenditure justified
• Land disputes referred to courts
Release of first tranche (60%)
Justification
Community and Farm Development Plan
• Group prepares detailed farm plan after relocating to the farm--or before, where feasible
• Group submits plan to DEC
• DEC approves plan
Land Acquisition
• Check in payment for land is issued to seller
• Settlement allowances are paid
• Transportation cost is paid to beneficiary groups traveling more than 50 kilometers
Requests for social infrastructure sent to MSAF and other donors
Opening of bank account in beneficiary group's name
First two projects from each district will require review by IDA before PS issues approval
LAFD Grant Agreement
• Financing agreement is signed
• Project is launched
NTAC Confirmation
• Considers and confirms project
• Trains PMCs
Sensitization
• Provide IEC on project, gender, and environmental issues
• Potential beneficiaries fill out individual expression-of-interest forms
• COCs and village headman verify forms
• Beneficiary group leaders fill out group expression-of-interest form and attach 20–35 individual member forms
• New COCs are formed
Desk Verification by LPO + 2 Specialists from DA
• Record, review, and verify group expression-of-interest form
Submission to LPO
Project Identification
• District PRA team conducts needs assessment and PRA
• Verify beneficiaries
• Communities endorse beneficiaries, COC, and oversee election of PMC
• Conduct COC training
• Form PMC
• Distribute group application form and list of estates for sale (prioritized by degree of impediments)
• Distribute VCT leaflets
Farm Identification, Purchase Negotiations, and Desk Appraisal
• Group identifies land and negotiates price
• Group identifies required key social infrastructure
• LPO confirms farm size in hectares, using handheld GPS device
• Group submits to the LPO its general farm plan and letter of agreement to buy land from the seller
• LPO circulates proposals to various sector specialists for desk review
• LPO issues a 21-day public notice announcing intended sale of a farm, and conducts field appraisal within that period
Field Appraisal
• LPO assesses eligibility of beneficiary group's application
• LPO constitutes a field appraisal team
• LPO leads field appraisal team in a field appraisal
• Originating and receiving communities participate in the field appraisal meetings
• LPO prepares a report for the DLC
District Approval
• DLC gives technical approval of projects and DA endorses at an appropriate time
PMU Review
• PMU verifies and vets projects
Preparation of Land Grant Agreement

Source: Adapted from Government of Malawi, Ministry of Lands, Physical Planning and Surveys (2004).
Note: COC = community oversight committee; DA= District Assembly; DEC = District Executive Committee; DLC = district lands committee; GPS = global positioning system; IDA = International Development Association; IEC = information, education campaign; LAFD = Land Acquisition and Farm Development; LPO = Lands Project Officer; MSAF = Malawi Social Action Fund; PMC = project management committee; PMU = project management unit; PRA = participatory rural appraisal; PS = principal secretary; VCT = voluntary counseling and testing.

size, encroachment status, suitability for agricultural production, and the availability of social infrastructure. Estates that are encroached, have dual ownership, or are not suitable for agricultural production cannot be purchased under this project. The PMU prepares for the beneficiary group a list of eligible estates and a set of negotiation guidelines that include indicative prices of agricultural land per hectare, given the prevailing economic trend. The group is advised to buy at least 2 hectares per beneficiary household, plus 3–5 hectares for communal use, such as afforestation and a school or playfield for children. Once the group chooses an estate it is interested in acquiring, its representatives negotiate the price with the owner. When agreement is reached, the owner issues a provisional letter of agreement to sell land to the group. Thereafter, with assistance from agricultural officers, the beneficiary group prepares a preliminary farm development plan. The group sends its application to the District Assembly where the estate is located, with individual and group expression-of-interest forms, the provisional letter of agreement, and the preliminary farm development plan attached.

Appraising and Approving

Upon receipt of the documents, the Lands Project Officer issues a 21-day public notice. The notice is posted on a public notice board at the District Assembly building and is published in newspapers. The submitted LAFD proposal is circulated to the field appraisal team for scrutiny before field appraisals are made. While the public notice is still in force, the field appraisal team evaluates the estate in the presence of members of the concerned project management committee, the receiving COC, and the general public. The field appraisal team prepares a report and recommendations that are presented to the District Executive Committee for approval. When that committee has approved that report and the team's recommendations, the LAFD proposal is sent to the PMU for consolidation and forwarding to the National Technical Advisory Committee for further review. Finally it goes to the Office of the Secretary for Lands and Natural Resources for final approval. To ensure compliance with guidelines set out in the *Project Implementation Manual* from each pilot district, the first two LAFD proposals had to be reviewed by the International Development Association before final approval was granted by the Secretary for Lands and Natural Resources.

Resettling and Developing Farms

When the LAFD proposal has been approved, the beneficiary group signs the LAFD grant agreement with the Malawi Social Action Fund (MASAF). For land purchases, MASAF transfers money directly to the seller. The amount transferred is equal to up to 30 percent of the LAFD grant. At the same time, the PMU advises MASAF to pay resettlement allowances (8 percent of the grant). If a beneficiary group travels more than 50 kilometers to the relocation site, its transportation cost also is paid in full. At this juncture, payment is made through the District Assembly because beneficiaries do not have bank accounts yet. Once resettled, beneficiaries open bank accounts into which the farm development funds will be transferred. The amount transferred into the account is equal to the remaining 62 percent of the LAFD grant. The funds are transferred in three tranches; the first tranche is 60 percent of the farm development funds. The second and third tranches are 20 percent each. Subsequent tranches are released when the Malawi Social Action Fund receives a satisfactory justification report. Release of the third part of the funding is tied to the District Executive Committee's approval of the farm development plan. The first tranche is higher because it is used to pay for the provision of water, construction of small culverts for access roads, and the purchase of farm tools and such inputs as seeds and fertilizers. Beneficiaries are advised by water technicians how to secure safe drinking water, either through a borehole or a protected shallow well. After the first season, the beneficiary group, with assistance from the agricultural extension staff, develops a detailed farm plan, taking into account environmental management concerns.

PROJECT ACHIEVEMENTS AND IMPACT

At the end of 2008, a total of 12,656 beneficiaries had been relocated on 27,988 hectares. Crop production has increased substantially, and the lives of the beneficiaries have improved.

Achievements and Challenges

When December 2008 ended, 84 percent of the 15,000 targeted beneficiary households had been relocated. Achievements to date are impressive, but with only six months to go until the end of the project—June 30, 2009—it is unlikely that the CBRLDP will fully reach its objective of resettling 15,000 households unless it is extended. The project also is facing a number of challenges, notably the slow pace of group title transfer and the provision of socioeconomic amenities by the state.

Resettlement Pace

The CBRLDP started slowly, with no households resettled in 2004, and 455 resettled in 2005. The pace eventually accelerated in 2006, resettling 4,052 households. Since that time, remarkable progress has been made. By the end of December 2008, a total of 12,656 beneficiaries had been resettled on 27,988 hectares. Because the project is tied to an agricultural calendar, beneficiaries can relocate only during the dry season (May to October). But the processing of LAFD proposals is continuous through the year, and a number of proposals are at different stages of the approval process at this moment. Notwithstanding significant progress made in the last 24 months, the project cannot achieve its initial objective of reaching 15,000 households by June 30, 2009. The first reason is that the remaining project period is largely outside the dry season. The second and even more critical reason is that funds for land acquisition and farm development have been exhausted. Some funds for resettlement were converted into an unallocated line item. This fact was discussed during a midterm review of the project in March 2007. During that review the government expressed interest in extending the project. Discussions on the issue are under way between the government of Malawi and the World Bank. Such an extension will ensure that there are impact data over three years and will help policy makers decide on the best way forward. The slow pace during the first two years was the result of issues specific to the project, including (1) delays in the approval of the first procurement plan, (2) delays in the mobilization of human and material resources, (3) underestimation of the time the PMU would require to master the procedures outlined in the *Project Implementation Manual,* (4) estate owners' skepticism that government would pay for their land, and (5) persistent misconceptions about the project, prompting the extremely cautious project staff to be afraid of making mistakes.

Land Acquisition

So far, 27,998 hectares have been acquired through the project. One of the major constraints keeping the exercise from moving forward is the unavailability of land in Mulanje and Thyolo districts.[8] In these districts, most private lands are held by multinational companies growing tea and other high-value tree crops. Until now, they have been unwilling to release land, and no land has been proposed to the project. As a result, beneficiaries from Mulanje (2,351 households) and Thyolo (2,265 households) had to be relocated in Machinga and Mangochi, while beneficiaries from Machinga (3,390 households) and Mangochi (4,126 households) were resettled in their district of origin. This interdistrict relocation created excessive demand for land in Machinga and Mangochi districts, thereby sharply increasing average land prices and relocation costs because beneficiaries have to travel frequently to other districts for farm identification and field appraisal. The project will continue interacting with estate owners in Mulanje and Thyolo, with the hope that some may see the importance of selling part of their land to the project for relocation of beneficiaries. Meanwhile, the government is said to be considering introducing an equitable land rent structure that could lead to the release of "excess" or unused/underused land (see box 14.2), while the expiration of land leases could result in an increase of land available for resettlement (see box 14.3).

In the districts of Balaka and Ntcheu, 264 and 260 households have been resettled, respectively. That the project was able to relocate 524 beneficiaries

Box 14.2 Land Rent Increase

Although in December 2004, the government increased land rent for agricultural land from MK 500 per hectare to MK 1,000 per hectare, collection of land rent has not been aggressive. Worse still, in 2005 the government imposed a moratorium on the collection of ground rent by the tobacco auction floors, arguing that the land rent targeted only tobacco farmers. Farmers producing other crops were not subjected to the same arrangement. The government reported that it was taking steps to normalize the situation. However, as of January 2009, no real progress has been made. In addition, the government is said to be considering introducing an equitable land rent structure that would take into account farm size and levels of input systems. Because of this inconsistency, the increase in land rent has not yet led to the release of "excess" or unused/underused land that could be used for the relocation of CBRLDP beneficiaries. Land planted with tea in Mulanje and Thyolo districts is on freehold, and currently is not subject to land rent. An increase in land rent would have no impact on a decision to sell or hold excess land.

Box 14.3 Expiring Leases

Expiring leases present both an opportunity and a risk. The opportunity is that owners whose lease payments are in arrears and/or who do not use their estates properly either may not apply for renewal of the leases or may find their applications rejected. Such land would then become public land. The risk arises because public land all over the world is occupied rapidly because there is no owner to protect it from illegal occupation, and governments rarely have the capacity to protect it. Therefore, settlement of these estates could turn into a free-for-all, with the land going to stronger and better-off people rather than to land-poor and food-insecure households. The government needs to study the operational modalities and capacities by which it could make use of such land for poverty reduction.

from the two districts within nine months is clear testimony that operations have been streamlined and that project staff have mastered them.

Land Transfer

To date, about 84 percent of the land acquired has been surveyed, 236 deed plans have been approved, and 211 group titles have been transferred. Out of a total of 551 beneficiary groups resettled by the CBRLDP, this represents a rate of 38 percent. Regardless of the amount of land offered, the pace of the land transfer has been seriously constrained by the low capacity of land agencies to establish the authenticity of the titleholders, check their indebtedness, and approve new deed plans. One of the main problems is that land records in Malawi are scattered and outdated. This hampers speedy land acquisition. In theory, leaseholders have to survey "their" estates; in practice, leases long have been issued on the basis of a simple sketch. That means each estate offered has to be surveyed.

To speed up the surveying process, the project had to replace the archaic survey equipment with modern instruments and had to procure software for verifying and approving deed plans. For its part, the government took corrective measures to facilitate examination of deed plans. As a result, the land acquisition process was streamlined and lead time was reduced from nine months to four months. Finally, another challenge faced by the project involves the concealment of indebtedness by willing sellers and the time required to clear debts before proceeding with a land transaction. This will be dealt with through information, education, and communication messages.

All of these issues suggest an almost dysfunctional legal and institutional framework for land administration in Malawi, and it is evident that reforming such a framework goes far beyond this project.

Socioeconomic Amenities

Providing beneficiaries with access to clean water and other socioeconomic amenities, such as schools and health centers, rapidly became one of the greatest challenges. At first, LAFD grants could not be used to provide socioeconomic amenities, but the grant agreement was amended so that beneficiary groups may use part of the farm development funds to drill boreholes or shallow wells. However, such use reduces the money available for farm development, especially for the small groups. In addition, the Malawi Social Action Fund provided MK 57 million for socioeconomic amenities in the relocation districts. To date, 38 boreholes and 30 protected shallow wells have been sunk and are in use. Five boreholes are yet to be drilled. Unfortunately, 27 protected shallow wells are dry because they were poorly located. (This happened before water technicians got involved.) Four junior primary schools are under construction. The fund also provided financing for 10 health packages for beneficiary groups and three maize mills for community-based organizations linked to beneficiaries. Through its various agencies, the government will strive to continue providing social amenities, and District Assemblies are required to include such services in their public sector investment programs. Finally, the beneficiary groups' limited access to extension services has had negative repercussions on technology adoption. Temporary consultants have been hired and advised to work closely with District Assembly officials.

Integrating Beneficiary Groups with Surrounding Communities

To accelerate the integration of beneficiaries with surrounding communities, beneficiaries are encouraged to participate in broader community development work; and local communities are urged to involve beneficiaries in local development structures, such as village and area development committees. Beneficiaries are advised to ensure that socioeconomic amenities provided by the project—such as boreholes drilled using project funds—also benefit surrounding communities. The project will continue sensitizing local chiefs, COCs, and project management committees to the importance of communities coming together. Despite such efforts, beneficiary groups and surrounding communities have had a number of disputes over boundaries and, in some cases, over the use of dambos (wetlands). Usually, surrounding communities do not recognize estate boundaries. The absence of survey beacons to mark estate boundaries intensifies the problem as local communities take advantage of the situation. Although most of the disputes have been resolved, some remain unsettled. District Assembly officials and traditional authorities have played leading roles in resolving these conflicts.

Working with NGOs

Although it has been the desire of the project to work with NGOs in serving beneficiaries, this took time to materialize—mainly because most NGOs work outside the relocation areas, and also because it was necessary to better define their specific involvement. The situation has changed. In Machinga, the Green Line Movement is providing extension services in natural resource management to the project beneficiaries at the time the NGO is servicing its usual clients. Their program is developed in close collaboration with CBRLDP and staff in district agricultural development offices. Another NGO, the Christian Service Committee, has supported one beneficiary group with a borehole, and has pledged to provide orientation on a farmer-to-farmer extension approach to staff from the project and district agriculture development offices.

Institutional Capacity Building

CBRLDP is enhancing institutional capacities through formal and informal training, by establishing community-based committees, and by recruiting project staff. It also directly provides resources to beneficiary groups, central and local government institutions, and other stakeholders to enable effective execution of operations. At the national level, the project is supporting staff development in the technical departments of the Ministry of Lands and Natural Resources and for other relevant stakeholders. Particular attention has been paid to developing technical capacities such as land administration, surveying, valuation, physical planning, monitoring and evaluation, and financial management. At the district level, the focus has been on strengthening the existing governance structures necessary for effective project implementation (for example, district assemblies and executive committees, area executive committees, and accounts personnel). At the local level, the project worked on training beneficiary groups, project management committees, and COCs.

Given the high prevalence of HIV/AIDS in Malawi, common activities include information on voluntary counseling and testing, antiretroviral therapy, and the national HIV/AIDS policy. Five thousand leaflets and 100 copies of a newsletter on HIV/AIDS also were distributed to potential beneficiaries. The materials came from the National AIDS Commission. In Machinga and Mangochi, special sensitization meetings on corruption were organized in collaboration with the Anti-Corruption Bureau of Malawi, and 26 traditional authorities participated. Finally, the interest in the project shown by the communities is a result of the sustained awareness-promoting efforts of the project's capacity-building team working closely with district assemblies.

Participation of Female-Headed Households

In a baseline array of 50 beneficiary groups, 99 out of 488 households are headed by women. A PMU head count of 72 groups also supports this finding. These figures are despite the considerable emphasis in the information, education, and communication training programs on gender inclusion and the mandatory inclusion of women on the oversight and project management committees in each community. However, lack of an effective management information system prevented early identification of this exclusionary trend. There has been no timely analysis of the difficulties encountered by female-headed households in the application and relocation processes. The PMU, however, has commissioned a study to assess the sociocultural reasons for the low participation levels of female-headed households.

Project Impact

The project is having a positive impact in terms of increasing agricultural production and income for the beneficiaries. Provision of socioeconomic amenities is another welcome development that has helped integrate the settlers with the surrounding communities.

Agricultural Production

Resettled households grow a wide range of crops, including maize, tobacco, groundnuts, sweet potatoes, cassava, and pigeon peas. For all these crops—especially maize and cassava—significant yield increases have been noted. Between crop years 2004/05 and 2005/06, the mean maize production by the beneficiary households increased from 902 kilograms per hectare to 2,269 kilograms per hectare (see table 14.2). This level of increase and the magnitude of production are far greater than those of the control groups. In Machinga, preliminary data on maize production for crop years 2006/07 already indicate higher yields than for 2005/06. By increasing the area under cultivation, using fertilizers and better seeds, and in the presence of favorable climatic conditions, many beneficiaries harvested 4 metric tons. Resettling beneficiary households in

Table 14.2 Beneficiary Households' Yield Changes for Principal Crops, Crop Years 2004/05 and 2005/06

Crop	2004/05 (Average Kilograms/Hectare)	2005/06 (Average Kilograms/Hectare)
Maize	962	2,269
Cassava	905	2,368
Sweet potatoes	864	1,006
Pigeon peas	232	543
Groundnuts	737	1,200
Tobacco	519	1,273

Source: PricewaterhouseCoopers 2007.

remote areas also has helped bring unutilized land into agricultural production, thereby improving the economic potential of the areas (see table 14.3).

Beneficiaries' Incomes

Mean gross margin for hybrid maize had increased from MK 2,625 per hectare prior to relocation (crop year 2004/05) to MK 27,265 per hectare one year after relocation (2005/06). The average annual beneficiary household income jumped from MK 54,000 before relocation to roughly MK 88,000 one year later. In addition to an increase in food security (from enough food to last only 3.6 months before relocation to enough to last 10.7 months the next year), many beneficiary households now own goats, chickens, and rabbits. The proportion of households with assets such as radios and bicycles also has increased. One beneficiary in Mangochi even bought a maize mill from tobacco proceeds.

Socioeconomic Amenities

The project has contributed directly and indirectly to the development of socioeconomic amenities, including boreholes, protected shallow wells, junior primary schools, and access roads. These amenities benefit both project households and surrounding communities. For instance, the several schools that are being built will enhance the human capital of many children in surrounding communities for whom schools were not accessible. Unfortunately, given the magnitude of the demand for socioeconomic amenities, existing problems cannot be resolved overnight. Some beneficiary groups will be disadvantaged for some time to come.

Land Prices

When relocating the first four beneficiary groups in 2005, the price of land was just over MK 8,000 per hectare. In 2006 and 2007, the price increased

Table 14.3 Comparison of Maize Production before and after Relocation, by Group

	Mean (kilograms)		Number (kilograms)		Minimum (kilograms)		Maximum (kilograms)	
Group	2004/05	2005/06	2004/05	2005/06	2004/05	2005/06	2004/05	2005/06
Beneficiary households	200	1,452	28	24	5	350	750	4,700
Surrounding communities	231	411	56	49	25	50	1,050	2,000
Households in vacated area	324	394	94	73	50	50	3,500	2,100
Long-term control group	207	267	101	78	25	50	850	1,350

Source: PricewaterhouseCoopers 2007.

rapidly and stabilized around MK 17,000 per hectare. Overall, the average land price is about MK 18,000 per hectare, although the average land price for the beneficiaries approved in September 2008 was MK 18,281. The relatively high land prices experienced so far are likely to be the result of localized demand for land. Most of the estates bought so far were undeveloped and lacked any infrastructure that would justify such prices. Some beneficiary groups appeared impatient to relocate and were prepared to pay more. However, this was noted during the approval process, and some groups were advised to renegotiate or look for other estates if prices were deemed to be unreasonable by either the District Executive Committee or the National Technical Advisory Committee.

Considerations for Scaling Up

Among the important lessons that can be learned form the CBRLDP experiences are these:

- With proper assistance, community groups can negotiate for land and relocate themselves, even across districts.
- The decentralized and participatory project implementation arrangements of the CBRLDP have the potential to be scaled up nationally.
- Districts differ sharply in the availability of land. Scaling up must carefully identify the most likely receiving districts and prepare their capacity for managing the influx of beneficiary groups.
- Inadequate capacity in land administration, surveying, and titling could become the major constraint to scaling up. The government needs to explore new ways to simplify procedures and requirements, and it must strengthen capacity at the central and decentralized levels.
- Provision of clean, potable water ought to have been made an integral part of the project rather than left to beneficiaries to request from district assemblies that usually do not have sufficient funds to invest in socioeconomic amenities.

CONCLUSION

Preliminary results of the project impact evaluation are promising. The project is having profound effects in the newly resettled areas. So far, 551 beneficiary groups—12,656 households—have been relocated, which means that they have acquired land and now are engaged in agricultural production. If farmers reinvest some of their proceeds into farm inputs, the current level of production can be sustained in the coming years. The benefits also have spilled over to the surrounding communities in the form of beneficiaries' demands for casual labor and their purchase of various goods and services. Some of the surrounding communities have gained access to the new water points put in place by the project.

If this trend is maintained, it will improve the quality of life significantly not only for the beneficiaries but also for the residents in contiguous neighborhoods.

Resettling landless and land-poor people does work, but it is a complex exercise. It becomes even more challenging when the legal and institutional frameworks for land administration are deficient (as in Malawi). For instance, in the absence of accurate and reliable land records, the exact amount of land under leasehold is unknown. There is an urgent need to conduct systematic cadastral surveys countrywide to obtain this information. Detailed assessments of landlessness, of the number of citizens who are land-poor, and of the amount of land available in different districts are needed if policy makers are to decide how a scaling up could be implemented. In any case, scaling necessarily entails committing more resources for resettlement processes and for the broader project of land reform. Ultimately, the decision to scale up the project will depend on political will to carry out land reform in general, and land resettlement to the benefit of the poor in particular.

As for the land transfer mechanism, preliminary results of the CBRLDP already show that in the current context, it is unlikely that the WSWB approach can deliver enough land for a large-scale land redistribution program. Similar experiences have been observed in several Southern African Development Community member-countries, including Namibia, South Africa, and Zimbabwe (chapter 5 of this volume; Moyo 2005; ANC 2007; Government of South Africa 2008). So far, indigenous Malawian estate owners have been more receptive to the approach than have foreign estate owners, who seem not to realize the severity of the land issue. The problem is that landowners usually are unwilling to sell their land or they offer it at exorbitant and exploitative prices that governments cannot afford. That situation seriously has undermined the current attempt to redistribute land and has produced undue pressure in the districts of Machinga and Mangochi.

Settler landlords or communities need to realize that they have contributed to the problem. As such they need to play a constructive role in resolving it. Skirting the problem is merely waiting for a time bomb to explode; and considering the observations made above, the need to broaden and diversity land acquisition mechanisms seems obvious. For instance, one could imagine a land reform scenario where the WSWB approach would be taken only as the entry point for land acquisition. Then, if necessary, a targeted land acquisition would be adopted. Estate owners with surplus land would be invited to sell part of their land at a "reasonable" price—that is, a fair and nonexploitative price. Should this approach fail, legal expropriation of under- or unused land would be pursued only as a last resort. In any case, the argument that legal expropriation is too costly to be employed at scale should not be overused to justify landgrabbing. It also will be necessary to stay the course in the event of some negative publicity generated by the settler-landlords. Finally, the importance of introducing a land tax as a way to fund land reform and discourage the underutilization of land should not be underestimated.

NOTES

1. From the late 1990s to the early 2000s, the price of tobacco was quite low, and growing tobacco was no longer economical. As a result, many farmers were forced to abandon the Industry.
2. With the establishment of a British colonial secretary of state in 1902, these rights were formalized through the publication of certificates of claim.
3. These acts were the Customary Land Development Act, the Registered Land Act, and the Local Land Boards Act.
4. A preliminary report for the 2008 Population and Housing Census gives the national population as 13,066,320, and states that the average population growth rate is 2.8 percent a year.
5. Participation in the project is on a voluntary basis, and beneficiaries have to take the initiative in forming a group, identifying land, and negotiating its price. Also, beneficiaries have to adhere to the principle of WSWB for land acquisition.
6. The districts of Balaka, Machinga, Mangochi, Mulanje, and Thyolo are in the southern region; Ntcheu is in the central region.
7. "Sensitization," in this context, involves passing out information about the project to the general public in the targeted districts so that would-be beneficiaries can make informed decisions about whether to participate in the project.
8. Malawian rural land markets are very unbalanced. The so-called estate crisis generated a growing supply of land. The farms are mostly unprofitable, poorly managed tobacco estates. In areas where the tobacco industry continues to face difficulties, more estates are being offered for sale. For instance, in the districts of Machinga and Mangochi, there is a vibrant land market. This contrasts with the situation in Mulanje and Thyolo where no land is offered. In any case, there are few buyers in any given area.

REFERENCES

ANC (African National Congress). 2007. Resolution. Presented at the 52nd National Conference, University of Limpopo, Polokwane, South Africa, December 16–20.

Government of Malawi. 1998. "Population and Housing Census." National Statistical Office, Zomba.

———. 1999. "Final Report of the Presidential Commission of Inquiry on Land Policy Reform." Volume 1. Lilongwe.

———. 2000. "Integrated Household Survey 1997–98, Statistical Abstract." National Statistical Office, Zomba.

———. 2008. "Population and Housing Census, Preliminary Report." National Statistical Office, Zomba.

Government of Malawi, Ministry of Lands, Physical Planning, and Surveys. 2002. "Malawi National Land Policy." Lilongwe. http://www.malawi.gov.mw/publications/landpol.htm [accessed January 8, 2009].

———. 2004. *Community-Based Rural Land Development Project: Project Implementation Manual.* Lilongwe.

Government of South Africa, Department of Agriculture. 2008. "The Land and Agrarian Reform Project (LARP) Concept Document." Pretoria.

Moyo, Sam. 2005. "Land Question and Land Reform in Southern Africa." Paper presented at the National Land Summit, Johannesburg, South Africa, July 27–31.

Ng'ong'ola, Clement. 1990. "The State, Settlers, and Indigenes in the Evolution of Land Law and Policy in Colonial Malawi." *International Journal of African Historical Studies* 23 (1): 27–58.

Pachai, Bridglal. 1973. "Land Policies in Malawi: An Examination of the Colonial Legacy." *Journal of African History* 14 (4): 681–98.

PricewaterhouseCoopers. 2007. "CBRLDP Impact Study Final Report."

van Donge, Jan Kees. 2002. "Disordering the Market: The Liberalisation of Burley Tobacco in Malawi in the 1990s." *Journal of Southern African Studies* 28 (1) special issue: 89–115.

World Bank. 2004. "Project Appraisal Document for the Community-Based Rural Land Development Project." Report No. 28188-MAI. Washington, DC. http://www-wds.worldbank.org/external/default/WDSContentServer/WDSP/IB/2004/04/02/000112742_20040402123117/Rendered/PDF/281880MAI0with0corrigendum.pdf [accessed January 8, 2009].

———. 2007. "Aide Memoire for Mid-Term Review Mission of Community-Based Rural Land Development Project." March 18–29. Washington, DC.

CHAPTER FIFTEEN

Monitoring and Evaluation of Land Policies and Land Reform

Klaus Deininger

Land policies can constitute a serious constraint on economic and social development in a number of respects that are of great relevance for developing countries. On one hand, insecure land tenure, outdated regulations, and slow or dysfunctional land institutions constrain private investment, undermine good governance, and reduce local government's ability to raise taxes. On the other hand, highly skewed distributions of land ownership and patterns of land access that discriminate along lines of gender or ethnicity limit the scope for decentralized market mechanisms to bring land to its best uses, constrain economic opportunities (including the ability to use land as collateral) for disadvantaged groups, and often foment social conflict and violence.

Because of differences in the historical evolution and actual patterns of land use and ownership, the nature of land rights and institutions tends to vary significantly across countries and even across regions within the same country. This fact implies that, more than in areas other than land rights, land policy and institutional reform (1) will involve a series of actions that need to be based on careful analysis of local conditions rather than on abstract principles; (2) will have to be sequenced in a way that combines objective need with political acceptability; and (3) often will need to be backed up by financial support to establish necessary infrastructure. These requirements increase the duration and complexity of formulating land policy and, because land often is closely linked to vested interests, generally make land policy reform politically controversial. The experience of many countries, however, illustrates that ignoring land issues will carry a very high cost and seriously may undermine development efforts in other sectors of the economy.

This chapter aims to provide practitioners with a quick reference to key policy issues, the way in which a poverty and social impact assessment (PSIA) can help address those issues, methodological considerations that will have to be included, analytical instruments that can be used to provide needed evidence, and ways in which the results can be communicated to different stakeholders so as to elicit the desired policy response. The discussion of substantive and methodological issues will be relatively brief because they are discussed in more detail elsewhere (Bourguignon and Pereira da Silva 2003; Deininger 2003). The rest of this chapter is structured as follows. The first section after this introduction discusses the impact of greater tenure security; ways to enhance it; and studies that have provided empirical evidence of its impact on investment, conflict, and land market participation. The second section covers key principles of land access, policies and regulations to enhance it, and empirical evidence and examples of the effects of land reform. Following that are a list of monitoring and evaluation principles and practical issues in the areas of sampling and questionnaire design and links to other areas of analysis that need to be considered in conducting a PSIA.

TENURE SECURITY

The importance of tenure security is widely recognized. Public provision of a framework that enables households (or individuals within those households) to have secure rights to land that they already use or occupy can provide obvious benefits: increasing investment incentives, reducing the conflict potential, possibly allowing the use of land as collateral, and improving social and economic equality by enhancing the bargaining power of those people who traditionally have been disadvantaged. Tenure security requires a legal framework that combines legal backing with social legitimacy; land institutions that are effective, accessible, efficient, and responsive to client demand; and incentives as well as structures to manage conflict and quickly deal with it before it escalates.

Principles

Land rights are multidimensional and complex constructs that determine the way in which the benefits from land use are distributed among different claimants. Control of and access to land historically have been major elements of economic power and social status. In fact, discriminatory land policies have been a crucial element in attempts by outside colonists to impose their economic control and to exclude parts of the population from economic opportunities. Such land policies have settled a number of countries—Brazil, Guatemala, the Philippines, South Africa, and Zimbabwe—with very high levels of land ownership inequality.

Another (and far more widespread) consequence of skewed access to land is a monopoly of bureaucratic control that negatively affects transparency and local accountability in a much larger number of countries. In addition to its economic dimensions, land access often performs an essential role as a social safety net. Where a safety net is important, land access generally is mediated through social structures such as tribes or clans, and the ability to access land forms an important part of people's social and cultural identity. All of this makes land much more than a commodity.

Whereas economists use the household as the unit of analysis, control of land often rests with individuals within the household or the clan. The way in which control of land (and other assets) is regulated within households or extended families will have consequences for members' long-term security and bargaining power that will affect socioeconomic outcomes such as different members' ability to control resources and the way in which the resources are spent. A number of studies show that greater bargaining power for women normally translates into higher spending on nutrition, education, and children's welfare. Moreover, women who can be sure that they securely can inherit their part of the household's land when their husbands die are more empowered to engage in independent economic activities, and thus to act as equal partners in supporting the sustenance of their families. Women's tenure security is of particular relevance in Africa, where customary institutions make independent control of land by women very difficult to achieve, even though the tragic consequences of rampant HIV/AIDS and its associated mortality greatly have increased the frequency of inheritance cases.

Land rights that provide tenure security for a period long enough to reap benefits from investment will provide an important incentive for households to make investments that enhance the productive capacity of their land, or to transfer land (for free or with compensation) to others who will be able to make better use of it. Studies show that shifting from insecure to more secure forms of tenure can more than double investment and increase land values by 30–80 percent (Jimenez 1984; Feder et al. 1988). Secure tenure (that is, the knowledge that tenants will not be able to claim the land as theirs) also is needed for landowners who wish to temporarily transfer their land to others (including outside investors) able to make better use of it while the landowners pursue activities that offer them greater economic benefits (for example, migration or local self-employment).

Because it is immobile and nearly indestructible in the short term, land is ideal collateral. The ability to draw on a formal registry to verify landownership dramatically can reduce the cost of providing credit, as compared to, say, microlending schemes that rely on social pressure or more costly forms of collateral to ensure repayment. If there is a latent demand for credit-financed investment, formal land title can improve the functioning of financial markets and producers' access to credit. At the same time, even though economic development generally is associated with a decline in the importance of land as an input to (agricultural) production, the importance of land as collateral for financial markets tends to increase with development. In developed economies, such as the United States, more than two-thirds of small-business loans are secured by land (Ibbotson, Siegel, and Love 1985). The ease with which the ownership of land can be verified and the cost at which it can be exchanged can have a major impact on the cost of credit and on the business environment for small- and medium-size enterprises, even in relatively developed economies.

Although private households and entrepreneurs normally are willing to spend scarce resources on defending property claims, doing so is often socially wasteful and detracts from more productive pursuits. Public provision of property rights to guarantee tenure security is justified by the high fixed cost of the infrastructure needed to establish and enforce property rights. However, what is important is not an abstract concept (for example, "private ownership" or "full marketability") but whether, in a specific context, the rights provided to households give them a sufficient level of tenure security at a low cost. This implies that the most appropriate land tenure system is likely to vary with time and space; that is, there is no single concept that would be relevant irrespective of specific needs and conditions.

In developing countries, rapid growth of population and nonagricultural demand for land increase the potential for land-related conflicts that are both unproductive and inequitable. Developing arrangements that enable societies to deal with such conflicts quickly and decisively will be advantageous for a number of reasons. First, conflict and its resultant loss of land prevent productive investment by land users and outsiders (often on the most productive land), and thus deprive the economy of much-needed growth potential. Second, if people do not trust the state to enforce their property rights or resolve conflicts, they will take measures to do so themselves, often in a way that is inefficient and draws resources from more productive activities (that is, they may build walls and fences instead of planting perennials and establishing irrigation). Third, conflicts favor powerful and wealthy people who normally have better access to information and the resources needed to sustain and resolve conflict. Finally, given that land access historically is linked closely to issues of race, ethnicity, gender, and class, conflict with origins traced to land easily can escalate and, even if land is no longer the main issue, give rise to large clashes (Colombia, Côte d'Ivoire, Zimbabwe) with far-reaching and very damaging social and economic consequences.

Specific Interventions

The discussion above illustrates that interventions that improve tenure security can provide significant and tangible benefits. At the same time, the context-specific nature of land rights implies that simply transferring specific interventions between countries rarely will be appropriate, especially if there are vast differences in culture or levels of economic development. In fact, unless they are adapted to local realities, interventions designed to enhance tenure security may be costly and ineffective, may bypass the poor, or even may increase insecurity by upsetting local customs that work reasonably well without offering a better alternative. Conducting a PSIA can help draw attention to how an appropriate legal framework can be established in a specific situation, how land administration institutions can implement needed measures effectively and efficiently, and how mechanisms to resolve conflict quickly and at low cost can be put in place. By demonstrating the costs and benefits of these efforts, an assessment can make an important contribution to advancing the policy dialogue.

Legal Interventions to Increase Tenure Security

Countries have a number of options to provide property rights that are defined in a way that makes them easy to observe, enforce, and exchange; and in a way that has a horizon long enough to provide investment incentives. Evidence has shown that, depending on their history and culture, the choices that countries make are very different (Di Tella, Galiani, and Schargrodsky 2007; Deininger and Ali 2008; Deininger, Jin, and Nagarajan 2008; Goldstein and Udry 2008). At the same time, it is critical that legal provisions be consistent with each other and unambiguous, and that they provide a menu of options with well-defined transitions between different arrangements (for example, between customary and private property rights). All over the world, ambiguous and unclear legislation is a major source of conflict and inequality because it enables people with sufficient resources to hire lawyers and bring lawsuits against others, often to settle private vendettas. That practice undermines the security of property rights and private investment, and it can force existing enterprises to eat up their productive capital to fend off unjustified claims.

In many developing countries, the state has limited outreach and the allocation of land is governed by traditional institutions, something that results in a gap between formal and informal systems that forces most of the poor into informality and deprives them of the ability to use their assets as "capital" (de Soto 2000). For example, only 2–10 percent of the total land area in Africa is formally recognized, and most urban and peri-urban settlements are in the informal sector (Oosterberg 2002). Although that should not be interpreted as indicating no demand for more secure tenure, responding to the need to secure large areas quickly and at low cost may require an array of options, some of which stop short of full title but can be upgraded if the need arises. To implement these options effectively, awareness campaigns and legal aid will be important.

The challenge there is to establish laws that combine legal backing with social legitimacy, and it can be met in a number of ways. In customary systems, legal recognition of existing rights and institutions, subject to minimum conditions, often is more effective than premature attempts to establish formalized structures. Legal recognition of customary land rights subject to a determination of membership and the codification or establishment of internal rules and mechanisms for conflict resolution can enhance occupants' rights significantly. At the same time, demarcating community lands can remove threats of encroachment by outsiders. Demarcating community lands, determining membership, and codifying or establishing rules and mechanisms for conflict resolution can provide significant benefits and remove threats of encroachment by outsiders. None of these actions requires private ownership rights. Lease terms can be increased and leases can be made inheritable. Admitting verbal evidence of ownership also can have big benefits for illiterate people while facilitating land-related investment for commercial exploitation, as in Mozambique (Tanner 2002). Publicly recording transactions, even if those transactions are informal, can remove a major source of uncertainty and reduce haggling over contract terms later. Conflicts often erupt in connection with land transfers, especially transfers to outsiders. Where such transfers occur and are socially accepted, the terms should be recorded in writing to avoid ambiguity that subsequently could lead to land-related conflict (Lavigne-Delville et al. 2002).

Occupants on state land often have made efforts to increase their level of security—in some cases through significant investments—but often they remain vulnerable to eviction threats. Because their land rights are limited, they often cannot make full use of the land they occupy. Giving them legal rights and regularizing their possession are important efforts, along with providing a means to resolve any conflicts that may arise in the process. Often, political or other considerations preclude the award of full private property rights. If existing institutions credibly can commit to honor lease contracts, giving users secure, transferable, long-term lease rights will permit realization of most, if not all, investment benefits of high tenure security. In these cases, recognizing long-term peaceful occupation in good faith (Baker 2001) and awarding long-term land leases with provisions for automatic renewal will be the most desirable options. However, if leases by state institutions are not credible, full privatization may be required. An indicator of leases' limited credibility is financial institutions' refusal to accept the leases as collateral, even where there is strong demand for credit.

In many developing countries, a surprisingly large amount of land that is suitable for private use remains in the hands of the state, which generally makes very poor use of it. By contrast, as noted above, occupants on such land often have tried to increase their tenure security—in some cases through significant investments—but they remain vulnerable to eviction threats. Giving them the right to formalize their possession (subject to bona fide occupation) of pieces of land that are sufficient to support a family but not large enough to encourage widespread corruption can have large benefits. It can increase households' welfare and enable them to obtain services or undertake other investments without necessarily requiring full individual ownership rights.

At the same time, in situations where central or local governments are not able or trustworthy to enforce leases, full privatization of ownership will be required. The importance of this principle, which rests on the assumption that land must be improved, is illustrated by the fact that most of the colonization of the western part of the United States occurred in this way.

Traditional tenure regimes often fail to recognize women's rights. Specific attention to these rights is warranted in at least two respects. One low-cost option that greatly can enhance the welfare of women is to provide a secure legal basis for spousal joint ownership of land, or at the very least to prevent disposition of a household's land assets by the husband without the wife's consent. A second area of concern relates to whether or how women can maintain their land rights when the spouse dies. As many of the social values governing land use and allocation are deeply ingrained in society, equality of women's land rights cannot be legislated from above or be imposed by the stroke of a pen. Instead, what is needed is to create the legal space (for example, writing gender equality into the constitution, thus superseding customary arrangements), raise awareness, and offer assistance where needed.

Enhanced Efficiency of Land Administration Institutions

Irrespective of the most desirable legal option to ensure tenure security, inefficiencies in the land administration institutions responsible for marking boundaries, registering and keeping records, adjudicating rights, managing conflicts, and resolving disputes can forestall realization of many of the benefits of secure tenure. In most developing countries, the institutions responsible for administering property rights to land are poorly coordinated and often have a reputation for being overstaffed, inefficient, and rife with corruption. If they are not working well or are poorly coordinated, inefficient, or corrupt, transaction costs will increase, thereby excluding the poor. In the extreme, lack of clearly assigned responsibilities or infighting between institutions will evolve into a major source of insecurity that undermines the value and authority of titles or certificates of land ownership. In such situations, institutional reform—including improved coordination within the government and with the private sector—will be a precondition for the state's ability to deliver property rights effectively. Drawing on the private sector (for example, for surveying services) can increase the efficiency of land administration institutions significantly if government establishes and enforces the needed regulatory framework.

Overlapping or ill-defined institutional responsibilities and the potential for discretionary behavior that arises if there are no clear boundaries to the role of bureaucracies also dampen confidence in land rights and the institutional framework. For example, one key reason for the limited effectiveness of land administration and for conflicts in many countries is that government expropriates land without adequate compensation; that different government institutions establish overlapping claims or regulations on the same piece of land; or that unclear responsibilities for resolving disputes cause conflicts to linger long and prompt litigious people to go "institution shopping"—that is, to search for institutions that are likely to be favorable to their case or to pursue several claims in parallel. Circumscribing the state's ability to intervene and clarifying different institutions' responsibilities will be crucial in avoiding these situations and their negative consequences. Interventions to improve tenure security will be appropriate in cases of high informality or extralegality, as in peri-urban areas of Africa and Asia where, respectively, more than 50 and 40 percent of the populations live under precarious informal arrangements that make it difficult to transfer land.

Lowered Levels of Existing Conflict and Potential for New Conflicts

A surprisingly high number of conflicts occur between members of the same household. Disputes related to inheritance or disposition of family land inundate land courts, which typically lack resources, enforcement capacity, or even consistent laws to settle such disputes. Instead of trying these cases, judicial systems often do better by putting their weight behind mediation among parties, encouraging negotiation based on compromise around mutual interests and formal recognition of the results. To deal with conflicts appropriately, three elements appear to be crucial: (1) the development of an incentive structure that rewards settlement of conflicts and an insistence on informal resolution as a first step, (2) the ability to give legal validity to agreements reached as a result of such informal settlements, and (3) a system of conflict monitoring and information dissemination to help establish norms of acceptable behavior to help affected individuals resolve conflicts among themselves.

Where land has been an important element contributing to conflict, attention to land issues will be required for postconflict reconciliation. A number of specific needs arise in such circumstances, namely (1) the need to use land to provide a livelihood for demobilized soldiers and displaced populations; (2) the need to deal with large numbers of refugees who may have been driven from their lands and whose documents may have been destroyed or lost; (3) the need to accommodate female-headed households and widows, who often account for 20–25 percent of all households, and orphans, all of whose land is particularly insecure; (4) the need to counter the breakdown of traditional social structures and the associated systems of informal secondary land and resource rights; (5) the need to manage rapid increases in the frequency and extent of land disputes, which often constitute about two-thirds of the civil caseload of a judiciary that is unable to cope with the demands; and (6) the need to contain and control continued interventions by the military, contamination of the land with land mines, and difficulties in physical movement.

Expected Impacts and Examples

The positive economic and social effects of improving tenure security, making institutions more accessible, and reducing the incidence and impact of conflict have been demonstrated by a number of studies. These studies also illustrate that, depending on the situation, a wide variety of arrangements can help bring about such improvements in tenure security. This section discusses some of these studies.

The World Bank's first self-standing project in support of land titling was implemented in Thailand, starting in the early 1980s. By awarding title to areas where there was great demand for credit that could only be satisfied by informal sources, the project helped increase credit access, land values, and investment (Feder, Onchan, and Raparla 1986). Following this, a large number of studies indicate that secure tenure can double investment and increase land values significantly (Deininger and Feder forthcoming). At the same time, there is growing evidence that full title is not always necessary to increase tenure security. In Ethiopia, for example, it was the perception of more secure tenure, rather than a formal title, that increased productivity-enhancing investments (Deininger, Ali, and Alemu 2008). That fact illustrates that formalizing ownership is not always needed to provide security, and that users' desire for more secure tenure often is expressed by their making investments (for example, in trees) that signal land ownership or by their willingness to pay for more secure arrangements (Deininger et al. 2003b). In all of these cases, it can be demonstrated that such investment translates into higher levels of productivity. The existence of significant benefits is supported by the fact that households would be willing to expend their own resources to increase tenure security (Deininger et al. 2008; Deininger, Ali, and Yamano 2008). This does not imply that title is irrelevant. For example, in Nicaragua—an environment characterized by high levels of tenure insecurity and pervasive land conflict—only a registered title, not less conclusive forms of evidence, significantly augmented the propensity to undertake productivity-enhancing investments and increased land values (Deininger and Chamorro 2004).

There is growing evidence in the literature that women's greater control of household assets affects consumption patterns, with households where women control greater shares of assets and land at marriage spending more on food and on children's welfare and education (de la Brière 1996; Doss 1996; Haddad, Hoddinott, and Alderman 1997; Fafchamps and Quisumbing 2002). Few studies, however, have focused explicitly on interventions specifically to enhance women's land access. In Honduras and Nicaragua, the amount of land women own has a significant and positive impact on food expenditure and on children's educational attainment (Katz and Chamorro 2002). The specific measures for giving women higher levels of tenure security often are quite simple technically, as in Vietnam (World Bank 2004), and they rely principally on effective dissemination and capacity building.

The ability to draw on a formal registry to verify landownership dramatically can reduce the cost of providing credit, compared with, say, microlending schemes. In the presence of effective demand for credit, formal land title that can be exchanged at very low cost (Brits, Grant, and Burns 2002) can improve landowners' access to credit (Feder et al. 1988). However, in view of the fact that the impact is likely to be differentiated by land size (Carter and Olinto 2003), the distributional aspects emphasized in a PSIA will need to be taken into account. The impact of more efficient means for transferring land title on the ability to access institutional credit in urban and peri-urban areas also is demonstrated impressively in transition countries. In the Kyrgyz Republic, for example, mortgage lending confined to urban areas has taken off quickly since land titling was initiated in 2001. Land-backed mortgages there already account for $4 million or 3 percent of GDP (Cook 2004).

There is growing consensus that, although giving land titles can reduce the cost of accessing credit for those with appropriate projects, it is by no means a silver bullet for everybody. Even if it will not affect the cost of getting credit, a higher level of tenure security can reduce a household's need to guard and secure its rights or to fend off conflicts. In Peru, greater security of informal rights increased participation in the formal labor market by as much as 50 percent, and it resulted in a sharp drop in household-based enterprises because it dispensed with the need for householders to stay at home as a precaution against others taking over their land (Field 2007). Evidence from Uganda illustrates that land-related conflicts impose high costs on society and land users in terms of foregone productivity and that, as is true in other African countries, legal and institutional innovations designed to reduce the potential for new conflicts and make it easier to resolve existing ones can have a high payoff, especially for women and widows who are much more likely to be affected (Berry 1997; Deininger and Castagnini 2006). In Mexico, establishing an accessible network of specialized courts to deal with land conflicts, together with strong emphasis on mechanisms for alternative conflict resolution, significantly helped reduce the number of conflicts and the danger that those conflicts would spill over into broader social and political unrest between communities (Zepeda 2000; World Bank 2001).

One factor that largely has been overlooked in the earlier literature on land issues is the contribution that even moderate improvements in land rights can make. Even though it gives neither unambiguous legal evidence nor precise boundary information, computerization of 20 million land records in Karnataka, India, helped reduce the scope for petty corruption and increased rural dwellers' confidence in government (Bhatnagar and Chawla 2004). The revenues obtained from the modest fees charged for copies of certified records enabled government to run a net profit, and the privately run e-kiosks used to retrieve land records have served as centers from which to provide a host of other services in rural areas. The fact that investments in securing tenure and facilitating land transactions can support themselves financially also has been illustrated in El Salvador where the registry generates significant profits.

The case of Mexico reveals the magnitude of the claims that can be involved and the attention that may need to be given to establishing appropriate mechanisms for conflict resolution, including informal ones. Following far-reaching legal changes, the government launched an intensive program to provide legal assistance that aimed to inform individuals and households affected by conflict or insecure land tenure about their rights. It also established a decentralized system of 42 agrarian courts covering the whole country. To make land conflict resolution more agile and accessible to beneficiaries, and at the same time preclude overburdening the judicial system, the court system was to accept only cases where prior efforts to arrive at a settlement using nonjudicial means of conflict resolution had failed. Despite the implied reduction in the number of cases, the judiciary spent more than four years dealing with the accumulated case backlog (Zepeda 2000). In fact, the ability to reduce the scope for arbitrary interference from village officials has been quoted as one of the key benefits to improving land registration in Mexico (World Bank 2001).

In Mozambique, the government could achieve the quick resettlement of only about 5 million people after the peace agreement because, instead of drawing up elaborate plans, it relied on local institutional mechanisms to resolve the conflicts that emerged. Subsequently, the right to occupancy by rural families, as well as a strong role for local institutions, was enshrined in the country's new land law (which was subjected to extensive public discussion and debate involving 50,000 individuals and 200 nongovernmental organizations) (Negrão 2002). Locals and outsiders recognized that the land law made a major contribution to social and economic stability (Tanner 2002). Similarly, in Ethiopia, the ability to redistribute land quickly made an important contribution to the rapid reintegration of demobilized soldiers into the economy (Ayalew, Dercon, and Krishnan 2000). Reliance on land rights granted through occupation and rapid resettlement was critical in Cambodia, where calls for land users to register their claims resulted in the lodging of almost 6 million initial claims. Observers repeatedly have identified the ability to deal with those claims quickly as an important element of postwar reconstruction (Zimmermann 2002).

LAND ACCESS AND LAND REFORM

Even though it also can contribute to better functioning of land rental markets, improving tenure security primarily will benefit those who already have access to land, thus providing limited benefits where the initial distribution of landownership is highly unequal. In such situations, greater emphasis on mechanisms to transfer land in a way that benefits the poor and helps bring land to better use will be important. Still, few topics have generated as passionate a discussion as the issue of land markets. To explore reasons and possible justifications for the intense interest, we consider rental and sales markets separately before focusing on redistributive land reform and appropriate land-use regulation.

Land Rental Markets

There is clear evidence in the literature that owner-operated family farms are more productive than wage labor–operated ones. Therefore, even though the desire to obtain an income comparable to the average in the nonagricultural sector will tend to increase average farm size over time as the economy grows, this implies that there may be less of a conflict between the objectives of equity and efficiency of land use than is commonly thought. In fact, the example of China, where the average household has a per capita endowment of less than 0.1 hectare distributed over 7–8 plots, demonstrates that small farmers can achieve very high levels of productivity and that broad land access can act as a social safety net that, in turn, helps drive growth in the nonfarm economy (Deininger and Jin 2005; Deininger, Jin, and Nagarajan 2009a). The superior performance of individual over collective ownership, irrespective of possible public goods that may be provided by the latter, has been demonstrated in the case of agricultural collectives throughout Eastern Europe before the 1990s (Lerman, Csaki, and Feder 2004).

Renting offers considerable opportunity to transfer land to more productive users. Because the adjustment costs are low, it is fairly easy to adjust the land area under cultivation to unexpected events without giving up ownership and the advantages associated with it. In addition to their low transaction costs, rental markets require only limited initial capital outlays, especially if rent is paid after the harvest or on a seasonal basis. Capital requirements of renting are thus relatively modest and can be adapted through a number of contractual arrangements (for example, sharecropping) to suit the needs of poor producers while providing them with working capital for production. Where owners are old, ill, without cash themselves, are noncultivating heirs, or want to take advantage of opportunities in nonagricultural markets or to migrate temporarily, renting can help ensure that the land freed up by such moves remains efficiently used. This tends to increase opportunities for landless or land-poor farmers, enabling them to gain access to land, accumulate experience, and possibly even make the transition to landownership. Even in situations where it was outlawed earlier, land rental can evolve rapidly if tenure security is high enough and opportunities exist. Renting is normally more effective in increasing productivity and targeting the poor than are government programs, and it can contribute to the evolution of nonfarm labor markets.

Although renting provides large productivity benefits, the associated equity benefits normally are lower than what could be obtained from landownership. In fact, policy makers have been concerned that rental opportunities may lead landlords to exploit tenants who have few alternative means of making productive use of their labor, offering them only the absolute minimum required to survive. Such behavior is well documented in history, although reductions in farm sizes through inheritance and government intervention as well as through economic growth and expansion of nonagricultural employment in many countries imply that the number of settings where a monopolistic landlord can drive down tenants' welfare to the absolute minimum may have decreased significantly. To prevent landlords from exploiting their tenants, governments in many countries impose limits on the amount of rent that can be charged by the landlord, or they protect tenants from eviction and strengthen their tenure security. To assess the potential impact of such interventions, three considerations are relevant.

First, implementing such restrictions is not easy. Rental restrictions obviously will work only if they combine limits on rents with protection of existing tenants. If they fail to do so, rent ceilings intended to improve the lot of poor tenants are likely to prompt landlords to evict them, and thus most probably worsen their situations—as was the case in Latin America and India following the imposition of tenancy laws there (Jaramillo 2001; Deininger, Jin, and Nagarajan 2008).[1] Although it has been shown that effectively implemented laws to increase the bargaining power of potential tenants (for example, by controlling rents and protecting them from eviction) have had a positive impact on equity and, in some cases, on productivity in the short term (Besley and Burgess 2000; Banerjee, Gertler, and Ghatak 2002), nothing in the literature accounts for reductions in land access as well as productivity that may arise from the fact that landowners who are concerned about potential loss of rights may keep land fallow or cultivate it with (less efficient) wage labor rather than rent it out.

A second consideration involves the impact produced by government-imposed rent ceilings and tenant security. Even if the laws have a positive impact in the short term, that impact may be confined largely to those people who are (or have been) renting at the time a law goes into effect, and over time the positive impact may be outweighed by a negative effect on land market activity and investment. Such negative effects occur because restrictions on land rental will reduce landlords' investment incentives and willingness to rent out their land. As a consequence, the laws will constrain access to land for farming and housing among those who did not have a contract when the legislation was enacted, thus reducing access to land by the landless and extremely poor.[2] Policies to increase the bargaining power of potential tenants by expanding the range of livelihood options available through access to infrastructure, nonagricultural labor markets, and so forth may be a more sustainable option for developing supportable growth in the long term.

Where rental restrictions continue to exist, a key policy issue is to find mechanisms that will help consolidate the equity gains without jeopardizing any future adjustments. Evidence from countries that have eliminated such restrictions suggests that doing so not only can improve access to land via rental, but also can increase households' participation in the nonfarm labor market and improve governance by reducing the discretionary power of bureaucrats.

The third consideration is that even where renting is unrestricted, the number of transactions, as well as their impact on equity and efficiency, will be affected by an array of factors. If households are not secure about their land rights or have limited information about land prices and contractual options, the "cost" of entering into rental contracts will increase (and thus reduce the number of transactions). Governments can help by increasing tenure security in a way that encourages rentals to nonrelatives, by educating households about the contractual options open to them, by reducing the cost of entering into rental contracts (for example, through standardized contracts), and by making information on prices in rental markets widely available to potential participants. Also, producers who rent land for only one year should not be able to make any significant investments or changes in land use. The fact that most rental contracts in developing countries are limited to the short term (that is, annual) reduces the scope for using land rental as an effective tool for generational and structural change in rural areas. Encouraging longer-term rentals will be an important avenue to bring about such change.

Land Sales Markets

Although transfer of land-use rights through rental markets can go a long way toward improving productivity and welfare in rural economies, the ability to transfer ownership is required to use land as collateral for credit and provides a basis for low-cost operation of financial markets. At the same time, many of the properties of land tend to increase its value above the present value of the profits earned from using it productively. For example, land values will increase with growing population density, the provision of public infrastructure, and greater land demand for nonagricultural purposes. Also, land is very useful as a real store of value in situations where the recurrence of inflation cannot be ruled out. All of those factors tend to cause land prices to deviate significantly from the "fundamental" present value of the profit stream derived from productive use of the asset.

If land commands a price that is higher than the present value of profits from its use, land sales transactions may be driven more by speculation than by the desire to improve concurrent productive use, implying that the scope for such markets to bring about productivity-enhancing land transfers will be more limited than is the case for rental markets. In particular, the potential for redistribution will be limited as poor people will not be able to finance mortgage-based land acquisition out of expected profits from agricultural production, even in the unlikely case that they are able to get access to a mortgage. This means that even if they have a productivity advantage over large operations based on wage labor, poor small farmers often are unable to translate their advantage into effective demand in land sales markets. All of these factors imply that land acquisition by the poor through the land sales market will be difficult. In cases where high inequality of landownership translates into large inefficiencies in land use together with marked inequality of opportunity, other types of intervention will be needed to bring about land redistribution.

Where they have neither neighbors and friends nor formal financial institutions to draw on, poor households hit by a sudden disaster or mishap (such as sickness, an accident in the family, or a bad harvest) may be forced to sell their land at prices below the fair market value just to ensure their survival. In the past, such "distress sales" have provided the mechanism through which unscrupulous moneylenders amassed vast amounts of land that they were not able to use productively. Even in today's developing countries, localized disasters can lead to sharp swings in land prices and can force those affected to sell their land at low prices during times of high supply and reduced demand, without being able to regain their assets when prices have recovered.

Those two factors imply that sales will be more affected by imperfections in other markets than rentals will be. Thus, in principle, government intervention to prevent outcomes that are undesirable could prevent losses by weak groups. In practice, however, it has been exceedingly difficult to implement such interventions for two reasons. First, distress sales of land and land price speculation are symptoms of broader structural issues. Passing legislation to make distress sales and speculation illegal without addressing their underlying causes may not prevent transactions, but may drive them into informality. Policies such as a general land tax, taxation of capital gains, or provision of safety nets in cases of distress will be more effective in addressing the root causes of distress sales and speculation, and thus are preferable to bans or restrictions on land markets if these are a concern and are to be prevented.

The second reason why governments may find it exceedingly difficult to implement interventions to prevent undesirable outcomes is that high levels of regulation may undermine the potential positive impact of land sales markets. Even if the imposition of regulations is well justified on conceptual grounds, restrictions will add to the transaction costs associated with land sales. In most developing economies, those land costs already are very high as a result of limits on private sector participation, lack of capacity, or the general level of implementation costs. Regulations thus may increase the cost of transferring land to a level that pushes transactions into informality, with all the associated undesirable consequences of such a move. Most restrictions on land sales also tend to undermine tenure security and investment incentives and to widen the scope for discretionary action by bureaucrats who can increase red tape significantly. The rationale for regulatory measures has to be weighed carefully, taking into account not only the conceptual justifications but also the ability to enforce the measures and the costs of compliance. As a consequence, trying to limit the operation of land sales markets often is unlikely to be the most effective means to achieve broader social objectives.

At the same time, in situations where local communities who are aware of the costs and benefits have imposed restrictions on the functioning of sales markets that are in compliance with the law (this is similar to condominium associations passing regulations that are binding on their membership), it will not be worthwhile to force liberalization because the benefits from doing so will be modest at best in most cases. Where such customary restrictions on land transfers to outsiders are maintained, often as a means to preserve identity and prevent members' landlessness, risks normally are high and there is little potential for efficiency-enhancing (as compared with speculative) land transactions. Once benefits from such restrictions decrease and cots of enforcing them consistently increase, the restrictions often are eliminated without the need for outside intervention.

Even where there are no restrictions on the operation of land sales markets, whether land sales to foreigners should be allowed is a hotly debated issue. Clearly, doing so offers a number of advantages, including better access to capital through foreign direct investment and the technology that normally comes with it. At the same time, there are many workable ways to obtain those advantages (for example, by offering long-term leases) without offering ownership; and if handled appropriately, those ways will not pose an obstacle to investment. Where issues of landownership are highly contentious politically, using such substitutes will be wiser than engaging in a very ideological debate that may detract from opportunities to improve the operation of land markets in other areas that are of greater importance for the poor.

Governments also have long been concerned about land fragmentation that increases the time it takes to get to plots and the amount of land needed for paths and roads. Plot sizes and access infrastructure can constrain the farmers' ability to mechanize their operations. To prevent fragmentation, minimum farm sizes and inheritance restrictions have been imposed, generally with little impact because they do not address the underlying reasons that lead farmers to fragment. Consolidation programs that aim to reduce the transaction cost that would arise if the affected parties were to resolve the issue based on bilateral negotiations (and that often provide infrastructure as well as spatial and land-use planning) have been successful, although extremely costly, in some developed countries and are now being experimented with in the European Union (EU) accession states. At lower levels of income, such programs are unlikely to have an important role to play. China provides an example: A family typically has eight to nine plots with an average per capita holding of 0.067 hectare. This high level of fragmentation has not prevented sustained growth in the past; in fact, administrative consolidation programs implemented in a number of places were not successful and quietly have been shelved (Deininger and Jin 2009). Reducing the transaction costs for sales by building capacity and allowing private sector participation will be a better option in such a situation.

Redistributive Land Reform

Where high levels of inequality in the landownership distribution and underutilization of vast tracts of productive land coexist with deeply rooted rural poverty, a case can be made for land redistribution to increase land-use productivity and provide poor people with greater access to land. As a number of successful land reforms show—for example, in Japan, the Republic of Korea, and Taiwan, China—the impact of such redistributive intervention can be far-reaching but also can meet political and practical obstacles. To maximize impact, it is important to choose appropriate instruments, normally relying on a combination of measures (such as divestiture of state lands, land taxation, expropriation with compensation, support for land markets, and direct negotiation) to maximize synergies, to be transparent about the cost, and to set clear goals and performance indicators that make it difficult to hijack the program for other ends.

Aware of the limited scope for sales markets to bring about improvements in equity or efficiency, policy makers often have tried to force the breakup of large farms by imposing ceilings on the amount of land that can be owned. If they could be enforced, such ceilings might help achieve redistribution in a decentralized fashion. In most cases, however, ceilings are circumvented easily. Especially if they stay in place for a long time, ceilings undermine financial markets because lenders who want to repossess land will be subject to similar restrictions; or if they are exempted from the restrictions, they will have greater difficulty disposing of the land. Ceilings also contribute to red tape and corruption. In India, ceiling legislation in place in most states for more than 30 years has failed to make available more than 2–3 percent of the total land area, even in the states that have the most land (Deininger, Jin, and Nagarajan 2009b). This implies that ceilings may have a useful role in increasing the cost of speculative land accumulation if they are set high enough (in thousands of hectares), as was the case in many countries of the former Soviet Union in the aftermath of decollectivization, but ceilings do not have a role in bringing about redistribution.

To maximize the possibilities for success while trying to minimize costs, land reform will have to complement—rather than try to substitute for—other avenues for accessing land. Governments that want to redistribute land will need to ensure that the poor can use rental and other mechanisms, ideally in a way that is integrated into the overall program design. For example, having rented land for one or two seasons could be made an eligibility requirement for a land reform grant. Imposing such a requirement could eliminate spurious claimants who later sell the land, and could give a boost to land rentals. Some African countries, including Zimbabwe, still have acts in force that prohibit or complicate subdivision of large farms—acts imposed by colonists as a means of preventing blacks from gaining access to land. Without scrapping that legislation, it will be much more difficult to use land reform as a catalyst for sustainable improvement in households' livelihoods.

If it is to be successful, land reform will need to give secure and transferable rights to land. Access to nonland assets, working capital, and a conducive policy environment are equally essential. The people who benefit from land reform need to be able to access output markets and credit, beneficiary selection needs to be transparent and participatory, and attention must be paid to the fiscal viability of land reform efforts (for example, by financing part of such reforms through proceeds from land taxation). Those requirements taken together imply (1) a need to integrate land reform into the broader context of economic and social policies intended to promote economic development and reduce poverty and (2) a need to implement programs in a decentralized way that encourages the maximum participation of potential beneficiaries and includes at least some grant element.

Given the relevance of the issue, the intense debate surrounding it, and the lack of recent success stories, the rigorous, open, and participatory evaluation of ongoing projects is particularly important. Evaluation, with proper capacity building and training, would be particularly important to assess the impact of different ways of making the land productive. The design of programs should be based on clear and transparent rules. It should provide incentives to maximize productivity gains—for example, by selecting underused lands or employing labor-intensive modes of land use. The rights given to beneficiaries need to be secure and unconditional to allow access to credit and the possible movement of beneficiaries' children out of agriculture as an occupation. Implementation of land reform programs should be decentralized, with potential beneficiaries and communities taking the lead in helping beneficiaries access social infrastructure, diversify against risks, and take advantage of other infrastructure (such as markets, technology, and credit). Efforts at land reform should complement existing mechanisms for land access, such as rental markets and nonland programs.

The cost of land reform can be substantial, with land itself normally accounting for only a faction (often about one-third) of the total cost. To justify such an expense, redistributive land reform needs to be viewed—and analyzed—as an investment in sustainable poverty reduction. There are many examples, especially in Latin America, where governments tried directly or indirectly to expropriate land from its owners and thus reduce the costs of land reform. Instead, such efforts often have reduced the sustainability of the reform by acquiring only marginal lands. In some cases, they have increased the cost of redistributive reform by reducing the overall security of property rights; lowering a country's attractiveness to foreign investors; and increasing rather than decreasing the level of social conflict, compared with the prereform level. In many of these cases, those results are likely to have increased the "cost" (including the losses sustained as a result of inappropriate policies) beyond what would have been required if the land had been compensated for directly, as in Nicaragua or Zimbabwe (World Bank 2003). This does not mean that landowners cannot be made to contribute to the cost of land reform, but a transparent way of doing so (perhaps a land tax) may be more acceptable than an indirect one.

During the last decades, efforts at land reform have transferred considerable amounts of land (table 15.1). Many countries have a legacy of unsuccessful or only partly successful attempts at land reform. Bringing to a good use the land

Table 15.1 Extent and Characteristics of Land Reforms

Economy	Area		Beneficiary households			
	Total area (thousands of hectares)	Arable land (%)	Number (thousands)	Rural households (%)	Area per household (hectares)	Period
Africa						
Egypt, Arab Republic of	390	15.4	438	10.0	0.89	1952–78
Kenya	403	1.6	34	1.6	11.85	1961–70
Zimbabwe	2,371	11.9	40	3.1	59.28	1980–87
Asia						
Japan	2,000	33.3	4,300	60.9	0.47	1946–49
Korea, Rep. of	577	27.3	1,646	45.5	0.35	1948–58
Philippines	1,092	10.8	1,511	24.2	0.72	1940–85
Taiwan, China	235	26.9	383	62.5	0.61	1949–53
Central America						
El Salvador	401	27.9	95	16.8	4.22	1932–89
Mexico	13,375	13.5	3,044	67.5	4.39	1915–76
Nicaragua	3,186	47.1	172	56.7	18.52	1978–87
South America						
Bolivia	9,792	32.3	237	47.5	41.32	1953–70
Brazil	13,100	11.3	266	5.4	49.32	1964–94
Chile	9,517	60.1	58	12.7	164.09	1973
Peru	8,599	28.1	375	30.8	22.93	1969–79

Sources: Scott 1976; Eckstein et al. 1978; McClintock 1981; Powelson and Stock 1987; El Ghonemy 1990; Grindle 1990; Hall 1990; Hayami, Quisumbing, and Adriano 1990; Prosterman, Temple, and Hanstad 1990.

that earlier was subjected to such efforts, dealing with the institutional legacy and the restrictions imposed by land reform legislation, and allowing beneficiaries from past land reforms to obtain working capital and skills that would enable them to make good use of their assets can produce a large payoff.

There are two reasons why careful monitoring and evaluation of land reform initiatives are warranted. First, even if the need for such initiatives is recognized, there are few good models on which to draw. To be most effective, interventions have to be refined and improved over time. Second, as history has clearly shown, land issues, and land reform in particular, are highly susceptible to political interference at all levels. Countering tendencies toward corruption by establishing a transparent and rigorous system of impact evaluation is the only way to ensure that corrupting forces are held in check, and it can inform program implementation on a continuing basis. Land reform also should avoid the temptation to focus only on beneficiaries; it should not neglect those people (such as farmworkers) who may be affected negatively by the reform. In Zimbabwe, for example, workers on farms that were subjected to redistribution constitute one of society's most vulnerable groups (Deininger, Hoogeveen, and Kinsey 2004). This suggests that it will be more important to monitor impacts on agricultural and nonagricultural activities and to be aware of direct and indirect effects beyond the range of direct beneficiaries.

Adopting Appropriate Land-Use Regulation

Governments have an array of fiscal and regulatory instruments at their disposal to promote land use that maximizes social welfare, to facilitate more effective public service provision, and to prevent harmful externalities (such as pollution) associated with specific land uses. The case for government intervention rests on its aggregate social benefit being larger than the cost of imposing such regulation, and on the presumption that public action can enforce regulations at minimum cost. This implies that zoning and other relevant land-use regulations will need to rely on a careful assessment of expected costs and benefits, based on local conditions, the way in which costs and benefits are distributed, and the implementation capacity available.

Concerning the distribution of costs and benefits, there are two considerations. On one hand, restrictions may be highly regressive, forcing small-scale landowners or the poor to make sacrifices (or even depriving them of their land) to the benefit of the wealthy. Foreign investment is one example of that. On the other hand, there may be longer-term effects that need to be taken into account.

Many developing countries still have regulations on their books that were imposed under completely different conditions (often by their colonial predecessors) and that may no longer serve their original purpose. Removing those laws may be opposed by comparatively small vested interests, possibly within the bureaucracy that uses them as a source of rents to derive handsome benefits.

Although it may require taking on these vested interests, doing away with outdated laws can produce significant benefits, especially for the poor.

Even if regulation is justified in some circumstances, it may not be necessary to implement it uniformly across all parts of a country. Attempts at land-use planning should start with mechanisms whereby costs will be borne and benefits obtained by local communities—a situation that might make a significant contribution toward more effective decentralization, especially because centralized bureaucracies often lack the level of local knowledge needed to provide services effectively or to monitor and supervise those people who are supposed to deliver them. Even where administrative capacity is lacking, many developing countries rely strongly on a regulatory approach, often with the result of encouraging discretionary bureaucratic behavior. Greater reliance on fiscal instruments, such as fees and taxes or tradable permits (possibly in collaboration with the private sector) can help reduce the requirements for compliance monitoring.

Provision of public infrastructure (roads, electricity, water, sewerage, and so forth) will increase land prices and thus benefit those who own the land. Providing these services is much cheaper in planned settlements than it is in unplanned ones. Therefore, zoning—especially in urban areas—whereby the government considers issues such as hydrology, congestion, air quality, traffic flow, and public safety is well justified. Governments also are justified in reaching decisions on such issues in an open and participatory manner and in using fees or other charges levied on landowners (for example, betterment levies) to finance public infrastructure.

Although fees can be assessed to pay for many such services, land taxes carry a number of conceptual advantages. Among other benefits, they cause minimal distortions and are less regressive than taxes levied on consumption, which normally hurt the poor; they tend to discourage speculative accumulation and encourage more intensive use of land; and they strengthen the accountability between local government and its constituency, thus enhancing fiscal discipline at the local level and making landowners pay for at least part of the benefits they receive from local government investments. Whereas the extent to which land taxes are used varies, revenues generally are well below their potential (Bird and Slack 2002). Greater emphasis on land taxes can have a significant impact on incentives for effective land use, on local government revenues, on the types and levels of public services provided, and on governance that helps prevent decentralization from degenerating into a competition for rents from the central level.

The state should have the right of compulsory land acquisition, with compensation, for broader public benefit (for example, to acquire land for roads). At the same time, the way in which many developing-country governments exercise this right—especially for urban expansion or to give to private entrepreneurs—can undermine existing and future owners' tenure security. In the many cases where little or no compensation is paid for the land taken, the equity impact is very negative, often leaving households landless. Anticipation of expropriation without compensation frequently leads landowners to sell their land in informal markets at low prices, thereby parting with a key asset at a fraction of its real value and encouraging unplanned development and urban sprawl that will make subsequent service provision more costly. Therefore, both the conditions under which land taking can be an option and the process for implementing it and determining compensation need to be defined clearly, and mechanisms for appeal must be available to prevent abuse.

Even though state ownership and management of land in many developing countries have failed to protect fragile lands or ensure optimal land management in peri-urban areas, large tracts of land continue to be held under such arrangements, with far-reaching implications. In peri-urban areas, unoccupied land of high potential often lacks investment and is subject to bureaucratic red tape, nontransparent processes of allocation, and corruption. Privatization of such land not only could yield significant amounts of resources for local governments, but also could increase investment and the effectiveness of land use. If public land has been occupied by poor people in good faith for a long time, and if significant improvements have been made, their rights should be recognized and formalized at a nominal cost. Where state land of high potential remains unoccupied, it should be auctioned off to the highest bidder, possibly with proceeds going to compensate original owners or to provide land and services to the poor.

Examples

Macroeconomic distortions have had a significant impact on land prices and activity in land rental markets. For example, land prices in Brazil dropped by as much as 70 percent in the early 1990s, thus making it easier to acquire land for productive purposes and providing the backdrop for a huge expansion in the government's land reform program that over a period of five years involved the purchase and redistribution of more land than had been acquired during the previous 30-year period (Reydon and Plata 2002).

In some developed countries, more than 70 percent of cultivated land is rented, partly because renting lowers capital requirements and offers users greater flexibility. Rental also was key for exchanging land in the initial phases of the transition to a market economy in Eastern European countries. It continues to have high potential where land plots were restituted to original owners who had little intention of farming, and where macroeconomic uncertainty and shallow financial markets slow the development of land sales markets. In most Eastern European countries, rental markets have achieved fundamental importance, especially where legal and institutional bases for land ownership are not in place. In Moldova, for example, the emphasis on leases enhanced the ability of the land market to develop rapidly (compared, for example, with Estonia, which had discouraged the use of leases). More than 80 percent of the 440,000 registered private farms in Moldova operate through some type of leasing arrangement (Lerman, Csaki, and Moroz 1998). At the same time, the purchase price of land is significantly above the capitalized value of agricultural profits because of government restrictions that drive up land prices, as well as speculation about the benefits of joining the EU and the demand by foreigners that might materialize with EU accession in both eastern and central European countries. Whereas peri-urban land markets and mortgage lending are starting to develop, agricultural land sales market activity remains low (Deininger, Sarris, and Savastano 2004).

In eastern Africa, temporary land transfers have a positive impact on equity, generally being pro-poor and beneficial for women (Place 2002). Both land sales and rentals appear to be relatively active and contribute to the equalization of operational or even ownership holdings of land, as confirmed in the case of Uganda (Carter and Wiebe 1990; Platteau 1996; Baland and Platteau 1998). Evidence from Uganda also suggests that activity in rental markets has increased sharply with economic liberalization and the associated growth of opportunities in the nonfarm economy; indeed, the share of households renting land increased from 13 percent in 1992 to 36 percent in 1999. In Uganda, by transferring land to more-productive producers, rental markets facilitate greater allocative efficiency in rural areas (Deininger and Mpuga 2009). Moreover, evidence from Ethiopia suggests that restrictions on land rental not only reduce the scope for more productive use of land, but also may constitute an effective obstacle to the development of the nonfarm sector because farmers who had taken on nonfarm jobs perceived a significantly higher risk of losing land through redistribution than did those who engaged in cultivation on their own land (Deininger et al. 2003a).

Rental markets, including those for long-term transactions that often are equivalent to sales, are active in West Africa, even though most are informal (Colin and Ayouz 2006). Land rental also has begun to emerge in Asian countries with egalitarian land distributions that recently liberalized land tenure, such as China and Vietnam. In China, where until recently rental was not needed because of frequent land reallocations, the share of households participating in land rental increased from 2.3 percent in 1995 to 9.4 percent in 2000. Moreover, 22.4 percent of households indicate that they would be willing to rent, given the current market rate; that implies that with economic development and the emergence of off-farm opportunities, there is considerable potential for further increases in rental market activity in China. Analysis illustrates that decentralized market transactions were better than state-sponsored redistribution in transferring land to households with higher productivity and, more surprising, they targeted the poor more effectively (Deininger and Jin 2002). The case of Vietnam, where similar increases in the incidence of land rentals are apparent, illustrates the differences between land sales and rental markets. The share of rural households who were renting increased from 3.8 percent in 1992 to 15.8 percent in 1998—an increase that was much more pronounced than the increase observed in sales markets. Although both renters and buyers were characterized by higher productivity, the magnitude of the effect was greater for the renters; and in situations where credit markets did not function well, there is some evidence of distress sales in that households who experienced significant income loss were more likely to sell land (Deininger et al. 2003b).

One would expect land rental markets to be particularly useful in equalizing land access in places such as Latin America, where the landownership distribution is known to be one of the most unequal in the world. To the contrary, in fact, rental activity in many countries of the region is quite limited. The low levels of rental activity may result from informational imperfections and the ensuing high transaction costs, as well as the impact of past restrictions on rental markets that have weakened landowners' perception of the security of their property rights. The impact of rental restrictions has been significant—in Colombia, for example, the amount of formally rented land decreased from 2.3 million hectares in 1960 to 1.1 million hectares in 1988, following the imposition of rent ceiling legislation (Jaramillo 2001). In 1998, more than a decade after rental restrictions had been lifted, tenancy rates in Colombia still were only about 11 percent, way below their 1960s level, highlighting the fact that restoring confidence in the property rights system takes time. Also, rental markets have been more effective than government-sponsored land reforms in bringing land to productive and poor producers (Deininger, González, and Castagnini 2004). That suggests that government-sponsored efforts at redistribution should try to build on complementary mechanisms rather than substitute for them.

Land sales markets in Latin America are relatively active, with average annual turnovers of 5.0 percent in Colombia, 2.0–3.5 percent in República Bolivariana de Venezuela,[3] 1.4–2.0 percent in Ecuador, and 1.0 percent in Honduras (Jaramillo 2001). Even in situations where activity is high, however, markets often are found to be highly segmented, which implies that sales transfer land either from large to large or from small to small producers but rarely across different farm-size groups. Such segmentation also is observed in Nicaragua (Carter and Chamorro 2002). In part, it results from the cost of subdividing large farms, high transaction costs, and credit market imperfections; in part, it is because of the lack of long-term financing available to the poor, which is associated with the continent's dualist landownership structure (Barham, Carter, and Sigelko 1995). What this tells us is that the purchase market does not operate as a mechanism of land access for labor-abundant, capital-constrained households, and that agents who are not capital constrained can translate relative technical efficiency into effective demand for more land (Carter and Salgado 2001).

Land reforms in Japan, Korea, and Taiwan, China—all of which were accomplished under external pressure—have helped improve welfare and often productivity (Jeon and Kim 2000). In India, abolition of the land rights of rent-collecting intermediaries is widely judged to have been very successful, in contrast to the more limited success of land ceilings and tenancy legislation (Appu 1997). In Kenya immediately after independence, the so-called One Million Acre Settlement Scheme distributed about 300,000 hectares of formerly white-owned large estates to small farmers, with positive economic results (Scott 1976). The program gathered momentum—for example, by farmers forming groups to purchase larger farms—but the government discontinued it, partly for political reasons (Kinsey and Binswanger 1993). Following independence in the early 1980s, Zimbabwe initiated a land reform program that redistributed about 250,000 hectares of land. Participation improved households' ability to accumulate assets, as well as their crop income, and reduced overall inequality (Gunning et al. 2000). The first phase of land reform in the Philippines, based on a 1972 law, benefited about 0.5 million households. Aided by the availability of green revolution technology, that measure led to significant improvements in household welfare (Otsuka 1991). Effects in terms of investment and human capital accumulation have been estimated as significant, positive, and long term (Deininger, Maertens, and Olinto 2001).

KEY CONSIDERATIONS FOR THE DESIGN OF MONITORING AND EVALUATION PROCESSES

The previous section outlined and exemplified general principles of land policy that can form the basis for a hypothesis to be explored quantitatively. To do so effectively, it will be necessary to take into account the explicit needs and priorities of stakeholders in an ongoing policy dialogue. It also will be necessary to rely on quantitative information that often is not available from standard household surveys. This section addresses both of these issues by first identifying some requirements to fit into an ongoing policy dialogue—or if there is no such dialogue, to generate discussion on a particular topic of high policy relevance. It then will discuss ways in which standard questionnaires can be enhanced and expanded to provide some of the information needed to make a meaningful and quantifiable contribution to such a dialogue.

Goals and Process Issues

A policy and social impact assessment can be part of a process. Given the political sensitivity of land issues, the fact that any reforms normally are perceived as a zero-sum game, and the desirability of having interventions backed by a consensus of the relevant stakeholders, monitoring and evaluation can perform a number of useful functions at different stages in the process of implementing land policy reform. The long-term nature of land-related interventions implies that, in some situations, analysis may be useful not only ex post (that is, after an intervention has been completed), but also at earlier stages so as to inform the policy dialogue.

Ex ante analysis of possible impacts can help assess the benefits to be expected from specific interventions, the way in which those benefits will be distributed among social groups, the existing demand for such interventions, and implications for cost recovery and institutional design. If accompanied by a broad and inclusive policy dialogue, analysis can help generate consensus and make it easier to implement reforms in a cost-effective fashion. In fact, existing analyses—for example, for Zambia (Jorgensen and Loudjeva 2004)—demonstrate the scope of evaluating the position of various stakeholders relative to various reform options and of using this analysis to explore new options that may not have been thought about earlier.

In preparation for interventions, an evaluation of pilot projects can help make the case for expansion of a particular model or can establish benchmarks for performance that can enhance accessibility and eliminate the opportunity for elite capture during full rollout. It also can enable policy makers to learn from differences in performance across regions or other units of analysis, to adjust implementation to fit realities on the ground, and often (as in the case of land reform) to improve the institutional design based on the innovations developed by beneficiaries.

Finally, ex post, it will be possible to draw broader lessons through rigorous quantitative assessment of costs incurred and benefits realized in a way that will improve the design of interventions in other settings or the integration of specific approaches into regular government programs (for example, to ensure the sustainability of titles that have been given out under a systematic program).

The examples of successful land policy reform noted above provide ample evidence that, despite popular perceptions to the contrary, land policy reform need not be a zero-sum game, an argument that analysis can strengthen by drawing on other countries' experiences. A legal basis that is less ambiguous and thus reduces conflict, the introduction of more efficient processes of land registration, and a reduction in the transaction costs of exchanging land or providing services related to it all are measures that will benefit those people who access land. Even redistributive land reform that helps make more productive use of land will leave society better off, and therefore it need not be a zero-sum game. Rigorous analysis can provide tangible evidence for such effects in a given country setting. Having a way to assess the impact during the implementation process based on demonstrated impact makes it easier to use political windows of opportunity, even with a less-than-perfect design, and to make corrections along the way. The methodology has to be rigorous but transparent and well communicated; especially in situations where local conditions differ significantly from those existing in other countries, analysis must incorporate the comparison of different design options as an integral element.

To make monitoring and evaluation as cost effective as possible, it will be necessary to build not only on other countries' experience and general principles, but also on existing survey data for the country under consideration. Fortunately, Living Standards Measurement Study–type surveys are now available for most of the countries where land-related analyses are likely to be undertaken. Even though the amount of land-related information in most of these surveys is limited, using such a survey can be helpful in a number of ways. First, it will enable policy makers to gather important prior information on the distribution of land among different income groups, the activity of land markets, and the productivity of land use in the country—data that can be used to guide the formulation of hypotheses and the design of the approach. Second, in some cases it may be possible to collaborate with national agencies to use existing samples as a basis for further analysis. One way to benefit from such a collaboration is to capitalize on natural complementarities between standard household surveys and analyses of land issues. Collecting good consumption data is very costly and cannot be done retrospectively. At the same time, given the importance of land in most households' asset portfolios, it will be quite easy to obtain information on land transactions and ownership some time earlier; in fact, most rural households know the amount of land they had when they started their families and are able to give a fairly accurate account of changes in ownership that have happened since then. An alternative is to build on the earlier survey to construct a panel, something that greatly enhances the scope for many types of analysis.

Even though preexisting data can help one understand the general situation in a country, quantitative and qualitative methods should be used in a way that reinforces each other. Because initial quantitative data need to be complemented by a much more detailed knowledge of the intervention concerned, interviews with focus groups and other types of qualitative information will be essential either to confirm or to formulate hypotheses on the potential and actual impact of a specific intervention (or the demand and need for it from different groups in the population) and to get a good understanding of the way things work in reality. To do so, it will be essential to obtain qualitative information from actual and potential beneficiaries in qualitative and focus-group interviews. Such assessments provide the flexibility to probe deeper into the reasons for certain patterns of behavior that appear to be inconsistent with expectations, and thereby to gain an understanding of "unexpected" behavior that cannot be obtained from only quantitative data (where it only would show up as "noise"). The areas selected for qualitative case study should be diverse enough to encompass the different segments of the target population (ethnic groups, large landowners, smallholders, and landless people; different types of land users, such as unreformed collectives and individual farmers; and so forth) and the intervention modalities that will be relevant for subsequent analysis. If combined with a stratification of interviews among groups who are likely to be affected by the intervention in different ways (for example, women and men, agricultural and nonagricultural workers), it will ensure that the research team gains an appreciation of an intervention's potential impacts, is able to formulate and prioritize hypotheses on this basis, and can identify questions that may be used to test these hypotheses quantitatively.

Two additional elements are critical and often overlooked in practical applications: (1) a thorough understanding of the local political economy and (2) knowledge of the proposed arrangements for implementing specific interventions. Unless evaluators clearly comprehend the outcomes expected from a specific intervention and (in the case of ex ante evaluation) the politically feasible ways of bringing the desired outcomes about or (in the case of ex post evaluation) the detailed procedures for project implementation (including how eligibility is defined and what application procedures have to be gone through), it will be difficult to conduct analysis that either will speak to the needs of policy makers or will provide a basis for robust methodological conclusions on project impact.

Methodological Considerations

For practitioners who may not be experts in land policy to use the opportunities to evaluate interventions fully in this area, the sections below contain a number of practical experiences and examples that can be helpful in translating general concepts into specific instruments and hypotheses.

Importance of a Baseline

It is now well understood that a solid baseline, comprising intervention and nonintervention areas, against which project outcomes can be compared is required if one is to have an understanding of an intervention's impact. In addition to providing a yardstick for assessing impact, the baseline also can help in designing strategies for intervention, in adapting them to conditions at hand, in assessing demand for intervention by different social groups, and in comparing different options to respond to this demand in the most effective way.

Need for a Control Group

The purpose of any good evaluation is to show that changes in outcomes observed among the target population can be attributed to a specific intervention rather than to other factors. For example, even if living standards, productivity, or other outcomes of interest may have declined among the target population during an intervention, the intervention may have helped beneficiaries avoid a greater decline (as observed in the control group) and thus had a positive impact. Similarly, even if one observes improved outcomes among the treatment group, these improvements may be attributable to a generalized increase in living standards or productivity, thus implying that the intervention had no impact. Naturally, members of the control group should be chosen to be as similar as possible to the group exposed to the intervention, something that will have to be reflected in the sample design adopted for the study.

Self-Selection of Beneficiaries

Many evaluations just compare the value of certain variables before and after an intervention, and fail to account for self-selection of beneficiaries—that is, the fact that programs are not distributed randomly among the eligible population. In the case of land titling, unless the program covers areas systematically and is based on random selection, it is likely that those who can benefit most from having a title (perhaps because they have high-quality land, have access to credit and other markets, or simply are more entrepreneurial and ready to take risks to reap higher rewards) are those who will make an effort to benefit from the intervention. This implies that any estimate of benefits that fails to control for such inherent differences will overstate the positive impact that can be obtained from expanding a project to other areas or groups who may lack such favorable initial conditions.

A number of options are available to deal with that issue. On conceptual grounds, if program implementation has not started already, the most rigorous way is to randomize—that is, to select beneficiaries/participants on a random basis among all of those who apply. Doing so is often not feasible in practice for political or ethical reasons. An attractive alternative if there is a limited overall budget is to decide ex ante about areas where a program will be introduced and other areas that will serve as a control. To some extent, such phasing also can work for interventions (such as changes to the law) that have national outreach but require complementary inputs (for example, specific dissemination or establishment of local offices or land tribunals). If the goal is to evaluate a program that already has been implemented without the possibility of generating additional data, instrumental variables techniques can be used. This approach requires evaluators to identify good instruments that are highly correlated with program participation but that do not affect outcomes—something that may be difficult if criteria for program eligibility are not tightly defined or enforced. Part of the challenge can be overcome by the method of propensity score matching that increasingly is being used for project evaluations in a wide range of settings (Ravallion 2001).

Questionnaire Design

Changes in rural households' ability to access land or changes in their tenure security will have an impact on labor market participation as well as other variables that at first sight may seem to be quite unrelated to land and in some cases may not have been anticipated by project staff. In Peru, for example, regularizing informal settlements had little impact on households' use of land as collateral (the main benefit expected from the project), but it significantly increased participation in formal labor markets—an impact that was rather unexpected (Field 2007). Households' labor market position and their ability to access other factors of production also have been shown to affect their decisions to participate in certain types of programs, such as farm privatization in countries of the former Soviet Union (Lerman, Csaki, and Feder 2002). Surveys that focus on land-related issues without putting them into a broader framework of household behavior may arrive at erroneous conclusions. Analysts will have to think at the outset about how expected impacts are likely to come about, and then adopt and implement a questionnaire that is broad enough to capture those variables in addition to ones that are narrowly related to land. If there is a need to trace the gender-differentiated impact of interventions, it may be necessary to split the household questionnaire into two parts, one administered to males and one administered to females in the household.

Also, to be able to draw out the distributional implications of different interventions, it is essential to have information on consumption that is detailed enough to allow construction of an expenditure aggregate that can be related to a nationally representative survey and to the poverty line. Collecting this information can increase the cost significantly, given the time involved in administering expenditure modules. If a household survey is available, it may be possible to reduce survey costs by using the information from that source to identify a set of variables that can predict consumption and to use those rather than include a full consumption module in the survey.

Sample Design

If the purpose is to evaluate the impact of an intervention targeted at a specific subset of the population, it may be more efficient to design the sample in a way that increases the probability of this subgroup being selected to economize on survey costs. Also, a number of phenomena that may be of interest (for example, land conflicts or land transactions) are infrequent in the overall population; with a limited budget, it often will be cost effective to stratify the sample into, say, households with and without conflict. Although doing so does not preclude use of standard procedures for selecting first-stage sampling units, it will require conduct of a listing in the selected primary sampling units, and the listing then will serve as the basis for selecting a household sample in given proportions and for constructing sampling weights.

Specific Elements of Questionnaire Design

The paucity of land-related surveys that can be drawn on may impose a constraint on the ability to design a good survey instrument and subsequently may limit the scope for policy-relevant analysis. To deal with this issue, the next subsections discuss the elements of a land-related questionnaire that will provide the information needed for much of the analysis discussed earlier. Because the design of standard household questionnaires is covered in great detail in the available literature (for example, Grosh and Glewwe 2000), we focus here on issues specifically related to land. Naturally, only some of the modules discussed will be of relevance in any given situation, so it is up to the team to make the appropriate selection and combine the information from the land modules with that from the rest of the instrument, particularly production and credit.

Household Questionnaire

- *Plot characteristics:* In most cases, there are significant differences between the types of tenure under which the land is held (leasehold, freehold, customary, without any certificate), the modalities through which it was acquired (purchased, inherited, cleared, or simply occupied), and the type of documentation that is available to demonstrate ownership (title, sales receipt, tax receipt). Therefore, it will be necessary to collect information on a plot-by-plot basis, that is, to create a "plot roster." If there are gender differences in land rights, this section of the survey also will need to discover in whose name documents to any specific plot are issued and if the current user (or the owner) has the right to transfer land through lease, sale, mortgage, and so forth. In addition to tenure characteristics, plot-wise information on land quality and topography will be of great importance. Of course, to the extent that one expects plot-specific land tenure arrangements to affect productivity, it will be essential to ensure that information on production is obtained at the same level of disaggregation and can be linked to specific plots.
- *Land-related investment:* Historically, one of the main reasons for introducing more secure property rights has been the incentives this provides for increased investment in maintaining the productivity of the land. At the same time, land-related investments such as fences or even trees can be used as a means to establish and secure property rights in an environment where enforcement by the state is perceived to be ineffective. Surprisingly, treatment of this issue in many questionnaires (and as a consequence, the analysis on the topic) is quite weak and could be strengthened considerably by observing a few basic principles. Even though the details of investments to be considered are likely to be specific to any given region or country, the basic categories of perennials, simple measures to maintain soil fertility for more than one year (establishing soil bunds to stop water runoff and erosion, leveling, drainage, irrigation, destoning, mulching), and the building of structures attached to a particular piece of land (animal sheds, processing facilities, wells, and so forth) are likely to apply for most situations. Also, it will be necessary to distinguish the stock of structures at any point in time from the amount of resources spent to maintain them, and to assess the two separately. Finally, especially if the aim is to assess the impact of an exogenous intervention on land-related investment, one will need to have information on at least two time periods. Crafting a good investment section in the questionnaire requires familiarity with local practices, but will enable the team to assess the impact of tenure security on different types of investment (for example, visible and invisible ones); and if an

appropriate production section is included, it will allow an empirical estimation of the impact of these investments on productivity.

- *Hypothetical question on land prices:* Even in environments where the frequency of land market transactions is limited, households normally have a good idea of the price they could receive if they were to sell or rent their land to others. This information then can be used to arrive at values for specific plot characteristics in a hedonic regression that would provide an estimate for the change in land values caused by restrictions on marketability or the benefits of having more secure tenure. This not only will provide a rough-and-ready estimate that can be of great interest to policy makers concerned about designing a system that is self-sustainable, but also will make it possible to assess variations in the ability to pay between different groups of the population. If a project is considering awarding or updating specific titles or certificates, it may be worth complementing this with direct questions about households' demand for (updated) certificates, and their willingness to pay for them at a plot level, in order to avoid some of the biases that may affect hedonic estimates.
- *Gender issues:* Women's rights to control land and benefit from the associated income streams often are constrained by law or, in cases where the law mandates gender equality, by actual practice on the ground. In situations where that is relevant, it will be important to gather more detailed information about who normally works on a plot, who determines what inputs to apply, and who decides how output is disposed of or benefits from the proceeds. If their spouse dies or divorces them, women in many customary systems will be unable to obtain ownership rights to their part of the land, or even to keep using it in some cases. Because this certainly will affect their longer-term economic security, and because there may be clear differences between the letter of the law and its actual implementation, including questions on what they perceive to be the situation under the current regime may be important. One way to check for differences in productivity between plots that are held by males and those that are held by females is to learn whether a piece of land that was inherited came from the husband's or the wife's side. However, systematically to uncover gender differences in inheritance and the extent to which these differences may be compensated by transfer of nonland assets, it will be necessary to ask about the actual and planned inheritance of all the parents' assets among all their children.
- *Land conflict:* As discussed above, to obtain reliable estimates of conflict-related issues with a reasonable sample size, oversampling of households affected by conflict will be necessary. In situations where the level of conflict is high enough, a simple question on whether a plot is currently under conflict can help the surveyor identify by how much conflict reduces land values, but it will not reveal too much about the dynamics of the phenomenon. To do the latter, additional information will be needed on whether there was ever a conflict, when it started, what the consequences were, how

it was tackled, what its formal and informal costs were, and when (if ever) the conflict was resolved. Again, this information necessarily will be plot-specific. Aggregating plot-level information to reveal the incidence of land-related conflict at the household level (for example, by gender or poverty status) can be a key contribution of land-related analysis. It will not be possible to ascertain the productivity impact of land conflict—something of great interest to policy makers—unless plot-level data are available.

- *Land accumulation trajectory:* Even in environments where land markets are thin, households' lifetime trajectories of land accumulation can provide a good source of at least descriptive information on how their land stocks have evolved over time. Although the econometric analysis that can be performed using this information will be constrained by the availability of other variables from the same time period, having this information will enable researchers to ascertain (1) how big macroshocks have affected landownership, (2) whether only those with higher levels of assets at the beginning of the period were able to accumulate land, and (3) the extent to which tenants were able either to accumulate land or to make the transition to landownership.
- *Current land rentals:* Information on land that is rented in and rented out can be collected quite easily using the same plot-level format that is used for or the land currently cultivated. For he former, obtaining characteristics of the current landlord (total amount of land owned, social stratum, residence, and occupation) and details of the rental contract (fixed or share rent, registered, duration, and date of inception) will provide the basis for a much richer characterization of land rental markets. Symmetrically, in the latter case it will be of interest to obtain details about the social and economic characteristics of the renter and when the land in question was leased out to this or other tenants. Having information on the title status of plots that were rented out, compared with plots that were self-cultivated, can be important in assessing whether insecure tenure limits households' abilities to engage in land transactions.
- *Current land sales:* Whereas plots that have been purchased automatically will appear in the "plot roster" unless they have been sold or otherwise lost in the meantime, this is not the case for land that has been sold or transferred in other ways. Even though meaningful analysis of land sales markets almost invariably will require panel data to control for initial conditions and characteristics, retrospective questions can provide some substitute, especially if it is possible to control for other variables (such as shocks).
- *Hypothetical land market transactions:* Although time limits on tenancy may lead to a "rotation" of tenants that is not consistent with maximizing productivity and investment, legislation that increases the security of sitting tenants while prohibiting them from subleasing may reduce the supply of land available for potential tenants. Similarly, high transaction costs resulting from cumbersome procedures that have to be complied with may drive

a wedge between what tenants pay and what landlords receive, thus possibly rationing out a significant number of potential tenants. Providing quantitative evidence on the impact of such restrictions (and thus the benefits of abolishing them) requires asking hypothetical questions on whether households have been trying to participate in rental markets but could not find any land on offer or whether they would change the amount of land rented if prices were to change. Similarly, if the government plans to conduct a program of redistributive land reform, exploring (1) potential beneficiaries' willingness to expend resources to obtain land; (2) whether they have a preference for land, compared with other assets that are of similar cash value; and (3) their plans for using such land can provide valuable insights regarding the design and targeting of such a program.

- *Land takings:* An issue of great importance (especially in peri-urban settings) that often has not been given the attention it deserves relates to the taking of land by the local or central bureaucracy. The lack of attention paid is partly because such takings can constitute a major source of revenue, if not corruption, and because one is unlikely to encounter a large number of such incidents in a simple random sample, which implies the need to draw a sample specifically from the cases where such taking occurred. If it is possible, however, obtaining information on the "transaction costs" involved (that is, the difference between the net value of compensation received by owners and the price paid by current users) and the use to which these lands are put currently could help (1) reduce the red tape outside investors have to battle, (2) enhance accountability and put local government finances on a sounder and more sustainable footing, (3) question the myth that the only way to attract outside investment is for government to expropriate (or nationalize) land, and (4) highlight to what extent disposal of land that already has been acquired by the state would provide an opportunity to meet needs for making land available to investors.
- *Administrative issues:* Considerable knowledge on the actual collection of land taxes and other fees can be gained by ascertaining the amount paid directly by the households concerned. Similarly, asking respondents whether under current circumstances they think it will be worthwhile to pay for updating registry records, surveys, and other land-related documentation can clarify the extent to which the services that should be provided by land administration respond to clients' needs and whether clients trust the land administration institutions. Such evidence can be invaluable in making the case for administrative simplification and streamlining based on client demand. If the interest is to assess ex post the impact of specific reforms that have been undertaken, asking households to describe their confidence in land certificates or the land administration institutions now and before the reforms can elicit very useful information for policy analysis. In environments where government still has the ability to redistribute land or to intervene in land markets in other ways, asking households about

their perceived level of tenure security (for example, whether they expect to have the same plot of land in five years' time) has helped complement more "objective" measures of tenure security (such as titles) and has revealed to what extent possession of such documents is associated with greater perceived tenure security.

- *Knowledge about laws:* One characteristic of many developing countries is that it is relatively easy to pass laws relating to land, but that there is often little attention to disseminating and implementing these laws or to ensuring that old legislation that may contain contradictory provisions is duly abrogated. A quick and simple way to expose such gaps is to assess households' understanding of the law—for example, by asking a series of simple questions concerning key provisions. Given that it is these beliefs that are likely to affect day-to-day behavior, showing that households (or men and women in specific households) either are not aware of or are confused about key provisions of land-related legislation can help demonstrate the need for increased dissemination and can help identify the target groups for such an effort. Moreover, having the same questions asked independently of leaders at the village level can offer valuable hints as to how such information-disseminating efforts should be structured.

Community Questionnaire

Given that there can be significant differences in the way in which regulations are implemented at the local level, a well-thought-out community questionnaire can elicit a wealth of information on the arrangements, regulations, and constraints that normally are taken as given by individual economic actors, and on recent changes in these. Information about the recent changes can be of great importance in explaining changes in behavior. From a more pragmatic perspective, comparing actual rules to households' perceptions about what those rules should be will make it possible to assess the extent to which individuals (or village officials) are aware of the legal provisions, thus enabling analysts to make the case for greater efforts at dissemination. We note that community surveys will be even more context-specific than are household questionnaires,[4] and again we limit discussion to variables that go beyond what is covered in standard reference works.

- *Institutional infrastructure for land administration:* Exploring the way in which land administration services are delivered at the local level (staffing, fee structures, accessibility) and how the quality of delivery is perceived will enable researchers to overcome the supply-side focus of many current studies that give scant, if any, attention to the user's perspective. Because only a fraction of households is likely to use these services at any point in time, a community survey is an appropriate tool for gathering this information. It can be complemented by questions on obligations incurred by property owners (for example, tax rates, the way taxes are assessed and change over time, zoning, and so forth) that are the same for all owners within the community. One particularly interesting point is that it will be relatively easy retrospectively to ascertain changes in these variables over time, something that will be especially relevant where there have been far-reaching shifts in social, political, and institutional environments. Identifying associated changes in the functions that are performed by local and central institutions, their staffing and funding, and the accessibility of these services to the local population can help paint a much more detailed picture of institutional change that is the precondition for gaining a more precise estimate of its impact.

- *Rules and land-related regulations:* Mechanisms for inheritance, land access for women, and conversion of land (from public to private or from agricultural to nonagricultural uses) normally vary significantly across localities, and in some instances, local communities impose restrictions on transferability (through rental or sale). The existence of such rules, and their changes over time, will have clear implications for land-use decisions by individual households. Exploring the impact of these rules often can be combined with a general assessment of the level of activity and direction of land market activity at the local level that can be compared with household-level assessments.
- *Administrative actions:* A household questionnaire normally will elicit information on whether a specific household was affected by redistribution, land taking, or conflict. However, even having only very few expropriations without compensation is likely to affect everyone's tenure security significantly. Because randomly administered household questionnaires may not give enough information on whether such events took place, it will be critical to seek information on them at the community level.
- *General governance:* In many settings, a key matter of interest is how the functioning of land administration institutions is affected by general administrative or institutional reforms (for example, higher levels of decentralization or having village leaders elected democratically rather than appointed by central government). Providing informed estimates of the impact of such measures will require greater familiarity with the underlying processes, but having information on what changes happened when (as can be obtained through a community questionnaire) is essential.
- *Leaders' knowledge about laws:* Local leaders frequently have considerable discretion in decisions regarding land management. Even though knowledge about the applicable legal provisions is not enough to prevent abuse, lack of such knowledge will make it very difficult to ensure that the laws are applied in a consistent manner, especially in situations where laws have changed recently. Testing leaders' knowledge with a number of straightforward questions is one way to discover whether there may be a need for greater efforts at dissemination and capacity building at the policy level.

Furthermore, because knowledge of or ignorance about legal provisions is likely to affect land-related actions without influencing economic outcomes, it can serve as an instrument.

CONCLUSIONS

Policy reforms in the area of land access and distribution are attractive candidates for analysis in a number of respects. They clearly have far-reaching distributional implications, and they consist of rather discrete interventions or policy changes that lend themselves to before-and-after analysis of the type that can be accommodated within the PSIA framework. Such reforms frequently are controversial politically and need to be sustained for a period of time that transcends the tenure of individual governments, which implies that information from PSIAs can be used to build consensus, establish clear performance indicators, and monitor these over time so as to limit the scope for using the program for political purposes.

To maximize the value and impact of land-related monitoring and impact evaluation, it will be important to be aware of the consensus on principles that has been reached and to observe a few basic methodological principles. Drawing on some of the policy design experiences discussed in this chapter can help policy makers reduce the costs and increase the credibility of whatever analysis is performed. To have an impact on policy, a PSIA will have to count on the input from various stakeholders to identify the "right" questions and to develop indicators that can command a broad consensus. It also will have to be conducted, and its results communicated, in a transparent and credible way, timed to fit into the broader policy discussion. Although it is a necessary condition, getting the methodology right is not sufficient to affect policy. If it enables task managers to focus more of their attention and energy on achieving the program goals, this chapter will have achieved its purpose.

NOTES

1. The numbers involved could be quite large. For example, tenancy reforms in India are estimated to have been associated with the eviction of more than 100 million tenants, causing the rural poor to lose about 30 percent of the total cultivated area (Appu 1997).
2. The impact is very clearly illustrated in the case of Mumbai, India. As a consequence of rent controls, Mumbai has the highest real estate prices in the world. These prices force people to make longer commutes (thereby raising their costs, adding to pollution, and so forth), and they make it more difficult for entrepreneurs to establish a business or create jobs. In rural areas, the poor and landless people are forced to rely on informal markets, possibly through subleasing from protected tenants, and that deprives them not only of the protection that the law intends to provide but also forces them into illegal activity (Bertaud, Buckley, and Owens 2003).

3. Activity varies considerably across regions. Annual turnover of land amounts to as much as 12.0 percent in recently colonized areas, but is about 2.5–3.0 percent for private lands and only 1.5–2.0 percent for lands that had been subject to agrarian reform (Delahaye 2001).
4. Survey instruments will need to be subjected to a thorough pretest. Whereas it is possible to obtain a surprisingly large and accurate amount of information even from retrospective questions in situations where the definition of community is unambiguous and there are administrative records on which respondents can draw to fill in the survey instrument, this will be impractical in situations where these conditions do not hold.

REFERENCES

Appu, Padma Bhushan P. S. 1997. *Land Reforms in India: A Survey of Policy, Legislation and Implementation.* New Delhi, India: Vikas Publishing.

Ayalew, Daniel, Stefan Dercon, and Pamila Krishnan. 2000. "Demobilisation, Land and Household Livelihoods: Lessons from Ethiopia." Working Paper WPS/00/25. Centre for the Study of African Economies, Oxford, U.K.

Baker, M. 2001. "Property Rights by Squatting: Land Ownership Risk and Adverse Possession Statutes." *Land Economics* 77 (3): 360–70.

Baland, Jean-Marie, and Jean-Philippe Platteau. 1998. "Division of the Commons: A Partial Assessment of the New Institutional Economics of Land Rights." *American Journal of Agricultural Economics* 80 (3): 644–50.

Banerjee, Abhijit V., Paul J. Gertler, and Maitreesh Ghatak. 2002. "Empowerment and Efficiency: Tenancy Reform in West Bengal." *Journal of Political Economy* 110 (2): 239–80.

Barham, Bradford, Michael R. Carter, and Wayne Sigelko. 1995. "Agro-Export Production and Peasant Land Access: Examining the Dynamic between Adoption and Accumulation." *Journal of Development Economics* 46 (1): 85–107.

Berry, Sara. 1997. "Tomatoes, Land and Hearsay: Property and History in Asante in the Time of Structural Adjustment." *World Development* 25 (8): 1225–41.

Bertaud, Alain, Robert Buckley, and Kathryn Owens. 2003. "Is Indian Urban Policy Impoverishing?" Unpublished manuscript. World Bank, Washington, DC.

Besley, Timothy J., and Robin Burgess. 2000. "Land Reform, Poverty Reduction, and Growth: Evidence from India." *Quarterly Journal of Economics* 115 (2): 389–430.

Bhatnagar, Subhash, and Rajeev Chawla. 2004. "Bhoomi: Online Delivery of Land Titles to Rural Farmers in Karnataka, India." Paper presented at the World Bank International Conference on Scaling Up Poverty Reduction, Shanghai, China, May 25–27.

Bird, Robert M., and Enid Slack. 2002. "Land and Property Taxation around the World: A Review." Paper presented at the World Bank Land Workshop, Budapest, Hungary, April 3–6.

Bourguignon, François, and Luis Pereira da Silva, eds. 2003. *The Impact of Economic Policies on Poverty and Income Distribution: Techniques and Tools.* New York: Oxford University Press.

Brits, Anne-Marie, Chris Grant, and Tony Burns. 2002. "Comparative Study of Land Administration Systems with Special Reference to Thailand, Indonesia and Karnataka (India)." Paper presented at the World Bank Regional Workshops on Land Policy Issues, Asia Program, Phnom Penh, Cambodia, June 4–6.

Carter, Michael, and Juan Sebastian Chamorro. 2002. "The Economics of Liberalizing Segmented Land Markets: Theory and Evidence from Nicaragua." Paper presented at the American Agricultural Economics Association Meeting, Chicago, IL.

Carter, Michael R., and Pedro Olinto. 2003. "Getting Institutions 'Right' for Whom? Credit Constraints and the Impact of Property Rights on the Quantity and Composition of Investment." *American Journal of Agricultural Economics* 85 (1): 173–86.

Carter, Michael R., and Ramón Salgado. 2001. "Land Market Liberalization and the Agrarian Question in Latin America." In *Access to Land, Rural Poverty, and Public Action*, ed. Alain de Janvry, Gustavo Gordillo, Jean-Philippe Platteau, and Elisabeth Sadoulet, 246–78. Oxford, U.K.: Oxford University Press.

Carter, Michael R., and Keith Wiebe. 1990. "Access to Capital and Its Impact on Agrarian Structure and Productivity in Kenya." *American Journal of Agricultural Economics* 72: 1146–50.

Colin, Jean P., and Mourad Ayouz. 2006. "The Development of a Land Market? Insights from Côte d'Ivoire." *Land Economics* 82 (3): 404–23.

Cook, Edward. 2004. "Kyrgyzstan Land and Real Estate Registration Project." Paper presented at the World Bank Workshop on Implementing Lessons from the Policy Research Report, Washington, DC.

Deininger, Klaus. 2003. *Land Policies for Growth and Poverty Reduction.* Washington, DC: World Bank.

Deininger, Klaus, and Daniel A. Ali. 2008. "Do Overlapping Property Rights Reduce Agricultural Investment? Evidence from Uganda." *American Journal of Agricultural Economics* 90 (4): 869–84.

Deininger, Klaus, Daniel A. Ali, and Tekie Alemu. 2008. "Impacts of Land Certification on Tenure Security, Investment, and Land Market Activity: Evidence from Ethiopia." Policy Research Working Paper 4764. World Bank, Washington, DC.

Deininger, Klaus, Daniel A. Ali, and Takashi Yamano. 2008. "Legal Knowledge and Economic Development: The Case of Land Rights in Uganda." *Land Economics* 84 (4): 593–619.

Deininger, Klaus, Daniel Ayalew, Stein Holden, and Jaap Zevenbergen. 2008. "Rural Land Certification in Ethiopia: Process, Initial Impact, and Implications for Other African Countries." *World Development* 36 (10): 1786–812.

Deininger, Klaus, and Raffaella Castagnini. 2006. "Incidence and Impact of Land Conflict in Uganda." *Journal of Economic Behavior & Organization* 60 (3): 321–45.

Deininger, Klaus, and Juan Sebastian Chamorro. 2004. "Investment and Income Effects of Land Regularization: The Case of Nicaragua." *Agricultural Economics* 30 (2): 101–16.

Deininger, Klaus, and Gershon Feder. Forthcoming. "Land Registration, Governance, and Economic Development: Evidence and Implications for Policy." *World Bank Research Observer.*

Deininger, Klaus, María A. González, and Raffaella Castagnini. 2004. "Comparing Land Reform and Land Markets in Colombia: Impacts on Equity and Efficiency." Policy Research Working Paper 3258. World Bank, Washington, DC.

Deininger, Klaus, Hans Hoogeveen, and Bill H. Kinsey. 2004. "Economic Benefits and Costs of Land Redistribution in Zimbabwe in the Early 1980s." *World Development* 32 (10): 1697–709.

Deininger, Klaus, and Songqing Jin. 2002. "Land Rental Markets as an Alternative to Government Reallocation? Equity and Efficiency Considerations in the Chinese Land Tenure System." Policy Research Working Paper 2930. World Bank, Washington, DC.

———. 2005. "The Potential of Land Markets in the Process of Economic Development: Evidence from China." *Journal of Development Economics* 78 (1): 241–70.

———. 2009. "Can Migration Be a Pathway Out of Poverty? Evidence from Rural China." Unpublished manuscript. World Bank, Washington, DC.

Deininger, Klaus, Songqing Jin, Berhanu Adenew, Samuel Gebre-Selassie, and Mulat Demeke. 2003a. "Market and Non-Market Transfers of Land in Ethiopia: Implications for Efficiency, Equity, and Non-Farm Development." Policy Research Working Paper 2992. World Bank, Washington, DC.

Deininger, Klaus, Songqing Jin, Berhanu Adenew, Samuel Gebre-Selassie, and Berhanu Nega. 2003b. "Tenure Security and Land-Related Investment: Evidence from Ethiopia." Policy Research Working Paper 2991. World Bank, Washington, DC.

Deininger, Klaus, Songqing Jin, and Hari K. Nagarajan. 2008. "Efficiency and Equity Impacts of Rural Land Market Restrictions: Evidence from India." *European Economic Review* 52 (5): 892–918.

———. 2009a. "Determinants and Consequences of Land Sales Market Participation: Panel Evidence from India." *World Development* 37 (2): 410–21.

———. 2009b. "Land Reforms, Poverty Reduction, and Economic Growth: Evidence from India." *Journal of Development Studies* 45 (4): 496–521.

Deininger, Klaus, Miet Maertens, and Pedro Olinto. 2001. "Redistribution, Investment, and Human Capital Accumulation." Unpublished manuscript. World Bank, Washington, DC.

Deininger, Klaus, and Paul Mpuga. 2009. "Land Markets in Uganda: What Is Their Impact and Who Benefits?" In *The Emergence of Land Markets in Africa: Impacts on Poverty, Equity, and Efficiency,* ed. Stein T. Holden, Keijiro Otsuka, and Frank M. Place. Washington, DC: Resources for the Future.

Deininger, Klaus, Alexander Sarris, and Sara Savastano. 2004. "Do Rental Markets Transfer Land to More Productive Producers? Evidence from 6 Central European Countries." *Quarterly Journal of International Agriculture.*

de la Brière, Bénédicte Leroy. 1996. "Household Behavior toward Soil Conservation and Remittances in the Dominican Republic." Unpublished manuscript. World Bank, Washington, DC.

Delahaye, Olivier. 2001. *Politicas de Tierras en Venezuela en el Siglo XX.* Caracas, República Bolivariana de Venezuela: Fondo Editorial Tropykos.

de Soto, Hernando. 2000. *The Mystery of Capital: Why Capitalism Triumphs in the West and Fails Everywhere Else.* New York: Basic Books.

Di Tella, Rafael, Sebastian Galiani, and Ernesto Schargrodsky. 2007. "The Formation of Beliefs: Evidence from the Allocation of Land Titles to Squatters." *Quarterly Journal of Economics* 122 (1): 209–41.

Doss, Cheryl R. 1996. "Testing among Models of Intrahousehold Resource Allocation." *World Development* 24 (10): 1597–609.

Eckstein, Shlomo, Gordon Donald, Douglas Horton, and Thomas Carroll. 1978. "Land Reform in Latin America: Bolivia, Chile, Mexico, Peru and Venezuela." Staff Working Paper 275. World Bank, Washington, DC.

El Ghonemy, Mohamad R. 1990. *The Political Economy of Rural Poverty: The Case for Land Reform.* New York: Routledge.

Fafchamps, Marcel, and Agnes R. Quisumbing. 2002. "Control and Ownership of Assets within Rural Ethiopian Households." *Journal of Development Studies* 38 (6): 47–82.

Feder, Gershon. 2002. "The Intricacies of Land Markets: Why the World Bank Succeeds in Economic Reform through Land Registration and Tenure Security." Paper presented at the Conference of the International Federation of Surveyors, Washington, DC, April 19–26.

Feder, Gershon, Tongroj Onchan, Yongyuth Chalamwong, and Chira Hongladarom. 1988. *Land Policies and Farm Productivity in Thailand.* Baltimore, MD: Johns Hopkins University Press.

Feder, Gershon, Tongroj Onchan, and Tejaswi Raparla. 1986. *Land Ownership Security and Access to Credit in Rural Thailand."* New York: Oxford University Press.

Field, Erica. 2007. "Entitled to Work: Urban Property Rights and Labor Supply in Peru." *Quarterly Journal of Economics* 122 (4): 1561–602.

Goldstein, Markus, and Christopher Udry. 2008. "The Profits of Power: Land Rights and Agricultural Investment in Ghana." *Journal of Political Economy* 116 (6): 980–1022.

Grindle, Merilee. S. 1990. "Agrarian Reform in Mexico: A Cautionary Tale." In *Agrarian Reform and Grassroots Development: Ten Case Studies,* ed. Roy L. Prosterman, Mary N. Temple, and Timothy M. Hanstad, 179–204. Boulder, CO: Lynne Rienner.

Grosh, Margaret, and Paul Glewwe, eds. 2000. *Designing Household Survey Questionnaires for Developing Countries: Lessons from Fifteen Years of the Living Standards Measurement Study.* Three volumes. Washington, DC: World Bank.

Gunning, Jan Willem, John Hoddinott, Bill Kinsey, and Trudy Owens. 2000. "Revisiting Forever Gained: Income Dynamics in the Resettlement Areas of Zimbabwe, 1983–96." *Journal of Development Studies* 36 (6): 131–54.

Haddad, Lawrence, John Hoddinott, and Harold Alderman. 1997. "Introduction: The Scope of Intrahousehold Resource Allocation Issues." In *Intrahousehold Resource Allocation in Developing Countries: Models, Methods, and Policy,* ed. Lawrence Haddad, John Hoddinott, and Harold Alderman, 1–18. Baltimore, MD: Johns Hopkins University Press.

Hall, Anthony L. 1990. "Land Tenure and Land Reform in Brazil." In *Agrarian Reform and Grassroots Development: Ten Case Studies,* ed. Roy L. Prosterman, Mary N. Temple, and Timothy M. Hanstad, 205–34. Boulder, CO: Lynne Rienner.

Hayami, Yujiro, Agnes R. Quisumbing, and Lourdes S. Adriano. 1990. *Toward an Alternative Land Reform Paradigm: A Philippine Perspective.* Quezon City, Philippines: Ateneo de Manila University Press.

Ibbotson, Roger G., Lawrence B. Siegel, and Kathryn S. Love. 1985. "World Wealth: Market Values and Returns." *Journal of Portfolio Management* 12 (1): 4–23.

Jaramillo, Carlos Felipe. 2001. "Liberalization, Crisis, and Change: Colombian Agriculture in the 1990s." *Economic Development and Cultural Change* 49 (4): 821–46.

Jeon, Yoong-Deok, and Young-Yong Kim. 2000. "Land Reform, Income Redistribution, and Agricultural Production in Korea." *Economic Development and Cultural Change* 48 (2): 253–68.

Jimenez, Emmanuel. 1984. "Tenure Security and Urban Squatting." *Review of Economics and Statistics* 66 (4): 556–67.

Jorgensen, Steen L., and Zlatina Loudjeva. 2004. "Poverty and Social Impact Analysis of Three Reforms in Zambia: Land, Fertilizer, and Infrastructure." Unpublished manuscript. World Bank, Washington, DC.

Katz, Elizabeth, and Juan Sebastian Chamorro. 2002. "Gender, Land Rights and the Household Economy in Rural Nicaragua and Honduras." Paper prepared for the Regional Workshop on Land Issues in Latin America and the Caribbean, Pachuca, Mexico, May 19–22.

Kinsey, Bill H., and Hans P. Binswanger. 1993. "Characteristics and Performance of Resettlement Programs: A Review." *World Development* 21 (9): 1477–94.

Lavigne-Delville, Philippe, Camilla Toulmin, Jean-Philippe Colin, and Jean-Paul Chauveau. 2002. "Negotiating Access to Land in West Africa: A Synthesis of Findings from Research on Derived Rights to Land." International Institute for Environment and Development/Groupe de recherche et d'échanges technologies, London.

Lerman, Zvi, Csaba Csaki, and Gershon Feder. 2002. "Land Policies and Evolving Farm Structures in Transition Countries." Policy Research Working Paper 2794. World Bank, Washington, DC.

———. 2004. *Agriculture in Transition: Land Policies and Evolving Farm Structures in Post-Soviet Countries.* Lanham, MD: Lexington Books.

Lerman, Zvi, Csaba Csaki, and Victor Moroz. 1998. *Land Reform and Farm Restructuring in Moldova: Progress and Prospects.* Washington, DC: World Bank.

McClintock, Cynthia. 1981. *Peasant Cooperatives and Political Change in Peru.* Princeton, NJ: Princeton University Press.

Negrão, José. 2002. "Comments: Land as a Source of Conflict and in Post-Conflict Settlement." Paper prepared for the World Bank Regional Workshop on Land Issues in Africa and the Middle East, Kampala, Uganda, April 28–May 2.

Oosterberg, Tommy. 2002. "Designing Viable Land Administration Systems." Paper prepared for the World Bank Regional Workshop on Land Issues in Africa and the Middle East, Kampala, Uganda, April 28–May 2.

Otsuka, Keijiro. 1991. "Determinants and Consequences of Land Reform Implementation in the Philippines." *Journal of Development Economics* 35 (2): 339–55.

Place, Frank M. 2002. "Land Markets in Africa: Preconditions, Potentials and Limitations." Paper prepared for the World Bank Regional Workshop on Land Issues in Africa and the Middle East, Kampala, Uganda, April 28–May 2.

Platteau, Jean-Philippe. 1996. "The Evolutionary Theory of Land Rights as Applied to Sub-Saharan Africa: A Critical Assessment." *Development and Change* 27 (1): 29–86.

Powelson, John P., and Richard Stock. 1987. *The Peasant Betrayed: Agriculture and Land Reform in the Third World.* Boston, MA: Oelgeschlager, Gunn, and Hain.

Prosterman, Roy L., Mary N. Temple, and Timothy Hanstad. 1990. *Agrarian Reform and Grassroots Development: Ten Case Studies.* Boulder, CO: Lynne Rienner.

Ravallion, Martin. 2001. "The Mystery of the Vanishing Benefits: An Introduction to Impact Evaluation." *World Bank Economic Review* 15 (1): 115–40.

Reydon, Bastiaan P., and Ludwig Agurto Plata. 2002. "Intervenção Estatal no mercado de terras: a experiência recente no Brasil." Universidade Estadual de Campinas and Instituto Nacional de Colonização e Reforma Agrária, Campinas, Brazil.

Scott, James C. 1976. *The Moral Economy of the Peasant: Rebellion and Subsistence in Southeast Asia.* New Haven, CT: Yale University Press.

Tanner, Christopher. 2002. "Law-Making in an African Context: The 1997 Mozambican Land Law." FAO Legal Papers Online 26. Rome. http://www.fao.org/Legal//Prs-OL/lpo26.pdf [accessed January 8, 2009].

World Bank. 2001. "Mexico Land Policy—A Decade after the Ejido Reforms." Report 22187-ME. Washington, DC. http://doc.politiquessociales.net/serv1/Mexico_Land_policy_A_decade_after_de_Ejido_reform.pdf [accessed January 8, 2009].

———. 2003. "Nicaragua Land Policy and Administration: Toward a More Secure Property Rights Regime." Report 26683-NI. Washington, DC.

———. 2004. "Agriculture Investment Sourcebook." Washington, DC. http://web.worldbank.org/WBSITE/EXTERNAL/TOPICS/EXTARD/EXTAGISOU/0,,contentMDK:20974103~menuPK:2802192~pagePK:64168445~piPK:64168309~theSitePK:2502781,00.html [accessed January 8, 2009].

Zepeda, Guillermo. 2000. "Transformación Agraria. Los Derechos de Propriedad en el Campo Mexicano bajo el Nuevo Marco Institucional." Central Independiente de Obreros Agrícolas y Campesinos, Mexico.

Zimmermann, Willi. 2002. "Comments on Land in Conflict and Post-Conflict Situations." Paper presented at the World Bank Regional Workshops on Land Policy Issues, Asia Program, Phnom Penh, Cambodia, June 4–6.

INDEX

Boxes, figures, notes, and tables are indicated by *b*, *f*, *n*, and *t*, respectively.

E

L

N

Q

R

ECO-AUDIT

Environmental Benefits Statement

The World Bank is committed to preserving endangered forests and natural resources. The Office of the Publisher has chosen to print ***Agricultural Land Redistribution*** on recycled paper with 30 percent postconsumer fiber in accordance with the recommended standards for paper usage set by the Green Press Initiative, a nonprofit program supporting publishers in using fiber that is not sourced from endangered forests. For more information, visit www.greenpressinitiative.org.

Saved:

- 11 trees
- 8 million British thermal units of total energy
- 980 pounds of net greenhouse gases
- 4,069 gallons of waste water
- 522 pounds of waste not generated

green press INITIATIVE

www.ingramcontent.com/pod-product-compliance
Lightning Source LLC
Chambersburg PA
CBHW060949280326
41935CB00009B/661
* 9 7 8 0 8 2 1 3 7 6 2 7 0 *